The Blackwell Guide to
Epistemology

Edited by
John Greco and *Ernest Sosa*

Copyright © Blackwell publishers Ltd, 1999

First published 1999

Reprinted 2001

Blackwell Publishers Inc.
350 Main Street
Malden, Massachusetts 02148
USA

Blackwell Publishers Ltd
108 Cowley Road
Oxford OX4 1JF
UK

All rights reserved. Except for the quotation of short passages for the purposes of criticism and review, no part of this publication may be reproduced, stored in a retrieval system, or transmitted, in any form or by any means, electronic, mechanical, photocopying, recording or otherwise, without the prior permission of the publisher.

Except in the United States of America, this book is sold subject to the condition that it shall not, by way of trade or otherwise, be lent, resold, hired out, or otherwise circulated without the publisher's prior consent in any form of binding or cover other than that in which it is published and without a similar condition including this condition being imposed on the subsequent purchaser.

Library of Congress Cataloging-in-Publication Data

The Blackwell guide to epistemology / edited by John Greco and Ernest Sosa.
  p. cm.
Includes bibliographical references and index.
ISBN 0–631–20290–0 (hc.: alk. paper). — ISBN 0–631–20291–9 (pbk. : alk. paper)
  1. Knowledge, Theory of. I. Greco, John. II. Sosa, Ernest.
BD161.B465 1999
121—dc21   98-23967
                                                       CIP

British Library Cataloguing in Publication Data

A CIP catalogue record for this book is available from the British Library.

Typeset in 10 on 13pt Galliard
by Graphicraft Limited, Hong Kong
Printed in Great Britain by Antony Rowe Ltd, Chippenham, Wiltshire

This book is printed on acid-free paper

Contents

Contributors	vii
Preface	viii
Introduction: What is Epistemology? *John Greco*	1

PART I   TRADITIONAL PROBLEMS OF EPISTEMOLOGY — 33

1	Skepticism *Michael Williams*	35
2	Realism, Objectivity, and Skepticism *Paul K. Moser*	70
3	What is Knowledge? *Linda Zagzebski*	92
4	The Dialectic of Foundationalism and Coherentism *Laurence BonJour*	117

PART II   THE NATURE OF EPISTEMIC EVALUATION — 143

5	Skepticism and the Internal/External Divide *Ernest Sosa*	145
6	In Defense of a Naturalized Epistemology *Hilary Kornblith*	158
7	Methodological Naturalism in Epistemology *Richard Feldman*	170
8	Contextualism: An Explanation and Defense *Keith DeRose*	187
9	Rationality *Keith Lehrer*	206

PART III   VARIETIES OF KNOWLEDGE — 221

10	Perceptual Knowledge *William Alston*	223
11	The A Priori *George Bealer*	243
12	Moral Knowledge and Ethical Pluralism *Robert Audi*	271
13	Epistemology of Religion *Nicholas Wolterstorff*	303

PART IV NEW DIRECTIONS — 325

14 Feminist Epistemology *Helen E. Longino* — 327
15 Social Epistemology *Frederick Schmitt* — 354
16 Procedural Epistemology – At the Interface of Philosophy and AI
    John L. Pollock — 383
17 Hermeneutics as Epistemology *Merold Westphal* — 415

Select Bibliography of Epistemology by Topic — 436
Index — 451

Contributors

William Alston, Professor Emeritus of Philosophy, Syracuse University
Robert Audi, Professor of Philosophy, University of Nebraska
George Bealer, Professor of Philosophy, University of Colorado
Laurence BonJour, Professor of Philosophy, University of Washington
Keith DeRose, Associate Professor of Philosophy, Yale University
Richard Feldman, Professor of Philosophy, University of Rochester
John Greco, Associate Professor of Philosophy, Fordham University
Hilary Kornblith, Professor of Philosophy, University of Vermont
Keith Lehrer, Regents Professor of Philosophy, University of Arizona
Helen Longino, Professor of Philosophy and Woman's Studies, University of Minnesota
Paul Moser, Professor and Chairperson of Philosophy, Loyola University of Chicago
John Pollock, Professor of Philosophy and Research Professor of Cognitive Science, University of Arizona
Frederick Schmitt, Professor of Philosophy, University of Illinois at Urbana-Champaign
Ernest Sosa, Romeo Elton Professor of Natural Theology and Professor of Philosophy, Brown University, and Distinguished Visiting Professor, Rutgers University
Merold Westphal, Distinguished Professor of Philosophy, Fordham University
Michael Williams, Morrison Professor of Humanities and Professor of Philosophy, Northwestern University
Nicholas Wolterstorff, Noah Porter Professor of Philosophical Theology, Yale University
Linda Zagzebski, Professor of Philosophy, Loyola Marymount University

Preface

This volume is part of a new series of *Blackwell Philosophy Guides*. It contains seventeen essays on central topics in epistemology, each by a leading author in the relevant topic area. The volume intends to be a valuable resource for both epistemologists and non-experts alike, including students, academics in other fields, and the educated public.

Each essay in the volume includes background material of an introductory nature. Such material will serve to introduce non-experts to the relevant topic, as well as clarify the history and logic of the topic for those who are already scholars in the field. The bulk of each essay, however, is devoted to arguments for the author's own views. In this respect each essay is an important contribution to ongoing scholarship.

Of course there is always a tension between the goals of important scholarship and accessibility. We have tried to address that tension in three ways. First, my introduction is specifically devoted to making the volume more accessible to non-experts. To this end I offer a general introduction to the main questions of epistemology, and I describe the central theses and arguments of each essay. Second, contributors have written their essays with non-experts in mind. In particular, they have emphasized giving context to questions and problematics, and motivations for answers. Finally, and most importantly, we have solicited contributors who continue to demonstrate that excellent scholarship is compatible with accessibility. The essays in this volume are in fact models in this respect.

A few words are in order regarding the way we have handled references. All essays contain full references in their notes. In addition to the references for individual essays, we have included a select bibliography by topic at the end of the volume. Contributors were responsible for the section of the bibliography that deals with their respective topic. There is inevitable overlap by doing things this way, but we thought that this option would be the most useful to readers. Finally, I have included a number of editor's notes referring readers to other essays in the volume. I have not done this every time an author discusses a topic that is

Preface

treated more fully in a different essay. Given the extent to which our authors are in conversation with each other, this would have been too cumbersome. Instead I have restricted such notes to places where I judged they would be especially helpful.

I would like to thank Brian Regan at Fordham University for help with various aspects of the volume.

John Greco

Introduction: What is Epistemology?

John Greco

The purpose of this volume is to provide a relatively complete guide to the current state of epistemology. To this end, each essay addresses some important issue in the theory of knowledge. Each provides some historical background or other contextual information so as to orient the reader to the problem at hand and to its current state of development. After this, each author provides an extended defense of his or her own position on the relevant topic. In this way the essays go well beyond simple introductions. They are attempts to (a) locate the current state of an important question in epistemology, and (b) move discussion forward from that point.

In this introduction I want to do two things, both aimed at making the volume more accessible to the non-expert. In section 1 I offer a general introduction to the theory of knowledge by discussing the main questions of the field, how they arise, and how they are related. I also look at how these questions give rise to the various subject matters treated herein, thereby giving a rationalization for the organization of the papers. In section 2 I give a short summary of each essay in the volume, identifying the central questions being asked and outlining the main arguments offered. Again, this is meant primarily to be of use to non-experts by providing a kind of map of each essay in the volume. However, experts in epistemology might find the section useful as well, insofar as it provides a précis for each contribution.

1. What is Epistemology?

Epistemology, or the theory of knowledge, is driven by two main questions: "What is knowledge?" and "What can we know?" If we think we can know something, as nearly everyone does, then a third main question arises: "How do we know what we do know?" Most of what has been written in epistemology over the ages addresses at least one of these three questions. For example, in the

Theaetetus, Plato considers the thesis that knowledge is true belief that can be backed up with an account or explanation. Rationalists like Descartes and empiricists like Hume have defended competing theses about how we know, and have also disagreed about what we can know. These three questions determine the basic organization of this volume.

Essays in the first part, entitled *Traditional Problems*, address each of our main questions according to some traditional formulation. Historically, these traditional formulations make up the "Big Questions" in the theory of knowledge, and they continue to occupy the field today. Essays in the next part, *The Nature of Epistemic Evaluation*, address different aspects of the question "What is Knowledge?" Specifically, these essays take a closer look at various dimensions of epistemic normativity, or the kind of normativity relevant to cognition. The essays in the third part, *Varieties of Knowledge*, address the question "What can we know?" Respectively, they investigate the possibility of perceptual knowledge, a priori knowledge, moral knowledge, and religious knowledge. Finally, the part entitled *New Directions* contains essays representing some recent trends in epistemology. As we shall see, it is fair to say that the main question occupying the authors of these essays is "How do we know what we do know?"

While it is useful to understand the organization of the volume in this way, it should be noted that the above characterization is limited. This is because our three questions are closely related, and so an epistemologist rarely addresses one of them without addressing the others, or without at least assuming something about the others. Accordingly, the organization of the volume according to our main questions is accurate only if we are thinking in terms of general focus. In fact, we will see that many of the essays overlap in the issues treated, and to a considerable extent our authors are in conversation with each other.

If we define epistemology in terms of its central questions then it is apparent that some recent objections to epistemology miss their mark. This is because the objections trade on implausible understandings of what epistemology is. For example, various objections caricature epistemology as (a) the quest for certainty, (b) the attempt to find absolute foundations, (c) the attempt to legitimate other disciplines, such as science, and (d) the project of refuting skepticism. The essays in this volume demonstrate that all of these conceptions of epistemology are parochial; at best, they describe the narrow projects of some very few philosophers. These conceptions are outdated as well, in that they describe projects that have been given up by their few adherents centuries ago. An adequate understanding of epistemology's questions, together with an informed view of the field today, makes this relatively easy to see.

2. Summary of Essays

I now turn to a summary of the essays. Following the organization of the volume, this part of the introduction is divided into four sections, as described above. Individual essays are treated in subsections, which are labeled according to topic.

Introduction

a. Traditional problems

Skepticism Again, one of the central questions of the theory of knowledge is "What can we know?" A person who gives a pessimistic answer to this question is called a skeptic. An entirely pessimistic and general skepticism denies that we can know anything at all. More commonly, however, the skeptic denies that we have knowledge of some particular kind, for example moral knowledge about right and wrong, or religious knowledge about God.

A very common character in the history of philosophy is the skeptic who denies that we can have knowledge of the material world. This includes a denial of scientific knowledge, but means to include a denial of "everyday" knowledge as well. For example, this kind of skeptic denies that we can know that there is a table in the room, or even that we ourselves have bodies. I say that this kind of skeptic is a common "character" because it is doubtful that many philosophers have actually held such a position. Rather, epistemologists have been concerned to show why such a position is wrong. In fact, it is quite common for epistemologists to *assume* that skepticism of this kind is wrong, and to concentrate on the question of *where* the skeptic goes wrong, or more exactly, where certain skeptical arguments go wrong. In this way, the motivation for engaging skeptical arguments is methodological. The point is to learn from them rather than to refute them, at least if "refutation" is understood to mean a rhetorically adequate refutation, for example one that would beg no question in a debate with a persistent skeptical opponent.

Michael Williams addresses what he calls "philosophical skepticism" in the lead essay of the volume. Philosophical skepticism is characterized by two main features: (a) it offers initially plausible arguments for its skeptical conclusion, and (b) its conclusion is radical in both its scope and its strength. Such arguments are not plausible in the sense that they are psychologically persuasive. As we said, almost no one actually holds the skeptical position. Rather, they are plausible in that each step of the argument seems intuitively correct. This is in fact what makes skeptical arguments philosophically interesting; they present us with a line of reasoning that we ourselves find intuitively plausible, but which leads to a conclusion that we find absolutely implausible. The task of the epistemologist is to identify and explain the mistake.

Williams argues that there are two broad families of skeptical argument. The first goes back to the ancient Greeks, and plays on a seemingly innocent fact about our concept of knowledge. Namely, we think that we should be able to give good reasons when we claim to know something. Moreover, we recognize that such reasons can provoke a new challenge, requiring that we give further good reasons for believing these. If we take this aspect of knowledge seriously, the skeptic argues, we will discover that our claims are not in fact well grounded. A persistent investigation into the reasons for our knowledge claims leads to either (a) an infinite regress, (b) a dogmatic assumption for which we are unwilling or unable to give further reasons, or (c) a repetition of some reason already given, and thus a circle in our reasoning. Williams calls this skeptical problematic "Agrippa's Trilemma," naming it after the ancient skeptic who first gave it clear articulation.

The second family of skeptical arguments is Cartesian. The most famous of these concerns our knowledge of the material world, but the basic pattern of the argument can be repeated for a variety of skepticisms, including skepticism about other minds, the past and the future. In the first step of the argument it is claimed that some targeted class of beliefs requires evidence of some nonproblematic kind (that is, nonproblematic for the sake of the argument at hand). For example, it is claimed that knowledge of the world must be inferred from knowledge of our sensory experience. Second, the skeptic argues that there is no good inference available, either deductive or inductive, from the relevant evidence to the targeted beliefs. Finally, the skeptic concludes that there is no way to justify the beliefs in question, and that therefore we lack the relevant kind of knowledge.

Williams reviews several traditional responses to the two families of skeptical argument and finds all of them to be inadequate. This is because traditional approaches share the mistaken assumptions that give rise to the skeptical arguments. Moreover, so long as these assumptions remain unchallenged, the skeptical reasoning will continue to seem intuitive and plausible, while traditional responses will seem forced and *ad hoc*. Williams' own diagnosis is that Agrippan arguments presuppose a widely accepted but ultimately misguided conception of epistemic justification. Namely, they suppose that *being justified* in one's beliefs, in the sense of being epistemically responsible, requires being able to *justify* one's beliefs by giving one's reasons on demand. This in turn assumes that all knowledge must have a prior grounding in reasons, and of a kind readily available to the knower. Without this "Prior Grounding Requirement," Agrippan-type arguments cannot get off the ground.

The problematic assumption behind Cartesian-type arguments is what Williams calls "epistemic realism"; the thesis that a belief's epistemic status depends on what kind of belief it is, rather than on contextual features of how the belief was produced or how it is held. Moreover, epistemic realism supposes that there is a hierarchy of epistemic priority, so that beliefs of some kinds always depend on beliefs of other kinds for their evidence, again independently of context. This is what allows the skeptic to insist that beliefs in some targeted class must be grounded in knowledge of some nonproblematic class, for example that beliefs about the world must be grounded in knowledge of sensory experience. The skeptic assumes, and we assume with him, that beliefs in the one class are and always must be epistemically prior to beliefs in the other.

Williams argues that a contextualist theory of knowledge and justification allows us to sidestep both Agrippan and Cartesian arguments. If justification depends on various features of context rather than attaching to absolute epstemic kinds, then both the Prior Grounding Requirement and epistemic realism can be rejected. For example, if context determines what kind of reason can provide appropriate grounding, or whether any further grounding is needed at all, then it is false that beliefs can be divided into privileged and problematic kinds. It will no longer be plausible, for example, that all beliefs about the world must be inferred from knowledge of sensory experience alone. Rather, adequate grounds for a given belief about the world will be determined by context, and will almost always include *other beliefs about the world* that are not challenged in that present context. In this way, the epistemologist is no longer faced with the impossible task of showing how knowledge of the world can be derived from knowledge of experience alone. That task seemed necessary so long as we assumed epistemic realism. But once that assumption is exposed, Williams argues, neither skeptical arguments nor traditional ways of responding to them seem compelling.

Realism and objectivity The essay on realism by Paul Moser also addresses the question "What can we know?" Here the issue is ontological realism, which is a thesis about the nature of the object known. More specifically, the question is this: "Can we know about the world as it really is, or are we restricted to knowledge of the world as it is shaped and colored by our own thoughts and experience?" Another way to put the question is to ask whether our knowledge can be objective, or whether, alternatively, our knowledge is restricted to our own subjective perspective on things. The moderate realist holds that at least some of our knowledge *is* objective. Moser defines moderate realism as "the view that what is represented by at least some of our beliefs is objective, that is, logically and causally independent of someone's conceiving of that thing."

In the first section of his paper Moser defends moderate realism against the objection that it is unintelligible. He concludes that moderate realism is at least intelligible, and so is the traditional quest for beliefs that represent how the world really is. The real issues concern whether moderate realism is true, or rationally acceptable, or otherwise epistemically adequate. In the second section of his essay Moser considers what he takes to be a serious skeptical challenge to moderate realism. In fact, we will see that Moser takes the challenge to be unanswerable. Specifically, the skeptic demands that the moderate realist provide non-questionbegging support for her position. The moderate realist should be able to argue for realism, but in such a way that she does not presuppose realism in making her argument. Moreover, the skeptic provides an argument that shows why this cannot be done. The problem is that, whatever reasons the moderate realist might offer, a question arises regarding the adequacy of those reasons: What non-questionbegging support do we have for the claim that those reasons are a reliable indication of how things objectively are? Since the skeptic is challenging the adequacy of our cognitive resources in general, the realist cannot invoke one kind of reason or ground to establish the adequacy of some previous reason or ground that she has given for her realism. Therefore, there is no argument for moderate realism available that does not beg the question against the skeptical challenge.

Even if this skeptical objection is correct it would not show that moderate realism is false, or even that beliefs about the objective world are irrational. Rather, it would show that moderate realism (and our beliefs about an objective world) lack a certain kind positive epistemic status; namely, they lack a kind of support that does not beg important questions about the truth of that position (or the truth of those beliefs). Moser points out that the present skeptical challenge cannot be dismissed in ways that are often supposed. For example, it does not presuppose some inordinately high standard for knowledge, or rational belief, or epistemic support. Rather, the challenge invokes a standard that the moderate realist already accepts: that one's support for a position should not beg relevant questions in an arbitrary way. It is this charge of epistemic arbitrariness that drives the current skeptical challenge, and which gives it its bite against the nonskeptic.

In the next two sections of the paper Moser considers several possible responses to the skeptical challenge discussed above. These include arguments to the best explanation in favor of realism, and the claim that science establishes realism. In response, Moser reminds us that the skeptical challenge is completely general, and so arguments to the best explanation and scientific inquiry get no special respect; we have no non-questionbegging support for the position that these kinds of grounds establish what is objectively the case. Moser also considers and rejects "pragmatic" responses to the skeptical challenge, including the view that we ought to ban questions about objectivity as useless. He concludes the essay by drawing some consequences from the discussion. If moderate realism cannot be given non-questionbegging support, it follows that human reasoning is limited in an important way, and that an appropriate humility about human reasoning is warranted.

What is knowledge? In the next essay Linda Zagzebski investigates what is perhaps epistemology's main question: "What is knowledge?" One way Socrates puts the question in the *Theaetetus* is to ask what distinguishes knowledge from mere opinion. It would seem that someone who knows is in a different and superior position to one who has only opinion, and even if the person's opinion happens to be true. If the person has the opinion they do because of a guess, for example, this is different from having knowledge. So what makes the difference?

The first two sections of Zagzebski's paper take care of some important preliminaries. She discusses why it is proper to think of knowledge as a form of belief (or assent), and she settles on a broad understanding of knowledge as believing something true in a good way. In the context of Plato's discussion, we can say that the person with knowledge believes in a good way, whereas the person with mere opinion assents in a way that lacks some relevant intellectual merit. Zagzebski argues that most of the difficulties and controversies concerning definitions of knowledge center around the concept of "in a good way." Giving an informative account of this normative dimension of knowledge poses the greatest task in stating an adequate definition.

After these preliminaries Zagzebski's argument can be divided into two main parts. First, she argues that any definition which says that knowledge is true belief plus something else, where that something else does not entail the truth of the belief in question, must fall prey to "Gettier counterexamples." This is especially important to realize, because nearly every definition of knowledge that *has* been offered by philosophers is of this sort. The second part of Zagzebski's argument is a defense of her own definition of knowledge, which she argues is not of the problematic sort described, and therefore has the resources to avoid Gettier counterexamples.

First, why are definitions of the sort mentioned vulnerable to counterexamples? If our general understanding of knowledge is that it is good true belief, then such definitions allow that some beliefs can be good in the sense required for knowledge, and yet nevertheless be false. For this is just to say that on such definitions, the "something else" in the definition does not entail the truth of the belief. Zagzebski argues that this gap between good belief and true belief guarantees that counterexamples can be generated to the definition that contains it.

For example, consider the definition of knowledge as true belief based on good reasons. If it is possible that someone have good reasons for her belief and the belief still be false, then a counterexample can be created by the following recipe. First, imagine that the person whose belief is based on good reasons runs into some bad luck – despite his best efforts, his belief turns out false. In a famous example, a person has excellent reasons for believing that one of his co-workers owns a Ford. But in reality it is all an elaborate deception and the co-worker does not in fact own a Ford. This is a case of epistemic bad luck. Second, add to the case an element of good luck that cancels out the bad luck. In our example, add that a different co-worker in the firm does own a Ford. In the case we have constructed, the person's belief that *One of my co-workers owns a Ford* is based on good reasons and is true. But it is clear that the person's belief does not amount to knowledge; the co-worker who owns the Ford isn't the one for whom the person has good reasons. Zagzebski argues that counterexamples involving this kind of double luck can be generated for any definition which allows the possibility of good but false belief. Therefore, she concludes, an adequate definition of knowledge must include a normative component that entails true belief.

In the second part of her argument she offers a definition of knowledge that does just this. A central concept in the definition is that of *an act of intellectual virtue*. In general, an act of virtue has several dimensions. It is one that (a) is properly motivated, (b) is what persons who have the relevant virtue would characteristically do in the circumstances, (c) is successful in achieving the end of the virtue in question, and (d) is successful because of the first two features of the act. For example, an act of kindness is an act that is motivated by the desire to be kind, is what a kind person would characteristically do in the circumstances, is successful in actually being kind to the someone in question, and is successful *because* the person was properly motivated and the act was characteristic of a person who is kind.

These considerations about acts of virtue in general can be applied to acts of intellectual virtue, where the kind of success that is aimed at is truth. If we define knowledge as belief arising out of acts of intellectual virtue, Zagzebski argues, we effectively avoid the above recipe for Gettier counterexamples. This is because an act of intellectual virtue, as here understood, entails that the person acting achieves true belief. Accordingly, Zagzebski has proposed a definition of knowledge in which the normative component of knowledge guarantees truth. It will be remembered that this is exactly what she promised. She ends by looking at some objections, and by raising some questions for future consideration.

Foundationalism and coherentism In Laurence BonJour's essay, the question "What is knowledge?" takes on a different dimension. The question becomes: "How must our total system of beliefs be structured in order for any of our beliefs to qualify as knowledge?" This question is closely related to Agrippa's Trilemma, reviewed in the section on Williams' essay above. That skeptical problematic arises, we saw, because it seems that knowledge must be grounded in good reasons. But where does such grounding in reasons come to an end? According to the trilemma there seem to be only three options: either (a) reasons goes on indefinitely; (b) reasons comes to an end, at which point no further reasons are available to support the last ones; or (c) reasons circle back on themselves. Foundationalism in epistemology agrees that options (a) and (c) are skeptical, but denies that option (b) is. Coherentism agrees that options (a) and (b) are skeptical, but denies that option (c) is. This controversy is taken up by BonJour.

BonJour's essay is divided into four main parts. First, he reviews the epistemic regress problem, or the problem of adequately grounding one's knowledge in good reasons. Second, he explores the foundationalist response to this problem. The main idea is that some beliefs can count as reasons for other beliefs, even though they are not backed up by further reasons themselves. Hence the regress of reasons stops with this "foundational" knowledge. Some objections to foundationalism concern the possibility of foundational knowledge: How can something serve as a reason, and even amount to knowledge, but not be in need of reasons itself? Other objections concern the relationship of foundational knowledge to non-foundational knowledge: Even if some narrow range of foundational knowledge exists, how can it be adequate to support all the other things that we seem to know?

Next BonJour considers the coherentist solution to the regress problem. This is the idea that reasons can be in a relationship of mutual support, so that an infinite number of reasons is avoided even though all knowledge must be backed up by good reasons. BonJour reviews some objections to coherentism and judges them to be fatal. One of these is that coherentism cannot account for the role of sensory experience in observational knowledge. The main strategy open to coherentists is to account for the role of experience by considering how beliefs *about* experience might give rise to observational knowledge. However, BonJour argues, this move does not allow a satisfactory answer to the problem at hand. This inspires the final part of the essay, which is a reconsideration of foundationalism.

We can see that the main argument of BonJour's paper is in the form of a dilemma: coherentism and foundationalism are the two best strategies for avoiding skepticism in the face of the regress problem; but there are fatal objections to coherentism, and therefore some form of foundationalism is most likely correct. The final sections of BonJour's paper consider the prospects for defending a viable foundationalism in the face of the objections that were raised at the beginning of the essay.

Another aspect of BonJour's argument is worth touching upon here. Namely, he tells us that the argument for his version of foundationalism presupposes an internalist theory of justification. As in Williams' essay, this is roughly the idea that knowledge must be grounded in reasons that are available to the knower. If this internalist constraint on knowledge is not presupposed, BonJour argues, then there is really nothing problematic about a straightforward foundationalist response to the regress problem. Since BonJour accepts the internalist constraint, he is faced with more formidable problems in defending foundationalism than there would be otherwise. This is noteworthy in that Ernest Sosa argues against any such internalist constraint in his essay on the internalism–externalism controversy concerning the nature of epistemic justification.

Finally, it will be fruitful to compare BonJour's response to the regress problem with the one defended by Williams. It seems clear that the two are at odds, since BonJour endorses an internalist version of foundationalism, whereas Williams endorses contextualism. However, we can detect two important points of agreement if we pay close attention to their terminology. First, Williams claims that "substantive" foundationalism should be rejected, because it presupposes the Prior Grounding Requirement and its attendant internalist constraint on the availability of adequate reasons. The contextualist alternative that Williams proposes is actually a version of what he elsewhere calls "formal foundationalism" and BonJour calls "foundationalism": the position that some beliefs can amount to knowledge even if they are not supported by further beliefs acting as their evidence.[1] Second, Williams call his contextualism "externalist" precisely because it does not require that one always be aware of one's grounds in the way that internalism requires. Hence, both authors agree that (a) formal foundationalism is the correct answer to the regress problem, and (b) an externalist version of foundationalism becomes plausible if an internalist conception of justification is rejected. They disagree over whether an internalist theory of justification should be rejected.

b. *The nature of epistemic evaluation*

Above we noted that knowledge seems superior to opinion, and we saw that knowledge can be broadly characterized as believing something true in a good way. Accordingly, to say that someone knows is to make a "value judgement." It is to attribute some positive evaluative character to the person's belief, or perhaps to the person herself. In this way, the question "What is Knowledge?" gives rise to questions about the nature of epistemic normativity and epistemic evaluation. This sort of question, in fact, has recently taken center stage in epistemology. Accordingly, the second part of the volume is devoted to questions of this kind.

Internalism and externalism As we have seen, internalists in epistemology take the view that epistemic justification is a function of factors that are relevantly "internal" to the knowing subject. For example, a common internalist position is that justification depends on having grounds that are easily available to the knower's perspective. Internalism is often tied to the view that epistemic evaluation is deontological, or duty-centered. The idea is that doing one's duty has to do with doing what is right from one's own perspective. Since internalists think that epistemic status has to do with doing one's cognitive duty, they reason that justification must be a function of what is easily available to that perspective. Externalists see problems with this set of views, and accordingly try to argue for a different account of epistemic evaluation.

Sosa begins his essay on the internalism–externalism controversy with a review of what he calls "Descartes's Paradox." The paradox takes the form of a skeptical argument, and is related to the Cartesian arguments that we saw in Williams' essay above. The reasoning is roughly as follows. To know that something is so, one must be able to rule out every possibility that one knows to be incompatible with one's knowing the thing in question. For example, to know that the animal in the distance is a husky, one must be able to rule out the possibility that it is a wolf. This principle seems to accurately reflect our working concept of knowledge. Notice, however, that it is a possibility that Descartes is dreaming, and that he does not actually perceive that he is, say, sitting by the fire. We can understand this possibility as a normal dream, as in one's sleep, or we can understand it more radically, as in Descartes's hypothesis of a powerful deceiving demon. Either way, the prospects for knowing that one is not dreaming seem slim, since it would seem that any attempt to know such a thing must already presuppose that one is not dreaming. It follows from this line of reasoning that Descartes does not know that he is sitting by the fire, and could not know anything on the basis of sensory experience compatible with his dreaming.

In the next section of the essay Sosa identifies what he takes to be an internalist assumption in the argument: that one can know through perception only if one knows that one is not dreaming. Externalists, he points out, would reject such an assumption, thereby enabling them to avoid Descartes's skeptical argument. This is because on an externalist view, one knows via perception so long as one's faculties of perception are *in fact* working well. One need not know that one's faculties are working well, or alternatively, that one is not dreaming rather than perceiving. This prompts the following question: What motivation is there for accepting the internalist assumption in question? Sosa goes on to identify two versions of internalism that would motivate the assumption, and to consider the relationship between them.

Cartesian internalism is the thesis that justification requires proper thinking, and that proper thinking is a function of things purely internal to the mind of the subject. Chisholmian internalism is the thesis that one can find out, merely by reflection, what one is justified in believing. If either of these theses were true then this would motivate the assumption of the skeptical argument above; i.e.,

Introduction

that one must know that one is not dreaming if one is to know anything else via perception. Next Sosa suggests a relationship between the two forms of internalism. Chisholmian internalism follows from Cartesian internalism, but only if we add two assumptions: that what is internal to one's mind is always accessible merely by reflection, and that the way in which such internal factors give rise to justification is always accessible just by reflection. Without these two assumptions, Sosa argues, it would not follow from Cartesian internalism that we can always tell by reflection whether our beliefs are justified. This prompts a second question: Why should we think that these latest assumptions are true?

As noted above, some philosophers have thought that internalism and a deontological conception of justification are closely related. Accordingly, in section three of his essay Sosa investigates whether the assumptions in question can be supported by a deontological, or duty-centered, understanding of epistemic justification. He concludes that they can be, but only by assuming Cartesian internalism as an independent premise. Therefore it is incorrect that, as some have thought, important kinds of internalism can be derived from a deontological conception of justification; one kind of internalism must be presupposed in order to derive the other.

Next Sosa moves to what is perhaps the main contention of his essay: that the deontological conception of justification, and therefore any internalism supported by it, is of limited value to epistemology. This is because this concept of justification fails to account for important aspects of epistemic excellence. He makes his case by considering several pairs of beliefs, each member of which would count as justified in the deontological sense. Each pair of beliefs, Sosa contends, is such that they differ in other important dimensions of epistemic excellence. Therefore, a duty-centered concept of justification fails to capture important kinds of epistemic evaluation. For example, consider two beliefs that are psychologically indubitable, and therefore justified in the sense that it is no violation of duty to believe them. But among indubitable beliefs, we want to distinguish those resulting from brainwashing and those resulting from sound mathematical intuition. Any important concept of epistemic justification must allow such a distinction.

In the final section of the essay Sosa considers pairs of beliefs that are ostensibly from deductive inference, reliable testimony, memory, and rational intuition. These are used to demonstrate that beliefs of different kinds can be internally on a par, and yet differ in important aspects of epistemic excellence. He concludes that, *contra* internalism, external factors such as the actual genesis of one's belief, including its social aetiology, can be relevant to its epistemic status. These results, Sosa concludes, leave it doubtful that there is any important sense of internalist justification.

Suppose someone were to accept an externalist view of epistemic evaluation. This would be a strong motivation for accepting naturalism is epistemology. According to externalism, positive epistemic status is at least partly a function of factors that are not internal to the knower's own mind, and therefore not recognizable just by reflection. Roughly, naturalism in epistemology is the view that epistemological questions can and must be answered by empirical means. Naturalism is therefore a methodological position that is quite naturally suggested by externalism; if important aspects of positive epistemic status are not accessible by reflection alone, presumably they are accessible by means of empirical investigation. The essays by Hilary Kornblith and Richard Feldman explore the prospects for a naturalized epistemology. Kornblith argues that nothing short of a fully naturalized epistemology can adequately address epistemology's main questions. Feldman argues that the claims of methodological naturalism are exaggerated. While empirical investigation can be relevant to some of epistemology's questions, those that define the central concerns of the field can only be addressed by more traditional, non-empirical modes of analysis.

For naturalized epistemology Kornblith's essay is divided into three main sections. In the first he reviews the Cartesian conception of epistemology as "first philosophy," arguing that it is concerned with three questions: (1) What is knowledge?; (2) How is knowledge possible?; and (3) What should we do in order to attain knowledge? In section two of the essay Kornblith presents a naturalistic alternative to the Cartesian approach, and argues that it is concerned with the same questions, although interpreted somewhat differently. In the third section of the paper he argues for the superiority of the naturalistic approach.

Kornblith argues that Descartes's foundationalism constitutes a unified theory that simultaneously answers the above three questions. Descartes proposes that a belief counts as knowledge if it is either foundational or appropriately derived from what is foundational. Moreover, a belief counts as foundational for Descartes only if it is inconceivable that it be mistaken. The criterion for appropriate derivation from such foundations is similar, requiring certainty of the highest grade. This answer to the question "What is knowledge?" gives Descartes an answer to the other two questions as well. Knowledge is possible, even in the light of skeptical challenges, if it can be derived from foundations that are immune from error. To achieve such knowledge we must first provide ourselves with adequate foundations, and then proceed from there by appropriate means of derivation.

On Descartes' view, epistemology is conceived as "first philosophy." In other words, the theory of knowledge is conceived as logically prior to empirical knowledge. In the context of skeptical doubts concerning the possibility of error, we first need to develop standards of belief that will safeguard against these. Only then are we in a position to appropriately form other beliefs, according to whether they meet our newfound standards. In this way epistemology must precede science, and in fact any empirical investigation whatsoever.

The naturalized alternative to this approach is to make epistemology continuous with the empirical sciences. Rather than preceding or guaranteeing the sciences, epistemology is conceived as addressing questions which themselves are open to empirical investigation. One way Kornblith makes the point is by arguing that epistemology ought to investigate the phenomenon of knowledge rather than our concept of knowledge. Just as our concept of aluminum may contain mistakes and be otherwise inadequate in capturing the nature of aluminum, our concept of knowledge might fail in various ways to explicate the nature of knowledge. But then epistemology should not proceed by conceptual analysis alone. The alternative is to treat knowledge as a natural phenomenon, to be investigated by whatever means are available, including empirical means. It is perfectly appropriate, for example, to investigate the psychological, physiological, and social mechanisms that give rise to paradigm cases of knowledge. By such means we might identify what features are common to all cases of knowledge, and thereby develop a more adequate account of knowledge than would have been possible by non-empirical modes of analysis alone.

Kornblith goes on to consider some naturalistic answers to the three questions above, although the questions take on somewhat different meanings within the context of the approach being advocated. "What is knowledge?" becomes a question about the nature of knowledge as a natural phenomenon. The latter two questions lose their connection to the project of answering the skeptic. They become questions about what cognitive and social mechanisms give rise to knowledge, and how we might improve upon these in order to better achieve our epistemic goals.

In the final section of the essay Kornblith identifies what he believes is the central issue between naturalists and traditionalists. It is not whether empirical enquiry can have some relevance to some of epistemology's main questions; that much is uncontroversial. The real issue is whether any such question lends itself to purely a priori (non-empirical) investigation. This issue ultimately rests on how we are to conceive the nature of epistemological inquiry, and specifically, how we are to interpret our three questions above. Traditionalists will want to interpret them in a Cartesian way, whereby empirical investigation is rendered inadmissible. Naturalists will want to interpret them in different ways, whereby empirical investigation is made essential. But how is this question of interpretation to be decided? Kornblith argues that there is no text to which we can refer, and no founding fathers to whom we can appeal. The question about interpretation is a question about what sorts of projects are interesting and fruitful. Accordingly, the case for naturalism rests largely on the fruitlessness of the Cartesian project, and on the better prospects for an empirical epistemology.

Against naturalized epistemology Feldman's essay responds critically to the position advocated by Kornblith. Feldman agrees that it is uncontroversial that empirical enquiry can have some relevance to some epistemological questions, especially if we define epistemology broadly. Like Kornblith, he thinks that the real issue is whether there are questions remaining which are properly investigated by non-empirical methods. He identifies three: (a) the analysis of important epistemic concepts like knowledge and justification; (b) the identification of epistemic principles stating sufficient conditions for justified belief; and (c) the response to arguments for skepticism.

Concerning the first, Feldman addresses the naturalist claim that scientific analysis of the phenomenon of knowledge is more useful than non-empirical analysis of the concept of knowledge. Here he insists on disanalogies between investigations of aluminum and of knowledge. For one, what we want from an investigation of aluminum is an account of its physical constitution, and it would be absurd not to rely on empirical methods for this. However, what drives our investigation of knowledge is a number of interesting conceptual puzzles, such as those concerning the conditions for justified belief, and those giving rise to difficult skeptical arguments. What is needed to address these is conceptual clarification of a traditional sort. Moreover, Feldman suggests, the naturalist's preference for reliabilist and causal accounts of knowledge is driven by just this sort of non-empirical analysis. For example, the definition of knowledge as true reliable belief is not accepted on the basis of empirical considerations, but because it is deemed to organize actual and possible cases in the right way. This mode of analysis, which arrives at a definition by considering how it handles actual and possible cases, is a paradigm case of non-empirical method.

Another task of epistemology is to identify epistemic principles, or principles that state sufficient conditions for some kind of positive epistemic status. Feldman argues that there are two sorts of issue here. One is the identification of general necessary truths that are supposed to explicate the nature of the property involved. The second is the identification of more restricted contingent truths, which are about how we actually satisfy, or fail to satisfy, the more general necessary principles. For example, the reliabilist about justification proposes that, necessarily, a belief is justified if it is formed by a reliable (i.e. truth-conducive) cognitive process. This is a general epistemic principle. But the reliabilist could go on to specify which of our cognitive processes are actually reliable, and thereby identify more restricted principles explaining how we actually arrive at justified belief. Feldman's point is that only the latter task requires empirical investigation. In fact, it is a purely empirical matter once the more general principles have been identified. Identification of the more general principles, however, is to be accomplished by "armchair" epistemology.

The above discussion can be applied to the final issue considered by Feldman; that of responding to skeptical arguments. Typically a skeptical argument will have a premise stating necessary conditions for knowledge, together with a premise stating that we fail to satisfy those conditions. Challenging the latter requires empirical investigation, since it will be at least partly an empirical matter whether we do or do not satisfy certain conditions laid down by the first premise. But challenging the first premise requires non-empirical investigation of the traditional sort. Only this mode of analysis is appropriate for investigating the necessary and sufficient conditions of our epistemic concepts. Feldman concludes that some of the traditional tasks of epistemology require or make use of empirical investigation of the sort associated with the natural sciences, but other central tasks do not.

Contextualism As we have seen above, there are reasons for thinking that various features of context are relevant to whether a person has knowledge or justified belief. In the most general sense of the term, "contextualism" in epistemology affirms that epistemic status is indeed relative to context. The essay by Keith DeRose explores contextualism in general and focuses on one version of the thesis. Specifically, he defends the position that (a) conversational context affects the truth-conditions of knowledge attributions, and (b) this happens by raising or lowering the standards of knowledge that are relevant for making a particular attribution true or false.

For example, suppose you are rushing an antidote to a dying poison victim and someone makes the claim that traffic is light on a particular route. Since you are in a situation where the person's being wrong would be disastrous, this makes the standards for knowledge very high. You would not assert that the person knows unless the grounds for her claim are excellent. In another context the same person's being right about the very same claim can be much less important. Suppose I am merely trying to decide which way to go home at the end of the day and I am not in any hurry. In this case I will be much more liberal about saying that the person knows. In this way, people who are ostensibly contradicting each other about whether someone knows can both be saying something true. If the conversational context of the first person sets higher standards than the conversational context of the second, then both can be right when one says "S does not know that P" and the other says "S does know that P."

DeRose argues that contextualism allows a powerful diagnosis of skepticism. Specifically, skeptical arguments manipulate the conversational context so as to drive standards for knowledge unusually high. Having done so, the skeptic is *correct* when she says that we don't know what we ordinarily claim to know. But conceding this to the skeptic turns out not to have general skeptical consequences. For in normal contexts (i.e., contexts other than highly specialized philosophical inquiry), the standards for knowledge are much lower, and so we do know many of the things we typically claim to know.

There is, however, an important objection to contextualism. Namely, it has been charged that the contextualist confuses two related questions: (a) whether a sentence such as "S knows that P" is true; and (b) whether the sentence is properly asserted. What varies according to context, the objection goes, is the latter rather than the former. DeRose explains that this kind of objection to contextualism involves a common maneuver in philosophy, what he calls a "warranted assertability maneuver" (or WAM). In general, WAMs try to explain away unwanted intuitions about truth and falsity in terms of what it is proper and improper to assert. For example, suppose that you are looking for Frick and Frack and you ask if they are with me. I reply that Frick is. If both Frick and Frack are with me then my reply seems wrong somehow. If you find out later that Frack was with me, you might even accuse me of lying to you. On the other hand, if it is true that both are with me then it must be true that Frick is. It is plausible to analyze this case by way of a WAM. Since Frick and Frack are with me, literally it is true that Frick is with me. However, if they are both with me then it is improper to assert only that Frick is; what is warranted in the context of your question is the assertion that *both* are with me.

In the above objection to contextualism a WAM is used to explain why intuitions about the truth of knowledge attributions vary according to context. The idea is that in some contexts where it is literally false that someone knows something, it is nevertheless proper to assert that the person does know. Other contexts call for a more literal assertion, and in these it is proper to assert that the same person does not know. Whether a given knowledge attribution is true or false is invariant across conversational contexts. What varies is assertability, and this makes it appear that truth conditions vary.

DeRose's strategy for responding to the present objection is to investigate some successful and unsuccessful examples of WAMs and to identify criteria for the proper use of WAMs in general. A central theme in his argument is that successful WAMs appeal to general conversational rules, and explain away intuitions about truth and falsity by means of these. For example, in the case above I violated the following quite general conversational rule: that if you are in a position to assert either of two things, then you should assert the stronger. Since I was in a position to assert that Frick and Frack were with me, and since the general "Assert the Stronger" rule was in place, my asserting that Frick was with me created the false implicature that Frack was not. DeRose argues that the WAM employed against contextualism does not work this way. It appeals to no general conversational rule, and to that extent it amounts to an *ad hoc* response to contextualism. For this reason, the most important objection to contextualism lacks plausibility.

Rationality In the final essay of this part Keith Lehrer considers the nature and ground of rationality. Here rationality is not conceived as an element of knowledge. Rather, it is a related normative property, which can apply to actions and preferences as well as to beliefs and reasonings. Being rational involves using one's reason with regard to what one does, intends, or prefers (practical rationality), and with regard to what one accepts and how one reasons (theoretical rationality). But what does it take for someone to be rational or reasonable in this sense?

According to a traditional view, rationality consists entirely in reasoning well about means for achieving ends. On this "instrumentalist" theory, to be rational is to be reasonable about how one goes about achieving one's purposes or goals. This view of rationality presupposes "the autonomy of ends." In other words, it presupposes that our goals and purposes cannot be evaluated as rational or irrational. Lehrer explains that some philosophers have held this view in order to avoid a regress problem. Specifically, if we say that some end is rational then this invites the question, "What makes it rational?" It would seem that any answer available must refer to some additional end: "It is rational to value X because I value Y." But of course this leads immediately to another question regarding the rationality of Y. On the other hand, the thesis of the autonomy of ends seems intuitively wrong. In other words, it seems wrong that someone's purposes and goals cannot themselves be rational or irrational. Lehrer interprets Aristotle as holding that ends can be rational or irrational, and he sets out to defend this Aristotelian alternative to the instrumentalist theory of rationality.

Introduction

According to Lehrer, the problem concerning the rationality of ends is answered by Aristotle's claim that man is a rational animal. By making the rationality of the person central we can explain why other things are rational, including the person's preferences concerning ends. Specifically, if we assume that a person is rational, then this gives us a reason for saying that her preferences are rational, via the following argument.

               1.   I am rational.
               2.   I prefer that A.
Therefore, 3.   I am rational in what I prefer. (From 1)
Therefore, 4.   I am rational in my preference that A. (From 2 and 3)

Lehrer explains that the inferences to 3 and 4 are not deductive. Rather, they are explanatory. It is because I have certain dispositions to be rational (this is what Premise 1 says), that I have a reason to think that my preferences are rational (this is what 3 and 4 conclude).

What reason do I have for accepting Premise 1? Since this is a question about what I should accept, it concerns theoretical rationality. In section two of the paper Lehrer turns to this topic, and suggests that I have a reason for accepting my own rationality via a similar looping argument. Roughly, the assumption that I am rational gives me a reason for thinking that I am rational in accepting the things that I do. Moreover, one of the things I accept is my own rationality. Therefore, my rationality explains why I am rational in accepting Premise 1 above, that I am rational. This sounds circular, and it is. But Lehrer argues that the circle is not vicious. On the contrary, it is central to the position being considered that personal rationality is explanatory of other kinds of rationality: it is because I embody certain dispositions regarding my acceptances that what I accept, including Premise 1, is rational. Of course this kind of looping argument does not allow us to prove that we are rational to a skeptic who denies it. But that is not what the argument is supposed to do. Rather, it is supposed to explain why Premise 1 is rational. In section three Lehrer argues that a similar line of reasoning solves the problem of induction, or the problem of explaining how inductive reasoning can be rational. What explains how I can be rational in my reasoning, including my reasoning to the conclusion that I am rational, is my rationality itself.

So far Lehrer has tried to explain (a) what makes a person's preferences, acceptances, and reasonings rational, and (b) what reasons one might have for accepting that these are rational. He next turns to the question, "What makes a *person* rational?". This becomes a question of first importance, since the rationality of the person is central to the Aristotelian account that Lehrer is defending. In the next two sections he approaches this question by exploring the nature of diachronic rationality (rationality regarding the way we change) and social rationality (rationality regarding the social group of which I am a part). He concludes that what makes a person rational importantly depends on these latter kinds of rationality. In sum, what makes me rational is my dispositions concerning what I prefer, what

I accept, how I reason, and how I change these in response to others. It is the character of these dispositions that *makes* me rational, although it is my rationality that explains and allows me to conclude that I am rational in these various undertakings. Lehrer invokes the metaphor of an arch to explain the relationship between my personal rationality and the rationality of my various undertakings. The first premise of my rationality is like the keystone of the arch, in that without it the arch collapses. But the keystone is supported by the other stones in the arch; I am a rational person because of my dispositions concerning what I prefer, what I accept, how I reason, and how I change.

c. *Varieties of knowledge*

We said that one of the main questions of epistemology is "What can we know?" The essays in the third part of the volume directly address this question by considering four varieties of (putative) knowledge: perceptual, a priori, moral, and religious.

Perceptual knowledge In the first essay of the part William Alston investigates the epistemology of perception. The essay begins with some preliminaries, including a distinction between two questions one might ask regarding perception. The first concerns the conditions for perceptual justification and/or perceptual knowledge in normal cases. This question asks about what conditions must actually be satisfied for a perceptual belief to be justified or qualify as knowledge. The second concerns how a philosopher might provide a justification for perception in general. This latter task is associated with proving the existence of an external world, perhaps in the context of replying to the skeptic. Although some philosophers have engaged in such a task, Alston makes it clear that his question is the first one. Alston also makes a distinction between externalist and internalist approaches to perception. He argues that externalist accounts of perceptual knowledge are plausible, but that perceptual justification has at least a weak internalist constraint. Namely, if a perceptual experience justifies me in holding some perceptual belief, I ought to have some insight into how this is so. I must have some idea, in other words, about why the particular experience I have ought to justify the particular belief I have.

The remainder of Alston's paper can be divided into three main sections. In the first he distinguishes four alternatives concerning the nature of perception and perceptual experience. In the second he argues that only one satisfies the internalist constraint set out above. In the final section he addresses the problem of hallucinations, which turns out to be an important concern for the account of perception he defends.

The account Alston defends is direct realism. On this view, perceptual consciousness is irreducibly relational in its nature; to have a perceptual experience is to have some object appear to you in some way, for example as being round or blue. This experience then acts as a justifier for the belief that the object is as it appears. The view is realist because the object that appears to the perceiver is understood to be extramental. It is direct because the manner in which we are held to perceive objects is not via some other object, such as a mental image or sense-datum.

A second view of perception is the sense-datum theory. Unlike direct realism, this view holds that what appears to us in perception is a mental object. Such mental particulars are held to be the direct objects of perception, by which we come to know extramental objects only indirectly. A third view is adverbialism, according to which perceptual experience is a way of being conscious rather than a conscious relation to some mental or extramental object. It is called "adverbialism" because varieties of perceptual experience must be described as different modifications of the way one is conscious, rather than as modifications of some perceived object. For example, the adverbialist understands perceiving blue as perceiving or sensing "bluely," as opposed to being aware of some object that is blue. Finally, the phenomenal quality view understands perceptual experience as an awareness of qualities of one's mental states. On this view we are aware of something mental, but it is one's mental states rather than mental particulars that have the perceived qualities.

Alston argues that only direct realism combines two important elements in its understanding of perceptual experience: it holds (a) that experience is a direct awareness of objects, and (b) that such objects are physical objects in the environment. All of the other views understand perceptual experience to be purely mental, or "in the head." For this reason, only direct realism makes it intuitively obvious how experience can justify perceptual beliefs. If by nature perceptual experience involves a direct awareness of a physical object as appearing a particular way, then intuitively this seems to be a good reason for believing that the object is as it appears. On the other hand, alternative views portray perceptual experience as purely subjective and involving no intrinsic relation to physical objects. Accordingly, these views do not make it clear why experience should justify beliefs about physical objects.

In the remainder of the paper Alston considers various strategies by sense-datum theorists, adverbialists, and phenomenal quality theorists for explaining why perceptual experience has justificatory force. He concludes that such attempts are inadequate, insofar as they either (a) simply lay it down in an *ad hoc* way that perceptual beliefs are justified, (b) invoke some discredited thesis about the ontology of physical objects, or (c) give up on the idea that justification has any connection to truth.

Alston ends by considering the problem of hallucinatory experiences. Such experiences are a problem for direct realism because they seem, at least in some cases, to justify beliefs about physical objects. On the other hand, hallucinatory experiences seem not to have the structure that the direct realist has described for justifying experiences: that of an object appearing to a subject in a particular way. Alston suggests two strategies that the direct realist might adopt in reply. One response is to bite the bullet and to hold that, despite appearances, hallucinatory experiences do not justify beliefs about physical objects. The other is to characterize the experiential justifier in terms of what perceptual and hallucinatory experiences have in common: that of seeming as if some physical object is appearing in a particular way. The direct realist may then hold that beliefs about physical objects can be justified by either kind of experience. Either way, Alston argues, the central contention of direct realism is preserved: that an object's appearing a particular way to a person justifies the person in believing that the object is that way.

A priori knowledge The varieties of knowledge have traditionally been divided into two main categories: a priori and a posteriori. We may understand the latter as knowledge which is evidentially grounded in sensory experience. Accordingly, perceptual knowledge is a paradigm case of the a posteriori. A priori knowledge can be understood as knowledge that is not grounded in experience. The evidence for a priori knowledge is not sensory experience, but intellectual (or rational) intuitions.

George Bealer begins his essay on a priori knowledge and evidence by addressing the source of some confusions. As Bealer explains, the a priori/a posteriori distinction has often been conflated with two others: (a) the distinction between analytic and synthetic sentences, and (b) the distinction between necessary and contingent truths. As we have seen, the a priori/a posteriori distinction is epistemic; it is a distinction between two kinds of knowledge, resting on a further distinction between two kinds of evidence. The latter distinctions, however, are logical or linguistic; they are about kinds of truth, or kinds of proposition, or kinds of sentence. Keeping these distinctions clear is important. For example, even if Quine's famous attack is correct and there is no tenable analytic/synthetic distinction, it does not follow, as many philosophers have thought, that we should give up the other two distinctions as well.

In the remainder of the essay Bealer defends an account of a priori knowledge and evidence. In section 1 he clarifies the notion of an intuition and defends the thesis that intuitions qualify as a kind of evidence. In section 2 he explains why intuitions count as evidence. The main idea is that basic sources of evidence must have an appropriate kind of reliable tie to the truth, and that intuitions are tied to the truth in this way. In section three Bealer explains why intuitions have this relationship to the truth. His explanation proceeds by way of an account of concept possession; given what it means to possess a concept, it follows that intuitions about the correct application of a concept are tied to truth in the required way.

First, what is an intuition? According to Bealer, it is nothing more than an intellectual "seeming." Just as a stick in the water can seem to be bent, a proposition can seem to be necessarily true. For example, consider one of de Morgan's Laws: that the sentence "P or Q" is true just in case the sentence "not-P and not-Q" is false. When most people first consider this law it does not seem true and it does not seem false. Upon further consideration, however, it not only seems true but necessarily true; it seems as though things could not be otherwise. This distinctive mode of consciousness is what Bealer calls an intellectual or rational intuition. It is different from belief, for one can believe that something is necessarily

Introduction

true without an accompanying intuition, and vice versa. Neither are intuitions infallible. It is possible for a proposition to seem necessarily true when it is not, and vice versa.

A review of our standard epistemic practices reveals that we use intuitions as evidence all the time. But are they really evidence, in the sense of being an effective ground of knowledge? Radical empiricism is a position in epistemology which allows only sensory experience as evidence, and therefore denies that intuitions can be evidence. Bealer defends the evidential status of intuitions against radical empiricism by means of an analogy. Suppose that the radical empiricist were confronted with a "visualist." The visualist accepts only visual experience as evidence and therefore rejects the radical empiricist's claim that auditory, tactile, and other kinds of sensory experience can be evidence. How could the empiricist defend her position that these other sources really are evidence? Bealer argues that there are various ways, but all are equally available to the intuitionist to be used against radical empiricism. Similarly, the radical empiricist might make various moves to block the defense of intuitionism, but all of these would be equally available to the visualist, allowing her to block a defense of radical empiricism. In other words, there is no relevant difference between (a) the visualist's rejection of nonvisual experience as evidence and (b) radical empiricism's rejection of intuitions as evidence. Since the former rejection is not justified, radical empiricism's rejection of intuitions is not justified either.

In the remainder of the paper Bealer argues that intuitions have a necessary but not infallible relationship to the truths they are about. The main idea is this: Having reliable intuitions about the correct application of a concept is part of what it means to have the concept in question. An example will illustrate this main idea. Suppose a woman uses the term "multigon" to describe various closed plane figures, but by chance has never considered whether triangles or rectangles are multigons. So far as we know, her concept of a multigon could be that of (a) a multi-sided closed figure or (b) a closed figure having more than four sides. Suppose now that she does consider whether a rectangle is a multigon. If she really does possess the concept of a multigon, then she will have the intuition that a rectangle can be a multigon only if the property of being a multigon is equivalent to the property of being a multi-sided closed figure. Alternatively, she will have the intuition that a rectangle cannot be a multigon only if the property of being a multigon is equivalent to the property of being a closed figure with more than four sides. In other words, what intuitions she has is partly constitutive of what concept she possesses. Of course people can fail to fully understand a concept. They can misunderstand it or their understanding can be incomplete. Nevertheless, even less than ideal concept possession implies some reliability in one's relevant intuitions; it implies this because such reliability is part of what it means to possess the concept in question.

Moral knowledge In the third essay of the part Robert Audi defends the possibility of moral knowledge. Audi's essay can be divided into two main sections. In the first he reviews four of the major positions available in moral epistemology, each of which has enjoyed some historical prominence. These are utilitarian empiricism, Kantian rationalism, Rossian intuitionism, and noncognitivism. In the second section of the essay he defends a reconstructed version of intuitionism.

Moral intuitionism has three main characteristics. First, it affirms an irreducible plurality of basic moral principles. Against Kantian rationalism and utilitarian empiricism, the position denies that there is one or few general moral principles from which all others can be derived. Second, each basic principle refers to some natural ground, which in turn implies some *prima facie* duty or obligation. For example: "If an injury occurs in one's presence, then one has a *prima facie* obligation to aid the injured party." *Prima facie* duty can be overridden by other factors, including other *prima facie* duties that one has in the circumstances. Third, intuitionism affirms that basic moral principles can be known intuitively. We will look more closely at what this means below, but one major idea is that the principles are known non-inferentially. Accordingly, intuitionism is a kind of foundationalism.

After describing intuitionism in outline Audi makes several important points by way of clarification and elaboration. First, we must distinguish between (a) apprehending the truth of a self-evident proposition, and (b) apprehending that the proposition is self-evident. For example, suppose that the proposition that *one plus one is two* is self-evident. A child might apprehend the truth of this proposition without understanding the notion of self-evidence at all. Intuitionism is committed to the thesis that a variety of basic moral principles are self-evident, and not to the thesis that it is self-evident that they are self-evident. Second, the intuitionist holds that the self-evidence of basic principles is defeasible. In other words, the positive epistemic status that basic principles initially have can be defeated by counter-evidence. For this reason it is wrong to think that the intuitionist must be closed off to arguments against her moral judgments, or that she must consider her moral judgments to be infallible or irrevisable.

Finally, intuitionism need not hold that basic moral principles are obvious. To make this point Audi considers the notion of self-evidence more carefully, and argues that there are two kinds. In general, a proposition is self-evident if adequately understanding it is sufficient to make one justified in believing it. Some propositions are immediately self-evident, in that they are adequately understood right away, at least by normal persons in normal circumstances. Other propositions are self-evident, but not immediately so. Instead, adequately understanding them requires reflection, and sometimes prolonged reflection. In the case of moral principles, reflection can involve applying a principle to possible cases, tracing possible consequences of adhering to it, and considering relations it has to other things one believes. In this way reflection can bring a proposition that is obscure into sharper focus, thereby creating the kind of understanding that self-evidence requires. Audi argues that basic moral principles enjoy this "mediate" self-evidence rather than immediate self-evidence. This is why basic moral principles are not obvious.

In the remainder of the essay Audi argues that intuitionism is compatible with a variety of epistemologies, including contextualist and socialist positions, that it does not require an implausible ontology or an implausible philosophy of mind, and that the position has resources for answering a variety of moral skepticisms. An interesting feature of the discussion is Audi's response to two objections typically brought against intuitionism. First, it is often argued that there is widespread disagreement concerning moral judgments, and that this makes the existence of self-evident moral intuitions implausible. However, this objection assumes that self-evident moral principles, if they existed, would have to be obvious. We have seen that intuitionism is not committed to this assumption. Second, it is commonly argued that intuitionism implies dogmatism. However, we have seen that intuitionism need only claim defeasible justification for basic moral principles. As such, intuitively known moral judgments are not closed off to relevant considerations against them.

Epistemology of religion   In his essay on the epistemology of religion Nicholas Wolterstorff explains that several aspects of religious practice fall within the domain of epistemology. For example, propositional attitudes such as belief, hope, and trust all qualify as important dimensions of a religious life, and all admit of various kinds of epistemic evaluation; they can be (or fail to be) rational, reasonable, reliably formed, warranted, and the like. A central issue in the epistemology of religion is whether religious beliefs have any important epistemic merit. Many philosophers have thought that they cannot. In a nutshell, their argument has been that there is no good evidence for God's existence, and therefore beliefs about God cannot have positive epistemic status. Others have responded to this skepticism by trying to construct sound arguments for God's existence: i.e., they have tried to provide the relevant evidence.

Recently, however, some philosophers responding to religious skepticism have taken a different tack: they have maintained that the arguments demanded by skeptics are not needed for positive epistemic status. On the contrary, religious beliefs can have a wide variety of epistemic merits even if they are not grounded in any argument at all. Perhaps the central thesis of Wolterstorff's essay is that this latter response to religious skepticism is in no way *ad hoc*. Rather, it is part of a recent revolution in epistemology. This revolution consists in the rejection of long held views about what is ideal for human cognition.

Wolterstorff's argument is in three main parts. First, he identifies an ideal held since Plato about the way humans ought best to form their beliefs, and he argues that this ideal can be found in both Aquinas's account of *scientia* and in Locke's account of entitlement (or rational belief). Second, he reviews some arguments from Hume and Reid which show that this ideal is inappropriate for human cognition in general; given the way human cognition is actually constituted, the ideal is largely irrelevant to beings like us. The conclusion is that many arguments against the epistemic merits of religious belief, insofar as such arguments presuppose this ideal, are likewise irrelevant. This does not show that religious beliefs do have important kinds of epistemic merit. But epistemology after the rejection of Plato's ideal must be open to this possibility. It becomes a major issue in the epistemology of religion to explore alternatives to the ideal that has been rejected, and to determine to what extent religious beliefs satisfy these alternatives.

Here I will look briefly at two issues: (a) the cognitive ideal that Wolterstorff identifies in Plato, Aquinas, and Locke; and (b) the main arguments against the ideal from Hume and Reid. To understand what Wolterstorff calls the "Doxastic Ideal" we need to understand the notion of acquaintance. Wolterstorff uses the example of dizziness to illustrate. Suppose you are riding a merry-go-round and you become dizzy. At this moment your dizziness is "present" to you. You are immediately acquainted with it in the sense we are trying to get at. Contrast this with your telling me later that you were dizzy. I can think about your dizziness as "the dizziness that you experienced yesterday." But my relationship to your dizziness is once removed; it is not something that is present to me or that I am acquainted with. And now for the Doxastic Ideal: the ideal way for us to form our beliefs is by way of acquaintance. This can happen in two ways. First, you can be acquainted with the very fact that your belief is about, as in the case of your belief that you are dizzy. In such a case, the content of your belief is read directly off the fact with which you are acquainted. Second, you can be acquainted with the fact that your belief is logically entailed (or at least made probable) by other things with which you are acquainted. In either case, your belief is fully grounded in things with which you are acquainted.

Wolterstorff argues that epistemology has recently undergone a "Humean–Reidian revolution." Due to arguments from Hume and Reid, epistemology has largely rejected the Doxastic Ideal. For example, Hume argued that we do not have any acquaintance with probability relations when we make inductive arguments to unobserved matters of fact, for example facts about the future. Rather, the cognitive mechanisms by which we make such inferences are in a sense blind; they serve us well and are in fact highly reliable, but they in no way involve acquaintance with logical or quasi-logical relations among the premises and conclusions of our inferences. Reid argued in a similar way regarding testimony. On the one hand, vast areas of our cognitive lives depend on beliefs formed through testimony. On the other, there is no good argument available to us to the conclusion that beliefs formed on testimony are probable in relation to other things we know more directly. Together the arguments from Hume and Reid show that beliefs formed by induction and testimony do not satisfy the Doxastic Ideal. At this point one might conclude that such beliefs therefore fail to have important kinds of positive epistemic status. Contemporary epistemology has drawn a different conclusion, however: that the Doxastic Ideal is irrelevant to human cognition, and that important varieties of positive epistemic status have little to do with it.

d. New directions

In recent years epistemology has been developed in a number of different directions. The essays in the last part of the volume look at four of these. The epistemologists pursuing these lines of inquiry are concerned with all of the discipline's main questions, but their emphasis is often on the question "How do we know what we do?"

Feminist epistemology In the first essay of the part Helen Longino looks at feminist epistemology. She does not use this term to identify any specific thesis within the theory of knowledge. Rather, she means to identify a certain way of doing epistemology. Longino's essay can be divided into three main sections. In the first section of her paper she gives the historical background for current work by feminists in epistemology. In the next two sections she reviews some distinctively feminist contributions to epistemology, regarding the nature of the knowing subject and the nature of epistemic justification, respectively. Here she argues that knowledge and justification are importantly contextual and social. At the same time, she defends her own version of these theses against alternatives put forward by other feminist philosophers. In the last section of the paper she addresses some objections to her own account. Some of these challenge her claim that justification and knowledge should be understood as social phenomena, while others challenge the very idea of a distinctively feminist epistemology.

Longino begins by explaining how current work by feminists in epistemology grew out of earlier feminist contributions to other disciplines. For example, feminists in both the natural and social sciences argued that gender biases have distorted scientific inquiry and thereby blocked progress in such diverse fields as primate studies, evolution theory, cell biology, genetics, anthropology, and sociology. Such distortions, they argued, have led to specific hypotheses such as that of a "master molecule" in biology, and have affected the very notions of objectivity and rationality at work in science. The notion that epistemic concepts are tainted by gender bias received further support from the history of philosophy. Various feminist philosophers analyzed the ways in which reason is masculinized in the history of Western philosophy, and argued that resulting epistemologies served political as well as philosophical purposes. Finally, work in educational psychology suggested that learning, problem-solving, and other cognitive activities might be gendered, giving rise to the idea that there are different "ways of knowing" for women and men.

Against the background of these developments, investigations into the nature of knowledge and related epistemic concepts became imperative for feminists. Feminist philosophers needed to ask what conceptions of knowledge and knowers facilitated gender biases in philosophy and the sciences, and whether alternative conceptions could block sexist thinking in these disciplines. Since gender bias in science and philosophy seems wrong from the point of view of truth and objectivity, another question arises: How much of our traditional epistemological thinking needs to be jettisoned and how much can be saved and used in the critique of our sexist traditions?

Feminist work regarding the nature of the knowing subject begins with a rejection of the traditional Cartesian understanding. On Descartes's view the mind is essentially distinct from the body, and the knowing subject is identified with the former. Against this, feminist philosophers have insisted on a conception of the knower as embodied. This move, Longino argues, gives rise to several consequences: (a) knowers must be understood as situated in specific times and places, and oriented in specific ways to their environment; (b) the knowing subject and the object of knowledge are no longer conceived as essentially distinct, and therefore knowing is no longer understood in terms of transcending bodily entanglements such as emotion and empathy; and (c) knowers are understood to be in various relations of interdependence, including ones concerning cognitive development, cultural training, intellectual responsibility, and various kinds of trust.

These changes in the way we understand knowers demand correlative changes in the way we understand epistemic justification. Specifically, we need to conceive justification as depending on various features of context. These include the interests and background assumptions of individuals, as well as the shared assumptions, methodologies, and norms of social groups. Moreover, Longino argues for contextualist dimensions of knowledge and justification similar to those we saw in Williams and DeRose; features of context determine which objections need to be met, and in general what standards need to be fulfilled, for a belief to qualify as justified or known.

An important part of Longino's position is that justification must be socialized as well as contextualized. Specifically, justification must be understood as arising out of social processes of critical interaction. Such interaction must take place both within communities and across them. First, the individual believer must be responsive to objections and critiques that come from within the group. Second, communities must develop means of critical discourse about their background assumptions and norms, both by incorporating diverse perspectives within the community and by engaging other communities whose shared background is different. By requiring these two kinds of critical interaction for justification, Longino argues, contextualism avoids subjectivism and relativism.

Social epistemology In the essay by Frederick Schmitt the topic of social epistemology is explored further. Like Longino, Schmitt understands social epistemology as the position that social features are importantly involved in the conditions for knowledge and justification. Schmitt explains that this is not a thesis about what is *causally* necessary for knowledge; the thesis that knowledge causally depends on social phenomena such as language acquisition, education, and various forms of social cooperation is not controversial. The socialist is saying more than that. A strong version of the thesis is that the conditions for justification actually refer to (or at least entail) social conditions. A weaker version is that the conditions for justification are "realized" by social conditions. Put another way, when a belief is justified, the conditions that make it justified are social conditions. All this is opposed to individualism in epistemology, which holds that positive epistemic status is entirely a function of properties of the individual.

Schmitt argues that a test case for socialism is the epistemology of testimony. On the one hand, testimonial justification is a plausible candidate for a socialist analysis. If individualism can be maintained even here, then knowledge in general must be seen as thoroughly individualistic. On the other hand, so much of our knowledge is directly or indirectly dependent on testimony. If testimonial justification is social, then knowledge in general must be understood as deeply social. Having identified this test case for socialism, the rest of Schmitt's argument can be divided into two main parts. First, he identifies what he considers to be the most plausible version of individualism regarding testimonial justification, and he raises objections to this view. Second, he identifies and defends his preferred version of socialism.

The most plausible version of individualism has also been the most historically prominent. On this view testimony is a causal instrument used to extend an individual's knowledge. Like a telescope, it can be a source of knowledge, but only after it has been established as accurate and reliable. According to this position, testimony is not a primary source of justification. Rather, it must be vindicated by primary sources and provides justification only on the basis of that vindication. What primary source of justification might vindicate the reliability of testimony? On the present view, it is an inductive argument mounted by the individual receiving the testimony, to the effect that testimony of the relevant kind has been a reliable source of information in the past. For example, I can gain knowledge about street locations from the testimony of my taxi driver, but only if I can establish the reliability of that information via an inductive argument; one to the effect that the testimony of taxi drivers concerning street locations is generally reliable. This position is in opposition to a socialist view, which holds that testimonial knowledge arises through the satisfaction of some set of social conditions.

Schmitt argues that the inductivist view of testimonial knowledge is implausible, since it is implausible that individuals typically possess the evidence for the required induction. To continue with the present example, my first-hand experience of testimony from taxi drivers is too limited to ground any but the weakest inductive argument. I could broaden my inductive pool if I were allowed to include other people's experiences, but this would sneak in testimony through the back door. The individualist needs to account for testimonial knowledge by grounding it entirely in nontestimonial sources of justification.

At this point Schmitt considers a possible reply on behalf of the individualist: that small-scale inductive arguments can be sources of justification. For example, consider that we can have knowledge about how a kind of fruit tastes after only one or two samples of the kind in question. If this is possible in general, it is possible with regard to inductive arguments regarding the reliability of kinds of testimony. By considering how Schmitt responds to this move by the individualist we also get the outline of his own socialist position.

Schmitt argues that there is a disanalogy between the way we select testimony and the way we make inductions about properties of natural kinds like fruits. Namely, the way we pick out natural kinds and their properties, and therefore the way we engage in small-scale inductions about them, can be understood entirely in terms of psychological processes of the individual. We are so constituted psychologically that we tend to select the right properties for our inductions, and as a result we are highly reliable at selecting reliable inductive arguments, even ones on a small scale. The case is different, Schmitt argues, with the way we select testimony. Namely, we are reliable at selecting reliable testimony due to a *social* process of learning. Small children are psychologically disposed to prefer their caretakers as sources of information in general, but also as sources of information about where to get information. Moreover, this social process by which the child learns to select reliable testimony is metareliable; for various reasons, parents and other caretakers tend to tell children the truth about where to find reliable testimony on various subject matters. Because the metareliable selection process for picking out testimony is social, testimonial justification is importantly social. Individualism about testimony cannot be maintained.

Epistemology and artificial intelligence In the next essay John Pollock argues for a close relationship between epistemology and work on artificial intelligence (AI). Specifically, he agues that epistemic theories ought to be tested by implementation in AI-type computer programs.

Pollock's motivations are essentially methodological. First, requiring implementation forces epistemologists to state their theories in precise and detailed fashion. This is important, he argues, because ideas that look good when painted in broad strokes often cannot be cashed out at the level of detail and precision demanded by computer programming. Second, implementation provides a test for correctness. Traditional methodology tests epistemic theories by trying to think of counterexamples. From her armchair, the epistemologist considers a variety of cases to see whether her theory gives intuitively correct results. Pollock argues that implementation is an improved version of the method of counterexample. In effect, the computer is a tool for considering a wide variety of complex, concrete test cases. Computer implementation of a theory outperforms armchair speculation in two ways. For one, a computer applies the theory to a test case mechanically, and so a theorist cannot be misled about what results her theory has for a particular case. Also, a computer can use test cases of greater complexity than those we can work through in our heads. This allows both a broader range of test cases, and ones that are closer to the complexity of real-life cognitive tasks.

In the first three sections of the essay Pollock discusses the proper subject matter for epistemology and defends a particular methodology for constructing epistemic theories. Here he argues that epistemology is driven by the question "How do you know?" Answers to this question can be formulated at different levels of generality. At the highest level, theories like foundationalism and coherentism try to describe the broad structure of cognition. At a lower level, epistemology tries to work out theories of particular cognitive procedures, such as inductive reasoning, memory, and perception. One adequacy condition for a high-level theory is that it is possible to construct and implement low-level theories that are compatible with it.

Pollock endorses a high-level structural theory of justification which he labels "direct realism." This position posits a similar structure to foundationalism: there is a foundational level of cognition, and beliefs are justified by virtue of an appropriate relationship to the foundations. But direct realism stresses that the foundational level consists of mental states rather than beliefs. For example, memory beliefs are justified by the having of recollections, and perceptual beliefs are justified by the experiencing of percepts. On this view, all justified beliefs are grounded in reasons, but not all justified beliefs have other *beliefs* as their reasons. (Note that Pollock and Alston mean different things by "direct realism," although their uses might be consistent.)

In the remaining sections of the essay Pollock illustrates the above methodology with an extended example. Specifically, he shows how a low-level theory of perception can be constructed and implemented in OSCAR, an artificial intellect being constructed on the assumption of direct realism. A fundamental thesis of direct realism is that perception involves a direct inference from percepts to beliefs about the world. Working out the nature of this inference quickly raises two problems. First, it is evident that having a percept with a particular content (e.g., that there is something red before you), is only a defeasible reason for believing that there is something red before you. In other words, having such a percept is a good reason, but one that evidence to the contrary could prevent from justifying your perceptual belief. An adequate theory of perception must accommodate the defeasible nature of perceptual reasons. A second problem that arises is showing how perceptual updating is possible. For example, my having a percept last week with the content that your house is blue is a good reason for a belief with the same content. But suppose I have a percept today with the content that your house is yellow. Clearly I should give up my previous belief and conclude that your house is now yellow, presumably because it has been painted a new color. An adequate theory must articulate how this can occur.

Pollock proposes a series of cognitive rules, or epistemic norms, to solve the above problems, and then shows how they are implemented in OSCAR. The idea is that a cognitive agent governed by these norms would successfully engage in defeasible reasoning and perceptual updating. An interesting feature of the discussion is that it does not remain at a general level. Pollock provides the actual steps that OSCAR runs through to arrive at perceptual judgments in two test cases.

Postmodernism and epistemology on the continent   In the final essay of the volume Merold Westphal investigates some prominent themes in contemporary continental philosophy. Specifically, he discusses Heidegger's hermeneutic theory, and then its "right-wing" and "left-wing" development in Gadamer and Derrida. One of Westphal's main theses is that hermeneutics is epistemology. Epistemology in general must be defined by its traditional task: an investigation into the nature and scope of human knowledge. But since hermeneutics addresses exactly these concerns, hermeneutics is epistemology.

Viewed this way, it is a mistake to identify epistemology in general with specific positions regarding the nature and scope of human knowledge. Rorty, for example, identifies epistemology variously with (a) the demand for absolute certainty, (b) the notion of a neutral, a priori tribunal for judging other disciplines, and (c) the search for absolute foundations. In sum, Rorty identifies epistemology with modernist epistemologies like those of Descartes and Locke; particularly strong versions of foundationalism, in which it is possible to ground certainty on theoretically neutral, unchallengeable foundations. Rorty advocates a shift from such Enlightenment pretensions to a hermeneutical philosophy that is holistic, historicist and pragmatic. But hermeneutics so conceived is not properly understood as a rejection of epistemology. Rather, it is a rejection of particular positions within epistemology in favor of others. Moreover, Westphal argues, the rejection of Enlightenment foundationalism is a prominent theme in both continental and anglo-american philosophy. In this sense, much of contemporary analytic epistemology is as post-modern as continental philosophy is.

After these preliminaries Westphal's essay can be divided into two main sections: an investigation into some central themes of Heidegger's epistemology, and then a shorter treatment of later developments in Gadamer and Derrida. An important theme in Heidegger's epistemology is that of the hermeneutic circle. This was originally an idea about the interpretation of texts: one comes to a text with a sense of the whole, but this must be revised in light of specific readings. The relationship between understanding the whole and understanding specifics is circular in that each is a function of the other. A similar idea is found in post-positivist philosophy of science, where theory is revisable in light of data, but data is understood as theory-laden, and so revision can go in the other direction as well. Heidegger turns such themes into a general epistemological position: all human understanding is interpretation, and all interpretation involves such hermeneutical circles.

Westphal proposes that Heidegger's epistemology is a revised Kantianism. It is Kantian in that it stresses the role of the a priori in all cognition; nothing is simply given, in that every cognitive act presupposes a prior understanding of the matter at hand. It is revised Kantianism in that the a priori elements that affect cognition are not universal or final, as were Kant's forms and categories. It is important to stress, however, that the lack of universality and finality do not make the hermeneutic circle vicious for Heidegger. On the contrary, the circular structure of interpretation makes knowledge possible.

Suppose we call the position that all data is theory-laden "theoretical holism." Heidegger's holism is theoretical, but pragmatic and affective as well. First, all knowledge at the level of assertion, or predicative judgment, is founded on a more basic kind of interpretation that expresses itself in actions rather than words. Our concerned involvement with things in the world, for example picking up a suitable tool or avoiding an angry bee, manifests a level of interpretation from which predication is a severe abstraction. Second, Heidegger stresses the function of passion or mood as an a priori condition of theoretical knowledge. Rather than interfering with thought, mood makes it possible for our thought to be directed toward anything at all. Once directed, predicative judgment again constitutes an abstraction from what is presented more fully in moods; a value-laden thing, "ready-to-hand."

Accordingly, Heidegger rejects the Enlightenment privileging of theory over practice and understanding over passion. Rather, theoretical understanding depends on practical understanding, which in turn rests on affective understanding. Gadamer continues this critique by attacking modernity's "prejudice against prejudices." Rather than inevitably distorting the truth, the "pre-judgments" inherited from tradition make understanding possible. In this sense, prejudices constitute the contingent and corrigible foundations of knowledge. Such foundations are subject to critique, but only by virtue of further presuppositions not yet subjected to criticism. Westphal ends by considering Derrida's claim that "There is nothing outside the text." On the one hand, this is simply an affirmation of the neo-Kantian claim we have already been discussing: that all knowledge is already interpretation. A second meaning, Westphal argues, is the Hegelian claim that the existence of things is constituted by their relations. More specifically for Derrida, there is no distinction between signs that signify and things that are signified; all reality points beyond itself as a sign for something else.

Note

1   *Unnatural Doubts* (Princeton: Princeton University Press, 1996), p. 114.

Part I

Traditional Problems of Epistemology

Chapter 1

Skepticism

Michael Williams

1. Philosophical Skepticism

Skepticism has been (and remains) a central concern of the theory of knowledge. Indeed, some philosophers think that, without the problem of skepticism, we would not know what to make of the idea of distinctively *philosophical* theories of knowledge.[1] However, a philosopher who thinks along these lines is likely to have in mind a rather special form of skepticism. Let us call it *philosophical skepticism*. Philosophical skepticism has a long history. Indeed, it is almost coeval with systematic philosophy itself.[2]

Skepticism is often associated with incredulity. A skeptic is someone with a skeptical attitude: he questions things (particularly, received opinions); he practices suspension of judgment. If he is uncomfortable with this inability to make up his mind, he will suffer from doubt or uncertainty, often regarded as the skeptic's characteristic state of mind.[3] Call this questioning outlook *practical skepticism*. Philosophical skepticism always involves more than this. Its essential element is a general view about human knowledge. In the broadest terms, the philosophical skeptic holds, or at least finds irrefutable, the view that knowledge is *impossible*.[4] Let us call this view *theoretical skepticism*. Philosophical skepticism's theoretical component *may* underwrite a skeptical attitude, though it need not. And even when it does, the theoretical and practical components need not be coextensive. Indeed, as we shall see, philosophical skepticism is such a strong form of skepticism that it is far from clear that anyone *could* act on it.

The philosophical skeptic is led to his theoretical skepticism by an array of skeptical arguments. Much theoretical work in epistemology is centered on coming to terms with these arguments: explaining how they go wrong, if they do, or where we are left, if they do not. Not that the mere existence of skeptical arguments creates a problem: one can argue for just about anything, but one's arguments might be in various ways unappealing. They might commit logical errors or depend on premises that nobody is tempted to accept. However, the best skeptical arguments are not like that. Not only do they display no obvious logical flaws, they seem to involve only the simplest and most mundane considerations. They appear to be highly "natural" or "intuitive." This apparent intuitiveness is crucial to skepticism's being such an intractable problem. If skeptical arguments were obviously dependent on controversial or implausible theoretical ideas, skepticism would not be a surprising verdict on our aspirations to knowledge but simply a consequence of some regrettable, theoretical missteps. Perhaps in the end it is. But if so, this will take some showing.

Not even powerful intuitive arguments for skepticism would present us with a problem if we were inclined to welcome their conclusions. There are forms of skepticism that a lot of us find congenial. Thus, according to one common definition, skepticism is the opposite of dogmatism. If we understand "dogmatism" in our current way, as indicating a blind adherence to a fixed set of beliefs, then some degree of skepticism is an essential component of any rational outlook. A related – and comparably benign – form of skepticism is indicated by the common contrast between skepticism and credulity. To be a skeptic, in this sense of "skeptic," is to take a tough-minded attitude towards standards of evidence and, as a result, to find oneself dubious about various commonly accepted claims. The skeptically minded person is unlikely to believe, on the basis of reports in the tabloid press, that every year hundreds of people are abducted by visitors from outer space. If this were all it meant to be "skeptical," it would be a good thing if some people were more skeptical than they are. However, two features of philosophical skepticism make it very different from such everyday "skeptical" outlooks.

The first has to do with its *strength*. The most interesting skeptical arguments do not seem to depend on imposing high standards for knowledge or justification. The skepticism they imply is *radical*. The radical skeptic is not someone who concedes that we have all kinds of good reasons for what we believe, though those reasons do not quite measure up to the standards required by genuine knowledge: radical skepticism raises the question of whether we ever have the slightest reason for believing one thing rather than another. We should beware, therefore, of reading too much into the claim that skepticism questions the possibility of *knowledge*. While most philosophers have taken knowledge to be true belief that is appropriately justified, they have agreed that not just any degree of justification, however slight, is sufficient for knowledge. Indeed, it is widely accepted today that even strong justifications can sometimes fail to yield knowledge.[5] If this is right, there are two ways of denying the possibility of knowledge. One way is to concede that we are often justified in believing this or that while denying that our justifications ever yield knowledge, properly so-called. Another, and much stronger skeptical thesis, is that we never even get to the point of justified belief, never mind whether our justifications are sufficient for knowledge, in some more restricted sense. This stronger thesis is radical skepticism.

It is particularly important to bear this distinction in mind because of the long philosophical tradition that connects knowledge with some kind of certainty. For large areas of inquiry – and perhaps for all – it is certainly possible to be dubious about claims to certainty. This could be thought of as a form of skepticism: indeed, in times when claims to certainty were taken very seriously indeed, it was often the important form of skepticism. However, it is not radical skepticism and, today, is perhaps better thought of as fallibilism, not skepticism at all. Historically, the skeptical tradition has played a crucial role in encouraging fallibilist epistemologies. This is much its credit. But to be problematic today, skepticism has to take a stronger form than this. In due course, we shall investigate the considerations that encourage philosophers to move from fallibilism to radical skepticism.

The second crucial feature of philosophical skepticism concerns its *scope*: the philosophical skeptic's negative verdict on human knowledge is highly general. The generality of the philosophical skeptic's theoretical skepticism explains why he formulates his challenge in terms of the *possibility* of knowledge. The philosophical skeptic does not hold merely that we *in fact* know a good deal less than we like to think (which is probably true) but rather that aspiring to knowledge – either everywhere or with respect to certain very broad domains of fact – is *inherently* problematic. The concern is not just that we *don't* know all that much (if anything) but that we *can't*. This challenge cannot be met by paying more attention or working longer hours. The strength and scope of philosophical skepticism are connected with the simplicity and intuitiveness of skeptical arguments, which are radical and general because they (apparently) exploit only "lowest common denominator" features of knowledge.

We can now see more clearly why philosophical skepticism need not have a practical component. Philosophical skepticism implies that, rationally speaking, we can believe anything or nothing. As Bertrand Russell once put it, the man who believes he is a boiled egg differs from the rest of us only by being in a minority. This brings out the enormous distance between philosophical skepticism and what is often thought of as a skeptical cast of mind. The ordinary (unphilosophical) skeptic typically thinks, not that the quest for knowledge is doomed from the outset, but rather that most peoples' standards of credibility are too low or too laxly applied. He will suspect that what are often advanced as items of knowledge are really just opinions held for no good reason at all. In consequence, his skepticism will be *demanding* and *selective*. But philosophical skepticism, as radical and general, undermines the very epistemological distinctions on which everyday skepticism depends. Accordingly, it is not simply different from but precludes skepticism of the ordinary kind.

Someone might object that the very extravagance of the philosophical skeptic's theoretical skepticism disqualifies it as a serious problem. As Hume put it, skeptical arguments "admit of no refutation but produce no conviction": so why waste time trying to refute a position which no one is able to take seriously? Certainly, we can treat skepticism as one of those theoretical problems that we do not have to solve for immediate practical purposes. But to anyone with a reflective turn of mind, there is something very unsatisfying in letting this be the last word on the subject. If theoretical skepticism is correct, our urge to believe far outstrips our ability to rationalize or justify: there are things that we simply cannot doubt but which we cannot defend. According to Hume – and various influential philosophers today – our everyday beliefs and epistemological attitudes cannot be reconciled with the (inevitably skeptical) results of philosophical reflection upon them. In everyday life, we operate effortlessly with various invidious (and important) distinctions. But when we step back to examine them, they blur and finally vanish. This paradoxical state of affairs cries out for further investigation.[6]

I said at the outset that, for many philosophers, the task of coming to terms with philosophical skepticism defines the theory of knowledge as a distinctively philosophical undertaking. However, there are others, notably Chisholm and his followers, who resist linking epistemology so closely with skeptical problems. The aim of epistemology, they say, is not to "refute the skeptic" but to construct an "analytic science of evidence" or "to show how knowledge is possible, given that it is possible." There is less at stake here than meets the eye, and our discussion of philosophical skepticism shows why. To make "refuting the skeptic" the central task of epistemology is not to imply that there are skeptics who need to be shown the error of their ways. The problem is that there are powerful and seemingly intuitive arguments for disastrously skeptical conclusions. We do not need to be in the market for these conclusions to take an interest in the arguments. Our interest in such arguments might be purely methodological: by seeing how such arguments go astray, we will learn something about knowledge. Thus we find that, in pursuing his science of evidence, Chisholm pushes questions of justification much harder than they would normally be pushed: that is, he proceeds as if he were arguing with a determined skeptic. Similarly with the project of showing how knowledge is possible: we understand what is involved in this only because there are powerful arguments for the conclusion that knowledge is impossible.[7]

To sum up, philosophical skepticism is a problem, demanding a theoretical response, because:

- Philosophical skepticism involves a theoretical component, a general view about human knowledge or human cognitive capacities.
- The arguments that support this view are "natural" or "intuitive" in the sense of not obviously dependent on contentious theoretical ideas. Thus they cannot be dismissed out of hand.
- But philosophical skepticism is unpalatable because of its strength and scope. So we cannot accept their conclusions either.

This said, we can turn to the arguments themselves.

2. Agrippa's Trilemma

There are two basic families of skeptical arguments, which I shall label "Agrippan" and "Cartesian." The Agrippan family is very ancient, going back to the classical Greek skeptics. I shall begin with it (but for theoretical reasons and not simply on account of its antiquity).[8]

Suppose I make a claim – any claim. You can ask me whether what I have said is something that I am just assuming to be true or whether I know it to be the case. If I reply that it is something I know, you are entitled to ask me *how* I know. I will therefore have to cite something in support of my claim: my evidence, my credentials, something. But now the question can be renewed: is whatever I cite in defense of my original claim something that I am just assuming or something that I know? If the former, it will not do the job required of it: you can't base knowledge on a mere assumption. But if the latter, it will in turn need to be backed up, and so on.

Obviously, in practice attempts to provide justification come to a halt. But how? The skeptic will say that we just run out of ideas: either we have nothing to say, or we find ourselves going back over old ground. As an implied claim to knowledge, every statement I make invites a new challenge; and in the face of these constantly renewed challenges, I can do only one of three things:

1. Keep trying to think of something new to say – i.e. embark on an infinite regress.
2. At some point, refuse to answer – i.e. make a dogmatic assumption.
3. At some point, repeat something I have already said – i.e. reason in a circle.

None of these gives us what we want.

We can call this set of options "Agrippa's Trilemma" after the ancient skeptic who seems first to have given it clear articulation. With options 2 and 3, the skeptic seems on strong ground. Surely, statements made in justification of an initial claim must themselves be justified: you can't base justifications on mere assumptions. So 2 is a dead letter. Equally, reasoning in a circle is a paradigmatically poor sort of reasoning: how can a statement support *itself*? To suppose that it could embodies a kind of pragmatic inconsistency, treating the same statement as needing support (in its role as conclusion) and as already in order (in its role as premise). So 3 is a dead letter too. However, we might wonder whether option 1 is so bad. To be sure, new claims can lead to new questions: but what is so terrible about that? This misses the skeptic's point, which is that the regress is *vicious*. The skeptic is not saying simply that justifications *can* always be questioned further, though they may be acceptable for the time being. His conclusion is rather that no claim is *ever* justified – to the slightest degree – unless, *per impossibile*, we first run through an infinite series of prior justifications. Option 1, then, fares no better than the others. The conclusion seems to be that justification is a complete illusion.

Agrippa's trilemma is commonly referred to as the problem of the regress of justification. I am not sure that this is such a good idea. For one thing, the trilemma represents an argumentative strategy, rather than a single problem. Thus there are many variations on it, depending on which of the unsatisfactory options gets emphasized. Here is an example. It is a version of what the ancient skeptics thought of as the "problem of the criterion": i.e. the problem of determining what should be the standard or method ("criterion") for distinguishing between genuine knowledge and mere opinion. Imagine a debate between a devout religious believer, who puts his faith in Divine revelation, and someone with a thoroughgoing scientific outlook, who thinks that all hypotheses need to be verified (or falsified) by systematic research involving observation and experiment. Two such opponents may well find themselves disagreeing, not just over particular facts, but over how the facts are to be determined. And how is such a disagreement to be resolved? By appeal to Divine revelation? By systematic observation? Some third way? (What would that be?) Here the danger of regress seems remote, but that of dogmatism or circularity very real. The fact that there are many ways of exploiting the Agrippan strategy is one reason for emphasizing the trilemma, which lies at the heart of them all. There is another, even more important, which we shall come to in due course.

Philosophical skepticism, according to my account, is intuitive, radical, and general. As we have just seen, the Agrippan strategy is not wholly presuppositionless: it exploits the idea that knowing differs from merely assuming or surmising and that this difference has something to do with an ability to back up or justify whatever can properly be said to be known. But this seems to be one of those lowest common denominator ideas that just about everyone who takes the concept of knowledge seriously is ready to concede. So far, so good.

Because the argument is intuitive, the skepticism it promotes is radical. Since the argument appears not to be committed to any particular view about what "back up" or "justification" consist in, it does not depend on setting high standards for knowledge. Its conclusion, therefore, is not that no one ever *really* knows anything, where really knowing means, say, being able to prove beyond a shadow of a doubt. The conclusion is that no one ever has the slightest reason to accept one thing rather than another. Historically, to be sure, the argument emerged when the dominant conception of knowledge linked knowledge with rational certainty. But nothing in the argument itself turns on that link. Accordingly, we cannot avoid the problem simply by opting for a more relaxed, fallibilist idea of knowledge.[9]

Generality is a little more problematic. Everyone will have experienced some arguments that run into an Agrippan dead end: for example disputes that engage deep political differences sometimes just get into a rut, where the parties end up shouting at each other, when not going round in circles. But does the problem arise only with respect to claims that are already controversial? It is possible that the ancient skeptics saw things this way. Sextus Empiricus presents the skeptical trilemma as three of Agrippa's "Five Modes of Suspension," the other two being "Discrepancy" and "Relativity." This suggests that the problem of justification arises only with respect to claims over which there is actual disagreement ("discrepancy") or which seem to reflect a particular perspective ("relativity"). Read this way, it is not clear how general a form of skepticism the Agrippan argument promotes.[10]

Having posed the Agrippan problem in terms of claims, challenges, and responses, I may have encouraged such a reading myself. On reflection, however, it seems that the Agrippan argument applies not just to things that anyone would agree are hard to know about but to anything whatsoever, no matter how obvious. If I claim to know something – that it is not just my opinion – it seems reasonable to ask how I know. If this is so, nothing of importance turns on the existence of challenges or challengers, or so the argument suggests. Moreover, the problem of justification is not confined to the context of public discussion. If, in a reflective moment, I take any belief I happen to hold and ask myself why I hold it, I am off and running. So the problem does not just concern public argumentation, or admittedly controversial opinions, but justified belief in general, whether actually challenged or not. Certainly, this is how the challenge of Agrippan skepticism is generally understood today.

3. Theoretical Responses

If the skeptic is right, *all* so-called knowledge is groundless belief. Supposing we decide not to throw in the towel right away, what are our choices? Assuming that requests for justification have to come to an end somewhere, we seem to have two, each defining a fundamental type of epistemological theory. This shows how important skeptical arguments are for the very idea of there being distinctively *philosophical* theories of knowledge: the ways in which such arguments can be met define the space of theoretical options.

One possible exit from the regress of justification would be to identify beliefs or judgments that bring requests for justification to a halt because, though they are not mere assumptions, they do not require, or perhaps even admit of, further justification. The quest for such "basic" beliefs is characteristic of *foundational theories* of knowledge and justification. There are many versions of foundationalism. They differ with respect to what beliefs they take to be basic as well as in their accounts of what being basic consists in. But they all share the idea of a privileged class of beliefs, the members of which are justified – rationally credible – without support from further beliefs. The regress comes to an end because some beliefs or judgments are intrinsically credible.

Of course, it is all very well to say that, if knowledge is to be possible, there *must* be such beliefs. But this does not mean that there *are* any. For foundationalism to look like a live option, we need some plausible examples of intrinsic credibility. One place we might locate epistemologically basic beliefs is in the realm of *a priori* knowledge, most obviously in our knowledge of elementary mathematical facts, such as "2 + 2 = 4." If you understand what it means to say that 2 + 2 = 4, you see that it is true. To say of such an elementary mathematical proposition, "I know what it means, it just doesn't seem very plausible to me" would be (at best) a bad joke. Or take sensations, such as pain. If you are in pain, you *just know* it. The question "How do you know?" has no clear application here. It is no surprise, then, that mathematics and immediate experience have both figured prominently in discussions of the foundational approach to the theory of knowledge.

Nevertheless, although the foundationalism is not obviously hopeless, it is difficult to develop foundational ideas in a fully convincing way. In particular, it is difficult to explain just how basic beliefs deserve their privileged status. Not even elementary mathematical judgments seem to be credible all by themselves: to grasp them at all, it seems, we need some understanding of a whole system of arithmetic. As for immediate experience, it cannot be the sensations themselves that constitute the foundations of knowledge. Lacking propositional content, sensations cannot stand in logical relations to beliefs and so can nether support nor falsify beliefs. But if we identify the foundations of knowledge with some type of judgment, we seem forced to acknowledge that, where there is description, there is the possibility of misdescription. If we are dealing with judgments that are suitably modest – judgments about how things look to me now, for example – it may well be that mistakes are rare. But if the judgments owe their credibility to our general reliability in making them, we have given up on the idea of their being intrinsically credible. We have explained their credibility in a way that invites reapplication of Agrippa's fatal trilemma.

Even if this difficulty could be resolved, it is not clear that much progress would have been made. No foundationalist has ever thought that just any belief can be plausibly represented as intrinsically credible. Even if there are such beliefs, they will form a severely restricted class. The burden then falls squarely on the foundationalist to show that his supposed foundations are adequate to support a workably extensive body of justified belief. This is no easy task, but failure to carry it through will commit the foundationalist to an extensive form of theoretical skepticism. Indeed, the foundationalist seems to be caught in a dilemma: the narrower his basis, the harder it will be to argue convincingly for its adequacy; but the broader he makes it, the harder it will be to defend the claim that the beliefs constituting it are genuinely foundational. Proponents of foundationalism tend to find themselves squeezed between the opposing requirements of security and adequacy.

Suppose, then, that we abandon the quest for basic beliefs, as many philosophers have come to believe that we should: the only remaining way of avoiding a skeptical conclusion seems to be to argue that circular reasoning isn't as bad as it looks. Surprisingly, perhaps, this idea too can be made to seem more promising than it first sounds. Philosophers attracted to it point out that our beliefs are not just a grab-bag of unrelated opinions. Rather, our beliefs about the world constitute an extensive and complicated *system*. Thus the fundamental idea behind *coherence theories* of knowledge and justification is that the members of such a system can give each other *mutual* support. Our beliefs are justified, not because they rest on a foundation, but because they are systematically interconnected.

Naturally, coherence has to be more than logical consistency or else, as critics have complained, any arbitrary belief could be "justified" by surrounding it with equally arbitrary beliefs that happen to be consistent with it. Coherence theorists typically deal with this problem by saying that justification depends on our belief-system's "hanging together" theoretically: coherence is explanatory coherence. Thus whereas foundational theories of justification tend to be atomistic – particular basic beliefs are credible all on their own, and they justify other particular non-basic beliefs – coherence theories are *radically holistic*. Not only are beliefs never justified singly (which I think is probably true), whether a particular belief is justified depends on how it fits into a whole system of beliefs (a much more dubious proposition).

This difference notwithstanding, it is far from clear that the coherence theory is really an alternative to rather than a variant of the foundations theory. First of all, such theories do not so much abolish the foundationalist appeal to epistemic privilege as relocate it: from particular beliefs to general criteria of "coherence," assumed to be truth-conducive.[11] Secondly, notice that to be able actually to produce a coherentist justification of any of our beliefs, we have to presuppose that we have some grasp of our whole system of belief: what beliefs in contains and how they are logically interconnected. But how is this presupposition to be justified? One recent theorist refers to the need to grant a "doxastic presumption." The skeptic is likely to reply that "assumption" would be a better word. Or are our doxastic judgments intrinsically credible, in which case we revert to the problems of foundationalism.[12]

Like foundationalism, the coherence theory is also in danger of encouraging skepticism. Suppose we grant the "doxastic presumption" to the extent that a person's beliefs about his beliefs are *prima facie* justified: we must still remember the coherence theory's commitment to radical holism. A given belief's being justified depends on its fitting in with a whole system of beliefs. To imagine that any of us has this kind of grasp of his or her beliefs and their endless logical interconnections is to assume an impossibly idealized view of our degree of cognitive self-awareness. To the extent that justification depends on such radically holistic considerations, none of us knows whether anything he or she believes is justified. Minimally, the skeptic triumphs one level up.[13]

In mentioning these problems facing foundational and coherence theories of justification, I have barely scratched the surface of the difficult theoretical issues that such theories raise. But I hope I have said enough to reinforce an earlier point about Agrippa's trilemma: that we should not think of it as "the regress problem." If we think of it this way, overstressing the need to avoid falling foul of a vicious regress, we will tend to assume that one of the remaining options *must* be defensible, so that some version of either foundationalism or coherentism *must* be correct. But none of this can be assumed. The Agrippan problem is to avoid the regress without lapsing into circularity or brute assumption. Although I cannot argue the case in detail here, it is my belief that no extant version of either foundationalism or the coherence theory comes close to meeting this demand.[14] This is why, in its recent history, epistemology has tended to swing between the twin poles of foundationalism and coherentism. Advocates of both strategies possess devastating critical weapons to deploy against their opponents. As a contemporary philosopher has remarked, we need to get off the seesaw.[15]

4. The External World

Whereas the family of Agrippan arguments goes back to the classical Greek skeptics, our next problem receives its first clear formulation in the writings of Descartes, around 350 years ago.[16] Despite the quantity of ink spilled over it, there is still no agreed solution.

We all take it for granted that we learn what is going on in our surroundings by way of our senses. Right now, I am sitting at a desk, looking at a computer monitor. How do I know? I can see that I am. But how do our senses convey this kind of information? The answer seems to be: they produce conscious awareness of the objects and events that we encounter. We are the subjects of a constantly changing stream of conscious experience: visual, tactile, olfactory, and so on. However, reflection on these seemingly obvious facts can lead to strange conclusions. We conceive our experience of the world as the end product of a rather complex chain of events. Take the case of visual experience: light of a certain wavelength is reflected off the surface of an object; it is focused on my retinae, where it sets off a certain pattern of neural excitation; impulses from the retinal neurons combine to produce a further pattern of firing in my optic nerve and, eventually, in the occipital region of my cerebral cortex; and the result is that I am aware of a red object, say an apple, a few feet in front of me. It seems to be a consequence of this picture, however, that the same result could in principle be produced by intervention at several points in the chain. And there do seem to be odd cases of illusions produced in just this way. In "phantom limb" cases, patients feel pain in limbs that have been amputated and so are no longer there. Presumably, the nerve impulses reaching the brain are the same as they would have been if they had originated in a more normal way. Descartes asks, in effect, the following question: if our awareness of the world is the end result of a complicated chain of events, and if the same result could in principle be produced in several different ways, why are we so sure that it is produced one way rather than another?

He presses this question by way of two vivid examples. The first appeals to the fact that we have dreams. Dreams are conscious experiences that we have while we are asleep. They do not correspond in any reliable way to ongoing events in our surroundings and so do not yield knowledge of those surroundings. (Presumably, they result from spontaneous brain activity.) But, Descartes suggests, there is no conscious experience that we have while awake that could not, in principle, be faithfully mimicked by a suitably vivid dream. So how do I know that I am not dreaming right now? How do I know that I am not dreaming all the time? We might say: I can pinch myself. But maybe that is just part of the dream. In fact, it seems that any test I could propose might just be part of the dream.

Descartes does not think that the dreaming argument pushes skepticism to the limit. He thinks that the argument raises a problem about how I know particular facts about my immediate surroundings but that it leaves my general conception of the world largely untouched. To be sure, strange things happen in dreams. Nevertheless, he thinks, even in the strangest experiences the imagination only produces unfamiliar combinations of familiar elements. To extend the argument, then, Descartes introduces his famous thought experiment of the Evil Deceiver. Imagine an all-powerful being bent on deceiving me. This being artificially induces in me all my experiences of the world. But my experiences bear no relation to reality. Not merely is the world, as it is in reality, nothing like the way I experience it to be, perhaps there is no "external world" at all, or at least no world of physical objects. What gives me the right to be so sure that there is?

A popular contemporary variation on Descartes's fantasy is the "brain in a vat" problem. Suppose that I were to be abducted by aliens, whose technological capabilities are somewhat in advance of our own. They capture me while I am asleep, drug me, and remove my brain, which they keep alive in a vat of nutrients. But they also implant microelectrodes in all the afferent nerve pathways going to my brain; and these electrodes are controlled by a supercomputer so as to exactly mimic the pattern of nerve-firing that would be produced if, say, I were sitting at a desk, looking at a computer screen and amusing myself with the thought of being abducted by aliens. . . . This story seems perfectly intelligible. Some readers may recall an episode of the television series, *Star Trek*, which is based on pretty much this idea. The original commander of the starship *Enterprise*, who has been horribly injured in an accident, emigrates to a planet whose inhabitants have mastered the technology of "virtual reality," where he can live the "life" that circumstances have robbed him of. There is also a film in which a company offers customers virtual reality holidays in the imaginary environment of their choice, and in which the hero ends up wondering when he is experiencing genuine, nonvirtual reality and when he isn't. And that of course is the question: how can he know? Indeed, how do *I* know that I am not a brain in a vat right now? We might even say that I *am* a brain in a vat, kept alive by circulating nutrients: for what, after all, is my skull? So perhaps the question should be, how do I know what kind of vat I am in? It is not easy to say, since anything that I experience could be part of the illusion.

Call these odd stories, like that of perpetual dreaming, the Evil Deceiver, or the brain in a vat, "skeptical hypotheses." Why "skeptical," given that no one actually believes them and there is no reason why anyone should? Because they seem to show that there are endlessly many ways that the world might be, even though my experience of it remains unchanged. Accordingly, my experience, though in the end all I have to go on, fails to provide an adequate basis for favoring my actual system of beliefs over alternatives which seem logically just as coherent. Someone will object: coherent maybe, but ludicrously far-fetched. However, what does "far-fetched" mean here, other than "different from what I ordinarily believe"? Again, it starts to look as though my beliefs about the world, however unshakable in practice, are, from a theoretical point of view, oddly groundless: *mere* beliefs rather than genuine knowledge.

5. Further Problems

The problem of our knowledge of the external world establishes a pattern for a variety of skeptical arguments. This is why I call them all "Cartesian" arguments, even though not all of them were recognized by Descartes himself.

Take our supposed knowledge of the thoughts and experiences of people other than ourselves. The starting point here is the essential *privacy* of experience. We can make judgments about the thoughts and experiences of others, but the only thoughts and experiences we can literally *have* are our own. A politician may say "I feel your pain." But he doesn't literally feel *your* pain: even if he is speaking truthfully, he means that it pains him to see that you are pained. When we form beliefs about what other people think or feel, then, all we have to go on is their outward behavior, including of course their speech: I see you wince or grimace; I hear you groan; I conclude that you are hurting. The inference is automatic, but does it have any rational basis? It seems not. A claim about your experiences is not logically implied by any claim about your outward behavior. It is a logical possibility, however remote, that your inner experiences are qualitatively entirely different from mine, or that you have no such experiences at all. But neither can I establish inductively that your outward behavior is a reliable indicator of your inner states: I cannot correlate your experiences with your behavior because your behavior is my only clue to your experiences. For all I know, then, *solipsism* – the thought that I am the only person with a conscious inner life, thus the only real *person* at all – may be true.

A similar argument can be constructed with respect to beliefs about the past. After all, our only access to the past is by way of things – records, artifacts, and so on – that have survived into the present. But what makes such things indicators of how things were in the past? Someone once tried to resolve the tension between geology and the Book of Genesis by suggesting that God created the world in 4004 BC complete with the fossil record. But why go back that far? How do we exclude the possibility that the world sprang into existence five minutes ago, complete with delusive "memories" implanted in the brains of its inhabitants?

What goes for the past goes for the future: this is the problem of induction. Our lives depend on complex expectations about how the world generally works: but the basis of these expectations is our experience of how it has worked up to now. What gives us the right to project these past regularities into the future? As Hume, the first to grasp the problem, observed: it is no contradiction to suppose that the course of Nature is subject to change, so the fact that things have happened a certain way up to now is no logical guarantee that they will continue to do so. But we cannot appeal to inductive inference here either, since the validity of induction, the practice of projecting known regularities into new situations, is the very thing in question. Earlier, and for the sake of argument, we allowed induction to be a defensible form of inference. This concession can now be withdrawn.

In developing these arguments, the point is not necessarily to suggest that anyone does or should accept skeptical conclusions. The question is whether there is any *reason* to ignore them? Or is it just – as Hume suggested – that skeptical worries are ignored, without reason? And if this is all we can say, aren't we admitting that skepticism is at least theoretically correct: that what we like to think of as knowledge is really, in the end, just assumption, however psychologically "natural" some of our assumptions may be? Some recent writers have been tempted to agree with Hume here. But I think that this is giving up too soon.[17]

6. More Theoretical Responses

Cartesian skeptical arguments go through four stages. I shall illustrate them using the problem of the external world, but their analogues for other skeptical problems are easily derived. They are:

1. Facts about the external world are the not the sort of thing that we "just know." Our knowledge of the external world is "inferential," in the sense that beliefs about the external world will amount to knowledge only to the extent that they can be justified by appropriate evidence. This evidence is provided by perceptual experience: that is to say, by how things look, sound, small, taste, and feel to us.
2. There is no deductive connection between our evidence and our desired conclusions. Our experiential beliefs never logically entail anything about the external world.
3. But there is no defensible inductive inference to bridge the gap either.
4. In consequence, there is no way to justify any belief about the external world, even that such a world exists.[18]

As in the case of Agrippan skepticism, the Cartesian pattern of argument appears to define the space of theoretical options available by way of response.

The first possibility is to deny the evidential gap. According to this "direct realism" facts about the external world are the sort of thing we just know. I know that there is a computer screen in front of me because I can see that there is: it isn't a matter of inference. But isn't it? After all, the skeptic will say, if I were a brain in a vat I would be every bit as confident that I could "just see" how things are in the world and yet I would be entirely deluded. The point is even clearer with respect to other minds and the past. We don't directly experience someone else's thoughts and experiences; nor can we summon up historical events for contemporary inspection. Furthermore, our everyday confidence in our perceptual abilities is not absolute: we believe ourselves to be reliable observers in some circumstances but not in others. This reflects a rather complex body of beliefs about ourselves and our environment: for example, what external conditions offer favorable viewing conditions for creatures like us. But this means that our ordinary, unreflective confidence in our perceptual judgments does not justify our knowledge of the external world: it takes such knowledge for granted.

Moving to the second stage of the argument, perhaps we were too hasty in conceding that there are no deductive links between experiential and worldly knowledge. Thus, according to *phenomenalism*, talk about the physical world is really just shorthand for logically complex claims about sensory experiences: claims about the experiences we do or, in various conditions, would have. In the context of our problem of other minds, *logical behaviorism* is the view that talk about mental states is a comparable way of talking about observable behavior. Given views like this, there is (allegedly) no unbridgeable gulf between, say, beliefs about the external world and the sensory evidence on which they ultimately rest.

Few philosophers, if any, these days are sanguine about actually translating talk about physical objects into talk about sensations. The problem is that no single statement about the external world seems to have any particular experiential consequences: how an object does or would appear seems to depend on indefinitely many further facts about the circumstances in which it is perceived.[19] Similar problems bedevil logical behaviorism. But these technical difficulties are perhaps not, in the end, the main reason for distrusting reductionist strategies. The fact is that, our beliefs about the external world are not, commonsensically speaking, just beliefs about what experiences we would have if . . . , any more than my views about your feelings are just views about what external actions you are performing or would perform in such and such circumstances. The external world is a world that exists and would exist whether or not there are or were human beings to experience it. This is the burden of common-sense *realism*, and no response to skepticism that does not respect it counts as salvaging our pre-theoretical aspirations to knowledge of the world. Thus, when the skeptic says that we have no knowledge of external reality, only of our own experiences, to be told that "external reality" is another way of describing patterns in our experiences seems less a refutation of skepticism than another way of making the skeptic's point.[20]

Philosophers who reject strict reductionism may still challenge the second step in the Cartesian strategy. Though no physical-object statements can be translated into experiential statements, they may say, it nevertheless belongs to the meaning of a physical-object statement that certain experiences count for or against it. It is part of the "logic" of such statements to be responsive to experiential "criteria." However, not only are many philosophers today dubious about such appeals to meaning, skeptical thought experiments seem to show that there is no particular a priori connection between appearances and reality, even of this weaker sort. If this is so, criterial theories are as much doomed as strict reductionism.

The remaining option seems to be to take issue with the third stage. Perhaps the skeptic's error is that he underestimates the resources of inductive inference. His argument identifies induction with extrapolation from observed correlations and he is quite right to point out that this type of induction is no help with the problems in hand. But there are other forms of inductive inference, notably what is sometimes called "inference to the best explanation." Thus we (justifiably) accept our common-sense beliefs about the external world because the existence of such a world offers the best explanation of certain features of our experience, which Hume called its "constancy and coherence." Our experience is not a phantasmagoria, a constant flux of colors, shapes, and sounds. Rather, experience presents us with what is apparently a world of stable objects, acting in predictable ways. The best explanation of this is that experience really does arise from our interaction with such a world. Descartes's Deceiver hypothesis, even if logically coherent, is thin and underdescribed, compared with our usual account of how experience arises. Accordingly, it is a worse explanation and may be justifiably dismissed.

There is something to this suggestion: skeptical hypotheses are thin and underdescribed. Nevertheless, it faces serious difficulties. First of all, in assuming the existence of stable patterns, it assumes a solution to the traditional problem of induction. My experience may have been stable enough up to now (assuming that my memory is reliable, which, given the problem of the past, is itself questionable); but this stability could disappear at any moment: for example, if the Evil Deceiver or the vat-experimenters decide to give me a shock. Secondly, it is not obvious that experience *is* coherent in the required sense. Certainly, there are all kinds of world-dependent experiential regularities: regularities in how external things appear under relevantly similar conditions of perception. But if we take ourselves to have knowledge of regularities of this sort, we are of course taking ourselves to be already in possession of extensive knowledge of the external world. What our "explanationist" justification of belief in the external world must presuppose, then, is that there are *purely experiential* regularities, of which the "hypothesis" of the external world is the best explanation. The problem is that, at this level of description, the flow of experience is disrupted by every blink of the eye and turn of the head. If we cannot allow for changes in the observer and the environment, it is wholly unclear whether his "experience" is stable or predictable at all.[21]

If all this is right, we end up in the same position with respect to Cartesian skepticism as we did in the Agrippan case. We find ourselves with a restricted range of theoretical options, none of which is really satisfactory. Again, we need a new approach.

7. Diagnostic Approaches to Skepticism

The antiskeptical strategies considered so far have all been *direct*. They take skeptical arguments at fact value, choosing as a point of attack some acknowledged premise or premises. By contrast, *diagnostic* responses treat skeptical arguments as deeply misleading. There are two broad diagnostic strategies, *therapeutic* and *theoretical*.

Therapeutic diagnosis treats skeptical problems as *pseudo-problems* generated by misuses or misunderstandings of language. First impressions notwithstanding, skeptical claims and arguments are less than fully intelligible. The problem is, we seem to understand such things well enough to appreciate how they generate a space of epistemological theories, structured by the possible forms of direct response. To philosophers impressed by skeptical arguments, it seems clearer that they do understand skeptical claims than that the views about meaning invoked to show otherwise are true.

Theoretical diagnosis treats skeptical arguments as misleading in a different way. The theoretical diagnostician suspects the skeptic of trading on theoretical commitments that he either does not acknowledge or tries to pass off as commonsense platitudes. The apparent simplicity and intuitiveness of skeptical arguments is a mask for contentious epistemological ideas.

Making good on this suspicion offers two sorts of gain. In the first place, skeptical problems gain an enormous dialectical advantage from their aura of naturalness, which makes them seem far more compelling than the arcane theories advanced to solve them. A convincing theoretical diagnosis will cancel this advantage. At the same time, it will deepen our understanding of skeptical problems and arguments by locating them in the network of theoretical ideas that generates both skepticism and the space of accepted theoretical responses. If these ideas can be argued to be optional, the need to choose between skepticism and one or other traditional theory of knowledge will lapse.[22]

8. Skeptical Commitments

Agrippa's trilemma seems to show that any attempt to justify a claim or belief leads to an infinite regress of supporting claims that can be cut off only either by making a brute assumption or by reasoning in a circle. The skeptic concludes that nothing we believe can ever really be justified.

Epistemological concepts, like that of justification, are not straightforwardly descriptive but evaluative or normative: to concede justification is to ascribe to a belief or a believer a particular normative status.[23] But justificational status has two dimensions. *Personal justification* has to do with whether, in holding a given belief, I am being epistemically responsible. For example, have I overlooked difficulties that I ought to have taken account of? *Evidential justification*, or groundedness, has to do with whether my belief is supported by adequate grounds: do I hold my belief on a basis that makes it likely to be true? Knowledge, as also justification *simpliciter*, requires justification along both dimensions. The issue between the skeptic and his opponent concerns the relation between them.

A view of this relation that has attracted many philosophers is that epistemically responsible believing is always and everywhere believing on the basis of adequate evidence. From this standpoint, personal justification is subject to the *Prior Grounding Requirement*. This *evidentialist bias* has two aspects. The first is the *dependence thesis*: the uniform subordination of personal to evidential justification. The second is *internalism*, according to which a person's "evidence" for a given belief is evidence in the strong sense: further beliefs – or if not beliefs, some other personal cognitive state – in virtue of which he holds the belief in question and which he can cite on demand. A person's belief may have been formed by a method that is *in fact* reliable. It may even have been the result of a process that, in the circumstances, ensures that it is true. But this does not make it "grounded." This form of grounding, in which a person is not necessarily aware of the factors that make his belief "truth-reliable," is *externalist*. The skeptic takes the Prior Grounding Requirement to exclude externalist validation.

The Agrippan argument must presuppose this conception of justification, *if it is to amount to an argument for radical skepticism*. The radically skeptical conclusion is that no one is ever justified, even to the slightest degree, in believing one thing rather than another. This is personal justification. What the skeptic argues, however, is that there are limits to our capacity to *give reasons* or *cite evidence*. This is a point about evidential justification. The skeptic tacitly relies on the Prior Grounding Requirement to get from what he argues to what he concludes. The skeptic must presuppose both that belief is epistemically irresponsible unless it rests on adequate grounds (the Dependence Thesis) and that no one's belief can rest on grounds of which he is unaware (internalism). Nothing less will do the job.

This is not the requirement's only function. It plays a crucial role in the argument itself. The skeptic assumes that, given any belief or claim, the question "How do you know?" or "Why do you believe that?" can *always* reasonably be entered. The skeptic implicitly denies that, if a knowledge-claim is to be reasonably challenged, the challenge itself needs to be motivated by reasons. The skeptic's position is that any claimant or believer with pretensions to epistemic responsibility accepts an unrestricted commitment to demonstrate entitlement to his opinion simply in virtue of entering a claim or holding a belief. Given the Prior Grounding Requirement, this position is entirely reasonable. If responsible believing is always and everywhere believing-on-evidence, the skeptic is entitled to ask for the evidence to be produced. Absent this requirement, however, his procedure is not reasonable at all.

The alternative is to see personal justification as exhibiting a "default and challenge structure."[24] The difference between the two conceptions of justification is like that between legal systems that treat the accused as guilty unless proved innocent and those that do the opposite, granting presumptive innocence and throwing the burden of proof on the accuser.[25] Adopting the second model, epistemic entitlement is the default status of a person's beliefs and assertions. One is entitled to a belief or assertion (personally justified) in the absence of reasons to think that one is *not* so entitled. Call such reasons "defeaters." Defeaters cite reasonable error-possibilities and work in various ways. Nonepistemic defeaters cite evidence that one's assertion is false: this evidence might be purely negative, or it might be positive evidence for the truth of some incompatible claim. Epistemic defeaters give grounds for suspecting that one's belief was acquired in an unreliable or irresponsible way. In the second case, the objector concedes that his interlocutor's claim or belief might be true but denies that it is justified. The types are not exclusive. Skeptical scenarios are meant to work both ways.

The default and challenge conception of epistemic responsibility does not imply that personal justification is completely independent of the ability to give grounds for what one believes. What it rejects, rather, is the idea that a responsible believer's commitment to *providing* grounds is *unrestricted*. As we saw, the Prior Grounding Requirement gives way to a limited *Defense Commitment*. An implicit claim to knowledge or justification involves a commitment to respond to any appropriate challenges that happen to emerge, or to withdraw the claim should no effective defense be available. The crucial difference is that, on this conception of justification, justificational commitments are shared with the challenger. The skeptic no longer enjoys a standing entitlement to demand backup for any and every assertion or belief. Rather, the entitlement to enter a challenge must itself be earned by finding specific reasons for questioning either the truth of a target belief or the claimant's entitlement to hold it.

Rejecting the Prior Grounding Requirement defangs Agrippa's Trilemma. There is no presumption that requests for further justification can be repeated indefinitely. At some point, they are brought to an end by default entitlements. Since these are genuine entitlements, and also subject to the Defense Commitment, they are not mere assumptions. But since they are *default* entitlements, they do not depend on any kind of grounding. In particular, they do not ground themselves, either immediately or indirectly, so the threat of circularity vanishes along with that of vicious regress.

Because default entitlement is always, in a sense, provisional, the default and challenge conception of justification is "skeptical" in the sense of "antidogmatic". But antidogmatism is fallibilism not radical skepticism. It may well be that *any* belief or claim can be challenged, given appropriate stage-setting, but if entitlements to challenges must themselves be earned, there is no possibility of judging our beliefs in the *collective* way that the philosophical skeptic aspires to. This is because a motivated challenge will itself presuppose a large background of default entitlements.

This diagnosis of the Agrippan problem implies that the relationship between personal and evidential justification is multiply *contextual*. In the first place, with respect to maintaining epistemic responsibility, the *existence* of a properly motivated challenge determines whether evidential justification is required *at all* to secure personal justification. In the second place, contextual factors fix the *adequacy conditions* on evidential justification's securing personal justification. Most importantly, they determine what potential defeaters ought to be excluded. These will never amount to every logically possible way of going wrong but will be restricted to a range of relevant alternatives.[26]

So much for personal justification. But for a person to be justified *simpliciter*, his belief must be adequately grounded (whether or not he is aware of its grounds). Here, too, contextual factors come into play. However, the factors involved are not restricted to the dialectical context: facts about the actual situations in which claims are entered or beliefs held are crucial. Thus the "adequate grounds" dimension of justification has a doubly "external" character. Because there is default entitlement, a claimant need not always be aware of the grounds for his belief, in order to be epistemically responsible. But the adequacy of his grounds – whether he is aware of them or not – will depend in part on what real-world possibilities those grounds need to exclude. I say "in part" because standards of adequacy are always standards that we fix in the light of our interests, epistemic and otherwise. This means that, even when considering the objective adequacy of grounds for a belief, questions of epistemic responsibility can never be wholly forgotten.

We must not confuse contextualism with relativism. Contextualism is not the view that epistemic evaluations come with implicit subscripts, so that "justified" really means "justified in context C." A belief is evidentially justified when it is supported by adequate evidence. But standards of adequacy depend on both the worldly and the dialectical environment and can shift with changes in either (and as a result of their interaction). Once-adequate evidence can lose its value in the light of new information, or with changes in our situation. Whether this fact itself has significant skeptical potential is a question we shall come back to.

9. Justification and Truth

What are the sources of traditional epistemology's evidentialist bias? One possibility is a misreading of ordinary justificatory practices. It is certainly true that *to justify* a belief is typically to marshal evidence, offer and defend one's credentials as a reliable judge in the matter in question, explain away apparent counter-evidence, and so on. *Justifying*, in other words, just is grounding, broadly conceived: showing that one's beliefs are likely to be true. But *being* justified is not always a matter of *having gone through* a prior process of justification. What is easy to overlook is that the practice of justifying is only activated by finding oneself in the context of a properly motivated challenge. It is easy to overlook this because claims are often advanced in the face of known problems or objections. Accordingly, since we do not go around stating the obvious, it may well be that, in the case of claims worth making, one does not normally have to wait for challenges to *emerge*, with the result that one's articulated claims are very often *not* justified by default. However, the fact that we often enter claims in the face of standing objections, so that they are entered in a context that automatically triggers the Defense Commitment, should not mislead us into overlooking the connection between the existence of motivated challenges and the obligation to produce positive evidence. Overlooking this connection will lead us to transform the ever-present possibility of contextually appropriate demands for evidence into an unrestricted insistence on grounds, encouraging us to move from fallibilism to radical skepticism.

To accept the Prior Grounding Requirement is to accept the priority of evidential over personal justification, grounding over responsibility. Both traditional foundationalism and the coherence theory make this commitment. This sharing of its unspoken presuppositions is what makes them direct responses to Agrippan skepticism. Contextualism makes the order of dependence go the other way: responsibility takes explanatory priority over grounding.

Traditionalists, whether foundationalists or coherence theorists, will reject this characterization of their common outlook. They will admit that entitlement to make a claim or hold a belief does not always depend on the possession of adequate evidence. In everyday situations, we often allow that a person is "justified" in taking for granted all kinds of things that he lacks the time or resources to investigate. But these are matters of practical exigency and have nothing to do with *epistemic* justification. The essential feature of epistemic justification is that it be *truth-conducive*: to justify a belief is to link it with some feature that increases the likelihood of its being true. An account of justification that does not make this aspect absolutely fundamental is therefore either not an account of epistemic justification at all or it is an account that makes epistemic justification purely dialectical. Either way, contextualism fails utterly as an answer to skepticism.

While contextualism *does* prioritize responsibility, it does *not* treat justification as purely dialectical. A contextualist can allow that knowledge and justification require both epistemic responsibility and adequate grounding. But rejecting the Prior Grounding Requirement allows him to give the grounding condition on knowledge and justification an *externalist* reading. A belief is adequately grounded when it is formed by a method that is in fact reliable: responsibility demands that we be able to demonstrate reliability only if reasons emerge for suspecting *unreliability*. However, although we do not have to demonstrate reliability to be entitled to make a knowledge-claim, in making such a claim we commit ourselves to our reliability. It is in virtue of this commitment that evidence of unreliability activates the Defense Commitment. Accordingly, a contextualist not only *can* but *should* insist that knowledge be grounded. Commitment to grounding is an important source of self-correction.

Contextualism articulates a competing methodological orientation, a different vision of how truth is to be pursued. The traditional outlook emphasizes *positive proof*: it is rational to believe only what you can show to be correct. Contextualism emphasizes openness to correction and error-elimination: to be rational is to be ready to defend or modify one's views as problems arise. For people like ourselves, who have seen even the most successful scientific theories fall by the wayside, the second conception is the more plausible and appropriate. I agree with Peirce and Popper that the first conception is ultimately rooted in a primitive picture of knowledge: knowledge as information issuing from some authoritative source: originally, the wisdom of one's ancestors or the Word of God; later, in more philosophical times, "the senses" or "Reason" or criteria of global coherence. But there are no finally authoritative sources. The great historical achievement of philosophical skepticism is to have helped us see this: to have moved us in the direction of fallibilism, hence eventually contextualism. However, because fallibilism has won the day, skepticism survives as a philosophical problem only if it goes beyond fallibilism to a radical and general repudiation of justification. This is not a step we are obliged to take.[27]

10. Skepticism and Epistemic Priority

Does the diagnostic strategy just sketched work against Cartesian skepticism too? Pursuing this question uncovers further theoretical presuppositions lurking in the skeptic's apparently intuitive arguments. To focus discussion, I shall concentrate on the problem of our knowledge of the external world. But what I have to say will apply, *mutatis mutandis*, to the entire range of Cartesian problems.

An obvious objection is that Cartesian arguments are compatible with the contextualist's distrust of "global" justification. Indeed, they exploit epistemic justification's default and challenge structure. Skeptical hypotheses, like that of the brain in a vat, are defeaters of ordinary knowledge-claims. Once we are aware of them, ordinary knowledge-claims no longer enjoy default justificational status. But because skeptical defeaters cannot be ruled out in any convincing way, we cannot give such claims an evidential grounding either.[28]

The response to this is that all the skeptic can show is that it is impossible to "rule out" the hypothesis that I am a brain in a vat on the basis of experiential evidence alone. But this affects my entitlement to believe that I am not a brain in a vat only if that entitlement is hostage to a prior commitment to provide every belief about the world with an experiential grounding. If I am justified in believing that I am sitting at a desk in Evanston, I am justified in believing that I am not a brain in a vat on Alpha Centauri.[29] Of course, if I am only justified in believing that *it seems to me* that I am sitting at a desk, matters are less clear. But given the availability of a contextualist approach to justification, that beliefs about the world – as such – need any basis, let alone the restricted basis that the skeptic offers, cannot be taken for granted.

As we have seen, Cartesian problems appear to depend on a partition of our beliefs into privileged and problematic classes. Given that contextualism gives us reason to be suspicious of such partitions, the conclusion seems to be that we are not vulnerable to Cartesian problems unless we first make ourselves vulnerable by becoming substantive foundationalists. However, this is not how matters have generally been seen. The most common view has been (and perhaps still is) that foundationalism is a response to skepticism, not its source.

It is often thought that the epistemological priority of experiential knowledge over knowledge of the world is too obvious to need arguing. Since the content of experiential knowledge is evidently more modest than that of any putative knowledge of the world, it is clear that the former is intrinsically less open to doubt, hence epistemologically more primitive, than the latter. But is it so obvious that knowledge of experience is always and everywhere less dubitable, more certain? A contextualist outlook leads us to question this. Aren't there many contexts where claims about the world are barely dubitable at all, so that they would be no more certain even if they could be experientially grounded? That there are no doubt some situations in which this is not so does not establish the general epistemological priority of experiential knowledge: only some equally general considerations would do that. But these considerations had better not be that there is a skeptical problem with respect to worldly knowledge that has no counterpart in the experiential case since, for all we have seen, that problem depends on *assuming* the general priority of experiential over worldly knowledge and so cannot be used to argue for it.[30]

Another common view is that the dependence of worldly on experiential knowledge follows from the undeniable fact that knowledge of the world depends on the "senses." This too gets us nowhere. Why should we suppose that all "the senses" ever really tell us is how things appear, never how they objectively are? Again, the reason had better not be that beliefs about the world are, by their very nature, especially vulnerable to skeptical challenge, or we will be going once more round the same small circle of ideas.

Some philosophers argue that the intuitive intelligibility of skeptical hypotheses establishes the priority of experiential knowledge over knowledge of the world. Because my experience could be just what it is although the objective world were very different, or even nonexistent, my knowing nothing about external reality would leave my experiential knowledge unscathed. But what does this have to do with priority, in the sense of general evidential dependence? Let us grant – what is not altogether obvious – that skeptical hypotheses represent genuine logical or conceptual possibilities:[31] we must conclude that there is a logical gap between experiential and worldly knowledge. Experience alone, we might say, is neutral with respect to the character and perhaps even the existence of the objective world. However, a logical gap is not in and of itself an epistemological asymmetry. The neutrality of experience cannot be equated with its priority.[32]

A much better suggestion is that what makes skeptical hypotheses into serious challenges is the skeptic's intention to raise certain very general questions about various kinds of knowledge. If, in some ordinary situation, we ask why a person is entitled to this or that particular belief about the world around him, then of course it will be appropriate to bring up further world-involving facts: that he was well-placed to see what was going on, is a generally reliable observer with respect to the matter in question, and so on. However, the skeptic means to step back from all such particular questions to reflect on our worldly knowledge as a whole. He wants to know what justifies us in believing *anything whatsoever* about the external world, even that there is one. This question is pointed because – as skeptical hypotheses show – there doesn't *have* to be an external world, at least not a world anything like the one we normally take ourselves to inhabit. But if this is the skeptic's question, it is simply begged if we answer it in ways that take knowledge of the world for granted. It seems to follow that, if the skeptic is allowed to ask his question in the way that he intends, we will be compelled to look for some more primitive evidential basis for our knowledge of the world; and what could this be if not experiential knowledge, however exactly such knowledge is understood? Thus the priority of experiential knowledge over knowledge of the world is a by-product of an encounter with skepticism, not a presupposition.[33]

As we know all too well, once we retreat to experiential knowledge as the only possible basis for knowledge of the world generally considered, the skeptic has powerful weapons at his disposal to block any future advance. The only possible basis for knowledge of the world turns out to be hopelessly inadequate. However, it now seems that the only way to avoid being forced into this retreat is to find fault with the skeptic's question: to attempt what I have called a therapeutic diagnosis, in the hope of finding the skeptic's question somehow less than fully intelligible. The trouble is, the skeptic's question does not seem to be defective in this way. For example, we all seem to understand it well enough to appreciate why it is so difficult to answer. In consequence, it is difficult to resist the suggestion that skepticism is at least conditionally correct in the sense that, if the skeptic is allowed to ask his intended question, it will be next-to-impossible to avoid returning his pessimistic answer.[34]

11. Epistemological Realism

In asking how we know, or justifiably believe, anything whatsoever about the external world, the skeptic imposes a *totality condition* on a properly philosophical understanding of such knowledge.[35] This explains why philosophical reflection demands detachment from ordinary practical concerns, which inevitably take all kinds of things for granted.

The generality of the skeptic's questions deserves a close look. We do not expect a general understanding of any arbitrary aggregate. There is no blanket explanation of how all the objects in my study got to be there. We expect general intelligibility only with respect to kinds that exhibit some kind of theoretical integrity. So what binds together the "kinds" of beliefs that interest the skeptic? Consider our "beliefs about the external world": these include all of physics, all of history, all of biology, and so on indefinitely, not to mention every casual thought about the world around us. There is no theoretical unity, no genuine totality, here, only a vague and arbitrary assemblage. The demand for a blanket explanation of "how we come to know such things" looks misplaced, if it is even intelligible.

There is only one way to escape this conclusion: the skeptic's kinds are epistemological kinds. What makes beliefs about the external world a theoretically coherent kind – and so makes sense of judging them as a whole – is their common epistemological status. "External" does not mean "in the environment," for even one's own body is, by the skeptic's standards, an "external" object. "External" means, in an old-fashioned phrase "without the mind." Knowledge of the external world contrasts with knowledge of the internal world: i.e. experiential knowledge. And the hallmark of knowledge of the internal world is its epistemic privilege.

This brings us back to (substantive) foundationalism, whose distinctive commitment is that every belief has an *intrinsic* epistemological status. On this picture, our beliefs fall into *natural epistemological kinds* standing in natural relations of epistemological priority. I speak of natural epistemological kinds to stress the point that the foundationalist's epistemological hierarchy cuts across ordinary subject-matter divisions and operates independently of all contextual factors. It answers to what Descartes called "the order of reasons": the fundamental, underlying, interest- and situation-independent structure of all empirical justification. Substantive foundationalism thus builds-in "epistemological realism": not realism as a position within epistemology (the view that we have knowledge of a "real" or objective world), but rather a form of extreme realism with respect to the typical objects of epistemological theorizing.

Foundationalism is much more deeply implicated in Cartesian skepticism than is generally recognized. Not only does foundationalism set the success-conditions for explaining how knowledge of the external world is possible, it is presupposed by the idea that there is such a "kind" of knowledge to examine. Our beliefs about the world can only be an epistemic kind. But to suppose that there are such kinds is to suppose that there are immutable epistemological constraints underlying the shifting standards of everyday justification: for example, the universal dependence of beliefs about the world on experiential evidence. On this view, context-sensitivity does not go all the way down, there being rather an underlying structure of justificational relations that philosophical reflection exposes to view and which allows us to determine, in some fully general way, whether we are entitled to claim knowledge of the world. Contextualism shows that commitment to such a structure is by no means mandatory. It shows how to sidestep Cartesian questions.

Faced with this diagnosis, some philosophers will deny that the Cartesian skeptic needs to begin with a general question. They will claim that the skeptic can reach his general conclusion by examining a single carefully chosen case of knowledge. This case will be a "best case": a case such that if knowledge fails here, it fails everywhere. So, for example, if I can't know that I am sitting at my desk right now (because, for all I know, I could be a brain in a vat) what can I know? Nothing.

This is a distinction without a difference. If my default entitlements include beliefs about the world, they rule out skeptical hypotheses. (I couldn't possibly be a brain in a vat on Alpha Centauri because I just got back from the office.) If I lack such default entitlements, ruling out skeptical scenarios may indeed be impossible. But then the argument assumes that, even in the best of cases, knowing about the world depends on experiential grounding, which is where we came in.

12. Skepticism in Context

Let us turn to the thought that contextualism itself invites Cartesian challenges to everyday knowledge. Certain aspects of contextualist epistemology suggest that this might be so. To begin with, there is the externalist dimension in the contextualist conception of adequate grounding. Not only does contextualism allow beliefs to rest on grounds of which we may be unaware, it makes the adequacy of grounds depend in part on the real-world environment.

Skeptical scenarios defeat ordinary knowledge in both a nonepistemic and an epistemic way: if I am a brain in a vat, most of my beliefs about the world will be false; but even if some of them happen to be true, they will not be properly grounded. In general, my beliefs about the world will be adequately grounded – by contextualist's standards – only if they were formed in a normal rather than a "vat" environment. But skeptical scenarios are only extreme illustrations of a general feature of contextualism or, in fact, of ordinary justification: that our grounds never rule out any and every error-possibility but only those that various contextual factors determine to be "significant" or "relevant." Nevertheless, we depend on certain possibilities *not* being realized. Knowledge and justification always involve, therefore, an element of *epistemic luck*. A belief whose truth is *wholly* accidental cannot count as knowledge. But, for a contextualist, getting things right is never wholly nonaccidental either.

The Cartesian skeptic will conclude from this that the contextualist, in taking himself to be epistemically lucky, is simply assuming that he does not live in a vat-world, and is therefore begging the question. This charge would be correct, if contextualism were meant to provide a direct response to Cartesian skepticism. But it isn't. Rather, contextualism is a view we are led to by a theoretical diagnosis of skeptical argumentation. We become contextualists by tracing the consequences of denying the skeptic's own presuppositions, notably the Prior Grounding Requirement and epistemological realism. Contextualism is acceptable because of a diagnosis that has already allowed us to sidestep skeptical problems.

Here is another slant on the same issue. No epistemology with important externalist elements can be a satisfactory response to the skeptic's demand that we explain how it is that we know *anything at all* about the external world. Any such response will be hopelessly conditional. It will explain how we know about the world, given that the world we inhabit is more or less normal. However, this objection depends on assuming the propriety of treating "our knowledge of the world" as a suitable object of wholesale assessment. Accordingly, it is no objection to contextualism, which grows out of a prior diagnosis of the skeptic's not-so-innocent questions.

With this in mind, let us look again at the "default and challenge" account of epistemic responsibility, which makes responsibility sensitive to the dialectical environment. Calling attention to overlooked error-possibilities, as a recent critic of contextualism puts it, raises the "level of scrutiny." We have to do more to maintain epistemic responsibility. Skeptical scenarios, brought up as overlooked error-possibilities, raise scrutiny to its maximal level, thereby defeating all ordinary knowledge-claims.

The contextualist will reply that skeptical hypotheses are not overlooked but reasonably disregarded because contextually irrelevant. The skeptic will deny this. He will admit that we are justified in ignoring skeptical possibilities for all *practical* purposes, but they are never strictly irrelevant. This sounds plausible but is actually quite wrong.

In a given context of inquiry, the *direction* of inquiry will require that certain propositions be treated as *not* in question. Contextual factors determine not only the *level* but also the *angle* of scrutiny. In conducting an experimental test of a scientific theory, we can raise the level of scrutiny indefinitely: we can insist on taking measurements to a further decimal point and narrowing the limits of error; we can repeat the experiment under more stringently controlled conditions, and so on. But if we start worrying whether our whole apparatus is part of a brain-in-vat illusion, we don't raise the level of scrutiny, we change the subject: from physics to general epistemology. There is no simple relation between level and angle of scrutiny and, consequently, no coherent idea of a maximal level.

It might seem that all this works to the skeptic's advantage. If the line between what is in question and what is not is fixed in part by the direction of inquiry, why can't the skeptic argue that the privileged status of experiential knowledge is fixed by his project of trying to understand our knowledge of the world *as a whole*? Or what comes to the same thing, how does the fact that skeptical scenarios change the angle of scrutiny, rather than the level, limit their capacity to undermine ordinary knowledge?

For the sake of argument, let us grant that simply calling attention to skeptical possibilities transforms the dialectical environment by shifting the angle of scrutiny. The most that this implies is something we have already conceded: the instability of knowledge. That we lose our ordinary justificational entitlements in the new environment does not show that we never had them in the old. To get from instability to impossibility, the skeptic must hold that the context he creates is privileged, that it reveals ultimate constraints on justification that are always in play, if ordinarily ignored. However, distinguishing between levels and angles of scrutiny blocks this move. Hume was right: skepticism belongs in the study, not the street. But this is a logical and not, as Hume thought, a psychological point.

Put it this way. The skeptic's "totality condition," which requires us to treat experiential knowledge as epistemologically prior to knowledge of the world, determines what it would be to understand knowledge of the world in a distinctively philosophical way. If we agree that no such understanding is attainable, the most this amounts to is the discovery that we cannot justify any beliefs about the world under the (self-imposed) conditions of philosophical reflection. What it does not amount to is the discovery, under the conditions of philosophical reflection, that no such beliefs are ever justified. To move to this truly skeptical conclusion, we must suppose that philosophical reflection reveals the final, context-independent constraints on justification with respect to our worldly beliefs. That is, we must take for granted epistemological realism.[36] If we reject epistemological realism, there are no such constraints for reflection to reveal.

Evaluative practices, including epistemic practices, are human constructions, designed to serve human purposes. We are therefore free to modify them in the face of unforeseen problems. Accordingly, if a certain picture of knowledge and justification leads to radical skepticism, thus erasing every important epistemological distinction, we have every reason to change the picture. However, neither the skeptic nor the traditional epistemologist sees things in quite this light. Behind both philosophical skepticism and traditional antiskepticism is a kind of naturalism: the wish to ground epistemological evaluations in a realm of epistemological fact, a natural order of reasons to which our reason-giving practices are ultimately answerable. Epistemic norms must be read off a hidden structure of epistemic fact.[37]

We have come full circle. The first skeptical commitment that we identified was the Prior Grounding Requirement, which prioritizes grounding over responsibility, an order of dependence that contextualism reverses. Now we see why the traditional vision seems so compelling and contextualism so perverse. If epistemological realism is assumed, the Prior Grounding Requirement follows automatically. If there is a structure of justificational constraints, existing independently of our interests and contingent situation, then of course responsibility demands that we respect it. Practical and other human limitations can excuse us from not always living up to its strictest demands, but if we fail to live up to them, from a purely epistemic standpoint – another element in epistemological realism's theoretical apparatus – the skeptic's negative verdict on our epistemic performance is entirely correct. However, if my argument is on anything like the right lines, skepticism is not detachable from this extraordinary metaphysics of knowledge. It is a picture that has held us captive too long. It is time to move on.

13. Epistemology after Skepticism

If epistemology has been centrally concerned with skeptical problems and if – as diagnostic responses suggest – such problems can be set aside, it seems to follow that epistemology can be set aside too. The thought that epistemology is dead, or deserves to be, is perhaps most associated with the writings of Richard Rorty. But Quine, too, though he thinks that epistemology can continue in a "naturalized" form, as a chapter of empirical psychology, agrees with Rorty that if epistemology tries to provide science with a "foundation" (which it will, if animated by a certain kind of methodological skepticism) we should have nothing further to do with it.[38]

Now, although skepticism has perhaps been the dominant problem for philosophers concerned with human knowledge, it has never been the only one. Indeed, even when philosophers have taken a serious interest in skepticism, it has often been because they have seen exploring the limits of skeptical argumentation as the key to solving other problems. The ancient skeptics thought of skepticism as a way of life: life without either theoretical convictions or definite claims to knowledge. The theories they eschewed included philosophical theories of knowledge. They propounded theoretical skepticism, neither to sow doubts about everyday beliefs nor to learn something about knowledge, but to combat dogmatic epistemologies.[39]

Philosophers have also taken a serious interest in skepticism out of motives that are not exclusively epistemological. For example, Descartes, who is generally credited with giving modern philosophy an epistemological turn, thought of exploring the limits of skepticism as a way to secure fundamental metaphysical as well as epistemological insights. In addition, there are epistemological concerns other than that of coming to a general understanding of the nature of knowledge or justification. One persistent concern has been with what we may call problems of demarcation. These problems concern "the scope and limits of human knowledge": are there principled reasons for thinking that knowledge, properly so-called, is a reasonable aspiration only in connection with certain kinds of inquiry? Or again, philosophers have often concerned themselves with what may broadly be called problems of method. What is the best way of trying to obtain knowledge? Are there different ways, depending on the subject (e.g. in the natural and the social sciences)? Can our methods be improved? Demarcational and methodological questions have often been linked with skeptical questions: we fix the bounds of knowledge by exploring the limits of skepticism. We could think of this as the Kantian strategy, mindful of Kant's claim to have limited Reason in order to make room for Faith. But another approach would be to examine the reasonableness of various cognitive aspirations in the light of our best scientific theories of the world and our place in it. Remembering the use Locke made of a generally mechanistic conception of nature, we could think of this as the Lockean approach. As for the problem of method, Descartes thought that a confrontation with skepticism was an essential component in his reconstruction of human knowledge. Bacon, by contrast, developed important ideas about scientific method without ever getting involved with general skeptical worries.[40] All this suggests that skeptically centered epistemology is one kind of epistemology, but not coextensive with epistemological theorizing as such.[41]

We should also recall my distinction between therapeutic and theoretical diagnosis. If we think that skeptical problems yield to a therapeutic diagnosis, and so were pseudo-problems all along, our hope is for them to disappear without residue. Naturally, the subject that devoted itself to solving them theoretically will disappear as well. However, if we approach them in the spirit of theoretical diagnosis matters are not so clear. A theoretical diagnosis denies the naturalness or intuitiveness of skeptical problems by linking them with unacknowledged theoretical ideas. Following a specific diagnostic hypothesis will lead to a new picture of knowledge and justification, in my case contextualism. But of course, the contextualist perspective is likely to raise problems of its own. Whatever its success as a response to traditional skeptical problems, it guarantees no permanent escape from epistemological concerns.

Notes

1 Thus A. J. Ayer in The *Problem of Knowledge* (London: Pelican, 1956), p. 78, having laid out a certain way of arguing for philosophical skepticism: "Concern with the theory of knowledge is very much a matter of taking this difficulty seriously. The different ways of trying to meet it mark out the different schools of philosophy...". Cf. Lawrence BonJour, *The Structure of Empirical Knowledge* (Cambridge, MA: Harvard University Press, 1985), pp. 14–15: "If skeptics did not exist, ... the serious epistemologist would have to invent them."

2 Historically, philosophical skepticism has taken various forms. A useful collection of essays on historical aspects of skepticism is M. F. Burnyeat, ed., *The Skeptical Tradition* (Berkeley: University of California Press, 1983). A groundbreaking work on the impact of the rediscovery of Greek skepticism on Western philosophical thought is Richard Popkin's *Scepticism from Erasmus to Spinoza* (Berkeley: University of California Press, 1979).

3 Sometimes, people have been called skeptics because they have been suspected not just of doubting but of actually *denying* important truths: for example, there have been times when "skeptic" and "atheist" were more or less interchangeable terms. In practical terms, the distinction between "not asserting" and "denying" can often seem rather forced.

4 In antiquity, there were two schools of skepticism: Pyrrhonian and Academic. The Pyrrhonian school traced itself to Pyrrho of Elis, a younger contemporary of Aristotle; the Academic to Plato's Academy. The Pyrrhonists claimed that the Academics were not true skeptics because they dogmatically asserted that knowledge is impossible. According to the Pyrrhonians, true skeptics suspend judgment on all questions, including that concerning the possibility of knowledge.

5 The idea that knowledge is justified true belief is often traced to Plato who, in his dialogue *Theaetetus* identifies knowledge with true belief plus an "account" (*logos*). That justified true belief is insufficient for knowledge, even when the justification is very strong, is the burden of what has come to be known as "the Gettier problem," after Edmund Gettier, "Is Justified True Belief Knowledge?", *Analysis* (1963). The best discussion of this problem, which has provoked an enormous literature, is in Robert Fogelin, *Pyrrhonian Reflections on Knowledge and Justification* (Princeton: Princeton University Press, 1994), Part 1.

6 David Hume, *Enquiry Concerning Human Understanding* in *Enquiries Concerning Human Understanding and the Principles of Morals*, ed. L. A. Selby-Bigge, 3rd edn, rev. P. H. Nidditch (Oxford: Oxford University Press, 1975), section XII. Today's neo-Humeans include Barry Stroud, *The Significance of Philosophical Scepticism* (Oxford: Oxford University Press, 1984); Thomas Nagel, *The View from Nowhere* (Oxford: Oxford University Press, 1986); and P. F. Strawson, *Skepticism and Naturalism: Some Varieties* (London: Methuen, 1985).

7 For Chisholm's approach, see Roderick Chisholm, *The Foundations of Knowing* (Minneapolis: University of Minnesota Press, 1982), ch. 1. The claim that epistemology aims at showing how knowledge is possible is advanced by John Pollock, "What is an Epistemological Problem?", *American Philosophical Quarterly* (1968), pp. 183–90.

8 Many ancient skeptics, including Pyrrho, did not write. In the case of others, such as the important Academic skeptic Carneades, their writings have not survived. Nevertheless, we know a good deal about ancient skepticism, largely owing to the encyclopedic writings of Sextus Empiricus, by far our most important source. See Sextus Empiricus, *Outlines of Pyrrhonism*, in *Sextus Empiricus*, vol. 1, Greek text with translation by R. G. Bury (London: Heinemann, 1933). A new translation of the *Outlines*, together with useful notes, has been prepared by Benson Mates under the title *The Skeptic Way* (Oxford: Oxford University Press, 1996). For an introductory account of ancient skepticism, in the context of Hellenistic thought, see R. W. Sharples, *Stoics, Epicureans and Sceptics* (London: Routledge, 1996).

9   There is a long tradition, going back at least to Plato's account of knowledge as an infallible mode of cognition, that associates knowledge with absolute certainty. The dominant articulation of this idea is the demonstrative ideal of knowledge: we can really know only what is either itself self-evident or what is logically deducible by self-evidently valid steps from self-evident premises. No doubt this ideal owes a lot of its appeal to the Greek discovery of the axiomatic approach to geometrical proof. It remains the dominant conception of knowledge in the Early Modern period in philosophy and is common ground between the "Rationalist" Descartes and the "Empiricist" Locke. Indeed, it persists well into the eighteenth century and is by no means dead even in Hume. The ancient skeptics, especially certain Academics, developed accounts of "skeptical assent," intended to show how a skeptic might regulate his opinions, while disclaiming any pretensions to knowledge. These could be seen as precursors of modern, fallibilist, theories of knowledge, which makes it questionable whether ancient skepticism is radical, in the sense proposed here. The important point, however, is that skeptical arguments seem to be readily adaptable to our contemporary and less demanding conception of knowledge. This protean character of skeptical arguments enables skepticism to become radical skepticism, thus to survive as a vital philosophical problem. For Carneades' account of skeptical assent, see Sextus Empiricus, *Against the Logicians* 1, 166–90, in *Sextus Empiricus*, vol. 2, trans. R. G. Bury (London: Heinemann, 1933).

10 The Five Modes are found at *Outlines*, Book 1, ch. XV. The question of what significance the ancient skeptics themselves saw in such arguments remains extremely controversial. See Julia Annas and Jonathan Barnes, *The Modes of Scepticism* (Cambridge: Cambridge University Press, 1985). Also, R. J. Hankinson, *The Sceptics* (London: Routledge, 1995). I give my own account of the ancient "modes" in "Scepticism without Theory," *Review of Metaphysics* (1988). A challenging update and defence of "Pyrrhonian" skepticism can be found in Fogelin's *Pyrrhonian Reflections*.

11 This is why coherence theories of *justification* are, historically, closely connected with coherence theories of *truth*. A coherence theorist who understands truth "realistically," as some kind of "correspondence" to an "independent" reality, faces the difficult, perhaps insuperable, problem of explaining why satisfying the criteria of coherence makes our beliefs likely to be true (hence why coherentist "justification" deserves to be thought of as justification at all). The standing temptation is to avoid this problem by identifying truth itself with idealized epistemic coherence. Whether this is an effective move is moot: for further discussion see my *Unnatural Doubts* (Princeton: Princeton University Press, 1996/original publication, Oxford: Blackwell, 1992), ch. 6. For readers unfamiliar with philosophical debates about the nature of truth, a useful introduction is Frederick Schmitt, *Truth: a Primer* (Boulder: Westview Press, 1995).

12 For a detailed defense of the claim that the coherence theory is a variant form of foundationalism, see *Unnatural Doubts*, ch. 7.

13 The view that foundationalism and the coherence theory themselves lead to skepticism is vigorously defended by Fogelin in *Pyrrhonian Reflections*, chs. 7–9.

14 Fogelin, *Pyrrhonian Reflections*, ch. 6.

15 John McDowell, *Mind and World* (Cambridge, MA: Harvard University Press, 1994). McDowell has an important and original view of the basis of the entire range of philosophical problems, including skeptical problems, that modern philosophy has come to treat as canonical. However, his writings are likely to prove challenging to

16 René Descartes, *Meditations on First Philosophy*, in Descartes, *Philosophical Works*, vol. 2, ed. J. Cottingham et al. (Cambridge: Cambridge University Press, 1984). On the novelty of Descartes's problem, see M. F. Burnyeat, "Idealism and Greek Philosophy: What Descartes Saw and Berkeley Missed," *Philosophical Review* (1982). While accepting Burnyeat's claim about Descartes's originality, I offer a somewhat different account of its character in "Descartes and the Metaphysics of Doubt," in A. O. Rorty, ed., *Essays on Descartes' Meditations* (Berkeley: University of California Press, 1986).

17 Their thought is that skeptical problems are *just* puzzles, interesting perhaps to those with the right turn of mind but safely ignored by everyone else. This is Strawson's position in *Skepticism and Naturalism*. However, I am not sure even about this, for I suspect that the effects of giving in to skepticism, even in its more bizarre forms, are not easily kept under control. See my *Unnatural Doubts*, ch. 13.

18 This analysis of Cartesian arguments is adapted from A. J. Ayer's classic account in *The Problem of Knowledge*, pp. 75–83.

19 The problems facing phenomenalism are ably reviewed by Ayer, who was once a leading phenomenalist himself: ibid., pp. 118–29.

20 For further development of this point, see Stroud, ch. V. There are extremely subtle discussions of realism and reductionism in the various papers by Michael Dummett. See for example "Realism" in his *Truth and Other Enigmas* (Cambridge, MA: Harvard University Press, 1978).

21 The idea that the "real world hypothesis" is a better account of the origin of experience than any skeptical alternative is defended by Jonathan Vogel, "Cartesian Skepticism and Inference to the Best Explanation," *Journal of Philosophy* (1990), pp. 658–66. This strategy receives a highly qualified endorsement from Strawson in *Skepticism and Naturalism*. Neither Strawson nor Vogel has much to say on the question of what it is *about* experience that calls for explanation in terms of an external origin.

22 The distinction between theoretical diagnosis and direct refutation is not a sharp one. Inevitably, what the skeptic acknowledges and what he leaves unsaid depends on how skeptical arguments are formulated. In practice, however, the distinction is clear enough. This is because the need for skeptical arguments to appear to be natural or intuitive sets limits to what the skeptic can afford to acknowledge. The danger of overexplicitness is that his skepticism will modulate from philosophical skepticism to skepticism about certain philosophical theories of knowledge. He will not show, in an unqualified way, that knowledge is impossible but only that it is impossible given certain adventitious standards, dictated by controversial epistemological ideas.

23 The evaluative/normative character of epistemological concepts has been stressed by many philosophers. The approach taken here follows the important recent work of Robert Brandom: see Brandom, *Making It Explicit* (Cambridge, MA: Harvard University Press, 1994), esp. ch. 4, sect. 1–4.

24 The phrase is Brandom's. There are, however, many prior articulations of this general conception. One of the most important is to be found in J. L. Austin's seminal essay "Other Minds," in Austin, *Philosophical Papers* (Oxford: Oxford University Press, 1961). I believe, however, that this conception of justification is very ancient, originating in Academic theories of "skeptical assent," particularly Carneades' doctrine of

the "tested impression." Since the ancient skeptics and their opponents contrast skeptical assent with knowledge, ancient attacks on the possibility of knowledge are not necessarily radical in my sense. However, it is notable that the Pyrrhonian skeptics attacked even "skeptical" epistemologies like that of Carneades. See note 8 above.

25 Default and challenge structures show up in nonepistemological accounting practices too. Consider a different sense of "responsibility": accountability for one's actions. Here, again, "responsibility" is the default position: one is accountable unless in possession of an appropriate excuse. This view of responsibility is taken by Austin in his famous paper "A Plea for Excuses," in Austin, *Philosophical Papers*. Austin's views on knowledge and freedom are importantly connected.

26 The relevant alternatives account of knowledge has its roots in Austin. It is further developed in papers by Fred Dretske. See "Contrastive Statements," *Philosophical Review* (1972) and "The Pragmatic Dimension of Knowledge," *Philosophical Studies* (1981). *Editor's note*: a contextualist view of justification is further explored in the essay by Keith DeRose, this volume.

27 See Charles Sanders Peirce, "The Fixation of Belief," in Justus Buchler, ed., *Philosophical Writings of Pierce* (New York: Dover, 1955). For Popper's views, see his collection *Conjectures and Refutations* (London: Routledge, 1963). Popper's great error is that, though he advocates a "trial and error" conception of rational inquiry, he accepts the Prior Grounding Requirement as definitive of epistemic justification. This is evident from his holding that the lesson of skepticism is that rationality has *nothing* to do with justification, that no theory can ever be justified, etc. Popper's agreement with the traditionalists leads him to concede far more to radical skepticism than he needs to.

28 Many philosophers, including of course Descartes himself, have connected skepticism with detachment from everyday practical concerns. See Thompson Clarke, "The Legacy of Skepticism," *Journal of Philosophy* (1972); Bernard Williams, *Descartes: The Project of Pure Enquiry* (Harmondsworth: Pelican, 1978), ch. 1; Marie McGinn, *Sense and Certainty* (Oxford: Blackwell, 1989), ch. 1. Stanley Cavell stresses the importance of the skeptic's apparent mimicry of ordinary patterns of claim–challenge–response in *The Claim of Reason* (Oxford: Oxford University Press, 1979). Clarke, Cavell, and McGinn all offer diagnostic responses to skepticism that merit serious consideration. I discuss Cavell in *Unnatural Doubts*, ch. 4 and Clarke, McGinn, and Williams in ch. 5. Stroud gives a skeptic's response to Clarke and Cavell in *The Significance of Philosophical Scepticism*, "Coda."

29 Some philosophers would deny this, notably Dretske. This is because Dretske connects the idea that justifying involves ruling out only certain relevant alternatives to the claim at issue with a much more problematic thesis: that knowledge is not "closed under known logical implication." The same idea is advanced – apparently independently – by Robert Nozick. (Arguably, the basic idea is present in Austin's "Other Minds" and Wittgenstein's *On Certainty*.) Epistemic closure is the principle that, if I know that P, and know that P logically entails Q, then I know that Q. This thesis is said to be presupposed by standard skeptical arguments. So, for example, suppose I know that I am now sitting at a computer screen; I know also that, if I am sitting at such a screen, I am not a brain in a vat; but I do not know, and can never know, that I am not a brain in a vat: therefore, I do not know that I am sitting at a computer screen. According to Dretske, however, I do know that I am sitting at a computer

screen, even though I do not know that I am not a brain in a vat. I know that I am sitting at a screen because I can rule out various relevant alternatives: e.g. that I am writing this footnote on a pad of paper, or dictating it into a microphone. I don't have to exclude the possibility that my whole experience is a vat-delusion. This is a relevant alternative, not to my specific belief about what I am doing right now, but only to some much more general claim: for example, that my experience reveals an external world that is pretty much what I take it to be. I can know specific facts without knowing more general facts that they logically imply. The principle of closure is false. Certainly, this is a dramatic diagnosis of how skeptical arguments go astray. For Dretske's views, see "Epistemic Operators," *Journal of Philosophy* (1972); and for Nozick's, *Philosophical Explanations* (Oxford: Oxford University Press, 1981), ch. 3. As my remarks in the main text will suggest, I think that the issue of closure is a red herring. Furthermore, contextualists are not committed to denying closure. Denial results from thinking that the range of relevant alternatives to a given claim are determined by the claim's propositional content alone, which no contextualist should suppose. For details, see *Unnatural Doubts*, ch. 8.

30 A *locus classicus* for this "argument from differential certainty" is H. H. Price, *Perception* (Oxford: Oxford University Press, 1932), ch. 1. I discuss Price in *Groundless Belief* (Oxford: Blackwell, 1977), pp. 43–6.

31 There have been many attempts to show that skeptical hypotheses do not really make sense. Mostly, they have taken for granted some kind of "verificationist" conception of meaning. A classic example is O. K. Bouwsma, "Descartes's Evil Deceiver," in Bouwsma, *Philosophical Essays* (Lincoln: University of Nebraska Press, 1969). This sort of response is not much in fashion at the moment. However, in what is perhaps something of the same spirit, Donald Davidson has argued that it is impossible for most of a person's beliefs to be false. Davidson's argument, which draws on his general idea about truth and meaning, is original and important, in part because it swings free of standard verificationism. See Davidson, "A Coherence Theory of Truth and Knowledge," in E. Lepore, ed., *Truth and Interpretation* (Blackwell: Oxford, 1986). Though Davidson's argument deserves serious consideration, coming to terms with it would require an exploration of fundamental issues in the philosophy of language which cannot be undertaken here. For some critical reactions, see Peter Klein, "Radical Interpretation and Global Scepticism," in Lepore. See also Bruce Vermazen, "The Intelligibility of Massive Error," *Philosophical Quarterly* (1983) and my own "Scepticism and Charity," *Ratio* (1988).

32 The position that what I am calling the "neutrality" of experience is the ground for its priority is taken by Stroud, *The Significance of Philosophical Scepticism*, p. 179. For more detailed criticism of this and other arguments for the priority of experience, see *Unnatural Doubts*, ch. 2. The classic attack on the whole idea of "basing" knowledge of the world on experience is J. L. Austin's *Sense and Sensibilia* (Oxford: Oxford University Press, 1962). Austin's writings are a major influence on the version of contextualism that I advocate as an alternative to traditional foundationalist and coherentists theories of justification.

33 This formulation is due to Barry Stroud, "Skepticism and the Possibility of Knowledge," *Journal of Philosophy* (1984), p. 550.

34 That skepticism is conditionally correct in this sense is the burden of Stroud's *The Significance of Philosophical Scepticism*.

35 The view that their distinctive generality is the key to the skeptic's questions is very interestingly developed by Barry Stroud in "Understanding Human Knowledge in General," in Marjorie Clay and Keith Lehrer, eds., *Knowledge and Skepticism* (Boulder: Westview Press, 1989). For further discussion, see Stroud's "Epistemological Reflection on Knowledge of the External World" and my own "Understanding Human Knowledge Philosophically," *Philosophy and Phenomenological Research* (1996).

36 In *Pyrrhonian Reflections*, Fogelin argues for what he calls "the fragility of knowledge." His thought is that, because ordinary justifications never rule out every logically possible way of being in error, a skeptic can always raise the "level of scrutiny" and so undermine claims to knowledge. He concludes from this that, although I may be right about Cartesian skepticism, Pyrrhonian considerational lead straight to radical skepticism, without reliance on controversial ideas such as foundationalism. However, I think that Fogelin's Pyrrhonian reflections lead only to a welcome fallibilism. Insofar as there is a hint of a stronger conclusion, his argument depends on the idea of a fixed hierarchy of "levels of scrutiny," with skeptical hypotheses moving us to the "highest" level. This is the epistemological-realist myth all over again. The most that the introduction of skeptical hypotheses can do is change the direction of inquiry, in a way that induces a temporary suspension of ordinary justifications. But I say "the most" because it isn't clear what induces such contextual shifts. There is room for further work here. The contextual variability of standards of justification is explored by David Lewis in "Elusive Knowledge," *Australasian Journal of Philosophy* (1996).

37 This makes skepticism result from something like the "naturalistic fallacy" of identifying an evaluative with a descriptive concept. Fogelin (*Pyrrhonian Reflections*, p. 39) finds something like the naturalistic fallacy in certain popular responses to Gettier's problem. I think that this insight invites wider application. It is tempting to speculate further about the basis of the reductive urge in epistemology. One possibility is a primitive picture of knowledge and justification: knowledge as issuing from one or more authoritative sources (originally, the words of the gods or the lore of one's ancestors). The naturalism I mention here is not, of course, what is typically thought of as epistemological naturalism today. Contemporary naturalists see themselves as opposed to "traditional" theories, such as standard versions of foundationalism. They also tend to be dubious about the problems, particularly skeptical problems, that such theories address. But these differences do not exempt contemporary naturalists from the danger of committing the epistemic analogue of the naturalistic fallacy. Contemporary naturalists advocate one or another version of the "reliabilist" account of knowledge: knowledge is belief produced by a truth-reliable process; and cognitive science will fill in the details as to what those processes are. However, whether a given method of belief-acquisition is reliable depends on the range of situations we apply it to. For example, reliabilists have divided over whether the way we form beliefs has to be reliable only in worlds very like the actual world, or whether they ought to be reliable in "skeptical" worlds too: e.g. for brains in vats. "Nature" does not determine the right answer to questions like this. For an illuminating discussion of this issue, see Brandom, *Making It Explicit*, pp. 206–13. On the general question of how skeptical problems appear to naturalistically inclined philosophers, see W. V. Quine, "The Nature of Natural Knowledge," in Samuel Guttenplan, ed., *Mind and Language* (Oxford: Oxford University Press, 1975); but see also Stroud's critical response in *The Significance of Philosophical Scepticism*, ch. VI. A provocative account of the revival of epistemological

naturalism can be found in Philip Kitcher, "The Naturalist's Return," *Philosophical Review* (1991).

McDowell, in *Mind and World*, also traces current epistemological perplexities to a pernicious naturalism. But what he has in mind is the "modern" naturalism that equates Nature with a "realm of law": roughly, a system of objects and events standing in exclusively causal relations. Since justification depends on logical relations, this naturalism makes it impossible to understand how our beliefs can be under "rational control" by the world. This diagnosis is quite different from the one I have in mind. I believe it reflects an undiagnosed urge to find an ultimate grounding for our knowledge of the world. So whereas McDowell thinks we need to expand our conception of Nature, I think we need to root out the last elements of naturalism in epistemology.

38 See especially Richard Rorty, *Philosophy and the Mirror of Nature* (Princeton: Princeton University Press, 1979). For Rorty, the emergence of epistemology is the precondition for the emergence of philosophy as a professionalized discipline from the natural sciences. Accordingly, the death of epistemology is tantamount to the death of philosophy itself. In Rorty's view, epistemology, at least as we understand it today, began to take shape in the seventeenth century and didn't attain its definitive form until Kant drew a sharp line between empirical and properly philosophical questions about knowledge. The idea that epistemology is such a novel subject strikes many philosophers as absolutely outrageous, as if there were anything wrong in discussing ancient epistemology. However, Rorty's position raises a number of subtle and important issues, both historical and theoretical, and embodies various defenses against summary dismissal. I discuss his "emergence thesis" in "Epistemology and the Mirror of Nature," in R. Brandom, ed., *Rorty and his Critics* (Oxford: Blackwell, forthcoming).

39 For a detailed defense of this interpretation, see my "Scepticism Without Theory." The French historian of philosophy, Pierre Hadot, claims that all ancient philosophy was concerned with how best to live and, indeed, that philosophy itself represented first and foremost a distinctive approach to living. Thus, for Hadot, philosophical writings are not, in themselves, "philosophy" but rather "discourse about philosophy." Though obviously controversial, this claim offers a very interesting slant on the skeptical writings of Sextus Empiricus. For Hadot's views, see his *Philosophy as a Way of Life* (Oxford: Blackwell, 1995) and *Qu'est-ce que la Philosophie Antique* (Paris: Gallimard, 1995). See also the discussion of ancient skepticism in Martha Nussbaum, *The Therapy of Desire* (Princeton: Princeton University Press, 1994).

40 One consequence of recent epistemology's fixation on Cartesian skepticism, hence on skeptically centred epistemology, is that Bacon's importance and originality is underrated. For example, very few undergraduate history of modern philosophy courses would bother to include Bacon on the list of required authors. For Bacon's ideas, see *Novum Organum*, in J. Spedding, R. Ellis, and D. Heath, eds, *The Works of Francis Bacon*, vol. IV (London: Longman, 1857–8). An introduction to Bacon's epistemological views can be found in Peter Urbach, *Francis Bacon's Philosophy of Science* (LaSalle, IL: Open Court, 1987).

41 For an example of how demarcational issues might be explored without the aid of methodological skepticism, see Crispin Wright, *Truth and Objectivity* (Cambridge, MA: Harvard University Press, 1992). That postskeptical epistemology might be refocused on the Baconian problem of method is the burden of Kitcher's argument in "The Naturalist's Return."

Chapter 2

Realism, Objectivity, and Skepticism

Paul K. Moser

Inquiring minds want to know, not merely to believe or even to believe truly. They want knowledge of "the facts," at least the facts in a relevant domain. Epistemology thus investigates and elucidates what inquiring minds want. So, epistemology is valuable to inquiring minds, whatever their domains of interest. A person might settle for true belief and remain lazily indifferent to knowledge, but this would be odd indeed. Inquiring minds seek something better grounded than true belief based just on lucky guesswork, for example. They want true beliefs grounded in adequate evidence, if only to avoid the vicissitudes of ungrounded belief.

Epistemology aims to characterize, among other things, adequate evidence and the way such evidence grounds true beliefs qualifying as knowledge. This aim resists easy satisfaction, owing to the complexities of evidence and knowledge, but this, of course, says nothing against the value of epistemology. The world resists easy explanation pretty much everywhere else, too. We thus should not fault epistemology, or any philosophical discipline, for its due complexities in explaining a theoretically demanding segment of the world.

Knowledge entails justified true belief, and more: more specifically, justified true belief undefeated by truths of the sort at work in Gettier-style counterexamples. We can set aside such counterexamples now, since our focus will not be the analysis of propositional knowledge. The focus will rather be on the kind of objectivity available to inquiring minds. In seeking adequately grounded true beliefs, inquiring minds want at least beliefs representative of how things really are. On what basis, if any, can they reasonably lay claim to such beliefs? This question motivates this chapter.

1. Objectivity and Intelligible Realism

In seeking beliefs representative of "how things really are," we pursue a kind of objectivity, and thereby tread on controversial philosophical ground. In particular, we invite controversy over realism about what our beliefs represent. Realism comes in many shapes and sizes; so a few distinctions may help. *Minimal* realism states that something exists objectively, that is, independently of being conceived of. *Ordinary* realism proposes that the tokens of most ordinary psychological and physical types (specified by ordinary language-use) exist objectively. *Scientific* realism holds that the tokens of most scientific types exist objectively.[1]

We shall examine *moderate* realism, the view that what is represented by at least some of our beliefs is objective, that is, logically and causally independent of someone's conceiving of that thing. (Let's render "conceiving" broadly, to encompass such psychological phenomena as assenting, believing, and perceiving.) For example, your belief that Lake Michigan is wet represents, plainly enough, Lake Michigan's being wet. Lake Michigan's being wet is objective now if and only if it does not now depend, logically or causally, on someone's conceiving of it. Even psychological phenomena, including events of conceiving, can be thus objective, so long as they are independent of someone's conceiving of them. Objectivity, then, derives from conceiving-independence of the sort noted. It can, at least in principle, characterize psychological as well as nonpsychological phenomena. Conceivers themselves, for example, might be conceiving-independent, that is, independent of being conceived of.

Put bluntly, talk of the objectivity of something is just talk of how that thing is independently of what any conceiver takes it to be. Some opponents of talk of objectivity have overlooked an important distinction between (a) the conceiving-dependence of one's *conceiving of something*, and (b) the conceiving-dependence of *what one's conceiving represents*. Your conceiving of Lake Michigan depends on conceiving, but it does not follow that Lake Michigan depends on conceiving. As for our *concept* of Lake Michigan, it evidently does not depend on our concept of conceiving. Conceivably, one could have the concept of Lake Michigan while lacking the concept of conceiving. The concept of conceiving is thus not a necessary ingredient of the content of a concept, even if concepts and events of conceiving depend for their existence on conceivers.

Some philosophers have questioned the intelligibility of any notion of objectivity relying on a concept of "how things really are," or "how things are independently of being conceived of." Richard Rorty, for instance, has spoken of "the sterility of attempts to give sense to phrases like 'the way the world is,'" adding that a notion of the world-in-itself is "completely unspecified and unspecifiable."[2] Similarly, in commenting on a Kantian notion of the thing-in-itself, Hilary Putnam has suggested that a concept of conceiving-independent reality "makes no sense."[3] They thus suggest that it is unintelligible to talk of objectivity in terms of how things really are, that is, how things are independently of being conceived of.

The claim that the notion of how things really are is unintelligible raises a notable self-referential problem. Let's ask whether that claim is itself a claim about how things really are. Either it is or it isn't. If it is, it is unintelligible given its own claim, as it implies that statements relying on the notion of how things really are qualify as unintelligible. If, alternatively, it is not a claim about how things really are, then we need an explanation of what kind of claim it is. Clearly, it will not help to reply that it is a claim about what we are *justified in claiming*, rather than a claim about how things really are. Given that reply, the view suggested by Rorty and Putnam is that we are justified in claiming that the notion of how things really are is unintelligible. The latter view fortifies rather than avoids our self-referential problem, because we can ask whether that view is itself a claim about how things really are, with respect to what we are justified in claiming. If it is, then given the very view in question, we are justified in holding that this view itself is unintelligible. If, alternatively, it is not a claim about how things really are, but only a claim about what we are justified in claiming (about what we are justified in claiming), a troublesome regress of increasing levels of supposed justification threatens. The threatening regress is troublesome if only because we seem not to have (and perhaps do not even understand) the kind of complex iterated justification it requires.[4]

We should doubt, then, the suggestion that the notion of how things really are is unintelligible. The suggestion of Rorty and Putnam about the notion of how things really are presupposes, on pain of implied unintelligibility or infinite regress, a realist notion of how things really are. Indeed, any truth-valued judgment presupposes a notion of how things really are and thereby illustrates the intelligibility of a notion of objectivity. So, moderate realism, implying that what is represented by at least some of our beliefs is objective, qualifies as intelligible. Semantically, in other words, moderate realism seems beyond reproach. Claims to the contrary have identifiable implications about how things really are, thereby testifying to the intelligibility (but not necessarily the truth) of moderate realism. (Section 4 will assess a more recent attempt by Rorty to eliminate issues central to traditional epistemology.)

The notion of how things really are enables us to introduce a minimal realist definition of truth. Using the term "proposition" to signify the content of a statement, we have this definition: the claim that a proposition, P, is true means that things really are as they are stated to be by P. This realist definition is a minimal correspondence definition in that it makes truth a function just of the statement relation between a proposition and how things really are. In addition, it can accommodate Tarski's necessary condition for any adequate definition of truth, namely, schema T: X is true if and only if P (where "P" stands for a declarative sentence, and "X" stands for the name of that sentence). The minimal realist definition of truth has the plausible implication that a person believes that a proposition is true if and only if she believes that the proposition states how things really are. It also supplies an important notion of *objective* truth.[5]

The intelligibility of a position does not, of course, entail its truth. Truth is not so easy to come by. The Ptolemaic model of the universe, for example, is intelligible but nonetheless false. Moderate realism, too, might be intelligible but false. That is, what is represented by a person's beliefs might not in fact be objective, even though it is intelligible that it is objective. In that case, moderate realism about the person's beliefs would be false but nonetheless intelligible. Given that moderate realism is intelligible, a quest for objectivity in what our beliefs represent is similarly intelligible. So, the familiar search in traditional epistemology for beliefs that are objective, in virtue of capturing conceiving-independent reality, is semantically acceptable, even if that search ultimately founders in light of some nonsemantical, epistemological problems. Let's turn to the latter problems.

2. Grounding Realism: From Intelligibility to Acceptability

Begging questions

Moderate realists want, of course, to maintain the truth and the (epistemically) rational acceptability of moderate realism, not just its intelligibility. Skepticism about moderate realism offers a dangerous obstacle. The central skeptical challenge is that moderate realists should deliver non-questionbegging epistemic support for moderate realism. In delivering such support, moderate realists will not beg relevant questions against their skeptical challengers. They will not simply assume any point needing defense in light of relevant skeptical questions. Otherwise, argument may become altogether superfluous in the exchange between realists and skeptics. A troublesome kind of epistemic arbitrariness would then threaten.

Given the permissibility of begging relevant questions, we can support *any* arbitrary position we like. We need only beg questions in a way that favors our preferred position. In that case, we would have intolerable epistemic arbitrariness in philosophical exchange. Cogent argument would be ultimately pointless, and doxastic caprice would threaten. Even though all arguments rest on premises, an argument's premises need not, of course, be questionbegging in a context of inquiry. So, the skeptical challenge at hand does not oppose argument in general. It opposes only arguments that beg relevant questions in a context of inquiry.

The skeptical challenge does not imply that moderate realism cannot be true or even that it is not true. So, the challenge does not require idealism of any sort. The main skeptical issue concerns not directly the objective truth or falsity of moderate realism but rather the kind of epistemic support available for it. Skeptics can acknowledge, if only for the sake of argument, that our representing any objective thing depends on such cognitively relevant processes as perception, introspection, memory, and testimony. The problem is that such processes apparently fail to yield non-questionbegging support for their own reliability or for the truth of the beliefs they deliver. Skeptics have asked, quite intelligibly, whether the processes in question create or at least decisively influence what is thereby represented. If they do, they risk being an unreliable means, even a completely unsuccessful means, to objectivity. In that case, our cognitive processes would function as producers or distorters rather than sound representers of their deliverances.

Skeptics, among others, doubt that we can avail ourselves of a position independent of our cognitively relevant processes to assess, in a non-questionbegging manner, either their general reliability in representing how things really are or the truth of the beliefs they yield. Skeptics, again among others, suspect that this is the unavoidable human cognitive predicament. Moderate realists seeking to avoid questionbegging reasoning will need either to offer a way out of this predicament or to show that the predicament is ultimately illusory.

William Alston has correctly noted that a threat of circularity, of the kind under scrutiny, "puts no limits whatever on the beliefs that can be justified, nor does it limit what can be known."[6] The skeptical problem at hand does not concern one's merely having justifying evidence for one's beliefs or even one's having true beliefs based on evidence resistant to Gettier-style problems. So, skeptics opposing circularity need not claim that we do not have justified belief or knowledge. Their challenge rather concerns one's producing, or at least having, *non-questionbegging epistemic support* for the truth of one's beliefs, given certain immediately relevant questions raised by skeptics. Since this challenge bears significantly, as noted previously, on the value of cogent argument over epistemic arbitrariness in philosophical inquiry, we do well to take the challenge seriously. We can pursue this challenge without digressing to controversy over the exact conditions for evidence, justification, or knowledge.

Skeptical questions

Consider the following familiar bases for beliefs entailing an objective world: (a) ordinary psychological processes, including perception, introspection, and memory, (b) suitable coherence among beliefs, (c) predictive success, and (d) widespread acceptance by one's community. Let's call such bases "grounding conditions" for beliefs entailing an objective world and, in turn, for moderate realism. Grounding conditions, according to many antiskeptics, can yield adequate epistemic support for beliefs entailing an external world and thus for moderate realism. We need to determine what kind of epistemic support is thereby yielded.

An essential feature of epistemic support for a proposition is that it provides a *truth-indicator* for that proposition. A truth-indicator can, of course, be fallible and probabilistic. Our epistemic support does not necessarily guarantee, or otherwise deliver, actual truth. For current purposes, we need not digress to debates over internalism and externalism concerning whether, and if so how, epistemic support must be accessible to a believer.[7]

In challenging moderate realism, skeptics inquire whether the available grounding conditions yield non-questionbegging epistemic support for such realism. They begin with a simple question: what non-questionbegging epistemic support have we to claim that moderate realism is objectively true? Realists typically reply by invoking some grounding condition for a belief entailing an objective world, often a member of the aforementioned options (a)–(d). Such a grounding condition, according to typical realists, yields the needed epistemic support for their moderate realism.

Skeptics will challenge any antiskeptical use of a grounding condition, as follows: what non-questionbegging epistemic support have we to claim that your preferred grounding condition is actually indicative of what is objectively the case? In other words, what non-questionbegging epistemic support have we to claim that a proposition (for instance, the proposition that mind-independent objects exist) warranted by your grounding condition is actually true? Realists who reply by invoking their preferred grounding conditions will beg this question against their skeptical challengers. The adequacy of those grounding conditions is being questioned now by skeptics, and begging their question will fail to deliver non-questionbegging support for moderate realism. Skeptics ban questionbegging reasoning, not fallibilism (the view that a well-grounded contingent belief can be false) or inductive inference in epistemic support. In addition, their ban on questionbegging reasoning remains neutral on issues about the exact conditions for epistemic justification and knowledge. So, skeptics are not relying on a special, self-serving account of justification, knowledge, or epistemic support.

Skeptics do not demand that realists argue for moderate realism without using premises. That would be absurd. They rather demand non-questionbegging epistemic support for moderate realism and for the common assumption that a preferred grounding condition is actually indicative of what is objectively the case. So, realists may offer premises in arguments whose conclusion is the truth of moderate realism. What they may not offer is a questionbegging premise given the skeptical challenge at hand. Such a premise would automatically fail to convince in a context of inquiry where it is itself under question, explicitly or implicitly. An argument using such a premise will be at best ineffective in the relevant context. Questionbegging thus makes argument superfluous.

The aforementioned human cognitive predicament suggests that realists will not meet the skeptical challenge. Epistemically significant access to anything by us apparently depends on such grounding conditions as perception, introspection, memory, testimony, and common sense. Since skeptics have questioned the reliability of such conditions in delivering objective truths, an appeal to such conditions will fail to yield the demanded non-questionbegging support. Whether *every* kind of cognitive being, including God, must beg questions against skeptics will remain open in this chapter. Even *if* cognition of every sort entails questionbegging against skeptics, owing to the nature of cognition itself, skeptics will be unmoved. They do not find the epistemic arbitrariness of questionbegging more acceptable in virtue of its allegedly being integral to cognition of any sort.

Skeptics are notorious for questioning our grounding conditions *on the whole*, that is, as a group. So, we cannot satisfy the skeptical challenge by invoking one preferred grounding condition to support another preferred grounding condition. The relevant challenge is *comprehensive*, bearing on grounding conditions, or supposed cognitive sources, *in general*. Any answer we give to such a comprehensive challenge will apparently rely on at least one of the grounding conditions being challenged. So, questionbegging seems to be our fate in competition with skeptics. Such, apparently, is the human cognitive predicament.

3. Realist Replies to Skepticism

Practical rationality

William Alston has replied to skeptical challenges to realism based on the threat of circularity, as follows:

> [It is] rational and proper to engage in our customary doxastic practices without having, or even being able to have, any positive noncircular reasons for supposing them to be reliable... [T]hese familiar practices [are] autonomous, acceptable on their own, just as such, without being grounded on anything external. Since any attempt to show one of these practices to be reliable will, in effect, assume the reliability of some other of our familiar practices there is no appeal beyond those practices.[8]

This reply has two important parts. First, it concedes that the skeptical challenge cannot be met, as we are unable to deliver noncircular (or, non-questionbegging) epistemic support for the cognitively relevant sources of our beliefs. So, the reply offers no threat to the main skeptical challenge. Second, the reply invokes a kind of rationality compatible with the unavoidable presence of epistemic circularity. What, however, does such rationality involve and what is its epistemic significance?

Alston's proposed rationality is "practical." It rests on the following rhetorical question offered by Alston: "Since we cannot take a step in intellectual endeavors without engaging in some doxastic practice(s) or other, what reasonable alternative is there to practicing the ones with which we are intimately familiar?"[9] Claiming that there is no such alternative, Alston follows Thomas Reid "in taking all our established doxastic practices to be acceptable as such, as innocent until proven guilty."[10] This talk of "established" doxastic practices is just talk of "customary" doxastic practices; it does not connote a special epistemic status. The core of Alston's practical rationality for doxastic practices is thus twofold: the thesis that there is no alternative to our customary doxastic practices and the thesis that such practices are innocent until proven guilty.

Skeptics can challenge the suggestion that there is no alternative to our customary doxastic practices, especially if our customary intellectual endeavors are optional. *Given* our customary intellectual endeavors (such as categorizing, explaining, and predicting), we perhaps have no easy alternative to our customary doxastic practices. Still, skeptics can challenge the epistemic significance of our customary intellectual endeavors. They can ask, quite intelligibly, whether those endeavors deliver accurate information about an objective world. In addition, they can intelligibly ask whether any non-questionbegging epistemic support indicates that practical rationality, of the sort recommended by Alston, yields reliability or objective truth in our resulting beliefs. If one concedes the lack of such support, then one's position is compatible with, and no challenge to, skepticism of the variety at hand. If, alternatively, one lays claim to such non-questionbegging support and offers a relevant grounding condition, then skeptics can challenge that grounding condition in the way indicated previously. The aforementioned human cognitive predicament offers no encouragement here.

Alston evidently agrees about the ineffectiveness of practical rationality in challenging shrewd skeptics. He concedes:

> We have shown, at most, that engaging in SP [= sense perceptual practice] enjoys a *practical* rationality; it is a reasonable thing to do, given our aims and our situation. But then it is only that same practical rationality that carries over, via the commitment relation, to the judgment that SP is reliable. We have not shown that it is rational in an *epistemic* sense that SP is reliable, where the latter involves showing that it is at least probably true that SP is reliable. . . . We have not shown the reliability attribution to be rational in a truth-conducive sense of rationality, one that itself is subject to a reliability constraint.[11]

So, we cannot invoke Alston's practical rationality to meet the skeptical challenge under examination. Skeptics will naturally ask what non-questionbegging epistemic support we have to suppose that practical rationality is actually indicative of objective truth. It seems doubtful that an answer favorable to moderate realism will avoid begging relevant questions against such skeptics.

An appeal to practical rationality for antiskeptical purposes resembles pragmatic defenses of realism. The latter defenses aim to rebut skeptical challenges on the basis of a belief's overall utility relative to set purposes, whether theoretical or practical. Skeptics will be unmoved, however, owing to the significance of this question: what non-questionbegging epistemic support have we to claim that a belief's overall pragmatic utility (of whatever degree or kind one prefers) is actually indicative of what is objectively the case? Resources for an adequate answer in favor of realism seem not to be readily available. It would not serve realists at all to claim that it is pragmatically useful to believe that pragmatic utility is indicative of objective truth. That move would only invite the skeptical challenge at a higher level, where it remains unanswered. Practical considerations, then, seem not to meet the skeptical challenge. As a result, they leave moderate realism inadequately defended.

Inference to best explanation

Many philosophers have tried to defend realism on the basis of explanatory considerations, specifically on the basis of an inference to best explanation.[12] A crucial assumption is that moderate realism is part of the best explanation of our overall perceptual experiences and thereby resists skeptical challenges. One might supplement this assumption with the claim that our perceptual inputs apparently are, at least for the most part, involuntary, unlike certain cases of active imagination. Typical perceptual inputs seem not to arise subjectively from our volitional activity.

However realists develop an argument from best explanation, skeptics can identify two problems. First, even *if* we have no indication in our experience of a subjective source of our object-like perceptual inputs, we likewise lack a non-questionbegging indication in our experience of an objective source of those inputs. In particular, we lack non-questionbegging epistemic support for the assumption that the absence of an indication of a subjective volitional source yields an indication of an objective source. Second, inference to be best explanation invites the same kind of challenge facing the grounding conditions noted above. In particular, what non-questionbegging epistemic support have we to claim that an inference to the best explanation (however elaborated) is actually indicative of how things really are, or of what is objectively the case?

The considerations raised in connection with the previous grounding conditions suggest, owing to the human cognitive predicament, that the support demanded by skeptics is not actually forthcoming. We apparently lack an independent standpoint for delivering the required support. At least, realists have not shown otherwise. Inference to the best explanation may be central to "justification" as commonly understood, but we have no reason to think that it delivers an adequate answer to the skeptical challenge.

Science, skepticism, and realism

Many realists hold that our best science lends support to their realism. For example, Michael Devitt has appealed to our best science to challenge skepticism, as follows:

> The thorough-going sceptic sets the standards of knowledge (or rational belief) too high for them ever to be achieved. Our best science shows us this. It shows us, for example, that if knowledge is to be gathered we must eliminate implausible hypotheses without being able, ultimately, to justify that elimination. It shows us that there is always an (empirical) possibility of error with any (normal) knowledge claim. Standards that our best science shows cannot be met short of instantaneous solipsism – a doctrine that is literally incredible – should be ignored. Scepticism is simply uninteresting: it throws the baby out with the bath water.[13]

Contrary to Devitt's suggestion, the skeptical challenge entertained in this chapter does not set excessively high standards for knowledge or justified belief. It grants realists their preferred standards for knowledge and justified belief. It even grants that people can have knowledge and justified belief by those standards. The central issue concerns the availability of non-questionbegging epistemic support for moderate realism. Realists cannot simply assume, by way of convincing reply to skeptics, that they actually possess such epistemic support. Even though moderate realism is nonepistemic in what it claims, proponents must, in a context of inquiry with skeptics, deliver the required non-questionbegging epistemic support for their realism or make a concession to the skeptical challengers.

Devitt calls his approach to epistemology "naturalized," because it recommends that "the epistemic relation between humans and the world itself becomes the object of scientific study."[14] He explains:

> Naturalized epistemology takes science and hence its posits pretty much for granted. And an obvious starting assumption is . . . that these posits exist objectively and independently of the mental. So it approaches epistemology from a Realist standpoint . . .[15]

Devitt claims that "once the sceptical problematic is abandoned in favour of a naturalized epistemology, arguments against Realism lack all cogency," adding that "Realism alone explains 'the regularities in our experience.'"[16] The latter point suggests a return to inference to best explanation (on which see the previous section of this chapter).

Two considerations raise problems. First, we have already raised doubts about the ability of explanatory considerations to answer the skeptical challenge. Even if realism has singular explanatory value, and thus achieves a kind of explanatory justification, it does not thereby gain non-questionbegging epistemic support. Hence, the skeptical challenge remains unanswered. Second, contrary to Devitt's suggestion, naturalized epistemology does not automatically block the cogency of arguments against realism. The skeptical challenge persists so long as (a) questionbegging is inappropriate in a context of debate with skeptics and (b) realism lacks non-questionbegging epistemic support. This challenge, we have seen, does not rest on excessively high standards for knowledge or justified belief. We can illustrate the second point in connection with W. V. Quine's naturalism about epistemology.

Quine maintains that skeptical doubt is "an offshoot of science" in that such doubt arises from simple physical science about the reality of bodies.[17] Simple physical science, Quine holds, is crucial to our distinction between reality and illusion. This view prompts Quine's suggestion that epistemology is "an enterprise within natural science."[18] Quine has motivated this suggestion in a manner favorable to realism, as follows:

> I also expressed, at the beginning, my unswerving belief in external things – people, nerve endings, sticks, stones. This I reaffirm. I believe also, if less firmly, in atoms and electrons and in classes. Now how is all this robust realism to be reconciled with the barren scene that I have just been depicting? The answer is naturalism: the recognition that it is within science itself, and not in some prior philosophy, that reality is to be identified and described.[19]

Evidently, Quine's naturalism relies on a principle of credulity regarding the reliability of our best science. This principle entails that we may reasonably assume the reliability of our best science in describing objective reality. Can such a principle disarm the skeptical challenge?

We may grant, if only for the sake of argument, that "simple" physical science is crucial to our having *the distinction* between what is real and what is illusory. Even so, our physical science, whether simple or complex, might still fail to deliver objectively true beliefs concerning what is real. The history of physical science bears witness to this. As a result, it is intelligible (but not, of course, thereby true) that most of the theses of our physical science are not objectively true. Principles of interpretive charity, including those offered by Quine and Donald Davidson, offer no serious challenge here, given a distinction between the conditions for the actual content of a belief and the conditions for *ascribing* a belief's content.[20]

The naturalist principle of credulity entails that we may reasonably assume the reliability of our best science in describing objective reality. Philosophers have rarely noted that this principle is not itself a hypothesis of our best science. Even if some scientists have adopted a principle of credulity, this principle is not a scientific hypothesis. It is rather a philosophical principle that goes beyond natural science proper. Witness the absence in natural science of a means of testing the principle of credulity. The crucial point, however, is that the principle of credulity does not enjoy non-questionbegging epistemic support of the kind demanded by skeptics.

The main question is: what non-questionbegging epistemic support have we for the claim that a belief satisfying the principle of credulity is objectively true? Let *scientific rationality* be the kind of rationality offered by belief-formation in accord with the principle of credulity. The question then becomes: what non-questionbegging epistemic support have we for the claim that scientific rationality is indicative of what is objectively the case? An appeal to our best science will be questionbegging in this connection, even if our best science delivers simplicity, comprehensiveness, and predictive success in belief-formation. Skeptics are equal-opportunity challengers of preferred grounding conditions. So, the sciences get no special respect in debates with skeptics. Naturalized epistemology thus fails to answer the skeptical challenge.

Perhaps, contrary to the available evidence, Quine does not actually hold a principle of credulity for our best science. In any case, this would not rescue him from the skeptical challenge, because questions about the reliability of our best science persist. Apart from a principle of credulity, Quine's naturalism slides dangerously toward skepticism. It would then lack a basis for its reliance on the reliability of prediction regarding sensory checkpoints as a guideline in the formation of theories. The naturalist would then be indistinguishable from the skeptic, at least relative to the skeptical challenge under examination.[21]

Circularity and intellectual satisfaction

Perhaps we have made too much of the skeptical challenge and thereby overlooked what really matters in an epistemology. Richard Foley has suggested as much, as follows:

> Inquiry requires a leap of intellectual faith, and the need for such faith cannot be eliminated by further inquiry, whether it be empirical or philosophical or whatever. ... Since we can never have non-question-begging assurances that our way of viewing things is correct, we can never have assurances that there is no point to further inquiry. The absolute knowledge of the Hegelian system, which requires the knowing mind to

be wholly adequate to its objects and to know with utter certainty that it is thus, is not a possibility for us.... For us there can be no such final resting spot.[22]

Many skeptics would welcome this attitude toward inquiry, given its concession that non-questionbegging assurances for the correctness of our beliefs are unavailable. The basis of this concession is evidently Foley's observation that "if a proposed method of inquiry is fundamental, then it cannot help but be used in its own defense if it is to be defended at all." Foley adds that "some questions deserve to be begged, [and that] questions about the reliability of our fundamental methods of inquiry are just such questions."[23]

Two questions arise. First, what can support an inference from the observation that we *cannot* avoid questionbegging regarding a fundamental method of inquiry to the view that some questions *deserve* to be begged? (I am not attributing this dubious inference to Foley; rather, I am considering how one might develop his remarks on questionbegging.) This question concerns epistemic support of a kind relevant to debates with skeptics. It is not about pragmatic expediency, but even if it were, skeptics could follow up with questions about the epistemic support for assumptions about what beliefs have pragmatic expediency. Skeptics will properly doubt that our inability to avoid begging skeptical questions *entitles* us as truth-seekers to beg those questions. Begging skeptical questions may obviously *hinder* our goal of acquiring truth and avoiding error (especially in cases where it fosters epistemic arbitrariness), and it will automatically leave skeptics unanswered. Our position will then seem epistemically arbitrary relative to intelligible skeptical questions. Second, what reason have we to link a demand for non-questionbegging epistemic support with a quest for *certainty*? The skeptical challenge under consideration has no conflict with the common assumption that the epistemic support for contingent propositions is typically fallible and defeasible and fails to yield epistemic certainty. We thus should separate a demand for non-questionbegging epistemic support from a demand for certainty.

Foley aims to liberate epistemology by linking it with "egocentric rationality," as follows:

> The prerequisite of egocentric rationality is not truth or reliability, not even in the long run; it is, rather, the absence of any internal motivation for either retraction or supplementation of our beliefs. Egocentric rationality requires that we have beliefs that are to our own deep intellectual satisfaction – beliefs that do not merely satisfy us in a superficial way but that would do so even with the deepest reflection. To be egocentrically rational is thus to be invulnerable to a certain kind of self-condemnation. It is to have beliefs that in our role as truth-seekers we wouldn't criticize ourselves for having even if we were to be deeply reflective.[24]

Egocentric rationality thus preserves our "role as truth-seekers," and thereby avoids collapse into merely pragmatic rationality. At the same time, it excludes truth as a "prerequisite," and thereby allows for fallibilism concerning rational belief. So far, so good.

The problem is that many of us truth-seekers, skeptics included, are not actually satisfied by questionbegging in the presence of skeptical challenges. In addition, this dissatisfaction endures even upon our deepest reflection, owing to the apparent epistemic arbitrariness in the relevant questionbegging against skeptics. Acknowledging this, we must deny that egocentric rationality liberates us from the skeptical challenge haunting us throughout this chapter. Foley himself does not pretend that egocentric rationality automatically saves a person from the threat of skeptical challenges. Rather, he properly reminds us that "many intellectually undesirable characteristics are compatible with being rational."[25] This is doubtless correct, but the skeptical challenge remains unanswered, and nonskeptics are still open to a charge of epistemically arbitrary questionbegging in the face of skeptical challenges. Skeptics will treat deep intellectual satisfaction as just another preferred grounding condition, and ask what non-questionbegging epistemic support we have to claim that it is actually indicative of how things really are. It is doubtful, then, that egocentric rationality will save moderate realism from the skeptical challenge.

4. Skepticism: Useless or Inconsistent?

Skepticism and eliminative pragmatism

Richard Rorty currently proposes that we reorient epistemology in a way that banishes questions about objectivity as "useless." Perhaps we can avoid the skeptical challenge of this chapter by simply eliminating traditional epistemological questions as altogether useless, even *if* they are intelligible.

Rorty proposes that any relevant constraint on inquiry will come from the remarks of fellow-inquirers in "our community," and his characterization of the members of our community is avowedly Darwinian. We humans are "animals with special organs and abilities," according to Rorty, but "they no more put us in a *representational* relation to an intrinsic nature of things than do the anteater's snout or the bower-bird's skill at weaving."[26] Rorty proposes, in addition, that "we should see what happens if (in Jean-Paul Sartre's words) 'we attempt to draw the full conclusion from a consistently atheist position', a position in which such phrases as 'the nature of human life' no longer distract us from the absence of a God's-eye view."[27] Rorty recommends that we "think of our relation to the rest of the universe in purely causal, as opposed to representationalist, terms," on the ground that Darwin, Dewey, and Davidson have made such a view promising.[28]

Rorty now confesses that many of his earlier criticisms of traditional philosophical distinctions and themes were misplaced:

> I should not have spoken of "unreal" or "confused" philosophical distinctions, but rather of distinctions whose employment has proved to lead nowhere, proved to be more trouble than they were worth. For pragmatists like Putnam and me, the question should always be, "What use it is?" rather than "Is it real?" or "Is it confused?"

> Criticism of other philosophers' distinctions and problematics should charge relative inutility, rather than "meaninglessness" or "illusion" or "incoherence."[29]

Rorty thus holds that *utility* rather than reality, or even evident reality, sets the standard for philosophical assessment. This fits well with Rorty's antiepistemological, antirepresentationalist pragmatism.

Rorty's main criticism now of various traditional distinctions pertinent to epistemology (for example, subject–object, scheme–content, and reality–appearance distinctions) is that they lack adequate utility. More generally, Rorty faults traditional epistemology (roughly, epistemology in the tradition of Plato's *Theaetetus*) for assuming that truth is something we can and should try to discover. He remarks:

> To say that we should drop the idea of truth as out there waiting to be discovered is not to say that we have discovered that, out there, there is no truth. It is to say that our purposes would be served best by ceasing to see truth as a deep matter, as a topic of philosophical interest, or "true" as a term which repays "analysis." "The nature of truth" is an unprofitable topic, resembling in this respect "the nature of man" and "the nature of God," and differing from "the nature of the positron," and "the nature of Oedipal fixation."[30]

Rorty urges that we replace the vocabulary of traditional epistemology with a new pragmatist vocabulary enabling us to "stop doing" traditional epistemology, including philosophical inquiry about skepticism. Rorty thus offers an epistemological analogue of eliminative materialism, the view that common psychological vocabulary should be replaced with a "better," materialist vocabulary.

Let's call Rorty's antiepistemological, antirepresentationalist view *eliminative pragmatism*. Its main negative thesis is that the vocabulary, problems, and goals of traditional epistemology are unprofitable and in need of replacement by pragmatist successors. Its main positive thesis is that "all philosophy should do is compare and contrast cultural traditions," that is, provide "a study of the comparative advantages and disadvantages of the various ways of talking which our race has invented."[31] Eliminative pragmatism endorses the philosophical dispensability of concerns about how the world really is, and recommends the central philosophical importance of what is profitable, advantageous, or useful. Rorty emphasizes *usefulness*, not majority opinion. As he says, "I do not recall that I have ever, even at my worst, spoken of either warrant or truth being determined by *majority* vote."[32]

A number of questions arise: Useful *for whom*? Useful *in what manner*? Useful *to what extent* and *for how long*? Since Rorty does not pursue these questions, his eliminative pragmatism resists precise formulation. The view raises, however, a more serious problem. Consider the implication of eliminative pragmatism that a claim is acceptable to us if and only if it is useful to us. (Let's allow Rorty to pick whatever notion of *useful* he finds useful.) This approach to acceptability is externalist in that it requires neither that we be aware of nor that we be able to access the usefulness of what is acceptable to us. Mere usefulness, rather than accessible usefulness, determines acceptability. Some philosophers, favoring internalism, hold that whatever confers rational acceptability for us must be accessible to us. This is not our problem now, however.

The problem is that if usefulness determines acceptability in the manner implied by eliminative pragmatism, then a view will be acceptable to us if and only if *it is true, and thus factually the case*, that the view is useful to us. The appeal to usefulness, then, entails something about matters of fact, and actual truth, regarding usefulness. Call this *the factuality requirement* on eliminative pragmatism. The factuality requirement, although neglected by Rorty, manifests that eliminative pragmatists do not – and, I suggest, cannot – avoid considerations about the real nature of things, about how things really are. Such implied minimal realism resists easy escape, even among pragmatists.

Pragmatists might counter the factuality requirement with the view that we need be concerned only with what it is useful for us (rather than true) to believe regarding what is useful for us. Such a reply may appear to advance pragmatism, but it is ultimately defective, if not useless. It generates a dilemma of either an unanswered important question or an implausible regress. The unanswered important question is: must it be *true*, in a particular case, that it is useful for us to believe something regarding what is useful for us? The implausible regress stems from applying the present reply to each level of questioning about whether it must be true that usefulness obtains. The result is an endless regress of increasingly complex claims about what is useful for us. Rorty himself has not embraced such a regress, and this is to his credit. The same threat of regress troubles any appeal to mere agreement about what is useful for us. If an actual fact about agreement has no place, we shall be left with a regress concerning agreement. As section 1 noted, the inevitability of making a claim regarding what is factual bears on *any* assertion, not just on the assertions of pragmatism.

Barring an implausible endless regress, the factuality requirement is unavoidable. It follows that eliminative pragmatism makes acceptability a function of how things really are, at least with respect to actual usefulness for us. Given the factuality requirement, we can easily raise traditional epistemological questions, including skeptical questions, about what is in fact useful. We can ask, for example, whether it is *true* that a particular view is useful for us, whether we have overwhelming *evidence* that this is true, and even whether we have non-questionbegging epistemic support that this is true. Traditional epistemology can thrive, then, even on eliminative pragmatism. Indeed, eliminative pragmatism invites the questions central to traditional epistemology, including skeptical questions. There is no problem here, then, for traditional epistemology or for the skeptical challenge of this chapter.

What about the status of eliminative pragmatism itself? Is it supposed to offer a *true* claim about acceptability? Does it aim to characterize the *real nature* of acceptability, how acceptability *really* is? Let's assume that it does. It then offers a characterization illicit by its own standard. In that case, it runs afoul of its own assumption that we should eliminate from philosophy concerns about how things really are. As a result, eliminative pragmatism faces a troublesome kind of self-defeat: it does what it says should not be done. It thereby violates its own normative standard for theories. Stable theories, in philosophy and elsewhere, avoid any such defect of self-defeat.[33] In keeping with the previous remarks, we can also raise traditional skeptical questions about eliminative pragmatism itself. For example, is the claim of eliminative pragmatism about acceptability epistemically supportable in a non-questionbegging manner?

If eliminative pragmatism does not offer, or even aim to offer, a characterization of the real nature of acceptability of belief, then why should we bother with it, if we aim to characterize acceptability of belief? Given the latter aim, we should not bother with it, as it is then irrelevant, *useless* to our purpose. Considerations of usefulness, ever significant to pragmatism, can thus count against eliminative pragmatism itself. Pragmatists have overlooked this potential difficulty for their pragmatism. If Rorty's pragmatism is indeed antirepresentational, it will have difficulty accommodating any talk of acceptability of belief, since belief is irredeemably representational. Perhaps, then, his pragmatism is altogether irrelevant to issues of rational belief or judgment.

We now have a simple dilemma for Rorty's antiepistemological position: either eliminative pragmatism is self-defeating or it is irrelevant to typical epistemologists seeking an account of epistemic acceptability or justifiability. This dilemma resists easy answers, and it indicates that eliminative pragmatism fails to challenge traditional epistemology and traditional skeptical worries. Many of us, in any case, do not find a self-defeating theory useful, given our theoretical aims concerning epistemic acceptability. So, by the very standards of Rorty's eliminative pragmatism, self-defeat is troublesome for us.

What exactly does Rorty mean in speaking of his eliminative pragmatism as "better" than traditional approaches to epistemology? He remarks:

> Let me just grant that, in some suitably broad sense, I *do* want to substitute new concepts for old. I want to recommend explaining "better" (in the context "better standards of warranted assertability") as "will come to seem better to *us*" ... Nor can I see what "us" can mean here except: us educated, sophisticated, tolerant, wet liberals, the people who are always willing to hear the other side, to think out all the implications, etc. – the sort of people, in short, who both Putnam and I hope, at our best, to be.[34]

If Rorty seeks "better standards of warranted assertability," he apparently will be committed to representational entities, such as beliefs. Only representational entities can have warranted assertability, at least as standardly characterized. Perhaps, then, Rorty's pragmatism is not antirepresentational after all. Even so, Rorty's characterization of "better" is defective, and perhaps even lacking in utility. It explains "better" in terms of "seems *better* to us," thereby using "better" (the very term needing elucidation) in the proposed explanans. In addition, it explains "us" in terms of the sort of people Rorty and others hope, at their *best*, to be, thereby relying on an obscure notion of bestness. One can, of course, be willing to "hear the other side" but then irrationally dismiss it. Certainly more is required of a group whose "seeming better" will determine what *is* better in standards of warranted assertibility. Epistemological betterness is much too easy to come by, given Rorty's weak social strictures. As a result, Rorty's standard for betterness is largely useless in resolving epistemological disputes. In addition, since there is no necessary connection between what "will come to seem better to us" and what is "actually useful" to us, Rorty's characterization marks a departure from pragmatism, contrary to its avowed aim.

Rorty apparently deems his pragmatism impervious to the sort of self-defeat identified previously. He claims: "My strategy for escaping the self-referential difficulties into which 'the Relativist' keeps getting himself is to move everything over from epistemology and metaphysics to cultural politics, . . . to suggestions about what we should try."[35] This move does not, however, escape the problem of self-defeat, because claims about what we *should try* are directly analogous to claims about what is *useful for us*. Rorty's attempted "pragmatic justification of [eliminative] pragmatism" generates the troublesome dilemma noted previously, unless some odd, hitherto unexplained approach to assertion is at work. Rorty favors a disquotationalist approach to truth, but he has not offered a theory of assertion that blocks the relevance of epistemological issues in light of the aforementioned dilemma for his pragmatism.

A pragmatist might recommend that we simply eliminate any talk of acceptable belief. Indeed, it is perhaps surprising that Rorty does not propose this, given (a) that he is an antirepresentationalist and (b) that belief is inherently representational. On this proposal, however, Rorty would be barred from offering his own pragmatism as acceptable and traditional epistemology as unacceptable. Rorty would then be left with a kind of evaluative nihilism. Anteaters perhaps do not evaluate in normative terms, but we humans do, and only a desperate theorist would suggest otherwise. In sum, then, Rorty's eliminative pragmatism does not improve on traditional epistemology, but rather suffers from self-defeat. It offers, in the end, no real difficulty for the skeptical challenge of this chapter.

Is skepticism inconsistent?

William Lycan has charged that a common skeptical demand is "contradictory." So, we need to ask whether this charge bears on the skeptical challenge under examination. Lycan has identified the general skeptical worry "that if the canons [of justification] are ultimate and cannot themselves be justified, then it seems that they are epistemically *arbitrary*; they are the rules that human beings happen to use, perhaps even the rules that human beings are built to use, but that does nothing to justify them in the normative sense appropriate to epistemology."[36] Note that Lycan has thus far identified a worry concerning *justification*, not questionbegging reasoning.

Lycan replies to the skeptical worry by rejecting an underlying contradictory demand:

On pain of circularity or regress, we know that some epistemic methods or procedures (whether explanatory methods or others) are going to be fundamental; so if a theorist is claiming to have discovered some such fundamental epistemic method, it is a fortiori inappropriate to respond by demanding a justification of it, in the sense of a deduction of it from some more fundamental principle – indeed, it is contradictory. Basic epistemic norms, like moral norms (and logical norms), are justified not by being deduced from more fundamental norms (an obvious impossibility) but by their ability to sort specific, individual normative intuitions and other relevant data into the right barrels in an economical and illuminating way. The present skeptical observation is tautologous, and the attendant demand is contradictory.[37]

Clearly, skeptics would be guilty of contradiction if they granted the existence of fundamental epistemic norms and demanded that those norms be deduced from more fundamental norms. The skeptical demand of this chapter, however, is that realists not beg questions against skeptics who have raised intelligible questions about the truth of moderate realism and the adequacy of grounding conditions for such realism regarding their being indicative of objective reality. The latter demand does not entail the contradiction just noted. Specifically, it does not entail that fundamental epistemic norms be deduced from more fundamental norms.

Lycan does consider a skeptic who (a) grants that beliefs warranted by particular methods are useful and conducive to success in goal-seeking but (b) asks the following question: what independent reason have we for thinking that they *correspond to reality?*"[38] Lycan mentions the observation that we cannot vacate our first-person perspective in order to compare our beliefs with objective reality, but he finds that "this observation seems pointless."[39] In keeping with the latter remark, Lycan identifies his explanationist epistemology with pragmatism, on the ground that explanatory virtues are pragmatic virtues making beliefs useful.[40] So, he may be suggesting a response to skeptical challenges that is similar to Rorty's aforementioned pragmatism. In particular, Lycan may share Rorty's view that the appropriate reply to some skeptical questions is just: those questions are not useful; they are pointless.

We have already seen some deficiencies in pragmatist attempts to disarm skeptical challenges. The central point now is that the skeptical challenge of this chapter may be very important, or "useful," in illuminating the limitations of human reasoning in debates with shrewd skeptics. More specifically, the challenge may illustrate that even though we have a principled opposition to questionbegging, owing to its attendant epistemic arbitrariness, we cannot avoid questionbegging in the face of some intelligible skeptical questions.

The fact that we cannot meet the skeptical challenge of this chapter does not show, or in any way indicate, that the challenge is useless, or pointless. On the contrary, the resulting lesson is very important for our understanding the limitations of human reasoning, especially in the context of debates with shrewd skeptics. What antiskeptics must explain is why questionbegging in the face of the skeptical challenge does not foster epistemic arbitrariness of the sort found, and generally opposed, in paradigmatic cases of circular reasoning. This is the key explanatory challenge raised by skepticism. Neither Lycan nor any other antiskeptic has delivered the needed explanation. Consequently, the skeptical challenge remains unscathed and directly relevant to moderate realism. Although the challenge focuses on circularity in defenses of moderate realism, it bears on any kind of first-order or higher-order support, or evidence, relevant to beliefs entailing moderate realism. Circularity arises in the presence of skeptical questions about the truth of beliefs based on one's preferred first-order or higher-order support, or evidence.

Aside from the views of Lycan and Rorty, a common antiskeptical ploy aims to show that skeptics themselves must assume a certain epistemic status for their premises and conclusions and thereby contradict their official position. (Such a result would concern what *skeptics must assume*, not skepticism itself as a thesis.) Sometimes this ploy comes with the charge that skepticism is self-referentially inconsistent or otherwise self-defeating. The truth of this charge would not by itself substantiate moderate realism, but it would disarm a serious challenge for philosophers aiming to defend realism. Perhaps the skeptical challenge of this chapter suffers from a kind of self-defeat, owing to some of its implications.

Two questions arise. First, must skeptics assume that their challenge to realism is non-questionbegging either relative to their own questions or relative to questions raised by realists? Second, is the skeptical challenge of this chapter itself questionbegging in a way that undermines its epistemic significance? Even a question can be questionbegging in virtue of its implications.

Let's distinguish two families of skeptics: skeptics who simply ask troublesome antirealist questions (such as those of this chapter concerning non-questionbegging epistemic support) and skeptics who offer antirealist theses and arguments. Call the former *interrogative* skeptics and the latter *declarative* skeptics. Declarative skeptics demanding non-questionbegging epistemic support from moderate realists offer intelligible theses and even arguments. So, we can ask whether declarative skeptics must presume that their theses are themselves non-questionbegging and, in addition, rest on non-questionbegging support. This question prompts another: must presume *for what*? A likely answer is: must presume for the skeptical challenge to succeed. Skeptics can, of course, offer theses just for the sake of argument, in order to elicit a troublesome result from an antiskeptical position.

Regarding this chapter's skeptical challenge, interrogative and declarative skeptics will succeed if and only if we have, in the wake of their antirealist challenge, no salient indication of non-questionbegging epistemic support for moderate realism. So, there is no requirement of a presumed or actual epistemic status inimical to skepticism. Is this, however, a principle of credulity for skepticism and therefore a double standard at work in the contest between skeptics and realists? Have we arbitrarily and unjustly shifted the epistemic burden away from skeptics to realists? Many realists will doubtless complain thus.

An interrogative skeptic, who issues challenging antirealist questions without offering theses or arguments, needs no principle of credulity for skepticism. Lacking a salient indication of non-questionbegging epistemic support for moderate realism, interrogative skeptics will leave their potential audience to draw the appropriate lesson from the unanswered skeptical challenge. Moderate realists, in contrast, offer a controversial ontological thesis about the objective world and thereby accrue a burden of epistemic support inapplicable to the interrogative skeptic. Moderate realists inherit a burden of epistemic support from their moderate realism. Interrogative skeptics have no corresponding disputed ontological position. Hence, they have no corresponding burden of epistemic support. Such asymmetry between the two camps makes all the epistemic difference in the world.

What about declarative skeptics? Aren't they promoting epistemic doubt while enjoying benefits thereby forbidden? Both declarative and interrogative skeptics may benefit from the fact that their skeptical challenge should not itself be a matter of dispute given our proper opposition to questionbegging in philosophica exchange. This opposition is proper owing to the threat of epistemic arbitrariness posed by questionbegging. Antiskeptics have not explained why questionbegging against the skeptical challenge does not condone epistemic arbitrariness of the sort found, and generally opposed, in typical cases of circular reasoning. We have already identified this key explanatory challenge raised by skeptics, and we can now see its role in answering the question about burden-shifting.

The skeptical challenge of this chapter does not introduce an epistemic standard foreign to moderate realists. It rather identifies a skeptical implication of an epistemic standard already (and properly) accepted by typical moderate realists. The antecedent role of this standard among realists is manifested in their attitude toward ordinary cases of circular reasoning, particularly the epistemic arbitrariness present in such cases. The skeptical challenge of this chapter is really nothing more than a call for epistemic consistency in the views of moderate realists. They properly oppose questionbegging elsewhere, but have no principled basis for making an exception in the case of the skeptical challenge. Skeptics exploit this consideration in their challenge concerning the absence of non-questionbegging epistemic support for moderate realism.

The skeptical challenge of this chapter would be ineffective if it were itself questionbegging against moderate realists. In that case, realists could plausibly challenge it as being epistemically arbitrary in the way that circular reasoning is. So, declarative skeptics do well not to challenge realists with questionbegging theses, and interrogative skeptics do well not to challenge realists with questions that are questionbegging in virtue of their implications. The skeptical challenge of this chapter illustrates that skeptics need not engage in such questionbegging. Of course, skeptics need not start with the assumption that there actually are moderate realists. They can run their story on the assumption of imagined moderate realists. The outcome would be the same: the skeptical challenge remains unchallenged and, therefore, the threat of epistemic arbitrariness persists.

5. Conclusion

Suppose that we cannot answer the skeptical challenge to deliver non-questionbegging epistemic support for moderate realism. What follows? First, realists cannot refute, or even defend themselves against, a notorious protagonist in the drama of Western epistemology, the shrewd skeptic. Second, human reasoning is more limited, less resourceful, than many epistemologists have assumed. Third, we need some way to bracket the skeptical challenge if we aim to proceed with constructive epistemology.[41] We cannot infer, however, that realism is false, unjustified, or not known to be true. Non-questionbegging epistemic support might not be a prerequisite for justification or knowledge. At least, nobody has shown that it is. Even so, we do well to take the skeptical challenge seriously, in order to identify the limitations of human reasoning. An important result will be increased wisdom and epistemic humility as well.

Notes

Thanks to Paul Abela, John Greco, and David Yandell for very helpful comments.

1. For further taxonomy for realism, see Michael Devitt, *Realism and Truth* (Oxford: Blackwell, 1984) and William Alston, *A Realist Conception of Truth* (Ithaca: Cornell University Press, 1996).
2. Richard Rorty, *Contingency, Irony, and Solidarity* (New York: Cambridge University Press, 1989), p. 20, and *Consequences of Pragmatism* (Minneapolis: University of Minnesota Press, 1982), p. 15.
3. Hilary Putnam, *The Many Faces of Realism* (La Salle, IL: Open Court, 1987), p. 36.
4. For further details on this problem, see Paul Moser, "A Dilemma for Internal Realism," *Philosophical Studies* 59 (1990): 101–6.
5. For elaboration and defense of this definition, see Paul Moser, *Knowledge and Evidence* (New York: Cambridge University Press, 1989), ch. 1; cf. Alston, *A Realist Conception of Truth*.
6. William Alston, "Epistemic Circularity," in Alston, *Epistemic Justification* (Ithaca: Cornell University Press, 1989), p. 349.
7. On such debates, see Moser, *Knowledge and Evidence*, ch. 2; Alston, *Epistemic Justification*, chs. 8 and 9; and Richard Fumerton, *Metaepistemology and Skepticism* (Lanham, MD: Rowman and Littlefield, 1995), chs. 3–7.
8. William Alston, *The Reliability of Sense Perception* (Ithaca: Cornell University Press, 1993), p. 124; cf. p. 125.
9. Ibid., pp. 125–6.
10. Ibid., p. 129.
11. Ibid., p. 133.
12. Some recent attempts can be found in James Cornman, *Skepticism, Justification, and Explanation* (Dordrecht: Reidel, 1980); Alan Goldman, *Empirical Knowledge* (Berkeley: University of California Press, 1988), chs. 9, 13; and Moser, *Knowledge and Evidence*, chs. 2–4.
13. Devitt, *Realism and Truth*, p. 63.
14. Ibid., p. 64.
15. Ibid.
16. Ibid., p. 68.

17 W. V. O. Quine, "The Nature of Natural Knowledge," in S. Guttenplan, ed., *Mind and Language* (Oxford: Clarendon Press, 1975), pp. 67–8.
18 Ibid., p. 68.
19 W. V. O. Quine, "Things and Their Place in Theories," in Quine, *Theories and Things* (Cambridge, MA: Harvard University Press, 1981), p. 21.
20 See W. V. O. Quine, *Word and Object* (Cambridge, MA: MIT Press, 1960) and Donald Davidson, "A Coherence Theory of Truth and Knowledge," in Dieter Henrich, ed., *Kant oder Hegel* (Stuttgart: Klett-Cotta, 1983). On the ineffectiveness of principles of charity against skepticism, see Paul Moser, *Philosophy After Objectivity* (New York: Oxford University Press, 1993), pp. 228–37, and Richard Foley, *Working Without a Net* (New York: Oxford University Press, 1993), pp. 67–73.
21 For more detail on this challenge to naturalism, as well as a serious self-referential problem for Quine's epistemological naturalism, see Paul Moser and David Yandell, "Against Naturalizing Rationality," *Protosociology* 8/9 (1996): 81–96.
22 Foley, *Working Without a Net*, p. 78.
23 Ibid., p. 77; ibid.
24 Ibid., pp. 78–9.
25 Ibid., pp. 80–1.
26 Richard Rorty, "Putnam and the Relativist Menace," *The Journal of Philosophy* 90 (1993): 449.
27 Ibid., p. 449.
28 Ibid. Cf. Richard Rorty, "Antirepresentationalism, Ethnocentrism, and Liberalism," in Rorty, *Objectivity, Relativism, and Truth: Philosophical Papers, Volume 1* (New York: Cambridge University Press, 1991), p. 7. For critical discussion of Rorty's current antirepresentationalist approach to realism, see Paul Moser, "Beyond Realism and Idealism," *Philosophia* 23 (1994): 271–88.
29 Rorty, "Putnam and the Relativist Menace," p. 445.
30 Rorty, *Contingency, Irony, and Solidarity*, p. 8.
31 Rorty, *Consequences of Pragmatism*, pp. xxxvii, xl.
32 Rorty, "Putnam and the Relativist Menace," p. 454.
33 For more detail on self-defeat, and an application to naturalized epistemology, see Moser and Yandell, "Against Naturalizing Rationality."
34 Rorty, "Putnam and the Relativist Menace," pp. 455, 451–2.
35 Ibid., p. 457.
36 William Lycan, *Judgement and Justification* (New York: Cambridge University Press, 1988), p. 134.
37 Ibid., pp. 135–6.
38 Ibid., pp. 136–7.
39 Ibid., p. 137.
40 Ibid., p. 134.
41 See Moser, *Philosophy After Objectivity*, for details on the latter point.

Chapter 3

What is Knowledge?

Linda Zagzebski

1. Introduction: The Object of Knowledge and the Components of Knowledge

Knowledge is a highly valued state in which a person is in cognitive contact with reality. It is, therefore, a relation. On one side of the relation is a conscious subject, and on the other side is a portion of reality to which the knower is directly or indirectly related. While directness is a matter of degree, it is convenient to think of knowledge of things as a direct form of knowledge in comparison to which knowledge *about* things is indirect. The former has often been called *knowledge by acquaintance* since the subject is in experiential contact with the portion of reality known, whereas the latter is *propositional knowledge* since what the subject knows is a true proposition about the world. Knowing Roger is an example of knowledge by acquaintance, while knowing *that* Roger is a philosopher is an example of propositional knowledge.[1] Knowledge by acquaintance includes not only knowledge of persons and things, but also knowledge of my own mental states. In fact, the knower's own mental states are often thought to be the most directly knowable portion of reality.

Propositional knowledge has been much more exhaustively discussed than knowledge by acquaintance for at least two reasons. For one thing, the proposition is the form in which knowledge is communicated, so propositional knowledge can be transferred from one person to another, whereas knowledge by acquaintance cannot be, at least not in any straightforward way.[2] A related reason is the common assumption that reality has a propositional structure or, at least, that the proposition is the principal form in which reality becomes understandable to the human mind. So even though my experience of Roger leads me to know Roger, and my experience of my own emotions leads me to know what it is like to have such emotions, as a theorist I am hard put to answer the question "What is knowledge?" about either of them. The object of knowledge is more easily explained when it is a proposition. In this paper I will follow the usual procedure of concentrating on propositional knowledge, but in doing so I recognize that the theoretical convenience of propositional knowledge does not necessarily imply its greater importance.

Propositions are either true or false, but only true propositions link the knower with reality in the desired manner. So the object of knowledge in the sense of most interest to philosophers is usually taken to be a true proposition. The nature of truth, propositions, and reality are all metaphysical questions. For this reason epistemologists generally do not direct their major effort to these questions when writing as epistemologists, and so discussions of knowledge normally do not center on the object of knowledge, but rather on the properties of the state itself that make it a state of knowing. Accounts of knowledge, then, direct their attention to the knowing relation and focus more on the subject side of the relation than on the object side.

So far we have seen that knowledge is a relation between a conscious subject and some portion of reality, usually understood to be mediated through a true proposition, and the majority of epistemological attention has been devoted to the subject side of that relation. In the state of knowledge the knower is related to a true proposition. The most general way of characterizing the relation between the knower and the proposition known is that she takes it to be true, and this relation is standardly called the state of belief. The idea that the knowing state is a species of the belief state undergirds the almost universal practice in epistemology of defining knowledge as true belief plus something else. But this view can be disputed since the history of epistemic concepts shows that belief and knowledge were sometimes regarded as mutually exclusive epistemic states. This was either because it was thought that knowledge and belief have distinct objects, or because it was thought appropriate to restrict the range of belief to epistemic states evaluatively inferior to the state of knowledge.[3] The first worry has been settled to the satisfaction of almost all contemporary epistemologists by the adoption of the widespread view that propositions are the objects of belief as well as of knowledge and, in fact, the same proposition can be either known or believed. So a person may know today what he only believed yesterday – say, that his favorite team would win the game today. If this is right, there is no objection to the idea that knowledge is a form of belief on the grounds of a difference in their objects. The second worry can be settled by stipulating that to believe is to *think with assent*, a definition that comes from Augustine.[4] Since it is indisputable that to know propositionally is, among other things, to take a proposition to be true, and if to assent to a proposition just *is* to take it to be true, then on the Augustinian definition of belief it follows that knowing is a form of believing.[5]

It is reasonable, then, to maintain that knowledge is a form of belief, but this is not necessarily helpful to a quest for a definition of knowledge since the concept of belief is itself in need of definition, and there are some philosophers who maintain that the concept has outlived its usefulness.[6] Still, it is widely assumed that the concept of belief is clearer and less controversial than the concept of knowledge. And this has to be the case if the common practice of defining knowledge as a form of belief is to be not only true, but illuminating. I think the assumption is correct but I will not defend it.

From what has been said so far it follows that knowledge is a form of believing a true proposition. At this point in the process of defining knowledge it becomes much more difficult and more open to debate. All parties agree that knowledge is a good state, good at least in the sense of desirable, and perhaps also good in the sense of praiseworthy. But there are different kinds of praiseworthiness. Good looks, wit, and strength are desirable qualities and we praise others for having them, but we typically do not blame them when they lack such qualities. In contrast, we praise persons for having qualities like courage, kindness, or fairness, and we also blame them for their absence. This suggests that it is a requirement of the moral sense of the praiseworthy that it is a quality whose presence is praised and whose absence is blamed. But this is only roughly right since blame for absence is also missing at the high end of moral praiseworthiness. We praise persons for being noble or saintly, but we do not blame them when they are not.

Now it is indisputably true that knowledge is desirable, but is it praiseworthy, and if so, in what sense? Is its praiseworthiness closer to the praiseworthiness of good looks, the praiseworthiness of kindness, or the praiseworthiness of saintliness? It is significant that knowledge has not traditionally been treated as a moral concept, yet it has had many of the trappings of the moral – for example, the connection with epistemic duty and responsibility, as when we criticize a person by saying she *ought* to know better, a criticism that is often accompanied by the type of distaste characteristic of the moral. Particular failings in knowledge are often attributed to qualities that have a decidedly moral tone, as when we say that a person is not fair to his intellectual opponents or is intellectually cowardly or is dogmatic. In each case the failing may be the explanation for the subject's lack of knowledge and he may be blamed for lacking knowledge because of this failing. Unfairness and cowardice are clearly qualities that have a moral sense, and dogmatism does also, although it is perhaps less obvious. A distinguishing feature of the dogmatic person is that he refuses to seriously entertain any evidence that might shake his belief; that is, nothing counts against it. But when we criticize a person for being dogmatic it is often very close to criticizing him for being a bigot. The response is akin to moral revulsion. In each of these cases, then, the failing is perceived to be like a moral one and if the subject lacks knowledge because of it, the lack of knowledge itself is perceived to be like a moral failing.

So sometimes the good of knowledge is treated like a moral good. A person is praised for its presence and blamed for its absence. But there are also instances of knowledge the lack of which is outside the realm of the blameworthy, and this indicates that moral concepts are not applicable. Obvious examples include perceptual and memory knowledge. It is usual these days to think that I know that I am looking at a yellow daffodil in ordinary circumstances in which I am looking at a yellow daffodil and form the belief that I am doing so, and all agree that that is a desirable state. It would be a stretch to say there is anything praiseworthy about it because it is so ordinary, and certainly the lack of perceptual knowledge in such circumstances due to a visual abnormality is pitied rather than blamed. Of course, cases of knowledge by extraordinary perceptual acuity are praised and deserving of it, but the lack of perceptual knowledge in such cases is surely not blamed. So certain kinds of knowledge seem to be far removed from the moral realm.

One problem for the theorist is to reconcile these different senses in which knowledge can be good. Sometimes the good of knowledge is like natural goods, sometimes it is similar to moral goods, and sometimes it may even be thought to be like the noble. Major disputes over the definition of knowledge may turn on contrasting senses in which knowledge is good. According to the contemporary theory of reliabilism knowledge is true belief arising from a reliable truth-producing mechanism. This proposal makes the good of knowledge a natural good like that of beauty, wit, or strength. The traditional proposal that knowledge is true belief based upon good reasons is associated with the ethical concepts of responsibility, praise and blame. One is praised for believing the truth upon good reasons and blamed for not doing so. The idea that knowledge is noble comes from Plato.[7] In my judgment no definition of knowledge can succeed if it does not incorporate or at least adjudicate the senses of good used in these opposing types of theory.

2. Desiderata in Defining Knowledge

In section 1, I have given a general characterization of knowledge as a state of believing a true proposition in a good way. This much is widely accepted, although some of the deepest disputes over the definition of knowledge turn on the sense of good intended in this loose, preliminary definition. But more has to be settled before proceeding. The question "What is knowledge?" is not a question with a single clear purpose. To ask the question and to give an answer are human activities that arise out of a variety of human needs. If the question is a request for a definition, what sort of definition is wanted? In this section I want to address this issue since some of the differences in accounts of knowledge arise from different aims in asking the question.

A definition can serve a number of different purposes, some practical, some theoretical. When we are defining knowledge one purpose might be the practical one of giving us directions for finding instances of knowledge in ourselves and in others, perhaps with the further aim of helping us to get it. A quite different purpose is the theoretical one of understanding where the *concept* of knowledge should be placed on a conceptual map that philosophers have already partially charted. This theoretical aim is intended to issue in a definition that is a necessary truth, whereas the practical aim may be satisfied by a contingent definition. Theoretical and practical purposes can sometimes be at odds.

A common theoretical purpose is to give what Locke called a *real definition*, a necessary truth that elucidates the nature of the kind of thing defined. Not all concepts defined by necessary truths have real definitions. For example, *bachelor* is defined as *an unmarried man*, and this is presumably a necessary truth, but no one thinks that bachelors constitute an independent kind of thing whose nature we want to investigate. In contrast, natural kinds like *human being*, *gold*, and *water* are thought to be good candidates for real definitions. In spite of the obvious dissimilarities between knowledge and these natural substances, it is common for philosophers to aim for a real definition of knowledge, although this is often not stated explicitly. I believe it is an aim that deserves attention, however, since it presupposes some disputable semantical and metaphysical views. Perhaps knowledge is not in an ontological category for which a real definition is possible. For example, no one would attempt a real definition of *rich*, *candy*, or *large plant*, and only some theorists would attempt a real definition of *food*, *intelligence*, or *virtue*. In some of these cases a contingent definition is probably sufficient, and it will be at least to some extent conventional. It is feasible to aim for a real definition of knowledge only if the concept of knowledge is not like the concept of a large plant. And even if it is closer to the concept of intelligence or of virtue, it is still undecided whether a real definition is attainable. In raising these questions about the purposes of definition my point is not to settle these matters, but to indicate how they prescribe what is wanted in an answer to the question "What is knowledge?"

The purpose of a definition might be reached by more than one method, so to criticize the method is not the same as to criticize the purpose.[8] The widespread purpose of giving a Lockian real definition issuing in a necessary truth can be attempted by more than one method. For decades the preferred method has been the method of truth condition analysis according to which putative necessary and sufficient conditions for being an instance of knowledge are proposed and tested by the method of counterexample (Chisholm, Klein, Plantinga, et al.). Recently this method has been under attack in general[9] and in the particular case of knowledge. For example, the recent theory of contextualism does not treat knowledge as a natural kind nor does it aim for a set of necessary and sufficient conditions.[10] Edward Craig seems to reject not only the method of truth condition analysis, but the purpose behind the method as well. Craig aims to identify the distinguishing features of knowledge by examining its pragmatic purpose in a community of informants. He seems to think of knowledge as closer to an artifact than a natural kind. He does not aim at a necessary truth and it does not bother him that not all knowers are good informants. The procedure of revising a definition by examining counterexamples is not part of his method.[11] Hilary Kornblith also rejects the method of truth condition analysis but not the purpose of giving a real definition. He sees knowledge as a natural kind, but he believes empirical investigation can result in a necessary truth about it just as empirical investigation can lead us to discover necessary truths about physical or biological kinds like gold or water. Alvin Goldman uses truth condition analysis of the concept of knowledge, but he sees empirical methods as applicable to it since he believes concepts are psychological structures the contents of which are subject to empirical test. He doubts that the resulting definition will be a necessary truth and he does not aim for a real definition.[12] Goldman therefore retains the method but not the purpose.

Aristotle identifies a kind of definition that is "a formula exhibiting the cause of a thing's existence." As an example he cites defining thunder by its efficient cause as what occurs "because fire is quenched in the clouds."[13] Aristotle contrasts this with the kind of definition that purports to give the essential nature of a thing, its formal cause, and he suggests that the same thing can be defined both ways. It is interesting to compare Alvin Goldman's early causal theory of knowledge and more recent forms of reliabilism with the Aristotelian procedure of defining a thing through its causes.[14] Unlike Aristotle, these philosophers take their definitions to be rivals to definitions such as *justified true belief* that aim to elucidate the nature of the knowing state itself. Goldman suggests that sometimes the nature of a thing just *is* to be (efficiently) caused a certain way, e.g. sunburn, and he thinks of knowledge as like sunburn. But the essential nature or formal cause of most things is distinct from their efficient cause, so if knowledge is like most things, it could be defined either through its nature or through its efficient cause, and the two definitions would not compete. I do not know of anyone who has pursued this possibility.

There is much to be said for each of the theoretical and practical purposes mentioned above, but reflection might show us that some purposes do not make good philosophical sense. At any rate, conscious consideration of the purpose and method of definition in general can lead us to see alternatives that might otherwise slip by us when attempting to define knowledge. It is particularly desirable to question whether we should aim for a real definition since it is hard to determine whether knowledge is a single kind of thing for which a real definition is possible. Epistemologists almost always have the aim Plato had in the *Theaetetus*, where he says he is setting out to "bring the many sorts of knowledge under one definition" (148e). But do we know this aim is attainable?

The attempt to give a real definition of knowledge can be challenged by the fact that the concept of knowledge has been treated in many different ways in different periods of philosophical history. Is there really a single target of analysis about which all these accounts differ, or are some of them simply talking about different things? This question is particularly striking when we look at the differences in the rigor of the requirements for knowledge throughout philosophical history. According to some theories the conditions for knowledge are narrow and strict, whereas in others they are broad and loose. The philosophical tradition leans to the rigorist side, although the contemporary trend is in the opposing direction. It is now widely held that ordinary cases of perception and memory yield knowledge and that small children and possibly even animals have knowledge in these ways. But it is worth noticing how much this differs from a long line of rigorist accounts starting with that of Plato in the *Phaedo* and the *Republic*. Plato made knowledge a much loftier state than the ordinary, and the difference between his rigorist conception and the more lenient contemporary one may make us doubt that a real definition of knowledge is possible.

These same worries also arise when we examine the sense in which knowledge is good, addressed in section 1. We saw there that perceptual knowledge seems initially to be good in a different sense from the good of the knowledge that requires reasons. Is it plausible to think that both phenomena are instances of the same kind of thing? Some philosophers have consciously divided the kinds of knowledge to reflect these differences.[15] The same problem arises with the treatment of skepticism. When the global skeptic says he does not know that he inhabits the planet Earth and I say he does know that he inhabits the planet earth, is it clear that we are disagreeing about something? Are we debating about the implications of a single concept or is there more than one concept that at times has gone by or has been translated by the term "knowledge"?[16] All of these worries may lead us to ask to what extent knowledge is a single phenomenon rather than a set of distinct phenomena, to what extent the boundaries of the kind are natural rather than set by convention, and to what extent "knowledge" is a term of philosophical art.

I believe we should begin by assuming that there is a single concept of knowledge about which philosophers have been debating for millennia and that we should aim for a necessary truth in our definition until forced to give up by continual failure in reaching the goal. I am less confident that knowledge is a single natural kind on a par with *water* or *gold*, but it is tempting to hope that that is the case. In any event, if knowledge is not a natural kind it is unlikely we will discover that unless we attempt to treat it as one. I will therefore tentatively accept the traditional aim of aspiring to a real definition of knowledge.

In addition to purposes and methods of definition, there are some common criteria for good definition that put limits on what will be acceptable, among them that a definition should not be *ad hoc*, that it should not be negative when it can be positive, that it should be brief, that it should not be circular, that it should utilize only concepts that are less obscure than the concept to be defined, and many others. I believe these criteria are good ones, although I will not examine them closely. Some of them serve the purpose of making a definition informative, a purpose that clearly goes beyond the aim of accuracy. The idea is that a definition is supposed to tell us something we didn't already know. We want a definition because of our failure to clearly grasp the concept to be defined. A circular definition does not do that since it uses the concept to be defined in the *definiens*, nor does one that uses other concepts as much in need of definition as the *definiendum*. Negative definitions fail in a more subtle way. They tell us what something is not, not what it is.[17] Of course, there are cases in which there is nothing more in a concept than the negation of another one. For instance, it is common to define *right act* as *an act that is not wrong*. In such cases we say that the negated concept in the *definiens* is conceptually more basic. I know of no reason to think that the concept of knowledge is like the concept of a right act, the negation of some other, more basic concept, so a negative definition of knowledge will probably be insufficiently informative.

The criterion that the concepts in the *definiens* should be less obscure than the *definiendum* may be one of the motives of those epistemologists who maintain that there should be no normative concept in the definition of knowledge. To be sure, they recognize that knowledge is good, but their aim is to define the sense in which knowledge is good in nonmoral and even nonnormative terms because of an assumption that nonnormative concepts are better understood than normative ones. This is often accompanied by worries about the ontological status of normative features of the universe. Normative facts and properties are thought to be puzzling in a way that descriptive facts and properties are not. I do not find this view plausible, but it is not a matter that can be settled without a deep investigation into the nature of normativity, and that would take us well outside the domain of epistemology. It is worth noting, however, that this criterion may be at odds with one of the theoretical purposes of a definition already mentioned. If we want a definition to connect the concept to be defined with other key concepts in well-developed philosophical theories, the concepts that have a central place in such theories might turn out to be normative ones. And since knowledge is a normative concept, that is just what we would expect. If so, it might actually be an advantage to use these concepts in the definition. If ultimately it turns out that normative concepts are reducible to nonnormative ones, the demonstration that that is the case would be work for a further project.

One of the requirements for a good definition I have mentioned is that it not be *ad hoc*. This requirement is particularly telling when the method used is that of truth condition analysis. That method aims to make a definition counterexample-free, but the procedure of proposing a definition and then repeatedly repairing it in response to counterexamples can sometimes lead to a definition that is too obviously a response to problems in some *other* definition. This is one way a definition can fail to be either theoretically illuminating or practically useful.

In my view there is nothing wrong with there being a number of different definitions of knowledge of differing sorts, and it is helpful to keep their different purposes and methods in mind when one is compared with another. It is also a good idea to be sensitive to the difficulty in satisfying all the desiderata in a single definition. One may have to be sacrificed for the sake of another. For example, precision is clearly better than vagueness, but sometimes precision results in a definition of knowledge that is so long, cumbersome, and hard to remember that it serves neither the purpose of giving us theoretical understanding nor the practical one of giving us guidance in achieving it.

In the next section we will look at an important set of counterexamples that attacked a long-standing definition of knowledge. It will be helpful to keep in mind the various desiderata in a definition of knowledge while addressing that problem, since one moral that might be drawn from it is that there is a problem with the method of counterexample itself.

3. The Traditional Definition of Knowledge and Gettier Objections

So far we have concluded that knowledge is *good true belief*. Nobody would consider this an acceptable definition, however, because it adequately serves neither a theoretical nor a practical purpose. The concept of good is at least as much in need of analysis as the concept of knowledge. The definition does not specify what sense of good is intended, and even if it did, it does not provide us with the means to apply it to cases. On the other hand, it is brief, it is noncircular, and within the bounds of extreme vagueness, it is accurate.

Since believing is something a person does, beliefs have customarily been treated as analogous to acts, so beliefs are good in the sense in which acts are right. Right believing has traditionally been identified with justified believing. So knowledge is *justified true belief* (JTB).[18] Sometimes, but not always, this has been understood to mean *true belief for the right reasons*. For several decades the concept of justification has received an enormous amount of attention since it was assumed that the JTB definition of knowledge was more or less accurate and that the concept of justification was the weak link in the definition. For the most part these discussions proceeded under the assumption that the aim was to arrive at a necessary truth and that the method to be used in doing so was that of truth condition analysis. An important set of counterexamples to the JTB definition of knowledge were proposed by Edmund Gettier (1963) and led to many attempts at refining the definition without questioning either the purpose or the method of definition. In this section we will look at the moral of Gettier's objection.

Gettier's examples are cases in which a belief is true and justified, but it is not an instance of knowledge because it is only by chance that the belief is true. Writers on Gettier normally do not say what they think is wrong with chance, but Aristotle does when he says, "To leave the greatest and noblest of things to chance would hardly be right."[19] Aristotle is here referring to *eudaimonia* or happiness, but his point is a general one about goods, at least great goods, and knowledge is surely a great good. It is incompatible with the value of knowledge that the aim of the knower, namely, getting the truth, occur by chance. This much has rarely been disputed even though, as we have seen, the sense of good intended has certainly been disputed.

In one standard Gettier example we are to imagine that Smith gives you plenty of evidence that he owns a Ford and you have no evidence against it. You then quite justifiably form the belief *Smith owns a Ford*. From that you infer its disjunction with *Brown is in Barcelona*, where Brown is an acquaintance whom you have no reason to believe is in Barcelona. Since the inference is justified, your belief *Smith owns a Ford or Brown is in Barcelona* is also justified. (Never mind what would possess you to form such a belief.) As it turns out, Smith is lying; he owns no Ford. But Brown is by chance in Barcelona. Your belief *Smith owns a Ford or Brown is in Barcelona* is therefore true and justified, but it is hardly something you know. Many examples of this kind have been proposed.[20]

As remarked above, it has often been noted that the problem in a Gettier case is that the truth is reached by chance; it is a kind of luck. But the structure of this case reveals that it is actually a case of double luck. It is mere bad luck that you are the unwitting victim of Smith's lies, and so it is only an accident that the kind of evidence that usually leads you to the truth instead leads you to form the false belief *Smith owns a Ford*. You end up with a true belief anyway because of a second accidental feature of the situation, a feature that has nothing to do with your cognitive activity. So an element of good luck cancels out the bad.

Some writers on Gettier have thought that the problem arises only for a restricted range of definitions, those according to which justified true belief means true belief based upon good reasons.[21] Since "justified" has sometimes *meant* "for the right reasons," this is understandable. Unfortunately, however, the problem is much more extensive than that. Given a couple of plausible assumptions already mentioned about what is required in an acceptable definition, it can be shown that Gettier problems arise for any definition in which knowledge is true belief plus something else that is closely connected with truth but does not entail it. It does not matter if the something else is a matter of believing for the right reasons or even if it is captured by the concept of justification. It need not even be anything accessible to the consciousness of the believer; for example, it may simply specify that the belief is produced by a reliable epistemic process or properly functioning faculties. All that is necessary is that there be a small gap between truth and the component of knowledge in addition to true belief in the definition. Call this component Q. In any such case a counterexample to the definition can be constructed according to the following recipe:

Start with a belief in the gap – that is, a belief that is false but is Q in as strong a sense of Q as is needed for knowledge. The falsity of the belief will not be due to any systematically describable element in the situation for if it were, such a feature could be used in the analysis of Q and then truth would be entailed by Q, contrary to the hypothesis. We may say that the falsity of the belief is due to some element of luck. Now amend the case by adding another element of luck, only this time one that makes the belief true after all. This second element must be independent of Q so that Q is unchanged. We now have an example of a belief that is Q in a sense strong enough for knowledge and that is true, but that is not knowledge. The conclusion is that as long as the concept of knowledge closely connects the component Q and the component of truth but permits *some* degree of independence between them, no definition of knowledge as true belief plus Q will succeed.

A well-known attempt to avoid Gettier problems without giving up the essence of the JTB definition is to add defeasibility conditions to the definition. This idea was proposed when it was noticed that in typical Gettier cases the justified belief depends upon or otherwise "goes through" a false belief. In any event there is a fact unknown to the subject which would defeat her justification should she discover it. In our example it is the fact that Smith does not own a Ford. With this observation in mind, defeasibility theories add to the components of true belief and justifiedness the requirement that there are no truths, qualified in various ways, which when added to the reasons justifying the belief would make it no longer justified. In the strong defeasibility theory a belief is not knowledge unless there is *no* truth which when added to the reasons justifying the belief make it no longer justified. But that, of course, makes Q entail truth, so it is not a case in which there is a small gap between truth and the other conditions for knowledge. Weaker defeasibility theories do not close the gap between Q and truth, and they are still vulnerable to Gettier-style problems using the recipe I have proposed. That procedure allows us to produce counterexamples even when the belief does not depend upon a false belief and even when there is no false belief in the neighborhood.

The nature of induction allows us to produce examples of this kind. Suppose that Dr. Jones, a physician, has very good inductive evidence that her patient, Smith, is suffering from virus X. Smith exhibits all of the symptoms of this virus, and laboratory tests are consistent with the presence of virus X and no other known virus. Let us also suppose that all of the evidence upon which Jones bases her diagnosis is true, and there is no evidence accessible to her that counts against the diagnosis. The conclusion that Smith is suffering from virus X really is extremely probable on the evidence. But even the strongest inductive evidence does not entail the conclusion and so it is possible to make a mistake. Let us suppose that this is one of those cases. Smith is suffering from a distinct and unknown virus Y. Dr. Jones's belief that Smith is presently suffering from virus X is false, but it is justified and undefeated by any evidence accessible to her.

Now the recipe for generating a Gettier-style example tells us to add an additional feature of the situation that makes the belief true after all but without altering the other features of the situation. Let us say that besides suffering from virus Y, Smith has very recently contracted virus X, but so recently that he does not yet exhibit symptoms caused by X, nor is the laboratory evidence upon which Jones bases her diagnosis produced by X. So while the evidence upon which Dr. Jones bases her diagnosis does make it highly probable that Smith has X, the fact that Smith has X has nothing to do with that evidence. In this case Dr. Jones's belief that Smith has virus X is true, justified, and undefeated, but it is not knowledge.

This same example can be used to generate counterexamples to a host of other theories. Since even the strongest inductive inference can lead to a false belief, that false inductive belief will satisfy any requirement for the normative element of knowledge that is not necessarily connected to truth. But then we can always describe a situation that is identical except that the belief turns out to be true after all due to some extraneous aspect of the situation. In such a case the subject will not have knowledge but will satisfy the conditions of the definition.

We may conclude that the prevalent method of defining knowledge as true belief plus something else cannot withstand counterexample as long as there is a small degree of independence between truth and that something else. It follows that there must be a necessary connection between truth and the other conditions of knowledge in addition to truth, whatever they may be. In the first section we saw that these other conditions can be loosely defined as believing in a good way. So the sense in which knowledge is believing in a good way must entail truth.[22]

It must be observed, however, that the conclusion of this section is correct only if we accept some plausible assumptions mentioned in section II about desired features in a definition. That is because the problem can be avoided by giving a definition that is either *ad hoc* or is too vague to be useful. For example, the definition *knowledge is justified true belief that is not a Gettier case* is obviously not susceptible to Gettier-style examples, nor is the very general definition we started with: *Knowledge is good true belief*. The first definition is clearly *ad hoc* as well as negative, and we have already said that the second is not only much too vague, it uses a concept in the *definiens* that is at least as obscure as the concept of knowledge.

Since Gettier cases are those in which accidentality or luck is involved, it has often been suggested that knowledge is *nonaccidentally true belief*. This definition also is vague as well as negative and it has little practical import. It is not a counterexample to the point of this section, though, since nonaccidental truth entails truth. However, it has been shown by the Howard-Snyders that the component of knowledge in addition to true belief can be defined in a way that uses the concept of nonaccidentality but does not entail truth. Their definition is this: Knowledge is *true belief which is such that if it were true it would be nonaccidentally true*.[23] The idea behind this definition is the observation that the nonaccidental connection between the way in which knowledge is good and the truth need only obtain in the cases in which the belief is true since false beliefs are not candidates for knowledge. A false belief can have the property of being such that if it were true it would be nonaccidentally true and, hence, this property does not entail truth. This definition highlights an assumption I have made in my recipe for generating Gettier-style counterexamples, the assumption that if a false belief has the property that converts true belief into knowledge – the property Q – it is always possible that there be a belief that has Q but that is accidentally true. The Howard-Snyders' idea is to rule out that possibility in the definition of property Q. The resulting definition combines the defects of the previous ones. Like the definition *nonaccidentally true belief* it is vague, negative, lacks practical import, and has little to recommend it theoretically. Like the definition *justified true belief that is not a Gettier case* it is *ad hoc*. In addition, it has the problems that come with interpreting the truth conditions of the subjunctive conditional *If it were true it would be nonaccidentally true*. On the other hand, it at least appears to be nonnormative, a feature that ought to please those philosophers who aim for a definition of knowledge that contains no normative element.

Nonaccidentality is not a desirable element in a definition of knowledge, but it shows us something interesting about the process of defining knowledge. Nonaccidentality has been suggested as a component of knowledge not because it has been identified as a feature of paradigm cases of knowledge, but because *accidentality* is a feature of certain well-known cases of *nonknowledge*. The trouble is that the observation that an accidental connection between truth and component Q is insufficient for knowledge does not tell us what *is* sufficient for knowledge. Of course, the connection between truth and component Q must be nonaccidental, but that is only the weakest thing we can say about it. Counterexamples are generally situations in which a defect in a definition is highlighted in an extreme form. But we should not conclude from that that anything less than the extreme defect is good enough. In this section we have seen that the connection between truth and the element of knowledge in addition to truth must be not only nonaccidental, there must be no possibility at all of a gap between them. Closing the gap can be done in a variety of ways, not all of which require entailment, and I suggest that we should choose a way that respects the other desired features in a definition.[24] To avoid a definition that is *ad hoc* it is preferable that there be a conceptual connection between truth and the other element of knowledge. That is, knowledge is not only a good way of cognitively grasping the truth, it is also one in which the truth and the good way in which it is achieved are intrinsically related. That intrinsic relation ought to be explicit in the definition. Theories that have this feature have been proposed, although they have usually not recognized that the moral of Gettier demands it.[25]

In this section we have seen that if we accept some plausible requirements for an acceptable definition, Gettier cases arise whenever there is a gap between the truth and the other conditions for knowledge. This means that knowledge is not merely a summation of the component of truth and the other components. I have drawn the conclusion that we want a definition that makes a conceptual connection between truth and the sense in which knowledge is good. However, our analysis might support a more radical conclusion. The discussion of Gettier cases arises within the context of certain assumptions about the purpose and method of the definition. The aim is to get a necessary truth, perhaps also to get to a real definition, and the method used is that of truth condition analysis. But as we saw in section II, it is not obvious that these assumptions are warranted. In particular, the method of truth condition analysis can be and has been disputed. The Gettier problem might be interpreted as exhibiting the defects of such a method, thereby supporting the move to a different method altogether. As I have already stated, however, my own preference is the more conservative one of retaining the method of truth condition analysis but without letting the aim to make the definition counterexample-free dominate the list of desiderata adopted in section 2.

4. A Definition of Knowledge

The conclusions of the first three sections of this paper give us a program for defining knowledge. Let us review them. In the first section I gave a rough definition of knowledge as believing a true proposition in a good way, and we saw that the sense of good intended in the concept of knowledge is a stumbling block to reaching a definition that encompasses both the cases of knowledge by perception or memory and the cases of knowledge that involve higher human abilities. The good of the former is similar to natural goods, whereas the latter are good in a sense that is close to the moral. The good of knowledge may sometimes even be like the most noble goods.

In section 2 I reviewed a number of different purposes and methods of defining knowledge and proposed that we try to satisfy as many of them as possible. But I will not try to satisfy the common purpose of eliminating all normative concepts from the definition. Since we know that the concept of knowledge is normative, it is a theoretical advantage if it can be related to central concepts in ethics since ethicists already have proposed theoretical structures in which these concepts have been analyzed. If it turns out that normative concepts are reducible to or supervene on nonnormative concepts, the demonstration that that is the case would be an independent project. Meanwhile, one of my purposes will be to integrate the concept of knowledge into a background ethical theory.

In section 3 we looked at the moral of Gettier examples and concluded that the normative component of knowledge, the component that makes knowledge good, must entail the truth. Success in reaching the truth must be an intrinsic part of the sense in which each instance of knowledge is good.

I will propose a definition that attempts to meet all of these criteria. It should be clear from what has been said, however, that there is no unique way of doing so. In particular, the successful attainment of the theoretical purpose of locating the concept of knowledge on a background conceptual map depends upon what concepts are thought to be most theoretically salient, and that, in turn, depends upon which background theories have the most importance in the eyes of those asking the question, "What is knowledge?" But that, in turn, depends upon the resolution of deep issues in metaphilosophy. Should we try to embed the concept of knowledge in a background normative theory because it is a normative concept? Should we instead embed it in a background metaphysical theory on the assumption that metaphysics is more basic than epistemology? Or should we embed it in a scientific theory on the grounds that knowledge is a natural phenomenon? I have already said that I will take the first of these alternatives, but I have not argued for it and I can see many advantages in defining knowledge in terms of very different concepts from the one I have chosen. In fact, even if the purpose is to embed the concept of knowledge in a background ethical theory, the choice of theory will obviously depend upon one's position regarding the kind of ethical theory most likely to serve our theoretical and practical purposes.

The definition I will propose arises from a virtue theory of ethics. The complete theory includes intellectual as well as moral virtues within the same theory and aims to give a unified account of the morality of believing as well as of acting, but I will discuss only that part of the theory that underlies the normative concept I use in defining knowledge.[26] This is the concept of *an act of intellectual virtue*.

The concept of a virtue has a number of theoretical and practical advantages. Its proposed advantages in ethics are well known and I have argued elsewhere (1996) that there are parallel advantages in epistemology. In the last section we saw that the definition of knowledge must make success in reaching the truth an intrinsic aspect of that which makes knowledge good. The traditional concept of justification cannot serve this purpose, nor can any concept of a property of a belief. That is because no normative property of a belief guarantees its truth, at least no property the concept of which already has a history. But in Aristotle the concept of a virtue combines that of an admirable internal state with external success. At least, that is one way of interpreting Aristotle, and in any event, the concept of a virtue as used in ethics can be adapted to our need for a concept that makes an intrinsic relation between the good of a person's internal state – in this case, belief – and its success – in this case, the truth. So I suggest that it will be beneficial to move back a step from properties of beliefs to properties of persons in our search for a concept that attaches the good of knowledge to its truth.[27]

Virtues are properties of persons. Intellectual virtues are properties of persons that aim at intellectual goods, most especially truth. Moral virtues are properties of persons that aim at distinctively moral goods such as the well-being of others.

Since the concept of a virtue already has a rich history, if we can connect knowledge to virtue, that would be a theoretical advantage. In addition, the concept of a virtue has practical uses. Ordinary people speak of such individual virtues as kindness, fairness, courage, open-mindedness, perseverance, generosity, discretion, and trust, and sometimes the same names are used for both moral and intellectual virtues. Furthermore, the evaluation of acts is often made in terms of the virtues or vices they express. The price of the practical usefulness of the concept of virtue and of the individual virtues may be a certain degree of conventionality in the application of the concept, although I will not discuss this aspect of the concept here. *Virtue* is not a technical concept, although it can be technically refined. I believe it is a virtue of the concept of virtue that it has both an extensive history in the philosophical literature and a wide use in ordinary discourse.

There are many accounts of the structure of a virtue. I will briefly summarize my own without argument.

A virtue has two components. The first is a motivational component and the second is a component of success in reaching the end of the motivational component. The motivational component of a virtue is a disposition to have an emotion that directs action towards an end. Each virtue has a distinctive motivational component with a distinctive end, but groups of virtues can be categorized by their ultimate ends. Most intellectual virtues have truth as their ultimate end.[28] Moral virtues have other ultimate ends. The success component of a virtue is a component of reliability in bringing about the end of the virtuous motivation. To take a few examples, the virtues of compassion, trust, and open-mindedness can be roughly defined as follows: The virtue of compassion is a trait that includes the emotion-disposition to alleviate the suffering of others and reliable success in doing so. The virtue of trust is the trait the includes the emotion-disposition to trust those and only those who are trustworthy, and reliable success in doing so. The virtue of open-mindedness is the trait that includes the emotion-disposition to be open to the views of others even when they conflict with one's own and reliable success in doing so. I suggest that the structure of all or, at least, most of the virtues can be defined by this pattern.

The concept of a virtue is important for character evaluation. When we say a person has a virtue we mean that she has a disposition to be motivated a certain way and to act a certain way in relevant circumstances, and in addition, is reliably successful in bringing about the end of her virtuous motive. But having a disposition to a motive does not mean she always has the motive in the relevant circumstances, and being reliably successful does not mean she is always successful. So the fact that she is virtuous does not entail that her individual acts and beliefs should be evaluated positively. At the same time, someone who is not virtuous may nonetheless be able to perform acts and have beliefs that are valuationally positive. The evaluation of acts and beliefs, then, requires further conditions.

Sometimes an act or belief has positive value simply because it is what a virtuous person would typically do in the circumstances, whether or not it is virtuously motivated. There is a sense of *right* in which we say a person has done the right thing in giving the correct change to a buyer even though he is not at all motivated by moral concerns. Similarly, there is a sense of *justified* in which we say a person has a justified belief in believing that the earth is a round even if he has not made the reasons for believing it his own. We also evaluate beliefs and acts from the aspect of the agent's motivation. An act or belief that is virtuously motivated deserves credit, although we almost always qualify it if it does not also involve doing/believing the right thing.

An act may be evaluated positively on both of these grounds and still not have everything we want morally in an act. So even when it is motivated properly and is what a virtuous person would do in the circumstances, it may fail in the aim of the act. When this happens the act lacks something morally desirable. Moral success is evaluated positively even though that is to some extent out of the hands of the agent. It is one of the ways in which we are all victims of moral luck. So, for example, a person might be motivated by generosity and act in a way characteristic of generous persons in some particular circumstances, say by giving money to a beggar on the street, but if it turns out that the beggar is really rich and is playing the part of a beggar to win a bet, we would think that there is something morally lacking in the act. This is not, of course, to suggest that we would withhold praise of the agent, but her *act* would not merit the degree of praise due it if the beggar really were deserving. The same point applies to intellectual acts. A person may be motivated by intellectual virtues and act in a way intellectually virtuous persons act in attempting to get knowledge, but if she fails to get the truth, her epistemic state is lacking something praiseworthy. This means there is a kind of epistemic luck analogous to moral luck. As Thomas Nagel has remarked, the Nobel Prize is not given to people who are wrong.[29] Getting knowledge itself is a kind of prize, and it is in part the prize of being right.

In addition, mere success in reaching the end of the virtuous motive in the particular case is not sufficient for the highest praise of an act or belief even if it also has the other praiseworthy features just identified. It is important that success in reaching the end is *due to* the other praiseworthy features of the act. The end must be reached *because of* these other features. This is because there are ethical analogues to Gettier cases, although as far as I know, ethicists have not noticed this. Let me describe one such case.

Suppose a judge, weighing the evidence against an accused killer, determines by an impeccable procedure and motivated by justice that the man is guilty. We may assume that the judge not only does everything he ought to do, but he exhibits all the virtues appropriate in this situation. Nonetheless, even the most virtuous can make a mistake, just as we saw that even the most intellectually admirable can fail in an inductive conclusion in the case of Dr. Jones. Suppose this is one of those times. The accused is the wrong man. The fact that the judge makes a mistake is not due to any defect in him, whether moral or intellectual; it is simply bad luck. Obviously things have gone wrong, wrong enough that we would call the act a miscarriage of justice. The judge's act is not *an act of justice* even though we would not blame him for the error and would even praise him for *acting justly*. Nonetheless, the act itself is not deserving of the highest praise. It is lacking something morally important.

To get a Gettier-style problem we added an additional element of luck, a feature of good luck that cancels out the bad, and we can use the same procedure here. Suppose that the actual killer is secretly switched with the man the judge thinks he is sentencing so that the judge ends up accidentally sentencing the right man. One accident cancels out the other so that the end result is the desired one of punishing the culprit. In this situation I believe we would not give the judge's act the praise that would be due it if he had found the right man guilty in the first place. Of course we are relieved that the innocent man is not punished, but even though the end result is the one at which the judge was aiming and he was praiseworthy in both his motive and his actions, that is not sufficient to make his act the kind of act that deserves the highest moral praise.

The foregoing considerations show us that we need the concept of an act that gets everything right, an act that is good in every respect. And we have seen the elements that must be right or good in order to merit that evaluation. I call the concept that of *an act of virtue*. The definition is as folllows:

> An act is *an act of virtue A* if and only if it arises from the motivational component of A, is an act that persons with virtue A characteristically do in the circumstances, and is successful in bringing about the end of virtue A because of these features of the act.

The motivational component of A is a disposition. An act that arises from that disposition need not be consciously motivated by A, but it must be such that the explanation for the act would refer to it. An act that is characteristic of virtue A is an act that is not only what persons with virtue A would probably do in the circumstances, but it is an act that is a mark of the behavior of persons with that virtue.[30] The third component specifies that success in reaching the end must be because of the other two components. This needs further analysis. I know of no account of the *because of* relation that fully captures it, but I will have a bit more to say about it in the next section. It is important to notice that on this definition it is *not* necessary that the agent possess virtue A in order to perform an act of virtue A. One of Aristotle's conditions for virtue possession is that the trait must be deeply entrenched. If so, persons who are virtuous-in-training do not possess a given virtue, yet I see no reason to think they cannot perform acts of virtue, that is, acts that are as praiseworthy as an act can be with respect to the virtue in question.

There are acts of moral virtue and acts of intellectual virtue. We are concerned here with the latter. An act of intellectual virtue A is one that arises from the motivational component of an intellectual virtue A, is an act that persons with virtue A characteristically do in those circumstances, and is successful in reaching the truth because of these other features of the act.

The definition of knowledge I propose is as follows:

Knowledge is belief arising out of acts of intellectual virtue.

At the beginning of this paper I mentioned that the common practice of concentrating on propositional knowledge in philosophical accounts of knowledge does not necessarily reflect its greater importance. All forms of knowledge involve contact of the mind with reality, however, and so a more comprehensive definition of knowledge that includes knowledge by acquaintance as well as propositional knowledge would be as follows:

Knowledge is cognitive contact with reality arising out of acts of intellectual virtue.

Knowledge is generally not reached through a single act, but through a combination of acts of one's own, as well as through the acts of others and cooperating circumstances. We tend to think of knowledge as our own accomplishment, but this is rarely the case. The fact that our knowledge depends upon the knowledge and intellectual virtue of a host of other persons in our intellectual community, as well as a cooperating universe, makes it clear that we cannot expect to isolate the conditions for knowledge in some set of independent properties of the knower, much less a set of properties over which the knower has control. Epistemic luck permeates the human condition whether for good or for ill.

5. Assessment of the Definition

A. *Resolving the sense in which knowledge is good*

At the end of the first section I said that no definition of knowledge can succeed unless it can resolve the different senses in which knowledge is good. Ordinary perceptual and memory knowledge seem to be good in a sense close to that of natural goods like beauty, wit, and strength. But sometimes knowledge is treated as a more elevated state, requiring effort and skill. In these cases it seems to be good in a sense close to the moral. If so, it might turn out that knowledge is not a natural kind for which a real definition is possible. Perhaps investigation will reveal that there really are two distinct kinds of knowledge, just as investigation into the nature of jade revealed that what is called "jade" is really two distinct substances: jadeite and nephrite. I have not eliminated the possibility that ultimately this may happen, but I do not think we yet have a reason to bifurcate knowledge into two distinct kinds with separate analyses. The definition proposed in the last section can cover both kinds. In fact, I think it can even cover the highest sort of knowledge that is arguably in the realm of the noble.

An act of intellectual virtue has been defined within a background ethical theory in which *virtue* is the primary concept. "Virtue" is a term flexible enough to apply to more than moral traits, although the moral sense is no doubt the paradigm.[31] The definition of "an act of virtue" stretches the moral sense of the term in another way. An act of virtue is an act in which there is an imitation of the behavior of virtuous persons and success in reaching the end for that reason. More importantly for our present interest in interpreting the concept of an act of *intellectual* virtue, there is nothing in the definition that precludes that property from attaching to acts that are more or less automatic, as typically happens in perception and memory. The virtuous motivation from which an act of virtue arises need not be either conscious or strong, so ordinary epistemic motives will often be sufficient. In fact, nothing in the definition prevents the motivational component from applying to motives that are almost universal in some situations. The second component specifies that the act must be something that a person with the virtue in question would typically do insofar as he is expressing the virtue. But virtuous persons do not necessarily act in a way that is out of the ordinary, although, of course, they certainly do so in some circumstances. A person who has the virtue of attentiveness is as attentive as is necessary in situations of a given kind in order to reach the truth. A person who has the virtue of thoroughness examines the evidence as thoroughly as is necessary for the particular circumstances, and so on. Suppose a person with all the intellectual virtues is looking at a white wall in ordinary circumstances. Does she stare for a long time before forming the belief that there is a white wall in front of her? Does she undertake an investigation of the possibility that she is hallucinating or under the influence of drugs? Does she question trustworthy authorities on the subject of the color of walls? Of course not. To do so would exhibit a degree of intellectual scrupulosity tantamount to paranoia. But she *is* sensitive to any evidence that would lead her to suspect a defect in her perceptual ability or any peculiarities of the circumstances that would suggest a non-cooperating environment. Fortunately, most of the time she need not follow up on these possibilities. So to act like a person with intellectual virtue acts when judging the color of a wall is not a very difficult thing to do. And the same point applies to ordinary cases of belief based on clear memory. Typical true beliefs by perception or memory, then, satisfy my definition of knowledge. It is even possible that young children satisfy the definition as soon as they are old enough to know there is a difference between truth and falsehood and to be motivated to get the former.

So the definition can handle cases on the low end of knowledge. Its real advantage over other accounts, however, is at the upper end of knowledge. Stunning intellectual discoveries yield knowledge is a way that needs to be captured by any acceptable definition of the knowing state. Such knowledge is not merely the result of reliable processes or properly functioning faculties or epistemic procedures that have no flaw, as some epistemologists have suggested. They are the result of epistemic activities that go well beyond the nondefective. They are, in fact, exceptionally laudatory. The concept of an intellectual virtue is well suited to the purpose of identifying knowledge in cases of this sort. A virtue is an admirable quality that goes beyond the minimum for being epistemically respectable. Some virtues go far enough beyond the minimum to reach the status of the highest goods. Creativity and originality of intellect are among those qualities associated with the high end of epistemic value, and an act of the virtue of originality is praiseworthy in the same way that acts of supreme generosity are praiseworthy. Such acts are truly exceptional. The definition of knowledge I have proposed, then, covers a range of cases from that of low-grade perceptual knowledge whose goodness is like natural goodness, to cases of beliefs based on evidence that are praised and blamed in the way we associate with the moral, to truly stellar intellectual achievements whose goodness is close to the noble.

B.   How it escapes Gettier problems

In section 3 I showed that unless we are willing to live with a very uninformative definition, Gettier problems result from any definition in which the sense in which knowledge is good does not entail truth. The concept of an act of intellectual virtue does entail truth, and so my definition is not guaranteed to fail in the way I have outlined for those theories susceptible to the double luck strategy. In the two cases we examined, that of the belief, *Smith owns a Ford or Brown is in Barcelona*, and the case of Dr. Jones and her diagnosis that Smith has virus X, the believer reaches the truth because of the feature of double luck I identified in these cases.[32] You and Dr. Jones do reach your respective beliefs because of your intellectually virtuous motivations and activities, but you do not reach the *truth* because of these features of the situation. This means that the concept of reaching *A because of B* is a key element of the definition. We all have intuitions about what it means for something to happen because of something else, but this concept is in need of further analysis and I do not know of one that is adequate. Some epistemologists have attempted counterfactual accounts of the component of knowledge in addition to true belief and, up to a point, whether the believer would arrive at the truth in close counterfactual circumstances can be used as a way of determining whether the truth is reached in the actual circumstances because of virtuous activity. So, for example, we might defend our claim that you do not get to the truth in the Ford and Barcelona case because of your virtuous motives and acts since in very similar circumstances you would have had the same motives and performed the same acts and failed to get to the truth. That would have been the case if Brown had not happened to be in Barcelona. Similarly, Dr. Jones would have reached a false belief in very similar circumstances even with her virtuous motives and acts. That would have happened if Smith had not happened to contract virus X just before she made her diagnosis. But looking at whether the believer reaches the truth in relevantly similar counterfactual circumstances is only a rough way of determining whether the truth is reached because of designated features of the act. It is certainly not a way of explaining what is *meant* by saying that the truth is reached because of these features. For example, there are no counterfactual circumstances in which a bachelor is not unmarried, but it would not be true to say that he is a bachelor *because* he is unmarried. The concept *A because of B* is not reducible to these counterfactual conditions. At best any such definition of *because of* will be a nominal definition.

C. *Issues for further inquiry*

In the method of truth condition analysis the principal question is whether the definition is too broad (weak) or too narrow (strong). John Greco has objected to me that the definition might be too weak in that it does not require the actual possession of intellectual virtue as a condition for knowledge. Since acts of intellectual virtue can be performed by agents whose virtuous behavior does not arise out of an entrenched habit, they cannot be trusted to act virtuously in similar circumstances in the future. Is it appropriate to attribute knowledge to them if they would not do the same thing in relevantly similar circumstances? I have said that to make the possession of the fully entrenched virtue a condition for knowledge is too strong since it rules out knowledge in children and unsophisticated adults, but Greco's point deserves further attention. It is likely that it would lead us into an investigation of the psychology of habit formation and the stability of the behavior of persons at early stages of acquiring intellectual traits. It also brings up the question of the extent to which we think an otherwise unreliable person can have knowledge because her behavior depends upon the reliability of other persons in her epistemic community.

It may also be objected that the definition is too strong. This is most likely to be raised against the motivational component of an act of intellectual virtue. Why think that the subject's motives have anything to do with whether she gets knowledge? This question highlights the differences between those who tend to think of knowledge as procedural and mechanical, and those who think of it as something for which we are responsible. My sympathies, of course, are with those in the latter category, but underlying the issue of whether responsibility extends to the cognitive sphere is a disagreement about the extent to which cognitive activity is voluntary. This suggests that deeper questions about human nature are at issue here.[33]

The definition as I have proposed it here meets many of the criteria for a good definition given in section 2, but it is vague and it clearly needs more extensive analysis. We have already seen the need for an account of the *because of* relation in the third component of the definition of an act of virtue. It also needs an account of motivation, as well as an account of acting in a way that is characteristic of a virtue, the first and second components of the definition. If an agent is doing what virtuous persons characteristically do in some circumstances, does that include having the relevant knowledge of the circumstances that virtuous persons have when they act? How far does that knowledge go? And if knowledge of circumstances is included in the account of the second component of an act of virtue, aren't we left with a circular definition since the concept of knowledge has been smuggled into the *definiens*?[34] There is also the matter of identifying and individuating the intellectual virtues. This is important not only because differing lists of the individual virtues and their analyses can result in accounts of knowledge that differ greatly in plausibility, but because it is possible that some of the virtues conflict. Virtue theories of ethics have this same problem. Aristotle's solution was to tie together the different virtues in the concept of *phronesis*, or practical wisdom, and I have attempted to use the same move with respect to the intellectual virtues.[35] But this move will not succeed unless it can be demonstrated that making every virtue relative to the judgment of a person with practical wisdom yields applications of the virtues to cases that are recognizably the same as the ones we have been using intuitively.

Many of these problems would have to be addressed by a detailed virtue theory of ethics anyway. There are, therefore, other motives in answering these questions besides the motive to define knowledge. A successful answer to them would serve a purpose in ethics as well as in epistemology. Other definitions of knowledge that meet the criteria I have described here would need to do the same thing, only they would refer to a different background theory in ethics, metaphysics, or cognitive psychology. The most detailed and advanced of such theories will always have the advantage in providing a theoretical background for the definition of knowledge.[36]

Notes

1. Some philosophers have tried to reduce one of these forms of knowledge to the other.
2. See Kierkegaard's notion of indirect communication for his view on the way to communicate truth or subjectivity, which he believes is nonpropositional. This idea appears throughout his writings, but particularly in *Concluding Unscientific Postscript*.
3. Plato used both reasons for his view that the objects of knowledge (*episteme*) and belief (*doxa*) differ. See particularly the line analogy in the *Republic* 509d–511e, and the famous Allegory of the Cave 514a–518d.
4. Augustine, *Predestination of the Saints*, 5, trans. Dods, reprinted in Oats, *Basic Writings of St. Augustine*, 2 vols. (New York: Random House, 1948).

    The definition of believing as *thinking with assent* seems to make beliefs conscious occurrences and so to rule out belief in the dispositional sense, the sense in which we sometimes attribute beliefs to a person even when he is not thinking of them. But the Augustinian definition of believing can be extended to include a dispositional sense. Believing p dispositionally would be defined as having the disposition to assent to p when thinking of it.
5. But see H. A. Prichard for the view that knowledge and belief are mutually exclusive states and that we can tell the difference by introspection. Prichard says: "We must recognize that whenever we know something we either do, or at least can, by reflecting, directly know that we are knowing it, and that whenever we believe something, we similarly either do or can directly know that we are believing it and not knowing it" (*Knowledge and Perception*, Oxford: Clarendon Press, 1950, p. 86).
6. Stephen Stich, *The Fragmentation of Reason* (Cambridge, MA: MIT Press, 1990).
7. Plato calls knowledge the most important element in life (*Protagoras* 352d) and says that the only thing truly evil is to be deprived of it (345b).
8. For an interesting discussion of the purposes and methods of definition, see Richard Robinson, *Definition* (Oxford: Clarendon Press, 1950).
9. See John Pollock, "A Theory of Moral Reasoning," *Ethics* 96 (April 1986): 506–23. Pollock argues that concepts are not individuated by truth condition analysis but by what he calls their conceptual roles.

10 For examples of contextualism see David Annis, "A Contextualist Theory of Epistemic Justification," *American Philosophical Quarterly* 15 (1978): 213–19; Keith De Rose, "Contextualism and Knowledge Attributions," *Philosophy and Phenomenological Research* 52 (1992): 913–29; David Lewis, "Elusive Knowledge," *Australasian Journal of Philosophy* 74, no. 4 (December 1996): 549–67.

11 I am not sure that Craig sees himself as offering a definition of knowledge in his book. Nonetheless, he is attempting to answer the question, "What is knowledge?" So the striking difference between his purposes and methods and those that are more common in contemporary epistemology is directly related to the topic of this paper.

12 In personal correspondence.

13 *Posterior Analytics* II, 94a1–5.

14 Goldman 1967, 1986.

15 Ernest Sosa distinguishes between animal knowledge and reflective knowledge in "Intellectual Virtue in Perspective" and in "Reliabilism and Intellectual Virtue," in Sosa (1991).

16 William P. Alston has raised these same worries about the concept of justification in "Epistemic Desiderata," *Philosophy and Phenomenological Research* 53 (Sept. 1993): 527–51. But he says that he believes there is more commonality in the concept of knowledge (n. 15).

17 Plato uses this criterion for a good definition in the *Theaetetus* where Socrates says: "But the original aim of our discussion was to find out rather what it is than what it is not; at the same time we have made some progress, for we no longer seek for knowledge in perception at all" (187a).

18 Sometimes the JTB definition of knowledge has been compared with that of Plato in *Theaetetus* 201d in which Socrates considers and then rejects the proposal that knowledge is true belief (*doxa*) with an account (*logos*). It seems unlikely, though, that what Plato meant by a *logos* is very close to what contemporary philosophers mean by justification. In addition, Plato is not discussing propositional knowledge in that dialogue, but rather knowledge of persons or things.

19 *Nicomachean Ethics* 1109b25.

20 Bertrand Russell proposes an example of a stopped clock that is similar to Gettier cases in *Human Knowledge: Its Scope and Limits* (New York: Simon & Schuster, 1948), p. 154. But Russell uses it as a counterexample to the proposal that knowledge is true belief. He does not seem to notice that if I have no reason to distrust my clock, my belief might be justified as well as true. This point was noticed by Israel Scheffler and is discussed by Robert Shope in *The Analysis of Knowing* (Princeton: Princeton University Press, 1983), pp. 19–20.

21 See Plantinga 1993: 36.

22 The argument of this section is taken from Zagzebski 1994 and Zagzebski 1996, part III, section 3.

23 Frances and Daniel Howard-Snyder, "The Gettier Problem and Infallibilism," paper delivered at the Central Division meetings of the American Philosophical Association, May 1996. Sharon Ryan makes a similar proposal in "Does Warrant Entail Truth?" *Philosophy and Phenomenological Research* LVI (March 1996): 183–92, but she puts the conditional in the indicative mood. This is at least misleading since it suggests she intends a material conditional.

24 I have argued here that there must be a necessary connection between the component Q and truth. As I have stated my conclusion, however, Q must entail truth, although I have not argued that the connection must be as strong as entailment. Peter Klein has pointed out to me that a relationship of nomic necessity between Q and truth might be sufficient to avoid the double luck problem. That is, it might be sufficient that the gap between Q and truth is closed in every possible world with our causal laws. I will not pursue this approach here, however, since the relationship of entailment is the most straightforward way to make the required connection of necessity between the two components of knowledge, and I do not see any reason to think that theories vulnerable to the double luck formula I have outlined here would be any better off with a requirement of nomic necessity instead of entailment.

25 Three examples are Chisholm's early theory, Goldman's causal theory, and the strong defeasibility theory, already mentioned. Chisholm used the concept of making p evident in the definition of knowledge he proposes in the first edition of *Theory of Knowledge*, and he says there that whatever makes p evident must not also make evident a false proposition. This precludes the falsehood of p. Goldman's causal theory of knowledge had the truth condition built into the causal condition because he required that the subject does not know p unless the state of affairs p is appropriately causally connected to the belief p. This puts the truth of p in the causal condition. Since Goldman's later reliabilism does not build in the truth in this way, I assume that he was not motivated by the considerations I am giving here. In the strong defeasibility theory as expressed by Klein a belief is an instance of knowledge only if there is no true proposition which when added to the reasons that justify the belief makes the belief no longer justified. This condition entails the truth of the belief since if a belief p is false, *not p* is true, so there is a true proposition which if added to the subject's reasons for p entails the falsehood of p, namely, *not p*.

26 I have outlined a background ethical virtue theory in part II of *Virtues of the Mind*.

27 The move to properties of persons rather than properties of beliefs had already been made by reliabilists and earlier virtue epistemologists for different reasons. See my entry, "Virtue Epistemology," in the forthcoming Routledge *International Encyclopedia of Philosophy* for a brief history of the development of virtue epistemology and its background in reliabilism.

28 There may be a few exceptions. Some virtues may aim at understanding rather than truth.

29 "Moral Luck," in *Mortal Questions* (Cambridge: Cambridge University Press, 1979), n. 11.

30 In *Virtues of the Mind* I expressed the second component of the definition as follows: "it is something a person with virtue A would (probably) do in the circumstances" (p. 248). But what a virtuous person would probably do may not have anything to do with the virtue in question.

31 In *Virtues of the Mind* I argue that intellectual virtues are best treated as forms of moral virtue. The definition of knowledge does not depend upon this point, however.

32 Not all counterexamples in the Gettier literature have the double luck feature, although, of course, I have argued that cases with this feature can always be produced whenever there is a gap between truth and the other component of knowledge. But in every Gettier case there is some element of chance or luck.

33 I have discussed the issue of the voluntariness of cognitive activity in *Virtues of the Mind*, pp. 58–69.

34 This potential problem has been pointed out to me by Peter Klein.
35 *Virtues of the Mind*, part II, section 5.
36 I am grateful to Peter Klein, John Greco, and Richard Feldman for comments on an earlier draft of this paper, as well as to Hilary Kornblith and Alvin Goldman for correspondence while the paper was in progress.

Chapter 4

The Dialectic of Foundationalism and Coherentism

Laurence BonJour

My aim in this paper is to explore the dispute between foundationalism and coherentism and attempt a resolution. I will begin by considering the origin of the issue in the famous epistemic regress problem. Next I will explore the central foundationalist idea and the most central objections that have been raised against foundationalist views. This will lead to a consideration of the main contours of the coherentist alternative, and eventually to a discussion of objections to coherentism – including several specific ones that I now judge to be clearly fatal, especially when taken together. This will motivate, finally, a reconsideration of foundationalism. I will argue that the dialectically most serious objection to foundationalism can be successfully answered. While the answer that I will suggest admittedly carries with it the price of aggravating certain other difficulties, especially the venerable problem of showing how belief in an external world of physical objects can be justified, it still seems to me to leave foundationalism as by far the more defensible and promising of the two alternatives.

For the purposes of this paper, I will make three rather large assumptions that I will not attempt to justify here. First, I will assume the correctness of the realist conception of truth as correspondence or agreement with the appropriate region or chunk of mind-independent reality (where the relevant sort of mind independence is only in relation to the specific cognitive act in question, thus allowing for the possibility that beliefs about mental matters may also be true in this sense). My own conviction is that there is no alternative to this conception of truth that is ultimately even intelligible, but those who do not agree can perhaps regard this assumption as merely a way of focusing the issue in a way that is adequately narrow to be reasonably dealt with within the present compass.

Second, I will assume that the subject of which foundationalism and coherentism are offering competing accounts is the fundamental structure of the epistemic justification of contingent or empirical beliefs, where what is distinctive about *epistemic* justification is that it involves an acceptably strong reason for thinking that the belief in question is true or likely to be true. This is not the only possible account of the subject matter of this dispute, but it is by far the most standard and straightforward.[1]

Third, I will assume that an *internalist* rather than an *externalist* conception of epistemic justification is correct, i.e., roughly, that a belief's being epistemically justified requires that the believer in question have in his cognitive possession or be suitably aware of such a reason or adequate basis for thinking that the belief is true. While I believe that this assumption is also correct, the main motivation for it in the present context is that it is needed in order for the foundationalism–coherentism issue to be even worth discussing. For if an externalist conception of justification were correct, there would then, in my judgment, be no serious objections to a foundationalist view and hence no dialectical motive for the complexities and difficulties of the coherentist alternative.

1. The Epistemic Regress Problem

As already remarked, the foundationalist–coherentist dialectic arises from the epistemic regress problem, and it is with that familiar problem that we must accordingly begin. Setting aside a general skepticism about reasoning, it seems highly plausible to suppose that many of a person's contingent or empirical beliefs are interrelated in such a way that if a particular belief of conjunction of beliefs were somehow known or assumed to be true, this would provide a good reason for thinking that some further belief was true. An explicit statement of such a reason would take the form of an argument or inference from the former belief or conjunction of beliefs as premise to the latter belief as conclusion. Such a putatively justifying reason may appropriately be referred to as a *conditional reason*. But it is obvious that the existence of a conditional reason of this sort can yield a reason or justification *simpliciter* for its nonconditional conclusion only if there is some further reason or justification, which must seemingly be epistemically prior, for accepting the truth of its premises.

In this way the issue of epistemic justification for one contingent or empirical belief may be in effect transmuted, via an appropriate conditional reason, into the issue of justification for one or more other contingent or empirical beliefs. Clearly this process can be repeated, in principle at least through many stages, yielding an epistemological tree-structure in which a belief at one level is conditionally justified in relation to those at a prior level, and so on.[2] Equally clearly, however, the delineation of an epistemological structure of this sort does nothing by itself to show that *any* of the beliefs that appear in it are true. It remains open to a would-be skeptic, even if he or she concedes all of the conditional reasons involved, to reject any belief in the structure simply by rejecting some or all of the premises upon which that belief's justification conditionally depends.

The foregoing picture leads directly to the epistemic regress problem. Suppose that at a particular node of the tree, the issue of justification for the premise beliefs is conditionally answered by appeal to a new set of premises; that at the next level, the issue of justification for those new premises is conditionally answered by appeal to yet further premises; and so on. The obvious problem is to say how this regress of levels or stages of justification, each dependent on the next, finally ends, assuming (as I shall here) that the finding of new sets of premise-beliefs (beliefs not appearing previously in the overall structure) that are adequate to conditionally justify the premise-beliefs of the previous stage cannot and does not go on infinitely. At first glance, at least, there seem to be only three general alternatives:

(i) The final stage of any particular branch of the regress may invoke premise-beliefs for which no further reason or justification of any sort is available. In this case, it seems to follow that the epistemological tree-structure, no matter how complicated and ramified it may be, offers no reason or justification for thinking that *any* of the component beliefs that are essentially dependent on those unjustified beliefs are true.[3] It tells us, in effect, only that some things would be true *if* other things were true, and that those other things would be true *if* still further things were true, and so on, ending with things that there is no reason to believe to be true.

(ii) The final stage of the regress may invoke premise-beliefs that have occurred earlier in the structure, so that the justificational structure in effect loops back upon itself in some fashion. In this case, assuming again that all relevant justificatory relations are captured by the structure, the justification for all of the components of the structure is apparently either directly circular or else dependent on premise-beliefs that are justified only in a circular and apparently questionbegging manner. Thus such a justificational structure again seems to present no reason for thinking that any of the component beliefs are true.

(iii) The only apparently remaining alternative is that though there is *some* sort of reason or justification for thinking that the premise-beliefs of the final stage are true, this reason is not of the conditional or inferential sort we have been discussing and hence avoids invoking new premise-beliefs that would themselves be in need of justification.[4] Thus such beliefs, if they exist, might be said to be *unconditionally justified*.

It is of course this third alternative that is advocated by foundationalism, with these unconditionally justified or "basic" beliefs constituting the foundation upon which the rest of contingent or empirical knowledge allegedly rests. The foundationalist's main argument is that only this alternative can avoid the highly implausible skeptical conclusion that no contingent or empirical belief is ever justified.

2. Foundationalism and its Problems

Given our earlier assumptions, the argument for foundationalism on the basis of the epistemic regress problem appears initially to be extremely compelling, indeed so much so that only very severe problems pertaining to the resulting foundationalist position could make it reasonable to resist it. In addition, the most standard version of foundationalism is extremely plausible from an intuitive or common-sense standpoint: it certainly seems as though we have many justified contingent or empirical beliefs that are not justified by appeal to other beliefs, but rather by appeal to sensory and introspective *experience*. Thus it is at least a bit surprising that a central theme of recent epistemological discussion, often the single point on which otherwise widely disparate philosophers find themselves in agreement, is the conviction that internalist foundationalism is an untenable, indeed hopeless position, one that must be abandoned if epistemological progress is to be made.

There are serious reasons for such a conclusion, the most important of which (in my judgment) will be considered momentarily. But it should also be noted that is doubtful that there is any very general agreement concerning the deficiencies of foundationalism; indeed, many of those who reject it do not seem to have any very definite argument in mind. Thus, as happens with rather alarming frequency in philosophy, the movement away from foundationalism in the last three decades or so often looks less like a reasoned dialectical progression than a fashionable stampede. And it is of course the rejection of internalist foundationalism that provides the main motivation for views like coherentism and externalism, neither of which could plausibly be claimed to be very attractive if it were not viewed by its proponents as the only remaining dialectical alternative.

What then are the alleged problems with internalist foundationalism? The most important ones fall into two main areas, the first pertaining to the relation between the supposed foundational beliefs and the other beliefs that are to be justified by appeal to them, and the second pertaining to the nature and justification of the foundational beliefs themselves.

The first kind of problem is concerned with the putative justificatory relation between the unconditionally justified foundational or basic beliefs and the nonbasic or "superstructure" beliefs, as those two components are specified by any particular version of foundationalism. The main issue here is whether it is possible on the basis of the foundation specified by such a position to provide an adequate justification for the other beliefs that we ordinarily regard as justified, or at least for a reasonably high proportion of such beliefs. A foundationalist view that falls seriously short in this area will itself amount to a fairly severe version of skepticism. Such a skeptical result is both implausible in itself and also tends to seriously undercut the foundationalist argument, discussed above, against other views.

It is obvious that the shape and seriousness of this first general sort of problem will vary widely among foundationalist views, depending in large part on just how much is included in the specified set of basic or foundational beliefs (which will depend in turn on the specific account of how those beliefs are justified). In particular, a view (e.g. Quinton's[5]) according to which at least some beliefs about physical objects count as basic or foundational will clearly have substantially less difficulty in giving a reasonably plausible account of the overall scope of nonfoundational knowledge than will a more traditional view (such as Lewis's[6]) that restricts the foundations to beliefs about subjective states of experience. Since, as will emerge later on, the general sort of foundationalist view that turns out, in my view, to be the most dialectically defensible is of the latter, more traditional sort, I believe that this issue has to be taken very seriously. More will be said about it toward the end of the paper, after the nature of the proposed foundation has emerged.

For the moment, however, I want to focus on a second and to my mind more dialectically fundamental kind of objection to foundationalism, one that asks how the supposedly basic or foundational beliefs are themselves justified or rendered epistemically acceptable. The basic beliefs in a foundationalist account of empirical knowledge are, after all, themselves contingent and presumably empirical beliefs, beliefs that are true in some possible worlds and false in others. It thus seems obvious that if they are to serve as the justificatory premises for all the rest of empirical knowledge, then some sort of justification is needed for thinking that they are themselves true or likely to be true. And the problem is that it initially seems impossible to explain how there can be such a reason or justification for basic beliefs that is internally accessible without at the same time impugning their status as basic.

Foundationalists have responded to this challenge, sometimes only by implication, in a variety of different ways. Some have claimed in effect that the issue of justification for the basic or foundational beliefs somehow does not arise or at least cannot be correctly or meaningfully raised, but this sort of view seems to me difficult or impossible to take seriously, given the already noted contingent and empirical character of the beliefs in question.

Others have appealed to the idea that such beliefs are somehow *self*-justifying.[7] This idea has a good deal of appeal in the area of a priori justification. It seems quite plausible to say of simple a priori beliefs that they are self-justified or, perhaps better, self-evident: that the intuitively apprehended necessity of their content provides a reason for thinking that they are true.[8] But whether or not this view of the a priori is correct, it is very hard to see how a belief that is contingent and empirical in character can have such a status. Since such a belief is not true in all possible worlds, some reason beyond its content seems needed for thinking that it is in fact true or likely to be true in the actual world.

But where then is the justification or epistemic authority of a basic belief supposed to come from? As already noted, the obvious appeal from an intuitive standpoint is to sensory and introspective experience. But it is not easy, from a structural and dialectical standpoint, to see how such an appeal is supposed to work, and foundationalists, despite the intuitive plausibility of their core idea, do not seem to me to have done very well in clarifying this critical point.

Clearly the experience that justifies a particular basic belief must have a correlative specific character. But the problem is to say how the specific character of the experience is itself apprehended in a way that makes it possible to appeal to it for justification within an internalist view. If that character is apprehended in an apperceptive belief (or belief-like state), the belief that I have such-and-such a specific sort of experience, then the original, supposedly basic belief appears to have lost that status, since its justification now depends on this further belief; and the issue of the justification of this new, apperceptive belief immediately arises and appears to be no easier to deal with. Whereas if the apprehension of the specific character of experience does not take the form of a belief or belief-like cognitive state, if when I apprehend my experience I am not thereby cognitively aware *that* it is of a certain specific sort, then any further issue of justification is perhaps avoided, but at the cost of making it difficult to see how such an apprehension can confer justification on the original, supposedly basic belief. In particular, if the apprehension of the experiential content is not in any way belief-like or propositional in character, how can there be any sort of inferential or quasi-inferential transition from the awareness of that content to the truth (or likely truth) of a supposedly basic belief?[9] And in the absence of such an inference, in what way does the experience or the apprehension thereof constitute a reason for thinking that the belief is true?

It is this fundamental dilemma pertaining to the apprehension of experiential content that seems to me to pose the most fundamental objection to the most obvious and otherwise plausible versions of foundationalism, thereby constituting a strong dialectical motive for considering the possibility of a nonfoundationalist alternative. We shall return to it later, following an extended look at the coherentist position.

3. The Coherentist Gambit

Even more obviously than in the case of externalism, where there are other, broadly "naturalistic" motivations at work as well, the main motivation for coherentism is the avoidance of foundationalism, rather than any initial plausibility attaching to coherentism itself. While it is very plausible that coherence or something like it is *one* important ingredient in empirical justification, it is initially *very* implausible that it is the whole story. The reasons here are both familiar and obvious: (i) a pure coherence theory seems to entail, paradoxically, that epistemic justification requires on input from or contact with the world outside the system of beliefs; (ii) it seems possible to invent indefinitely many alternative systems of belief in a purely arbitrary way and yet make each of them entirely coherent; and, in part because of these two previous objections, (iii) there seems to be no clear connection between the coherence of a system of beliefs and the cognitive goal of truth.

In fact, of course, largely for the reasons just noted, probably no one has ever seriously advocated a *pure* coherence theory of empirical justification, one in which the coherence of a set of beliefs is claimed to be by itself sufficient for justification. The coherentist project has rather been in effect to supplement the appeal to coherence in a way that avoids or at least mitigates the foregoing objections, while at the same time avoiding a relapse into foundationalism. Given this essentially negative aim, it is not surprising that the details of the various positive coherentist and quasi-coherentist positions vary quite widely, so much so that it is far from clear that there is very much common ground that can be identified as the core coherentist position.

I will attempt nonetheless in the present section to identify and explain in a necessarily schematic way the main elements that are arguably essential to any developed coherentist position that purports to be an account of a notion of epistemic justification that is both internalist in character and plausibly conducive to finding truth (understood in the realist way indicated above). There are, I will suggest, four such elements, elements that are needed to stave off the most obvious problems and define a relatively clear and specific position.[10]

(i) Of the three alternatives with regard to the outcome of the epistemic regress that were outlined above, the coherentist clearly opts for the second, the idea that the chains of justification for particular contingent, empirical beliefs circle or loop back upon themselves. Incautious advocates of coherentism have sometimes seemed to endorse the idea that such a picture is acceptable if only the circles are "large enough." But the obvious objection to circular chains of justification, to which the size of the circle seems irrelevant, is that they involve circular reasoning and hence have no genuine justificatory force.

The only very clear coherentist response to this objection, stemming originally from Bosanquet,[11] is that it depends on the mistaken idea that relations of justification fundamentally involve a *linear*, asymmetrical order of dependence among the beliefs in question. The contrary suggestion is that justification, when properly understood, is ultimately *nonlinear* or *holistic* in character, with all of the beliefs in the system standing in relations of mutual support, but none being epistemically prior to the others. In this way, it is alleged, any true circularity is avoided. Such a view amounts to making the system itself the primary unit of justification, with its component beliefs being justified only derivatively, by virtue of their membership in an appropriate sort of system. And the property of the system, in virtue of which it is justified, is of course specified as coherence.[12]

(ii) But what exactly is coherence? The second component of any serious coherence theory will be some relatively specific account of this relation. On an intuitive level, coherence is a matter of how the beliefs in a system of beliefs fit together or "dovetail" with each other, so as to constitute one unified and tightly structured whole. And it is clear that this fitting together depends on logical, inferential, and explanatory relations of many different sorts among the components of the system. But spelling out the details of this idea, particularly in a way that would allow reasonably precise assessments of comparative coherence, is extremely difficult, at least partly because such an account will depend on the correct account of a number of more specific and still inadequately understood topics, such as induction, confirmation, probability, explanation, and various issues in logic (such as those connected with "relevance logic").

Some points are, however, relatively clear. First, any conception of coherence that is even *prima facie* adequate as a basis for epistemic justification must require more than logical consistency; indeed, in light of general human logical fallibility and more specific problems such as the paradox of the preface (pertaining to the case in which an author prefaces a complicated discussion by saying that he is sure that some of the claims in it are false), it seems a mistake to view logical consistency as even an absolutely necessary requirement for a significant degree of coherence. Second, coherence requires a high degree of inferential interconnectedness in the system of beliefs, involving relations of necessitation, both strictly logical and otherwise, together with probabilistic connections of various kinds. One important aspect of this is what might be called probabilistic consistency, i.e. the minimizing of relations between beliefs in the system in virtue of which some are highly unlikely to be true in relation to others. Third, while some recent positions have emphasized explanatory relations as the basis for coherence,[13] it seems reasonably clear that this cannot be the whole story. The coherence of a system of beliefs is surely enhanced to the extent that some parts of the system are explained by others, thus reducing the degree to which the beliefs of the system portray unexplained anomalies. But not all relevant sorts of inferential connections are explanatory in character.[14]

As the foregoing very sketchy account suggests, the precise nature of coherence remains a largely unsolved problem, making it reasonable to ask why this lacuna isn't in itself a sufficient basis for dismissing such theories. A partial response to this objection is that difficulties in this area cannot yield anything like a decisive argument against coherence theories and in favor of their foundationalist rivals, because the concept of coherence, or something so similar to it that it will be capable of playing essentially the same role and will involve the same problems, is also an indispensable ingredient in virtually all foundationalist theories: coherence must seemingly be invoked to account for the relation between the basic or foundational beliefs and other nonfoundational or "superstructure" beliefs, in virtue of which the latter are justified in relation to the former.[15] For this reason, giving an adequate account of coherence should not be regarded as exclusively the responsibility of coherentists, despite the central role that the concept plays in their position. But while there is something clearly right about this point as a dialectical response to the use of this problem as an argument for foundationalism, it does not alter the fact that without further clarification of its central concept, coherentism remains an essentially schematic view, rather than a developed position.

(iii) It is a seemingly obvious fact, one that few if any coherentists have seriously attempted to deny, that sensory observation or perception plays a central role in empirical justification. Any coherence theory that even hopes to be viable must thus explain how such observation can be understood in a nonfoundationalist way.

Here the main coherentist claim is that while observational beliefs are indeed a *causal* result of sensory experience, rather than being arrived at inferentially, this does not account for their *justification*, for the reasons outlined above in connection with the second main objection to foundationalism. And thus it seems open for the coherentist to hold that the justification of such a belief can still depend on coherence with the background system of beliefs. It is crucial here, however, that the justification in question still depend also in some way on the fact that the belief was a result of perception, since justification that depended only on the coherence of the belief's propositional content with the rest of the cognitive system would make the observational status of the belief justificationally irrelevant.

My own previously held version of this general gambit[16] attempts to provide for observational input by appealing to the slightly more specific idea of a *cognitively spontaneous belief*: one that simply strikes the observer in an involuntary, coercive, noninferential way, rather than arising as a product of any sort of inference or other discursive process, whether explicit or implicit. That a belief has this status, however, says nothing so far, according to the coherentist, about how or even whether it is justified; indeed, there is no reason to think that all cognitively spontaneous beliefs *are* justified, or even necessarily that most of them are, since the category would include hunches and irrational spontaneous convictions, as well as beliefs resulting from perception. The suggestion is then that certain cognitively spontaneous beliefs are justified from within the system, by appeal to: (i) the fact of their spontaneous occurrence; and (ii) the apparent track record of spontaneous beliefs of those specific kinds (identified by such things as their general subject matter, their apparent mode of sensory production, as reflected in the content of the belief, and concomitant factors of various kinds) as regards frequency of truth (under specified conditions), all this being assessed, of course, from within the system.[17]

It this way, it seems possible for there to be a justifying reason for such a cognitively spontaneous belief that appeals to its status as cognitively spontaneous and thus putatively observational, but still does so in a way that makes the resulting justification dependent on the fact that the claim that a belief of this kind and produced in this way is likely to be true stands in a relation of coherence with the background system of beliefs. Such a belief would thus be *arrived at* noninferentially, but still *justified* by appeal to inference relations and coherence. It would thus seem to provide a kind of input from the nonconceptual world that is still recognizably coherentist in character.

There are two further important points about coherentist observation that need to be mentioned briefly. First, the other beliefs needed to give a justifying reason for a particular observational belief must themselves be justified in some way that does not amount to a relapse into foundationalism. Included here will be: (i) beliefs about the specific conditions under which the cognitively spontaneous belief in question occurred; (ii) the belief that cognitively spontaneous beliefs of the specific kind in question are likely, under those conditions, to be true; and (iii) beliefs pertaining to that specific belief and its occurrence, including the belief that it was indeed cognitively spontaneous, together with further beliefs that are relevant to determining the particular kind of belief in question. The justification for (i) will in general have to include other observational beliefs, themselves justified in the same general fashion, so that any case of justified observation will normally or perhaps always involve a set of mutually supporting observations. The justification for (ii) will appeal inductively to other cases of correct observation, as judged from within the system, as well as to more theoretical reasons for thinking that beliefs of the kind in question are generally produced in a reliable way. The justification for (iii) will appeal to introspective beliefs, themselves constituting a species of observation, and ultimately to the believer's comprehensive grasp of his or her overall system of beliefs – the status of which is the focus of the fourth of the main elements, to be discussed next.[18]

Second, the bare *possibility* of coherentist observation is pretty obviously insufficient to accommodate the role that observation (apparently) plays in our cognitive lives. Our intuitive conviction is that perceptual observation is not only possible but pervasive and that an appeal to observational evidence, whether direct or indirect, is essential for the justification of at least contingent beliefs about the world. Thus a coherence theory that does not do violence to these intuitions must *require* and not just allow that a substantial observational element be present in any justified system that includes such contingent beliefs. It must, that is, impose something akin to what I have elsewhere called the Observational Requirement,[19] to the effect that any justified system of putatively empirical beliefs must contain a reasonable proportion of cognitively spontaneous beliefs that according to the system itself are likely to be true.

(iv) Like the other elements already discussed, the last is also in effect a response to an objection that threatens to derail the coherentist position before it even gets off the ground. If it is by appeal to coherence with one's system of beliefs that all issues of empirical justification are to be decided, then an *internalist* coherence theory requires that the believer have an adequate grasp or representation of his system of beliefs, since it is with respect to this system that issues of coherence and so of justification are to be decided. Such a grasp would presumably take the form of a set of metabeliefs (or one comprehensive metabelief) specifying the contents of the system of beliefs. And the seemingly glaring difficulty is that the coherentist view also seemingly precludes there being any way for the metabeliefs that constitutes this grasp to themselves be justified. Such beliefs are obviously empirical and contingent in character; and yet any appeal to coherence for *their* justification would seem to be plainly circular or questionbegging, since what is at issue is the specification of the very system of beliefs in relation to which coherence is to be assessed. Most coherentists have failed to explicitly acknowledge this problem, but it still strikes me as obviously one that a coherentist position must somehow deal with.

In my own version of coherentism, I appeal at this point to what I call the "Doxastic Presumption." Though this move now strikes me as pretty desperate (a view that many others no doubt arrived at much more swiftly than I did), I still know of no better way to handle the issue in question. The idea is to mitigate the foregoing objection by treating the metabelief in question as an unjustified hypothesis in relation to which issues of justification are *conditionally* assessed, yielding results of the general form: *if* my representation of my system of beliefs is correct, then such-and-such a particular belief is justified in the sense of being likely to be true. The metabelief in question would presumably still in fact be a product of introspection, even though there is no way within a coherentist position for this most fundamental result of introspection to be justified.[20]

This completes my enumeration of the main elements that any coherentist position must arguably include. All of them are responses to deep-seated problems, and this highlights again the dialectically defensive and reactive posture that seems inevitable for a coherence theory. It is, moreover, more than a little uncertain that any of these elements is really adequate to deal with the specific problem that motivates it. But there is worse to come, as we will see in the next section.

Before turning to further objections to coherentism, however, there is one modest point to be made in the opposite direction, one that has at least some tendency to mitigate the problems faced by the coherentist view. The foregoing account of coherentism follows the trend of virtually all coherentist positions in construing the holistic element in an extreme way in which the unit of justification is the person's entire system of beliefs. Such a view seriously aggravates both the problem that gives rise to the Doxastic Presumption, as discussed above, and also other issues pertaining to the access to coherentist justification. It also yields the highly questionable result that the justification of a belief in one area could be undermined by an incoherence in one's beliefs in a completely unrelated area. And such an extreme holism is in any case quite unnecessary. We have not yet considered the question of just why the coherence of a group of beliefs is supposed to be an indication of its truth, but if there is a defensible answer to this question, there is no apparent reason (and in fact none will emerge) as to why it would not work just as well for a coherent set of beliefs that is much smaller than one's complete belief system (as long as the set in question is not so small as to raise a serious possibility that its apparent coherence is merely a matter of coincidence).

4. Objections to Coherentism

The three historically most standard objections to coherentism have already been briefly enumerated above. There is, first, the so-called "isolation problem" or "input objection," which claims that an account of justification that depends entirely on coherence will have the absurd consequence that contingent or empirical beliefs might be justified in the absence of any informational input from the extraconceptual world that they attempt to describe. This would seem to mean in turn that the truth of the component beliefs, if they happened to be true, could only be an accident in relation to that world, and thus that there could be no genuine reason to think that they are true and so no epistemic justification.

As already discussed above, the primary motivation for the coherentist account of observation is to meet this objection by showing how observational beliefs that are causally generated by the world might nonetheless be given a coherentist justification, and how an observational requirement of this sort can be made a necessary condition for empirical justification within a coherentist framework.[21] In this way, the input objection might seem, at least *prima facie*, to be met – though we will have to reconsider below whether this attempted answer really succeeds.

The second standard objection is what may be called the alternative coherent systems objection: Even given a relatively demanding conception of coherence, there will still be indefinitely many different possible systems of beliefs, each as internally coherent as the others. Thus, each of these systems will seemingly be equally justified according to a coherentist view. And this is surely an absurd result, especially since *any* belief that is not internally incoherent will be part of one or more such systems.

The coherentist's main attempted response to this objection also depends crucially on the idea of observation. If the existence of a substantial observational component is, as suggested above, made a necessary condition for empirical justification, then, it is claimed, there is no longer any reason to think that such alternative systems can be freely invented, and hence no longer any obvious reason why they should be thought to exist. The point here is that there is no reason to think that the cognitively spontaneous beliefs that are judged as likely to be true by an arbitrarily invented system of beliefs will in fact cohere with that system over time, and thus no reason to think that such a system will remain coherent.[22] Here too the coherentist seems to have at least the gist of a *prima facie* adequate response to the objection in question, though this issue too will be reconsidered below.

The third and most fundamental of the standard objections is in effect a challenge to the coherentist to give a reason for thinking that adopting beliefs on the basis of coherentist justification is likely to lead to believing the truth, which is obviously essential if coherence is to be genuinely a basis for epistemic justification. One response to this problem, one which I have already rejected by implication, is the adoption of a coherence theory of truth. The only apparent alternative is for the coherentist to offer an argument from the (empirical) premise that a given system of beliefs is coherent (and satisfies the requirement of observation) to the conclusion that the component beliefs are likely, to an appropriate degree, to be true. Such an argument will apparently have to itself be a priori in character, since any empirical appeal (beyond the premise that the system is and remains coherent) would have to be itself justified by appeal to coherence, thereby rendering the argument viciously circular.[23] I have elsewhere attempted such an a priori "metajustificatory argument,"[24] centering around the idea that only approximate truth could *explain* the fact of long-run coherence (given the satisfaction of the requirement of observation), but the details of that attempt cannot be gone into here. Whether or not it is defeated by other problems, the coherentist version of such an argument now seems to me to be decisively undercut by the more specific objections to coherentism that are discussed further on in this section.[25]

Coherentism emerges from the foregoing discussion as a shaky and problematic position at best, dialectically on the defensive from the beginning and afflicted with a multitude of problems and objections that can seemingly at best be only staved off, but rarely if ever decisively answered. Given the apparent strength of the arguments against foundationalism, together with the unacceptability (in my judgment) of externalism, coherentism seemed a project worth attempting, albeit one that clearly faced pretty long odds from the very beginning. Now, however, it seems to me time to concede that it has not succeeded and almost certainly cannot succeed. This result is perhaps already obvious enough in light of the foregoing discussion, but I will support it a bit more by discussing three further objections to coherentism that seem to me pretty clearly fatal. These are not unrelated to the problems and objections already discussed, but they are somewhat narrower and more focused.

First. The most obvious objection pertains to the so-called Doxastic Presumption. We have already taken note of the problem of access to the system of beliefs in relation to which coherence is to be assessed, and of the Doxastic Presumption as the only response that is apparently available. But it must be admitted that the result of this move, as many have taken pains to point out, is a very deep and troubling version of skepticism, albeit not perhaps quite the version that philosophical responses to skepticism have been mainly concerned with: a skepticism according to which no one has *any* justification *simpliciter* for *any* empirical belief, but only at best for the conditional claim that *if* a certain unjustified and unjustifiable presumption is correct, then various empirical beliefs are likely to be true.[26] And while it still seems to me that some forms of skepticism are unavoidable and will simply have to be lived with, I find it more and more implausible to suppose that this is one of them.

Second. A less obvious but equally serious objection pertains to the coherentist's attempted account of observational input. It still seems to me that something like the account sketched above succeeds in showing how there can be a kind of input that is justified in a coherentist way. But it is less clear that such input can be effectively recognized or identified as such in an internalistically acceptable way. In particular, the attempt, discussed above, to make the existence of such input a requirement for empirical justification does not succeed, so long as this requirement is construed in such a way that its satisfaction is internalistically recognizable.[27] The reason for this is that the alternative coherent systems objection, which this account of input is aimed in part to meet, recurs all over again: as long as it is only specified *within the system* that cognitively spontaneous beliefs occur and that the Observation Requirement is satisfied, there will be indefinitely many other competing coherent systems containing analogous specifications but characterizing the world in more or less any arbitrarily chosen way one likes.

In my earlier discussion of this issue, I attempted to meet this objection by saying that in order to genuinely be justified, such a system must actually be believed and applied,[28] with the suggestion being, as we saw above, that an arbitrarily constructed system would not remain coherent in actual use, and in particular that its allegedly cognitively spontaneous beliefs would not genuinely be found to occur in a cognitively spontaneous way. Unfortunately, however, as I somehow managed not to see, this sort of response seems to succeed only because it tacitly appeals to a direct awareness of one's own actual beliefs and their occurrence that is not legitimately available to a coherentist. As long as the occurrence of cognitively spontaneous beliefs and the satisfaction of the Observation Requirement is assessed only in terms of the coherence of beliefs that these conditions are satisfied with the rest of the system, which is all that the coherentist legitimately has to go on, the objection stands.

I note in passing that it would of course be possible to avoid this second objection by construing the Observation Requirement as an *externalist* requirement, one whose satisfaction does not need to be internally assessable. But externalism, for reasons that I do not have space to detail here, seems to me equally unacceptable; and in any case, as already noted above, an externalist version of coherentism would have no dialectical point, since if externalism were otherwise acceptable, a foundationalist version would be much more straightforward and easier to defend.

Third. The third objection pertains to a topic that has not emerged at all explicitly in our discussion of coherentism so far, but which is nonetheless vitally related to the tenability of the view. As was implicit in the discussion of the alternative coherent systems objection in section 3, a coherence theory must appeal, not just to coherence at a moment, but to coherence over a period of time and indeed over at least a relatively long run. It takes time for the coherence of an arbitrarily invented system to be destroyed by new observations; and in attempting to argue for the connection between coherence and truth, it is only long-run or at least relatively sustained coherence that might seem to demand truth as an explanation.[29] But then the issue arises of how, according to a coherence theory, the memory beliefs upon which any access to the fact of *continued* coherence must rely are themselves to be justified. Many philosophers have offered coherence theories of the justification of memory beliefs, but such an account seems clearly to be involved in vicious circularity if the only reason for thinking that coherentist justification is conductive to truth, and so that the memory beliefs in particular are true, relies on the existence of coherence over time and so on those very memory beliefs themselves. The upshot is that there is no noncircular way for a coherentist to appeal to sustained or long-run coherence, making it even more difficult or, I think, impossible to respond to the alternative coherent systems objection or to argue for the connection between coherence and truth.

Even the foregoing does not exhaust the litany of objections to coherentism, but it surely suffices to make quite clear the untenability of the central coherentist view.

5. Back to Foundationalism

Supposing that I am right in thinking that coherentism is thoroughly untenable – and also, though I have not argued the point here, that externalism is equally unacceptable – the obvious question is why such views have been taken so seriously and fairly widely adopted, especially since the problems that I have pointed to are in the end, and perhaps even in the beginning, relatively easy to spot? The answer, of course, is that coherentism, like externalism, was viewed by its proponents as the only remaining dialectical refuge, given the perceived untenability of classical internalist foundationalism. The problems that we have found with coherentism thus provide a powerful motive for reconsidering the case against foundationalism to see if it is really as powerful as it has often seemed to be.

Here the crucial objection to be reconsidered, I suggest, is the dilemma posed in section 2 with respect to the apprehension of the character of experience: if the character of experience is apprehended in a belief-like or propositional state, then it seems capable of providing a reason for thinking that further propositional beliefs are true, but is also itself in need of justification; whereas if the apprehension of the character of experience is not a belief-like or propositional state, where this is construed as its not involving any apprehension *that* the experience in question has one sort of character rather than another, the need for justification is avoided, but at the cost of rendering the apprehension seemingly incapable of providing justification for any further belief-like or propositional claim. It is this dilemma that has always seemed to me to constitute the most fundamental objection to the foundationalist appeal to experience and thereby to internalist foundationalism itself. Is there any way to respond to it?

The move that I want to suggest will be at least a bit easier to see if we focus for a while on the specific case where the (alleged) basic belief in question (though this label will turn out in fact to be something of a misnomer) is the metabelief that I have a certain specific occurrent belief. The natural place to look for justification for such a metabelief is to the experience of having the occurrent belief in question. And here the crucial fact that, I will suggest, allows an escape between the horns of the dilemma just discussed is that my most fundamental experience or awareness of one of my own occurrent beliefs is *neither* an apperceptive belief or belief-like state that would itself require justification *nor* a noncognitive awareness of some sort that fails to reflect the specific character of the apprehended state, i.e., in this case, the propositional content of the belief. Instead, I suggest, to have an occurrent belief is *ipso facto* to have an awareness of the content of that belief (and also of one's acceptance of that content), an awareness that is not reflective or apperceptive in nature, but is instead partly *constitutive* of the first-level occurrent belief state itself. My suggestion is that it is by appeal to this nonapperceptive, constitutive awareness that an apperceptive metabelief can be justified – though we now see that it is this nonapperceptive awareness rather than the metabelief that finally deserves to be called "basic."

The crucial point here is simply that occurrent belief is, after all, a *conscious* state, and that what one is primarily conscious of in having such a belief is precisely its propositional content (together with one's acceptance of that content). This awareness of content seems obviously to constitute in and by itself, if other things are equal, a justifying reason for the metabelief that I have an occurrent belief with that very content. But because of its nonapperceptive, constituent character, this "built-in" awareness, as it might be described, neither requires any justification itself, nor for that matter even admits of any. Indeed, I submit, such a nonapperceptive, constituent awareness of content is strictly *infallible* in essentially the way that foundationalist views traditionally claimed, but which most have long since abandoned. Because it is this constitutive or "built-in" awareness of content that *gives* the belief its specific character, that *makes* it the particular belief that it is with the specific content that it has (rather than some other belief or some nonbelief state), there is apparently no way in which this awareness could be mistaken, simply because there is nothing independent of the awareness itself for it to be mistaken about.

This infallibility does not, of course, extend to an apperceptive metabelief: it would still be possible to apperceptively misapprehend one's own belief, i.e., to have a metabelief that does not accurately reflect the content contained in the constitutive or "built-in" awareness. Such a mistake might be a case of mere inattention, or it might result from the complexity or obscurity of the belief content itself or from some further problem. But unless there is some reason in a particular case to think that the chances of such a misapprehension are large, this possibility of error does not seem to prevent the metabelief from being justifiable by appeal to the constituent awareness.

The foregoing provides at least a sketch of how a certain specific sort of belief, viz. an apperceptive metabelief about an occurrent belief of one's own, can be basic in the sense of there being an internally available reason why it is likely to be true without that reason depending on any further belief or other cognitive state that is itself in need of justification – though, as we have seen, it is really the constitutive awareness of content rather than the metabelief that ultimately turns out to be foundational. It seems plausible to suppose that it is this sort of non-apperceptive, constituent awareness of the content of a conscious state that earlier epistemologists and some more recent ones have had at least primarily in mind in their use of the notion of "direct acquaintance" (or "immediate awareness"). But if this is right, then many discussions of direct acquaintance were needlessly obscure, suggesting as they did some sort of mysteriously authoritative or infallible apprehension of an independent cognitive object, rather than an awareness that is simply constitutive of the conscious state itself. And the occasional suggestions that one might possibly be directly acquainted with physical objects, suggestions that simply make no sense on the present account of what direct acquaintance amounts to, seem to me to show clearly that at least some of the proponents of direct acquaintance did not fully understand what they were dealing with. I also think that it is this sort of constitutive awareness of the content of a conscious state that Chisholm had in mind in speaking of states that are "self-presenting,"[30] a terminology that seems rather more appropriate to the phenomenon in question than "acquaintance."

Where, then, does this leave us? Even this much of a foundationalist ingredient seems enough, when combined with the other elements of a coherentist view as discussed above, to yield a significantly more plausible and defensible position. Though there is still a problem of what to say about nonoccurrent beliefs, to which the account sketched so far is not directly applicable, the problem that created the need for the Doxastic Presumption is at least mitigated. And even a foundational knowledge restricted to my own beliefs is enough to substantially reduce the force of the input objection and the alternative coherent systems objections. Occurrent beliefs are after all states that genuinely occur in the world and of whose occurrence is incompatible with the vast majority of arbitrarily invented coherent systems, so long as these include some specification of the person's system of beliefs. It is still questionable, however, whether knowledge merely of one's own beliefs, even if worries stemming from the occurrent–dispositional distinction are set aside, is enough by itself to provide an adequate basis for knowledge of the objective physical world. And in any case, having shown how a foundational grasp of the content of one's own beliefs is possible, there is an analogous, albeit some-what more complicated and problematic possibility with respect to the contents of other kinds of experience, mainly sensory or perceptual experience, that needs to be considered.

Consider then a state of, e.g. visual experience, such as the one that I am presently having as I look out of the window in my study. Like an occurrent belief, such an experience is of course a conscious state. This means, I suggest, that, in a way that parallels the account of occurrent belief offered above, it automatically involves a constitutive or "built-in," nonapperceptive awareness of its own distinctive sort of experiential or phenomenal content. And, again in parallel fashion, such an awareness is in no need of justification and is indeed infallible in the sense that there is no sort of mistake that is even relevant to it. Thus this awareness of sensory content is also apparently available to play a foundational role.

Before we embrace this idea too eagerly, however, there is a further objection that needs to be addressed, one that applies at least much more straightforwardly to the case of sensory experience than it does to the case of belief. This objection, which is present with various degrees of explicitness in the thought of philosophers as different as Popper, Davidson, Sellars, and Rorty,[31] begins with the idea that the distinctive content of a perceptual experience, that content the awareness of which makes the experience the very experience that it is, is nonpropositional and nonconceptual in character. Exactly what this means is more than a little obscure, but it means at least that this most basic awareness is not itself in general or classificatory terms, is not a propositional awareness *that* the experience falls under general categories or universals. And from this the conclusion is drawn that such an awareness cannot stand in any intelligible justificatory relation to a belief formulated in propositional and conceptual terms, and hence that the relation between the two must be merely causal. As Davidson puts it:

> The relation between a sensation and a belief cannot be logical, since sensations are not beliefs or other propositional attitudes. What then is the relation? The answer is, I think, obvious: the relation is causal. Sensations cause some beliefs and in *this* sense are the basis or ground of those beliefs. But a causal explanation of a belief does not show how or why the belief is justified.[32]

And if this were correct, what I have been calling the constituent or built-in awareness of perceptual content, even though it undeniably exists, would be incapable of playing any justificatory role and thus would apparently have no real epistemological significance.

The premise of this argument, viz. the claim that sensory experience is essentially nonconceptual in character, seems to me to be both true and important, even though it would be nice to have a fuller understanding of it. At least part of the point is that the content of, for example, the visual experience that I am having as I look out of my window is far too specific, detailed, and variegated to be adequately captured in any conceptual or propositional formulation – or at least in any that I am presently able to formulate or even understand.

But although many epistemologists, myself included, have been influenced by this argument, it now seems to me clear that its conclusion simply does not follow from its premise. For even if we grant that the specific experiential or phenomenal content of my visual experience is itself nonpropositional and nonconceptual, I am, as already argued, nonetheless aware of that specific content simply by virtue of having that experience. And thus if (i) an apperceptive belief that I entertain purports to describe or conceptually characterize that perceptual content, albeit no doubt incompletely, and if (ii) I understand the descriptive content of that belief, i.e., understand what an experience would have to be like in order to satisfy the conceptual description, then I seem to be in a good, indeed an ideal, position to judge whether the conceptual description is accurate as far as it goes; and if it appears to be accurate, to be justified on that basis in accepting the belief.

Here indeed we seem to have exactly the sort of "confrontation" between a conceptual description and the nonconceptual chunk of reality that it purports to describe which many philosophers, myself again alas included, have rejected as impossible. Such a confrontation is only possible, to be sure, where the reality in question is itself a conscious state and where the description in question pertains to the conscious content of that state, but in that very specific case it seems to be entirely unproblematic. In this way it turns out to be possible for nonconceptual experience to yield justification for beliefs about the experienced content itself. I conclude that the given is not after all a myth!

6. The Problem of the External World Returns

But this result does not by itself take us very far, for it leaves two large questions still outstanding. The more obvious and ultimately more important question is whether and how the given content in question can play an epistemic role in justifying beliefs about the external material world, thus yielding a response to the other main line of objection to foundationalism discussed earlier (in section 2). But a prior question that must be dealt with first is how the given nonconceptual perceptual content is to be correctly described or formulated, as it seemingly must if it is to play a justificatory role in the person's overall cognitive economy. Granted that our built-in awareness of this nonconceptual content is capable in principle of justifying apperceptive beliefs that purport to describe it, what kinds of apperceptive beliefs are in fact thus justified? In the remainder of the present paper, I will focus mainly on the latter of these two questions, returning to the former only briefly at the very end.

The question at issue would be relatively simple to deal with if it were plausible to suppose that we are able to conceptually formulate the given content in phenomenological terms that are as close as possible to the apparent character of the given experience itself – in something like the pure sense-datum language or concepts envisaged by various philosophers earlier in this century. The advocates of such views have usually assumed that the resulting description of, e.g., visual experience would be in terms of patches of color arranged in a two-dimensional visual space, and I have no desire at present to quarrel with such a picture. And while there are many philosophers who would reject the idea that such a purely phenomenological description could accurately capture the content of experience as wrong-headed in principle,[33] I can find no very compelling argument for such a view, no reason why it would not be possible for us to have the conceptual resources to provide such a phenomenological description of experience to any level of precision and accuracy desired (even though it seems obvious that we would always fall short of an ideally complete description).

But even if it represents a theoretical possibility, the idea that our main conceptual grasp of the content of experience is in phenomenological terms faces two severe difficulties of a more narrowly practical sort. First, we clearly do not in fact possess the needed conceptual resources, even if I am right that it would be possible in principle to possess them. It is important not to exaggerate this point. Most people are capable of giving reasonably precise and accurate phenomenological or at least quasi-phenomenological descriptions of some aspects of their experience, and a person who cultivates this ability, such as an artist or a wine taster, can often do a good deal better. It is doubtful, however, if even those whose abilities of this sort are the best developed are in a position to conceptually formulate a strictly phenomenological characterization of sense experience that is sufficiently detailed and precise to capture all or even most of its justificatory significance for claims about the physical world (assuming for the moment that it has such significance). And in any case, it is clear that most of us do not even begin to approach such a capacity. Second, even if we did possess the needed conceptual resources, it seems abundantly clear that the time and effort required to formulate such a justificatorily adequate description in such terms, either overtly in language or internally to oneself, would be prohibitive.

But if our conceptual formulations of the given content of sensory experience are not, at least for the most part, couched in purely phenomenological terms, the only very obvious alternative is that we conceptually grasp such content in terms of the physical objects and situations that we would be inclined on the basis of that experience, other things being equal, to think we are perceiving. Thus, for example, my primary conceptual grasp of my present visual experience characterizes it as the sort of experience that in the absence of countervailing considerations would lead me to think that I am perceiving an expanse of grass, several large trees, the corner of a house, etc., with all the parts of this description capable of being spelled out at much greater length. The usual way of putting this is to say that what I am conceptually aware of is certain physical-object *appearances* or apparent physical objects – or, in a slightly more technical terminology, of ways of being "appeared to."

But although this is the obvious answer to the question of how we grasp sensory content in conceptual terms, the potential for misunderstanding its significance is very serious, and many philosophers seem to me to have succumbed to this danger. In particular, it is crucially important to distinguish a description of experience that merely indicates what sort of physical objects and situations seem or appear, on the basis of that experience, to be present from one that embodies some further causal or relational claim about the connection between experience and the physical realm, one whose justification would clearly have to appeal to something beyond the experienced content itself.

A useful example of the sort of danger that I am warning against is provided by Susan Haack in her recent book on epistemology, in the course of which she attempts to give a specification of the evidential force of a state of perceptual experience. Her suggestion is that this can captured by a set of propositions ascribing the perceptual states to the subject in question. Thus, for example, such an ascription might say that the subject "is in the sort of perceptual state a person would be in, in normal circumstances, when looking at a rabbit three feet away and in good light" or "is in the sort of perceptual state a normal subject would be in, in normal circumstances, when getting a brief glimpse of a fast-moving rabbit at dusk."[34] Haack's discussion of this point is not as clear or full as one might like, but the specific formulations offered make it reasonable to suppose that these characterizations are intended to describe the experience in terms of the physical situations that are *causally* or *lawfully* connected with it, rather than in terms of its intrinsic content. This, however, is precisely the sort of description that cannot be justified by appeal to the experienced content alone. My experience may incline me to think that a rabbit is present, but the experience cannot by itself reveal that it is of the sort that is normally *caused* by rabbits. A useful way of putting the point is to say that the claims about physical appearances or ways of being appeared to that constitute our primary conceptual formulations of sensory experience must be understood in something like what Chisholm has called the "descriptive, noncomparative" sense of the terms or concepts in question,[35] for only in that sense can the claim to be "appeared to" in a certain way be adequately justified simply by appeal to our primary nonconceptual awareness of sensory content.

It seems quite obvious that we have the ability to grasp or represent the character of our perceptual experience fairly accurately, albeit somewhat obliquely, in terms of such physical object appearances. But once illegitimate construals like

Haack's are set aside, it is far from obvious exactly what such characterizations of experience really amount to. In giving them, we seem to be relying on a tacitly grasped and, we think, mutually understood correlation or association of some sort, perhaps learned or perhaps at least partially innate, between experiential features and the physical situations of which they are taken to be appearances, one that we are confidently guided by in the vast majority of cases, even though we are unable to even begin to formulate it explicitly.[36] Whatever this correlation ultimately amounts to, however, the important issue is whether beliefs adopted on the basis of it are at least likely to reflect in an accurate way what is really going on in the physical world, something that cannot be simply assumed without begging the most important philosophical question in this area.

This brings me then to the second main issue that arises for this sort of position: if the foregoing is at least approximately the right way to understand our primary conceptual representations of the given content of sensory experience, how, if at all, do such representations contribute to the justification of beliefs about the physical world? In particular, how does the fact that my given sensory experience can be correctly described, in light of the tacit correlation, as the appearance of a certain sort of physical object or situation, contribute to the *justification* of the claim that such an object or situation is actually present and being perceived? This is of course the ultimate question in this general area, one that would take far more space than is available in the present paper to deal with adequately. For the moment, I will therefore have to be content with a brief canvassing of the main alternative possibilities for a nonskeptical solution.

First. Perhaps the most historically standard solution is the reductive phenomenalist attempt to define physical object concepts in terms of sensory appearance concepts. Though there are difficult issues of conceptual priority involved,[37] it seems to me that this approach is likely to succeed for the specific case of secondary qualities. But the problems afflicting a more global phenomenalist approach are both well known and, in my judgment, clearly fatal.

Second. A quite different solution is advocated by H. H. Price[38] and, in what seems to be a rather seriously qualified form, by Chisholm, among others. The core idea of this view is that the mere occurrence of a physical appearance or state of being appeared to confers *prima facie* justification on the corresponding physical claim. Chisholm's own version of this solution, presented in the most recent edition of *Theory of Knowledge*,[39] appeals to a logical relation of "tending to make evident" that is alleged to exist between claims or beliefs about sensory appearances and the corresponding claims or beliefs about the actual perception of physical objects. Thus my belief that my present visual experience involves appearances of an expanse of grass, several large trees, and the corner of a house, all of them fairly detailed and distinctive, or my belief that I am being appeared to in the corresponding ways, *tends to make evident* my belief that I am perceiving such an expanse of grass, such trees, and such a corner of a house (and thus that that these items really exist in the physical world). Such a tendency is, on Chisholm's view, capable of being defeated by countervailing evidence, but where no such defeater is present, the claim of genuine perception (and so of the existence of the object in question, is allegedly justified).

The main problem with this sort of view is that it is quite doubtful that such a logical relation of "tending to make evident" or "tending to justify" genuinely exists between an individual belief about physical appearances and the corresponding belief about physical reality. To be sure, Chisholm's claim is not that any such relation is discernible a priori in itself, but only that it is an a priori consequence of the "general presupposition" or "faith," roughly, that epistemological success is possible.[40] And the skeptical implications of ascribing no stronger epistemic status than this to the claim that such a connection between appearances and physical reality really exists seem pretty serious in themselves. But over and above that, if the belief about appearance is construed, as I have argued that it must be construed, as merely a useful though oblique way of describing the nonconceptual experiential or phenomenal content of sensory experience, then there is no apparent way that it could by itself have any direct bearing on the truth or likely truth of the corresponding physical claim, as long as that claim is nonreductively understood – and thus no way that there could be any such relation of "tending to make evident" or "tending to justify," whether a priori knowable or not.

One way to argue this point is to notice that if descriptions of the given content of experience in terms of physical object appearances are understood in the way just indicated, rather than as embodying some further claim or inference for which additional justification would be required, then it would be a mistake to think that they have any epistemological, as opposed to practical, advantage over descriptions of such experience in purely phenomenological terms. The experiential content being described is the same in either case, and its justificatory capacity is not somehow enhanced by failing to conceptualize it in the terms that would be most explicitly descriptive of it. But the idea that a purely phenomenological description of the same experience that is in fact conceptualized as a particular physical object appearance (or state of being appeared to) would by itself have any tendency to justify or render evident the corresponding claim about the physical world seems to have no plausibility at all. At the very least, some much more specific and detailed account would have to be given of why this is supposed to be so.

Third. My own fairly tentative suggestion would be that the basis for the needed inference between sensory appearance and objective fact is to be found in two further fundamental facts about such appearances: first, their involuntary, spontaneous character; and second, the fact that they fit together and reinforce each other in, dare I say, a *coherent* fashion – though the primary sort of coherence in question here pertains only to sensory appearances or the beliefs that they directly justify, rather than extending to other sorts of beliefs, and is realized in relatively limited perceptual situations, especially those involved in a series of perceptions of what we think of as an individual physical object, rather than being more global in character.[41] These two fundamental facts are, of course, the central ones appealed to by Locke, in justifying his inference from sensory ideas to the external world;⁴² and by Berkeley, in justifying his inference to the God who is supposed to produce our ideas.⁴³ In both cases, the underlying idea, rather more explicit in Berkeley, is that some *explanation* is needed for the combination of involuntariness and coherence, and that the conclusion advocated by the philosopher in question is thereby justified as the best explanation of the facts in question.⁴⁴ My own conviction is that such an inference, to Locke's conclusion rather than Berkeley's, is ultimately cogent and can be justified on a priori grounds. But how such a justification might go in detail is a long story that there is no space to consider here.⁴⁵

My conclusion for the moment is twofold: (i) coherentism is pretty obviously untenable, indeed hopeless; and (ii) a very traditional version of experiential foundationalism can be successfully defended against the most immediate and telling objection, even though it then faces a very familiar and serious problem for which no developed solution is yet available.

Notes

1. I say "contingent or empirical" to indicate an approximate target, since what it means for a belief to be *empirically* justified is of course one key facet of the overall issue. There is also a somewhat analogous issue and accompanying dialectic for a priori justification, but it differs too greatly, in my judgment, to be capable of being considered within the bounds of the present paper. For a discussion and defense of a foundationalist conception of a priori justification, see my book *In Defense of Pure Reason* (London: Cambridge University Press, 1997).
2. For a clear elaboration of such a picture, see Ernest Sosa, "How Do You Know?" *American Philosophical Quarterly* 11 (1974): 113–22.
3. I ignore here the possibility of epistemic overdetermination.
4. Obviously a particular epistemological structure might partially realize two or even all three of the alternative outcomes of the regress to be discussed. Explicit consideration of these further possibilities will be left to the reader.
5. See Anthony Quinton, *The Nature of Things* (London: Routledge & Kegan Paul, 1973).
6. See C. I. Lewis, *An Analysis of Knowledge and Valuation* (LaSalle, IL: Open Court, 1946).
7. See Roderick Chisholm, "Theory of Knowledge in America," reprinted in Chisholm, *The Foundations of Knowing* (Minneapolis: University of Minnesota Press, 1982), pp. 109–93.
8. For a defense of this view, see my paper "Toward a Moderate Rationalism," *Philosophical Topics* 23 (1995): 47–78; and my book *In Defense of Pure Reason*.
9. For a more elaborate development of this basic objection to foundationalism, see my book *The Structure of Empirical Knowledge* (Cambridge, MA: Harvard University Press, 1985), ch. 4. This book will henceforth be cited as *SEK*.
10. Perhaps not surprisingly, the elements that I regard as essential are realized most fully and explicitly in my own former coherentist position, developed in *SEK*. But it is my belief (which cannot be fully defended here) that any coherentist position that has even a *prima facie* chance of meeting the indicated constraints will have to involve

at least a close approximation to these elements, and that at least all but the fourth can be discerned (with varying degrees of clarity) in the main historical examples of coherentism.

11 See Bernard Bosanquet, *Implication and Linear Inference* (London: Macmillan, 1920).
12 For a further development of this idea, see *SEK*, pp. 89–93.
13 This is true, e.g. of Gilbert Harman's view in *Thought* (Princeton: Princeton University Press, 1973); and is at least strongly suggested by Wilfrid Sellars, in such papers as "Givenness and Explanatory Coherence," *Journal of Philosophy* 70 (1973): 612–24.
14 For some further discussion of the concept of coherence, see *SEK*, pp. 93–101.
15 See e.g. Lewis, in *Analysis of Knowledge and Valuation*, ch. 11 (who uses the term "congruence"); and Chisholm, *Theory of Knowledge*, 2nd ed. (Englewood Cliffs, NJ: Prentice-Hall, 1977), ch. 4. The basic point here is that strictly deductive or even enumerative inductive inference from the foundational beliefs does not suffice to justify most of the superstructure beliefs that the foundationalist typically wants to claim to be justified.
16 See *SEK*, ch. 6.
17 Something like this idea seems implicit in Blanshard's talk of "beliefs about the technique of acquiring beliefs" and in Sellars' talk of "language-entry transitions"; see Brand Blanshard, *The Nature of Thought* (London: Allen & Unwin, 1939), pp. 285–6, and Wilfrid Sellars, "Some Reflections on Language Games," reprinted in his *Science, Perception and Reality* (London: Routledge & Kegan Paul, 1963), pp. 321–58. It seems also to be hinted at, though less explicitly, in various other coherentist views.
18 For more detail, see *SEK*, pp. 124–38.
19 See *SEK*, pp. 140–3.
20 For more extended discussion, see *SEK*, pp. 101–6 and 147–8.
21 See *SEK*, pp. 139–40.
22 For more discussion, see *SEK*, pp. 143–6.
23 It might be suggested that there is nothing objectionably circular about a coherence theory appealing to coherence to justify the claim that coherence is truth conductive, and indeed that *any* theory of justification must make an analogous appeal to its fundamental standard (on pain of abandoning its claim to be a comprehensive account of justification). One way to see that there is something wrong with this response is to note that such a self-invoking justification of the claim of truth conduciveness is equally available for many obviously unsatisfactory views of justification (consider the view that belief by me is the standard of justification, where I also believe that all of my beliefs are true). The proper conclusion, I think, is that only a view that appeals to a direct insight into or grasp of truth can avoid this problem – which is what paradigmatically foundationalist views, like the one offered later in this paper, attempt to do. A coherentist view could appeal to such a direct insight into truth only by adopting the sort of coherence theory of truth that is briefly mentioned in the text. (I am indebted to John Greco for calling this issue to my attention.)
24 *SEK*, ch. 8.
25 Rescher attempts to give a *pragmatic* argument that the practical success that results from the employment of the coherent system makes it likely that the beliefs of the system are at least approximately true. See Nicholas Rescher, *Methodological Pragmatism* (New York: New York University Press, 1977). But the relation of this argument to the coherence of the system is less than clear, and in any case the obviously

empirical claim of pragmatic success would, for a coherentist, have to be itself justified by appeal to coherence, again making the argument viciously circular.

26 I have sometimes suggested that *if* this presumption is in fact true, then the various empirical beliefs *are justified*, since there is a reason why they are likely to be true. This, however, is a mistake, since though such a reason would, as it were, exist in the abstract, it would still be inaccessible to the believer – or to anyone else. (It was Richard Fumerton's gentle insistence that finally led me to see this pretty obvious point.)

27 I am assuming here that the satisfaction of this requirement is part of the overall coherentist reason or justification for *any* empirical claim, i.e., that one who has no access to the fact that this requirement is satisfied fails to really possess a reason for thinking that a belief that satisfies the rest of the coherentist account is likely to be true. For only a justification that includes the satisfaction of this requirement can withstand the input and alternative coherent systems objections. (I am indebted to John Greco for pointing out the need to be more explicit on this point.)

28 *SEK*, pp. 149–50.

29 See *SEK*, ch. 8.

30 See e.g. Chisholm, *Theory of Knowledge*, 3rd ed. (Englewood Cliffs, NJ: Prentice-Hall, 1989), pp. 18–19.

31 See Karl Popper, *The Logic of Scientific Discovery* (New York: Harper, 1959), §§ 25–30; Donald Davidson, "A Coherence Theory of Truth and Knowledge," in Dieter Henrich, ed., *Kant oder Hegel* (Stuttgart: Klett-Cotta, 1983), pp. 423–38; Wilfrid Sellars, "Empiricism and the Philosophy of Mind," reprinted in his *Science, Perception and Reality* (London: Routledge & Kegan Paul, 1963); and Richard Rorty, *Philosophy and the Mirror of Nature* (Princeton: Princeton University Press, 1979), pp. 182–92.

32 Davidson, "A Coherence Theory," p. 428.

33 See e.g. P. F. Strawson, "Perception and Its Objects," in G. F. Macdonald, ed., *Perception and Identity* (Ithaca: Cornell University Press, 1979), pp. 41–60.

34 Susan Haack, *Evidence and Inquiry: Towards Reconstruction in Epistemology* (Oxford: Blackwell, 1993), p. 80.

35 See Chisholm, *Theory of Knowledge*, 3rd ed., p. 23.

36 To speak here of a "correlation" might suggest that it is a *mere* correlation, that the experiential content and the corresponding propositional claim about physical objects are only externally coordinated, without being connected with each other in any more intimate way. This, however, seems to me to be mistaken. While the issue is very hard to get a confident grip on, it seems intuitively pretty clear that the experiential content is in itself *somehow* strongly suggestive of the correlative physical object claims.

37 See e.g. the discussion of this issue in the first of Sellars' Carus lectures, "The Lever of Archimedes," *Monist* 64 (1981): 3–36.

38 See H. H. Price, *Perception*, 2nd ed. (London: Methuen, 1950), ch. 7.

39 *Theory of Knowledge*, 3rd ed., pp. 46–54, 64–8, 71–4.

40 Ibid., pp. 4–6, 72–3.

41 As was pointed out to me by John Greco, "coherence" here cannot be understood in the way discussed above if it is to be a relation among sensory appearances themselves. Nonetheless, it seems clear that such appearances do fit together or fail to fit together in ways for which the term "coherence" is intuitively appropriate; and also that this fitting together is something for which some explanation seems intuitively required. While recognizing that more needs ultimately to be said about this relation,

I am content to leave matters at this intuitive level for the purposes of the present paper.

42 John Locke, *An Essay Concerning Human Understanding*, ed. P. H. Nidditch (Oxford: Oxford University Press, 1975), book IV, ch. xi.

43 George Berkeley, *The Principles of Human Knowledge*, in *Principles, Dialogues, and Philosophical Correspondence*, ed. C. M. Turbayne (Indianapolis: Bobbs-Merrill, 1965), §§ 28–30.

44 For a useful discussion and elaboration of Locke's argument, see J. L. Mackie, *Problems from Locke* (Oxford: Oxford University Press, 1976), ch. 2.

45 But see *SEK*, ch. 8, for some of the ideas that I take to be relevant, even though they are couched there in terms of a coherence theory of justification.

Part II
The Nature of Epistemic Evaluation

Chapter 5

Skepticism and the Internal/External Divide

Ernest Sosa[1]

1. Descartes's Paradox

"A belief is knowledge only when proof against all doubt, even the most hyperbolic" – so premises Descartes. If unable to rule out the possibility that one is deceived by a demon (or is embodied in an envatted brain), therefore, one knows neither what one ostensibly sees, nor the truth of any conclusion one may infer from such "data," or at least it cannot be any such inference that gives one knowledge of the truth of its conclusion.

This skeptical argument is naturally dismissed for imposing an unreasonably high requirement. Ordinarily we require nothing nearly so stringent, but only well-justified beliefs, based perhaps on less-than-conclusive reasoning. We do not require apodictic reasoning beyond any possible doubt, from axioms infallibly known.[2]

How superficial that dismissal seems, however, in light of the following: Newly-arrived in Alaska, I spot a husky as such, even though from my distance and angle no feature or circumstance distinguishes it from the many wolves in that vicinity. You believe Tom stole a book because Dick tells you so, and in fact you are right, but when Dick is accused of slander you have no basis to rule that out. Thirst-crazed by the desert sun, you hallucinate an oasis where, by coincidence, there happens to be one just as pictured in your feverish imagination. Such cases plausibly suggest this "principle of exclusion":

> PE To know a fact X, one must rule out every possibility one knows to be incompatible with one's knowing that fact X (with one's knowing that X is so).

None of your three beliefs – about the husky, about Tom's honesty, about the oasis – satisfies this requirement, which explains why none amounts to knowledge.

We may now understand the inadequacy of the above dismissal of Descartes's skepticism. Consider some fact F that you can know only by knowing it perceptually

(Descartes's situation as he sits before a fire). Take now any scenario – evil demon, brain in a vat, etc. – in which, through direct stimulation of one's brain, or through direct control of one's experience by the demon, one has fully detailed and rich experience as if fact F were the case, although one's experience is quite independent of F. One knows that such a skeptical scenario is incompatible with one's knowing F. Unable to discern the veridical experience that would enable one to know F from the delusive experience that fools one in a skeptical scenario, one cannot know F perceptually, and cannot then know F.

A version of the argument (supplemented) may be laid out as follows:

a. All your sensory experience and information at a given time is compatible with your dreaming at that time.

b. So you need some test which "indicates" that you are not then dreaming, such that you know, first, that the test is satisfied and, second, that when it is satisfied you are not dreaming.

c. But how could such a test ever be available to you, how could you ever reasonably rely on any such test, if it is a condition of your knowing (perceptually) *anything* beyond your experience that you know yourself *not* to be dreaming, not-D? If so, you could not know perceptually that you satisfy the test unless you (already?) on some occasion knew (the likes of) not-D. And how could you have satisfied such a requirement except, at least in part, *perceptually*? Besides, how could you know that if the test is satisfied then you are awake, except by relying on being awake (not-D) either at that time or at some earlier times (when you gathered the data, presumably observational and perceptually gathered, enabling your conclusion that in general one satisfies the test only when awake)?

This nowhere assumes that in order to know that p one must be *absolutely* and justifiably *certain* that p. We are not setting the standards too high and then complaining we cannot meet them. Our argument is designed to show rather that, when compared with the possibility that we are just dreaming, our thought that we really see is based on *no good reason whatever*. The dismissal above overlooks this argument.

2. Epistemic Externalism and Internalism

A famous Moorean dialectic consists of three theses:

MD a. Knowing that here is a hand requires knowing that one is not dreaming.
     b. I know that here is a hand.
     c. I do not know that I am not dreaming.

Moore and the skeptic both accept MDa, but then part ways, the skeptic rejecting MDb, while Moore rejects MDc instead. Given Moore's commitment to the given, it is not surprising that he accepts MDa. Contemporary externalists share no such commitment, and join in rejecting MDa along with other traditional assumptions.[3] How can one be justified in one's belief about the hand, however, except by relying on an assumption that one is awake and not dreaming? And how could this assumption ever get justified? It is not something that could be known just a priori, nor is it directly introspectable. It pertains rather to a certain contingent causal relation between oneself and one's surroundings. What could be one's basis for thinking that such a relation in fact obtains? If it is not known a priori and is not known through any kind of direct perception or introspection, then how is it known? More specifically, if one's epistemic justification is not of the armchair variety, nor of the introspective or perceptual variety, then how *is* one justified in believing oneself causally connected with one's surroundings in the ways required for epistemically justified beliefs, e.g. as to how it is out there on the basis of how it seems from here? This prompts questions about the nature and status of such epistemic justification. What reason might be offered in support of an internalism such as Moore's? Here are two familiar supports.

Cartesian Internalism of Justification
Justification requires only really proper thought on the part of the subject: if a believer has obtained and sustains his belief through wholly appropriate thought, then the believer is justified in so believing – where the appropriateness of the thought is a matter purely internal to the mind of the subject, and not dependent on what lies beyond.

Chisholmian Internalism of Justification
The "concept of epistemic justification . . . is *internal* . . . in that one can find out directly, by *reflection*, what one is justified in believing at any time" (*Theory of Knowledge*, 3rd ed., p. 7).

The appropriateness of one's thought is "purely internal to one's mind" only if what makes and *would* make (would make by necessity if ever it occurred) one's thought appropriate – that *in virtue of which* it is and would necessarily be appropriate – involves only matters "internal to one's mind." And these are matters constituted by mental properties of the subject's, including relations intrinsic to that mind, as when one introspects one's headache, and also "propositional attitudes."

How are these forms of internalism related?
Thesis: that Chisholmian internalism follows from Cartesian internalism, given only the following assumptions:[4]

AI *The Accessibility of the Internal*
   Matters purely internal to one's mind, such as one's occurrent mental properties and one's propositional attitudes, are always open to discovery by one's own reflection.

AES *The Accessibility of Epistemic Supervenience*
   If a belief attains, and would necessarily attain, a particular epistemic status in virtue of certain nonepistemic properties of it, that it *would* do so is open to discovery by one's own reflection.

Here again is how Chisholm himself sees the matter:[5]

> The usual approach to the traditional questions of theory of knowledge is properly called "internal" or "internalistic." The internalist assumes that merely by reflecting upon his own conscious state, he can formulate a set of epistemic principles that will enable him to find out, with respect to any possible belief he has, whether he is *justified* in having that belief. The epistemic principles that he formulates are principles that one may come upon and apply merely by sitting in one's armchair, so to speak, and without calling for any outside assistance. In a word, one need consider only one's own state of mind.

But what justifies this assumption? Why assume with Chisholmian internalism that unaided armchair reflection could always reveal whether or not one is justified? An answer to that question has been proposed by Alvin Plantinga. An answer is needed since, for one thing, neither assumption AI nor assumption AES seems just obvious on inspection. Take AI. Even if individual mental states are always transparent to reflection, which may be doubted, complex combinations of them might not be transparent. As for AES, who knows how complex the ways of supervenience might be, or how open to discovery by our limited minds?

3. Chisholmian Internalism

What does it take for a belief to be epistemically justified? What sort of status does a belief have in being epistemically justified? Deontology, (epistemic) justification, and internalism are said to be closely connected, and Chisholm's internalism has been explicated by means of these connections.[6] By "internalism" we shall mean mostly Chisholmian, epistemic internalism, i.e., the view that we have armchair access to the epistemic status of our beliefs (or at least to their status of being justified).

According to the deontological view of epistemic justification, such justification consists in an appropriate relation to one's epistemic obligations or duties. Thus:

(Epistemic) Deontologism
One is epistemically justified (and one is not blameworthy) in ø'ing if and only if in ø'ing one does one's epistemic duty – or, at least, that is so for a large, important, and basic class of epistemic duties.

The plausibility of *Deontologism* depends on how we interpret "epistemic justification." On a strong deontological interpretation:

Deontological Conception of Epistemic Justification
S is epistemically justified at t in believing that p IFF S at t freely opts to believe that p, while justifiedly aware that he ought then to believe that p.[7]

The large and important class of cases involved in *Deontologism* would be those in which one would know one's duty and would be free to abide by it. With ignorance and compulsion ruled out, one would be justified if and only if one did as required by duty.

Suppose we combine thus the doctrine of (Epistemic) Deontologism with the Deontological Conception of Epistemic Justification. Even on this combined account, where's the internalism? For example, how do we arrive at the result that when one knows what one ought to believe one knows it by reflection? (Only if one can know this by reflection, presumably, can one know by reflection that one *is* epistemically justified.)

The beliefs of the evil demon's victim might be held here to be be no less and no more justified than our own ordinary beliefs, and on the same basis. Since the victim must be justified in virtue of properties *ontologically* internal to him, and since for any actual thinker there is such a victimized double, therefore the justification of actual people must also derive from properties internal to them.

If the victim knows himself to be justified, he must know this by knowing of certain ontologically internal properties of his. But why must this knowledge be by *reflection*? Well, "reflection" usually means: "some combination of introspection and memory, along with intuition and inferential reason." It is not unreasonable, then, that if the victim knows what makes him justified, he knows it through these reflective faculties. Even if not irresistible, the argument does seem moving.

This line of reasoning from a deontological account of epistemic justification to an epistemic internalism *assumes* ontological internalism. It assumes both that the demon's victim would be no less and no more justified than his flesh and blood counterpart, and that the victim's justification would derive from his internal properties. Only on such assumptions can we thus derive epistemic internalism: the doctrine that one could always know *by reflection* whether one is epistemically justified. On this line of reasoning, therefore, one could not start with a deontological account of epistemic justification, and derive *either* or *both* of epistemic internalism *and* ontological internalism from that. On the contrary, it is only by first assuming ontological internalism that one could then derive epistemic internalism from a deontological account of justification.[8] What is more, we still face (a) how unobvious it is that one's mind should be *wholly* transparent to one's own reflection, as required by AI, and (b) how unobvious it is that the supervenience base of one's epistemic obligation must always be simple enough that its identity would be accessible to our unaided reflection, as required by AES.

Moreover, our account of epistemic justification as deontological has further limitations. Most epistemologists, of whatever persuasion, externalist or not, will surely grant that for a large and important class of cases, what has been claimed on behalf of the internalist is likely to be true. Take any case where one knows something or one is epistemically justified in believing something purely on the basis of reflection. Many epistemologists, externalist or not, will agree that in any such case one can know internalistically, by reflection, that one's belief has its positive epistemic status. Real disagreement will arise, however, concerning knowledge that either is itself perceptual or depends essentially on such knowledge. Of course, even here perhaps one must be able to know or believe correctly, simply on the basis of reflection, that one's belief is justified, but now the argument for this will have to rely on an independently held *ontological internalism*; or so it was argued above.

In addition, the conception of epistemic justification as deontological is also limited in other ways. The problem is not so much that there isn't such a notion, nor is it that the scope of such epistemic justification is too narrow, given our limited control over what we believe. These are problems, I believe, but my main problem here is rather this: Does the defined notion of "epistemic justification" capture an epistemic status of primary interest to epistemology, *even to "internalists" generally*? Don't we fall short in our effort to throw light on internalist epistemic justification if we stop with the explicated notion of deontological justification? After all, there are other desirable statuses for our beliefs to attain. Thus it is good that one's beliefs not derive from a deliberate effort on one's part to believe what is false, from a sort of "epistemic masochism." And it is a good thing that one's beliefs not derive from uncaring negligence. These are moreover sorts of things that one could know about the derivation of one's beliefs on the basis of armchair reflection. So one could secure internalism, and define a sort of "epistemic justification" even without invoking the full deontological machinery. But surely we would then fall short in our attempt to throw light on matters epistemic. Avoiding epistemic masochism and uncaring negligence are only two of the things involved in epistemic excellence. And a similar question could now be pressed against the deontologist: In opting for a deontological conception of epistemic justification, are we capturing all relevant aspects of "internal" epistemic excellence that we wish to illuminate? Or are we falling short in ways analogous to the ways in which we fall short if we stop with mere masochism-avoidance or negligence-avoidance conceptions of justification?

If we focus on the concept of epistemic justification defined, I believe we can see that it will inevitably miss respects of epistemic excellence, of internal epistemic excellence.

Consider our correct beliefs about what duty requires in various circumstances, and our correct beliefs about the particulars of our own situation which determine the call of duty for that situation. These beliefs must also be assessable as epistemically justified or not. What is more, one could hardly attain deontological *epistemic* justification if the duty-specifying beliefs that govern one's epistemic choice are wholly *unjustified*. So, these beliefs must themselves be epistemically justified in some sense. But, on pain of vicious circularity, the sense involved cannot be that of deontological epistemic justification. For we would then be involved in a circular definition: thus justified belief would be defined, in brief, as belief that is enjoined by the principles of required belief that one *justifiedly* believes pertinent to one's situation. This would assume that we already understand a notion of belief justification, whereas that is supposed to be the notion being defined.

Secondly, what are we to say of beliefs that do *not* result from a knowledgeable choice on the part of the believer? Some beliefs one either could not have avoided, *or* could not have known to be wrong beliefs to hold in the circumstances. Either way one bears no responsibility for one's lack of pertinent control *or* knowledge or correct belief. This could perhaps happen even with wholly internal beliefs that are introspective or reflective and independent of perception. If we restrict epistemic justification to our deontological concept, then all such beliefs turn out to be indistinguishable in respect of epistemic justification – none can be said to be justified.

That consequence is hard to accept. A belief unavoidable upon consideration can still amount to certainty of the highest grade: the belief that $1 + 1 = 2$, for example, or the belief that one has a headache, when one has a migraine, beliefs one cannot help having – and the great class of such obvious, nonoptional beliefs. Compare the convictions of someone brainwashed, however, or the beliefs of a *naif* with a crude conception of what justification requires in a certain ambit, who acquires his beliefs in ways that he is convinced are methodologically sound, simply because he was raised in a culture where such ways are instilled, so that now, through no fault of his own, our *naif* does not properly know what to believe and what not to believe in that ambit.

Is there a sense of justification in which these two classes of belief are on a par? If so, can that be a sense of much importance for epistemology? Clearly, at a minimum we would need to go beyond our account of epistemic justification as deontological, if we wished to explicate the fact that some indubitable truths are epistemically justified while other beliefs are not, despite being equally indubitable at least to the brainwashed or naive. The claim is *not* that there is *no* sense in which both sets of beliefs are on a par in respect of internal justification. The claim is *rather* that there is likely some further important sense of internal justification that remains uncaptured by our account of justification as deontological. With this deontological account we fall short, in a way in which we would fall short in our effort to explicate internal justification if we were to stop with the notion of belief non-negligently acquired and sustained. The broader account of internal justification would perhaps need to take account both of the avoidance of negligence and of the securing of deontological justification – these would both be relevant, in different ways, to internal epistemic justification. But, as we have seen, the broader account would need to go beyond these as well. The contours of that broader account have yet to be traced.[9] Nevertheless, to the extent that we find it plausible that a belief can be irresistible without being epistemically justified, we should be willing to hold open the possibility, worth exploring, that there is such a broader account, even if its contours remain obscure. We next explore that possibility.

4. Justification and the Internal

Compare yourself with a counterpart victim of the evil demon. Suppose the two of you indistinguishable in every current mental respect whatsoever: if you are having a current sensory experience, so is your counterpart; if you have a certain belief, so does your counterpart; if you would defend your belief by appeal to certain reasons, so would your counterpart; etc.; and vice versa. The two of you are thus point by point replicas in every current mental respect whatsoever; not only in respect of occurrent mental events, but also in respect of deeply lodged dispositions to adduce reasons, etc. Must you then be equally epistemically justified, in some relevant sense, in each of those beliefs that by hypothesis you share? If either of you is epistemically justified in believing that you face a hand, must the other be equally justified in holding that same belief? What could a difference in justification derive from? Each of you would have the same fund of sensory experiences and background beliefs to draw upon, and each of you would appeal to the same components of such a cognitive structure if ever you were challenged to defend your belief that you then face a hand. So how could there possibly be any difference in epistemic justification? All of this jibes with Chisholm's internalism, as we have seen. For Chisholm, justification is a matter of the rational-cum-experiential structure of one's mind. It is constituted by one's experience together with one's dispositions to respond in certain ways under sustained Socratic dialectic.

According to Chisholm, for every epistemically justified belief, there must be a rational structure whose presence in the subject's mind yields that justification. This rational structure may be brought to light through a process of Socratic dialectic, which will press for the reasons one might have for believing as one does, and for the reasons for those reasons, and for deeper reasons in turn, until one reaches a bedrock where one can only repeat oneself, saying "What justifies me in believing that p is just the fact that p," or the like. In other words, subjects alike in their dispositions to respond to Socratic dialectic, to demands for a display of one's justification, will be alike in their attained justification (so long as their bed-rocks are equally secure). But your demonic counterpart is imagined to be like you precisely in such underlying rational structure: you each would adduce the same reasons in response to challenges (and your experiential bedrocks are equally secure). Each of you will hence share the same epistemic justification for your corresponding beliefs. Call this "Chisholm-justification," a sort of present-moment justification.

Compare this: Mary and Jane both arrive at a conclusion C, Mary through a brilliant proof, Jane through a tissue of fallacies. At present, however, they both have forgotten the relevant stretches of their respective reasonings, and each takes herself to have established her conclusion validly. What is more, each of their performances is uncharacteristic, Jane being normally the better logician, while Mary is a normally competent but undistinguished thinker, as they both well know. The point is this: Jane would seem currently only better justified in taking herself to have proved C, as compared with Mary. As of the present moment, therefore,

Jane might seem to some as well justified as is Mary, in believing C. We know the respective aetiologies, however; what do *we* say? No doubt we normally would grant Mary justification and withhold it from Jane. Would we not judge Jane's belief unjustified since based essentially on fallacies? If so, then a belief's aetiology can make a difference to its justification. Call this sort of justification PA-justification ("personal aetiology justification").

Mary and Jane are equally Chisholm-justified, then, but only Mary is PA-justified. Chisholm-justification depends just on your present ability to adduce reasons, and on your present structure of experiences and beliefs. So it depends on present-time-slice, internal faculties such as introspection and current ability to adduce reasons. By contrast, PA-justification goes beyond that to encompass also the operation of past sensory experience and introspection, along with pertinent temporally extended reasoning and the operation of memory. Although we have extended our scope to encompass also one's mental past, however, there is a clear sense in which PA-justification is still internal to the subjectivity of the subject, past as well as present. What reason might there be for preferring one over the other of these concepts of justification, the Chisholmian present-restricted one or the past-encompassing one? We leave this question open for now.

Suppose a teacher lapses into reasoning that $(x^n)^n = x^{n+n}$, and on that basis reports that $(2^2)^2 = 2^4$. You, a schoolchild, believe accordingly, just on the teacher's say-so. Are you then justified in so believing? Suppose the conditions for acceptance of testimony to be optimal: the teacher is normally exceedingly reliable, and the circumstances are otherwise unremarkable; it's just a normal school morning in every other relevant respect. Are you then well justified in your belief? You *are* Chisholm-justified, and also PA-justified. But is there any sense in which you are not as well justified as you might be? If so, then a belief's justification would seem to depend on factors that go beyond its present-time-slice profile, and even beyond its personal aetiology, to encompass also the quality of the information derived from testimony. This sort of justification is "social-aetiology justification", since it depends not only on the quality of the belief's present supporting rational structure, and not even just on that together with the quality of its personal aetiology, via such faculties as memory and reasoning, but also on its social aetiology, wherein testimony may figure crucially.

How far might justification depend on the external? Consider some examples. Suppose you face a friend named "Mary" believed by you to be so named; your counterpart will then face a counterpart "friend" and will believe her to be so named. What if you remember her name because she is a lifelong friend, however; whereas your counterpart is oblivious to having been just created by a playful demon with just that set of beliefs and experiences (and, let's say, either there is no "friend" there at all, or if there is one it just derives from the demon's caprice). Are you equally well justified in your respective beliefs?

Second case: You remember having oatmeal for breakfast, because you did experience having it, and have retained that bit of information through your excellent memory. Your counterpart self-attributes having had oatmeal for breakfast, and may self-attribute remembering that to be so (as presumably do you), but his beliefs are radically wide of the mark, as are an army of affiliated beliefs, since your counterpart was created just a moment ago, complete with all of those beliefs and relevant current experiences. Are you two on a par in respect of epistemic justification?

Here is a third case. You believe C as a conclusion of long and complex deductive reasoning, but your counterpart believes it only due to the demon's caprice, although you both would now report having deduced C through complex reasoning, and each of you could now produce on demand some limited fragment of such reasoning. A relevant difference between you, compatible with your remaining perfect mental twins as of the present moment, is this: you have deduced that conclusion through a flawless proof; your counterpart is far from having done so. Are you both equally well justified?

Return now to that innermost sanctum of rationalist internalism which includes rational intuition itself. Given the human mind's liability to fall into paradox, wherein reason itself apparently leads us astray, how are we to think of the justification provided by intuition? In the throes of paradox, reason delivers beliefs $B1, \ldots, Bn$, but also the belief, $Bn + 1$, that the earlier n beliefs are logically incompatible. At least one of these beliefs must be false. Such paradoxes show, therefore, that rational intuition leads us astray in the sort of way in which perception sometimes leads us astray, through illusion of one or another sort.

Of the paradox-enmeshed beliefs, let Bi be the one that is false. Is belief Bi justified? It seems as well justified as any of the other, true, beliefs; assent to Bi is not some special mistake that some particular subject has fallen into, through inattention or intellectual negligence or special deficiency. It is a mistake to which the human mind itself is inherently subject. It is like a perceptual illusion such as the Müller–Lyer lines, or the "bent" stick in water, or the oasis in the distance. Subjects unaware of the special circumstances – inexperienced children, for example – would *not* seem "unjustified" in "trusting their senses" when thus misled. Collateral information normally prevents such mistakes, but may be missing through no fault or defect of one's own, as with the inexperienced child. So in some sense one is then epistemically justified in assenting. And assenting to the deliverances of rational intuition when in the grip of paradox seems quite analogous. But there is an alternative reaction; one is also pulled in the opposite direction (paradoxically?).

Recall that fallacious reasoning does not plausibly justify, even if one may be justified in believing the reasoning to have been valid and sound. That is so *in some natural sense, even though in the Chisholmian present-time-slice sense, despite the faults in one's reasoning (or in one's memory), one may still be fully justified.* Apply that now to our case of paradox-enmeshed intuition. Can't we appropriately distinguish two corresponding senses? Of course, the distinction must now be made *within the present time slice*, since there is here no time-encompassing faculty at work, unlike our earlier cases of inferential reason or memory. Here is a way to draw the distinction. Let Bi be the one false belief contained in the paradox-constituting set $\{B1, \ldots, Bn, Bn + 1\}$. Let Bj be a true belief in that set. Bi and Bj are alike in being, let us say, *subjectively* justified, but only Bj might be *objectively* justified. What is this difference? Bi is a belief that gives every appearance of being justified. The human mind (and not just our subject's mind) is drawn to affirm Bi just on the basis of understanding its content. And the human mind is, let us suppose, quite reliable in what it accepts on such a basis, and that it is thus reliable is itself believed justifiedly by our subject, or so we may suppose. In such circumstances, our subject is "subjectively" justified in assenting to Bi. He takes himself to be justified, or may be supposed to do so, in a way that coheres with his intellectual self-conception. But there is still something importantly wrong with his assent to Bi. People are presumably reliable in what they assent to just on the basis of understanding it, as we are thereby nonaccidentally put in touch with what is true (either because such assent is truth-constituting, or because such assent in such circumstances is reflective of what is independently true). Nevertheless, in accepting Bi specifically, one *fails* to be thus nonaccidentally in touch with the truth: Bi being false, one is thereby not at all in touch with the truth.

More revealingly, through Bi one fails to be appropriately sensitive to the truth: in assenting to its content one is not believing something in such a way that one would not go wrong. One would not go wrong either when one's believing as one does is, in the circumstances, truth-constituting, or when one's so believing is in the circumstances truth-reflecting, i.e., reflective of a fact of the matter, a fact independent of the current state of one's mind. In neither way is one's assent to the content of Bi correlated or in step with the truth, however, since Bi is not so much as true.

Something goes wrong, then, with one's assent to the content of Bi, but it is something in a natural sense *external* to one's mind, something pertaining to a fact that in some way goes beyond what is determined by the contents of one's mind, because it is independent of that, either in the way the roundness of the Earth is thus independent, or in the way community rules are independent of any one mind. Nevertheless, it is not something that need go beyond the present time, for it is at this present time that Bi is false and (hence) fails to mirror or track the truth. Although the rationally intuitive belief Bi is thus different from mistaken beliefs attributable to memory or inference in that temporal respect, the three sorts of belief are also importantly alike: In each of our three cases – faulty "memory," faulty "inference," and faulty "intuition" – a normally reliable faculty is ostensibly operative, but is not *really* operative.[10] Regarding memory and inference, there is a strong pull in opposite directions: towards the verdict that the subject is justified and also towards the verdict that the subject is not really well justified. This suggests an ambiguity: the subject is *subjectively* justified, but *objectively* unjustified. The subject is subjectively justified in that he quite reasonably attributes the belief to the operation of a normally reliable faculty of his own. This applies in all three cases: that of memory, that of inference, and that of intuition. But the subject is objectively unjustified in that the relevant faculty is not really properly operative in the case at hand. It is not really true memory, or true deductive inference, or true intuition that is at work.

If that much is right, it prompts two questions. First, is there an important externalist element even in the faculties of reflection: namely, those of memory and reason, deductive and intuitive (along, perhaps, with introspection)? Second, if the external is thus involved in such justification, why stop with these as faculties that provide justification? Why not include also environment-involving perception, and even neighbor-involving testimony? Concerning epistemic justification, the importance of any intuitive internal/external divide is thus put in question.[11]

Notes

1. My thanks to John Greco, Jennifer Lackey, Matthew McGrath, and Baron Reed for helpful comments or discussion.
2. The term "justified" is not widely applied to beliefs in ordinary discourse. It may be a philosophers' term of art, meaning: "belief not defectively formed or sustained in a way that reflects poorly on the believer's mind." Of evaluative terms ordinarily applied to beliefs, "reasonable" comes perhaps closest to this.
3. Let "dreaming" here stand for "philosophically dreaming" defined as follows: S philosophically dreams that p iff S experiences as if p, but *unveridically* so (and the same goes for all of S's sensory experiences at the time).
4. The demonstration is left to the interested reader. By definition, "reflection" involves either (i) introspection, (ii) rational intuition, (iii) memory, (iv) deduction, or (v) induction or ampliative reason which builds only on materials provided by (i)–(iv) above.
5. R. M. Chisholm, *Theory of Knowledge*, 3rd ed. (Englewood Cliffs, NJ: Prentice-Hall, 1989), p. 77.
6. Cf. Alvin Plantinga, *Warrant: the Current Debate* (Oxford: Oxford University Press, 1993), chs. 1–3. My discussion of Plantinga's critique of Chisholmian internalism (from which I draw in the present piece) is "Plantinga on Epistemic Internalism," in J. Kvanvig, ed., *Warrant in Contemporary Epistemology* (Lanham, MD: Rowman and Littlefield, 1996).
7. The present account is viciously circular as it stands. I had pointed to this problem in my "Plantinga on Epistemic Internalism," in Kvanvig (ed.), and to this Plantinga replied (ibid., pp. 366–7) that the account of justification is too demanding; thus he is inclined to think that "what objective justification requires is that [one] ... be nonculpable in not believing that the action in question is wrong," the implied suggestion re epistemology being that perhaps epistemic justification for believing that p requires only that one be nonculpable in not believing that the belief in question is unjustified. However, this is not clearly adequate as a response to my objection. My objection was that the "deontological conception" would be circular; my objection was not, as Plantinga supposes explicitly in his reply, that the "deontological conception" would involve an infinite regress. My problem of circularity is that the definition of epistemic justification in the "deontological conception" is viciously circular because it appeals in the definiens to the concept under definition. And we do not clearly escape the problem if, in keeping with Plantinga's reply, we replace the requirement that one be justifiedly aware that one ought to believe that p with the

8   requirement that one justifiedly (nonculpably) *not* believe that one would be (epistemically) wrong to believe that p. The whole question will be whether we can explain a concept of justification for not believing that will be different enough (though presumably in relevant respects it would have to be an *epistemic* concept of justification) from justification for believing, different enough that it can be used in the definiens of an illuminating account of such justification for believing without falling into vicious circularity.

8   Actually, it is not ruled out that ontological internalism receive some independent support; the important point is that, so far as we have been able to determine, it seems needed as a prior premise for any discernible argument that moves from deontologism of justification to epistemic internalism.

9   Some suggestions towards this project may be found in chs. 8 and 16 of my *Knowledge in Perspective* (Cambridge: Cambridge University Press, 1991).

10 Not that these faculties could not on occasion really be operative while still misleading us. I simply have in mind our specific examples (such as the oatmeal case) where by hypothesis memory is ostensibly operative but is not really operative.

11 So I have raised doubts not only about Chisholmian and deontological internalism but about internalism more generally, and even about ontological and Cartesian internalism. The paradox-enmeshed false intuition is justified in one sense, "subjectively," while not quite justified in another sense, "objectively." This latter is the sense in which fallacious reasoning fails to justify, however Chisholm-justified its conclusion may be for its proponent.

Chapter 6

In Defense of a Naturalized Epistemology

Hilary Kornblith

Naturalism in philosophy has a long and distinguished heritage. This is no less true in epistemology than it is in other areas of philosophy. At the same time, epistemology in the English speaking world in the first half of the twentieth century was dominated by an approach quite hostile to naturalism. Now, at the close of the twentieth century, naturalism is resurgent.

This rebirth of naturalism in epistemology has its source in the work of W. V. Quine, especially his 1969 essay "Epistemology Naturalized."[1] Quine there argued that epistemology, and indeed all of philosophy, is inevitably continuous with the sciences. Descartes's view of epistemology as first philosophy was doomed to failure, Quine argued, but this should not be seen as the end of epistemology. Instead, a proper epistemology would be empirically informed, of a piece with the scientific enterprise, and not somehow independent of it.[2]

Precisely what such an epistemology would look like Quine did not say. But many have now taken up the banner of naturalized epistemology and tried to fill out the Quinean picture.[3] No single approach has gained universal acceptance among naturalists, and there are many who believe that the move to naturalize epistemology is founded on a mistake.[4] Whether to naturalize epistemology, and if so, just what such a move would involve, is now a subject of great controversy.

In this essay, I offer an explanation and defense of a naturalistic epistemology. To that end, I begin in section 1 with a characterization of the Cartesian tradition and its difficulties. Section 2 presents a naturalistic alternative to the Cartesian approach, and discusses the extent to which traditional epistemological questions are addressed by naturalism. Finally, section 3 argues that nothing less than a fully empirical epistemology can address the epistemological problems which have rightly concerned philosophers for centuries.

1. The Cartesian Tradition

Descartes's foundationalism provides a unified theory which simultaneously answers three central questions in epistemology:

(1) What is knowledge?
(2) How is knowledge possible?
(3) What should we do in order to attain knowledge?

In answer to question (1), Descartes proposed that a belief counts as knowledge if it is either foundational – that is, on Descartes's view, a belief about which mistake is inconceivable – or derived from foundational beliefs by appropriate principles of inference. Descartes argued that beliefs about one's own mental states meet the requirements for foundational beliefs,[5] and he proceeded to argue that this provides a sufficient foundation for knowledge of the existence of God and the external world.

The demonstration that so much could, allegedly, be derived from so certain a foundation served to explain how knowledge is possible. Indeed, for Descartes, the question about the possibility of knowledge was viewed as requiring a response to skepticism. The skeptic wonders whether knowledge of the external world is even so much as possible in light of the apparent possibility of error in each of our beliefs about the external world. But in deriving such beliefs from a foundation immune to error, skeptical doubts are fully allayed.

Finally, in response to question (3), Descartes provides a recipe for attaining knowledge. We must begin by giving up all of our beliefs about the external world, since each is susceptible to doubt, and accept beliefs only if they meet foundational requirements. Then, having provided ourselves with an adequate foundation, we may build upon it by using appropriate principles of inference. Our process of belief acquisition is thereby assured of meeting the requirements for knowledge.

On Descartes's view, epistemology is "first philosophy"; our theory of knowledge is logically prior to any empirical knowledge. The reason for this is not far to seek. We should have no confidence in any of our pretheoretical beliefs, according to Descartes, because we have reason to believe that any of them might be false. The only rational course is thus to reject all beliefs about which we might be mistaken, and rebuild our body of beliefs from the very beginning. We need first to develop appropriate standards for belief – this is where we construct our epistemological theory – and then form beliefs if and only if they meet appropriate standards. Epistemology must therefore precede science, and, indeed, precede any empirical belief whatsoever. No empirical belief may be rationally formed without our first having an epistemological theory to guide our belief formation.

Descartes's answer to the first of our three questions thus provides him with the means for answering all three. This unifying feature of Descartes's approach is surely one of its most attractive features. At the same time, Cartesian epistemology is fraught with difficulties. Descartes's standards for knowledge seem impossibly high, since he required not only that the foundation for knowledge provide immunity to doubt, but that the principles of inference from the foundation guarantee the truth of the conclusions inferred. Philosophers sympathetic with Descartes's foundational account of knowledge have sought to weaken the standards required for knowledge in order to avoid the skeptical consequences which seem inevitably to follow from the standards he laid down.

The difficulties here, however, are not merely ones of detail. Philosophers who have sought to weaken the standards for the principles of inference from the foundation, or for the foundation itself, or both, while simultaneously maintaining a commitment to the foundationalist structure for knowledge, have faced difficulties as well. While any such proposal needs to be examined in detail, it is fair to say that there is a worry that the constraints imposed by the foundational structure itself may lead to skepticism.[6] The history of foundationalist proposals does not encourage optimism on this score. Perhaps most importantly, any attempt to avoid skepticism seems inevitably to undermine the very unifying power of the original Cartesian program.[7]

On Descartes's view, a fully adequate response to the skeptic would be possible precisely because his standards for knowledge were so remarkably high. The philosopher who seeks to weaken Cartesian standards for knowledge precisely in order to show that knowledge, suitably understood, does not present an unattainable ideal, thereby undermines Descartes's answer to question (2). Of course knowledge is possible if we weaken the standards for knowledge far enough, in particular, if we weaken them until we can show that many of our beliefs then pass the standards. But this seems to be nothing more than an exercise in self-congratulation. Why should we care about knowledge so defined? On Descartes's view, it was at least clear why knowledge was something worth caring about.

Descartes's approach to question (3) is undermined as well by the foundationalist philosopher who simply weakens Cartesian standards until our ordinary beliefs may be shown to meet them. Descartes sought to give advice about how to arrive at our beliefs which was, at least potentially, quite revolutionary. Many of our current beliefs might be deeply mistaken; indeed, our unreflective standards for belief acquisition may well be far short of what they should be. A proper epistemology ought at least, as Descartes's did, leave room for the possibility that our body of beliefs might require substantial revision. But if our standards for knowledge are merely designed to allow us to attach the epithet "knowledge" to whatever it is we pretheoretically believe, then this potentially revisionary role for epistemology is thereby undermined. Epistemology ought to be in a position to correct the mistakes in our pretheoretical views. But when we hold on to Descartes's foundationalist structure and revise the standards for foundational knowledge and proper inference until they endorse our pretheoretical beliefs, the result is an uncritical endorsement of the epistemological status quo. Foundationalism is thus preserved at the cost of undermining the very point of engaging in epistemological theorizing.

Descartes's foundationalism failed because the task of reconstructing our knowledge from an indubitable foundation proved impossible. More recent versions of foundationalism may face a similar problem, but in weakening the standards for knowledge in the way they do, they run into an additional problem as well: they rob epistemological theorizing of its significance. What is needed is an approach to the theory of knowledge which gives substantive answers to legitimate intellectual problems, an approach which allows us to explain why it is that theorizing about knowledge is an enterprise worthy of our attention. This is precisely what a naturalized epistemology attempts to provide.

2. A Naturalistic Theory of Knowledge

The goal of a naturalistic theory of knowledge, as I see it, is not to provide an account of our concept of knowledge, but instead to provide an account of a certain natural phenomenon, namely, knowledge itself.[8] Our concept of knowledge, like our concepts of various other natural phenomena, may be defective in important ways. Consider, for example, the concept of aluminum. Many people have a concept of aluminum which is little more than a reflection of their ignorance about that metal: they think of aluminum as a gray metal, but they know little more about it. Their concept does not include enough information to pick out aluminum from many other metals, and indeed, may include some misinformation as well. This is not merely true of laypeople; even experts, at various points in history, have concepts which do not fully, or even accurately, characterize the things of which they are concepts. Indeed, developing concepts which accurately characterize various natural phenomena is one of the hard-won achievements of science; it is not a starting point for scientific investigation.

The same may be said of knowledge. What we seek is an adequate account of knowledge, and in order to develop such an account we must investigate the phenomenon of knowledge itself. We may do this by examining apparently clear cases of knowledge to see what it is that they have in common, just as an attempt to understand what aluminum is would begin by collecting apparently clear cases of the stuff in order to see what it is that they have in common. Along the way, as our theoretical understanding of the phenomenon increases, cases which initially seemed clear may come to be reclassified. What once seemed to be a clear case of knowledge may come to be regarded as no kind of knowledge at all. Moreover, what initially seemed to be a defining feature of knowledge may come to seem merely incidental; the true nature of knowledge, like the true nature of aluminum, may not lie in its most salient features.

Let me say a bit about what I regard as the clearest cases of knowledge, and also something about the appropriate method for investigating the phenomenon. First, cases of scientific knowledge are surely among the most clear-cut examples of knowledge we are likely to find. The advance of our scientific understanding of the world surely marks one of the greatest intellectual achievements of the human species, and it is here that knowledge is to be found, if anywhere. At the same time, knowledge seems very much a part of our everyday life as well, in simple perceptual encounters with physical objects and in more complicated inferential judgments of many kinds. What is needed here is not a precise characterization of cases of knowledge, for that can only come later; at this point we simply provide a rough and ready account of some of the clearest cases of knowledge as input to our theoretical investigation of the phenomenon.

But what does the theoretical investigation look like? It seems to me that this investigation must take place at a number of different levels. We must examine the various psychological mechanisms by which knowledge is produced and retained in order to see what, if anything, they have in common.[9] In addition, as many have argued, there seems to be an important social element in knowledge. In many of the most central cases, social factors play a role in the production, retention, and dissemination of knowledge. Investigation of these social factors is likely to reveal features of knowledge that are easily overlooked in the investigation of the psychological mechanisms of individual knowers.[10] One promising line of investigation suggests that our Darwinian heritage sheds an important light on the investigation of our cognitive lives.[11] Others have suggested that work in neuroscience provides deep insight into the nature of cognition.[12] These different avenues of investigation need not be seen as competitors; they may prove to be complementary to one another. Which, in the end, will provide the greatest insight into the phenomenon of knowledge cannot be determined in advance. We must simply wait and see which of these various investigations prove to be fruitful in understanding the phenomenon of knowledge in general.

It is a presupposition of this investigation that there is something which cases of knowledge have in common, that there is some theoretical unity to the phenomenon of knowledge. This presupposition is by no means trivial, and it could well turn out to be false. If there were no such unity to the phenomenon of knowledge, if cases of knowledge turned out to be nothing more than a heterogeneous mishmash, then we would have to say that a presupposition of the use of the term had been undermined and that the very idea of knowledge had turned out to rest upon a mistake. But there is little reason for such pessimism now, I believe; indeed, there is every reason to be optimistic about the prospects for knowledge.

The account of knowledge I favor, due to Alvin Goldman, is that knowledge is reliably produced true belief.[13] What cases of knowledge have in common is a relational property: it has to do with how our beliefs are produced. Unlike some accounts of knowledge, this account does not require that the agent be able to produce any kind of argument in favor of his or her belief; the ability to defend one's beliefs, while a useful cognitive skill, is not a constituent of knowledge. Instead, what is required is a certain sensitivity to features of the environment. Our cognitive processes result in knowledge when they manifest a certain stable disposition: the disposition to produce beliefs which are an accurate reflection of the agent's environment.

Such an answer to question (1) has important implications for question (2). If we wish to know how knowledge is possible, then, given the above account of knowledge, we need to know how it is that our cognitive equipment allows for the possibility of reliably produced belief. All of the different theoretical investigations outlined above – neurological, psychological, biological, and social – are relevant to this question. Thus, there are interesting questions about the sensitivity of our perceptual mechanisms and the extent to which they natively tend to produce true belief. Similarly, we have certain native inferential tendencies whose connection with true belief is a subject of intense investigation. At the social level, it is quite clear that the social organization of scientific institutions may either contribute to, or detract from, the production and dissemination of true belief, and there are interesting questions here about the extent to which the current social structure of science plays a constructive role in knowledge production. The question about how knowledge is possible is thus understood in this project as a question about the extent to which creatures with our physiological, psychological, biological, and social condition may be attuned to their environment.

Such an investigation has straightforward implications for what we should be doing in order to attain knowledge, thereby allowing us to answer question (3) as well. An understanding of the various mechanisms by which our beliefs are produced will clearly highlight both our strengths and weaknesses. The only way in which useful epistemic advice can be attained is by way of such detailed knowledge. If the ways in which we unreflectively arrive at our beliefs were extremely reliable, then the only epistemic advice which would be called for might well be to keep on doing whatever it is that we are already doing. Reflection on our epistemic condition might be interesting in its own right, but it would be unnecessary for the betterment of our epistemic condition; our epistemic condition would not need to be bettered. Similarly, if our epistemic condition were sufficiently bad, if there were reason to think that our epistemic powers are simply not up to the job of reliably producing true beliefs, then little change in our epistemic practices might be called for, since any change we were capable of making would be of no use in attaining knowledge. But these two extreme pictures are each implausible. Instead, there is every reason to think that our epistemic situation is quite good, that we can and do know a great deal about the world, but that we also are capable of grave error, and that unreflective belief acquisition is, in many cases, extremely unreliable. By investigating the various mechanisms of belief production and retention, we may determine where we are most in need of guidance, and what steps can be taken, given our capabilities, to overcome our shortcomings.

Just as Descartes's foundationalist program provided a unified perspective on our three fundamental epistemological questions, the naturalistic program unifies our approach to these three questions as well. While Descartes viewed epistemology as first philosophy, however, naturalists see epistemology as very much a part of the scientific enterprise. Epistemology does not precede science, and indeed, it is not required that it do so if it is to provide the kind of epistemic guidance which Descartes rightfully sought. We do want epistemology to provide us with advice in revising our methods of belief acquisition, but the best way to provide constructive epistemic advice is under the guidance of the best current scientific understanding of the mechanisms of belief production. Rather than simply bracket our best available information and proceed in ignorance, naturalists would have the important task of devising epistemic advice informed by the best available information that bears on it.

Descartes was not foolish to seek an epistemology which was insulated from the best available science of his day. What he rightly appreciated was that the best available science of his day was not good enough. Indeed, the state of science in Descartes's time could not have informed the epistemological project outlined above; there was little in the way of successful science to draw upon. Descartes's motivation, in the *Meditations*, as he informs us on the first page of the first meditation, was to find "anything at all in science that was stable and likely to last." Nothing less than the scientific revolution of the seventeenth and eighteenth centuries was required to provide that. But Descartes, whose work preceded that revolution, had to look elsewhere, outside of science, for epistemic guidance.

Extrascientific insight into our epistemic situation has not been forthcoming. We, who do have a successful science to draw upon, should not follow Descartes's lead and seek epistemic insight uninformed by scientific understanding. If we follow Descartes's lead and attempt to engage in epistemological theorizing without the benefit of science, we thereby show a failure to appreciate the extent to which our epistemic situation has changed since the 1600s.

3. Why Nothing Less than a Fully Empirical Epistemology Will Do

Those who prefer a more traditional approach to epistemology are not likely to object to the projects outlined above. Certainly there is nothing wrong with investigating the various mechanisms by which knowledge is produced, nor is it inappropriate to seek to discover the strengths and weaknesses of our current cognitive condition. Such projects could, without doubt, serve as a useful source of epistemic advice. Nevertheless, it will be objected that these are scientific projects; they are not a part of philosophy.[14]

Naturalists of course do not believe that there is a sharp distinction to be drawn between scientific and philosophical projects. Traditionally, it was held that the sciences are a product of empirical investigation, but philosophy is properly pursued a priori. This account of the distinction between philosophy and science, however, is one which naturalists reject.[15] Epistemology, conceived of as first philosophy, is regarded by naturalists as ill-advised – because it would insulate epistemology from information relevant to its projects – and impossible to carry out in any case. The debate over whether naturalistic epistemology is any kind of philosophy at all thus seems unproductive. Naturalists will claim that they are simply addressing philosophical questions by empirical means; more traditional philosophers will argue that insofar as empirical methods are used, the investigation being carried out is not philosophical.

There is, however, an important question at issue between naturalists and their opponents, and debate over this issue need not be entirely sterile. If the opponents of naturalism are correct, then there are legitimate epistemological questions which are susceptible to a priori investigation; these questions, they would argue, are rightly regarded as purely philosophical. The projects which naturalists undertake may be regarded as "applied philosophy," and now whether one regards these applied projects as part of philosophy or not seems to be of no real interest; that would be a trivial terminological dispute. The real question at issue between naturalists and their more traditional opponents is whether a legitimate area of a priori epistemological investigation really exists.

There are two ways to approach this issue. First, there are arguments of principle on either side: naturalists will argue that empirical information will inevitably be relevant to epistemological questions, while more traditional philosophers will argue that certain questions which can only be settled a priori must be addressed before any empirical questions about knowledge can be dealt with. We will want to look at these arguments of principle on both sides of the issue. Second, there is a more direct approach. Opponents of naturalism have engaged in apparently a priori epistemological theorizing, and have claimed to gain some insight thereby. We will need to look at the result of this kind of work to see what insight it offers. If either of these approaches reveal that there is promise in a priori methods for addressing epistemological issues, then naturalists will need to concede that the case for a fully naturalized epistemology has yet to be made out.

The argument of principle for naturalism has already been briefly presented. Our three fundamental questions of epistemology are all such that empirical information is directly relevant to them. Nothing is gained, and everything is lost, by pursuing them in a way which insulates our investigation from relevant empirical information.

But the way in which naturalists understand these questions is not uncontroversial. Many opposed to naturalism believe that the proper way to investigate the first of our questions is by way of conceptual analysis.[16] The question about what knowledge is, they will say, is not a question about features of the phenomenon in the world, but rather it is a question about our concept of knowledge, that which allows us to recognize that certain things are, and others are not, instances of the concept. Similarly, opponents of naturalism will argue that the second question, about the possibility of knowledge, is misunderstood by naturalists. This is a question about how to respond to skepticism, a question which requires a logical reconstruction of knowledge; it is not, as naturalists claim, a question about the various mechanisms which make knowledge nomologically possible. Finally, the third question as well is misinterpreted by naturalists, it will be said. While there are legitimate empirical questions about how best to train individuals so that they will be able to surmount their cognitive shortcomings, the distinctively philosophical question here is quite different. The third question, understood philosophically, is really one about the cognitive goals which need to be attained if one is to have knowledge. After all, if we wish to implement some program for attaining a set of goals, we need first to identify what those goals are, and it is here that philosophy goes to work. The naturalistic reinterpretation of the third question makes it look empirical only by taking for granted that we have already answered the distinctively philosophical question about the goals of cognition.

Now there is no text to which we can refer, no founding fathers' original intentions to which we can appeal, to settle the meaning of our three questions. The issue here is not about which questions some philosopher or group of philosophers have thought to be important, or about which questions have historically been regarded as important. Instead, the issue concerns the very nature of epistemological inquiry. Each side here has views about which questions are genuinely interesting or genuinely important, and each side has expectations about the research programs that are most likely to bear fruit.

Naturalists should, I believe, reject any account of the first question which attempts to secure its solution by way of conceptual analysis.[17] Just as an account of our concept of aluminum is of little interest to chemistry, an account of our current concept of knowledge, I believe, should be of little interest to epistemology. Precisely because the concept of knowledge currently at work may be founded on a good deal of ignorance and mistake, even if there is some real understanding of the phenomenon built into it as well, we do best when we investigate the phenomenon of knowledge itself rather than our current conception of it. As with science, the point of philosophy is not to understand our concepts but to change them.

The project of responding to skepticism – which is how the antinaturalist addresses our second question – is one which naturalists regard as a dead end. Naturalists will argue that this project has a history of failure, and the manner in which the project has failed calls the very point of the project itself into question. There are, from a naturalistic perspective, interesting questions about how knowledge is possible, and none of these involve attempts to respond to the total skeptic. Instead, they are empirically based questions about the extent to which our cognitive faculties are apt for the production of true belief.

Finally, the question about cognitive goals is also viewed by the naturalist as one which must be empirically based if it is to make contact with the phenomenon of knowledge. What we need to do is look at the knowledge gathering enterprise and see what goals are embedded in it, what goals make sense of our practice. Moreover, the project of providing epistemic advice, which must quite clearly be empirically based, is one which the naturalist will want to insist is central to epistemological inquiry, for it is here that epistemology may prove useful to the project of inquiry. This critical role for epistemology, and indeed, for philosophy generally, is one we should not be willing to abandon.

Is there some limit to the amount of empirical information on which the naturalistic project must draw? For example, can we limit the inquiry to using information generally available to circumspect agents, so that in practice we need not engage in any empirical investigation even if in fact we are drawing on a certain measure of empirical knowledge? I don't see how the investigation can be limited in any such way. Once we allow that empirical investigation is relevant to epistemological inquiry, it will be impossible, I believe, to draw a principled line which marks off some empirical information as automatically irrelevant. In addition, it should be noted that quite a bit of information not generally available to circumspect agents, information which is the result of substantive empirical inquiry, has had an important impact on epistemological theorizing. For example, work on the psychology of human inference shows pervasive patterns of reasoning which, on their face, seem quite irrational.[18] This work has rightly received a good deal of attention not only from psychologists, but from philosophers as well.[19] It raises interesting questions about the nature of epistemic ideals, and about the relationship between such ideals and what is humanly attainable. Such questions are precisely the kind, according to naturalists, which further our understanding of knowledge. But if we attempt to delimit, in advance, the kind of empirical information which might be allowed to bear on epistemological inquiry, we risk barring information of this sort, the very kind of information which is most likely to inform epistemological inquiry. We must allow the inquiry itself to dictate what is relevant as our investigation unfolds, rather than seek to limit, in advance, precisely what kind of information may be drawn upon.

I thus conclude my brief for a naturalized epistemology. In the end, it is the most fruitful research project which will win the day. But I believe that the case for a naturalistic approach to the field, and against more traditional conceptions of it, is currently quite strong.

Notes

1 In W. V. Quine, *Ontological Relativity and Other Essays* (New York: Columbia University Press, 1969), pp. 69–90.

2 The extent to which epistemology should be informed by science is a subject of some debate, even among naturalists. In the text, I defend the extreme position that epistemology is fully continuous with science, but there are some naturalists who would allow scientific input to epistemological projects, while allowing that there are parts of epistemological inquiry which are largely, or wholly, independent of science. I discuss such a view briefly in section 3 below. For a nice discussion of the range of different epistemological positions which fall under the heading of naturalism, see James Maffie, "Recent Work on Naturalized Epistemology," *American Philosophical Quarterly* 27 (1990): 281–93.

3 See, for example, D. M. Armstrong, *Belief, Truth and Knowledge* (Cambridge Cambridge University Press, 1973); Christopher Cherniak, *Minimal Rationality* (Cambridge, MA: MIT Press, 1986); Fred Dretske, *Knowledge and the Flow of Information* (Cambridge, MA: MIT Press, 1981); Alvin Goldman, *Epistemology and Cognition* (Cambridge, MA: Harvard University Press, 1986) and *Liaisons: Philosophy Meets the Cognitive and Social Sciences* (Cambridge, MA: MIT Press, 1992); Gilbert Harman, *Change in View: Principle of Reasoning* (Cambridge, MA: MIT Press, 1986); Hilary Kornblith, *Inductive Inference and Its Natural Ground: An Essay in Naturalized Epistemology*

(Cambridge, MA: MIT Press, 1993) and Kornblith, ed., *Naturalizing Epistemology*, 2nd ed. (Cambridge, MA: MIT Press, 1994); William Lycan, *Judgment and Justification* (Cambridge: Cambridge University Press, 1988); Alvin Plantinga, *Warrant and Proper Function* (Oxford: Oxford University Press, 1993); Ernest Sosa, *Knowledge in Perspective: Selected Essays in Epistemology* (Cambridge: Cambridge University Press, 1991); Edward Stein, *Without Good Reason: The Rationality Debate in Philosophy and Cognitive Science* (Oxford: Oxford University Press, 1996); Stephen Stich, *The Fragmentation of Reason: Preface to a Pragmatic Theory of Cognitive Evaluation* (Cambridge, MA: MIT Press, 1990). For an especially valuable account of the history, motivations, and development of naturalized epistemology, see Philip Kitcher, "The Naturalists Return," *Philosophical Review*, CI (1992): 53–114.

4 See especially George Bealer, "The Incoherence of Empiricism," in S. Wagner and R. Warner, eds., *Naturalism: A Critical Appraisal* (Notre Dame: University of Notre Dame Press, 1993), pp. 163–96; Laurence BonJour, "A Rationalist Manifesto," in P. Hansen and B. Hunter, eds., *Return of the A Priori* (Calgary: University of Calgary Press, 1992), pp. 53–88 and "Against Naturalized Epistemology," *Midwest Studies in Philosophy* XIX (1994): 283–300; Richard Foley, "Quine and Naturalized Epistemology," *Midwest Studies in Philosophy* XIX (1994): 243–60; Mark Kaplan, "Epistemology Denatured," *Midwest Studies in Philosophy* XIX (1994): 350–65; Jaegwon Kim, "What Is 'Naturalized Epistemology'?," in Kornblith, ed., *Naturalizing Epistemology*, pp. 33–55; Barry Stroud, *The Significance of Philosophical Skepticism* (Oxford: Oxford University Press, 1984); Bas van Fraassen, "Against Naturalized Epistemology," in P. Leonardi and M. Santambrogio, eds., *On Quine: New Essays* (Cambridge: Cambridge University Press, 1995), pp. 68–88.

5 But not only beliefs about one's own mental states; certain necessary truths meet this requirement as well.

6 For a particularly useful statement of this position, see Michael Williams, *Groundless Belief: An Essay on the Possibility of Epistemology* (New Haven: Yale University Press, 1977).

7 The argument presented for this claim is largely due to Mark Kaplan, "Epistemology on Holiday," *Journal of Philosophy* 88 (1991): 132–54, and Stephen Stich, *The Fragmentation of Reason* See also Kornblith, "Naturalistic Epistemology and Its Critics," *Philosophical Topics* 23 (1996): 239–57.

8 The present account will not be endorsed by all naturalists. Alvin Goldman, in particular, is an important dissenting voice here; see note 14 below. For further development of the view presented in the text of this paper, see Kornblith, "The Role of Intuition in Philosophical Inquiry: An Account with No Unnatural Ingredients," in M. DePaul and W. Ramsey, eds., *Rethinking Intuition*, forthcoming.

9 This is the focus of most of the works cited in note 2 above.

10 See e.g. the essays in F. Schmitt, ed., *Socializing Epistemology: The Social Dimensions of Knowledge* (Lanham, MD: Rowman and Littlefield, 1994).

11 See L. Cosmides and J. Tooby, eds., *The Adapted Mind: Evolutionary Psychology and the Generation of Culture* (Oxford: Oxford University Press, 1992).

12 Patricia Churchland, *Neurophilosophy: Toward a Unified Science of the Mind/Brain* (Cambridge, MA: MIT Press, 1986); Paul Churchland, *The Engine of Reason, The Seat of the Soul: A Philosophical Journey into the Brain* (Cambridge, MA: MIT Press, 1995).

13 See Goldman, *Epistemology and Cognition*.
14 This very sentiment is expressed in Laurence BonJour, "Against Naturalized Epistemology"; Mark Kaplan, "Epistemology Denatured"; and Barry Stroud, *The Significance*, ch. 6.
15 Indeed, most naturalists, following Quine, reject the distinction between a priori and a posteriori knowledge as itself founded on a mistaken view about language and knowledge.
16 Some naturalists accept this as well, but believe that conceptual analysis is itself an empirical investigation. See Alvin Goldman, "Psychology and Philosophical Analysis," *Proceedings of the Aristotelian Society* 89 (1989): 195–209, and Alvin Goldman and Joel Pust, "Philosophical Theory and Intuitional Evidence," in DePaul and Ramsey, *Rethinking Intuition*. The position in these two papers marks a change from Goldman's view in *Epistemology and Cognition*.
17 But see the work of Goldman, and Goldman and Pust (cited in note 14 above) for dissenting voices on how to develop a naturalistic epistemology.
18 See the papers collected in D. Kahneman, P. Slovic, and A. Tversky, *Judgment under Uncertainty: Heuristics and Biases* (Cambridge: Cambridge University Press, 1982).
19 See much of the work cited in note 2 above.

Chapter 7

Methodological Naturalism in Epistemology

Richard Feldman

I. Introduction

Epistemologists often attempt to analyze epistemological concepts and to formulate epistemic principles. A common way to proceed is to propose analyses and principles and then revise them in the light of potential counterexamples. Analyses and principles not refuted by counterexamples are judged to be correct. To evaluate potential counterexamples, epistemologists rely upon their ability to make correct reflective judgments about whether there is knowledge or justified belief in the situations described in the proposed examples. For these purposes, it does not matter how people actually form beliefs, since the analyses and principles are supposed to be adequate to all possible cases. As long as an example is possible, adequate philosophical principles must get it right. Since this methodology does not depend upon information about how people actually reason, its practitioners can proceed in ignorance of the results of the sciences that study human cognition. Consequently, we can call what they do "armchair epistemology."

In what appears to be a revolt against armchair epistemology, in recent years many epistemologists have claimed that results in psychology concerning human cognition and reasoning are in some way essential to or useful for progress in epistemology.[1] I will call this view "Methodological Naturalism." This is but one of numerous doctrines that goes under the name "Naturalism." In this paper I will not attempt to describe or discuss any of the other views among the confusing array that go under the same name.

Methodological naturalism has many advocates, as can be seen from the following claims:

> "Thus, a mix of philosophy and psychology is needed to produce acceptable principles of justifiedness."[2]

> "... any epistemologist who rejects skepticism ought to be influenced in his or her philosophical work by descriptive work in psychology."[3]

"... the results from the sciences of cognition may be relevant to, and may be legitimately used in the resolution of traditional epistemological problems."[4]

"[Philosophers] ... ignore [recent experimental work about human reasoning] at their own peril."[5]

"[I]t is hard to come up with convincing normative principles except by considering how people actually do reason, which is the province of descriptive theory."[6]

No doubt these philosophers were engaged in different epistemological projects and their views about the exact role psychology might play in their efforts differed accordingly.[7]

In this paper I will examine some of the arguments designed to support methodological naturalism. My discussion will, I hope, dampen some of the enthusiasm of the more extreme methodological naturalists. On the other hand, I will argue that some defenders of the traditional armchair methodology have also overstated what can be established without the input of science.

II. Clarifying the Issue

As soon as one begins thinking about the connection between epistemology and psychology, one is confronted with a difficult question: What counts as epistemology? The answer affects the plausibility of methodological naturalism considerably. There is no doubt that if epistemology is as expansive a discipline as some think, then methodological naturalism is true. Philip Kitcher, another advocate of methodological naturalism, asks, "How could our psychological and biological capacities and limitations *fail* to be relevant to the study of human knowledge?"[8] Obviously, empirical work is relevant to "the study of human knowledge." But this shows its relevance to epistemology only if epistemology is as broad as the study of human knowledge. The complete study of human knowledge would, presumably, include historical studies of what people knew when; studies in neuroscience concerning the ways the brain processes information; sociological studies about the ways knowledge is transmitted in societies, and so on. While some philosophers may think that they have something to say from their armchairs about many of these topics, no sensible person could think that all such inquiries can succeed without scientific input. So, it is hard to imagine any disagreement with the view that methodological naturalism is true given such a broad interpretation of what counts as epistemology.

Another account of what epistemology includes also makes methodological naturalism unquestionably true. If epistemology is or includes a systematic effort to help people to reason better, then there is no doubt that it must rely on empirical results concerning the sorts of errors in reasoning that people make and the techniques that might help them improve. Notably, several years ago when Alvin Goldman wrote a paper urging that this project be given serious attention, he chose to call the proposed discipline "epistemics."[9] I think that this was in recognition of the fact that it was a departure from the central issues taken up in epistemology.[10]

Arguing about which of the issues just described count as epistemology strikes me as a dull and futile enterprise. What is clear is that there are certain traditional and characteristic epistemological matters, such as the effort to understand or analyze what knowledge and rational (or justified) belief are, to identify specific principles or methods that yield knowledge and justification, and to defend or respond to arguments for skepticism. There is no doubt that these are traditional questions of epistemology, and it is the value of psychology for the study of these questions that is the topic of this paper.

III. Psychology and the Analysis of Epistemic Concepts

Although there is disagreement about exactly what is required of an adequate philosophical analysis, it is widely agreed among armchair epistemologists that a successful analysis of knowledge or justification will provide necessary and sufficient conditions for knowledge or justification. Some candidate answers are that beliefs are justified when they are reliably caused, when they are responsibly formed, when they cohere with the believer's other beliefs, or when they are well supported by the believer's evidence. Candidate analyses of knowledge hold that knowledge is justified true belief, or justified true belief that meets some additional condition designed to deal with Gettier cases. On some views, knowledge does not require justification, but is instead reliably caused true belief, although this no doubt needs refinement. Some methodological naturalists seem to think that psychological results concerning human reasoning will play an important role in developing and evaluating these analyses. We'll consider three reasons for this claim.

1. Adequate analyses use concepts from psychology

One potential reason for thinking that results from psychology are needed to analyze knowledge or justification is based on the fact any adequate analysis will invoke concepts from psychology. This is not a promising line of defense for methodological naturalism, but examining it briefly will provide some useful background for what follows.

In his paper "The Naturalists Return" Philip Kitcher argues that recent epistemology displays a return by epistemologists to theories importantly similar to those prominent prior to the antinaturalist and antipsychologistic views he thinks have been dominant in this century. In the first part of his paper, he describes one way (but not what he regards as the most important way) in which psychology has reentered epistemology in recent years. Current epistemological folk wisdom holds that prior to 1963 an almost universally held view was that knowledge is justified true belief. Edmund Gettier showed that justified true belief is not sufficient for knowledge.[11] A flurry of analyses of knowledge ensued, as did increased attention to the justification component. According to Kitcher, the apsychologistic tradition denied that "the concepts of psychology are needed to understand what differentiates cases of knowledge or of justification" from their opposites.[12] What he sees as a significant development in this period is the realization that knowledge and justified belief must be analyzed in causal terms, more specifically in terms of the properties of the cognitive processes that cause beliefs. The reliability of such processes came to seem important to many epistemologists and reliabilism became a leading contender among the proposed analyses of knowledge and justification. These newer analyses are to be contrasted with traditional analyses according to which knowledge was understood in terms of good reasons or adequate evidence.

Kitcher sees significance in these developments because with them psychological concepts entered into previously apsychologistic accounts of knowledge and justification, and thus "psychology re-entered epistemology." While the development of causal and reliabilist analyses of knowledge and justification is surely significant, their significance can't derive from the fact that they *introduced* psychological concepts into epistemology. Traditional, noncausal analyses included psychological concepts as well. They said that knowledge was justified true belief, and surely the concept of belief is as psychological a concept as one can find. Furthermore, traditionalists typically said that whether a belief was justified depended upon the evidence a person had. And, surely, the concept of having evidence is another psychological concept. Furthermore, traditionalists often said that to have a justified belief or knowledge one must base one's belief on adequate evidence. The basing relation also seems to be a psychological relation. Thus, the new naturalists and the old "nonnaturalists" all make use of psychological concepts in their analyses. If appealing to psychological concepts in an analysis of knowledge or justification makes one a naturalist, the naturalists have not recently returned. They never left.[13]

There are differences between the newer causal theories and many of their predecessors that are noteworthy. The newer ones often make reference to belief-forming processes, whereas the older analyses did not. There is, then, an added explicit reference to certain things that are likely to figure prominently in psychological theories. Furthermore, some (but not all) causal and reliabilist theories attempt to analyze knowledge or justification in completely naturalistic terms. That is, they attempt to state conditions of knowledge or justification entirely in terms that would find legitimacy in the sciences. Concepts such as the concept of good evidence or the concept of an adequate reason have no place in these analyses. The goal here, presumably, is to fit knowledge and justification into the natural world, to tie these epistemological concepts down to the real world.

Whatever the merits of these causal and reliabilist analyses, for present purposes what is crucial is that they have no important connections to methodological naturalism. From the fact that an epistemologist refers to psychological concepts in her analysis of epistemic concepts, it does not follow that psychological results imply that theory or that the epistemologist must or can use such results to support that theory. The new theories are versions of what Alvin Goldman calls "substantive naturalism," a view that has no clear-cut connection to methodological naturalism.[14]

2. Empirical results can lead to modifications of analyses

A second argument for methodological naturalism is based on the idea that empirical results from psychology can induce epistemologists to modify or abandon their analyses of knowledge or justification. Both Hilary Kornblith and Alvin Goldman have defended arguments along these lines. Both illustrate their point by showing how results from psychology will lead reliabilists to modify their theory.

Suppose a reliabilist begins by defending a simple version of reliabilism, such as the following:

(R) A belief is justified if and only if it is caused by a generally reliable process.[15]

Kornblith reasons as follows. Suppose that a reliabilist who endorses (R) also accepts "ballpark psychologism," the view that "the processes by which we arrive at our beliefs are at least roughly like the processes by which we ought to arrive at our beliefs."[16] If ballpark psychologism is true, then we can test (R) by seeing if the processes we actually use are generally reliable. If they aren't, then (R) must be wrong. Somewhat similar reasoning could be used to reject other proposed analyses of justification. Thus, psychological results can be used to falsify epistemological theories.[17]

This argument relies on the truth of ballpark psychologism. But can it be defended, especially in light of the grim assessments some people are inclined to make of the way people actually think and in light of what's said on talk radio? The most obvious way we might defend ballpark psychologism is to first analyze justification and then notice a pleasant fact: our beliefs often do meet the conditions for justification. If this is how we learn that ballpark psychologism is true, then ballpark psychologism is a consequence of an independently established epistemological theory. The psychological results are thus not useful in analyzing justification. We have here no good defense of methodological naturalism. To support methodological naturalism we need a defense of ballpark psychologism that does not depend upon a prior analysis of justification.

It is possible that ballpark psychologism is not a thesis one argues for but rather a starting point or assumption for building an epistemological theory. It is true that many philosophers who seek analyses of knowledge and justification do seem to assume the falsity of skepticism. And something like ballpark psychologism is a consequence of this antiskeptical assumption.[18] Kornblith gives an example to illustrate the way in which he thinks psychological results will influence epistemology given this assumption. Suppose that one is a reliabilist who endorses something like (R). Kornblith says that recent empirical results seem to show that we are bad inductive reasoners.[19] If reliabilists were to hold that there is one process

– inductive reasoning – that is invoked in all cases of inductive reasoning, then, since that process is not reliable,[20] reliabilists are stuck with the skeptical conclusion that we have no justified beliefs as a result of inductive reasoning. But this conflicts with the ballpark psychologist assumption that we do have inductive knowledge. Kornblith concludes that in this case epistemologists must modify or abandon reliabilism. So, their epistemology is influenced by empirical results.

Alvin Goldman argues in a similar way. He cites empirical results showing that visual object recognition is more reliable in some circumstances than in others.[21] This leads him to reject (R) and to consider instead:

(R1) A belief is justified iff the cognitive process that caused it is reliable when it operates under the parameter values in which it caused the belief.

Thus, we need not say that beliefs resulting from a single process are all justified or all unjustified. Kornblith's point about induction might lead to a similar revision of simple reliabilism. In light of his arguments, nonskeptical reliabilists ought either to say that there are many different inductive processes, or else relativize reliability to circumstances, as (R1) does.

In these cases, knowledge of contingent facts – the fact that people sometimes make bad inductive inferences, the fact that people are able to identify objects better in some circumstances than in others – may influence one's epistemology. The way this knowledge influences epistemology is to make one aware of actual, and thus possible, examples that an analysis of justification must accommodate.

However, these cases do not provide the materials needed for a defense of methodological naturalism. Neither argument shows that we really need results from empirical science in order to formulate versions of reliabilism that are good enough to meet the objections raised to (R). Since the analyses are supposed to be adequate to all possible cases, these cases need only be possible in order to show that (R) needs revision. Since it is easy to figure out from our armchairs that the examples like these are possible, it is easy to figure out from our armchairs that (R) needs revision. We don't need results from psychology to tell us this.

A further criticism of this argument for methodological naturalism depends upon what information is available to us from our armchairs. If armchair epistemologists are allowed to assume that ballpark psychologism is true (or that skepticism is false), then surely they are also entitled to assume that some inductive beliefs are not justified. That is, they are equally entitled to assume that we can (and do) sometimes generalize on the basis of too few examples, ignore relevant information, or let our emotions influence our inferences. So, not only is the fact that it is possible that some inductive beliefs are not justified available to us in our armchairs, so also is the fact some actual inductive beliefs are not justified. So, if the point of the induction example was to make us see that we should reject (R) in favor of something like (R1), then it fails to show that results from scientific psychology are particularly useful. Essentially the same point applies to Goldman's example. The research he mentions may help to make it clear that our perceptual beliefs are better justified in some circumstances than in others, and this requires that reliabilists introduce some sort of relativization to context within their theory. This is the proposal found in (R1). But whatever sort of information allowed us to assume that we do have some knowledge, and thus entitles us to ballpark psychologism, entitles us to the assumption that we do better perceptually in some situations than others. We don't need cognitive psychologists to tell us that we can's see in the dark or to tell us that not all our inductive inferences are reasonable. We learned that in our armchairs.

Similar points apply, I believe, to other empirical considerations sometimes used to evaluate proposed analyses of knowledge or justification. For example, some versions of coherentism require for the justification of any belief that it be part of a fully coherent system of beliefs. Psychological results seem to show that people typically don't have fully coherent systems of belief. Given ballpark psychologism, then, this empirical result shows that versions of coherentism with this requirement must be wrong.[22] It seems to me that it is rather easy to see, without the aid of empirical results, that a person can have a justified belief about one topic while having incoherencies in distant areas of her system of beliefs. So, the possibility of this sort of case is readily available to us in our armchairs. Perhaps the fact that such cases are actual may also be available to us in our armchairs, depending again upon exactly what sort of information armchair epistemologists are allowed to use.

Even if we assume the truth of ballpark psychologism, then, the case has not been made for methodological naturalism with respect to the project of analyzing the concepts of knowledge and justification. This does not rule out the possibility that psychologists could describe actual examples of a sort epistemologists had not previously considered. If they did, it would be foolish for epistemologists not to test their theories with them. But there's nothing in what's been presented so far to warrant advertisements for naturalistic revolutions in epistemology. The evidential relevance of psychology to the effort to analyze knowledge and justification is, as the arguments and examples considered so far suggest, quite modest.[23]

3. *Scientific analysis is more useful than conceptual analysis*

In a recent paper, Kornblith argues in a rather different way for the conclusion that empirical results must play a central role in figuring out the nature of knowledge. He begins by disparaging conceptual analysis:

> Analyzing our concept of knowledge, to the extent that we can make sense of such a project, is no more useful than analyzing the ordinary concept of, say, aluminum. The ordinary concept of aluminum is of little interest for two reasons. First, most people are largely ignorant of what makes aluminum the kind of stuff it is, and so their concept of aluminum will tell us little about the stuff itself. Second, most people have many misconceptions about aluminum, and so their concepts will reflect this misinformation as well . . . Now, the same may be said, I believe, of knowledge.

Epistemologists ought to be interested in the study of knowledge itself. If we substitute a study of the ordinary concept of knowledge, we are getting at knowledge only indirectly; knowledge is thereby filtered through a good deal of ignorance about the phenomenon, as well as a good deal of misinformation.[24]

I take Kornblith to be arguing here that armchair methods introduce errors into our account of knowledge, and these errors can only (or can best) be avoided by an empirical study of "knowledge itself." This argument raises several questions. First, is it true that our armchair methodology leads us to introduce errors and misinformation into our account of knowledge? Second, how will the empirical study of "knowledge itself" proceed?

It is surely true that people may have many false beliefs about aluminum. Whether these false beliefs affect their concept of aluminum depends in part upon exactly what enters into a concept. But no matter what concepts are like, were we to try to figure out "what makes [aluminum] the kind of stuff it is" – its physical constitution – using armchair methods, it would be miraculous if we got it right. Surely, empirical science is the only sensible way to learn about the physical nature of aluminum. Kornblith's case for a scientific study of "knowledge itself" would be strong if there were some errors about knowledge that armchair thinkers tend to make which affect their analyses and would be avoided by his proposed replacement. What are the alleged errors that we make about knowledge?[25]

Oddly, Kornblith never says what the errors are. The closest thing to an answer that I can find in Kornblith's essays is in section I of "In Defense of a Naturalized Epistemology." This section, entitled "The Cartesian Tradition," purports to reveal the failures of Cartesian approaches to epistemology. According to standard accounts of Descartes, he is a foundationalist. He holds that a person's knowledge is limited to what is foundational for the person or what can be derived from what is foundational. The foundations are limited to propositions about which the person can't be mistaken. These standards are extraordinarily high. Armchair philosophers have long realized that they leave us with precious little knowledge. Various accounts of knowledge with standards that are more readily met have been proposed. However, without discussing any such accounts in detail, Kornblith dismisses them. He writes,

Of course knowledge is possible if we weaken the standards for knowledge far enough, in particular if we weaken them until we can show that many of our beliefs then pass the standards. But this seems to be nothing more than an exercise in self-congratulation. Why should we care about knowledge so defined?[26]

Kornblith also claims that weakening the standards for knowledge below the Cartesian standards undermines epistemologists' ability to give useful advice. He writes, "But if our standards for knowledge are merely designed to allow us to attach the epithet 'knowledge' to whatever it is we pretheoretically believe, then ... the result is an uncritical endorsement of the epistemological status quo."[27]

There is an extraordinarily wide gap between demanding Cartesian certainty in order to have knowledge and weakening the standards so far as to be merely performing "an exercise in self-congratulation" in which we endorse "whatever it is we pretheoretically believe." One will search in vain in the epistemological literature for blanket endorsements of our actual beliefs and inferential practices. Few armchair epistemologists say that "whatever it is we pretheoretically believe" amounts to knowledge. Virtually all defenders of foundationalism, coherentism, reliabilism, and their rivals agree that many everyday beliefs fall short of what's needed for justification and knowledge. Even those who assume that any general form of skepticism is false agree that superstition, wishful thinking, and hasty generalization may be prevalent, and where they are, the resulting beliefs are not knowledge. Armchair epistemologists typically pick and choose among realistic and fanciful examples, identifying some as cases of knowledge and some as not. Many conclude that knowledge is less common than one would initially think. By reflecting carefully on what they take to be realistic examples, they attempt to identify what is good about possible ways of reasoning. By calling our attention to the reasoning that withstands scrutiny and reflection, they can contribute to an effort to help us improve. It is a mistake to characterize this as an exercise in self-congratulation.

It is worth clarifying the role examples play in armchair epistemology. Some armchair epistemologists begin by describing realistic cases that they take to be cases of, for example, perceptual knowledge. Kornblith and others may think that these philosophers are assuming that actual cases like these count as knowledge no matter what else it true of them. It may be that some armchair epistemologists do proceed in this way. They think that actual typical cases of, say, perceptual belief, count as knowledge *no matter what else is true of them*. Since empirical science may show that what occurs in these actual cases differs significantly from what we think occurs in them in our armchairs, empirical science may uncover information that undermines any proposed analysis of knowledge.

I believe that this mischaracterizes the role that examples play, or should play, in armchair epistemology. I think that the assumption standardly made, or at least the one that should be made, is that *if* our perceptual systems are at least roughly like we take them to be and the world is at least roughly like the way we think it is, then many of our ordinary perceptual beliefs amount to knowledge. It's consistent with this that our actual perceptual beliefs rarely or never amount to knowledge.[28] So, armchair epistemologists, even when they use realistic examples as their starting point, are not proceeding in a way that guarantees that the resulting theories will imply that these are cases of knowledge or justification.

There is, then, no merit in the charge that armchair epistemology is based on mistaken assumptions about knowledge or in the contention that armchair epistemology is committed to a mindless ratification of common-sense views of the world. So, these are not good reasons to think that there is anything defective about the methodology of armchair epistemology. Nevertheless, it could still be the case that a scientific study of knowledge would be preferable in some way. In the case of aluminum, even if our ordinary thoughts about aluminum were not seriously mistaken, it would still be absurd to try to understand what aluminum is by engaging in armchair analysis of our concept of aluminum rather than by engaging in scientific study of aluminum. So, why isn't the same thing true of knowledge?

It's difficult to see, however, exactly why we should think that knowledge is relevantly like aluminum. For one thing, what we seek in the case of aluminum is an understanding of its physical constitution. We want to know what it is made of, how it interacts with other materials and why, and what we can use it for. Our analysis of knowledge does not call for an account of its physical constitution. It's doubtful that there is any such thing. We might also seek scientific analyses of physical processes, such as cell division. But knowledge isn't a substance like aluminum or a process like cell division. So, analogies such as these don't provide reasons to seek naturalistic analyses of knowledge.

More importantly, however, is the fact that there are conceptual puzzles about knowledge that many people find interesting. These puzzles lead to arguments for skepticism and questions about what epistemic justification requires. Study of these puzzles requires conceptual clarification. Part of Kornblith's case for naturalized epistemology rests on the contention that our ordinary concept of knowledge is "of little interest." I think that it is a good idea to be wary of philosophical arguments based on claims about what is of "interest." Different people find different things interesting, but the conceptual questions about knowledge and justification have a long track record. There are no comparable puzzles about aluminum.

Some topics and questions are amenable to armchair methods and some are not. It would be foolish to extend Kornblith's line of thinking to logical concepts such as validity or conjunction, to modal concepts such as necessity, or, I believe, to moral concepts such as obligation. Some concepts have a richer conceptual structure than others.[29] The fact that knowledge requires true belief seems beyond dispute, and this shows that it has at least this much conceptual complexity. What else it requires continues to be in dispute. Whether anything of interest will emerge from further analysis remains to be seen. In any case, the alleged analogy to aluminum provides no basis for thinking that armchair epistemology should be replaced by an empirical study of knowledge.

Even if the arguments against armchair epistemology considered here all fail, it could nevertheless be true that an empirical investigation of the nature of knowledge would be preferable. Suppose we were to attempt to study knowledge empirically. What would we do? Kornblith gives a brief description of an answer. He says that an empirical study of knowledge will begin with the assumption that we can identify some clear cases of knowledge. Having done that, "We must examine the various psychological mechanisms by which knowledge is produced and retained in order to see what, if anything, they have in common."[30] But why should we look at these mechanisms? Why not look at the diets of people who have the most knowledge or look at the color of the socks they are wearing when they get knowledge? Why think the psychological mechanisms that caused the beliefs are of any significance at all to understanding the nature of knowledge? Kornblith does not explicitly answer this, but a reason is suggested when he says, "The account of knowledge I favor, due to Alvin Goldman, is that knowledge is reliably produced true belief."[31] I take it that this "account of knowledge" states Kornblith's view of the nature of knowledge. Kornblith announces that he "favors" this "account" without reliance on any scientific information. And it's noteworthy that Goldman's defense of reliabilism that Kornblith cites is as clear an example of armchair methodology as one can find.[32] Kornblith provides no explanation of how empirical information could possibly lend support to his account of the nature of knowledge.

There are, of course, fascinating empirical questions about how people form beliefs. Nothing said here is intended to suggest otherwise. But this fact, and the analogy to aluminum, provides neither the basis for rejecting armchair epistemology nor reason to think that a naturalistic study of knowledge will provide a better account of the nature of knowledge.

None of the reasons for rejecting armchair epistemology in favor of methodological naturalism that we've considered succeeds. To the extent that epistemology is involved in coming up with general analyses of knowledge and justification, the need for scientific input is yet to be established.

IV. Psychology and Epistemic Principles

In addition to analyzing knowledge and justification, armchair epistemologists often attempt to identify epistemic principles which typically state sufficient conditions for a belief's being justified. Some proposed epistemic principles state that if certain beliefs are justified, then certain other beliefs are justified. For example, one much discussed principle of this sort says that if each of two beliefs is justified, then so is the conjunction of the two. Another proposed principle says that if a person is justified in believing one proposition, then the person is justified in believing all the logical consequences of that principle. Epistemic principles of another kind state sufficient conditions for justification that are not other justified beliefs.[33] These principles identify the ultimate sources of justification for beliefs. It is principles of this second kind that will be our focus here.[34]

Epistemic principles about sources of justification often emphasize the role sources such as perception, testimony, or memory play. A simple example of such a principle about perceptual evidence might be:

> For any sensory quality P and any person S, if S is appeared to P-ishly, then S is justified in believing that there is something with property P present.

According to this, "being appeared to redly" (seeming to see something red) justifies one in believing that there is something red present. Similar principles about testimony, memory, or other potential sources of justification can be formulated.

A crucial aspect of the common armchair epistemologist's view is that these principles about evidential support are necessary and a priori.

The closest thing to this sort of principle that a reliabilist or causal theorist is likely to formulate is a claim about which processes or mechanisms are reliable. Any such claim will be the product of psychological results, even if we do have some general information about this available to us in our armchairs. There appears to be, then, a significant difference between armchair epistemologists who formulate these a priori principles and reliabilists who use empirical evidence to formulate contingent claims about reliable processes. As Goldman puts it, evidentialists are apt to claim "that knowledge, justification, and rationality arise primarily from evidential relations between sentences or propositions, abstract subject matter that can be studied by logic and probability theory," whereas reliabilists think that we learn about such matters through "the study of biological or psychological systems in the natural (physical) world."[35] So evidentialists seek a priori principles about quasi-logical relations among propositions, where reliabilists seek contingent truths about reliable processes. It appears, then, when it comes to formulating specific principles of the sorts described here, methodological naturalism is correct given reliabilist theories but perhaps not given traditional theories that focus on evidential support.

It is surely true that many evidentialists have attempted to formulate epistemic principles without the aid of information from science. Whether this is a project with any chance of success depends in large part upon exactly what the epistemic principles they formulate are supposed to be like. It is surely true that for most of us, when we are appeared to redly, we are usually justified in believing that there is something red before us. But this is a contingent truth. The sensory experiences people have are only contingently related to the external objects that we (properly) take them to be evidence for. Had our eyes been different, the sort of experience we actually get when in the presence of something red might have been caused by things that were not red. In that case, that sort of experience might have been part of one's evidence for the presence of some different sort of thing. In fact, that sort of experience could have had no interesting relationship to external objects at all. It could instead have been, like some twitches and tingles, not evidentially relevant to the existence of external objects of any sort. This suggests that there are no a priori evidential principles linking specific kinds of perceptual experiences with the presence of objects of specific kinds.

One might instead propose a somewhat more general principle about perceptual evidence, such as that if a kind of perceptual experience is regularly caused by a certain kind of object, then the occurrence of the experience in a person provides the person with at least some reason to believe that an object of that kind is present. But principles along these lines are dubious, since any such regular causal connection could be entirely beyond the grasp of the people having the experiences. If it turns out that sunspots cause experiences of a certain sort, say a particular kind of headache, and no one has the slightest inkling that this is the case, having such a headache does not provide evidence for the occurrence of sunspots.

Perhaps a true principle concerning perceptual evidence is that if one has a perceptual experience of a certain sort, and one has evidence that experiences of that sort are normally caused by objects of a certain sort, and one lacks evidence that one's current experience is abnormal, then one is justified in believing that an object of the stated kind is present. Even if some such principle is true, it hardly counts as a special principle about perceptual evidence. It is equally true that if one has a twitch, a tingle, or telepathic experience of a certain sort, and one has evidence that experiences of that sort are normally caused by objects of a certain kind, and one lacks evidence that one's current experience is abnormal, then one is justified in believing that an object of the specified kind is present. These principles are just instances of a very general principle about evidential support. There is no special truth about perception here.

Similar points apply to testimonial evidence. Armchair epistemologists might think that people are typically better justified in believing things that they read in newspapers such as the *New York Times* than they are in believing things they read in supermarket tabloids. If this point is elevated to the status of an epistemological principle, then evidentialists should hold that such principles are contingent and dependent upon empirical evidence about the accuracy and integrity of these newspapers. However, I doubt that many epistemologists would say that a principle about specific newspapers counts as a principle of epistemology. They seek something more general. But what? A possibility might be that one is justified in believing things, all else being equal, that come from reputable sources. If by "reputable sources" we mean sources that have a generally strong reputation, then the principles is not true. One might have reason to distrust a source that has a generally good reputation. "Reputable sources" might mean trustworthy sources, sources one has reason to believe. But this is just another way of saying that if one is told something by a source one has reason to believe, then one has reason to believe what one was told. And this just seems to be a special case of the analysis of justification that holds that one is justified in believing what is supported by one's evidence.

My own hypothesis is that there are no true special epistemic principles about sources of evidence of the sort epistemologists have often sought. Any proposed principle will turn out to be either false or else just a restricted version of a very general epistemic principle. An analogy to ethics might be instructive. Act utilitarians – those who hold that in any circumstance one ought to do that action among one's alternatives that maximizes utility – will hold that the there are no true special moral principles about promise-keeping, truth-telling, or even taking lives. One ought to do those things when and only when they maximize utility. The only true general principles about these kinds of actions are simply special cases of the wholly general utilitarian rule. There are, however, useful rules of thumb, to the effect that certain sorts of actions typically do or don't maximize utility. Such rules of thumb may be helpful guides to life.

I suspect that the epistemic case is similar. The overriding rule is that one is justified in believing what is supported by one's evidence. This is a rough statement of what I believe is a correct analysis of justification.[36] One is justified in accepting testimony or forming a perceptual belief when, and only when, so doing is supported by one's overall evidence. There may be useful rules of thumb about when that will be the case. There are some general things one can say about the notion of evidential support, but what can be said will not be the more specific principles about particular sources of evidence like those many armchair epistemologists have sought.[37] If this view about epistemic principles is correct, then the traditional search for such principles is bound to fail. The only principles are very abstract general principles about evidential support.

Are things importantly different if one holds a reliabilist or causal theory? Suppose one comes up with a reliabilist theory along the liens of (R1). It is possible to formulate principles about perception or memory that are, in effect, instances of this. For example, one might hold that memory is reliable for beliefs of such-and-such a kind in such-and-such circumstances. It is surely correct to say that philosophers need help from psychologists in developing principles such as this. But, as I see it, saying this is something like saying that philosophers need help from plumbers in fixing their leaking faucets. Figuring out which processes are reliable in which circumstances is an entirely empirical matter. The psychologists, like the plumbers, don't need any help from the epistemologists in this project. There's not much for the epistemologists to do other than stand around and watch.

Thus, for both reliabilists and defenders of more traditional evidential theories, information of two sorts is needed to assess the epistemic status of beliefs resulting from perception, memory, or testimony. We need to know what the general standards for such evaluations are. And we need empirical information about either the reliability of processes or the evidence people actually have about those sources. The latter is a purely empirical matter. Theorizing about the first topic is the province of armchair epistemology, and we haven't seen good arguments for the role of psychology in identifying and clarifying these general standards. Empirical information is needed to determine if the standards are met in particular kinds of cases.

V. Evaluating Arguments for Skepticism

The role of natural science in evaluating arguments for skepticism can easily be determined, based on the conclusions reached in previous sections of this paper and a brief account of what skeptical arguments are like. Arguments for skepticism almost always involve premises of two sorts. Premises of one sort say that knowledge has some necessary condition. Premises of the other sort say that people's beliefs never, or rarely, satisfy that necessary condition, or perhaps that they can't satisfy that condition. To the extent that an evaluation of the skeptical argument focuses on a premise of the first sort, armchair epistemologists will be in a position to carry out the task. A good analysis of knowledge will enable us to determine whether knowledge really does have the necessary condition the argument requires. To the extent that the evaluation focuses on a premise of the second sort, it will typically require empirical information, often information that will come from natural science. Of course, sometimes that empirical information will also be available to intelligent epistemologists in their armchairs, since it may not depend on technical results from psychology.

VI. Conclusion

The resulting picture, then, is this: some projects some would call epistemological, such as the study of human knowledge and reasoning or the effort to help people to reason better, undoubtedly do require empirical input. In spite of arguments to the contrary, there's not much reason to think that psychological results will play any significant role in efforts to construct general abstract theories about or analyses of knowledge and justification. The formulation of specific principles about perception, testimony, memory, and other potential sources of knowledge and justification either amounts to specifying mere special cases of the abstract general principles or else is a purely empirical matter. Finally, whether responses to skepticism require input from science depends entirely upon the nature of the response.[38]

Notes

1 I refer here and throughout the paper explicitly only to psychology. In all cases, however, I intend my remarks to apply to all sciences that study reasoning and cognition.
2 Alvin Goldman, "Epistemic Folkways and Scientific Epistemology," reprinted in *Naturalizing Epistemology*, 2nd ed., ed. Hilary Kornblith (Cambridge, MA: MIT Press, 1994), pp. 291–315. The quotation is from p. 314.
3 Hilary Kornblith, "Introduction: What is Naturalized Epistemology?" *Naturalizing Epistemology*, pp. 1–14. The quotation is from p. 14.
4 Susan Haack, *Evidence and Inquiry* (Oxford: Blackwell, 1993), p. 118.
5 Stephen Stich and Richard Nisbett, "Justification and the Psychology of Human Reasoning," *Philosophy of Science* 47 (1980): 188–202. The quotation is from p. 188.
6 Gilbert Harman, *Change in View: Principles of Reasoned Revision* (Cambridge, MA: MIT Press, 1986), p. 7.
7 Haack, for example, is generally less enthusiastic about naturalism than the other authors cited.
8 Philip Kitcher, "The Naturalists Return," *The Philosophical Review* 101 (1992): 53–114. The quotation is from p. 58.
9 Alvin Goldman, "Epistemics: The Regulative Theory of Cognition," *Journal of Philosophy* 75 (1978): 509–23.
10 I think that if you are seriously interested in helping people to reason better, the branch of philosophy that you'd work in is "critical thinking" ("informal logic"). I see this as a kind of applied epistemology, related to epistemology in something like

the way applied ethics is related to theoretical ethics. Oddly, advocates of methodological naturalism often don't seem to think that such applied work is central to epistemology at all. Their emphasis is usually cognitive psychology or cognitive science.

11 "Is Justified True Belief Knowledge?" *Analysis* 23 (1963): 121–3.
12 "The Naturalists Return," p. 60, n. 20.
13 It is important to emphasize that Kitcher's main reason for thinking that naturalism has returned is not the one discussed here.
14 See Goldman's "Naturalistic Epistemology and Reliabilism" in *Midwest Studies in Philosophy* XIX, eds. Peter A. French, Theodore E. Uehling, Jr., and Howard K. Wettstein (Notre Dame: University of Notre Dame Press, 1994), pp. 301–20.
15 For discussion of some of the troubles reliabilism faces in identifying the processes mentioned in (R), see Earl Conee and Richard Feldman, "The Generality Problem for Reliabilism," *Philosophical Studies*, 89 (1998): 1–29.
16 "Introduction: What is Naturalized Epistemology?" p. 10. It will simplify matters, and cause no problems for present purposes, to identify what one is justified in believing with what one ought to believe.
17 Of course, one could equally well argue from ballpark psychologism and (R) to the conclusion that the psychologists must be wrong about which processes we actually use.
18 Whether the assumption that skepticism is false implies ballpark psychologism depends on several points, including: (i) exactly how much knowledge we are assumed to have, (ii) what ballpark psychologism implies about how similar our belief-forming processes are to the ones we ought to use, and (iii) whether knowing a proposition to be true implies arriving at one's belief in the proposition by means of a process similar to one we ought to use. It's worth noting that philosophers who assume that skepticism is false need not assume that nearly all, or even most, of our beliefs amount to knowledge.
19 "Introduction: What is Naturalized Epistemology?" pp. 12ff.
20 It's a bit of a stretch to say that empirical results show that inductive reasoning is not generally reliable. At most, they show the existence of widespread errors. But that's far short of showing a lack of general reliability.
21 See "Epistemic Folkways and Scientific Epistemology," pp. 304–6.
22 This argument was suggested to me by John Greco.
23 My discussion so far has been about attempts to analyze what is allegedly a standard concept of knowledge and justification. I think that we'd reach a similar conclusion if the goal were to elucidate some other conception of epistemic value. So, I don't think my points are affected by the arguments of those who think our conceptions of epistemic value are somehow suspect or unimportant.
24 "Naturalistic Epistemology and Its Critics," *Philosophical Topics* 23 (1995): 237–55. The quotation is from pp. 243–4. Kornblith makes essentially the same points in "In Defense of a Naturalized Epistemology," this volume, p. 159.
25 People may routinely have some false beliefs about knowledge. They may, for example, think that they know more than they do. What's crucial here is whether there are errors that get in the way of successfully analyzing knowledge.
26 "In Defense of a Naturalized Epistemology," this volume, p. 158. Stephen Stich makes a somewhat similar point in *The Fragmentation of Reason* (Cambridge, MA: The MIT Press, 1990), ch. 4. Stich asserts that our concept of justification is culturally acquired and that there is no reason to think that it is any better than alternative concepts. He

then asks "why we should care one whit whether the cognitive processes we use are sanctioned by" our concept of justification? (p. 92).

27 "In Defense of a Naturalized Epistemology," this volume, p. 158.
28 Thus, I think that armchair epistemologists who seem to assume that skepticism is false typically aren't making (or shouldn't make) that assumption. The assumption they are making is the conditional assumption just mentioned.
29 For a defense of the use of intuitions about examples in doing philosophical analysis, see George Bealer, "The Incoherence of Empiricism," in Steven Wagner and Richard Warner, eds., *Naturalism: A Critical Appraisal* (Notre Dame: Notre Dame University Press, 1993), pp. 163–96.
30 "In Defense of a Naturalized Epistemology," this volume, p. 160.
31 "In Defense of a Naturalized Epistemology," this volume, p. 160.
32 See *Epistemology and Cognition* (Cambridge, MA: Harvard University Press, 1986), part I, "Theoretical Foundations."
33 Probably the most influential armchair epistemologist who attempts to develop principles of the sort described here is Roderick Chisholm. See e.g. *Theory of Knowledge* (Englewood Cliffs, NJ: Prentice-Hall, 1989), chs. 5 and 6.
34 One reason for thinking that empirical input is needed when formulating epistemic principles of the first kind has to do with human limitations. Some take the rules in question to state what one is *required* to believe if one has certain other justified beliefs. Given that one isn't required to believe what one can't believe or, perhaps, what is extremely hard for one to believe, the rules must conform to human limitations. This sort of point is made by Goldman in "Epistemics: The Regulative Theory of Cognition," pp. 510 and 514, and by Stich in *The Fragmentation of Reason*, ch. 2. A quick response to this point is to take the relevant rules to state what one is permitted to believe rather than what one is obligated to believe. Another response is to modify the principles by adding to their antecedents the requirement that one is able to form the belief in question.
35 "Naturalistic Epistemology and Reliabilism," p. 302.
36 This analysis is developed and defended in Richard Feldman and Earl Conee, "Evidentialism," *Philosophical Studies* 48 (1985): 15–34.
37 I suspect that advocates of other general epistemic principles, such as Bayes' theorem, are likely to agree that there aren't any special epistemic principles about perception, testimony, or other sources of evidence.
38 Previous versions of this paper have been presented at the State University of New York at Geneseo, Rutgers University, The American Philosophical Association (Pacific Division), and the Central States Philosophical Society. I thank the participants in the discussions at all those sessions for their comments. I am also grateful to Earl Conee, John Greco, and Peter Markie for helpful comments and discussion of these issues.

Chapter 8

Contextualism: An Explanation and Defense

Keith DeRose

In epistemology, "contextualism" denotes a wide variety of more-or-less closely related positions according to which the issues of knowledge or justification are somehow relative to context. I will proceed by first explicating the position *I* call contextualism, and distinguishing that position from some closely related positions in epistemology, some of which sometimes also go by the name of "contextualism." I'll then present and answer what seems to many the most pressing of the objections to contextualism as I construe it, and also indicate some of the main positive motivations for accepting the view. Among the epistemologists I've spoken with who have an opinion on the matter, I think it's fair to say a majority reject contextualism. However, the resistance has to this point been largely underground, with little by way of sustained arguments against contextualism appearing in the journals,[1] though I have begun to see various papers in manuscript form which are critical of contextualism. Here, I'll respond to the criticism of contextualism that, in my travels, I have found to be the most pervasive in producing suspicion about the view.

1. What Is Contextualism?

As I use it, and as I think the term is most usefully employed, "contextualism" refers to the position that the truth-conditions of knowledge ascribing and knowledge denying sentences (sentences of the form "S knows that P" and "S doesn't know that P" and related variants of such sentences) vary in certain ways according to the context in which they are uttered. What so varies is the epistemic standards that S must meet (or, in the case of a denial of knowledge, fail to meet) in order for such a statement to be true. In some contexts, "S knows that P" requires for its truth that S have a true belief that P and also be in a *very* strong epistemic position with respect to P, while in other contexts, the very same sentence may require for its truth, in addition to S's having a true belief that P, only that S meet some lower epistemic standards. Thus, the contextualist will allow that one speaker can truthfully say "S knows that P," while another speaker, in a different context where higher standards are in place, can truthfully say "S doesn't know that P," though both speakers are talking about the same S and the same P at the same time. The "invariantist" – Peter Unger's good name for one who denies contextualism[2] – will have none of this. According to her, there's a single, invariant set of standards which, at least as far as truth-conditions go, govern the use of knowledge attributions regardless of the context in which they're uttered; thus, our two speakers can't both be speaking a truth.

I am not alone in endorsing contextualism so construed; other contextualists prominently include Stewart Cohen, David Lewis, Gail Stine, and Peter Unger.[3]

Now it should be, and I think it largely is, fairly uncontroversial that in different conversational contexts, quite different standards govern whether ordinary speakers *will say* that someone knows something: What we're happy to call knowledge in some ("low-standards") contexts we'll deny is knowledge in other ("high-standards") contexts. The invariantist needn't deny this, and if she's wise she won't deny it. Nor need she or should she deny that this is a very useful feature of our use of the relevant sentences. What she must deny is that these varying standards for when ordinary speakers *will* attribute knowledge, and/or for when they're in some sense *warranted* in attributing knowledge, reflect varying standards for when it is or would be *true* for them to attribute knowledge, for, again, according to the invariantist, the *truth-conditions* of the relevant sentences do not vary in the relevant way.

Contextualism, so understood, then, is a position about knowledge attributions (sentences attributing knowledge to a subject) and denials of knowledge – precisely, a thesis about their truth-conditions. This has been known to give rise to the following type of outburst: "Your contextualism isn't a theory about *knowledge* at all; it's just a theory about *knowledge attributions*. As such, it's not a piece of epistemology at all, but of the philosophy of language."

Of the many things that can be said in response to this type of charge, let me limit myself here to just this. To the extent that contextualism/invariantism is an issue in the philosophy of language, it's a piece of philosophy of language that is of profound importance to epistemology. How we should proceed in studying knowledge will be greatly affected by how we come down on the contextualism/invariantism issue. For contextualism opens up possibilities for dealing with issues and puzzles in epistemology which, of course, must be rejected if invariantism is instead the correct position. And how could it be otherwise? Those who work on the problem of free will and determinism should *of course* be very interested in the issue of what it means to call an action "free." If that could mean different things in different contexts, then all sorts of problems could arise from a failure to recognize this shift in meaning. If there is no such shift, then that too will be vital information. In either case, one will want to know what such claims mean. Likewise, it's important in studying knowledge to discern what it means to say someone knows something. If that can mean different things in different contexts, all sorts of problems in epistemology, and not just in philosophy of language, will arise from a failure to recognize such shifts in meaning. If, on the other hand, there is no such shift, then we're bound to fall into all sorts of error about knowledge, as well as about "knows," if we think such shifts occur.

2. Contextualism regarding Other Epistemic Terms

Contextualism, as described above, is a thesis about knowledge attributing and denying sentences. But, since there are other terms with analytic ties to the concept of knowledge, we should expect that if contextualism about knowledge is true, there should be corresponding shifts in the content of sentences containing those other terms. To use David Lewis's words (though he wasn't writing about "knows" when he used them), we should expect the content of knowledge attributing sentences and the sentences containing the other terms to "sway together."[4] For instance, to a first approximation, at least, "It's possible that P_{ind}"[5] is true if and only if the speaker of the sentence doesn't know that P is false.[6] Given contextualism, then, we should expect that, as the standards for knowledge go up, making it harder for belief to count as knowledge, it should become easier for statements of possibility to be true.[7] And, since "It's certain that P" is the dual of "It's possible that P_{ind}" ("It's certain that P" is true if and only if "It's possible that not-P_{ind}" is false), we should expect that as the standards for knowledge go up, making it harder for knowledge attributions to be true, it should also become harder for such expressions of impersonal certainty to be true.[8]

We can construe contextualism regarding *justification* as an analogue of what we're calling contextualism about knowledge: According to the contextualist about justification, the standards for justified belief that a subject must meet in order to render true a sentence describing a belief of hers as justified vary with context. The relation between knowledge and justification is controversial, and neither of these forms of contextualism clearly implies the other. If one holds that a belief's being justified is a necessary condition for its being a piece of knowledge, then one may believe that the two contextualisms are closely related: Perhaps it's *because* the standards for justification vary with context that the standards for knowledge so vary. However, it's widely accepted today that more is needed for knowledge than simply justified true belief, and it may be varying requirements for that something more that's reflected in the varying standards for knowledge – in addition to, or instead of, varying standards for justification.

In what follows, when I write simply of "contextualism," I will mean contextualism regarding knowledge; when I mean to refer to contextualism about justification or some other epistemic term, I will explicitly state so. To the best of my knowledge, neither I nor any of the contextualists mentioned above in section 1 have either endorsed or rejected contextualism about justification.[9]

3. Contextualism is Not a Thesis about the Structure of Knowledge or Justification

In his influential paper, "A Contextualist Theory of Epistemic Justification,"[10] David Annis presents what he calls "contextualism" as an alternative to both foundationalism and coherentism in the issue of the structure of justification. Now, I think that even Annis's "contextualism" is not a structural alternative to those two theories, but is rather best construed as a form of foundationalism. But the vital point to be made now is that "contextualism" as *I* am construing it here, is certainly not a thesis about the structure of knowledge or of justification. It is, in fact, consistent with either foundationalism or coherentism.

If you're a foundationalist, then if you're also a contextualist, you may well come to think of the issue of which beliefs are properly basic (i.e., the issue of which beliefs are justified to a degree sufficient for knowledge independent of any support they receive from other beliefs), and/or the issue of how strongly supported a belief in the superstructure must be in order to count as knowledge or as a justified belief, to be matters that vary according to features of conversational context. And if you're a coherentist, then if you're also a contextualist, you'll probably want to hold that how strongly beliefs must cohere with one another in order to count as knowledge (if they're true), or to count as justified, is a contextually variable matter. So contextualism will certainly color the theories of either structural camp. But contextualism is not itself a structural alternative. Nor does it in any obvious way favor one structural alternative over the other.

4. "Subject" vs. "Attributor" Contextualism

Some distinguish between "subject contextualism" and "attributor contextualism," or use slightly different titles to mark the same distinction.[11] The basic issue here is whether the varying standards a subject must live up to to count as knowing are relative to the context of that subject, or rather to the context of the attributor – the person describing the subject as a knower or a nonknower. I should be clear that what *I* am calling "contextualism" is a form of what these folks call "attributor contextualism." But it is worth briefly describing what these views call "subject contextualism" to distinguish it from what I am here calling "contextualism."

Some "subject contextualists" point to examples in which features of the surroundings of the putative subject of knowledge which don't constitute any part of his evidence for the belief in question, and which the subject may even be completely oblivious to, impact on whether the subject knows. For instance, in Carl Ginet's much-discussed fake barn example,[12] if a subject is driving through a region teeming with fake barns, deceptive enough that they would have fooled him if he had come across them, but is luckily encountering the only real barn anywhere about, and he confidently believes that he is seeing a barn, most respond that the subject doesn't know that what he's seeing is a barn. Presumably, though, he would have known it was a barn in a normal situation in which there are no fakes about. Here the presence of fakes in the region seems to rob the subject of knowledge, even if the subject doesn't know about the fakes and hasn't even encountered one. Now, I endorse the intuitions appealed to here: You don't know with the many fakes about, but do know in the normal situation. So, in this way, questions of knowledge are relative to the subject's "context," where "context" is being used to describe such extraevidential features of the subject's situation. So if accepting this is tantamount to being a subject-contextualist, then sign me up. But I think it's better to reserve the label "contextualism" for the more controversial thesis described in section 1, above.

Other "subject contextualists" point to features of the subject's *conversational* context: How important is it that the parties to the discussion in which the subject may be engaged be right on the matter in question (how high are the stakes for them)? What has transpired in the conversation in which the subject may be engaged? In what "community" is the subject operating, and what epistemic standards are appropriate to that community's intents and purposes? Now, I think that the conversational features that these subject contextualists point to are the kinds of features which affect whether attributions of knowledge are true, but I think it's these features of the *attributor's* context that are important. Suppose that you and I are in a discussion in which we're employing very high epistemic standards. Perhaps we're discussing a matter of great importance which calls for great caution, and we've made it clear by what we've said that we're employing such very high standards. So, though we have enough evidence for the belief in question that we'd have claimed to know it if we were in a more ordinary context, we've each denied that we know the item in question. Now, suppose I raise the question of whether Mary, a friend of ours who is not present at our conversation, knows the item in question. And suppose that you know that Mary has precisely the same evidence for the belief that we have, but that the issue isn't important to her or to those with whom she's presently speaking, and that she is in a context in which quite lax epistemic standards are being employed. Should you describe Mary as a knower? It seems that if you're not willing to call *us* knowers, then you shouldn't call Mary, who's in possession of the same evidence we have, a knower either. Here, the standards are set by the features of the attributor's setting. Of course, for certain purposes, we may wish to evaluate a subject's belief relative to standards set by features of her context. But there's nothing in attributor contextualism to rule this out: among the many standards a speaker's context may select are those relevant to the subject's context.

5. A Brief History of Contextualism

Theories according to which there are two senses of "know" – a "low," "weak," or "ordinary" sense on the one hand, and a "high," "strong," or "philosophical" sense, which is much more demanding, on the other – can be viewed as limiting cases of contextualist views. Such a view was prominently defended by Norman Malcolm in his 1952 "Knowledge and Belief."[13] For reasons I'll touch on in section 7, below, current contextualist theories don't hold that there are just two different sets of epistemic standards governing the truth-conditions of knowledge attributions, but rather posit a wide variety of different standards.

In important work on knowledge and skepticism in the early and mid-1970s, which culminated in his 1975 book *Ignorance*,[14] Peter Unger argued that, in order to really know something, one must be in a *very* strong epistemic position with respect to that proposition – so strong, in fact, that it would be impossible for anyone ever to be better positioned with respect to any matter than you are now with respect to the matter in question. Though the terminology wasn't in place yet, largely because the contextualist alternative to it wasn't in place yet, what Unger was there defending was *skeptical invariantism*. It was a form of invariantism because, so far as their truth-conditions go, Unger claimed that a single set of epistemic standards governed attributions of knowledge, in whatever context they were uttered. And it was *skeptical* invariantism because those standards were held to be very demanding. (Nonskeptical invariantism, then, is invariantism that keeps the standards governing the truth-conditions of knowledge attributions constant, but meetably low.) And Unger drew the skeptical conclusions that were naturally implied by such a stance. Importantly, Unger *did* admit that varying standards for knowledge govern our use of sentences of the form, "S knows that P," but did not endorse contextualism, because Unger claimed that these varying standards were only standards for whether it was *appropriate* to *say* that S knows; the truth-conditions for the sentence, as I've already noted, were, according to Unger, constant, and *very* demanding. Thus, the skeptic is right when she says we don't know, and we are saying something false (though perhaps appropriate) when, even in ordinary, nonphilosophical discussions, we claim to know this or that. This position, invariantism about truth conditions (whether this invariantism is skeptical like Unger's or nonskeptical), combined with variable standards for warranted assertability, is the great rival to contextualism. The "rival" came first, however: It was largely in response to this "invariantist" theory of Unger's that the early contextualist views of the late 1970s and early 1980s – like that expressed by David Lewis in a short section of his 1979 "Scorekeeping in a Language Game" (see note 3, above) and in contextualist versions of the Relevant Alternatives approach – were developed.

Later, Barry Stroud, in chapter 2 of his prominent 1984 *The Significance of Philosophical Scepticism*,[15] while not advocating skeptical invariantism, did seek to defend the view by appealing to the idea that the varying standards which can seem to govern the truth conditions of knowledge attributions might instead just govern their conditions of warranted assertability.

According to the very prominent "Relevant Alternatives" (RA) account of knowledge, which came to the fore during the middle and late 1970s, the main ingredient which must be added to true belief in order to yield knowledge is that the believer be able to rule out all the relevant alternatives to what she believes.

The range of alternatives to, or contraries of, what one believes that are relevant is held to be sensitive to a variety of factors. Many relevant alternativists held that the matter of which alternatives are relevant can be sensitive to the conversational context of the attributor of knowledge. This yields a contextualist version of the Relevant Alternatives theory. Among the most prominent examples of RA in the mid-1970s, Stine clearly held a contextualist version of RA, and in his important "Discrimination and Perceptual Knowledge," Alvin Goldman, while he sketched both a contextualist and an invariantist version of RA, expressed his preference for the contextualist version. Later, Stewart Cohen developed a version of RA that was explicitly a contextualist one, though Cohen used a different term: He called his an "indexical" version of RA.[16] But while the most frequently held and probably most defensible manifestation of the RA approach is the contextualist version of the theory, RA can be held in an invariantist form. If you hold that the range of relevant alternatives is not sensitive to the conversational context of the attributor of knowledge, but only to factors about the putative subject of knowledge and her surroundings, the result is an invariantist form of RA. (Some will call such versions of RA instances of "subject contextualism," but, as noted in the previous section, what I am calling "contextualism" is only what makers of such distinctions call "attributor contextualism.")[17]

Unger's 1984 book *Philosophical Relativity* contained what was at that time – and for some time to come, for that matter – easily the most complete exposition of the contextualist view. But while this book represented a change of mind for Unger from his skeptical writings of his *Ignorance* period, he was not advocating contextualism in *Philosophical Relativity*. Instead, he defended the "relativist" conclusion that contextualism and his earlier invariantist views which led to skepticism were equally good theories, and that there simply is no fact of the matter as to which view is correct. Unger's relativism, defended, as it is, by parity considerations, according to which the advantages and disadvantages of contextualism and invariantism balance each other out in such a way that there is no winner, is a precarious view to defend: Any contextualist who succeeds in defeating invariantism will conquer Unger's relativism as an automatic corollary, and the same will happen for any invariantist who produces a successful argument against contextualism. But here Unger laid out very carefully the invariantist rival to contextualism, together with an argument that it was, while not superior to contextualism, at least an equal of it. With his 1986 "The Cone Model of Knowledge" (see note 3), Unger finally joined the ranks of the contextualists, but did not counter his earlier arguments that invariantism is superior to or at least the equal of contextualism. Struggling against the invariantist rival that Unger set up remains a main task of contextualism.

6. Contextualism and Skepticism

Contextualist theories of knowledge attributions have almost invariably been developed with an eye toward providing some kind of answer to philosophical skepticism. For many of the most powerful skeptical arguments threaten to show that we just plain don't know what we ordinarily think we know. They thus threaten to establish the startling result that we never, or almost never, truthfully ascribe knowledge to ourselves or to other mere mortals.

But, according to contextualists, the skeptic, in presenting her argument, manipulates the semantic standards for knowledge, thereby creating a context in which she can *truthfully* say that we know nothing or very little. Once the standards have been so raised, we *correctly* sense that we could only falsely claim to know such things as that we have hands. Why then are we puzzled? Why don't we simply accept the skeptic's conclusion and henceforth refrain from ascribing such knowledge to ourselves or others? Because, the contextualist continues, we also realize this: As soon as we find ourselves in more ordinary conversational contexts, it will not only be true for us to claim to know the very things that the skeptic now denies we know, but it will also be *wrong* for us to *deny* that we know these things. But then, isn't the skeptic's present denial equally false? And wouldn't it be equally true for us now, in the skeptic's presence, to claim to know?

What we fail to realize, according to the contextualist solution, is that the skeptic's present denials that we know various things are perfectly *compatible* with our ordinary claims to know those very propositions. Once we realize this, we can see how *both* the skeptic's denials of knowledge *and* our ordinary attributions of knowledge can be correct.

Thus, it is hoped, our ordinary claims to know can be safeguarded from the apparently powerful attack of the skeptic, while, at the same time, the persuasiveness of the skeptical argument is explained. For the fact that the skeptic can install very high standards which we don't live up to has no tendency to show that we don't satisfy the more relaxed standards that are in place in more ordinary conversations and debates.

The success of such an approach to skepticism hinges largely on the contextualist's ability to explain how the skeptic raises the standards for knowledge in the presentation of her argument. If such an explanation can be successfully constructed, such a solution to skepticism can be very attractive, and can provide a powerful motivation for accepting contextualism.[18]

7. The Contextualist Approach to Skepticism and to What Goes On in Conversation

But while philosophical skepticism has drawn much of the attention of contextualists, support for contextualism should also – and perhaps primarily – be looked for in how "knows" is utilized in nonphilosophical conversation. For as I've already noted, we do seem to apply "knows" differently in different contexts, a phenomenon that, at least on the surface, seems to promise significant support for contextualism. And the contextualist's appeal to varying standards for knowledge in his solution for skepticism would rightly seem unmotivated and *ad hoc* if we didn't have independent reason to think such shifts in the content of knowledge attributions occur.

Additionally, the contextualist solution to the skeptical puzzles might fail to do justice to the impact the skeptical arguments can have on us if it were only in the presence of such arguments that the standards for knowledge were shifted upward. Why? Well, it is a fairly natural reaction to the skeptical arguments to suppose that they induce us to raise the standards for knowledge. In most classes of any size in which I've first presented skeptical arguments to introductory students, some of them will pursue such an analysis of the argument's force. Usually, they propose a version of the "Two Senses of 'knows'" theory I mentioned in section 5. Students sometimes label the two senses they posit "weak" and "strong," or sometimes "low" and "high," and once "regular" and "high octane." But though many will suspect that the skeptic is somehow "changing the subject" on us, she certainly isn't doing so in any very obvious way – as is shown by the fact that some students in most introductory classes will reject the suggestion that any such thing is going on. Yet, if there were just two senses of "Knows" – one normal and quite common, and the other very strong and brought on only in contexts in which philosophical skepticism is being discussed – it would probably be quite clear to us that the skeptic was doing something fairly new and different when she started using "knows" in the "high octane" sense, and it would probably be pretty obvious she was "changing the subject" on us, and the arguments wouldn't seem to be a threat to our ordinary knowledge. On the other hand, if, as current contextualists hold, the standards for knowledge vary with context even in ordinary, nonphilosophical conversations, and the skeptic is utilizing mechanisms for the raising of epistemic standards that we're familiar with from such ordinary conversations, then it would seem much more likely that the skeptic's argument would strike us as threatening our knowledge ordinarily so-called, since the skeptic's use of "knows" would much more likely pass for what ordinarily goes on with the use of the term. As Stine writes: "It is an essential characteristic of our concept of knowledge that tighter criteria are appropriate in different contexts. It is one thing in a street encounter, another in a classroom, another in a court of law – and who is to say it cannot be another in a philosophical discussion? . . . We can point out that some philosophers are very perverse in their standards (by *some* extreme standard, there is some reason to think there is an evil genius, after all) – but we cannot legitimately go so far as to say that their perversity has stretched the concept of knowledge out of all recognition – in fact they have played on an essential feature of the concept" (Stine, p. 254).

8. The Warranted Assertability Objection

As already mentioned in section 1, the issue dividing invariantists and contextualists is not whether in different conversational contexts, quite different standards govern whether ordinary speakers *will say* that someone knows something. *Of course*, what we're happy to call knowledge in some ("low-standards") contexts we'll deny is knowledge in other ("high-standards") contexts. The issue is whether these varying standards for when ordinary speakers *will* attribute knowledge, and/or for when they're in some sense *warranted* in attributing knowledge, reflect varying standards for when it is or would be *true* for them to attribute knowledge.

The contextualist will appeal to pairs of cases where the standards for knowledge seem to vary: Low-standards cases in which a speaker seems truthfully to ascribe knowledge to a subject will be paired with high-standards cases in which another speaker in a quite different and more demanding context seems truthfully to describe that same subject as a nonknower. If the contextualist has chosen her pair of cases well, there will be a quite strong intuition about each assertion, at least when it is considered individually, that it is true. The invariantist, of course, cannot accept that both of the speakers' assertions are true, and so must deny a quite strong intuition. But it is often argued, the idea of varying standards for the warranted assertability of knowledge attributions can help the invariantist explain away the intuition that is hostile to her.

How so? Well, it has proven generally fruitful in philosophy to explain away certain intuitions by means of what we may usefully call *warranted assertability maneuvers* (WAMs). Such maneuvers involve explaining why an assertion can seem false in certain circumstances in which it's in fact true by appeal to the fact that the utterance would be improper or unwarranted in the circumstances in question. The idea behind the maneuver is that we mistake this unwarranted assertability for falsehood. Alternatively, but less commonly, an intuition that an assertion is true can be explained away by means of the claim that the assertion, while false, is warranted, and we mistake this warranted assertability for truth. Either way, the maneuver is based on the correct insight that truth-conditions and conditions of warranted assertability are quite different things, but that we can easily mistake one for the other. According to perhaps the most common objection to contextualism – the warranted assertability objection – the contextualist has confused a variance in the warranted assertability conditions of knowledge for a variance in their truth conditions.

To assess the power of this important objection, we should try to develop guidelines for the proper use of WAMs. Toward that end, in the next section, we'll examine a successful and then a patently unsuccessful example of such maneuvers. In section 10, then, we'll seek to draw some general lessons about the conditions under which such maneuvers should be taken seriously. We'll then be in a position, in section 11, to assess the power of the invariant's use of the warranted assertability objection against the contextualist.

9. Warranted Assertability Maneuvers, Good and Bad

When a speaker knows that P, it can seem somehow wrong, and to some it can seem downright false, for her to say "It's possible that P_{ind}." Suppose, for instance, that Kelly knows full well that a certain book is in her office. Suppose

Tom wants to borrow the book, and he asks Kelly whether the book is in her office. Here, it seems somehow wrong for Kelly to assert, "It's possible that the book is in my office." Indeed, pre-theoretically, there's some tendency to think she'd be saying something false. Such tendencies, if unchecked, could tempt one toward a "Don't Know Either Way" (DKEW) account of "It's possible that P_{ind}," according to which:

DKEW: S's assertion, "It's possible that P_{ind}" is true iff (1) S doesn't know that P is false and (2) S doesn't know that P is true.

But this temptation should be resisted, I think, for the correct account lies down the "Don't Know Otherwise" (DKO) path:

DKO: S's assertion, "It's possible that P_{ind}" is true iff (1) S doesn't know that P is false.[19]

According to DKO, Kelly is asserting the truth in our example. The tendency to think she's saying something false can be explained away as follows. Both "P" and "I know that P" are stronger than – they imply but are not implied by – "It's possible that P_{ind}," according to DKO. And there's a very general conversational rule to the effect that when you're in a position to assert either of two things, then, other things being equal, if you assert either of them, you should assert the stronger. Now when someone like Kelly knows that P, then they're usually in position to assert that they know that P, and they're always in a position to assert P itself. Thus, by the "Assert the Stronger" rule, they should assert one of those two things rather than the needlessly weak "It's possible that P_{ind}." To say the weaker thing is to make an inappropriate assertion, and it's this unwarrantedness of the assertion that we're mistaking for falsehood. In the following section, we'll see reasons for thinking that this example of a WAM is quite credible. But even before such reasons are given, I hope you will be able to sense that this maneuver is more successful than the WAM we're about to consider.

Suppose a crazed philosopher of language were to defend the view that the truth-conditions of "S is a bachelor" do not contain any condition to the effect that S be unmarried; rather, the sentence is true iff S is a male. You might think this view is refuted by such facts as that we speakers of English have strong intuitions that assertions of the form "S is a bachelor" are false when they're said of married men, and that, in our linguistic behavior, we'll refrain from saying of any male that we believe is married that he's a bachelor, and in fact will go so far as to deny that he's a bachelor. But our imagined philosopher, though crazed, is not without resources. Suppose he attempts to explain away such facts as follows: "When S is married, it is inappropriate or unwarranted to assert 'S is a bachelor.' We mistake this unwarranted assertability for falsehood. That explains why we find such assertions false when made of married men and why we won't make such assertions about married men."

10. Conditions for Successful Uses of Warranted Assertability Maneuvers

The second WAM above – the one made in defense of the weird theory about the meaning of "bachelor" – is, I hope you can sense, wildly unsuccessful. That's no doubt partly because it's being offered in defense of such a loser of a theory – a theory for which it's difficult to imagine what possible positive support it might have. But it's important for our present purposes to notice the deeper reason why the defensive maneuver has no force here. It's an instance of a general scheme that, if allowed, could be used to far too easily explain away the counterexamples marshalled against *any* theory about the truth-conditions of sentence forms in natural language. Whenever you face an apparent counterexample – where your theory says that what seems false is true, or when it says that what seems true is false – you can very easily just ascribe the apparent truth (falsehood) to the warranted (unwarranted) assertability of the sentence in the circumstances problematic to your theory. If we allow such maneuvers, we'll completely lose our ability to profitably test theories against examples. It would be disastrous to let theories off the hook with respect to putative counterexamples so easily.

Does that mean that we should generally stop putting any faith in WAMs? No. A number of contrasts between the first and the second example of WAMs from the above section will provide some guidelines for when such maneuvers can be accorded some legitimacy. Consider, then, the following features of the first example – the maneuver made on behalf of the DKO approach to "It's possible that P_{ind}."

First, where a speaker knows that P, while it does indeed seem wrong, and may even seem false to some, for her to assert "It's possible that P_{ind}," it seems just as bad – in fact, worse – and certainly seems false, for her to instead say "It's *im*possible that P_{ind}" or "It's *not* possible that P_{ind}." But it seems quite unlikely that *both* "It's possible that P_{ind}" and "It's *not* possible that P_{ind}" are false, so we have good reason to believe that *something* is not as it seems here. So we're going to have to explain away the misleading appearance of falsehood of something. By contrast, in the problem cases for the crazed theory of bachelor (cases involving married males), there's no such pressure to have to explain away any appearances: It seems false to say of married men that they are bachelors, and it seems true to say of them that they are not bachelors. So there appears to be no problem. Given just this, we can see already that the intuition of falsehood that some have about "It's possible that P_{ind}" where the speaker knows that P is a better candidate for explaining away via a WAM than are the intuitions of falsehood regarding the application of "S is a bachelor" to married men.

Second, and closely related, the maneuver used in defense of DKO can appeal to the generation of a *false implicature* to explain the appearance of falsehood. Given that there is an "Assert the Stronger" rule, asserting "It's possible that P_{ind}"

will generate what, following H. P. Grice, has come to be called an *implicature* to the effect that the speaker doesn't know that P.[20] An implicature is not part of "what is said," to use Grice's favorite phrase, in making an assertion, but it is something conveyed by the making of the assertion. In the case of "It's possible that P_{ind}," the listener can, on the assumption that the speaker is following the "Assert the Stronger" rule, calculate that the speaker does not know that P, since if he did, he would have said that he knew that P, or at least would have said that P, rather than the needlessly week "It's possible that P_{ind}." Thus, if a speaker breaks that conversational rule, and asserts "It's possible that P_{ind}" where he knows that P, while he won't have said anything false, he will have conveyed a false implicature to the effect that he doesn't know that P.

Most of the clearly effective WAMs involve explaining away apparent falsehood of an assertion by appeal to the generation of a false implicature. This is not surprising. Where *something* false *is* conveyed by the making of an assertion, it's not surprising that we might mistake that for the assertion's itself being false.

What of the defense of the crazed theory about "bachelor"? As it stands, it doesn't appeal to the generation of a false implicature to explain away apparent falsehood. It's rather an instance of what we may call a "bare warranted assertability maneuver" – a WAM that simply explains away the problematic intuitions of falsehood by claiming the assertions in question are unwarranted or explains away intuitions of truth by appeal to the warranted assertability of the relevant assertions, without further explaining *why* the true assertions are unwarranted or the false ones warranted.

But that's just the explanation as it now stands. It could be beefed up to appeal to the generation of implicatures. Suppose our crazed philosopher were to get even more resourceful, and argue as follows: "There's a conversational rule to the effect that you shouldn't assert 'S is a bachelor' where S is married. Thus, when you make such an assertion, your listener, assuming that you're following the rule, will gather that S is unmarried. Thus, making such an assertion will generate an implicature to the effect that S is unmarried. Where S is married, this implicature is false. That explains why we find such assertions to be false when they're made of married men: We mistake the falsehood of the implicature that the assertion generates for the falsehood of the assertion itself." So the crazed theory regarding "bachelor" can be defended by appeal to implicatures.

But there are two problems with this strategy. The first problem is closely associated with our first contrast between our two WAMs. Our crazed philosopher doesn't only have intuitions of falsehood to explain away, but also intuitions of truth which are problematic to his theory. When we say of a married man that he is not a bachelor, that seems true, but is false according to the crazed theory. Even if you can come up with a good explanation for why the assertion would generate some true implicature, this wouldn't seem to help much. For don't we want to avoid falsehood both in what we implicate and (especially!) in what we actually say? So, it would seem that it would be unwarranted to assert a falsehood, even if doing so generates a true implicature. Thus it's no wonder that most clearly successful WAMs involve explaining away apparent falsehood by appeal to the generation of a false implicature; none I know of involve explaining away apparent truth by appeal to the generation of true implicatures.

Finally, a vitally important contrast between our two WAMs involves *how* they explain the generation of the implicatures to which they appeal. They defense of DKO utilized a very general rule of conversation – "Assert the Stronger" – which applies to assertions of any content.[21] This general rule, together with DKO's account of the content of "It's possible that P_{ind}," generates the implicate that S doesn't know that P. By contrast, the defense of the crazed theory of "bachelor" resorted to positing a *special* rule attaching only to assertions involving the term "bachelor." Again, the danger of making it too easy to sweep away intuitions emerges. *Any* theory which omits what is in fact a truth-condition for a type of assertion could just admit the missing condition, not as a truth-condition, but rather as a condition for warranted assertability that's generated by some special rule that attaches only to assertions containing the relevant term, and then go on to explain away the intuitions of falsehood that the theory will inevitably fall prey to. If such moves are allowed, it's difficult to see how we could ever discern truth-conditions from conditions of warranted assertability. But it's not so easy to generate the implicatures you need to deflect the apparent counterexamples to your theory by means of *general* conversational rules. If your theory is subject to apparent counterexamples where the relevant sentences seem false though your theory says they're true, but if your proposed truth-conditions, together with general rules of conversation, which can be tested on very different sentences, predict that false implicatures will be generated in the circumstances that generate the apparent counterexamples, that seems to have significant potential to mitigate the damage of the apparent counterexamples.

In summary, then, the rather successful defense of DKO starts out with a better candidate for WAMming: An intuition that an assertion is false, where the opposite assertion also seems false, indicating that some intuition here has to be explained away. It then explains away the apparent falsehood of "It's possible that P_{ind}" where the speaker knows that P by means of an appeal to the generation of a false implicature. And it explains how this implicature is generated by means of a very general rule of conversation together with the DKO account of the content of the assertions in question. By contrast, the lame defense of the crazed theory of "bachelor" starts with a bad candidate for WAMming: An intuition that an assertion is false, where the opposite assertion appears to be true, so that our intuitions about both the assertion in question and its opposite would have to be explained away. To the extent that it appeals to the generation of implicatures in its explanations, it has to generate these implicatures by means of special rules that apply only to assertions involving the terms in question. And even then, it runs into trouble with intuitions of truth, where it seems to involve itself in claims that false assertions can be warranted if they generate true implicatures.

11. Evaluation of the Invariantist's Warranted Assertability Maneuver

We can now evaluate the warranted assertability objection to contextualism. If our above investigation of the conditions under which to give credence to WAMs is at all on the right track, then this objection to contextualism is a prime example of a WAM we should *not* give any credence to, since it fails every test we discerned above.

First, in the "high-standards" contexts, we don't just refrain from ascribing knowledge to the same subjects we're happy to call knowers in more lenient contexts; rather, we go so far as to appropriately *deny* that those subjects know. In the "low-standards" contexts, it seems appropriate and it seems true to say that certain subjects know and it would seem wrong and false to deny they know, while in the "high standards" context, it seems appropriate and true to deny that similarly situated subjects know and it seems inappropriate and false to say they do know. Thus, whichever set of appearances the invariantist seeks to discredit – whether she says we're mistaken about the "high" or the "low" contexts – she'll have to explain away both an appearance of falsity and (much more problematically) an appearance of truth. Like our imagined philosopher who defends the crazy theory about the truth conditions of "bachelor" sentences, our invariantist about "knows" is trying to employ a WAM on a set of data that doesn't seem a good candidate for WAMming.

Next, it's difficult to see how the invariantist could appeal to general rules of assertability to explain why the misleading appearances she alleges are generated. Truth be told, the warranted assertability objection against contextualism usually takes the form of a *bare* warranted assertability objection: It's simply claimed that it's the conditions of warranted assertability, rather than of truth, that are varying with context, and the contextualist is then accused of mistaking warranted assertability with truth. To the extent that invariantists go beyond such bare maneuvers, with an exception I'll present in the next paragraph, they seem to appeal to *special* rules for the assertability of "knows," like "If someone is close enough, for present intents and purposes, to being a knower, don't say that she doesn't know, but rather say that she knows." Of course, if he's allowed to appeal to the bare possibility that warranted assertability is being confused with truth or to special rules about the term in question, even our theorist about "bachelor" can rebut the evidence against his theory.

The exception I alluded to is Unger's defense of skeptical invariantism in *Ignorance*, which does a bit better by our criteria for successful WAMs. While Unger didn't appeal there to a fully general conversational rule like "Assert the Stronger," he did attempt to treat "knows" as an instance of a *fairly* wide group of terms which he called "absolute" terms. A precise exposition of where and how Unger drew the line between absolute and other terms is beyond the scope of the present short paper. It will suffice for our purposes to note that it was indeed a fairly wide group of terms, that included among their number such terms as "flat," "dry," "straight," "empty," and "square." Thus, while Unger held the skeptical invariantist position that for any assertion of "S knows that P" to be true, S must be in such a strong epistemic position with respect to P that it is impossible that anyone should be better positioned with respect to any proposition than S is positioned with respect to P, with the result that none or almost none of our attributions of knowledge are true, he did not thereby make "knows" an "isolated freak" of our language, as he put it. For he held similar views about other absolute terms like "flat," according to which surfaces had to meet very stringent, absolute standards of flatness for a sentence describing them as "flat" to be true. In general, then, according to this view, positive assertions containing absolute terms (like "S knows that P" or "X is flat") have incredibly demanding truth-conditions, making most of our uses of such assertions false, but, in general, when the person, object, or situation being described comes *close enough* for present conversational intents and purposes to satisfying the demanding criteria for the application of the relevant absolute term, it is warranted for one to falsely assert that the surface is flat, that the person knows, etc.

The Unger of *Ignorance*, then, is not subject to the charge of appealing to a special rule for the warranted assertability of "knows." Consequently, Unger's defense of invariantism is on firmer ground than the WAMs that are typically leveled against contextualism. However, several features of Unger's old invariantism work together to make it unattractive.

First, Unger's invariantism is a *skeptical* invariantism. Most who reject the contextualist's varying standards, I think, don't imagine that the constant standards they endorse will be so demanding as to be unmeetable by mere mortals. However, it's unclear, to say the least, that a general invariantism about absolute terms of the kind Unger mounts could be used in defense of a moderate or nonskeptical invariantism, according to which the constant standards that govern the truth-conditions of sentences containing absolute terms will be meetably low, for such a moderate account will not be able to utilize Unger's account of assertability going by whether the belief in question is *close enough* to being knowledge to be appropriately called such. Second, the cost of the generality of Unger's account is that the impossibly demanding standards and the resulting systematic falsehood in what we say spreads to a large stretch of our language. Thus, we end up speaking falsely whenever we describe a physical surface as "flat," or when we apply any number of "absolute" terms in the way we're accustomed to applying them. I'm fairly confident that most would find a general contextualist approach to absolute terms far more plausible than such a relentlessly demanding invariantist approach. Finally, by not utilizing a thoroughly general rule which has clearly correct applications like "Assert the Stronger," the Unger of *Ignorance* loses a lot of leverage in advocating his view. His rule of assertability would be something like: "When x is close enough, for present conversational intents and purposes, to satisfying the semantic requirements for 'F,' where 'F' is an absolute term, it is appropriate to describe x as being F." But a general contextualist account of the use of what Unger calls "absolute" terms which avoids the systematic falsehood is available, and so it's difficult to see where the pressure to accept a demanding invariantist account will come from. By contrast, a WAM that utilizes a rule like "Assert the Stronger," will have the advantage of being based on a rule that we are independently motivated to accept. Thus, I don't think many will be tempted by Unger's old approach.

Most who let considerations like those embodied in the Warranted Assertability Objection dissuade them from accepting contextualism don't see themselves as accepting anything so radical as Unger's general approach of relentless stringency and systemic falsehood for large stretches of our language. But then, as far as I can see, they are being moved by nothing more than a bare WAM that miserably fails to meet all the reasonable criteria we can discern for what it would take for a WAM to be successful. Of course, some invariantist may be able to more successfully explain away the facts supportive of contextualism in a way that I can't see. But to date, there's been no such explanation that I am aware of. And even if a general rule can be found to do *some* of the damage control that the invariantist needs done, the generation of implicatures seems to hold promise only for explaining away the intuitions of falsehood that the invariantist must reject, and seems powerless against the intuitions of truth that any invariantist will find lined up against his position, for reasons we have already seen. The Warranted Assertability Objection to contextualism, in short, seems to be a paradigm case of a powerless WAM.

Notes

1 A notable exception to this is Stephen Schiffer's "Contextualist Solutions to Scepticism," *Proceedings of the Aristotelian Society* 96 (1996): 317–33. I do not here respond to Schiffer's criticisms. Schiffer's criticisms raise important issues about the viability of what he calls "hidden indexical" accounts of various types of sentences. I am eager to defend not only contextualism about knowledge attributions, but also hidden indexical accounts of attitude ascriptions, from Schiffer's attacks (see esp. pp. 510–19 of Schiffer, "Belief Ascription," *Journal of Philosophy* 89 (1992): 499–521), but such a defense, if it were to be at all adequate to the task, would be far too extensive for the present paper.
2 See Peter Unger, *Philosophical Relativity* (Minneapolis, MN: University of Minnesota Press, 1984).
3 See Cohen, "Knowledge, Context, and Social Standards," *Synthese* 73 (1987): 3–26; Cohen, "How to be a Fallibilist," *Philosophical Perspectives* 2 (1988): 91–123; DeRose, "Contextualism and Knowledge Attributions," *Philosophy and Phenomenological Research* 52 (1992): 913–29; DeRose, "Solving the Skeptical Puzzle," *Philosophical Review* 104 (1995): 1–52; Lewis, "Scorekeeping in a Language Game," *Journal of Philosophical Logic* 8 (1979): 339–59, esp. Example 6, "Relative Modality," pp. 354–5; Lewis, "Elusive Knowledge," *Australasian Journal of Philosophy* 74 (1996): 549–67; and Unger, "The Cone Model of Knowledge," *Philosophical Topics* 14 (1986):

125–78. Gail Stine advocates a contextualist version of the "Relevant Alternatives" theory of knowledge in Stine, "Skepticism, Relevant Alternatives, and Deductive Closure," *Philosophical Studies* 29 (1976): 249–61. Fred Dretske is another prominent relevant alternativist, but whether he's a contextualist is extremely difficult issue. I won't here go into a long, inconclusive story about this matter, but will content myself with pointing the reader to the most enlightening material on it: See pp. 191 (starting with the paragraph that begins "This brings me to the very important distinction...") –196 of Dretske, "Dretske's Replies," in Brian P. McLaughlin, ed., *Dretske and His Critics* (Cambridge, MA: Blackwell, 1991). *Editor's note*: versions of contextualism are also endorsed by Williams and Longino in their essays in this volume.

4   Lewis, *Counterfactuals* (Cambridge, MA: Harvard University Press, 1973), p. 92; the full sentence, and the sentence which precedes it, which are about the link between similarity and counterfactual conditionals, read: "I am not one of those philosophers who seek to rest fixed distinctions upon a foundation quite incapable of supporting them. I rather seek to rest an unfixed distinction upon a swaying foundation, claiming that the two sway together rather than independently."

5   The subscript "ind" indicates that the embedded P is to be kept in the indicative mood: very different possibilities are expressed where the P is subjective. The subjunctive, "It's possible that I should not have existed," is just plain good sense, while the indicative "It's possible that I don't exist" is bizarre.

6   A more exact analysis of the sentence would still involve the concept of knowledge in a way that, though more complicated, doesn't ruin the point I'm making. See DeRose, "Epistemic Possibilities," *Philosophical Review* 100 (1991): 581–605 for such a more exact analysis.

7   For more on contextualism and statements of possibility, see ch. 2, section V ("Contextualism and Epistemic Modal Statements") of my *Knowledge, Epistemic Possibility, and Scepticism* (Ph.D. diss., University of California, Los Angeles, 1990; University Microfilms International order number 9035253), and my "Simple *Might*'s, Indicative Possibilities, and the Open Future," *Philosophical Quarterly*, 1998, especially section 3 ("The Second Problem, the Context-Sensitivity of Knowledge, and the Methodology of Flat-Footed, 'All-in-One-Breath' Conjunctions").

8   Though "It's certain that P" *is* the dual of "It's possible that P_{ind}," it doesn't mean just that the speaker knows that P, because the provisional analysis of "It's possible that P_{ind}" as simply being a matter of the speaker not knowing otherwise is just a first approximation, and so isn't exactly correct. For a more exact account of the meaning of "It's certain that P," see my "Simple *Might*'s," esp. section 8 ("It's Certain That"). Expressions of the form "S is certain that...", where S is a subject – expressions of *personal* certainty – of course, are a completely different matter.

9   In "Elusive Knowledge," Lewis explicitly denies that justification is even necessary for knowledge. It's still open to him, of course, to be a contextualist about justification, but if he were to go that route, this contextualism would be independent from his contextualism regarding knowledge.

10 David Annis, "A Contextualist Theory of Epistemic Justification," *American Philosophical Quarterly* 15 (1978): 213–19.

11 As of now, I haven't seen this in print, though I've read several papers in manuscript that mark this distinction, some of them with exactly those labels. (When those exact labels are used, their use *may* derive from my distinction between "subject

factors" and "attributor factors" in part II of DeRose, "Contextualism and Knowledge Attributions.")
12. This case appeared prominently in Alvin Goldman, "Discrimination and Perceptual Knowledge," *The Journal of Philosophy* 73 (1976): 771–91. On p. 252 of Stine, "Skepticism, Relevant Alternatives, and Deductive Closure," it is reported that Goldman attributes the example to Ginet.
13. Norman Malcolm, "Knowledge and Belief," *Mind* 51 (1952): 178–89.
14. Peter Unger, *Ignorance: A Case for Scepticism* (Oxford: Oxford University Press, 1975). This book incorporates, with some improvements, Unger's important journal articles from the early 1970s, while adding new material as well.
15. Barry Stroud, *The Significance of Philosophical Scepticism* (Oxford: Oxford University Press, 1984).
16. See especially Cohen, "How to be a Fallibilist."
17. For more on the relationship between RA and contextualism, see part II of DeRose, "Contextualism and Knowledge Attributions," and also DeRose, "Relevant Alternatives and the Content of Knowledge Attributions," *Philosophy and Phenomenological Research* 56 (1996): 193–7.
18. For much more on the contextualist approach to skepticism, see DeRose, "Solving the Skeptical Problem."
19. This account is on the right path (the DKO path), but is not correct as it stands. See DeRose, "Epistemic Possibilities," for my best attempt at the truth conditions of "It's possible that P_{ind}."
20. See esp. "Logic and Conversation," in H. P. Grice, *Studies in the Way of Words* (Cambridge, MA: Harvard University Press, 1989).
21. Don't mistake generality for exceptionlessness. Though the rule is very general, there are occasions on which one should not assert the stronger, as is pointed out in section 2 of Frank Jackson, "On Assertion and Indicative Conditionals," *Philosophical Review* 88 (1979): 565–89.

Chapter 9

Rationality

Keith Lehrer

Man is a rational animal, or so says Aristotle.[1] But what is rationality? It is the use of reason to reach a certain level of reasonableness or unreasonableness. To be rational is to be extremely reasonable as to be irrational is to be extremely unreasonable. The varieties of rationality and distinctions about rationality are many. First of all, there is a distinction between practical and theoretical rationality. Secondly, there is a distinction between synchronic or static rationality and diachronic or dynamic rationality. Thirdly, there is a distinction between personal rationality and interpersonal rationality. Combinations of these kinds of rationality yield eight kinds of rationality:

Practical, personal, static
Practical, personal, dynamic
Practical, interpersonal, static
Practical, interpersonal, dynamic
Theoretical, personal, static
Theoretical, personal, dynamic
Theoretical, interpersonal, static
Theoretical, interpersonal, dynamic.

Other distinctions and refinements are possible, but the understanding of these must suffice here. Let us begin our account with the personal synchronic form of rationality. There is no assumption that this form of rationality is philosophically prior to the others, but it is a traditional starting point and an illuminating one.

1. Practical Rationality

Let us consider personal practical rationality at a moment in time. This is ordinarily rationality about what one does, intends to do, or simply prefers to do. Practical rationality of this kind as well as of other kinds is concerned with evaluation in terms of reason. Evaluations are based on some objective, the objective of obtaining something that has worth, merit, or is simply desirable. A person incapable of evaluating in terms of reason may act as a rational person would act, he may act as if he were himself rational, but he would be neither rational nor irrational. A rational person is one who follows reason, and the role of reason is to evaluate what one does or would do.

The traditional view of this role of reason is one that considers reason as reflective activity. Reason sorts beliefs into those that are rational and those that are irrational, allowing, perhaps, for some that are neutral. This activity of reason involves thinking about beliefs which transcends the first level of belief to a higher level, a metalevel, of thought about them. That is a view I embrace, but I think it should be left open whether reason must always operate at the metalevel or whether it can operate at the first level alone.[2] In the latter case, one belief would lead us to revise others by a sequence of reasoning all on one level.

One standard view of rationality, advanced most notably by Hume, might be called the instrumental theory of rationality. It affirms that reason is only an instrument serving some end or other.[3] A person is rational in preferring or doing something on the instrumental view of rationality if and only if what is preferred or done is a rational means to an end, that is, a means one would adopt to reason in pursuit of an end. There are two immediate objections to such a view. In the first place, what is preferred or done might be preferred or done as an end, not a means to an end. Secondly, a question of the rationality of pursuing the end remains open. The two objections are closely connected. If what is preferred or done is preferred or done as an end, it would not be rational on the instrumental view. That does not, of course, mean that it is irrational, for it may be that things preferred or done as an end are neither rational nor irrational. Yet if the end is not rational, then it seems as though the adoption of a means to purse it might fail to be rational as a result, even though it was an effective means for attaining the end.

The instrumental theory of rationality implies another thesis advanced by Hume; that reason only serves our ends and, thus, cannot evaluate them. I will refer to this thesis as that of the autonomy of ends.[4] Ends are autonomous in the life of reason and not subject to evaluation of reason to ascertain whether they are rational or not.

Why should a philosopher subscribe to the thesis of the autonomy of ends? There are two reasons. The first is what one might call the incompleteness of judgments of rationality. When a person is judged by another to be irrational in what they have done, one might be inclined to inquire for what purpose the person acted before accepting the judgment. A person might seem irrational until we know what they sought and then seem irrational no longer. A person might seem irrational to fill a drawer with candy wrappers until one learns that after accumulating ten thousand one may receive a trip to Hawaii.

The other reason for accepting the autonomy of ends is the regress argument. One may do one thing to obtain a second, the second to obtain a third, and so forth, but eventually it appears that the sequence must terminate in some end one seeks for itself. That end must be valued in itself or one will be led into an infinite regress in the life of reason. There are other reasons that might be offered in defense of the autonomy of ends, but these two are the most salient. Whether one is rational on the instrumental theory, depends on what one is seeking, and what one seeks must end with something one seeks as an end in itself.[5]

Must we agree to the instrumental theory of rationality and to the implied autonomy of ends? Notice that the incompleteness of judgments of rationality only reveals that the rationality of what we do depends upon what ends we seek, but it does not prove that a person cannot be irrational to pursue some ends. A person who does something in pursuit of some irrational end, if such there be, may be judged irrational in what she does even if what she does is a rational means to the attainment of her irrational end. So the incompleteness argument is, itself, incomplete.

Can it be supported and sustained with the regress argument? This is a more difficult question, but once again the answer must be negative. A person cannot run through an infinity of reasons for doing something, to be sure, but the rationality of pursuing some end might be the result of some system of preferences providing a reason for seeking each thing that one seeks.

Standard expected utility maximization accounts of rationality such as Jeffrey's may be considered as offering such a system.[6] Suppose that a person has pairwise preferences that are complete and coherent over all alternatives. This implies that for any two alternatives, a person either prefers one to the other or is indifferent. From such preferences, using Bayesian methods, one can extrapolate a utility function over alternatives and a probability function over propositions. A rational person on such an account is one who maximizes expected utility. The details of such accounts take us beyond our current study, but the intuitive idea is that being able to compare pairwise enables one to extrapolate to degrees of preference, utilities, and to degrees of belief, probabilities. The choice that maximizes expectation, measured as a product of utility and probability of attaining it, is rational. Other less idealized mathematical accounts are possible based on comparative preferences. If I prefer some alternative to any that competes with it, then, in terms of those preferences, it is rational for me to choose the preferred alternatives. To say that does not commit one to the view that every preference is based on some set of ends valued in themselves. It only requires that I be able to coherently systematize my preferences.

Such a view faces an objection, however. It is that the preferences, the basic pairwise comparisons, may themselves be irrational. If a person maximizes expected utility when the preferences of the person, though coherent, are irrational, then the utilities and probabilities on which the maximization of expected utilities is based might be irrational, indeed, they might be quite mad. It is important, however, to realize that an appeal to some ends valued in themselves is not the remedy for this defect, and the reason is obvious. What is valued in itself by someone who is irrational may yield coherent preferences but still be quite mad.

I might prefer some end to all others, the end of collecting used chewing gum and pasting it in an album, for example, and be quite mad to do so. The conclusion is that mere instrumental rationality, whether conceived of in terms of a traditional conception of means and ends or in a modern version of expected utility, has a defect concerning the rationality of what we seek, the rationality of our preferences, and that is the problem which must be solved. An appeal to what is valued in itself does not solve the problem. The problem only reiterates at the level of ends valued in themselves. Why are they rational? If you answer, "They just are!," admitting there is no rational explanation of why it is rational to pursue what are valued as ends, you have only replaced a regress with a surd.

The foregoing reflections may reveal why philosophers have been instrumentalists concerning reason and embraced the doctrine of the autonomy of ends. They have thought it hopeless to attempt to provide an account of the rationality of ends, for, whatever end might be proposed, like the preferences based upon them, raises the question of rationality anew. Why is that end rational? And what could one do by way of answering other than to appeal to yet another end which will only lead to another question of the same sort. Rather than seeking ends that are rational in themselves, which we can never establish, it is better to admit that reason can only serve as an instrument for the adoption of means or, in modern dress, the maximization of expected utility. Why begin asking questions that can never be answered? Better to admit the limitations of reason than set it an impossible task.

There is, however, an alternative to instrumentalism which may have been chosen by those who are often cited as advocates of it, Aristotle, for example, who championed the practical syllogism as a source of rational choice.[7] The alternative avoids the regress and the surd. It is Aristotle who said that man is a rational animal. The theory that avoids the regress and the surd is contained in this simple claim, for it places the rationality of the person in a central position. Suppose we begin with the assumption that the person is rational. This provides us with a reason for concluding that the ends or preferences of the person are rational, namely, that the person is rational. One may, of course, inquire why the person is rational, and part of the answer, naturally, is that the evaluations of the person in the use of reason are rational. So the preferences are rational because the person is rational, and the person is rational, in part, because the preferences are rational. The noose of the circle is so tight it threatens to strangle the life of reason in a loop.

We can loosen the loop quite readily, however. The rationality of the preferences is explained by the rationality of the person.[8] It is the rationality of the person that makes the preferences rational and is explanatory. Of course, a rational person must make rational evaluations, but it is the rationality of the person that explains the rationality of all the rest. Though the rationality of the preferences confirms the conclusion that the person is rational, and other preferences would have disconfirmed it, it is the rationality of the person that explains the rationality of the preferences and not vice versa. As an analogy, consider the fact that the law of gravitation explains the motion of two bodies, though the motion of the two bodies confirms the law.

Consider the following argument for the rationality of preference:

1. I am rational.
2. I prefer that A.
3. I am rational in what I prefer. (From 1)
4. I am rational in my preference that A. (From 2 and 3)
5. I prefer that A as a means to end E.
6. I am rational in my preference of A as a means to E. (From 4)

It is clear that premise 1 is the master premise. There are questions raised by the inferences from this premise. Premise 3, for example, is not a valid deductive consequence of premise 1, for even if I am rational, it would be a rash conclusion that I am rational in everything I prefer. The inference is nondeductive, it is inductive and explicative, but the most fundamental question is how we can justify the acceptance and deployment of the premise. Is it just a surd? When I am asked why I accept that premise, must I reply, "I just do!" or be lost in an infinite regress? To answer these questions we must turn from a discussion of practical rationality to theoretical rationality, for the question of why it is rational to accept a premise is a theoretical question.

2. Theoretical Rationality

The questions about theoretical rationality resemble those of practical rationality with, perhaps, one difference. Practical rationality is concerned with preference and action. Theoretical rationality is concerned with reasoning and acceptance. Just as we ask about the purposes of preference and action of a person and withhold judgment of rationality until we understand what the person seeks in preference and action, so we ask about the purposes of reasoning and acceptance of a person and withhold judgments of rationality until we understand what the person seeks in reasoning and acceptance. The difference is that one purpose is assumed in reasoning and acceptance when none is specified, and that is the purpose of reaching what is true by reasoning and accepting it as well. It would be a mistake, of course, to suppose that the objective of accepting what is true, of accepting something if and only if it is true, is one that naturalizes rationality, for truth is part of semantics, not natural science, and is problematic from a naturalistic standpoint in the same way that rationality is.

Nevertheless, the sematicizing of rationality in terms of the truth objective is a natural one. As a result, the end of reasoning and acceptance and, hence, of theoretical rationality, is often assumed to be truth in a way that closes the question of the end of theoretical rationality and escapes the regress of ends at the outset. Moreover, given truth as the end, reason becomes an instrument to that end and an instrumental view of theoretical rationality is assumed. This view has not taken the field in philosophy without dispute, however, and this reveals a secret in the heart of theoretical reason.

Some have thought other things more worthy than truth as an objective; explanatory power and informative content are two salient examples.[9] In fact, we often risk error for these other purposes in what we accept in scientific contexts. The history of scientific theories would teach us that the primary theory of the day, even that advanced by Newton, turned out to be false, and, by reasoning, we should conclude that the theory of our day will also turn out to be false. But we accept it, nonetheless, admitting the high probability of error, for the explanatory power and informative content of it. If our only goal is to accept a theory if and only if it is true, it looks as though we should suspend judgement when we reflect on the part of the objective that directs us to accept something only if it is true. We might try to escape the objection by affirming that the goal contains two subgoals, (a) accepting something if it is true, and (b) not accepting it if it is not true, which draw us in opposite directions. Part (a) would lead us to venture acceptance freely to capture truths while part (b) would lead us to always withhold acceptance to avoid error, but to pursue both we need to balance our interest in these two parts of the truth objective. Once we join this path of reflection, however, we note that there is more to the objective of theoretical rationality than we at first suppose.

Our theoretical goal is, in fact, to reason and accept what is worth concluding and accepting, and, though it is often the truth that is worth accepting and concluding, that is not all there is to the matter. First of all, as we have noted, risking the truth for other theoretical purposes cannot be ruled illegitimate at the outset. Secondly, and perhaps crucially, there is more to rationality than simply accepting what is true. Suppose we accept what is true but for the wrong reasons, for reasons not worthy of our trust. Then, though we may be successful in the quest for truth, we may be irrational. If I believe someone I know to be a fool, who happens in one bit of foolish luck to be right, I may be irrational to accept what I do, what the fool tells me, though I believe what is true. Moreover, the single instance of unreasonably accepting what is true may be multiplied with a bit of imagination. Imagine a foolish enthusiast of philosophical study, Cardupe by name, who reads the *Meditations* of Descartes.[10] Where Descartes describes the powerful demon to aid the hyperbolic doubt, Cardupe thinks Descartes is claiming there is such a demon, and, enthralled with Descartes, concludes Descartes is right. He resolves to formulate all his beliefs to accommodate this marvelous insight, and, when he is inclined to believe something, is careful instead to prefix his belief with the demonic prefix, "The demon is deceiving me into believing that . . ." Cardupe is diligent in his consistency, as the foolish may be, and always adds the cardupian prefix. If there were a demon of the sort that Descartes described, Cardupe would be right always and we wrong, but he would not be rational in what he accepts with all his prefixes no matter what the truth of the matter.

The fact is that we seek to reason and accept what is worth concluding and accepting in a way that is worthy of our trust. To put the matter in the first person, I seek to reason and accept what is worth concluding and accepting. In many cases, truth coincides with what is worth accepting. False explanation and false information are often unworthy of our reasoning and acceptance, though not always, as Newton illustrates; but the examples we have considered show that there is no simple reduction of theoretical rationality to reasoning and acceptance directed at truth.

Are we left with the choice of the regress or the surd as we confront the problems attached to theoretical rationality? We can avoid both. Again, let me take the first-person perspective and begin with the assumption that I am rational. The argument concerning theoretical rationality proceeds as follows:

1. I am rational.
2. I accept that P.
3. I am rational in what I accept. (From 1)
4. I am rational in my acceptance that P. (From 2 and 3)
5. I accept that P as a means to truth.
6. I am rational in my acceptance that P as a means to truth. (From 4)

The argument depends primarily on premise 3 which is inferred from premise 1. This inference, like the inference from 2 and 3 to 4, is inductive and explicative and not deductive for reasons that are soon to be explained. It is clear, however, that premises 1 and 3 are key premises. These premises are ones that are themselves accepted, of course, and the question arises as to whether it is rational to accept them and why it is rational to accept them. Must we reply when asked why it is rational to accept 1, "It just is!" and remain content with an unexplained surd?

We may, in fact, avoid the surd. Suppose that the variable P in the argument is replaced with premise 1 in the argument. We then obtain the following sequence:

1. I am rational.
2. I accept that I am rational.
3. I am rational in what I accept. (From 1)
4. I am rational in my acceptance that I am rational. (From 2 and 3)
5. I accept that I am rational as a means to truth.
6. I am rational in my acceptance that I am rational as a means to truth. (From 4)

What the argument shows, is that if I am rational, then I am rational to accept that I am, and, in fact, my rationality explains why I am rational to accept that I am. My rationality in accepting that I am rational is explained by my rationality in what I accept. This explanation contains a loop to be sure. My rationality in accepting that I am rational is ultimately explained by my rationality itself. Is that a critical defect in the argument?

The explanation, though circular, avoids the surd. The rationality of accepting what I accept is not something assumed without explanation. Moreover, explanation must either be regressive, looping, or end with a surd. The argument exhibits the advantage of the loop. My use of the premise of my rationality in the argument yields the conclusion that it is rational to accept the premise along with other things that I accept. Finally, this feature of the premise of rationality is not shared by premises in general. My use of the premise that I am Keith Lehrer does not yield the conclusion that it is rational for me to accept the premise. To reach that, I require the first and third premises in the argument above. The loop implicit in premise 1 yields an explanation of why it is rational to accept that premise. Of course, the loop in the argument implies that it is ineffective against a skeptic who denies that I am rational, for it would beg the question against the skeptic to argue in a circle. But we are here concerned to explain why we are rational, not to prove the skeptic wrong.

We noted that in both arguments, the argument of practical rationality and the argument of theoretical rationality, there are inferences that are nondeductive. The inference from

I am rational

to either

I am rational in what I prefer

or

I am rational in what I accept

Is not deductive because my being rational does not logically entail that I am rational in everything I do. My being rational describes a disposition to be rational in what I do. Thus, the conclusions that I am rational in what I do, in what I accept, in what I prefer, are inferred inductively, not deductively, from the premise describing the disposition. Similarly, the inference form

I am rational in what I prefer

and

I prefer that P

to

I am rational to prefer that P

and from

I am rational in what I accept

and

>I accept that P

to

>I am rational to accept that P

are not deductive for the same reason. The premises

>I am rational in what I prefer

and

>I am rational in what I accept

describe dispositions to be rational in my preferences and acceptances respectively but do not logically entail that I am rational in everything that I prefer or accept.

3. The Rationality of Reasoning

This reflection reveals the relationship between rationality and reasoning. The conclusions of both arguments are, of course, the result of reasoning and assume the rationality of my reasoning. This leaves me with the problem of explaining the rationality of reasoning, and it raises the same problem of the regress or the surd concerning the rationality of reasoning that we faced concerning the rationality of preference and acceptance. Happily, the solution to the problem is again found in a loop.

I again begin with the premise of my rationality and reach the conclusion of the rationality of how I reason, including how I reason to the rationality of the premise of my rationality. Consider the argument for the rationality of how I reason as follows:

1. I am rational.
2. I reason that P.
3. I am rational in how I reason. (From 1)
4. I am rational in my reasoning that P. (From 2 and 3)
5. I reason that P as a means to reaching truth.
6. I am rational in my reasoning that P as a means to reaching truth. (From 4)

Now, if it is inquired whether I am rational in reasoning from 1, which is part of my reasoning, I can substitute for the variable P premise 1 itself and reach the conclusions

>I am rational in my reasoning that I am rational

and ultimately

> I am rational in my reasoning that I am rational as a means to reaching the truth.

This argument is a solution to the problem of induction and the problem of deduction as well, for these are the problems of explaining how reasoning is rational.[11] What explains why it is rational for me to reason to the conclusion that I am rational is my rationality itself. It is my rationality that explains why I am rational in what I prefer, accept, and how I reason. Of course, the rationality of instances of my acceptance, preference, and reasoning confirm the conclusion of my rationality, but it is my rationality that explains my rationality of preference, acceptance, and reasoning.

4. Diachronic Rationality

The preceding argument reaches to practical and theoretical rationality that is personal and synchronic. We immediately see the need for transcending this level of argumentation when we ask what makes a person rational. For it is immediately clear that the arguments presented above, though they yield conclusions about my rationality, cannot explain what makes me rational. The arguments yield the conclusion that I am rational in what I accept and prefer and how I reason, but arguing in this way is not sufficient to make me rational. Indeed, the argument depends on the premise of my rationality. A person who was not rational might argue in this way as well as a person who is. So what makes a person rational? The answer must take us beyond the synchronic to the diachronic, and leads immediately to a paradox.

Diachronic rationality is rationality in the way in which we change what we prefer, accept, and how we reason. Moreover, our synchronic rationality obviously depends on our improvement in the way in which we do these things which results from the way in which we change how we do these things. Our ability to correct our errors and learn from experience by reflection upon it explains how we acquire the disposition to be rational in what we do, in what we prefer, in what we accept, in how we reason, at present. This immediately leads to the paradox of diachronic reason. For we assume at each time, including the present time, that we are rational, but each time we have assumed this in the past as the first premise of the argument for rationality we have subsequently changed our disposition concerning what we prefer, accept, and how we reason. If, however, we change our disposition, then it appears as though we were not rational before changing and, therefore, that the first premise of our rationality is false each time we use it. The paradox is that it appears that we assume that we are rational to reach the conclusion that we are not.

The solution to the paradox depends on realizing that our synchronic rationality depends on our commitment to the rationality of the way in which we change, indeed our synchronic rationality consists, in part, of our rationality in the way in which we change what we prefer, what we accept, and how we reason. Our disposition to change in these ways is essential to our rationality. I am, to return to the first person, committed to the principle:

> I am rational in the way I change what I prefer, what I accept and how I reason.

Synchronic rationality includes dynamic rationality and is impossible without it.

That is not the end of the diachronic problem, however. For just as I change what I prefer, what I accept, and how I reason, I also change my method of change, that is, I change the way I change. I am, therefore, committed to the further simpler and more general principle:

> I am rational in the way I change.

Notice the looping character of this principle. For it yields not only the preceding principle concerning the rationality of change of preference, acceptance, and reasoning but also contains a principle of rationality in the way in which we change these, the way in which we change how we change. Synchronic rationality depends upon and is explained by dynamic rationality. It is this principle of dynamic rationality that avoids paradox and regress in an explanatory loop of rationality.

My being rational consists in part of a disposition to prefer, accept, and reason in specific ways at the present moment but also, and most fundamentally, of a disposition toward change. Diachronic rationality incorporates the dynamic rationality of change. The paradox of diachronic reason is solved by including the dynamic rationality of change in synchronic rationality. I am now rational if and only if I am rational in what I now do (what I prefer, what I accept, how I reason) and rational in the way I change (what I prefer, what I accept, how I reason). Synchronic rationality must include diachronic rationality. We are rational because we are rational in how we change. It is the rationality of the way we change that rescues rationality in the moment, in the evanescent present, from its present errors and defects by self-correction and improvement.[12]

5. Social Rationality

Having moved from personal synchronic rationality to diachronic rationality, we must now go beyond the individual to society and find the proper connection between them. My being rational depends on the rationality of others, for they inform and correct what I prefer, what I accept, how I reason, and even how I change the way I do these things. At the same time, I must evaluate the rationality of others and be rational in how I do this, or I will be misinformed and led into error. Thus, I need the principle:

I am rational in how I evaluate the rationality of others.

This leaves us with a principle of the personal rationality of the evaluation of the rationality of others and does not take us beyond that to interpersonal rationality. We need the principles:

We are rational

and

We are rational in how we change

to reach the conclusions that we are rational in what we prefer, what we accept, how we reason, and in the way we change the way we do these things. But what is the connection between the personal first premise

I am rational

and the interpersonal first premise

We are rational?

As soon as we attempt to explain the connection we reach a paradox of interpersonal rationality. For if the group referred to by *we* prefers, accepts, or reasons in a way contrary to the way in which I reason, and I am a member of that group, then my personal first premise of rationality seems refuted by the rationality of the group. Now, if the group does not include me, then I can remain an outsider and an iconoclast. But the use of *we* is a problem, for that includes me, for I am one of us. This is more than a grammatical point. The dispositions of a group which make them rational must be an amalgamation of the dispositions of individuals composing it, of that there can be no doubt. On the other hand, the dispositions of individuals reflect their social evaluations and commitments. The social mind is an aggregation of individual minds, while individual minds are essentially social.

The individual and society compose a kind of dynamic duo. Individuals reasonably evaluate the rationality of each other, and the amalgamation of the process of evaluation yields a common or consensual disposition.[13] Thus, in the simplest case, the disposition of the group, of us, is the simple sum of the dispositions of members of the group. There is an exact coincidence between the personal and the interpersonal. But there are often times at which consensus fails, the process of evaluation is incomplete and yields a decomposition of dispositions into the dissenting dispositions of individuals. And yet, we are rational, for we may be rational to disagree and to accept our disagreement.

Is there, nonetheless, some rational summary of what we accept or prefer in the case of decomposition of the group into dissenting dispositions of individuals? All that is left is a kind of fictional *we* based on an averaging of the members of the group. We are like the average person in a society and so is our rationality. There are, nevertheless, truths about us, about that social fiction, as there are about the average person, though they are truths about no single person. No one in a group may have the character of the average person. No one, for example, may have 2.1 children. There is, therefore, a truth about dispositions of the fictional *we* which constitute our rationality even when we fail to achieve consensus.[14] We may be more rational than any one of us considered alone.

Looked at from the first person in the present moment, I proceed to prefer, accept, and reason as I do, and reasonably so, for I am rational in the present moment. I know, however, that my rationality commits me to dynamic change correcting and improving what I now do as past changes corrected and improved what I did to yield what I now do. Similarly, I know that my rationality commits me to social change correcting and improving what I now do as the past social changes corrected and improved what I did to yield what I now do. My relationship to others resembles my relationship to the future. There is a continuing interaction between the present and future, between the personal and the interpersonal, that creates and recreates what it is for me to be rational and for us to be rational. It is, finally, my and our commitment to prefer, accept, and reason about our rationality that makes us rational as well, thus revealing the loop of reason and rationality.

I have spoken of the first premise of our rationality. But this is not a foundation on which all is built. It is an explanatory premise confirmed by other premises, for I am rational because of my disposition concerning what I prefer, accept, how I reason, how I change, and how I evaluate others. The first premise of my rationality allows me to conclude that I am rational in these undertakings and explains my rationality in them, but it is the character of my disposition toward these undertakings that makes me rational. The premise of my rationality is like a triangular keystone set in the top of an arch. Without it the arch collapses, but the keystone is supported by the other stones in the arch. The first premise of my rationality is supported by what I prefer, what I accept, how I reason, how I change, and how I evaluate others. To be rational, I must be worthy of my trust in all these undertakings, disposed in a way that makes me trustworthy in them all, including the conclusion of my rationality in what I prefer, what I accept, how I reason, how I change, and how I evaluate others.

That is the story of my and our rationality.

Notes

1 Aristotle, *Nicomachean Ethics*, trans. David Ross (Oxford: Oxford University Press, 1991), I.7 ff., and *On the Soul*, trans. W. S. Hett (Cambridge, MA: Harvard University Press, 1986), 414a ff.
2 Keith Lehrer, *Self-Trust: A Study of Reason, Knowledge and Autonomy* (Oxford: Clarendon Press, 1997), esp. ch. 1. Keith Lehrer, *Metamind* (Oxford: Clarendon Press, 1990), Introduction.

3 There are many supporters of the instrumental view. David Hume, in *A Treatise Of Human Nature* (Oxford: Clarendon Press, 1978), offers one of the most historically important formulations of this view: "Reason is, and ought only to be the slave of the passions, and can never pretend to any other office than to serve and obey them," p. 415. For the view that instrumental rationality is the default theory, see Robert Nozick, *The Nature of Rationality* (Princeton: Princeton University Press, 1993), p. 133. A recent instrumentalist view may be found in David Gauthier, *Morals By Agreement* (Oxford: Clarendon Press, 1986).

4 Again, Hume offers a classic statement on reason's inability to fix ends: "'Tis not contrary to reason to prefer the destruction of the world to the pricking of my finger.... 'Tis as little contrary to reason to prefer even my own acknowledge'd lesser good to my greater, and have amore ardent affection for the former than the latter" (*A Treatise*, p. 416). A more recent statement can be found in Herbert Simon, *Reason In Human Affairs* (Stanford: Stanford University Press, 1983), pp. 7–8: "reason...cannot tell us where to go; at best it can tell us how to get there" (cited in Harold I. Brown, *Rationality* (London: Westview Press), p. 78).

5 Brown (*Rationality*, passim) also demonstrates concern about a regress.

6 Richard Jeffery, *The Logic of Decision* (New York: McGraw-Hill, 1965). Gauthier (*Morals By Agreement*, p. 22 and passim) offers a modified expected-utility account of rationality.

7 Aristotle, *Nicomachean Ethics*, III.iii., VI.ii., *On the Soul*, III.xi.

8 The rationality of the person may be found in the discussion of the third antinomy in Immanuel Kant, *Critique of Pure Reason*, trans. Norman Kemp Smith (New York: The Humanities Press, 1950), pp. 409–15.

9 Gilbert Harman, *A Change in View* (Cambridge, MA: MIT Press), chs. 4–7, and Karl Popper, *The Logic of Scientific Discovery* (New York: Basic Books, 1959), ch. 10.

10 René Descartes, *First Meditation*, in J. Cottingham *et al.*, trans., *The Philosophical Writings of Descartes*, vol. II (Cambridge: Cambridge University Press, 1993), p. 15.

11 Max Black, "Self Supporting Inductive Arguments," *Journal of Philosophy* 55 (1958): 718–25.

12 David Schmidtz pointed this out to me in conversation.

13 Adrienne Lehrer and Keith Lehrer, "Fields, Networks and Vectors," in F. Palmer, ed., *Grammar and Meaning* (New York: Cambridge University Press, 1995), pp. 26–47.

14 Keith Lehrer and Carl Wagner, *Rational Consensus in Science and Society* (Dordrecht: Reidel, 1981), pp. 65–72.

Part III
Varieties of Knowledge

Chapter 10

Perceptual Knowledge

William Alston

i

This essay deals with epistemological issues concerning perception. These can be briefly indicated by the question: "How, if at all, is perception a source of knowledge or justified belief?" To keep a discussion of a very complex subject matter within prescribed bounds, I will mostly focus on the "justified belief" side of the above disjunction, bringing in questions about perceptual *knowledge* only when dealing with a position that is specially concerned with knowledge. There are some other housekeeping moves to be made before we can get under way.

(1) First a couple of points about epistemic justification. (a) Justification comes in degrees. I can be more or less justified in supposing that Yeltsin will resign the presidency, depending on the strength of my reasons for this. The epistemological literature mostly treats "justified" as an absolute term. Presumably this is because some minimal degree is being presupposed. I will follow this practice. (b) For most of our beliefs, including perceptual beliefs, what we typically identify as a justifier provides only *defeasible, prima facie* justification. Thus the way something looks to me *prima facie* justifies the belief that it is an elephant. That is, this belief will be justified, all things considered, provided there are no sufficient overriders of this *prima facie* justification, for example, strong reasons that there could not be an elephant in this spot, or reasons for thinking that my visual apparatus is malfunctioning. I will be thinking of *prima facie* justification in this essay.

(2) What sorts of beliefs are we to think of as candidates for being justified by perception? Perceptual beliefs, of course, i.e., beliefs that are given rise to by perception. But there is an important distinction between two sorts of beliefs that satisfy this condition.

A. Beliefs about what is putatively perceived – *The tree in front of me is a maple.*
B. Beliefs to the effect that one is perceiving something – *I see a maple tree* or *I see that this tree is a maple.*

It is beliefs of the A sort that are at the heart of the epistemology of perception, just because they constitute the most fundamental doxastic perceptual output – most fundamental in two ways. First, they are ontogenetically and phylogenetically most basic. Even the least sophisticated cognitive subjects – lower animals and very young infants who have no language – get information about the environment from perception. But it takes greater cognitive sophistication to form propositions to the effect that one is perceiving so-and-so. Second, it seems that the primary function of perception is to give the subject information about the environment, rather than information about the subject's perceptual activity and accomplishment. Hence this essay will deal with issues concerning how perception serves as a source of justification for beliefs about what is putatively perceived.

(3) Here, as elsewhere in epistemology, there is an important distinction between two enterprises. (a) We can raise the radical question as to whether we have any knowledge (justified belief) in the domain in question. This amounts to deciding how to react to a certain kind of scepticism. (b) Assuming that we do have knowledge (justified beliefs) of the relevant sort, we can try to understand that – determine what the conditions are under which one has knowledge (justified beliefs) in that domain, make such internal distinctions in the domain as seem called for, clarify the basic concepts involved in carrying out these tasks, and so on. In the history of epistemology (a) has bulked large. With perception in particular, many philosophers talk as if the concern with skepticism exhausts the subject. But, again in order to keep this essay within reasonable limits, I will forgo grappling with scepticism, which in any event is treated elsewhere in this volume, and focus on (b). [*Editor's note*: skepticism regarding perception is treated in the essay by Williams, this volume.]

(4) Philosophers have been concerned both with the epistemology of perceptual belief and the nature of perception. Under the latter heading we can distinguish two main interrelated problems, (a) what it is to perceive an object (event, situation, state of affairs), and (b) what is the nature and structure of perceptual experience (consciousness). The positions taken on these issues, especially the second, have a crucial bearing on epistemological issues. It seems obvious that perceptual experience plays a major role in determining the epistemic status of beliefs based on it. But what kind of role it plays depends on what it is like. If we think of perceptual experience as purely internal, just a subjective state of the perceiver, its epistemic role *vis-à-vis* beliefs about the environment will be different from what it is if it involves some direct awareness of extramental reality. Again, if, as it is fashionable to think nowadays, perceptual experience is essentially propositionally structured, then it may be that it already contains perceptual beliefs of the sort we are concerned with here, in which case the experience is in need of epistemic support, instead of or as well as being an ultimate source thereof.

(5) It is obvious that one's general epistemological orientation has an important influence on one's epistemology of perception. This relevance will obtrude itself throughout the essay. But at this point I will set aside one branch of a major

divide in epistemology, that over whether any belief can be justified otherwise than by its relation to other beliefs. Most of those who answer this question in the negative espouse some form of coherentism, the view that particular beliefs are justified or not by how they fit into some total system of belief, and how internally coherent that system is. A coherentist will have no use for the idea that perceptual beliefs can be justified by experience, whereas those who take a more "local" view of justification are free to allow this. This difference in general epistemology makes an enormous difference to the epistemology of perception. It seems to me incontestable that coherentism can't be the right way to approach perception. If I look out my window and see snow on the ground, and everything is working normally, then surely I am amply justified in believing there is snow on the ground, even if this does not fit coherently in my total belief system, and even if that system exhibits a very low degree of coherence. Hence I will exclude coherentist approaches from consideration.[1] [*Editor's note*: coherentism is treated in the essay by BonJour, this volume.]

ii

(6) Another preliminary point that needs more extensive consideration is the difference between the following questions. (1) How, if at all, are perceivers (sometimes) justified in their perceptual beliefs? (2) How, if at all, is it *possible* to justify perceptual beliefs? (1) is addressed to the (typical or frequent) situation of real-life perceivers. It tries to determine what, if anything, in their actual situations renders their perceptual beliefs justified. (2) is a question about what considerations could be adduced to justify perceptual beliefs, whether or not this is something that perceivers typically, or ever, adduce or are aware of. Thus (2) could be answered by spelling out some elaborate philosophical argument that is so complex as to be available only to a select few. But (1) restricts itself to justificatory factors that are widely distributed, even though most perceivers might not be clearly aware of them or of their bearing. (2) is the enterprise often called "proving the existence of the external world."

One reason this distinction is important is that if we are not aware of it, as philosophers often are not, we will wind up arguing past each other. Thus Price, Broad, and others, object to a "causal theory of perception" that perceivers rarely if ever carry out a causal inference from perceptual experience to external cause when they form perceptual beliefs. But when Locke or Descartes or Russell or Lovejoy, or more recently Moser, defend the epistemic credentials of perceptual beliefs by appealing to causal arguments, they are best read as engaging not in (1) but in (2).

As intimated above, even if (2) could be successfully carried out, it would leave (1) without a satisfactory answer, provided that the success depends on argumentation that few if any perceivers can be aware of. Nevertheless, (2) is not totally irrelevant to (1). Suppose we carry out (2) by showing that whenever one has a perceptual experience of a certain sort, a certain kind of fact obtains in the external world. That would show that having an experience of that sort confers a positive epistemic status (justification or knowledge) on a belief in that fact that stems from that experience. At least it would show this on an externalist account of justification or knowledge.[2] We will look at some externalist accounts in section iv.

Partly because of this relevance, and partly for its intrinsic interest, it is worth glancing at some attempts to carry out (2). These are usefully divided into a priori and empirical arguments. The former try to show that it is logically or conceptually impossible that perceptual beliefs should not often be true. An example is the claim that concepts of perceivable kinds and properties consist of "criteria" (Wittgenstein) or "justification conditions" (Pollock) in terms of sensory experience, so that it is conceptually necessary that when one is having a certain kind of sensory experience one is *prima facie* justified in supposing there is an object, or an object with a property, for which that experience is a justification condition.[3] Here I will concentrate on empirical arguments.

These typically proceed by assuming that it is unproblematic that perceivers have knowledge of the character of their own perceptual experiences. They then look for some way of making cogent inferences from that knowledge to the propositional contents of typical perceptual beliefs (for example, *there is a robin on my lawn*). But a survey of such arguments affords little ground for optimism about the prospect of success.[4] Look first at a very simple example. One might try to construct an enumerative induction from correlations of experience type and external fact. If experience of type e is conjoined in many cases with external putatively perceivable fact of type f, we can infer that they are generally correlated and hence be justified in inferring from an e to an f. But, as Hume and many others have noted, this runs into the difficulty that to get knowledge of particular instances of such pairings, we would already have to have perceptual knowledge of the external perceived objects, the very thing that is in question.

A somewhat more elaborate example is an argument to the best explanation. It is contended that there are various features of our experience that are best explained by the usual supposition that this experience has among its causes the physical objects we normally suppose ourselves to be perceiving in these experiences. Such considerations are found in the work of C.D. Broad.[5] The features in question can be illustrated as follows.[6] (1) It often happens that whenever I look in a certain direction I undergo sensory experiences of pretty much the same sort. This can be explained by the supposition that there are physical things of the sort I believe myself to be perceiving that remain in that location and contribute to the production of similar experiences. And when I receive significantly different experiences from looking in that direction, this is plausibly explained in terms of physical changes in that location. (2) If I move from point a to point b my experiences undergo a characteristic continuous change that, again, is of roughly the same sort over a considerable period, and this is best explained by supposing that the objects I seem to be perceiving along the route remain relatively stable over the period of time in question. And again, when the sequence is different from what it had been, this can be plausibly explained by differences in the physical constituents along the route. Explanatory arguments like this are subject to two difficulties. (a) No one has ever succeeded in making a plausible case for the superiority of this "standard" explanation to its alternatives, like the self-generation of sensory experiences or their direct production by a Cartesian demon or a Berkeleian God. (b) More crucially, the patterns in experience cited as the explananda involve suppositions about the physical en-vironment we could only know about through perception, thus introducing a circularity in the argument. In these cases those suppositions include my repeatedly looking in a certain (physical) direction, and my physically moving from one location to another. If we were to make the explanandum purely phenomenal, we would not be able to find patterns that it is plausible to explain in terms of the putatively perceived external objects, as I argue in *The Reliability of Sense Perception*.[7]

iii

With these preliminaries out of the way I am ready to explore various ways in which philosophers have tried to understand the conditions of justification of perceptual belief. A good starting place is the intuitively plausible idea that when I form the visual belief that a robin is on my front lawn, that belief is justified, if at all, by my current visual experience. The experience, which, as we might say, is as if I am seeing a robin on the lawn, gives rise to the belief and thereby renders it justified. It is plausible to suppose that the experience has this epistemic efficacy because it consists in, or involves, a direct awareness of the robin and its position on the lawn. My visual experience justifies the belief because the latter is simply the conceptual encoding of the realities that are directly presented to my awareness in the visual experience. This is the so-called "naive" direct realism that is one of the perennial answers to our central question of how perceptual beliefs are justified. I shall be contending that it is, in essentials, the correct answer, though to make it adequate we will have to go some distance beyond this crude formulation.

We must distinguish two ways in which perceptual experience might be involved in the justification of perceptual beliefs. (a) The belief might be justified by the experience itself, or by the fact that the belief stems from the experience, as the last paragraph suggested. (b) The belief might be justified by the subject's *knowledge* (justified belief) that she has an experience of that kind. I have already hinted at reasons for rejecting (b) as an account of real-life justification of perceptual beliefs. For one thing, perceivers typically have no actual knowledge of the character of their experiences. Even if they could always acquire such knowledge by attending to the matter, they rarely so attend. Their attention is almost always fastened on the external (putatively) perceived scene, not the experience by virtue of which they perceive it. Second, if they had such knowledge it would play that role by functioning as an adequate reason for the perceptual belief. And that in turn would require a successful inference from the fact that the experience is of a certain sort to the perceptual belief, or at least the possibility of such an inference. But, as I suggested above (but by no means proved), it looks as if no such inference is possible. Hence for this reason (b) cannot be successfully carried through.[8]

Before leaving this approach I should mention one consideration that has made (b) seem an attractive or even compelling prospect. Traditional foundationalism in epistemology (q.v.) has supposed that all knowledge (justified belief) must rest on foundations that are absolutely certain. It seems that if there are such foundations of empirical knowledge, they consist of one's knowledge of one's own conscious states. And so, on such a view, we must show that whatever empirical knowledge one has of other matters is derived from one's knowledge of one's own conscious states. But the difficulties that have attended attempts to develop this kind of foundationalism weaken any support it gives to (b).

Turning now to (a), before considering how, if at all, a perceptual belief might be justified by an experience on which it is based, we must consider the idea that even if that is part of the story it is not all of it, at least not always. It seems that other knowledge of the subject sometimes makes a contribution. I am looking for Bernice's house. I've been to her house a number of times and I recognize it by its appearance. If the look of the house is all that I go on, then my belief that this is Bernice's house is based solely on the character of the visual presentation. But is that so? For all I know, there are many other houses that look just like this, given the distance and angle and lighting with respect to which I am viewing it. It is reasonable to think that I am also taking into account my current location – that I am on a certain block of a certain street, or at least in a certain part of a certain town, whether I explicitly think about these matters or not. In that case my belief would be justified partly by the character of the visual presentation and partly by my knowledge of my current location.

Some philosophers think that all cases of perceptual recognition exhibit this mixed character. If so, the doxastic conditions will often have to be more hidden from the subject's awareness than the location beliefs in the above case. One candidate is what we might call "adequacy conditions." It might be thought that whenever I perceptually recognize x as P on the basis of a certain perceptual appearance, a belief that such an appearance is an adequate sign of P is also part of what justifies the belief. But the trouble with this is that it leads to an infinite regress. If for any basis, B_1, of a belief there is a further basis, B_2, which consists of a justified belief that B_1 is an adequate basis, then the same principle will apply to B_2, and so on ad infinitum. At some point we must take it as sufficient that the basis *is* adequate, without also requiring that the subject justifiably believe this. Another candidate for an omnipresent doxastic basis is the justified belief that one's perceptual apparatus is working normally. But one can recognize the relevance of this consideration without supposing that a justified belief in normality has to figure as part of the justification of the perceptual belief. One can hold, rather, that the experience suffices to justify *in the absence of any sufficient reasons to suspect abnormality*. That is, normality considerations can figure as possible overriders of *prima facie* justification, rather than as part of what confers *prima facie* justification.

If we can generalize from the disposal of these two candidates, we need not worry about the possibility that perceptual beliefs *always* draw their justification, at least in part, from other justified beliefs. Nevertheless, there is a strong case for the thesis that this is not infrequently the case, as my example of house identification indicates. Hence doxastic contributors to justification will figure in any comprehensive epistemology of perceptual belief. But in the space at my disposal here I will concentrate on the experiential contribution, which deserves to be called the heart of the matter, both because that is always involved and because it is distinctive of perceptual justification.

iv

When we begin to think about how to specify the conditions under which an experience provides support for a perceptual belief, two other oppositions in general epistemology become relevant. (In the ensuing discussion I will use "evidence" in a broad sense for anything that has the potentiality of increasing the justification of a belief, whether it is reasons, other things the subject knows or justifiably believes ("evidence" in a narrow sense), or experience.) First, there is the question whether it is sufficient for justification that one simply *has* evidence, or whether it is required that the belief is *based* on that evidence. Though a decision on this point will pervasively affect the shape an account of epistemic justification takes, it is not crucial for the present topic just because it is plausible to restrict perceptual beliefs to those *based on* perceptual experience, apart from questions about their justification. Hence there is little or no chance of a perceptual belief's not being based on experience that constitutes evidence for it.[9]

The second opposition is between internalism and externalism in epistemology (see ch. 5 above). These terms are used variously, but I will understand them here as follows. Internalism restricts factors bearing on epistemic status to those to which the subject has some high grade of cognitive access, typically specified as knowable just on reflection. While externalism, though not excluding such factors, does not enforce any such restriction. The most important divergence between these orientations concerns certain truth conducive conditions which a subject cannot be expected to ascertain just on reflection. Two of these have been prominent in the epistemology of perception – reliability of belief formation and the truth indicativeness of the experience on which the belief was based. Externalist accounts of the epistemology of perceptual beliefs can feature one or the other of these. I begin with an account of the latter sort by Fred Dretske.[10] This concerns knowledge specifically; Dretske deliberately ignores justification.

First, Dretske's epistemology of perceptual belief is based on a direct realism of object perception. He argues, successfully in my opinion, that at the heart of perception is an awareness of objects that does not involve belief (judgment) in any way. He calls this "non-epistemic seeing" and abbreviates it as "see$_n$".[11] Here are the conditions he lays down for a bit of visual knowledge ("*S* sees that *b* is *P*").

(i)   *b* is *P*. (the truth condition)
(ii) *S* sees$_n$ *b*.
(iii) The conditions under which *S* sees$_n$ *b* are such that *b* would not look, *L*, the way it now looks to *S*, unless it was *P*.
(iv) *S*, believing the conditions are as described in (iii), takes *b* to be *P*.[12]

(Dretske explains that the belief that (iii) which he requires in condition (iv) can be more or less implicit.) What this account amounts to is that when I base a true belief that *b* is *P* on the way *b* looks, that belief counts as knowledge provided the look is an adequate indication of *b*'s being *P*. And it is an adequate indication provided that *b* wouldn't look that way if it were not *P*. My visual belief that the tree is a maple, a belief based on the tree's looking a certain way, counts as knowledge provided that the tree wouldn't have looked that way (in these circumstances) if it weren't a maple.

This account is externalist, not only because of the truth condition (1), but, more distinctively, because the truth of the crucial counterfactual, (iii), is not the sort of thing one can ascertain just on reflection. And, like most externalists, Dretske, by condition (iv), requires that the belief be *based on* the relevant evidence in order that it achieve the positive epistemic status in question.

I find Dretske's view very attractive as an account of perceptual knowledge,[13] though, as I will bring out shortly, it, or rather suitable parts of it, is less promising as an account of justification. I will now say a few words about a *reliabilist* approach. The general idea of a reliabilist approach to knowledge or justification is that a belief gets one or another positive epistemic status by being formed in a way that is generally reliable, one that would yield mostly true beliefs in a suitably large and varied range of cases in conditions of the sort in which we typically find ourselves.[14] The relation of this to Dretske's "adequate indication" account depends on how this "way of being formed" is thought of. If we spell it out in terms of the way the belief is based on features of experience (way of looking), then it turns out to be another formulation of the same basic idea. For if the way of looking would not occur in those circumstances without the belief's being true, as Dretske requires, then forming the belief on the basis of that way of looking, in those circumstances, would be a reliable way of forming it. But if, with Goldman and many other reliabilists, we do not wish to restrict perceptual belief formation to any such formula, then the reliabilist approach would apply more widely. In any event, reliabilism is externalist for the same reason as Dretske's account: the general reliability of the mode of belief formation exemplified in this case is not something that one could be expected to ascertain just on reflection.

It is plausible to suppose that if we can handle Dretske's counterfactuals successfully, and if we can assign particular processes of belief formation to general "ways of forming beliefs" that can be assessed for reliability in epistemically useful ways, then either externalist approach identifies an important epistemically positive feature of beliefs, one that, together with truth, bids fair to be a sufficient condition of knowledge. The main dissatisfaction with such accounts is that they give us no hint as to how we tell whether their conditions are satisfied in a particular case. If we are interested not just in understanding the *concept* of perceptual knowledge but in finding out where we have it and where we do not, we are likely to feel let down. That is not to say that we have no capacity at all to determine when a Dretske-type counterfactual is true or when a way of forming a perceptual belief is of a reliable type. But it would obviously be desirable to have more of a general method for achieving this, and externalist epistemologists are not forthcoming on this point. They bend over backwards to make the (correct) point that knowing (being justified in believing) that b is P, on the basis of perception, does not require being able to know or show that one is. But being able to tell whether one is or not is obviously a cognitive desideratum. Moreover, if as I argue in *The Reliability of Sense Perception*, we cannot construct a noncircular successful argument that what we ordinarily take as experiential bases of perceptual beliefs yield mostly true beliefs, this is a serious problem for externalists, for on their view one has perceptual knowledge only if the perceptual belief in question is based on experience in such a way as to generally yield true beliefs. It is worth noting that they seem mostly untroubled by this. Since they typically adopt the nonskeptical approach to epistemology in terms of which this essay is written, they feel warranted in assuming that our usual ways of forming perceptual (and other) beliefs are truth-conducive until we have reasons in particular cases to abandon that assumption.

V

There is a reason for holding that even if externalist accounts like these are adequate accounts of perceptual knowledge (not thought of in terms of justification), they are deficient as accounts of the justification of perceptual belief.[15] That is because there is an internalist constraint it is plausible to apply to justification but not to knowledge, viz., that in order for something to justify a belief the subject must have the capacity for some insight into its doing so. This is weaker than requiring a capacity to ascertain justificatory efficacy just by reflection. But it is sufficiently strong to rule out typical externalist accounts. It is clear that a case of perceptual belief formation can satisfy Dretske's conditions without the subject having any insight whatsoever into this. This is presumably the case with lower animals and small children, and may well be the case with many unsophisticated normal adult humans. I will now explore the ways in which the justification of perceptual beliefs might be construed from this kind of internalist perspective.

But first I should mention a recently prominent view that there is something fundamentally wrong-headed about the idea of a belief being justified by an experience. Davidson, after opining that "nothing can count as a reason for holding a belief except another belief," acknowledges that the only alternatives to this worth taking seriously attempt to ground beliefs on experience. But this won't do, he says. "The relation between a sensation and a belief cannot be logical, since sensations are not beliefs or other propositional attitudes. What then is the relation? . . . the relation is causal. Sensations cause some beliefs and in *this* sense are the basis or ground of those beliefs. But a causal explanation of a belief does not show that or why the belief is justified."[16] To be sure, Davidson offers this argument as a support for coherentism, and I have already excluded coherentism from consideration. Nevertheless, I want to say why I think that this argument doesn't do the job. In a word, it is much too heavy-handed. It question-beggingly assumes that only *logical* relations can carry justificatory force. Moreover it undiscriminatingly takes causation and justification to be mutually exclusive. But before swallowing this, we should reflect that there are causes and causes. Whether the kind of cause a visual experience is can confer justification on the kind of effect a perceptual belief is depends on the details of what these causes and effects are like and further facts about their relationship. (*Of course*, the abstract fact that *x* causes *y* has no implications for justificatory efficacy.) That is, it depends on the outcome of the kind of exploration on which I am about to embark.

When we try to give an internalist account of the way perceptual experience confers justification on perceptual beliefs, we are forced to attend to the differences between ways of construing that experience. These differences do not make an important difference for externalist accounts, since those accounts do not trade on connections between the intrinsic character of experiences and the content of beliefs. So long as the experience wouldn't be formed in those circumstances without the belief's being true, or so long as the belief results from the experience in a way that is generally reliable, it doesn't matter how the experience is constituted. No doubt, we would have to attend to that if we tried to *explain* the truth of the counterfactual or to explain the reliability; but no such explanation has to enter into the externalist account of what it is to know (justifiably believe) something perceptually. But since the internalist enterprise requires us to find a way in which it can be apparent to the subject how the experience renders the belief justified, there seems to be no place to look for this except in some connection between the intrinsic character of one's perceptual consciousness and the content of the belief. And what connection there is depends on both ends of the link.

Turning then to the main alternatives for a characterization of the intrinsic nature of perceptual experience, I assume that even if that experience is by its very nature conceptually, propositionally, or judgmentally structured (none of which I accept), we are concerned here with that aspect of the experience that makes it distinctively perceptual, an aspect we are assuming to be non-conceptual, non-propositional. Hence we can ignore the question of whether conceptualization is essentially involved. Proceeding on that basis, and painting the picture in broad strokes, we can discern four main accounts.

1. *Direct realism*. This takes perceptual consciousness to consist, most basically, in the fact that one or more objects *appear* to the subject *as so-and-so*, as

(restricting ourselves to vision) round, bulgy, blue, jagged, etc. In other terms, they *present* themselves to the subject as so-and-so. This view takes perceptual consciousness to be irreducibly relational in character. And, where one is genuinely perceiving objects, situations, and events in the external environment, it takes the relation to have an external object as its other term. This distinguishes it from its rivals, all of whom take perceptual experience to be (intrinsically) purely intramental.

2. *The sense-datum theory.* This agrees with 1. in taking perceptual consciousness to consist in an awareness of objects, to have an "act–object" structure. But the objects in question are never the familiar denizens of the physical world, but are instead special, nonphysical objects of a markedly peculiar character. They have the special role of bearing the qualities that putatively external perceived objects sensorily appear to have.

3. *The adverbial theory.* Perceptual consciousness is simply a *way* of being conscious; it does not display any sort of "act–object" structure. Just as a mode of consciousness, it is not a cognition of objects of any kind.

4. *Phenomenal quality view.* This is a position that I think is rather widely held but has not received the systematic development of the first three. It agrees with 2. in taking perceptual experience to be a direct awareness of something "mental," something private, but it differs in construing these private objects as qualities of mental states, which you could term sensations, rather than as subsistent nonphysical particulars.[17]

Thus direct realism is distinguished from the other alternatives by insisting that perceptual consciousness is essentially, in itself, an *awareness of* objects, which are, in normal cases, *physical objects in the environment*. Unlike the other views, it does not regard perceptual experience, in normal cases, to be purely "inside the head."[18] When I take myself to be seeing a red apple, the direct realist will say that I am directly aware of something (an apple if things are going right) that looks red and apple-shaped to me. Sense-datum theory will say that I am directly aware of a red, apple-shaped sense datum that is a special nonphysical particular that exists only as a bearer of sensory qualia like color and shape. The phenomenal quality view will say that I am directly aware of sensory qualia of (some of my) current mental states, qualia like redness. And the adverbial theory will say that I am sensing in a red, apple-shaped *way* or *manner*.

To avoid misapprehension, let me make it clear that direct realism, as I construe it, does *not* hold that presented objects always are what they present themselves as. It is compatible with recognizing a considerable amount of misleading appearance. X can look like a cow when it is an automobile. A tower in the distance can look round when it is square. And so on. To be sure, if perceptual appearances were always or usually misleading, they would be of much less value epistemically than I take them to be. But that value does not require infallibility.

Reflecting on the bearing of these differences on perceptual epistemology, one can hardly avoid being struck by the apparent superiority of direct realism. On that view perceptual experience in itself involves, in normal cases, a cognitive relation with external objects that perceptual beliefs are about. Hence it seems obvious how an experience could be a source of knowledge (justified belief) about such objects. If the leaf looks yellow to me or the house visually presents two front windows, that is an obvious basis for supposing the leaf to be yellow or the house to have two front windows (a *prima facie*, defeasible basis of course). But with the other construals, according to which the experience involves no intrinsic cognitive connection with the external world, there is no such intuitive justificatory force. Perceptual experience is a purely subjective affair, and as such it wears on its face no (even apparent) information about the external environment. Why should we suppose that sensing in a certain way, or being aware of a nonphysical sense datum or a phenomenal quality of a mental state, should tell us anything about what there is in the immediate environment of the perceiver and about what that is like? Of course, there may be *externalist* connections of the sort envisaged by the counterfactual or reliabilist approaches. It may be that sensing in a certain way is a reliable indication of the presence of a maple tree, or that the way in which a certain sensing gives rise to a belief that a car is driving down the street is a reliable way. But we are currently exploring the possibility of a more internalist perceptual epistemology, according to which a perceptual belief is justified only if the perceiver has, or can have, some insight into how her experience provides justification for the belief about the external environment to which it gives rise. And the direct realist construal would seem to provide that in a way its alternatives do not. The supposition that a leaf's looking yellow supports the belief that that leaf is yellow is just as clear as the plausibility of the supposition that, by and large and in the absence of sufficient reasons to the contrary, perceived things are as they perceptually appear to be. Whereas on the other construals it is difficult to see how perceptual experience confers any such *prima facie* credibility. Later we will see that things are not so rosy for direct realism as this preliminary statement suggests. But for now I want to explore what happens when advocates of the other views of perceptual experience address the epistemological problem. Since 4. has not been prominent in this literature, I will confine the discussion to the sense-datum and adverbial theorists.

My sample sense-datum theorists will be Broad, Price, Moore, Russell, and C. I. Lewis, while adverbial theory will be represented by Chisholm. The first point to note is that they all agree with me that there is a major problem in building an intuitively plausible bridge between perceptual experience, as they conceive it, and putatively perceived facts about the external environment. They all reject simple inductive arguments for general experience–external fact correlations, for reasons like those I gave in section ii. But when it comes to attempting to show how experience provides a basis for beliefs about the physical world, they divide into two groups on the question of the proper construal of those beliefs. Some of them, including Broad, Moore, Price, and Chisholm are *realists* on this point. They accept the common-sense view that the physical world we take ourselves to perceive is of a radically different ontological nature from sensory experience itself and is what it is independently of our experience. *Phenomenalists* like C. I. Lewis and Russell (at a certain stage) advocate construing physical objects in terms of what sensory experiences a subject would have under certain conditions. To say that there is a plate on the table is to say something about what visual, tactual, and other experiences a percipient would have under certain conditions, *and that's all there is to it*. That's what there being a plate on the table consists in. Physical objects, to use a favorite term of Russell's, are "logical constructions" out of sense data (or sense experiences).[19]

Let's first look at how realist sense-datum theorists approach the epistemology of perceptual belief. Broad and Price, as we saw earlier, discuss various ways in which sense data are patterned, ways which suggest an explanation in terms of the influence of objects we suppose ourselves to perceive.[20] But they reject the claim that anything about the putatively perceived world can be established in this way. Broad goes so far as to say that if the "external world" hypothesis had a finite initial probability, its explanation of these facts would increase that probability, though he sees no grounds for such an initial probability. Price goes further than Broad in discerning the circularity involved in the argument, the ways in which the allegedly pure starting points are actually infected with all sorts of suppositions about the physical world, e.g., that the subject is or is not moving in a certain direction. They agree that one cannot successfully establish putatively perceived facts about the external world from premises concerning sense data or our experiences. And Chisholm, from the adverbial side, agrees with this.[21]

So what positive view do these philosophers have of the epistemic status of perceptual beliefs? The one favored by Price and Moore, and Chisholm part of the time, constitutes a sort of cop-out.[22] Having despaired of finding any reason for supposing that a certain kind of experience indicates the truth of a certain perceptual belief about the external world, they simply lay it down that perceptual beliefs are to be taken as *prima facie* credible just by virtue of being formed. They are, as we might say, *prima facie self-warranted* just by being perceptual beliefs. To quote Chisholm, "if he takes there to be a tree, then . . . this intentional attitude, this taking, tends to make it probable that the taking has an actual object."[23] And Price: "the existence of a particular visual or tactual sense-datum is prima facie evidence (1) for the existence of a material thing such that this sense-datum belongs to it, (2) for the possession by this thing of a front surface of a certain general sort."[24] I call this a "cop-out" because it abandons the attempt to find any kind of intelligible connection between the character of the experience and the content of the perceptual belief formed on its basis, such that this connection would enable us to understand how the experience can provide support for the belief. This position is just as neutral with respect to the constitution of the experience as the externalist positions we surveyed earlier.

What basis, if any, is there for this *prima facie self-warrant* principle? Here attitudes vary. Chisholm sometimes takes it to be directly known a priori, sometimes to owe its status to the fact that it is part of a system of principles that best accommodates particular intuitive cognitions of particular cases of justification, sometimes to be the only way of escaping skepticism. Price, after surveying various alternatives, opts for the view that "perceptual consciousness is an *ultimate* form of consciousness not reducible to any other; and further, it is an *autonomous* or self-correcting form of consciousness." In other words, the principle needs no external support, even though it is not self-evident. It is clear that these theorists are settling for less than what they were hoping and aiming for initially, and finding ways to make do with what they have found.

As for phenomenalists, they are not faced with an ontological gap between experience and the physical world, but that does not mean that they are home free on the epistemological question. Even if there is nothing to physical things or facts other than what sense experiences would occur under certain conditions, we are still faced with the problem of how we know something about an unlimited number of such contingencies from a particular sense datum or sensation, or some limited number thereof. Phenomenalists generally claim that this is a matter of induction, a mode of inference that, even if not without its problems, is crucial in many other spheres of thought. They thus take themselves to have shown at least that there are no special epistemological problems about perception. But a more serious difficulty for their position concerns their phenomenalist account of physical objects. Chisholm showed, in a classic article, that one cannot begin to formulate a set of propositions concerning the conditions under which a subject S would have an experience of type E, a set that it is at all plausible to take as equivalent to a certain physical fact, without including physical facts in the antecedents of the conditional propositions.[25] Hence the project of reducing propositions about physical objects to propositions that are solely about experience cannot be carried through.

The difficulties that the likes of Price and Broad have with constructing a plausible view of how perceptual experience can *justify* beliefs about the external world depend, *inter alia*, on their taking epistemic justification to be essentially truth-conducive. This means that it is part of the concept of epistemic justification that if a belief is justified to a high degree, it thereby is likely to be true. As many epistemologists have persuasively argued, if we don't conceive epistemic justification in that way, why should we care so much whether our beliefs are justified?[26] It is combining this conviction with their sense-datum construal of perceptual experience and realism about physical objects that drives them to what I termed a "cop-out." But another reaction to the problem is to abandon truth-conducivity as a constraint on justification. This is what we find in Chisholm. He takes us to have an intuitive idea of a belief's being more or less justified, an idea that is conceptually independent of truth or probability of truth. He thinks that we know intuitively, a priori, in many cases that a given belief enjoys a certain degree of justification or not, and that we can inductively generalize from such cases to principles that lay down conditions for justification.[27] Thus, though he believes that having justified beliefs is the best way of getting the truth, he feels confident that he can tell when a belief is justified without showing that it is likely to be true.

Another way of divorcing justification from truth-conducivity is the Wittgensteinian idea that our concepts contain *criteria* of their correct application.

> The fluctuation in grammar between criteria and symptoms makes it look as if there were nothing at all but symptoms. We say, for example: "Experience teaches that there is rain when the barometer falls, but it also teaches that there is rain when we have certain sensations of wet and cold, or such-and-such visual impressions". In defense of this one says that these sense-impressions can deceive us. But here one fails to reflect that the fact that the false appearance is precisely one of rain is founded on a definition.[28]

This idea has been developed by John Pollock in his view that the meaning of many of our concepts, including concepts of perceivable objects, is given by "justification conditions" rather than by "truth conditions."[29] Thus it is part of our concept of a bird that such-and-such visual experiences count as justifying the belief that what one sees is a bird. If this view can be successfully carried through, it obviously gives us an insight into how and why the kinds of experiences we ordinarily take to justify perceptual beliefs with a certain content really do so. There are problems with the approach. For example, it seems to require that we ascribe a concept of epistemic justification to all perceivers, at least all perceivers who have justified perceptual beliefs, and this seems questionable. But the main point I want to make in this context is that since the concept of justification has been cut loose from truth, by both Chisholm and Pollock, it runs up against the question of why we should be so concerned with how justified our beliefs are.

vi

So the sense-datum and adverbial views, which construe perceptual experience as purely intramental, run into difficulties in forging an account of the justification of perceptual beliefs by experience that gives us insight into how and why it works. I believe that the phenomenal qualities view, when combined with realism about the physical world and a truth-conducivity conception of justification, will run into similar problems. But before we award the palm to direct realism, we must surmount two obstacles.

First, we must confront the considerations that have seemed to most philosophers in the modern period to show conclusively that perceptual experience cannot essentially involve any cognitive relation to an extramental object. Here some historical background would be useful. An Aristotelian form of direct realism was dominant in the high Middle Ages, but it was widely abandoned at the beginning of the modern era because of its connection with Aristotelian physics. That physics took "secondary" qualities like color, and felt heat and cold, roughness and smoothness, to be objectively real and even, in some cases, physically efficacious. Thus the Aristotelians felt justified in supposing that when something looks red or feels cold, objective physical properties are presenting themselves to us perceptually.

But with the rise of the new mathematical physics, secondary qualities were banished from the physical world because they were not susceptible of mathematical treatment. And since nothing perceptually appears to us as solely bearing the "primary," mathematicizable properties like size, shape, and motion, thinkers rejected the view that we are directly aware of external physical reality in perception. Perceptual experience, being rife with secondary qualities, had to be construed as purely intramental, as, in the current jargon, an awareness of "ideas".

There are considerations independent of the shape of physical science that convince most current philosophers that perceptual experience does not consist of any cognitive relation to the extramental. The crucial point is that there are hallucinatory experiences in which the supposed external perceived object does not exist, and these are introspectively indistinguishable from veridical perception. Case studies of psychotics present examples aplenty. Such experiences have been taken to support a stronger or weaker objection to direct realism. The stronger is that perceptual experience never includes a direct awareness of an existent external object. This is supposed to be shown by the intrinsic indistinguishability of hallucinations and the real thing. It need not be alleged that they are never phenomenally distinguishable; that is clearly false. It is enough that they sometimes are not. The argument is that since veridical perceptual experience is of just the same sort, experientially, as (some) hallucinations, then since the latter involves no awareness of an external object, neither does the former. Thus we are driven to some kind of purely subjective construal of all perceptual experience.

The Achilles heel of this argument is the supposition that the ontological constitution of an experience is completely displayed to introspection. Why suppose that? Why suppose that there are no differences in ontological structure that are not revealed to the subject's direct awareness? Why couldn't an experience in which something genuinely is presented to one be phenomenologically just like one in which nothing is? Once we ask these questions, we see that the above argument rests on groundless prejudices. If the demands of theory require it, we are free to take phenomenologically indistinguishable states of affairs as significantly different in ontology. Moreover, we need not confine ourselves to appeals to abstract possibilities. The persistent disputes about the constitution of perceptual experience are eloquent testimony to the point that our direct awareness of our experiences does not suffice to settle the question. If perceptual experience wears its ontological structure on its sleeve, how could many philosophers be confident that it consists of awareness of nonphysical sense-data and many others be equally sure that it does not? The fine ontological structure of perceptual experience is a matter for theory, not one's normal awareness of one's own conscious states.

But even if hallucinations do not prove that perceptual experience is never a direct awareness of external objects, they certainly prove that it isn't always that. And this is enough to show that direct realism, as so far presented, cannot be a comprehensive account of perceptual experience. We might take it as a correct account of veridical perceptual experience, but there are strong motivations for finding a single unified account. The best strategy for the direct realist would be to find some other kind of entity that is directly presenting itself to the subject's awareness as so-and-so when no physical object is available. In some cases this might be the air or the space in a certain area of the environment. But another alternative that would seem to cover all hallucinations (and dreams as well if they are to be ranged under perceptual experience) would be a particularly vivid mental image. This suggestion would not commend itself to materialists and many other contemporary philosophers as well. But there is, in fact, considerable psychological evidence that mental images are perceived in something like the way external objects are. We cannot pursue this issue here, beyond pointing to the necessity of some such development to enable direct realism to handle hallucinations.

More to the present purpose, the fact of hallucination complicates the application of direct realism to the question of how an experience can justify a perceptual belief. As I have been presenting this, a direct realist account of perceptual experience gives us real insight into how an experience can justify a perceptual belief in the following way. Since the experience just *is* a matter of an object, *o*, presenting itself to one's experience as *P*, that confers *prima facie* justification on the belief that *o* is *P*, on the enormously plausible principle that it is *prima facie* credible to suppose that things are as they experientially appear to be. But now we are forced to confront the fact that not all perceptual experiences *are* a matter of an object of the sort they seem to be perceptions of presenting itself as so-and-so. Suppose I have an hallucinatory experience of a computer that, so far as I can tell just by having the experience, is a case of a computer's visually presenting itself with the word "externalism" displayed on the screen? Does this experience provide *prima facie* justification for the belief that there is a computer in front of me with "externalism" displayed on the screen? On the one hand, it seems that I must hold that it does, so long as there is no way in which I can tell that I am not aware of a real computer. But then I must abandon the simple epistemological application of direct realism for which I have been commending it. Justification of perceptual beliefs by experience would no longer be confined to cases in which the object the belief is about directly appears to the subject as so-and-so. Indeed, it is beginning to look as if direct realism is in no better position than its rivals on this issue. For here too we are in the position of providing insight into how a purely intramental experience can confer justification on a belief about something extramental.

There are two positions direct realism can take on this issue, one more externalist and one more internalist. On the former, we stick to the original unqualified position. Perceptual experience justifies beliefs only about what the subject is thereby directly aware of. If in hallucinations it is visual images that appear so-and-so to the subject, it is the false belief that some image has sentences (really) appearing on its (real) screen that is *prima facie* justified by the experience. Since the subject has no direct cognitive access to the hallucinatory character of the experience, she doesn't realize that her belief is about a mental image; but that is what is more externalist about the position. On the latter, more fully internalist position, we limit our construal of the justifying experience to what is directly accessible to the subject. Since whether the experience is veridical or hallucinatory is not directly accessible, we limit the specification of the experiential justifier to what is neutral between those alternatives – something like *it is (experientially) just as if a computer is presenting itself to me as having "externalist" on its screen*. And what we can take to be *prima facie* justified by the experience is dictated by that description, viz., a belief that a real computer in front of her has "externalist" on its screen.[30] This *prima facie* justification will be overridden if the subject comes to know or justifiably believe that the experience is hallucinatory. Note that both of these positions are internalist in restricting the justifier, what does the justifying, to experiences that are directly accessible to the subject. They differ in that the former position takes the justification to accrue to a belief about what is actually appearing to the subject, while the latter takes it to accrue to a belief about what seems to the subject to be presenting itself to her.

Note that both positions enjoy the advantage I have attributed to the direct realist epistemology of perceptual belief. For they are both squarely based on the idea that X's appearing P to S provides *prima facie* justification for believing that X is P. The more externalist version preserves this idea unmodified, at the cost of leaving the subject unable to tell with certainty, from the inside, just what belief is so justified. The more internalist position extends the range of justifying experiences to include introspectively indistinguishable lookalikes, but their characterization is parasitic on the characterization of the real article. And so the original idea – that X's looking ø to S *prima facie* justifies S in supposing that X is ø – is still at the heart of the account.

Notes

1 For an interesting coherentist attempt to handle perceptual belief see Laurence BonJour, *The Structure of Empirical Knowledge* (Cambridge, MA: Harvard University Press, 1985), ch. 6. For extensive criticism of coherentism see John W. Bender, ed., *The Current State of the Coherence Theory* (Boston: Kluwer, 1989).
2 For an explanation of the distinction between externalism and internalism in epistemology see section iv and the essay by Sosa in this volume.
3 I briefly discuss this argument at the end of section v.
4 For an extensive critique of both a priori and empirical arguments see William Alston, *The Reliability of Sense Perception* (Ithaca: Cornell University Press, 1993).
5 C. D. Broad, *Scientific Thought* (London: Routledge & Kegan Paul, 1923), chs. 9 and 10, and *The Mind and Its Place in Nature* (London: Routledge & Kegan Paul, 1925), ch. 4.
6 Broad, *The Mind and Its Place in Nature*, pp. 196–8.
7 William Alston, *The Reliability of Sense Perception* (Ithaca: Cornell University Press, 1993).
8 At least his second reason holds on an internalist account of justification, on which the subject must have some insight into that and how a reason is adequate in order that the belief for which it is a reason be thereby justified. An externalist account of justification or knowledge is a different ball game, as I will note shortly. But even for

externalism the first consideration, the typical absence of knowledge of the character of one's sensory experience, is applicable.
9. To be sure, even if a perceptual belief must be based on some experience, there may be experience that is fitted to be evidence for it on which it is not based. But that combination is not likely enough to warrant consideration.
10. Fred Dretske, *Seeing and Knowing* (London: Routledge & Kegan Paul, 1969).
11. Ibid., ch. 2.
12. Ibid., pp. 79–88.
13. There are problems, as usual, with the counterfactual involved. Dretske has insightful things to say about how to interpret it, but I can't go into that here.
14. See Alvin Goldman, "What is Justified Belief?", *Journal of Philosophy*, 73 (1979), and *Epistemology and Cognition* (Cambridge, MA: Harvard University Press, 1986).
15. Needless to say, anyone who is thoroughly convinced that justification of belief is necessary for knowledge will not find any account of knowledge more attractive than a parallel account of justification, since she will hold that the former must go through the latter. It should also be noted that although Goldman takes reliability as what confers justification on beliefs, Dretske's account of perceptual knowledge spelled out above needs a bit of jimmying to turn it into an account of justification. (I), the truth requirement has to be dropped of course, and since (iii), as stated, implies that, it has to be weakened, by making it a high probability claim, for example.
16. Donald Davidson, "A Coherence Theory of Truth and Knowledge," in Ernest LePore, ed., *Truth and Interpretation: Perspectives on the Philosophy of Donald Davidson* (Oxford: Blackwell, 1986), p. 310.
17. My colleague, Jonathan Bennett, has forced me (by rational argument, not threats) to acknowledge 4. as a serious alternative.
18. This, of course, raises the question of how direct realism treats complete hallucinations where no direct awareness of an external object is involved. I will come to that later.
19. See "The Ultimate Constituents of Matter" and "The Relations of Sense-Data to Physics," both in Bertrand Russell's *Our Knowledge of the External World as a Field for Scientific Method in Philosophy* (Chicago: Open Court, 1914). (Beginning in the 1920s Russell took an increasingly realist approach to the physical world.) For C. I. Lewis's phenomenalism see his *An Analysis of Knowledge and Valuation* (La Salle, IL: Open Court, 1946), chs. 7–9.
20. Broad, *The Mind and Its Place in Nature*, ch. 4, and H. H. Price, *Perception* (London: Methuen, 1932), ch. 4.
21. Roderick Chisholm, *Theory of Knowledge* (Englewood Cliffs, NJ: Prentice-Hall, 3rd ed. 1989). Cf. G. E. Moore, *Philosophical Studies* (London: Routledge & Kegan Paul, 1922), chs. 2, 5, 7; and *Some Main Problems of Philosophy* (London: Allen & Unwin, 1953), chs. 2, 5, 7.
22. Broad seems content with the "would increase the initial probability if it had any" position hinted at above.
23. Chisholm, *Theory of Knowledge*, p. 47.
24. Price, *Perception*, p. 185.
25. Roderick Chisholm, "The Problem of Empiricism," *Journal of Philosophy* XLV (1948).
26. An incisive formulation of this argument if found in BonJour, *The Structure of Empirical Knowledge*, ch. 1.

27 Though the priority of particular cases is the dominant strand in his writings, he sometimes suggests, as noted earlier, that general principles of justification are directly known a priori.
28 Ludwig Wittgenstein, *Philosophical Investigations*, tr. G. E. M. Anscombe (Oxford: Blackwell, 1953), no. 354.
29 John Pollock, *Knowledge and Justification* (Princeton: Princeton University Press, 1974).
30 I would prefer not to say that she is justified in a singular belief about a particular object, because there is no object of the sort she believes herself to be directly aware of that is appearing to her in this case. Since there is a reference failure, no singular proposition forms that content of any belief of hers, and hence the question of whether a belief with such a content is justified, and if so how, does not arise. However, an existentially quantified belief, *there is a computer in front of me with "externalism" on its screen*, could still be *prima facie* justified.

Chapter 11

The A Priori

George Bealer

In the history of epistemology, discussions of the a priori have been bound up with discussions of necessity and analyticity, often in confusing ways. Disentangling these confusions is an essential step in the study of the a priori. This will be the aim of my introductory remarks. The goal of the remainder of the paper will then be to try to develop a unified account of the a priori, dealing with the notions of intuition and a priori evidence, the question of why intuitions qualify as evidence, and the question of how they can be a reliable guide to the truth about a priori matters.

Three traditional distinctions

The a priori/a posteriori distinction is epistemological whereas the necessary/contingent distinction and the analytic/synthetic distinction are arguably logical (or perhaps linguistic or metaphysical). Despite this, in the first half of the twentieth century many philosophers (especially among the logical positivists) treated these three distinctions as equivalent. They held: (1) p is necessary iff p is analytic; (2) p is knowable a priori iff p is analytic; (3) p is necessary iff p is knowable a priori.[1] But each of the implications from left to right has been convincingly challenged: (1) Not every necessary truth is analytic. For example, various supervenience principles and transitivity principles are necessary but not analytic.[2] (2) Not everything that is knowable a priori is analytic. For example, the indicated supervenience and transitivity principles are all knowable a priori but are not analytic. (3) Not every necessary truth is knowable a priori. Scientific essentialism teaches us, for example, that it is necessary that water = H_2O but that this identity is knowable only with the aid of empirical science.[3]

The remaining three implications (those from right to left) have also been challenged: (1) It has been claimed that not every analytic truth is necessary; for example, assertions of certain indexical sentences such as "I am here" have been alleged to be analytic but contingent.[4] (2) On the assumption that definitions are analytic and that scientific definitions are definitions, then not every analytic truth would be knowable a priori. Scientific definitions (e.g., water $=_{def} H_2O$) would be an exception. (3) It has been claimed that not everything that is knowable a priori is necessary. For example, it has been claimed that the man who introduced the term "meter" for the length of the standard meter-bar knew a priori that the length of that bar was one meter, but it is contingent that the length of that bar was one meter.[5] While the success of these three challenges is less clear,[6] the former three challenges are very convincing. And that is all it takes to show that each of the three equivalences fails.

Quine's attack

At mid-century W. V. Quine launched his famous attack on the analytic/synthetic distinction. Much in the spirit of Berkeley's skepticism about the meaningfulness of "substance" and Hume's skepticism about the meaningfulness of "necessary connexion" ("in all these expressions, *so apply'd*, we have really no distinct meaning, and make use only of common words, without any clear and determinate ideas"), Quine held that there was no sense to the terms "analytic" and "synthetic." Quine's argument is an enthymeme with roughly the following form: there is no noncircular, purely *empiricist* clarification of the distinction, and therefore there is no distinction at all: "That there is such a distinction to be drawn at all is an unempirical dogma of empiricists, a metaphysical article of faith."[7]

Quine's attack did not stop with analyticity. Reminiscent of the philosophers who believed that the three traditional distinctions were equivalent, Quine seems to suppose that, *if there were such distinctions*, the analytic/synthetic distinction would be the same as the necessary/contingent distinction, which in turn would be the same as the a priori/a posteriori distinction. So, for Quine, since there is no analytic/synthetic distinction, there is no necessary/contingent distinction and no a priori/a posteriori distinction either. But since these distinctions are not equivalent, these further conclusions would not follow even if Quine were right about the analytic/synthetic distinction.

Although Quine's attack on the analytic/synthetic distinction has had many followers, his attack on the necessary/contingent distinction has had much less effect. Most philosophers accept the distinction and invoke it in their work; modal logic and modal metaphysics are thriving subjects. Can we give noncircular characterizations of our modal notions? Although some have been suggested,[8] there would be nothing unreasonable in holding them to be primitive.[9] After all, everyone must take *some* notions to be primitive. But what evidence (or reasons) do we have for our positive modal *assertions* (that this or that is necessary, possible, or contingent)? No doubt Quine was right that we cannot defend such assertions using exclusively empirical evidence: when one brings to bear all the ingenious Quinean techniques of regimentation, the simplest theory based solely on empirical evidence will not affirm any positive modal assertions; it simply leaves them out. For evidence (reasons) sufficient to defend such assertions, we must turn to the a priori, specifically, to our intuitions. Evidential use of intuitions is standard practice in logic, mathematics, and philosophy (Quine himself follows this practice in logic and set theory). Defending the legitimacy of using intuitions as evidence will be the primary goal of section 1. We can then give a straightforward defense of the necessary/contingent distinction: we have a very wide range of robust modal intuitions (e.g., the intuition that it is contingent that the number of planets is greater than seven; there could have been fewer); when such intuitions are taken as evidence, the simplest theory is one which accepts the necessary/contingent distinction at face value. Of course, once the distinction is defended in this way, we will be entitled to make use of it in our positive theoretical account of the a priori.

What about the analytic/synthetic distinction? There are reasons for thinking that no single notion can play all the theoretical roles – logical, linguistic, metaphysical, epistemological – which "analytic" has traditionally been asked to play.[10] It might well be that there is no good way to bring order to the diverse uses of the term and that it should simply be eschewed for sake of clarity. Even so, there is no good reason to abandon our relatively pretheoretic notion of a *definition*. To do so would fly in the face of standard practice in mathematics, science, and philosophy. Again, once we have established that intuitions are evidence, it will be straightforward to defend various definitional assertions and to incorporate them in our final positive account of the a priori.

Although our modal notions and the notion of a definition might well lack a noncircular characterization, it is easy to give a noncircular characterization of our notions of the a priori and the a posteriori, at least as they arise in connection with the topic of evidence: a posteriori evidence is that which is imparted through experiences; a priori evidence is that which is not imparted through experiences but rather through intuitions.[11] One of the reasons Quineans have been suspicious of the a priori is that they have wrongly supposed that a priori evidence (if it existed) would need to be infallible and unrevisable. But both infallibilism and unrevisability are mistaken (as I will explain in the course of the paper). One of the main traditional lines of thought on the a priori – from Plato to Gödel – recognizes that a priori evidence (intuition) is fallible and revisable and that conclusions based on it are holistic, relying on dialectic or a priori theory construction. The views developed in this paper should be thought of as continuing in this tradition.

Knowledge and evidence

We began by considering three alleged equivalences, (1)–(3), and reasons for rejecting them. There are two other alleged equivalences which have been even more prominent in the history of epistemology: (a) x knows p iff x has a justified true belief in p; (b) x is justified in believing p iff x has good evidence for p. If correct, these two equivalences would make the tie between knowledge and evidence very close indeed. But in contemporary epistemology this close connection has been challenged. Gettier examples have been used convincingly to show that good evidence plus true belief is not sufficient for knowledge.[12] And various reliabilists and coherentists have questioned whether good evidence is even necessary for knowledge. Although debate about the latter challenge continues, there is significant agreement that good evidence is required for the high grade of theoretical knowledge sought in science, mathematics, and philosophy. It certainly is required for *critical* understanding.

Our strategy

These remarks suggest that a promising approach to the a priori is through the topic of *a priori evidence*.[13] This is the plan I will follow. The paper will have three parts. First, a brief discussion of our standard justificatory procedure and the phenomenology of intuition, followed by a defense of the thesis that intuitions are indeed evidence. Second, an explanation of *why* intuitions are evidence. The explanation is provided by *modal reliabilism* – the doctrine that there is a certain kind of attenuated modal tie between intuitions and the truth.[14] Third, an explanation of why there should be such a tie between intuitions and the truth. According to the explanation, the tie does not have a mysterious, or supernatural, source (as perhaps it does in Gödel's theory of mathematical intuition[15]); rather, it is simply a consequence of what, by definition, it is to possess – to understand – the concepts involved in our intuitions. Taken together, these three parts form the basis of a unified general account of the a priori, an account which promises to clarify the relation between the a priori disciplines – logic, mathematics, and philosophy – and the empirical sciences.[16]

1. Intuition and Evidence

Our standard justificatory procedure

I begin by reviewing some plain truths about the procedure we standardly use to justify our beliefs and theories. The first point is that we standardly use various items – for example, phenomenal experiences, observations, testimony – as evidence. Now, as we indicated above, at one time many people accepted the doctrine that knowledge is justified true belief, but by using Gettier examples we can show this to be mistaken. Specifically, we find it intuitively obvious that situations like those described in the Gettier examples could occur, and we find it intuitively obvious that in such a situation the person would not know the thing at issue despite having a justified true belief. These intuitions – that such situations could occur and that in them the person would not know – are our evidence (reasons for believing) that the traditional theory is mistaken. This sort of evidential use of intuitions is ubiquitous in philosophy; recall just a few further examples:

Chisholm's perceptual-relativity refutation of phenomenalism, the Chisholm, Geach, and Putnam refutations of behaviorism, Putnam's twin-earth examples, Burge's arthritis example, multiple-realizability, etc., etc. The use of intuitions is equally prevalent in logic, arithmetic, set theory, etc. Clearly, it is our standard justificatory procedure to *use* intuitions as evidence (or as reasons). This, of course, does not entail that intuitions *are* evidence; showing that comes later.

Phenomenology of intuitions

By intuition, we do not mean a magical power or inner voice or a mysterious "faculty" or anything of the sort. For you to have an intuition that A is just for it to *seem* to you that A. Here "seems" is understood, not as a cautionary or "hedging" term, but in its use as a term for a genuine kind of conscious episode. For example, when you first consider one of de Morgan's laws, often it neither seems to be true nor seems to be false; after a moment's reflection, however, something new happens: suddenly it *seems* true. Of course, this kind of seeming is *intellectual*, not sensory or introspective (or imaginative). For this reason, intuitions are counted as "data of reason" not "data of experience."

In our context when we speak of intuition, we mean "rational intuition." This is distinguished from what physicists call "physical intuition." We have a physical intuition that, when a house is undermined, it will fall. This does not count as a rational intuition, for it does not present itself as necessary: it does not seem that a house undermined *must* fall; plainly, it is *possible* for a house undermined to remain in its original position or, indeed, to rise up. By contrast, when we have a rational intuition, say, that if P then not not P, this presents itself as necessary: it seems that things could not be otherwise; it must be that if P then not not P.[17]

Intuition must also be distinguished from belief: belief is not a seeming; intuition is. For example, there are many mathematical theorems that I believe (because I have seen the proofs) but that do not *seem* to me to be true and that do not *seem* to me to be false; I do not have intuitions about them either way. Conversely, I have an intuition – it still *seems* to me – that the naive truth schema holds; this is so despite the fact that I do not believe that it holds (because I know of the Liar paradox).[18] There is a rather similar phenomenon in sensory (vs. intellectual) seeming. In the Müller–Lyer illusion, it still *seems* to me that one of the arrows is longer than the other; this is so despite the fact that I do not believe that it is (because I have measured them). In each case, the seeming (intellectual or sensory) persists in spite of the countervailing belief. It should be observed at this point that the existence of the paradoxes shows that the infallibilist theory of intuition is mistaken: for example, the Liar Paradox shows that either our intuition of the naive truth schema or one or more of our intuitions about classical logic must be mistaken.

This brings up a closely related difference between belief and intuition. Belief is highly plastic. Using (false) appeals to authority and so forth, you can get a person to believe almost anything, at least briefly. Not so for intuitions. Although there is disagreement about the degree of plasticity of intuitions (some people believe they are rather plastic; I do not), it is clear that, *collectively*, they are inherently rather more resistant to such influences than beliefs.

Similar phenomenological considerations make it clear that intuitions are likewise distinct from judgments, guesses, hunches, and common sense. My view is simply that, like sensory seeming, intellectual seeming (intuition) is just one more primitive propositional attitude. I should note, finally, that the work of cognitive psychologists such as Wason, Johnson-Laird, Nisbett, Kahneman and Tversky tells us little about intuitions in our sense; they have simply not been concerned with them.

The argument from epistemic norms

So far we have seen what intuitions are and that we *use* them as evidence. But using something as evidence does not show that it really is evidence; for example, simply using astrology charts as evidence for what will happen is hardly enough to make them evidence for what will happen.

One way to show that intuitions are truly evidence is to invoke various intuitions which imply that intuitions are evidence. While this direct route is entirely correct, it does not convince the skeptic. To do that, one needs a special form of argument which is designed to persuade, on their own terms, people who are in the grip of a view which interferes with the effectiveness of ordinary, direct arguments. Self-defeat arguments fall into this category. In "The Incoherence of Empiricism"[19] I gave three distinct self-defeat arguments showing that radical empiricists, who reject intuitions as evidence, find themselves with a self-defeating epistemology. To give a feel for this style of argument I will now sketch one of these arguments against radical empiricism, the view that *only* phenomenal experiences and/or observations have genuine evidential weight.[20]

Consider an absurd position like *visualism* – the view that, among our phenomenal experiences, only visual experiences are evidence, arbitrarily excluding nonvisual experiences (tactile, auditory, etc.). How is radical empiricism relevantly different from visualism? To avoid begging the question, radical empiricists must answer *from within* the standard justificatory procedure. The question to consider is this: when one implements the standard justificatory procedure's mechanism of self-criticism, does intuition – in contrast to nonvisual experience – get excluded as a source of evidence?

In relation to the "three *c*'s" – *consistency, corroboration*, and *confirmation* – intuition is quite unlike spurious sources of evidence such as astrology charts, tea leaves, tarot, oracles, birds, and the like. First, a person's concrete-case intuitions are largely consistent with one another. (We confine ourselves to concrete-case intuitions, for it is to them that the standard justificatory procedure assigns primary evidential weight.) To be sure, a given person's concrete-case intuitions occasionally appear to be inconsistent with one another, but so do our observations and even our phenomenal experiences. This is hardly enough to throw out observation and experience as sources of evidence. Moreover, for each of these sources – including intuition – most apparent conflicts can be reconciled by standard rephrasal techniques. Second, although different people do have conflicting intuitions from time to time, there is an impressive corroboration by others of one's elementary logical, mathematical, conceptual, and modal intuitions.[21] The situation is much the same with observation: different people have conflicting observations from time to time, but this is hardly enough to throw out observation as a source of evidence. Third, unlike astrology charts, intuition is seldom, if ever, disconfirmed by our experiences and observations. The primary reason is that the contents of our intuitions – whether conceptual, logical, mathematical, or modal – are by and large independent of the contents of our observations and experiences. The one potential exception involves our modal intuitions, but virtually no conflicts arise here because our intuitions about what experiences and observations are logically (metaphysically) possible are so liberal.

There is another kind of conflict, namely, conflict between certain *theories* and certain intuitions (e.g., intuitions about simultaneity and Euclidean geometry). Do such conflicts overturn intuition as a source of evidence? No, for there are analogous conflicts between certain theories and certain observations (e.g., observations that the sun is about the same size as the moon and that it moves across the sky). Likewise, phenomenal experience, memory, and testimony come into conflict with certain theories. Such conflicts are not enough to overturn any of these sources of evidence. As a matter of fact, however, most of our elementary conceptual, logical, and numerical intuitions are not in conflict with, but are actually affirmed by, our empirical theories. And modal and higher mathematical intuitions, while not affirmed by purely empirical theories, are for the most part not inconsistent with them. Moreover, our simplest comprehensive theory based on *all* standard sources of evidence, *including intuition*, affirms most of our modal and higher mathematical intuitions. This should be no surprise since it begins by including intuitions as evidence.

If radical empiricists are to try to overthrow intuition by means of the standard justificatory procedure's mechanism for self-criticism, there is only one remaining alternative, which goes as follows. First, one formulates one's simplest comprehensive theory on the basis of the standard sources of evidence that one is not challenging. Then, if the resulting theory does not deem the omitted sources to be reliable, they are discounted as sources of evidence. This method is appropriate in some cases, for example, to challenge as a source of evidence the hitherto uncritically accepted pronouncements of an established political authority (reminiscent of the Wizard of Oz). However, there are cases in which this method does not work. For example, it may not be used by our imagined proponents of visualism to challenge other modes of phenomenal experience (tactile, auditory, etc.) as sources of evidence. Neither vision nor touch may be used in this way to override the other as a source of evidence. To be a source of evidence, neither requires affirmation by the simplest comprehensive theory based on other sources of evidence.

The difference between the political-authority case and the visualism case is clear. The political authority is *intuitively not as basic* a source of evidence as the sources of evidence that are being used to challenge it (i.e., experience, observation, etc.). By contrast, vision and touch are *intuitively equally basic* sources of evidence. The standard justificatory procedure permits us to apply the present method against a currently accepted source of evidence if and only if it is intuitive that the source is not as basic as the sources of evidence being used to challenge it.[22]

So in the radical empiricists' effort to eliminate intuition as a source of evidence, the standard justificatory procedure would warrant this move only if we had intuitions to the effect that intuition is a less basic source of evidence than experience and/or observation, one requiring auxiliary support from the best comprehensive theory based exclusively on other sources of evidence.[23] But when we consider relevant cases, we see that we do not have such intuitions. For example, suppose a person has an intuition, say, that if P then not not P; or (in your favorite Gettier example) that the person in question would not know; or that a good theory must take into account *all* the evidence; and so forth. Nothing more is needed. Intuitively, these intuitions are evidentially as basic as evidence gets. They are intuitively as basic as experiences, much as tactile experiences are intuitively as basic as visual experiences. In consequence, the present method for challenging a source of evidence cannot be used against intuition, any more than it can be used against, say, touch or vision.

In reply, someone might hold that being intuitively basic is necessary but not sufficient for a candidate source to withstand critique. For sufficiency, something additional is required, namely, that our best *explanation* of the candidate source should entail that its deliverances have an appropriate tie to the truth. Using this idea, radical empiricists might hold that, although the best explanation of our (reports of) experiences and/or observations entail that they have an appropriate tie to the truth, this is not so for intuitions and, accordingly, intuition does not withstand critique. This reply, however, is questionbegging. Advocates of intuitions may counter that the best explanation of intuition must invoke the analysis of what it takes to possess concepts determinately (see section 3 below), and, according to that analysis, it is constitutive of determinate concept possession that intuitions have an appropriate tie to the truth. Why accept this explanation? Well, if (certain compelling) intuitions are admitted as evidence, its superiority over competing explanations can be shown. Given this prospect, it would be questionbegging for radical empiricists to reject this explanation in favor of their own candidate: their candidate could be defended only by disregarding a significant body of evidence (or at least what is counted as evidence according to our standard procedure). Their candidate could be defended only if they had *already* (i.e., independently of their candidate) shown intuition not to be a source of evidence. As we have shown, however, they are unable to do this. Absent a reason for departing from our standard procedure, we are therefore entitled – indeed, obligated – to continue using intuitions as evidence.

The upshot is that intuition survives as a genuine source of evidence when one applies the standard justificatory procedure's mechanism for self-criticism. We have not been able to find a relevant difference between radical empiricism, which excludes intuition as a source of evidence, and various preposterous theories (e.g., visualism) that arbitrarily exclude other standard sources of evidence (e.g., touch). But, surely, these preposterous theories are not justified. So radical empiricism is not justified, either.

There is a way to strengthen this argument. Suppose that in our justificatory practices we were to make an arbitrary departure from our epistemic norms. There would then be reason to doubt that the theories we would formulate by following the nonstandard procedure are justified. Since radical empiricists make an arbitrary departure from our epistemic norms, what can they do to overcome this reasonable doubt in their own case? They are caught in a fatal dilemma. On the one hand, they could invoke theories arrived at by following the standard justificatory procedure, with its inclusion of intuitions as evidence. But, by the radical empiricists' own standards, these theories are not justified. So this avenue is of no help. On the other hand, they could invoke theories arrived at by following their radical empiricist procedure. But this would be of no help, either. For, as just noted, there is reasonable doubt whether, by following that procedure, one obtains justified theories. To overcome this doubt, one may not invoke the very theories about whose justification there is already reasonable doubt. That would only beg the question. Either way, therefore, radical empiricists are unable to overcome the reasonable doubt that their procedure leads to justified theories. So the reasonable doubt stands.

Our epistemic situation is in this sense "hermeneutical": when one makes an arbitrary departure from it, reasonable doubts are generated, and there is in principle no way to overcome them. This is the fate of radical empiricism. Only the standard justificatory procedure escapes this problem: because it conforms to – and, indeed, constitutes – the epistemic norm, there is no reason to doubt that the theories it yields are justified; so the problem never arises.

2. Modal Reliabilism: Why Intuitions are Evidence

What explains why intuitions are evidence? In "Philosophical Limits of Scientific Essentialism" I argued that the only adequate explanation is some kind of truth-based (i.e., reliabilist) explanation. In *Philosophical Limits of Science* I develop this argument in detail, dealing there with various alternative explanations – pragmatist, coherentist, conventionalist, contextualist, and rule-based (or practice-based). In the present context, I will assume that these arguments are successful and that we must turn to a truth-based explanation. This assumption will appeal to many readers independently of the indicated arguments.

Reliabilism has been associated with analyses of knowledge and justification, analyses which most philosophers today reject. Our topic, however, is not knowledge or justification but rather evidence. This difference is salutary, for here reliabilism is more promising. But not as a *general* theory of evidence: sources of evidence traditionally classified as *nonbasic* (or *derived*) sources are subject to counterexamples much like those used against reliabilist theories of justification. For example, testimony would still provide an individual with evidence (reasons to believe) even if the individual has been exposed to systematic undetectable lying. So reliability is not a necessary condition for something's qualifying as a source of evidence. Nor is reliability a sufficient condition for something's qualifying as a source of evidence: as in the case of justification, such things as nomologically reliable clairvoyance, etc. are *prima facie* counterexamples.

The natural response to these counterexamples is to demand only that *basic* sources of evidence be reliable: something is a basic source of evidence iff it has an appropriate kind of reliable tie to the truth. Then we would be free to adopt some alternative treatment of nonbasic sources; for example, something is a nonbasic source of evidence relative to a given subject iff it would be deemed (perhaps unreliably) to have a reliable tie to the truth by the best comprehensive theory based on the subject's basic sources of evidence.[24] If we accept the traditional thesis that phenomenal experience and intuition are our basic sources and that all other sources are nonbasic,[25] then the above counterexamples would not fault this analysis of nonbasic sources of evidence. In the case of undetectable lying, testimony would now rightly be counted as a source of evidence, for the best comprehensive theory based on the individual's basic sources (experience and intuition) would deem it to have a reliable tie to the truth (even if it in fact does not because of the envisaged lying). In the case of spurious nonbasic sources (reliable clairvoyance, etc.), if their reliability is not affirmed by the best comprehensive theory based on the individual's basic sources, their deliverances would rightly not qualify as evidence.

Let us therefore agree that reliabilism should be restricted to basic sources of evidence: something is a basic source of evidence iff it has an appropriate kind of reliable tie to the truth. The fundamental question then concerns the character of this tie. Is it a contingent (nomological or causal) tie? Or is it some kind of necessary tie?

Contingent reliabilism

On this account, something counts as a basic source of evidence iff there is a contingent nomological tie between its deliverances and the truth. This account, however, is subject to counterexamples of the sort which faulted the original sufficiency condition above (nomologically reliable clairvoyance, etc.). Consider a creature who has a capacity for making reliable telepathically generated guesses. Phenomenologically, these guesses resemble those which people make in blindsight experiments. The guesses at issue concern necessary truths of some very high degree of difficulty. These truths are known to the beings on a distant planet who have arrived at them by ordinary a priori means (theoretical systematization of intuitions, proof of consequences therefrom, etc.). These beings have intelligence far exceeding that of our creature or anyone else coinhabiting his planet. Indeed, the creature and his coinhabitants will never be able to establish any of these necessary truths (or even assess their consistency) by ordinary a priori means. Moreover, none of these creatures has any beliefs whatsoever about the superior beings and their intellectual accomplishments. Finally, suppose that the following holds as a matter of nomological necessity: the creature guesses that p is true iff p is one of these necessary truths and the superior beings telepathically induce the creature to guess that p is true when the question arises. But, plainly, guessing would not qualify as a basic source of evidence for the creature, contrary to contingent reliabilism.[26] Would you say that, by virtue of just guessing that Fermat's Last Theorem is true, the creature has evidence (reason to believe) that it is true?!

Modal reliabilism

Given that contingent reliabilism fails, we are left with modal reliabilism, according to which something counts as a basic source of evidence iff there is an appropriate kind of modal tie between its deliverances and the truth. This formula provides us with a general scheme for analyzing what it takes for a candidate source of evidence to be basic. It is not itself an analysis: it is not intended that *just any* strong modal tie be necessary and sufficient for something's being a basic source of evidence. Rather, this scheme provides us with an *invitation* to find the weakest modal tie that does the job – that is, the weakest modal tie which lets in the right sources and excludes the wrong ones.[27] The explanation of why intuition is a basic source of evidence then goes as follows. By definition, a candidate source of evidence is basic iff it has *that* sort of modal tie; intuition does have that sort of modal tie; therefore, intuition is a basic source of evidence. Likewise for phenomenal experience: it too has that sort of modal tie and so is a basic source of evidence. And we have an explanation of why other candidate sources are nonbasic: they lack that sort of modal tie.

We thus have an invitation to find the weakest modal tie that does the job. One candidate is the kind of modal tie posited by traditional infallibilists. The resulting analysis would be: a candidate source is basic iff, necessarily, all of its deliverances are true. But this is not satisfactory for two reasons. First, we have good reasons to reject infallibilism both in the case of intuition (e.g., the logical paradoxes) and in the case of phenomenal experience (e.g., Russell's locally uniform color spectrum), so the infallibilist analysis would wrongly exclude intuition and phenomenal experience as basic sources of evidence. Second, as we will see, there are weaker modal ties that do the job.

One candidate is an infallibilist tie which is relativized to ideal cognitive conditions. On this analysis, a candidate source is basic iff, necessarily, for anyone in ideal cognitive conditions, the deliverances of that source would be true. Accordingly, for anyone in ideal cognitive conditions, basic sources provide a guaranteed pathway to the truth regarding the deliverances of the source. Of course, we humans are not in *ideal* cognitive conditions, so there is no guarantee that the deliverances of *our* basic sources are always true. But, if we limit ourselves to suitably elementary propositions, then relative to them we *approximate* ideal cognitive conditions. For suitably elementary propositions, deliverances of our basic sources would therefore provide in an approximate way the kind of pathway to the truth they would have generally in ideal conditions. For those of us capable of real theorizing – that is, subjects whose cognitive conditions (intelligence, memory, attentiveness, constancy, etc.) are good enough to enable them to process theoretically the deliverances of their basic sources – the size of the class of relevantly elementary propositions would not be inconsiderable.[28]

While this relativized infallibilist analysis is an improvement, it too posits a very strong modal tie. Our larger analytical strategy, however, invited us only to posit the weakest modal tie that does the job, and there is indeed a weaker one. It is a tie which is holistic in character and which holds, not with absolute universality, but as Aristotle would say *for the most part*. To wit, a candidate source is basic iff for cognitive conditions of some suitably high quality, necessarily, if someone in those cognitive conditions were to process theoretically the deliverances of the candidate source, the resulting theory would provide a correct assessment as to the truth or falsity of most of those deliverances. Whereas the previous analysis required that the deliverances of a basic source themselves be true, this weaker analysis requires only that most of the theoretical assessments as to the truth or falsity of those deliverances be true.[29] The previous remarks about approximations then carry over *mutatis mutandis*. For subjects (like ourselves) capable of processing their basic sources theoretically, the result of that processing would, for elementary deliverances, provide in an approximate way the kind of pathway to the truth it would provide generally in the indicated high quality cognitive conditions, a pathway whose reliability increases the more elementary those deliverances are.

This analysis does the job. It tells us in a natural and non-*ad-hoc* way what is common to the traditional basic sources of evidence – intuition and phenomenal experience.[30] And it tells us what is lacking in all other candidate sources – those which are nonbasic and those which are not even sources of evidence, basic or nonbasic. Moreover, I can think of no weaker modal tie that does the job. Finally, although there might be still weaker modal ties that do the job, it is plausible that they would at least resemble the foregoing.

Review

A shortcoming of traditional empiricism was that it offered no explanation of why phenomenal experience is a basic source of evidence; this was just an unexplained dogma. By the same token, traditional rationalists (and also moderate empiricists who, like Hume, accepted intuition as a basic source of evidence) did not successfully explain why intuition is a basic source of evidence. Modal reliabilism provides a natural explanation filling in these two gaps left by the traditional theories.

The explanation is in terms of the indicated modal tie between these sources and the truth. But why should there be such a tie to the truth? Neither traditional empiricism nor traditional rationalism provided a satisfactory explanation. The theory of concept possession promises to fill in this gap.

3. Concept Possession

Our theory presupposes three realisms: realism about the modalities (possibility, necessity, contingency), realism about concepts and propositions, and realism about the propositional attitudes – including, in particular, intuition. In the way outlined in our introduction, modal intuitions yield a straightforward defense of the first of these realisms. Other intuitions yield related defenses of the other two realisms.

We will begin by isolating two different but related senses in which a subject can be said to possess a concept. The first is a nominal sense; the second is the full, strong sense. The first may be analyzed thus:

> A subject possesses a given concept at least nominally iff the subject has natural propositional attitudes (belief, desire, etc.) toward propositions which have that concept as a conceptual content.[31]

Possessing a concept in this nominal sense is compatible with what Tyler Burge calls misunderstanding and incomplete understanding of the concept.[32] For example, in Burge's arthritis case, the subject misunderstands the concept of arthritis, wrongly taking it to be possible to have arthritis in the thigh. In Burge's verbal contract case, the subject incompletely understands the concept of a contract, not knowing whether or not contracts must be written. (Hereafter I will use "misunderstanding" for cases where there are errors in the subject's understanding of the concept and "incomplete understanding" for cases where there are gaps – "don't knows" – in the subject's understanding of the concept.) Possessing a concept in the nominal sense is also compatible with having propositional attitudes merely by virtue of the standard attribution practices of third-person interpreters. For example, we commonly attribute to animals, children, and members of other cultures various beliefs involving concepts which loom large in our own thought. We do so without thereby committing ourselves to there being a causally efficacious psychological state having the attributed content which plays a role in "methodologically solipsistic" psychological explanation. Our standard attribution practices, nonetheless, would have us deem such attributions to be appropriate. Advocates of this point of view hold that these attribution practices reveal to us essential features of our concept of belief (and, indeed, might even be constitutive of it). Everyone should at least agree that people could have a word "believe" which expresses a concept having these features. In what follows, the theory I will propose is designed to be compatible with this practice-based view but will not presuppose it. These, then, are some weak ways in which a person can possess a concept. And there might be others belonging to a natural similarity class. This, too, is something which our theory will be designed to accommodate but not to presuppose.

With these various weak ways of possessing a concept in mind, we are in a position to give an informal characterization of possessing a concept in the full, strong sense:

> A subject possesses a concept in the full sense iff (i) the subject at least nominally possesses the concept and (ii) the subject does *not* do this with misunderstanding or incomplete understanding or just by virtue of satisfying our attribution practices or in any other weak such way.

In ordinary language, when we speak of "understanding a concept," what we mean is possessing the concept in the full sense. In what follows, this ordinary-language idiom will help to anchor our inquiry, and I will use it wherever convenient.[33] It will also be convenient to have available the technical term "possessing a concept determinately," which is just another way of expressing the notion of understanding a concept (i.e., possessing a concept in the full sense).

Now just as a person can be said to understand a concept (to possess it in the full sense), a person can be said to misunderstand a concept or to understand a concept incompletely and so on. Similarly, a person can be said to understand a proposition, to misunderstand a proposition, to understand a proposition incompletely, and so forth.

We have characterized determinate possession informally – negatively and by means of examples – and we evidently have an ordinary-language idiom for this notion. We readily see what the notion is, and it seems important theoretically. A legitimate philosophical project would therefore be to give a positive general analysis of the notion. Indeed, it cries out for one.

My strategy will be to begin with a series of intuitive examples which serve to isolate some ideas which will play a role in the eventual analysis. The first two examples are designed so that neither features of other people nor of the larger social or linguistic context are relevant. Nor are features of the environment. Nor are features such as salience, naturalness, or metaphysical basicness.

The multigon example

Suppose that a sincere, wholly normal, attentive woman introduces *through use* (not stipulation) a new term "multigon."[34] She applies the term to various closed plane figures having several sides (pentagons, octagons, chiliagons, etc.). Suppose her term expresses some definite concept – the concept of being a multigon – and that she determinately possesses this concept. Surely this is possible. By chance, however, the woman has neither applied her term "multigon" to triangles and rectangles nor withheld it from them. The question has not come up. But eventually she does consider the question of whether it is possible for a triangle or a rectangle to be a multigon. When she does, her cognitive conditions continue to be normal – she is intelligent, attentive, possessed of good memory, free from distraction, and so forth – and she determinately understands the question. Now let us suppose that the property of being a multigon is either the property of being a closed straight-sided plane figure or the property of being a closed straight-sided plane figure with five or more sides. (Each alternative is listed under "polygon" in my desk *Webster's*.) Then, intuitively, when the woman considers the question, she would have an intuition that it *is* possible for a triangle or a rectangle to be a multigon if and only if the property of being a multigon = the property of being a closed straight-sided plane figure. Alternatively, she would have an intuition that it is *not* possible for a triangle or a rectangle to be a multigon if and only if the property of being a multigon = the property of being a closed straight-sided plane figure with five or more sides. Intuitively, if these things did not hold, the right thing to say would be that either the woman does not really possess a determinate concept or her cognitive conditions are not really normal.[35]

The chromic example

Suppose a woman has through use (in, say, her diary) introduced a new term "chromic." She applies the term to phenomenal qualia, specifically, to shades of phenomenal color – red, blue, purple, etc. – but withholds it from phenomenal black and phenomenal white. Suppose the term "chromic" expresses some definite concept – the concept of being chromic – and that she determinately possesses this concept. Again, this is surely possible. Suppose, however, that the woman has not yet experienced any shades of phenomenal gray. When she finally does, it is a central shade of phenomenal gray, and the experience of it is clear and distinct – vivid, unwavering, and long-lasting. During the course of the experience, the question whether the shade is chromic occurs to her. When it does, her cognitive conditions are wholly normal (she is fully attentive, etc.), and she determinately understands the question. Suppose, finally, that the property of being chromic is either the property of being a nonblack nonwhite phenomenal color or the property of being a nonblack nonwhite nongray phenomenal color. In this case, intuitively, the following would hold: the woman would have the intuition that the shade *is* chromic iff the property of being chromic = the property of being a nonblack nonwhite phenomenal color. Alternatively, she would have the intuition that the shades is *not* chromic iff the property of being chromic = the property of being a nonblack nonwhite nongray phenomenal color. That is, just as in the multigon case, the woman's intuitions would track the truth *vis-à-vis* the relevant test question. As before, if this were not so, we should say instead that the woman does not really possess a determinate concept or her cognitive conditions are not really normal.

What is distinctive about the chromic example is that the woman determinately possesses the concept of being chromic at a time when the decisive cases involve items – namely, shades of phenomenal gray – which lie beyond her experience and conceptual repertory. She determinately possesses the concept of being chromic even though, prior to experiencing phenomenal gray, she cannot even entertain the relevant test questions, let alone have truth-tracking intuitions regarding them. Surely such a thing is possible. There is no requirement that, in order to possess a concept determinately, a person must *already* have experiential and/or conceptual resources sufficient for deciding the possible extensions of the concept. Determinate concept possession is in this sense "Hegelian" – a present feature revealed only in the future.

Here is a variant on the example. It might be that it is *nomologically impossible* for the woman (or, for that matter, anyone else) to experience phenomenal gray: as a matter of nomological necessity, attempts to overcome this deficiency (e.g., electrodes, drugs, neurosurgery, etc.) only lead to irreversible coma and death. But this would not prevent the woman's term "chromic" from determinately expressing a definite concept, the concept of being chromic. Consistent with all of this, there is a certain *metaphysical possibility*, namely, the metaphysical possibility that the woman – or someone whose epistemic situation is qualitatively identical to hers – might have an increased potential for phenomenal experiences (viz., for phenomenal gray). This could be so without there being any (immediate) shift in the way the woman (or her counterpart) understands any of her concepts or the propositions involving them. In this improved situation, there would be no barrier to the woman's coming to understand and to consider the test question determinately. Intuitively, it is metaphysically possible for all this to happen.[36] And, intuitively, if it did, then just as in the original example, the woman (or her counterpart) would have truth-tracking intuitions *vis-à-vis* the test question.

Of course, the same sort of thing could happen in connection with nomologically necessary limitations on aspects of the woman's cognitive conditions (intelligence, attentiveness, memory, constancy, etc.): it could be that, because of such limitations, it is nomologically impossible for her to have truth-tracking intuitions *vis-à-vis* relevant test questions. It would nonetheless be metaphysically possible for her (or a counterpart whose epistemic situation is qualitatively identical) to have improved cognitive conditions. Intuitively, in such a situation, she would then have the relevant truth-tracking intuitions. She would determinately possess the concept iff such intuitions were metaphysically possible.

Finally, all this would hold *mutatis mutandis* if the examples concerned, not a solitary person (as above), but whole groups of people who determinately possess relevant concepts. These people would determinately possess a given target concept iff it were metaphysically possible for them to have the associated truth-tracking intuitions.

The moral is that, even though there might be a nomological barrier to there being intuitions of the sort we have been discussing, there is no metaphysically necessary barrier. (Remember: these intuitions need not be those of the original subjects; they may be those of people whose epistemic situation is qualitatively identical to that of the original subjects.) This leads to the thought that determinate concept possession might be explicated in terms of the metaphysical possibility of relevant truth-tracking intuitions (in appropriately good cognitive conditions and with appropriately rich conceptual repertoires). The idea is that determinateness is that mode of possession which constitutes the categorical base of this possibility. When a subject's mode of concept possession shifts to determinateness there is a corresponding shift in the possible intuitions accessible to the subject. In fact, there is a shift in both *quantity* and *quality*. The quantity grows because incomplete understanding is replaced with complete understanding, eliminating "don't knows." The quality improves because incorrect understanding is replaced with correct understanding.

Using these ideas, I will now formulate a progression of analyses, each beset with a problem which its successor is designed to overcome – converging, one hopes, on a successful analysis.

a. *Subjunctive analyses*

Our discussion of the multigon example suggests the following:

> x determinately possesses the concept of being a multigon iff:
> x would have the intuition that it is possible for a triangle or a rectangle to be a multigon iff it is *true* that it is possible for a triangle or a rectangle to be a multigon.

In turn, this suggests the following:

> x determinately possesses the concept of being a multigon iff:
> x would have intuitions which *imply* that the property of being a multigon = the property of being a closed straight-sided plane figure iff it is *true* that the property of being a multigon = the property of being a closed straight-sided plane figure.

We have been assuming that in the example x possesses the target concept determinately in all respects except perhaps those which would decide this sort of test property-identity. Suppose, however, that we remove this background supposition. We would then want to generalize on the above idea. The natural generalization is the following:

> x determinately possesses a given concept iff, for associated test property-identities p:
> x would have intuitions which imply that p is true iff p is true.

If f is the given concept, the associated test property-identities p are propositions to the effect that the property of being f = the property of being A, or the denials of such propositions (where A is some formula).[37] When we transform this proposal into a direct definition of *determinateness*, the mode of understanding involved when one understands determinately, we obtain the following:

determinateness = the mode m of understanding such that, necessarily, for all x and property-identities p which x understands m-ly,
   p is true iff x would have intuitions which imply that p is true.

The intention here is that "m" ranges over *natural* modes of understanding (i.e., non-*ad-hoc* modes of understanding).

b. A priori stability

A problem with this analysis is that it relies on the subjunctive "would," but there are well-known general objections to subjunctive analyses. The solution is to replace the subjunctives with a certain ordinary modal notion. I will call this modal notion *a priori stability*. Consider an arbitrary property-identity p which someone x understands m-ly. Then, x settles with a priori stability that p is true iff, for cognitive conditions of some level l and for some conceptual repertoire c, (1) x has cognitive conditions of level l and conceptual repertoire c and x attempts to elicit intuitions bearing on p and x seeks a theoretical systematization based on those intuitions and that systematization affirms that p is true and all the while x understands p m-ly, and (2) necessarily, for cognitive conditions of any level l' greater than l and for any conceptual repertoire c' which properly includes c, if x has cognitive conditions of level l' and conceptual repertoire c' and x attempts to elicit intuitions bearing on p and seeks a theoretical systematization based on those intuitions and all the while x understands p m-ly, then that systematization also affirms that p is true.[38] A diagram can be helpful here (figure 11.1).

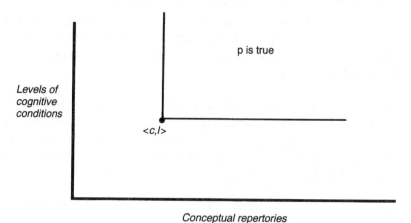

Figure 11.1

The idea is that, after x achieves $<c,l>$, theoretical systematizations of x's intuitions always yield the same verdict on p as long as p is understood m-ly throughout. That is, as long as p is understand m-ly, p always gets settled the same way throughout the region to the "northeast" of $<c,l>$. When this notion of a priori stability replaces the subjunctives in our earlier analysis, we arrive at the following:

determinateness = the mode m of understanding such that, necessarily, for all x and property-identities p which x understands m-ly,
   p is true iff it is possible for x to settle with a priori stability that p is true.

The biconditional has two parts:

(a) p is true *if* it is possible for x to settle with a priori stability that p is true.

and

(b) p is true *only if* it is possible for x to settle with a priori stability that p is true.

The former is a *correctness* (or soundness) property. The latter is a *completeness* property. The correctness property tells us about the potential *quality* of x's intuitions: it is possible for x to get into a situation such that from then on x's intuitions yield only the truth regarding p, given that x understands p m-ly. The completeness property tells us about the potential *quantity* of x's intuitions: it is possible for x to have enough intuitions to reach a priori stability regarding the question of p's truth, given that x understands p m-ly. According to the analysis, determinateness is that mode of understanding which constitutes the categorical base for the possibility of intuitions of this quantity and quality.

A qualification is in order. As the analysis is stated, x must be able to go through the envisaged intuition-driven process arriving at the conclusion that p is true. It is enough, however, that *an epistemic counterpart of* x (i.e., someone in qualitatively the same epistemic situation as x) be able to go through the envisaged process with that outcome, while understanding p m-ly. Let us understand the proposal and its sequels in this way.

c. *Accommodating scientific essentialism*

Even with this qualification, however, there is a problem with the completeness clause: it conflicts with scientific essentialism – the doctrine that there are property-identities that are essentially a posteriori (e.g., the property of being water = the property of being H_2O). Plainly, the completeness clause in the analysis goes too far, for it requires that such things can be settled a priori. The completeness clause thus needs to be weakened.

Granted, we do not have a priori intuitions supporting such scientific essentialist property-identities. Even so, whoever determinately understands these property-identities should at least have associated twin-earth intuitions, that is, intuitions regarding twin-earth scenarios of the sort which underwrite arguments for scientific essentialism. For example, if someone determinately understands the proposition that the property of being water = the property of being H_2O, that person ought to have the following twin-earth intuition: if all and only samples of water here on earth are composed of H₂O, and if the corresponding samples on a macroscopically identical twin earth are composed of XYZ (≠ H₂O), then those samples would not be samples of water.

If the person has intuitions of this sort, the person also ought to have various modal intuitions concerning the sorts of *counterpart entities* that are possible. For example, the person ought to intuit that it is possible for there to be a twin earth on which there is a counterpart of water whose composition consists of counterparts of hydrogen, oxygen, and the sharing of two electrons. Naturally, this generalizes.

These considerations lead to the following idea. Although a person who determinately understands a given natural-kind property-identity cannot settle a priori whether it is true, nonetheless the person ought to be able to settle a priori whether there is at least a *counterpart* of the property-identity which is true. Being able to settle such things a priori is a necessary condition for understanding the *categorial content* of the constituent concepts. And, of course, understanding the categorical content of a concept is a necessary condition for determinately possessing it. The idea is that this condition, taken together with the correctness condition, is jointly necessary and sufficient for determinateness.

This suggests the following analysis in which the completeness clause (b) is weakened so that it only requires categorical understanding:

determinateness = the mode m of understanding such that, necessarily, for all x and property-identities p understood m-ly by x,
(a) p is true *if* it is possible for x to settle with a priori stability that p is true.
(b) p is true *only if* it is possible for x to settle with a priori stability that p has a counterpart which is true.[39]

Before proceeding, I should note that there is an important family of test propositions p which are entirely immune to scientific essentialism, namely, those which I call *semantically stable*: p is semantically stable iff, necessarily, for any population C, it is necessary that, for any proposition p' and any population C' whose epistemic situation is qualitatively identical to that of C, if p' in C' is the counterpart of p in C, then p = p'. (There is of course an analogous notion of a *semantically stable concept*.[40]) Thus, if p is a semantically stable property-identity, the weakened completeness clause in the revised analysis entails the strong completeness clause of the earlier analysis:

(b) p is true *only if* it is possible for x to settle with a priori stability that p is true.

This fact is significant for epistemology, for most of the central propositions in the a priori disciplines – logic, mathematics, philosophy – are semantically stable and, therefore, immune to scientific essentialism.[41]

d. *Accommodating anti-individualism*

To avoid the clash with scientific essentialism, we weakened the completeness clause so that it bears on only the categorial content of our concepts. This weakening, however, creates a predictable problem having to do with the *noncategorial* content of our concepts. Suppose x is in command of nothing but the categorial content of a certain pair of concepts, say, the concept of being a beech and the concept of being an elm. He would then be in a position resembling that of Hilary Putnam, who was entirely unable to distinguish beeches from elms. In this case, x certainly would not possess these concepts determinately (although the above analysis wrongly implies that he would). A symptom of x's incomplete understanding would be his complete inability – *without relying on the expertise of others* – even to begin to do the science of beeches and elms. What is missing, of course, is that x's "web of belief" is too sparse. An analogous problem of misunderstanding would arise if x were too often to classify beeches as elms and/or conversely.

In order for x to achieve determinate possession, x's web of belief would need to be improved. But how? We can answer this question by making use of the idea of *truth-absorption*. If x were to absorb ever more true beliefs related to beeches and elms (perhaps including relevant social and linguistic facts), eventually x's incomplete understanding (or misunderstanding) would shift to determinate understanding. And, in general, if an arbitrary person x has categorial mastery of certain of his concepts but nonetheless does not understand them determinately, then by absorbing ever more true beliefs x eventually will switch out of his deficient mode of understanding and thereby come to possess the relevant concepts determinately. By contrast, people who already determinately possess their concepts can always absorb more true beliefs without switching out of their determinate possession.

These considerations suggest a final revision in our analysis:

> determinateness = the mode m of understanding such that, necessarily, for all x and all p understood m-ly by x,
> (a) p is true *if* it is possible for x to settle with a priori stability that p is true.
> (b.i) p is true *only if* it is possible for x to settle with a priori stability that p has a counterpart which is true. (for property-identities p)
> (b.ii) p is true *only if* it is possible for x to believe m-ly that p is true. (for p believable by x).[42]

Why do improvements in the web of belief suffice to eliminate indeterminateness in the usual beech/elm cases? The reason (given the truth of scientific essentialism) is that there can be nothing else in which determinateness could consist in cases like this; the question of whether this is a beech or an elm is simply beyond the ken of a priori intuition. Absent intuition, web of belief is the default position on which determinateness rides. But on questions for which there is a possibility of a priori intuitions, they are determinate.

e. The final analysis

In the course of our discussion, we found it convenient to shift our focus from determinate understanding of *concepts* to determinate understanding of *propositions*. The analysis of the former notion, however, has always been only a step away:

> x determinately possesses a given concept iff$_{def}$ x determinately understands some proposition which has that concept as a conceptual content.

This analysis invokes the notion of determinately understanding a proposition. To understand a proposition determinately is to understand it in a certain *mode* – namely, determinately. The hard problem is to say what distinguishes this mode from other natural modes of understanding. My strategy for answering this question was to quantify over natural modes of understanding, including determinateness itself (much as in nonreductive functional definitions of mental properties one quantifies over properties, including the properties being defined). The goal in this setting was to isolate general properties which determinateness has and which other natural modes of understanding lack. My proposal was the following:

> determinateness = the mode m of understanding with the following properties:
> (a) correctness
> (b.i) categorial completeness
> (b.ii) noncategorial completeness.

(a) A mode m has the correctness property iff, necessarily, for all individuals x and all propositions p which x understands in mode m, p is true *if* it is possible for x (or someone initially in qualitatively the same sort of epistemic situation as x) to settle with a priori stability that p is true, all the while understanding p in mode m. (b.i) A mode m has the categorial completeness property iff, necessarily, for all individuals x and all true (positive or negative) property identities p which x understands in mode m, it is possible for x (or someone initially in qualitatively the same sort of epistemic situation) to settle with a priori stability that there is some true twin-earth style counterpart of p, all the while understanding p in mode m. (b.ii) A mode m has the noncategorial completeness property iff, necessarily, for all individuals x and all true propositions p which x understands in mode m and which x could believe, it is possible for x to believe p while still understanding it in mode m.

Of course, this analysis might need to be refined in one way or another.[43] The thesis I wish to be committed to is that some analysis along these general lines can be made to work.[44]

Let us close by indicating how this analysis of concept possession completes the account of the a priori which we have been developing. In the course of our discussion of the evidential force of intuitions, we noted a shortcoming in traditional empiricism and traditional rationalism, namely, that neither successfully explains why intuition and phenomenal experience should be basic sources of evidence. Modal reliabilism filled this explanatory gap: the explanation is that these two sources have the right sort of modal tie to the truth. We saw, moreover, that neither traditional empiricism nor traditional rationalism successfully explains why there should be such a tie between these basic sources and the truth. The analysis of determinate concept possession fills this gap: In the case of intuition, determinate possession of our concepts entails that there must be such a tie. But determinate concept possession also guarantees that there be a corresponding tie in the case of phenomenal experience. Our intuitions are what seem to be so concerning the applicability of concepts to cases presented to pure thought. If our intellectual seemings have the indicated modal tie to truth, then we could hardly be mistaken regarding what seem to be the contents of our phenomenal experiences. In this way, the analysis of determinate concept possession promises to complete the picture begun by our two main epistemological traditions – rationalism and empiricism. If this is so, the fact that one and the same analysis can play this dual role provides additional reason to accept it.

If correct, the analysis of concept possession serves as the cornerstone of a unified account of a priori knowledge. On the one hand, the correctness property provides the basis of an explanation of the *reliability* of a priori intuition and, in turn, a priori knowledge itself. On the other hand, the completeness property provides the basis of an explanation of the *scope* of a priori intuition and, in turn, a priori knowledge. Taken together, the correctness and completeness properties also answer Benacerraf's question of how, absent a supernatural source, mathematical knowledge is possible – and, more generally, they explain how knowledge of Popper's Third World (the realm of abstract objects) is possible. Finally, in view of our earlier remarks about semantic stability, these properties of determinate concept possession imply a qualified authority and autonomy for logic, mathematics, and philosophy *vis-à-vis* empirical science.

Notes

1 Cautious advocates of these equivalences restrict p to *knowable* propositions. I will take the equivalences this way.
2 E.g., the transitivity of the part/whole relation over the field of regions is necessary but not analytic. Here is another kind of counterexample: for arbitrary contingent propositions p, the fact that p is contingent is itself necessary but not analytic.
3 Saul Kripke, "Naming and Necessity," in *Semantics of Natural Language*, Davidson and Harman, eds., Dordrecht: Reidel, 1972, pp. 253–355 and pp. 763–9. Reprinted as *Naming and Necessity*, Cambridge, Mass.: Harvard, 1980. Hilary Putnam, "The Meaning of 'Meaning'," in *Language, Mind, and Knowledge*, Minnesota Studies in the Philosophy of Science, vol. 8, Minneapolis: University of Minnesota Press, 1975, pp. 131–91.

4. David Kaplan, "On the Logic of Demonstratives," *Midwest Studies in Philosophy* 4, 1979: 401–14.
5. Kripke, *Naming and Necessity*.
6. I personally am more moved by the second than the first and third.
7. P. 37, W. V. Quine "Two Dogmas of Empiricism," *From a Logical Point of View*, Cambridge, Mass.: Harvard, 1953, pp. 20–46.
8. Alonzo Church, "A Formulation of the Logic of Sense and Denotation," in *Structure, Method, and Meaning: Essays in Honor of Henry M. Scheffer*, P. Henle, H. H. Kallen, S. K. Langer, eds., New York: Liberal Arts Press, 1951, pp. 3–24. George Bealer, "Necessity," *Quality and Concept*, Oxford: Clarendon, 1982.
9. A. N. Prior and Kit Fine, *Worlds, Times and Selves*, London: Duckworth, 1977.
10. See my "Analyticity," *Routledge Encyclopedia of Philosophy*.
11. I am not claiming that this is a good definition but only that it serves to clarify the notion in a noncircular fashion.
12. Edmund Gettier, "Is Justified True Belief Knowledge?", *Analysis*, 23, 1963: 121–3. *Editor's note*: see also the essay by Zagzebski, this volume.
13. In this paper I will not have time to discuss the topic of a priori concepts (vs. empirical concepts), though this too is a worthy topic.
14. So, even if reliabilists are right that evidence is not a necessary condition for knowledge, the reliabilist's demand that knowledge have a reliable tie to the truth will be satisfied in cases of knowledge which are based on a priori intuitions.
15. Kurt Gödel, "What Is Cantor's Continuum Problem?", *Collected Works*, vol. II, Solomon Feferman et al., eds., New York: Oxford, 1990, pp. 254–70 and "Some Basic Theorems on the Foundations of Mathematics and Their Implications," *Collected Works*, vol. III, 1995, pp. 304–23.
16. The views presented in this paper are developed and defended in greater detail in my book *Philosophical Limits of Science* (New York: Oxford, forthcoming) and in various papers cited below and in the Select Bibliography at the end of this volume.
17. Incidentally, as indicated earlier, Kripke believes that there is a kind of a priori knowledge of certain contingent facts (e.g., the length of the standard meter bar) which is associated with stipulative introductions of names. If this is right and if there are rational intuitions associated with this a priori knowledge, these remarks would need to be refined.
18. I am indebted to George Myro, in conversation in 1986, for a kindred example (the comprehension principle of naive set theory) and for the point it illustrates, namely, that it is possible to have an intuition without having the corresponding belief.
19. *The Aristotelian Society, Supplementary Volume* 56, 1992: 99–138. Reprinted in *Rationality and Naturalism*, Steven J. Wagner and Richard Warner, eds., Notre Dame: University of Notre Dame Press, 1993.
20. Unlike radical empiricism, Hume's more moderate empiricism deems intuitions of relations of ideas to be evidence. It is a scholarly question whether Hume's relations of ideas include only analyticities. If so, his view is also self-defeating (but for somewhat different reasons). If not, it resembles the sort of moderate rationalism which I am defending here.
21. It is often claimed that there are widespread conflicts among moral intuitions and among aesthetic intuitions. Two comments are in order. First, people making this claim usually make no effort to distinguish genuine intuitions from beliefs and feelings.

Although we have genuine evaluative intuitions about various general conditionals (e.g., if on balance one ought to do p, then it is not the case that on balance one ought not to do p), it is less clear that we have them about concrete cases. But the supposed conflict usually concerns concrete cases. Second, suppose, however, that there really are such conflicts. This would not call into question the evidential status of intuitions generally, for there is not widespread conflict among non-evaluative intuitions. At most, our concrete-case evaluative intuitions would lose their evidential status. Naturally, it would be good to explain why these intuitions are in conflict. One explanation is that emotions and desires have a corrupting influence on them; if so, perhaps cognitive conditions superior to ours would be sufficient to overcome the conflicts. But maybe even that would not be enough; maybe there is a further source of the conflict. Two such sources come to mind. (1) Like the concept of being big, perhaps evaluative concepts are not genuine concepts. (2) Perhaps we do not possess our evaluative concepts determinately (see the theory of concept possession given below); perhaps the understanding is always dancing around a cloud of relevant concepts, never permanently coming to rest on any one of them. (Analogy: there are certain conflicting intuitions in the foundations of set theory; one plausible explanation is that we do not express a single determinate concept with "is an element of.")

22 See note 24 for more on the notion of basic sources of evidence. Incidentally, someone might think that, rather than consulting intuition on the question of relative basicness, one should consult the simplest overall theory that takes as its evidence the deliverances of all of one's currently accepted sources of evidence. But this approach yields the wrong results. For example, with minor sophistications, the political authority case would still be a counterexample.

23 Note that intuitions are not being used here as evidence but rather as a component of the standard justificatory procedure's mechanism for critically assessing candidate sources of evidence.

24 This account of nonbasic sources is perhaps only an idealization. See Christopher Peacocke ("Rationality Requirements, Knowledge and Content," *Thoughts: An Essay on Content*, Oxford: Blackwell, 1986) for a suggestive discussion of how idealizations might function in epistemology. Note that I need not commit myself to the account of nonbasic sources in the text. For an alternative account, see note 25 in my "On the Possibility of Philosophical Knowledge," *Philosophical Perspectives* 10, 1996: 1–34. What is important for the present argument is that there be *some* account consistent with a reliabilist account of basic sources.

This notion of a basic source of evidence is an intuitive notion which can be picked out with the aid of examples and rough-and-ready general principles. The following examples are typical. Depending on one's epistemic situation, calculators can serve as a source of evidence for arithmetic questions; tree-rings, as evidence for the age of trees; etc. It is natural to say that these sources are not as basic as phenomenal experience, intuition, observation, and testimony. By the same token, it is natural to say that testimony is not as basic as observation, and likewise that observation is not as basic as phenomenal experience. Phenomenal experience, however, is as basic as evidence can get. Here are some typical rough-and-ready principles. A source is basic iff it has its status as a source of evidence intrinsically, not by virtue of its relation to other sources of evidence. A source is basic iff no other source has greater authority. A source is basic iff its deliverances, as a class, play the role of "regress stoppers." Although examples and principles like these serve to fix our attention on a salient intuitive notion, they do not constitute a definition. That is our goal in the text.

25 Might intuition be a nonbasic source? No. First, in section 1 we already elicited concrete-case intuitions supporting the thesis that intuition is as basic as experience (or any other source of evidence). Second, as Quine has shown us, our best overall purely empirical theory does not affirm that our modal intuitions have a reliable tie to the truth and, hence, fails to explain the evidential status of these intuitions. So within the present explanatory strategy, we have no alternative but to identify intuition as a basic source of evidence. This point is developed in greater detail in section 6 of my "Philosophical Limits of Scientific Essentialism," *Philosophical Perspectives* 1, 1987: 289–365.

26 An analogous counterexample could be constructed around "hardwired" dispositions to guess. One way of trying to rule out these counterexamples would be to add to contingent reliabilism a further requirement involving *evolutionary psychology*: in the course of the evolution of the species, a cognitive mechanism's contingent tie to the truth must have been more advantageous to the survival of the species than alternative sources which would not have had a tie to the truth. But this additional requirement does not help. Each of the examples can be adapted to yield a counterexample to the revised analysis. Specifically, we need only make the examples about a hypothetical species in whom the extraordinary powers for making true guesses have played a positive (but always undetected) role in the species' evolution.

27 It is understood here that something can be a basic source only if it is a natural (i.e., non-Cambridge-like) propositional attitude. For example, intuition, appearance, belief, desire, guessing, wondering, etc. This requirement serves to block various *ad hoc* counterexamples, e.g., the relation holding between x and p such that x believes p and p is the proposition that there is no largest prime. Plainly, this relation is not a natural propositional attitude.

28 For the sort of theorizers who are able to engage in end-game self-approving theorizing, these cognitive conditions would perhaps need to be even higher, and so in turn the class of relevantly elementary propositions would be larger. Of course, what counts as "elementary" and "approximate" is vague. Even though the lines are fuzzy, the larger explanatory point stands.

29 I allow for the possibility that many particular deliverances of a basic source be false. What makes something a basic source is not the truth of its individual deliverances but rather that, taken together, the deliverances provide a pathway to the truth. How many individual deliverances can be mistaken while, collectively, still preserving the indicated pathway to the truth? There need not be a determinate answer, but certainly not too many.

Note also that I require only that *most* of the indicated assessments made by this a priori theory be true. I do not say *all*, for I do not want to rule out the possibility of in principle unresolvable logical and philosophical antinomies. Nor do I want to rule out the possibility that Burge-like incomplete understanding might contaminate selected intuitions. What is ruled out is that these sorts of things could be the norm.

30 Likewise, one may use the analysis to explain why basic sources of evidence have the informal features invoked in note 24 to help single out the intuitive concept of a basic source of evidence.

Incidentally, a review of our larger dialectical strategy will make it clear that our defense of the reliability of intuition is not caught in the pernicious sort of epistemic circularity that William Alston attributes to defenses of the reliability of observation. See his *Perceiving God*, Ithaca: Cornell, 1991.

31 This notion of conceptual content is defined in *Philosophical Limits of Science*. In the simplified setting in which all propositions are hyper-fine-grained we would have the following more familiar analysis: x possesses a given concept at least nominally iff x has natural propositional attitudes (belief, desire, etc.) toward propositions in whose logical analysis the concept appears. Incidentally, if you question whether there really is this weak, nominal sense of possessing a concept, you may treat the analysis just given as a stipulative definition of a technical term. Doing so makes no difference to the larger project.

32 Tyler Burge, "Individualism and the Mental," *Midwest Studies in Philosophy* 4, 1979: 73–122.

33 It is not essential to our inquiry that the ordinary-language idiom fit exactly the informally characterized notion of possessing a concept in the full sense. If it does not, my eventual proposal should be viewed as an analysis of the informally characterized notion.

34 This example is taken from my "Philosophical Limits of Scientific Essentialism."

35 What would happen if the person had one of these intuitions – say, that a triangular multigon is not possible – but upon seeing a triangle the person formed a perceptual belief that the presently seen triangle *is* a multigon? Would this go against what I say in the text? No. For the person's cognitive conditions would clearly be *abnormal*.

36 In the present example we can be sure that the envisaged conditions are metaphysically possible, for *we* are beings in such conditions. But this is only an artifact of the example. When we generalize on the above set-up, facts about actual human beings drop out. Thinking otherwise would be a preposterous form of anthropocentrism.

37 There is a residual question regarding the restriction to property-identities p. Concerning this restriction, the formulation might be exactly right just as it stands. On a certain view of properties, however, an additional qualification would be needed. I have in mind the view according to which (1) all necessarily equivalent properties are identical and (2) for absolutely any formula A (no matter how *ad hoc* and irrelevant A's subclauses might be), a property is denoted by all expressions of the form: the property of being something such that A. If this view were correct, there would be true property-identities of the following sort: the property of being f = the property of being f such that P, where P is any arbitrary necessary truth. In this case, the proposed analysis would commit us to the possibility of settling a priori *every* necessary truth. This is too fast. This consequence can be avoided in one of two ways. The first is to deny (1) or (2) or both; there are some interesting arguments supporting this move. The second way is to accept (1) and (2) but to adopt an enriched logical theory which is able to mark the distinction between property-identities which are *ad hoc* in the indicated way and those which are not. There are already several logical theories of this sort in the literature. In what follows I am going to assume that the unwanted consequence can be avoided by one or another of these means.

38 When I speak of higher level cognitive conditions, I do not presuppose that there is always commensurability. In order for the proposal to succeed, I need only consider levels of cognitive conditions l' and l such that, with respect to *every* relevant dimension, l' is definitely greater than l.

39 The notion of counterpart is defined as follows: p′ is a counterpart of p iff$_{def}$ it is possible that there is a population C such that it is possible that, for some population C′ which is in qualitatively the same epistemic situation as C, p′ plays the same epistemic role in C′ as p does in C.

40 These notions were isolated in "Mental Properties" (*The Journal of Philosophy* 91, 1994: 185–208) and examined further in "*A Priori* Knowledge and the Scope of Philosophy" (*Philosophical Studies* 81, 1996: 121–42) and "On the Possibility of Philosophical Knowledge."

41 This theme is explored further in the papers just mentioned and in *Philosophical Limits of Science*.

42 Perhaps "believe" should be strengthened to "rationally believe" and p restricted to propositions which x can rationally believe. In this connection, bear in mind that the testimony of a trusted informant is often sufficient for rational belief.

43 We have identified determinateness as *the* mode m of understanding that has both the correctness and completeness properties. Plausibly, there is not just one mode m like this. (For example, if there is a relation of acquaintance like that posited in traditional epistemology, there is presumably an associated mode of understanding; if so, it would have both the correctness and completeness properties.) But such modes of understanding would be species of a genus, and that genus would be the general mode of understanding, determinateness. This would lead us to revise the analysis one last time as follows: determinateness = the genus of modes m of understanding with the correctness and completeness properties.

44 If you have doubts about the analysis, bear in mind that the analysis is compatible with the idea that determinateness might come in degrees, achieved to a greater or lesser extent. What the analysis aims at is the notion of completely determinate possession. If you find yourself disagreeing with the analysis on some point or other, perhaps the explanation is that you have in mind cases involving something less than completely determinate possession.

Chapter 12

Moral Knowledge and Ethical Pluralism

Robert Audi

Moral epistemology is central to ethical theory and, after a period of some neglect, is currently receiving much attention.[1] Discussion of the subject suffered no small setback from the influence of positivistic noncognitivism. Nor was moral epistemology a main object of the narrowly metaethical focus that dominated much of ethical discussion between the Second World War and the early 1970s; the concern during that period was mainly semantical and metaphysical. Even now, many writers in ethics who tend to take for granted that there is much scientific knowledge are skeptical about the possibility of any moral knowledge; and some of them accept the view, especially common in university communities, that moral judgments represent at best cultural assumptions having no claim to truth.

The aim of this essay is both to indicate the scope of some major positions in moral epistemology and to defend, at least in outline, my own view in this field. There are many significant positions to consider, but a reasonable selection can be made by taking account of both rationalism and empiricism as general epistemological outlooks and, in ethics specifically, of utilitarianism, Kantianism, intuitionism, virtue ethics, and noncognitivism. These are perhaps the dominant approaches in current ethical theory.

1. Four Basic Approaches in Moral Epistemology

If we distinguish approaches in moral epistemology sharply, we find a great many. But if we think in terms of major positions in general epistemology and connect those with historically influential theories in ethics, at least four approaches in moral epistemology deserve emphasis: empiricism, rationalism, intuitionism, and noncognitivism (I take virtue ethics to be combinable with any of these). It is useful to begin with empiricism and the most closely associated version of utilitarianism.

Utilitarian empiricism

The most prominent empiricist position in moral epistemology is linked to utilitarianism.[2] For purposes of discerning the moral epistemology appropriate to utilitarianism, we might work from a formulation of utilitarianism that roughly captures the (or a) central principle common at least to Bentham and Mill. I refer to the following act-utilitarian formulation: an act is right if and only if it contributes at least as much to the proportion of (nonmoral) good to evil (say, happiness to unhappiness) in the relevant population (say, human beings) as any available alternative (where the criteria for availability are nonmoral[3]). The good (or evil) in question is most plausibly taken to be intrinsic: good in itself, independently of what it leads to. For act-utilitarians, the truth or falsity of a moral judgment concerning the rightness of an action is knowable on the basis of factual knowledge about how the action does or would contribute to intrinsic goodness. This epistemological claim is a *consequentialist thesis*, since it characterizes the rightness of actions in terms of their consequences.

Mill and other utilitarians have maintained, in addition, a *valuational thesis*: that only pleasure and freedom from pain are good in themselves. Mill believed that both theses can be known and that they justify holding, as one's fundamental moral principle, roughly the following hedonistic utilitarian view: that an action is right if and only if it contributes at least as much to pleasure (and freedom from pain) in the world as any alternative available to the agent.[4] (I ignore the points Mill raises later about qualities of pleasure.[5]) Since, on Mill's view, a combination of common-sense and scientific procedures can identify these utility-maximizing acts, moral judgments are in principle knowable roughly in the same way as the common-sense and scientific propositions that ground them.

The epistemological question that now arises for Mill (among others who regard pleasure as a source of basic reasons for action) is how we know that pleasure – or anything else – is intrinsically good. Mill argued, apparently following Aristotle, that we can know what is intrinsically good by determining what people naturally desire for its own sake. But the utilitarian approach is by no means committed either to that epistemic license to move from the natural to the normative (a move that many philosophers and commentators on Mill find unwarranted) or even to hedonism. For instance, it might be argued that the intrinsically good is what people would want for its own sake provided their wants are adequately rational, say held in the light of reflection that is logically and scientifically rational, vivid, and appropriately focused on the nature of what is wanted.[6]

If any approach in moral epistemology can claim to be scientific, utilitarianism surely can. This is one reason for its wide appeal. Given the crucial (and to be sure controversial) assumption that we can have scientific or at least "factual" knowledge of what has intrinsic value – as we apparently can of what conduces to pleasure and to reduction of pain – the question of what actions are right is itself scientific, or at least factual. We can rank our options in terms of their expected value, and we may flip a coin whenever two or more are equally valuable. The task is often difficult, but much scientific knowledge is not easily acquired either. Utilitarians tend to take it as a great benefit of their view that it provides a factual criterion (in the sense of a test) of moral rightness.

Kantian rationalism

If utilitarianism is the most prominent ethical view whose moral epistemology is empiricist, Kantianism is the most prominent ethical position whose moral epistemology is rationalist. Very roughly, Kantianism takes actions to be right provided they conform to a maxim (roughly, a first-person principle of action) that passes the test set by the categorical imperative. Kant formulated this imperative in several ways. In one version of his universality formulation, the imperative says that we are to act only on principles which we can (rationally) will to be universal laws of nature (hence obeyed by us all). But Kant regarded this imperative as equivalent to the "intrinsic end formulation," the principle that we are always to treat people as ends in themselves, never merely as means.[7] He apparently took his principle to be knowable a priori in either formulation.

To see how this approach might yield moral knowledge, take the apparently uncontroversial principle that flogging infants for pleasure is wrong. There is much plausibility in saying that we know this principle to be true. Kantians would hold that we know it through an obvious application of the categorical imperative. The principle seems plausible in the light of even brief reflection on what it is to flog infants, and it is at least difficult to conceive circumstances that would lead rational persons not to endorse it provided they are taking either the point of view of universalizability or (assuming this is not equivalent) that of treating people as ends and never merely as means.

Consider another example, a modest version of something more powerful – call it the *equality principle*: we ought to treat people equally in matters of life and death (say, in regard to eligibility for organ transplants) unless they differ in some relevant way (and not merely in being different people). This is a kind of principle of consistency (not logical consistency, but something like consistency in roughly the sense of always using a principled policy or procedure in deciding important matters). It implies that differential treatment in these mortal matters is wrong unless it is justifiable by a difference between the persons in question. It does not specify what kind of difference is relevant, for example that the health of candidates for transplant is and their skin color is not. Specifying relevant differences is a further step. But the principle is still a moral one, and it implies the important requirement that any indicated differences in treatment be justifiable by a reason. Particularly since it is a kind of (moral) consistency principle, there is some reason to think that if it is true, it is deducible from, or at least supportable by, the categorical imperative and perhaps also knowable a priori. Establishing these points would be a major task; I present them only as plausible hypotheses.

The contrast between Kantian and utilitarian approaches to moral knowledge is nicely parallel to differences between Kant's and Mill's general epistemologies.

On Kant's rationalistic epistemology, substantive propositions can be a priori, and moral principles in particular are synthetic a priori. On Mill's empiricist view, moral principles are both empirical and inductively knowable.[8]

There is a further epistemologically interesting contrast. On Kant's approach, or at least on some similar rationalistic approaches, such as the most common kinds of intuitionism, there can be direct (non-inferential) moral knowledge. On these views, at least one moral principle is so basic that knowledge of it need not be inferentially grounded in knowledge of any other propositions. Even the categorical imperative, in its intrinsic end formulation, may be argued to specify at least two act-types – avoiding treating people merely as means and treating them as ends – that can be non-inferentially known to be at least *prima facie* obligatory. On a utilitarian approach, there cannot be direct moral knowledge except in special cases. The main and perhaps only cases seem to be these two. First, such knowledge may be only *memorially direct*, that is, direct (non-inferential) as preserved in memory, but originally indirect and now direct just by virtue of one's having forgotten one's evidential grounds for it, as one forgets the steps in proving the Pythagorean theorem and remembers only the theorem. Second, one's moral knowledge may be only *testimonially direct*: non-inferentially grounded in testimony, but such that (as a utilitarian would require) at some time *someone* (say, the attester) knew the truth inferentially.

Both the memorial and the testimonial cases would be *secondary knowledge*, since the knowledge depends on other knowledge of the same proposition and is not primary in the way that, say, perceptual knowledge is. Secondary knowledge need not, however, be inferential, since it need not at the time in question be based on other knowledge. On Mill's view, knowledge that, for instance, keeping one's promises is obligatory would ultimately depend on someone's knowing a good deal about the effects of promise-keeping on happiness. One could know the principle through parental teaching experienced during one's moral education; one could also establish it for oneself by studying human behavior and then retain one's knowledge of it after forgetting one's grounds. But no one could know it directly unless someone knew it inferentially, through evidence.[9]

This difference between Kant and Mill – the former providing, as do intuitionists, for direct (primary) moral knowledge and the latter not – is no accident. On the kind of view Mill and at least most other utilitarians hold, moral properties, such as obligatoriness, are unlike sensory properties in not being directly experienced or otherwise objects of direct – say, intuitive – knowledge. As an empiricistic, and thus experience-based, moral theory, it must treat primary knowledge of moral truths as ultimately indirect (unless, as has occasionally been done, it posits moral experience as a source of knowledge that grounds knowledge rather in the way perception does). Thus, even if, by memory, I have some direct moral knowledge, no moral knowledge is *independently basic*, in the sense that it need not at any time be inferentially grounded in another kind of knowledge. If I know that cruelty to children is wrong, it is by virtue of my (or someone's) knowing that (e.g.) it does not contribute optimally to happiness in the world. I cannot reach such an epistemic height without a ladder, though once having climbed up on it I no longer need it to remain there.

For a broadly Kantian view, by contrast, we can rationally grasp that cruelty to children is wrong, at least as a consequence of a more general moral principle. We can thus have moral knowledge which is direct *and* independently basic. Even if Kant is best interpreted as taking the most general moral knowledge to depend on nonmoral premises, and thus to be indirect, he apparently took all knowledge of general moral principles to be deductively derivable from (and only from) a priori premises and thus itself a priori (at least on the assumption that the derivations are self-evident throughout and short enough not to render one's knowledge of their conclusions dependent on memory).

This perspective on such moral propositions as the principle of equality suggests that we might take the Kantian view to be *internalist* in its moral epistemology: it is only by using reason, and hence through internally accessible grounds – roughly grounds accessible to reflection (including introspection) – that we have a basis for knowledge or justified belief of moral truths. We may need much experience to understand moral concepts; but once we properly understand them, sufficient reflection on them provides justification for basic principles of action, including moral principles. Unlike Kant's moral epistemology, Mill's is *externalist*: we have a basis for knowledge or justified belief of moral truths only through external considerations about the consequences of actions for pleasure and pain, and those considerations require observational evidence or other inductive grounding not accessible to reflection.

Intuitionism

The most prominent intuitionist views share with Kantianism a commitment to rationalism; but by contrast with both utilitarianism and Kantianism, ethical intuitionism has been put forward quite explicitly as centered largely in a moral epistemology, and by contrast with Kantianism an intuitionist view can (for reasons set out below) be empiricist.[10] To see the main epistemological thrust of intuitionism, consider how one might explain the justification of an ordinary moral principle such as the proposition that we should (*prima facie*) keep our promises. Why believe this? I could explain why I do; but explaining need not justify, and perhaps I cannot justify the principle by appeal to any more fundamental proposition. According to intuitionism, this would not show that I do not know or justifiedly believe it. At some point or other in defending a factual (say, perceptual) judgment, I may be equally incapable of giving a further justification. It would not follow that the judgment I am defending does not express knowledge or justified belief.

The issue should be explicitly considered in the light of a general commitment of most (and arguably the most plausible) intuitionist ethical theories: epistemological foundationalism. This view (in a generic form) says above all that if there is any knowledge or justification, it traces to some non-inferential knowledge or justification.[11] A foundationalist may say that (with some special exceptions) the principle that one should keep one's promises, or at least some more general principle, such as that people should be treated with respect, is self-evident, hence intuitively knowable, and needs no defense by derivation from prior principles. Intuitionism so viewed does not claim that *everyone* who considers the relevant principle will find it obvious (especially immediately); but that will hold for certain theorems in logic, the kind that are initially hard to understand but, when they are finally understood, are comfortably accepted as self-evident, or at least as logically true.[12] The appeal to self-evident propositions, then, should not be assimilated to the appeal to obviousness nor expected to be made with a view to cutting off discussion.

Foundationalists will tend to argue that an appeal to what is self-evident can be warranted when we get to certain stages in a process of justification. For they take some beliefs (including many that lack self-evident propositions as objects) as foundational in a way that warrants holding them without having prior premises. Self-evident propositions are paradigms of appropriate objects of foundational beliefs. For foundationalism, if there were no non-inferentially justified beliefs, then we would not be justified in holding anything. A coherentist seeking to justify the promising principle may be willing to go on arguing, perhaps pointing out that if we do not keep promises life will be unbearable, and then, for each thesis attacked, defending it with respect to one or more others that can support it. A skeptic may not be pacified by either approach. But neither can simply be rejected out of hand. To be warranted in rejecting either approach, one must have a plausible alternative conception of knowledge and justification. What would it be?

One might seek an answer by joining virtue ethics to a similarly inspired virtue epistemology. Virtue ethics has appealed to many who reject all three epistemological approaches so far sketched but are nonskeptics who believe that some general account of ethics and moral knowledge or justification is possible. If, however, we take Aristotle's moral theory as a paradigm of a virtue ethics, I believe we find little explicit moral epistemology but instead a pervasive presupposition that the virtuous agent has ethical knowledge appropriate to the exercise of virtue. A courageous person, e.g., as opposed to one who is cowardly or foolhardy, should have an adequate knowledge of the kinds of risks one should take for various ends, and a just person should have an adequate knowledge of what a just person should do in adjudicating a dispute. I find this presupposition quite plausible. But far from requiring a specific moral epistemology (such as one grounded in a virtue epistemology), it can be accounted for by adapting to virtue ethics any of the positions in moral epistemology so far considered.[13]

Since virtue theory has been applied to general epistemology and, as developed there, may yield an approach useful in moral epistemology, we may learn something from considering a generic version of virtue epistemology. Perhaps the broadest idea common to such approaches is that knowledge is a manifestation of the functioning of an epistemic virtue. The virtue might be, say, perceptual, memorial, or ethical. For instance, in the moral sphere, an epistemic sense of veracity (as opposed to the motivational and affective sides of this trait) might be understood as a stable capacity for reaching true belief within a certain range, say in situations calling for communication with others or for appraising their representations to oneself. More generally, an epistemic virtue is, roughly, a cognitive trait apt for producing true beliefs.[14] The idea that knowledge is a manifestation of an epistemic virtue can be developed in many ways, for instance along externalist lines, in which case the crucial feature of the relevant (epistemic) moral virtue would be producing a favorable ratio of true to false moral beliefs, or along internalist lines, in which case the crucial feature would be either producing such a ratio on the basis of internally accessible grounds or – if justification rather than knowledge is the epistemic target – producing a suitable ratio of moral beliefs that are at least internally justified.

A virtue ethics that is close to utilitarianism or some naturalistic ethics, say in conceiving virtues as traits whose exercise properly promotes happiness, would be likely to take the first, externalist line. Kantians and other rationalists, including most intuitionists, would be likely to take the second, internalist line in accounting for the place of virtue in ethics. Given the rationalism of the Kantian view, Kantians would also likely argue that the grounds, such as our rational apprehension of concepts, which, in virtuous moral agents, yield justified beliefs of moral principles, also typically yield knowledge of them.

Virtue ethics can also be developed in other ways, but in its most plausible forms it provides for (if it does not in fact presuppose) the possibility of moral knowledge or justification. It apparently does this chiefly by drawing on one of the other approaches in moral epistemology considered here, particularly the empiricist, the rationalist, and the intuitionist, but perhaps also the virtue-theoretic.[15] The tentative conclusion that seems warranted, then, is that a virtue epistemology will contribute to understanding moral knowledge more as an adjunct to the kinds of approaches just described than as independent epistemological theory.

Noncognitivism

Without further development, the three basic approaches to moral knowledge just described, utilitarian empiricism, Kantian rationalism, and intuitionism, do not go as far as one might like in supporting the possibility of moral knowledge and justification, and even apart from that some philosophers and others might be skeptical about the possibility. Skepticism, and particularly general skepticism, is too large a topic to address directly here.[16] But there is a major position in ethical theory that we should locate in relation to skepticism, in part because it is so easily thought to imply moral skepticism. I refer to noncognitivism.

For noncognitivism, broadly understood, moral judgments, including moral principles as well as moral judgments of particular actions, are not true or false but rather expressive, say of pro or con attitudes or of commitments to norms.[17] If knowledge is of truths, then it plainly follows that moral judgments do not constitute expressions of knowledge; and if moral sentences are not cognitive at all, then (on the assumption that knowledge and belief are sententially expressible) there is presumably neither moral knowledge nor justified moral belief. This is not the sweeping skeptical view it may appear to be. There may still be rational and indeed justified moral attitudes, say those based on a balanced (or virtuous) appraisal of the facts.

Noncognitivists may even allow that so far as propriety of language goes, we may say of moral judgments "That is true" or "I know that his judgment on that matter was correct". The claim is roughly that such a "statement" is neither an empirical nor an a priori truth or falsehood; it is not a kind of truth or falsehood at all, as it would be for the other views we have explored. But that alone does not entail a global ethical skepticism, in part because such normative notions as justification and rationality can apply to non-truth-valued items, such as actions.[18] If a moral judgment can be rational and can guide rational action, then one kind of skepticism is mistaken even if skepticism about moral knowledge strictly construed is true.

To be sure, if we can go as far as this toward knowledge and justification, then, depending on our metaphysics – above all on whether we think there are any moral properties for actions to have or lack – we might reject moral skepticism altogether and avoid having to posit a separate, nonpropositional category of uses of "true," "false," and other apparently cognitive terms of appraisal applicable to moral judgments. But to pursue that issue would take us too far into moral ontology, and at this point our main purposes are better served by exploring a quite different approach to the epistemology of ethics.

2. The Epistemological Resources of Moderate Intuitionism

Of the moral theories just considered – utilitarianism, Kantianism, intuitionism, virtue theory, and noncognitivism – it is in my judgment intuitionism that is at once least discussed and, in its moral epistemology, perhaps most promising. This section will set out a moderate version of intuitionism, a version intended to improve on the one proposed by W. D. Ross in *the Right and the Good* (1930), which remains the statement of intuitionism most often illustratively referred to by writers in ethical theory.

Rossian intuitionism

As Ross portrayed it, intuitionism as a kind of ethical theory has three main characteristics. (1) It affirms an irreducible plurality of basic moral principles. (2) Each principle centers on a different kind of ground, in the sense of a factor, such as an injury occurring in one's presence, implying a *prima facie* moral duty, say a duty to aid someone just injured. (3) Each principle is in some sense intuitively (hence non-inferentially) known by those who appropriately understand it. All three points seem appropriate to any full-blooded version of intuitionism.

On the normative side, Ross proposed, as fundamental both in guiding daily life and in articulating a sound ethical theory, a list (which he did not claim to be complete) of *prima facie* duties: duties of fidelity (promise-keeping, including honesty conceived as fidelity to one's word); reparation; justice (particularly rectification of injustice, such as exploitation of the poor); gratitude; beneficence; self-improvement; and non-injury.[19]

Epistemologically, Ross emphasized the self-evidence of the propositions expressing our *prima facie* duties:

> That an act, *qua* fulfilling a promise, or *qua* effecting a just distribution of good ... is *prima facie* right, is self-evident; not in the sense that it is evident from the beginning of our lives, or as soon as we attend to the proposition for the first time, but in the sense that when we have reached sufficient mental maturity and have given sufficient attention to the proposition it is evident without any need of proof, or of evidence beyond itself. It is evident just as a mathematical axiom, or the validity of a form of inference, is evident ... In our confidence that these propositions are true there is involved the same confidence in our reason that is involved in our confidence in mathematics ... In both cases we are dealing with propositions that cannot be proved, but that just as certainly need no proof.[20]

In explaining how we apprehend the self-evident, unprovable moral truths in question, Ross appealed to something like what we commonly call intuitions (his term here is "conviction" and apparently designates a cognition held at least partly on the basis of understanding its propositional object[21]). He said, e.g., that if someone challenges

> our view that there is a special obligatoriness attaching to the keeping of promises because [according to the challenger] it is self-evident that the only duty is to produce as much good as possible, we have to ask ourselves whether we really, when we reflect, *are* convinced that [as he takes G. E. Moore to hold] this is self-evident ... it seems self-evident that a promise simply as such, is something that *prima facie* ought to be kept ... the moral convictions of thoughtful and well-educated people are the data of ethics, just as sense-perceptions are the data of a natural science. Just as some of the latter have to be rejected as illusory, so have some of the former; but as the latter are rejected only when they conflict with other more accurate sense-perceptions, the former are rejected only when they conflict with convictions which stand better the test of refection.[22]

I want to stress that Ross speaks here not only of our grasping (or apprehending) the truth of the relevant moral and mathematical propositions, but also of what I think he conceives as our apprehending their self-evidence. One indication of this latter focus is his taking us to be aware that we are dealing with propositions which are not in need of proof – *proof-exempt*, we might say. He is influenced, I believe, by the dialectic of argument with other philosophers about what is self-evident, and he is here not concentrating on the more basic question of how we can know the truth of first-order moral propositions. Such a shift of focus is particularly easy if one thinks that the relevant *kind* of proposition, if true, is self-evident. For then one does not expect to find cogent premises for such a proposition – or, like Moore and Ross, thinks there can be none – and, as a philosopher, one will want to explain *why* one has none by maintaining that the proposition is self-evident.

Whatever the reason for it, Ross does not always distinguish (or does not explicitly distinguish) apprehending the truth of a proposition that *is* self-evident from apprehending *its self-evidence*.[23] This is a point whose significance is easily missed. The truth of at least some self-evident propositions is easy to apprehend. Self-evident propositions have even been thought to be so luminous that one cannot grasp them *without* believing them.[24] But the epistemic *status* of propositions, for instance their justification or self-evidence, is a paradigm source of disagreement. Two people attending to the same proposition can agree that it is true but differ concerning its status, one of them thinking it self-evident and the other taking it to be merely empirical. Intuitionism as most plausibly developed does not require positing non-inferential knowledge of the self-evidence, as opposed to the truth, of its basic principles. If I am correct, then one apparently common view of intuitionism is a mistake. Let me clarify the crucial distinction.

We might know that a moral principle, say that promise-keeping is a *prima facie* duty, is self-evident only on the basis of sophisticated considerations, say from knowing the conceptual as opposed to empirical (e.g., observational) character of the grounds on which we know that principle to be true. We would know its truth *on* these grounds; we would know its self-evidence through knowledge *about* the grounds. It is, however, that first-order proposition, the principle that promise-keeping is a duty, not the second-order thesis that this principle is self-evident, which is the fundamental thing we must be able to know intuitively if intuitionism (whether in Ross's version or any other plausible one) is to succeed.

One might indeed consider the concept of self-evidence, by contrast with that of truth, to be an epistemically explanatory notion more appropriate to the metaethics of intuitionism than to its basic formulation as a normative theory. Its application to a proposition explains both how it can be known (roughly, through understanding it in its own terms) and why knowing it requires no premises. Ross naturally wanted to indicated why his principles are true and how they are known, not just *that* they are true; but one might surely know their truth, intuitively or otherwise, without knowing either why they are true or how they are known.

Granted, then, that intuitionists hold that moral agents need and have intuitive knowledge of their duties, neither intuitionists as moral theorists nor we as moral agents need intuitive knowledge of the status of the principles of duty. Nor need an intuitionist hold that conscientious moral agents must in general even know that they know the moral principles that guide them. The first-order knowledge does the crucial day-to-day normative work.

These reflections bring us to another major element in the most common conception of intuitionism: the idea that, for cognition grounded in genuine intuition, intuitionism implies *indefeasible justification* – roughly, justification that cannot be undermined or overridden. Intuitionism (even in Ross) is not committed to this general idea, though he may have accepted it for certain cases. For ethical intuitionism as a normative theory, the primary role of intuition is to give us direct, i.e., non-inferential, knowledge or justified belief of the *truth* of certain moral propositions. It is not, as one might think from reading Ross and some other intuitionists, to provide either knowledge of the self-evidence of basic moral propositions (especially certain moral principles) or what one might naturally take to follow from the existence of such knowledge – indefeasible justification for believing those propositions. Intuition can yield a kind of insight into, and non-inferential knowledge of, first-order propositions without yielding such knowledge of or any insight into second-order propositions about their status.

What reason remains, then, to think that intuitively grounded beliefs of moral principles are indefeasibly justified? To be sure, self-evidence apparently entails necessity; but even the necessary truth of a principle would not imply that one's *justification* for believing it is indefeasible. Clearly, we can cease to be justified in believing even a genuine theorem that is necessary and even a priori, because our "proof" of it is shown to be defective.

Conclusions of inference versus conclusions of reflection

If I have eliminated one significant element from Ross's view and thereby provided a more moderate intuitionism, on a related matter I want to claim somewhat more than he did. In a sense, an intuition (or intuitive judgment) *can* be a conclusion formed though rational inquiry or searching reflection, and when this is understood it will be apparent that there is room for a still wider intuitionism than so far described. Consider reading a poem to decide whether the language is artificial. After two readings, one silent and the other aloud, one might judge that the language is indeed artificial. This judgment could be a response to evidential propositions, say that the author has manipulated words to make the lines scan. But the judgment need not so arise: if the artificiality is subtler, there may just be a stilted quality that one can hardly pin down. In this second case, one judges from a global, intuitive sense of the integration of vocabulary, movement, and content. Call the first judgment of artificiality a *conclusion of inference*: it is premised on propositions one has noted as evidence. Call the second judgment a *conclusion of reflection*: it emerges from thinking about the poem, but not from one or more evidential premises. It is more like a response to viewing a painting than like an inference from propositionally represented information. You respond to a pattern: you notice a stiff movement in the otherwise flowing meter; you are irritated by an inapt simile; and so on. The conclusion of reflection is a kind of wrapping up of the question, akin to concluding a practical matter with a *decision*. One has not added up the evidences and inferred their implication; one has obtained a view of the whole and broadly characterized it. Far from starting with a checklist of artificialities, one could not even compose the relevant list until after studying the poem.

By no means all moral intuitions are conclusions of reflection (and the point apparently holds for intuitions in general); and in this respect, as in other aspects of intuitive reactivity, people differ and may themselves change over time, even in relation to the same proposition. Moreover, there is no need to deny that in principle, where one arrives at such a conclusion, one *could* figure out why and *then* formulate, in explicit premises, one's basis for the conclusion. But that a ground of judgment can be so formulated does not entail that it must do its work in that inferential way. An intuitive judgment or belief may not emerge until reflection proceeds for some time, even when inference is not a factor in the formation of that judgment or belief. This delay is particularly likely when the object of judgment is complicated. Such an intuition can be a conclusion of reflection, temporally as well as epistemically; and in content it may be either empirical or a priori.

On the conception of intuition I am developing, then, it is, in the "faculty" sense, chiefly a non-inferential cognitive capacity, not a nonreflective one. The cognitions in question – intuitions – instantiate intuition in what we might call the experiential sense: they are cognitive responses to the relevant object, such as a moral assessment. Understanding of that object is required for these cognitions to possess intuitive justification or constitute intuitive knowledge, and, often, understanding comes only with time.[25] Achieving understanding may be so labored that even a self-evident truth it finally reveals, even non-inferentially, *seems* not to be self-evident and is either not believed or not believed with much conviction. Let me develop this idea.

Self-evidence and understanding

The contrast between conclusions of inference and conclusions of reflection is related to a distinction that is highly pertinent to understanding intuitionism. It is between two kinds of self-evidence. Let me first sketch a general conception of self-evident propositions; we can then distinguish two kinds. Taking off from the idea that a self-evident proposition is one whose truth is in some way evident "in itself," I propose the following sketch of the basic notion of self-evidence. A self-evident proposition is (roughly) a truth such that an adequate understanding of it meets two conditions: (a) in virtue of that understanding, one is justified in believing the proposition (i.e., has justification for believing it, whether one in fact believes it or not) – this is why such a truth is evident *in itself*; and (b) if one believes the proposition on the *basis* of that understanding of it, then one knows it.[26] Thus (abbreviating and slightly altering the characterization), a proposition is self-evident provided an adequate understanding of it is sufficient for being justified in believing it and for knowing it if one believes it on the basis of that understanding. Three clarifications are needed immediately.

First, as (a) indicates, it does not follow from the self-evidence of a proposition that if one understands (and considers) the proposition, then one believes it.

Self-evident propositions may be *withholdable* and indeed *disbelievable*: there are some that one might fail to believe or even believe false. This non-belief-entailing conception of self-evidence is plausible because one can fail initially to "see" a self-evident truth and later grasp it in just the way one grasps the truth of a paradigmatically self-evident proposition: one that is obvious in itself the moment one considers it. Take, e.g., a self-evident proposition that is perhaps not immediately obvious: the existence of great-grandchildren is impossible apart from that of at least four generations of people. A delay in seeing a truth (such as this) need not change the character of what one sees. What is self-evident can be justifiedly believed on its "intrinsic" merits, but they need not leap out immediately. Granted, rational persons tend to believe self-evident propositions they adequately understand when they comprehendingly consider them. In some cases, however, one can see *what* a self-evident proposition says – and thus understand it – before seeing *that*, or how, it is true.[27]

Second, though I offer no full analysis of adequate understanding, I have several clarifying points. It is to be contrasted with mistaken or partial or clouded understanding. Adequate understanding of a proposition is more than simply getting the general sense of a sentence expressing it, as where one can parse the sentence grammatically, indicate something of what it means through examples, and perhaps translate it into another language one knows well. Adequacy here implies not only seeing what the proposition says, but also being able to apply it to (and withhold its application from) an appropriately wide range of cases, and being able to see some of its logical implications, to distinguish it from a certain range of close relatives, and to comprehend its elements and some of their relations. An inadequate understanding of a self-evident proposition is not sufficient for knowledge or justified belief of it.

Third, there is both an occurrent and a dispositional use of "understanding." The former is illustrated by one's comprehension of a proposition one is considering, the latter by such comprehension as is retained after one's attention turns elsewhere. A weaker dispositional use is illustrated by "She understands such ideas," uttered where one has in mind something like this: she has never entertained them, but would (occurrently) understand them upon considering them.

Leaving further subtleties aside, the crucial point is that in the above characterization of self-evidence, "understanding", in clause (a), may bear any of the suggested senses so long as justification is construed accordingly. If you have occurrent understanding of a self-evident proposition, you have occurrent justification for it; if you have strong dispositional understanding of it, you have dispositional justification; and if you have weak dispositional understanding, you have only *structural justification* for it: roughly, there is an appropriate path leading from justificatory materials accessible to you to an occurrent justification for the proposition but you lack dispositional justification.[28] (I shall assume that when knowledge of a self-evident proposition is based on understanding it, the understanding must be occurrent or strongly dispositional, but even here one could devise a conception of knowledge with a looser connection to understanding.)

Two kinds of self-evidence

Given the points about self-evidence expressed in (a) and (b), we may distinguish those self-evident propositions that are readily understood by normal adults (or by people of some relevant description, e.g. mature moral agents) and those they understand only through reflection on them. Call the first *immediately self-evident* and the second *mediately self-evident*, since their truth can be grasped only through the mediation of reflection (as opposed to inference from one or more premises.[29] This is not a logical or epistemological distinction, but a psychological and pragmatic one concerning comprehensibility to a certain kind of mind. It will soon be clear why the distinction is nonetheless important for understanding intuitionism.

The reflection in question may involve drawing inferences, say about what it means, for both perpetrator and victim, to flog an infant for pleasure. But the role of inferences is limited largely to clarifying what the proposition in question says: as self-evidence is normally understood, a self-evident proposition is knowable without relying on inferential *grounds* for it. One may require time to get it in clear focus, but need not reach it by an inferential path from one or more premises. To see one kind of role inference *can* have, however, consider the proposition that if p entails q and q entails r and yet r is false, then p is false. One may instantly just see the truth of this; but even if one must first infer that p entails r, this is not a ground for believing the whole conditional proposition. It is an implicate of a part of it (of the if-clause) that helps one to see how it is that the whole conditional is true. Even if such *internal inference* is required to know the truth of a proposition, it may still be mediately self-evident.

Internal inferences may also be purely clarificatory, say semantically, as where, from the proposition that there is a great-grandchild, one infers that there are parental, grandparental, and great-grandparental generations. We might say, then, that knowledge of a self-evident proposition (and justification for believing it) may depend *internally* on inference, above all where inference is needed for understanding the proposition, but may not depend *externally* on inference, where this is a matter of epistemic dependence on one or more premises (the kind of dependence entailing independent evidential support for the proposition in question).

In the light of the distinction between the mediately and the immediately self-evident, the characteristic intuitionist claim that basic moral principles are self-evident can be seen to require only that a kind of reflection will yield adequate justification for them – the kind of justification that yields knowledge when belief of a true proposition is based on such reflection. Given how much time and thought this reflection may require, the intuitionist view may be seen as closer to Kant's moral epistemology than one might think, at least assuming that for Kant it is the apriority of the categorical imperative itself that is epistemologically most important, as opposed to the inferential character of our knowledge of it.

Even supposing that it is crucial for Kant that knowledge of the categorical imperative be inferential (as one might think from his arguing for it from considerations about the nature of practical reason), it should be stressed that the Rossian principles of duty, as first-order moral principles, need not be in the same epistemic boat. If they are even mediately self-evident, they may be taken to be non-inferentially knowable. Still, surely any (or virtually any) proposition that can be known non-inferentially can also be known inferentially. Ross, apparently following Moore and Prichard, implicitly denied this,[30] but there is no need for a intuitionism, either as a moral epistemology positing intuitive knowledge of moral principles or as an ethical pluralism, to deny it.[31]

As long as basic moral principles *can* be known (or at least justifiedly accepted) independently of relying on grounding premises, morality can be understood and practiced as intuitionists understand it. Life would be very different if we could not move our legs except by doing something else, such as activating a machine that moves them; but we *can* do such things and at times may find it desirable. The possibility of moving our legs in a secondary way does not change the nature of our primary leg movements. So it can be with knowledge of basic moral principles. It is only ethical theory (of a certain kind) that must provide for the possibility of overdetermined justification or knowledge of moral principles by virtue of their being supported independently by both intuitive and inferential grounds. Providing for this possibility is in no way hostile to any major intuitionist purpose.

3. Some Prospects and Problems for Moderate Intuitionism

If the arguments of this chapter indicate how intuitionism as broadly characterized in the previous section can be plausible, they also show how an overall rationalist intuitionism like Ross's can be strengthened. Intuitionism can be defended, however, apart from rationalism. Let me suggest some of the defenses and liaisons possible for intuitionism.

The possibility of an empiricist intuitionism

Historically, intuitionism is strongly associated with rationalism. But suppose intuitionism is taken in the minimal (and rough) sense of the view that an irreducible plurality of basic moral judgments can be intuitively and non-inferentially justified. Then an intuitionist view could be empiricist, taking intuitions to be non-inferential responses to experience and thereby capable of providing experiential, inductive grounds for moral judgments or principles.[32] Intuitions might, e.g., be construed as deliverances of a moral sense, regarded as much like a perceptual faculty. (Moral principles would likely be taken to be justified inductively on the basis of intuitions and would not be construed as self-evident, so on that score an empiricist intuitionism would contrast with a Rossian version.)

Intuitionists characteristically hold that moral knowledge as well as moral justification can be intuitive, but (for reasons indicated earlier) the major ones are not committed to holding, and tend to deny, that this justification or knowledge is indefeasible. This removes a further apparently insurmountable obstacle to considering them empirical. Moral knowledge could be held to come from a broadly perceptual faculty (perhaps an empathic one), from an intuitive sense of obligatoriness, or from some other empirical source sensitive to moral properties.

One way in which moral knowledge could be quasi-perceptual is by way of morally sensitive agents responding to the natural properties that are (I shall assume) the base on which the relevant moral properties supervene, or are, in Ross's perhaps preferable terminology, "consequential." For instance, for a sensitive moral agent, just seeing someone gleefully flog an infant would evoke some negative judgment – say that the act is an outrage – and doubtless also moral indignation. Moral indignation and other emotions may also have non-inferential evidential value. The sensitivity that yields intuitive judgment need not be geared directly to a base property; it may also be a response to something that is produced by one or more base properties in a way that adequately evidences the moral property in question, as indignation might. Granted, indignation can have some other genesis, such as a prejudiced assessment leading to a mistaken moral judgment; it can still have *some* evidential value. Given that it is (arguably) a necessary truth that such a flogging implies wrongdoing, the judgment that it is wrong is well-grounded and can express justified belief and indeed knowledge.

There are at least two ways to conceive the justification of a judgment that is evidenced by a direct or indirect responsiveness to the kinds of natural properties that underlie moral properties. On reliabilist lines, the judgment that the flogging is wrong is well-grounded because it is produced by a reliable belief-generating process: roughly one with a high (possibly perfect) ratio of true to false beliefs as outputs. One might, for instance, judge an action on the basis of a sensitivity to the property of producing a negative balance of happiness to unhappiness. On internalist lines, the judgment might be well-grounded by virtue of being based on a ground accessible to introspection or reflection, such as a sensory experience that, through an appropriate connection with moral standards, justifies believing that the flogging is wrong. Thus, given a visual experience characteristic of seeing a flogging, one might accordingly judge the act wrong.

The difference between the two epistemological approaches here is mainly in the internalist's but not the externalist's requiring accessibility. The former appeals to an experience that is not necessarily veridical and so does not by itself entail the truth of the belief it grounds; reliabilism appeals to a ground that is not necessarily experienced and so, even if it more often than not produces true beliefs, can apparently also produce justified beliefs – even beliefs of certain generalizations – without the agent's having a sense of any factor that justifies beliefs, including supporting premises.[33] If one brain can reliably "read" another in a way that generates true moral judgments of the person in question, the agent with the neural detectors can have moral justification or knowledge even apart from having any sense of what justifies the judgments. The reliabilist's intuitions might thus be less articulate than the internalist's, but both kinds would be non-inferential.

In the light of the ways in which both epistemically externalist and epistemically internalist moral epistemologies can exploit supervenience as providing for an objective non-inferential ground for moral knowledge, we can see in more detail how intuitionism can be developed along empiricist as well as on rationalist lines. (I have in mind a strong supervenience relation such that the base properties *determine* the supervening ones, in a sense implying some degree of explanatory power.[34]) Empiricist versions take the supervenience relation to be empirical; rationalist versions take it to be a priori.

There are related metaphysical considerations. Although the supervenience of moral on natural properties might be thought to constitute a nonreductive naturalism, its nonreductive character is of paramount importance: it allows a nonnaturalist like Ross to exploit the objectivity of the supervenience relation to argue for the possibility of genuine moral knowledge without either construing that knowledge as empirical or taking the properties that are the primary object of moral knowledge to be (in any straightforward way) perceptual or even natural. Injustice, for instance, can be objectively grounded in unequal treatment even if the property of injustice is not a natural one and even if the knowledge that the kind of unjust act in question is *prima facie* wrong is not empirical. Rationalists and empiricists tend to disagree not on the objectivity of this relation but on its modality. The former take it to be conceptual and a priori; the latter, whether they think it conceptual or not, conceive it as empirical.[35]

Contextualist intuitionism

One could also defend a form of intuitionism along contextualist lines. Here the central point would be that contextual features of a cognition determine its justification. Since there is no a priori requirement that these features all operate through inference, intuitive non-inferential justification and knowledge are not precluded.[36] For instance, in a context in which a friend asks me to help load a car, I may be justified without further reflection in believing I should, whereas I might need deliberation and inference if the friend meant to abandon spouse and children. My justification is, as for Rossian intuitionism, defeasible.

The defeasibility of such singular moral judgments can be missed if one does not keep in mind that for intuitionism, it is basic moral principles and not singular moral judgments that are considered self-evident. For contextualism, even the former might be contextually grounded (say in terms of prevailing social practices) rather than a priori. As with Rossian intuitionism, a contextualist version may hold that singular moral judgments need not always be intuitive or otherwise non-inferential, say because some of them arise only through comparing conflicting obligations. In some cases, one might have little confidence in such a judgment; in others, it might come to seem intuitive as one reviews the various considerations that led one to make it.

The defeasibility of moral judgments, however, implies not that they are justified by inferential grounds – foundations that may crumble, one might think – but instead that they may loose their justification through (at least) such grounds, say where one acquires justification for an incompatible position that overturns the judgment. Compare the case of action again: through external forces, I can loose the ability to move my legs; this does not imply that it is through external forces that I move them now.

If a contextualist understanding of the basis of moral knowledge is promising, one could take a social practice approach. For a social practice view, moral justification accrues to cognitions, say moral judgments, when they meet the requirements of a suitable social practice or, in perhaps equivalent Wittgensteinian terms, of a moral language-game.[37] This view, depending on how it is developed, may or may not also be contextualist, and in either case it can be combined with an empiricist or rationalist account of what it is about a practice or context that renders it justificatory.

Just as a linguistic practice is governed by rules that allow us to say some things and not others without objection, a moral practice can impose similar immunities and liabilities: it might, e.g., embody the Rossian duties as bases for non-inferential ascriptions of duties. Social practices, such as morally criticizing people for lying, are perhaps the most promising sources of normativity to account for the plausibility of contextualism, though that view need not make them central. Plainly, a moral judgment that needs no explanation, and seems intuitive, in one society or subculture, say that bull-fighting is wrongful treatment of animals, would need explanation or defense or both in another. The familiarity and historical entrenchment of the practice of attending and applauding such activities is, on the social practice approach, a crucial contextual feature of judgments appraising those activities.

Rationalist intuitionism

Although intuitionism in moral epistemology can be defended along these and other non-rationalist lines, it is best conceived, given the overall views of Ross and its other major proponents, as a rationalist position, and in answering some objections to it I will stress the rationalism of the reconstructed Rossian intuitionism developed above – in outline, the view that we have intuitive justification for both some of our particular moral judgments and a plurality of mediately self-evident moral principles.

A common objection to intuitionism centers on the claim that the basic principles of ethics are self-evident. If so, why is there so much disagreement on them? I suggest three points in reply.

First, if mediate self-evidence is the only kind that need be claimed for basic moral principles, such as Ross's principles of *prima facie* duty, there is no presumption that there should be consensus on them, even after some discussion or reflection. Indeed, given the complexities of the notion of the *prima facie* justified (and even of the notion of justification itself), some people may be expected to have difficulty understanding Ross's principles in the first place.

Second, some of the apparent hesitation in accepting the truth of the principles may come from *thinking* of their truth as a kind requiring endorsement of their self-evidence – the status intuitionists have prominently claimed for them – or of their necessity, a property that, at least since Kant, has commonly been taken to be grasped *in* seeing the truth of an a priori proposition. But I have stressed that the second-order claim that they are self-evident need not also be self-evident in order for them to have this status themselves, and, unlike Ross, I argue that it should not be expected to be self-evident. Seeing its truth requires some theoretical premises.

Third, even if there should be persisting disagreement on the truth or status of the Rossian principles, there need not be disagreement about the basic moral force of the considerations they cite. For instance, whether or not we accept Ross's principles concerning promising and non-injury, we might, both in our abstract thinking and in regulating our conduct, take our having promised to do something as a basic moral reason to do it, or the fact that leaving now would strand a friend about to be attacked by a mad dog, as a basic reason not to do that. Such agreement *in* reasons for action – *operative agreement*, we might call it – does not require agreement *on* them, for instance on some principle expressing them, or on their force. We can agree that a factor, such as avoidance of abandoning a friend, is a good reason for action even if we cannot formulate, or cannot both accept, a principle subsuming the case.

More commonly, we agree on the positive or negative relevance of a reason yet differ on its force; this may occur even where we can agree on a principle subsuming the case, and it can lead to at least temporary disagreement on the final resolution of a moral issue. If there is the kind of wide agreement in moral practice that I think there is among civilized people, then the most important kind of consensus needed for the success of intuitionism as a moral theory is in place. It can at least be argued that the truth and non-inferential justifiability of the relevant principles best explains the high degree of consensus among civilized people in wide segments of their everyday moral practice.[38]

Incommensurability as a problem for intuitionism

Supposing this threefold reply to the first objection succeeds, we must acknowledge a further problem for intuitionism – though it besets virtually any pluralistic ethical view. Non-inferential knowledge or justified belief that a consideration morally favors an action is one thing; such knowledge or justification for taking it as an overriding reason for action is quite another. One might speak of an *incommensurability problem*, since intuitionism grants that there are irreducibly different kinds of moral grounds. Intuitionists deny that there are, say, just hedonic grounds that can be aggregatively assessed to determine what our obligations are. There are at least three crucial points here.

First, intuitionism does not imply that we typically have non-inferential knowledge of *final* duty. We may, for instance, have to compare the case at hand with earlier ones or hypothetical cases and then reason from relevant information to a conclusion. Thus, we might note that if we submit a certain appraisal we may be accused of bias, and we may begin to see the question in relation to conflict of interest. Our final judgment may arise from formulating a sufficient condition for a conflict of interest and judging that the prospective action satisfies it and is thereby impermissible.

Second, it is essential to distinguish higher-order knowledge (or justification) regarding the overridingness of a duty (or other kind of reason) from the first-order knowledge that a given action, say keeping one's promise in spite of a good excuse for non-performance, is obligatory (or otherwise reasonable in some overall way). One can know what one is obligated to do, even in a situation of conflicting duties, yet lack the kind of comparative knowledge one might get from, say, a utilitarian calculation or a Kantian deduction. Perhaps if I know that I should wait for a distressed friend, in a case where I realize this means missing an appointment, I am in a *position* to figure out that one of the two duties is overriding, or even to reach the second-order knowledge that I know this comparative proposition. But I do not in such cases automatically know either of these propositions; and if I am not skilled in moral reasoning, it may be hard for me to do any more than sketch an account of why one duty is overriding. That we easily make mistakes in such sketches is one reason why knowledge of overridingness, and particularly of just *why* it obtains, is often hard to come by.

Third, the difficulty of achieving knowledge or justification in the fact of conflicting grounds is not peculiar to ethics. Consider divided evidence for a scientific hypothesis. Sometimes we must suspend judgment on a hypothesis or cannot reasonably choose between two alternative ones. This does not imply that we never have grounds good enough for knowledge; and the conditions for a degree of justification sufficient to warrant acceptance of a hypothesis are less stringent than the conditions for knowledge. So it is in ethics, sometimes with lesser justification than is common in rational scientific acceptance, but in many cases with greater: even when lying would spare someone pain, it can sometimes be utterly and immediately clear that we should not do it. If there is incommensurability, in the sense of the absence of a common measure for all moral considerations, there is nonetheless *comparability* in the sense implying the possibility of a rational weighting in the context of the relevant facts.

Intuitionism can also maintain (though it may leave open) that final duty is like *prima facie* duty in supervening on natural facts. This plausible view implies that, even where there is no single quantitative or otherwise arguably straightforward basis for comparing conflicting duties, it is possible to describe the various grounds of duty in each case, to compare the cases in that respect with similar cases resolved in the past, bring to bear hypothetical examples, and the like. This is the sort of stuff on which practical wisdom is made.

The charge of dogmatism

Because the controversy between empiricism and rationalism as epistemological perspectives is apparently very much with us in ethical theory, despite how few ethical theorists avowedly maintain either perspective, I want to examine some plausible objections to the intuitionism developed here that are either motivated by empiricism or best seen as objections, not to appeal to intuitions, but to the underlying rationalism of the prominent intuitionist views: roughly, to their taking reason, as opposed to observation, to be capable of grounding justification for substantive truths, such as (arguably) Ross's moral principles of *prima facie* duty.

Is intuitionism dogmatic, as some have held?[39] It might well be dogmatic to claim both that we have intuitive, certain knowledge of what our *prima facie* duties are *and* cannot ground that knowledge on any kind of evidence or in some way support it by examples. But I have argued that a plausible intuitionism, including Ross's, is not committed to our having "certain knowledge" here – where such certainty implies indefeasible justification. Moreover, dogmatism – as distinct from mere stubbornness – is a second-order attitude, such as believing, on a controversial matter, that one is obviously right. Even holding that basic moral principles are self-evident does not entail taking a dogmatic attitude toward them or one's critics. The self-evident may not even be readily understood, much less obvious. A related point is that intuitionism also does not invite moral agents to be dogmatic. Moral principles can *be* basic in our ethical life and non-inferentially justified for us, even if we do not take them to be self-evident (or perhaps even true).

Despite Ross's in some ways unfortunate analogy between moral principles and elementary logical and mathematical ones, he provides a place for reflective equilibrium, which is roughly a kind of fairly stable balance among one's principles and one's judgments about particular cases, to enhance – or for its unobtainability to undermine – our justification for an "intuitive" moral judgment. Nor does anything he must hold, *qua* intuitionist, preclude his allowing a systematization of his moral principles in terms of something more general. Indeed, in at least one place he speaks as if one of the *prima facie* duties might be derivable from another.[40] If such systematization is achieved, then contrary to what the dogmatism charge suggests, that systematization might provide both reasons for the principles and a source of correctives for certain false intuitions or for merely apparent intuitions. An intuition can be mistaken, and a mere prejudice can masquerade as an intuition.

Suppose, e.g., that one uses the categorical imperative to systematize first-order moral principles like Ross's.[41] This would enable one to justify them with whatever force that higher-order principle transmits. Suppose that principle is itself either non-inferentially knowable – in which case intuitionism might claim to encompass among self-evident principles a higher-order moral standard as well as its typical workaday ones – or well justified by arguments from premises, say general truths about practical reason. In either case, it is a good premise for first-order principles of duty. And might it not follow from the categorical imperative that there is (e.g.) *prima facie* moral reason to keep promises? After all, breaking them is *prima facie* something the intrinsic end formulation explicitly forbids: treating people merely as means – giving them an expectation and then, for one's own ends, letting them down.[42] Quite apart from how successful such a unifying enterprise is, if it is even possible as a critical and clarificatory perspective on first-order intuitive principles, this reduces the plausibility of claiming that positing such principles invites dogmatism.

Moreover, given how intuitions are understood – as deriving from the exercise of reason and as having evidential weight – it is incumbent on conscientious intuitionists to factor into their moral thinking, particularly on controversial issues, the apparent intuitions of *others*.[43] If mine have evidential weight, should not others' too? Ross appealed repeatedly to "what we really think" and drew attention to the analogy between intuitions in ethics and perceptions in science. Intuitions, then, are not properly conceived as arbitrary. Many have a basis in reflection and are shared by people of very different experience. Moreover, any rule of conduct arbitrarily posited or grounded in the special interests of its proponents would be hard-pressed to survive the kind of reflection to which conscientious intuitionists will subject their basic moral standards. Thus, even if an apparent intuition might sometimes arise as an arbitrary cognition, it would not necessarily have even *prima facie* justification; and, where a genuine intuition, which presumably does have some degree of *prime facie* justification, is misleading, it can at least normally be defeated by other intuitions that reflection might generate or by those together with further elements in the reflective equilibrium a reasonable intuitionist would seek.

Some philosophical commitments of intuitionism

Something should also be said about the philosophy of mind associated with intuitionism, though the chief issue here applies to philosophy in general. I do not see that a rationalist epistemology entails an implausible philosophy of mind. The view does not, so far as I can see, presuppose either a mysterious mental faculty or a scientifically unlikely mode of access to entities that cannot causally affect the brain. It *may* be that we can have a priori knowledge or a priori justification only if we can in some sense grasp abstract entities, such as the concept of a promise, where this grasp is conceived as something more than having a set of behavioral tendencies, including linguistic ones, and requires a kind of apprehension of abstract entities that do not figure in causal relations. But if this kind of apprehension is required for a priori knowledge and justification, it is not obvious that the apprehension is either obscure or scientifically unlikely, or in any event not required for a grasp of elementary arithmetic truths and other apparently a priori propositions essential in both everyday reasoning and scientific inquiry.

It is perhaps true that we will have a simpler philosophy of mind, at least ontologically, if we can avoid positing any "non-empirical" objects, such as numbers or propositions or concepts. But if properties are abstract entities, as many philosophers hold, then it is not clear that even generalizations about the physical world can be known apart from some kind of grasp of abstract entities. I believe it is fair to say that there is at present no clearly adequate, thoroughly empiricist account of justification in general, applicable to logic and mathematics as well as to epistemic principles.

I turn now to the matter of epistemic principles, roughly principles indicating the grounds or nature of knowledge and justification, say that if, on the basis of a clear visual impression of print on paper, I believe there is printed paper before me, then I am justified in so believing. Is moderate intuitionism (Rossian or other) committed to implausible epistemic principles? I have already suggested that intuitionists as such need not take a self-evident proposition to be incapable of being evidenced by anything else. I now want to suggest that, quite apart from whether they can be evidenced by something else, Ross's basic principles of duty are at least candidates for a priori justification in the way they should be if they are mediately self-evident.

Keeping in mind what constitutes a *prima facie* duty, consider how we would regard some native speaker of English who denied that there is (say) a *prima facie* duty not to injure other people and meant by this something which implies that doing it would not in general be even *prima facie* wrong. This is not amoralism, in the most common sense – the point is not that the person would not be *moved*. Rather, such a person apparently exhibits a kind of *moral deafness*. As with any denial of a clearly true a priori proposition, our first thought might be that there is misunderstanding of some key term, such as "prima facie". Apart from misunderstanding, I doubt that anyone not in the grip of a competing theory would deny the proposition, and I believe that any plausible competing theory would tend to support the same moral judgment, perhaps disguised in different clothing. To be sure, it may be that some skeptical consideration could lead someone who adequately understands a properly formulated Rossian principle to deny it. But some skeptical considerations can be brought against nonmoral a priori propositions and in any event are not necessarily good reasons to doubt either the truth or the a priori status of the challenged proposition.

What is perhaps less controversial is that if we do not ascribe to reason the minimal power required in order for a moderate intuitionism of the kind I have described to be epistemologically plausible, then we face serious problems that must be solved before any instrumentalist or empiricist ethical theory is plausible.[44] For one thing, instrumentalists must account for their fundamental principle that if, on our beliefs, an action serves a basic (roughly, non-instrumental) desire of ours, then there is a reason for us to perform the action. This proposition seems a better candidate for mediate self-evidence than for empirical confirmation.[45] None of this entails that a moderate intuitionism is true; the point is that unless reason has sufficient power to make principles like Ross's plausible candidates for truth, then it is not clear that instrumentalist principles are plausible candidates either.

4. The Gap between Intuitive Moral Judgment and Rational Action

It may easily seem that to show that moral knowledge is possible is to vanquish moral skepticism. But if moral skepticism includes the full range of skeptical positions in ethics, this is not so. Granted that general moral knowledge, say of principles expressing basic *prima facie* duties, is significant, it can exist quite apart from knowledge of singular moral judgments – even the self-addressed, action-guiding kind that moral life depends on. I have argued that despite the problem raised by the plurality of values, such singular judgments can express knowledge, and certainly justified belief. But is either moral knowledge or justified moral belief extensive enough to give us moral guidance in daily life?

A related question arises when we realize that *nonmoral* values can conflict with moral ones, and that it cannot simply be assumed that the latter must always prevail.[46] A third problem concerns the gap between moral judgment (or any moral cognition) and action: even on the controversial assumption that holding a moral judgment entails motivation to act accordingly,[47] such action may be inhibited or may occur for another reason, say out of self-interest. The action then deserves no moral credit and may not even be rational (depending on whether the nonmoral explaining factor suffices to render it rational). Let us pursue these three problems.

Some challenges of moral skepticism

On the first question, concerning the possibility of knowledge or justified belief regarding the moral status of individual actions, I maintain that although singular moral judgments should not be considered self-evident, they may still be non-inferentially knowable (or justified). This point may be obscured because it may seem that intuitionism requires self-evidence for justified belief of singular as well as certain general moral propositions. But it does not and in fact cannot plausibly require this if I am right in taking self-evident propositions to be knowable on conceptual grounds. Nor does intuitionism imply that only self-evident propositions are intuitively knowable. A singular moral judgment about a particular person can be intuitively knowable, especially when it is an application of a principle of *prima facie* as opposed to final duty.

One may also be tempted to think that if, in making singular moral judgments, we are guided by moral principles, and if, afterwards, we can frame a principle to cover the action in question, then we should be able to see the relevant judgments as derivable from principles in a way that as it were certifies them as knowledge. This idea neglects a point essential to a particularist intuitionism such as Ross's: at least some intuitions regarding concrete cases are epistemically more basic than, or in any event indispensable to, intuitive knowledge of the corresponding generalizations. It may be only when we think of a deed concretely and realize it is wrong that we see (or are justified in believing) that all deeds of that kind are wrong.

The idea that singular moral judgments are knowable only as applications of generalizations may also arise from the correct point that in many cases one must be able to see two or more conflicting (*prima facie*) generalizations to apply to one's options before one can tell what, overall, one should do. Still, the applicability of several generalizations to a case does not imply that one's final obligation therein is determined by applying a further, reconciling generalization. That point holds even if such a generalization is in principle formulable after the fact.

To be sure, supposing that (all) moral properties supervene on a finite set of natural ones and that the relevant natural ones and their grounding relations to the moral ones are discernible by ordinary kinds of inquiry, then in principle one can, given a good grasp of a sound moral judgment in a case of conflicting obligations, formulate a generalization that nontrivially applies to similar cases. For the overall obligatoriness one discerns will be based on natural properties that one can in principle discriminate and appeal to in framing a generalization. But this generalization possibility is not a necessary condition for one's forming a justified judgment (or one expressing knowledge), say a judgment that one must rectify an injustice. One can achieve a sound result whether or not one generalizes on it or is even able to do so. It could be, for instance, that overall obligation is *organic*, and that given the sense in which it is, we can have no guarantee of being able to specify just what properties are the basis of it. Even if *prima facie* obligation is entailed by certain natural properties (a view that intuitionists commonly hold), overall obligation apparently requires a more complicated account.

A further point concerning the epistemic resources of the intuitionism I am developing is that in many cases of a singular judgment settling a conflict of duties, there is the possibility of reaching a reflective equilibrium between this judgment and various moral principles and other singular judgments. This equilibrium may contribute to the justification of that judgment; the former or elements in it may even produce the latter. Here, then, is one way a judgment that begins as a hypothesis can graduate to the status of justified belief or even knowledge.

As to the problem of possible conflicts between moral and nonmoral values, it should first be said that this can affect any plausible ethical theory. If it warrants skepticism about intuitionism, it warrants it for other plausible theories. To be sure, Kant treated ethical considerations as basic in the theory of practical reason and regarded the categorical imperative as grounding absolute moral obligations. But suppose for the sake of argument that it does ground some absolute obligations; this does not entail that there is no possibility of anyone's ever rationally (and knowingly) doing something that morality does not permit. Regarding utilitarian theories, if (as I shall assume) they ground all reasons for action in whatever they take to have intrinsic value, then unless (implausibly) a utilitarian view considers *only* one quite specific kind of value to be basic, something like an incommensurability problem can arise. Even if, e.g., some pleasures are not better than others, there are problems weighing promotion of pleasure against reductions of pain. To say, however, that the problem besets other views is not to answer the skeptical claim that it is devastating. Let me briefly address that problem.

If the (ideally moderate) foundationalism that I suggest is crucial for a plausible intuitionism is sound, we can make at least two significant points here. First, if we distinguish between rebutting a skeptical view – showing that the case for it is unsound – and refuting it, which is showing it false by establishing that there *is* the relevant kind of knowledge or justification, then there is reason to think rebuttal is possible. What we can do, I contend, is consider the various epistemic standards the skeptic says moral judgment cannot meet and argue that either the standard is too high or the judgment can meet it.[48] Second, although refuting skepticism is harder than rebutting it, it may yet be possible given epistemic standards that are not unrealistically high. For one thing, there is a chance that some paradigms will simply be more intuitive than any competing intuitions that serve skepticism. Surely it is more intuitive that we are justified in judging that flogging infants for pleasure is wrong than that no one is justified in holding moral judgments. Perhaps we can exhibit or argue for our justification here in a compelling way that counts as showing that we have moral justification.

The gap between moral reasons for action and action for moral reasons

The third problem mentioned at the beginning of this section is the logical gap between moral judgment expressing knowledge or justified belief and, on the other hand, rational action in accordance with it. More generally, there is a gap between having an adequate moral reason to do something and doing it for that reason. Call it *the cynic's gap*, since cynics typically grant that there are moral reasons but tend to hold that we rarely act on them and that in general we do not know we do.

Why, however, should we assume, as skepticism characteristically does, that a logical gap is intrinsically unbridgeable by rational considerations? In this case, the skeptic notes that one can justifiedly judge that one should A, yet end up A-ing for a selfish reason and in a way that prevents the action from being rational: the deed might be neither based on the justified judgment calling for it nor rational on any other ground. This is surely possible; and as Kant saw regarding moral actions,[49] we cannot always know that vitiating motivation has not operated. But again, we may resist the skeptical claim that if a thing is possible, we can know that it has not occurred only on grounds entailing it has not. Sometimes we are – and have good reason to believe we are – wholehearted in wanting to do a duty, and we can sometimes tell that the sense of this duty is a sufficient motivator of our action.[50] Suppose, however, that we cannot tell. At worst (as where prejudice motivates us), in virtue of holding a moral judgment expressing knowledge or justified belief calling for the action, we *have* justification for the action but it does not transfer from our judgment to our action. This is at least better than acting neither with justification nor even having it.

There is far more to say about the dimensions and prospects of moral skepticism. Here I have simply suggested along what lines, given the moderate intuitionism presented here, moral skepticism may be at least rebutted. I have said too little to accomplish such a rebuttal, but I have indicated a strategy of rebuttal (and perhaps of refutation) one might take given the position I am defending. The appropriate attitude to adopt in the light of all this is a fallibilist humility. It permits moral conviction, but forswears ethical dogmatism.

We have seen in outline how some basic approaches in moral epistemology account for – or deny, in the way noncognitivism does – the possibility of moral knowledge. Among these, it is a reconstructed intuitionism that seems to me most promising. If I have been roughly correct about this view, a moderate intuitionism in moral epistemology is a candidate for a leading place in contemporary ethical theory. For many of the same reasons, there is more room for a rationalist moral epistemology than is generally realized. Once it is seen how reflection is central in ethical theorizing, some of the major obstacles in the way of a rationalist account of the foundations of ethics are eliminated. Other obstacles may be cleared away by noting how a moderate intuitionism conceives self-evidence, distinguishes it from obviousness, and brings to bear the distinction between conclusions of inference and conclusions of reflection. There is much to commend a fallibilist, intuitionistic moral rationalism that uses reflection as a justificatory method in the ways described here, encompassing both intuitions as *prima facie* justified inputs to ethical theorizing and reflective equilibrium as a means of extending and systematizing those inputs. This moderate intuitionism gives a good account of the data to which ethical theory is responsible, comports well with a plausible epistemology and philosophy of mind, and provides a fruitful approach both to ethical theory and to everyday moral practice.[51]

Notes

1 A sampling of the positions is found in Walter Sinnott-Armstrong and Mark Timmons, eds., *Moral Knowledge?* (New York and Oxford: Oxford University Press, 1996).
2 Noncognitivism may also be empiricist – and (non-reductively) naturalistic – but since it denies that there is moral knowledge in the ordinary sense, I treat it separately.
3 One could delete this clause on the ground that there *is* no morally neutral way to specify what counts as an available alternative; then failures to maximize due to overlooking an alternative may always yield objectively wrong action, but may or may not deserve disapproval, depending on one's theory of excuses.
4 This is quite different from the puzzling formulation Mill gives in the first paragraph of ch. 2 of *Utilitarianism*, where he says acts are "right insofar as they tend to promote happiness" (by which he means "pleasure and the absence of pain"). He never countenances degrees of rightness, as this formulation might lead one to expect, and my formulation fits much of his presentation of his theory.
5 In ch. 2, shortly after introducing his utilitarian principle, Mill contends that some pleasures are preferable to others, offers an empirical way to determine which of two pleasures is better (para. 5), and attempts to provide a similar way to weight quality of pleasure against quantity (para. 8). All this complicates his moral epistemology but does not alter the basic features in question.
6 Mill's attempted proof that pleasure is good is in ch. 4 of *Utilitarianism*; for an account of the view that goodness is to be determined by seeing what one would desire given adequate information and suitable reflection, see Richard B. Brandt, *A Theory of the Good and the Right* (Oxford: Oxford University Press, 1979). Cf. Peter

Railton's version of a similar approach in "Alienation, Consequentialism, and the Demands of Morality," *Philosophy & Public Affairs* 13 (1984): 134–71.

7 Kant gave other universality formulations, but all seem to presuppose that the universalizability is subject to a rationality constraint, which I add for clarity though Kant did not put it into his formulations. We may here leave aside the issue of whether the universality and intrinsic end formulations are equivalent.

8 In the *Groundwork of the Metaphysics of Morals* Kant emphasizes the synthetic a priori character of the categorical imperative. In *Utilitarianism* Mill is rarely explicitly epistemological, but when he is most so, in his "General Remarks," he attacks Kant and other "a priori moralists," and his pervasive empiricism is evident; in the third paragraph, e.g., he calls right and wrong "questions of observation and experience." For him not even logic and mathematics are a priori.

9 An exception might be made, perhaps even by an empiricist, for an infinite being of a certain sort: given a kind of omnipresence, non-inferential knowledge of every truth about the world might be thought possible.

10 There is also the metaphysical nonnaturalism important for intuitionism, and it is an interesting question whether this or the moral epistemology – if either – is primary. For discussion of how intuitionism has been conceived, see my "Intuitionism, Pluralism, and the Foundations of Ethics," in Sinnott-Armstrong and Timmons, esp. section 1. Cf. William K. Frankena, "Obligation and Value in the Philosophy of G. E. Moore," in Paul Arthur Schilpp, ed., *The Philosophy of G. E. Moore* (New York: Tudor Publishing Co., 1952), and *Ethics*, 2nd ed. (Englewood Cliffs, NJ: Prentice-Hall, 1973).

11 Foundationalism in this moderate form is widely held, though in many cases only implicitly. For an account of its status see "The Foundationalism–Coherentism Controversy: Hardened Stereotypes and Overlapping Theories," ch. 4 in my *The Structure of Justification* (Cambridge and New York: Cambridge University Press, 1993). *Editor's note*: see also the essay by BonJour, this volume.

12 This is the kind of thing W. D. Ross and other intuitionists have said about basic moral principles: they are intuitively knowable and self-evident, though seeing their truth may take a good deal of reflection. See e.g. Ross's *The Right and the Good* (Oxford: Oxford University Press, 1930), esp. ch. 2. The point is developed below.

13 This is confirmed by the partial account of virtue ethics given in my "Acting from Virtue," *Mind* 104 (1995): 449–71.

14 Recent treatments of virtue epistemology are given in Ernest Sosa, "Knowledge and Intellectual Virtue" and "Reliabilism and Intellectual Virtue," both in *Knowledge in Perspective* (Cambridge: Cambridge University Press, 1991); Jonathan L. Kvanvig, *The Intellectual Virtues and the Life of the Mind* (Lanham, MD: Rowman and Littlefield, 1992); James Montmarquet, *Epistemic Virtue and Doxastic Responsibility* (Lanham, MD: Rowman and Littlefield, 1993); and Linda Zagzebski, *Virtues of the Mind* (Cambridge and New York: Cambridge University Press, 1996). For a recent critical study indicating different forms a virtue epistemology can take see John Greco, "Virtues and Vices of Virtue Epistemology," *Canadian Journal of Philosophy* 23 (1993).

15 I say "perhaps" because it is not clear that the virtue-theoretical approach in epistemology is basic or instead a way of understanding and applying such views as rationalistic intuitionism or empiricistic reliabilism.

16 I have discussed it in some detail in "Skepticism in Theory and Practice," ch. 3 in my *Moral Knowledge and Ethical Character* (Oxford and New York: Oxford University Press, 1997).

17 For a sophisticated contemporary statement of noncognitivism see Allan Gibbard, *Wise Choices, Apt Feelings* (Cambridge: Harvard University Press, 1990). For criticism of Gibbard's position, see Walter Sinnott-Armstrong's "Some Problems for Gibbard's Norm-Expressivism," *Philosophical Studies* 69 (1993), and Mark van Roojen's "Expressivism and Irrationality," *Philosophical Review* 105 (1996): 311–33 (a critique of Gibbard and Simon Blackburn).

18 For a case against the implication of global skepticism by noncognitivism as just characterized, see Simon Blackburn's "Securing the Nots," in Sinnott-Armstrong and Timmons; and Timmons' *Morality Without Foundations* (forthcoming). Detailed critical discussion of Blackburn's expressivism is given in the paper by van Roojen cited above.

19 See Ross, p. 21.

20 Ibid., pp. 29–30. Cf. H. A. Prichard, "Does Moral Philosophy Rest on a Mistake?" (1912), in his *Moral Obligation* (Oxford: Oxford University Press, 1949). The mistake is "supposing the possibility of proving what can only be apprehended directly by an act of moral thinking" (p. 16).

21 A brief account of what constitutes an intuition in the relevant sense is given in my "Intuitionism, Pluralism, and the Foundations of Ethics," cited above.

22 Ross, pp. 39–41.

23 This may be in part what leads R. B. Brandt (among others) to consider intuitionism committed to the possibility of intuitively grasping self-evidence, as opposed to truth. See *Ethical Theory* (Englewood Cliffs, NJ: Prentice-Hall, 1959), ch. 8. Cf. Jonathan Harrison: "According to this view [intuitionism], a person who can grasp the truth of ethical generalizations . . . just sees without argument that they are and must be true, and true of all possible worlds." See "Ethical Objectivism," *The Encyclopedia of Philosophy* (New York: Macmillan, 1967). Cf. Laurence BonJour's construal of the "traditional rationalist account of *a priori* knowledge as the intuitive grasp or apprehension of necessity." See *The Structure of Empirical Knowledge* (Cambridge: Harvard University Press, 1985), p. 207. BonJour's view is helpfully discussed by Paul Tidman in "The Justification of A Priori Intuitions," *Philosophy and Phenomenological Research* 46, 1 (1996): 161–71.

24 As Alvin Plantinga puts it, "the tradition . . . held that self-evident propositions – simple truths of arithmetic and logic, for example – are such that we can't even grasp or understand them without seeing that they are true . . . A better position, I think, is that a self-evident proposition is such that a *properly functioning* (mature) human being can't grasp it without believing it." See *Warrant and Proper Function* (Oxford and New York: Oxford University Press, 1993), pp. 108–9. The view developed in this paper differs from both positions.

25 I speak here only of intuitions *that*, as opposed to property intuitions, intuitions *of* or regarding something; the latter do not admit of justification or knowledge in the same way.

26 Three qualifications will help. First, if the belief is based on anything *other* than understanding the proposition, that understanding must still be a sufficient basis (in a sense I cannot explicate now). Second, I take the relevant basis relation to preclude

a wayward causal chain: the understanding must not produce the belief in certain abnormal ways. Third, there may be a non-truth-entailing use of "self-evident" that allows for false and hence unknowable self-evident propositions; but I assume any such use is at best nonstandard. What is more controversial about my characterization is that – apparently – only a priori propositions satisfy it. Note, however, that the analysandum is self-evidence *simpliciter*, not self-evidence *for S*. There is some plausibility in saying that it is self-evident, for me, that I exist. I leave open whether such cases illustrate a kind of self-evidence, but the relevant proposition asserting my existence is surely not self-evident.

27 Granted, a rational person who adequately understands a self-evident proposition at least tends to believe it. But even with adequate understanding some self-evident propositions seem disbelievable by rational persons.

28 I explicate structural justification in a paper of that title in my *The Structure of Justification* (Cambridge and New York: Cambridge University Press, 1993).

29 The term 'normal adults' is vague, but the problem is largely eliminable by relativizing, making the basic notion that of the mediately self-evident *for S*, or for adults with a certain conceptual sophistication.

30 Ross said (e.g., in the quotation given from pp. 29–30) that his principles do not admit of proof, and Moore went so far as to say that in calling propositions intuitions he means "*merely* to assert that they are incapable of proof; I imply nothing whatever as to the manner or origin of our cognition of them." *Principia Ethica* (London: Cambridge University Press, 1903), p. x. See also p. 145.

31 I defend this claim in "Intuitionism, Pluralism, and the Foundations of Ethics," cited above, and more concretely in ch. 12 of *Moral Knowledge and Ethical Character*. A different and largely compatible kind of defense is given by Brad Hooker in "Ross-style Pluralism versus Rule-consequentialism," *Mind* 105 (1996): 531–52.

32 The relevant kind of induction must not be the intuitive kind Ross took to occur, since that is roughly a process of coming to know, through a kind of conceptual insight, something non-empirical. Jonathan Dancy, in *Moral Reasons* (Oxford: Blackwell, 1993) is probably best considered to be developing an empiricist intuitionism.

33 I have critically compared these two approaches to justification in "Justification, Truth, and Reliability," in *The Structure of Justification*, cited above. *Editor's note*: see also the essay by Sosa, this volume.

34 I have discussed the supervenience of moral on natural properties in "Ethical Naturalism and the Supervenience of Moral Properties," ch. 5 in *Moral Knowledge*.

35 I discuss this issue in detail (and briefly defend the rationalist view) in ch. 5 of *Moral Knowledge*. For detailed discussion of supervenience see Jaegwon Kim, "Supervenience as a Philosophical Concept," *Metaphilosophy* 21 (1990), and, particularly on the appraisal of positions like nonreductive naturalism, "The Myth of Nonreductive Materialism," *Proceedings and Addresses of the American Philosophical Association* 63, supplement to no. 1 (1989). Nonreductive naturalism is arguably unstable for the same reasons he takes nonreductive materialism to be. For criticism of Kim and a case for nonreductive naturalism see John F. Post, "Global Supervenient Determination: Too Permissive?", in Elias Savellos and Umit Yalcin, eds., *Essays on Supervenience* (Cambridge and New York: Cambridge University Press, 1995).

36 For a portrait and defense of contextualism in moral epistemology see Mark Timmons, "Outline of a Contextualist Moral Epistemology," in Sinnott-Armstrong and Timmons.

Cf. the contextual particularism of Jonathan Dancy's view in *Moral Reasons*, esp. chs. 4–6.

37 For discussion of the epistemology of social practices, see W. P. Alston, *The Reliability of Sense-Perception* (Ithaca and London: Cornell University Press, 1993).

38 Compare Judith Jarvis Thomson's distinction between explanatory and object-level moral judgments, e.g. between the judgment that capital punishment is wrong because it is intentional killing of someone who poses no threat, and the judgment that capital punishment is wrong. See *The Realm of Rights* (Cambridge: Harvard University Press, 1990), p. 30. I suspect that some resistance to Rossian intuitionism may derive from insufficiently detaching his object-level principles of *prima facie* duty from his explanatory gloss – prominent in his introduction of the basic duties – construing each as having a particular ground.

39 Mill is a source of a vivid statement of this objection:

> The notion that truths external to the mind may be known by intuition or consciousness, independently of observation and experience, is, I am persuaded, in these times, the great intellectual support of false doctrines and bad institutions. By the aid of this theory, every inveterate belief and every intense feeling, of which the origin is not remembered, is enabled to dispense with the obligation of justifying itself by reason, and is erected into its own all-sufficient voucher and justification. There never was such an instrument devised for consecrating all deep seated prejudices.

See John Stuart Mill's *Autobiography*, ed. Jack Stillinger (Boston: Houghton Mifflin Co., 1969), p. 134. BonJour, p. 209, notes a similar range of objections.

40 He says that "[E]ven before the implicit undertaking to tell the truth was established [by a contract] I had a duty not to tell lies, since to tell lies is *prima facie* to do a positive injury to a person," *The Right and the Good*, p. 55. This seems to countenance a derivation of a duty of fidelity (Ross conceived honesty as fidelity to one's implicit agreement in speaking) from one of non-injury.

41 This is a project I do in outline in ch. 12 of *Moral Knowledge*.

42 The case for such an entailment may depend on carefully distinguishing overridden from canceled, nullified, or otherwise "neutralized" or "invalidated" promises, as well as on distinguishing promises from certain statements of intention. If, having promised to do something for Louise, I discover that she has dropped the plan calling for it but I must decide whether to do it before I can speak to her, my promise seems nullified.

43 On the importance of this in ethics see Margaret Walker's "Feminist Skepticism, Authority, and Transparency," in Sinnott-Armstrong and Timmons.

44 I neglect noncognitivism here; I believe that it encounters serious problems of its own, but it is a significant contender. I also neglect R. B. Brandt's modified instrumentalism; see his *A Theory of the Good and the Right* (Oxford: The Clarendon Press, 1979). I have appraised Brandt's overall view of rationality in "An Epistemic Conception of Rationality," in *The Structure of Justification*, cited above.

45 Some empiricists might claim that it is analytic, say because to have a reason for action *is* to have such a basic desire and set of beliefs. But this is at best highly controversial, in part because it begs the question against intuitionism and other prominent views.

46 For a plausible case that rational judgment and action can go against morality, see Bruce Russell, "Two Forms of Ethical Skepticism," in Louis P. Pojman, ed., *Ethical Theory* (Belmont, CA: Wadsworth, 1989). Cf. Bernard Gert's view, in *Morality: A New Justification of the Moral Rules* (Oxford and New York: Oxford University Press, 1988), that even if moral action is not always rationally required it is always rationally permitted (see e.g. p. 227).

47 This motivational internalist assumption is appraised in detail and with many references to the relevant literature on the question, in my "Moral Judgment and Reasons for Action," ch. 10 in *Moral Knowledge*.

48 In ch. 10 of *Epistemology* (London and New York: Routledge, 1998), I offer arguments of this kind concerning some representative skeptical theses.

49 In the *Groundwork of the Metaphysics of Morals* Kant claims or at least implies that except where one is acting against inclination, one cannot know one is acting from duty. See e.g. sect. 407.

50 Unlike Kant, I unequivocally allow that one can be acting from duty even if a different motive cooperates, provided one's motive of duty actually explains the deed. If overdetermination is ruled out, the skeptical view is more difficult to resist. I discuss this range of issues in "Causalist Internalism," in my *The Structure of Justification*, cited above.

51 This essay has benefited from presentations of earlier versions at the Association for Informal Logic and Critical Thinking, where Julia Driver and John Post gave provocative commentaries, and at Brown University, Carleton College, MIT, St. Cloud State University, St. Olaf College, and Wayne State University. For detailed comments at different stages I am grateful to Terry Horgan, Stephen Kershnar and, especially, John Greco and Bruce Russell. Parts of the essay are revisions of earlier work of mine, mainly "Intuitionism, Pluralism, and the Foundations of Ethics," in Sinnott-Armstrong and Timmons, and "Moderate Intuitionism and the Epistemology of Moral Judgment," forthcoming in *Ethical Theory and Moral Practice*.

Chapter 13

Epistemology of Religion

Nicholas Wolterstorff

Adherence to a religion, and participation therein, typically involve worship, the reading and interpretation of sacred scripture, prayer, meditation, self-discipline, submission to instruction, acts of justice and charity. Typically they involve allowing certain metaphors and images to shape one's actions and perception of reality. They incorporate such propositional attitudes as hoping that certain things will come about, trusting that certain things will come about, regretting that certain things have come about, and accepting various things, in the sense of playing the role of one who believes those things. And typically they involve believing various things – about God, about the sacred, about humanity, its past and future, glory and misery, and about the world. Sometimes what evokes and sustains adherence to, and participation in, a religion is religious experience of one sort and another – mystical experience, uncanny experience, a sense of cosmic security, the experience of something *as created by God*, usually this being something amazing in its minuteness, its immensity, or its intricate and improbable workings. The phrase Wittgenstein made famous is appropriate here: participation in a religion is a form of life.

What, in all this, falls within the domain of the epistemologist? The *experiences*, naturally: the epistemologist will want to understand the structure of religious experience. He will try to identify the object of the acquaintance which is ingredient in the experience. Is mystical experience simply an inner state, of which one is aware and from which one draws various inferences, or is it itself constituted of one's acquaintance with something external to the self – God, perhaps, or more generally, the divine? And the epistemologist will try to understand what it is to be aware of something *as created by God*, or *as revelatory of God*, or whatever.

Likewise the *beliefs* ingredient in religion fall within the domain of the epistemologist. A good deal of the task of general epistemology is to understand the nature of the various truth-relevant merits which beliefs can possess, the necessary and sufficient conditions for beliefs to possess those merits, and the virtues of mind and practice requisite and apt for their presence: merits such as being reliably formed, being warranted, being entitled, being scientific, being rational, being justified – and, indeed, being true. In developing his analysis, the epistemologist will want to keep an eye on religious belief; for an account, say, of entitlement, which is offered as a general account but fails to fit religious belief, is so far forth a failure. But also, conversely, the epistemologist who has developed a general account of entitlement may want to show how his account applies to the specific case of religious belief.

Let me highlight an assumption in what I have just said. Until rather recently, analytic epistemology in the twentieth century was conducted as if there were – apart from truth itself – just one truth-relevant merit in beliefs, that one typically called either "justification" or "rationality." It was asked what was necessary and sufficient for a belief to be *justified*, or *rational*; and since there was a great deal of disagreement on the answer to that question, there was a great flowering of theories of justification, or theories of rationality. My contention, to the contrary, is that there is a large number of distinct truth-relevant merits in beliefs, and that neither "justification" nor "rationality" picks out any single such merit; both are highly ambiguous terms, each picking out a number of distinct merits. A corollary of this point is that a good many philosophical disputes over justification and rationality have had their source in the fact that philosophers, with their eye on distinct merits, have offered accounts of those different merits, rather than in the fact that, with their eye on the same merit, they have offered different accounts of that single merit. The way forward is to acknowledge this fact, and to be clear on which merit it is that one wishes to discuss. The enterprise of offering an account of entitlement is different, say, from the enterprise of offering an account of warrant.[1]

A good many of the truth-relevant merits possessed by beliefs are possessed as well by other propositional attitudes, such as hoping that, expecting that, and trusting that. Some of our hopes are hopes that we are not entitled to; some of our trustings have not been reliably formed. From among the considerable diversity of propositional attitudes, epistemologists in our century have concentrated almost entirely on beliefs. Given the fact that a good many of the truth-relevant merits present in beliefs which have been of interest to philosophers are present in other propositional attitudes as well, that limitation of focus seems groundless. It seems especially groundless in the case of epistemology of religion; for in many religious forms of life (in contrast, perhaps, to science), hoping, trusting, regretting, accepting, and so forth, are as prominent as believing. Thus epistemology of religion, though it certainly comprises epistemology of religious belief, is not to be identified with that.[2] That said, however, I propose on this occasion to follow the convention and to single out belief for attention, from all the other propositional attitudes to be found in religion.

1. The Doxastic Ideal

Ever since Plato, a certain picture of *the ideally formed belief* has haunted Western philosophy, and in particular, the epistemology of religion. Sometimes the picture has been incorporated within a theory of knowledge, at other times, within a theory of science, on yet other occasions, within a theory of entitlement – and over and over, within an account of certitude.

Here is the picture. Fundamental in the life of the mind is *acquaintance* with entities, and awareness of having acquaintance with entities. What I call "acquaintance" is what Kant called *Anschauung* – standardly, though not very adequately, translated in the English versions of Kant as "intuition." Or to look at the same thing from the converse side: fundamental in the life of the mind is presence – entities presenting themselves to us, putting in their appearance to us. Consider the definite description: "the dizziness you felt when you rode that merry-go-round yesterday." If you did in fact feel dizzy when riding that merry-go-round yesterday, then I can use that phrase to pick out that particular dizziness – to pick it out well enough to make assertions about it, for example. Nonetheless, that particular dizziness was never part of the intuitional content of *my* mind; I was never acquainted with it, it was never presented to me. My contact with it is – and was – very different from my contact with the dizziness *I* felt when *I* rode that merry-go-round yesterday. *That* dizziness was present to me; I was acquainted with it.

To say it again: acquaintance, and its converse, presence, are in their various modes fundamental to the life of the mind. Perception has intuitional content, memory has intuitional content, introspection has intuitional content, intellection (reason) has intuitional content. Surely there could be no human mind devoid of all these; perhaps there could be no mind at all. (To assure oneself that the four activities just mentioned do all have an intuitional component, contrast picking out some entity by means of a definite description, with perceiving, remembering, introspecting, or intellecting that entity, or an entity of that sort.)

Among the entities with which we have acquaintance, are facts: I perceive *that the sun is rising*, I introspect *that I am feeling rather dizzy*, I remember *that the ride made me dizzy*, I intellect *that the proposition, green is a color, is necessarily true*. And now for the picture of the ideally formed belief: sometimes, so it has been claimed and assumed, one's acquaintance with some fact, coupled, if necessary, with one's awareness of that acquaintance, produces in one a belief whose propositional content corresponds to the fact with which one is acquainted. My acquaintance with the fact that I am feeling rather dizzy produces in me the belief that I am feeling rather dizzy. The content of my belief is, as it were, read directly off the fact with which I have acquaintance. How could such a belief possibly be mistaken? It must be the case that it is certain.

That's one type of ideally formed belief, the *first grade*, as it were: the belief formed by one's acquaintance with a fact to which the propositional content of the belief corresponds. There is a second type, of a somewhat lower grade: the belief formed by one's acquaintance with the fact that the propositional content of the belief is logically entailed by propositions corresponding to facts of which one is aware. In such a case, the certainty of one's belief concerning the premises, coupled with the certainty of one's belief concerning the entailment, is transmitted to one's belief of the conclusion; it too is certain for one. What accounts for the fact that such a belief will typically be of a lower grade than the highest is that one may have acquaintance with the facts corresponding to the premises in an argument, and acquaintance with the fact that those premises deductively support the conclusion, without having acquaintance with the fact corresponding to the conclusion. Indeed, therein lies the point of such arguments. Deductive arguments, if grounded in acquaintance, carry us beyond acquaintance while yet preserving certitude.

Is there a third grade of ideally formed belief, viz., the belief formed by one's acquaintance with the fact that the propositional content of the belief is *probable* relative to facts with which one has acquaintance? The issue has been a matter of controversy; accordingly, it's best for our purposes to leave it an open question whether there is this third type and grade. John Locke, as we will see shortly, thought there was. He recognized that such arguments are incapable of transmitting certainty to the conclusion; hence beliefs thus formed are of a lower grade than the others. Nonetheless, Locke quite clearly regarded probabilistic arguments as like deductive arguments in that, if one has collected a satisfactory body of evidence as premises, and if one is acquainted with the facts corresponding to the premises and with the fact that the conclusion is more probable than not on those premises, then one's acceptance of the conclusion is entirely grounded in acquaintance. Hume challenged – decisively so, to my mind – this assumption of Locke concerning those probabilistic arguments which are inductive in character. Inductively arrived at beliefs cannot be entirely grounded in acquaintance, Hume argued. Though many such beliefs are beyond reproach, nonetheless, in the very nature of the case they fall short of the ideal of having one's beliefs entirely grounded in acquaintance with facts.

Let us henceforth alternate between speaking of "the ideally formed belief" and "The Doxastic Ideal." The central theme in my subsequent discussion will be the role of this Ideal in epistemology of religion. But before we get to that, let's observe that the question posed above, "How could such a belief possibly be mistaken if it is formed by acquaintance with a fact to which the propositional content of the belief corresponds?" though meant to be purely rhetorical, proves, on close scrutiny, instead to be beside the point in a fundamental way. It's true, of course, that a belief evoked by (one's awareness of) one's acquaintance with a fact to which the propositional content of the belief corresponds, will never be false; it will be certain for one. But an all-too-pervasive feature of our mental life is that a belief, rather than being evoked by acquaintance with some fact which corresponds to the belief's propositional content, is evoked instead by what might be called a "mimic" of that acquaintance.

It's a fact that it's necessarily true that green is a color, I'm acquainted with that fact, I'm aware that I'm acquainted with it; and that awareness-of-acquaintance evokes in me the belief that it's necessarily true that green is a color. So the belief is certain: I couldn't have that acquaintance and the belief be false. All very elegant. But now and then we have an experience which is a *mimic* of acquaintance with the fact that some proposition is necessarily true – just as we now and then have an experience which is a mimic of acquaintance with some external object. One is acquainted with some proposition, indeed; but the proposition is not necessarily true, so one cannot be acquainted with the fact that it is necessarily true. Yet it *seems* necessarily true; it has that "look" about it. What one is introspectively aware of is not intellective acquaintance with some fact of necessary truth, but only of a mimic thereof. But since the experience does mimic acquaintance with some fact of necessary truth, one's awareness of the experience produces the *belief* that the proposition, with which one *is* acquainted, is a necessary truth – provided, of course, that one doesn't believe that the experience is a mimic. What establishes that it is a mimic is that the proposition in question does not have the relations to other propositions that it would have if it were necessarily true. If one knows, or believes, that it doesn't have those relations, then one will recognize the experience for what it is, namely, a mimic, and one's acquaintance with it will no longer produce the belief that the proposition is necessarily true. Any logical paradox – the Russell Paradox, for example – illustrates the point. For at least one of the premises in such a paradox, what one is introspectively aware of when considering the premise is not acquaintance with some fact of necessary truth, but only a mimic thereof.

Back, then, to certainty: what good is the explained sense of certainty to us, if there are these mimics in our experience and we don't recognize them as such – the consequence of our failure to recognize their mimicry being that they produce false beliefs in us?

2. The Role of The Doxastic Ideal in the Medieval Understanding of *Scientia*

The medieval philosophers produced little that could be called, by our lights, "epistemology of religion." Not until the Enlightenment did epistemology of religion enter its majority. It was about theology, not religion, that the medieval philosophers, and philosophical theologians, raised epistemological questions. Nonetheless, for our purposes here it will be instructive to look briefly at one aspect of the thought of the medieval philosophers. As already mentioned, the role of The Doxastic Ideal in epistemology of religion will be the central theme in my subsequent discussion; that Ideal played a role in the medieval reflections on theology. For the medievals regarded theology as a science, a *scientia*; and central to their understanding of a *scientia* was The Doxastic Ideal. Let us see how they worked these ideas out, taking Aquinas's explanation of *scientia* as paradigmatic.[3]

Two ideas were central in Aquinas's adaptation of the Aristotelian concept of *scientia*. *Scientia* is a community enterprise; and in that community enterprise, the phenomenon of a proposition or argument being *evident* to a person plays a central role. In a few of his formulations, Aquinas allows propositions which have been "evident to the senses" of some person or other as premises for *scientia*. But though it becomes clear from his discussion what he would cite as examples of this category – the proposition that *some things change*, for instance – he never tells us what exactly the concept comes to, and it becomes clear that it is only with reluctance that he allows propositions evident to the senses among the premises for *scientia*. Ideally, *scientia* would have as premises only propositions which are *self-evident* to someone or other.

Aquinas's notion of the self-evident was traditional. The explanation comes in two stages: first, self-evidence *per se*, then, self-evidence to a specific person. A proposition is self-evident *per se* if it is impossible that a person should grasp it without both "seeing" that it is true and believing it. The explanation makes use of ideas which we explored just a few pages back. Let's reformulate it to make that explicit: a proposition is self-evident *per se* if it is impossible that a person, when acquainted with it and aware of being acquainted, should understand it and not both be acquainted with the fact that it is true, and form the belief whose propositional content corresponds to that fact. Though it was not built into the traditional concept of the self-evident that self-evident propositions are *necessarily* true, it was always, to my knowledge, assumed that this is the case. A proposition, then, is self-evident *to* a specific person if it is self-evident *per se*, and if that person has acquaintance with it and understands it. It follows, of course, that the person will then also both be acquainted with the fact that the proposition is true, and form the belief whose propositional content corresponds to that fact.

Scientia includes the conclusions of all those arguments whose premises and deductive validity are, or have been, self-evident to someone. On account of *scientia*'s communitarian character, however, it comprises much more than this. The physicist – to use one of Aquinas's own examples – makes use of the results of the mathematician. That is to say: the physicist does not himself develop the mathematics he needs by starting from premises self-evident to himself and constructing arguments such that it is self-evident to himself that they are deductively valid. The mathematician reports what he has found self-evident and what he has deductively proved from that; and the physicist, rather than replicating the work of the mathematician, trusts him and employs the mathematician's results among the premises for his own argumentation. Accordingly, many of the premises of the physicist's arguments will not be self-evident to him, the physicist. Some of the propositions which are self-evident to the mathematician may not be self-evident to the physicist; and the conclusions of the mathematician's arguments will typically not be self-evident to the physicist. Indeed, typically they will not even have been self-evident to the mathematician. For, as we saw above, an argument whose premises are self-evident to a person, and is such that it's self-evident to that person that the argument is deductively valid, will often have a conclusion which is not self-evident to that person.

It's tempting to offer the following as a formulation of Aquinas's full concept of *scientia*: *scientia* consists of the conclusions of arguments each of which is such that each premise has been self-evident to someone or other, and each of which is such that the fact of its deductive validity has been self-evident to someone or other. But this won't do, since, for the reason just indicated, some of the mathematical propositions that the physicist uses in his argumentation may not have been self-evident to anyone at all, including the mathematician who proved them. The way to put it then is this: *scientia* consists of the conclusions of those deductively valid arguments each subargument of which (if any) is such that its deductive validity has been self-evident to someone or other, and each of whose noninferred premises has been self-evident to someone or other. It will be the case that most of these arguments will never have been seen whole by any human being.

The overarching aim of the medieval philosophical theologians was to develop theology as a *scientia*. They regularly divided the enterprise into two parts: natural theology and sacred theology. In natural theology, one made use only of the deliverances of natural human reason; in sacred theology, one was allowed, in addition, to use as premises propositions revealed by God. The obvious question is how the use of such propositions as premises could possibly be allowed if it was a *scientia* one was trying to develop – since at every point self-evidence shapes the character of *scientia*. Aquinas's answer is both ingenious, and for us, unexpected. The membership of the scientific community is not limited to human beings dwelling on earth; it includes, as well, God and the blessed. Now the contents of revelation are self-evident to God – and to the blessed. Accordingly, just as the physicist is allowed to use as premises, in his own argumentation, what the mathematician reports as having been self-evident to him or deductively proved from such, so the scientific theologian is allowed to use as premises what *God* reports as self-evident to Him – in particular, the contents of scripture.

Many of us in the modern world are haunted by such questions about religious belief as whether we are entitled to hold such beliefs, whether any of them are warranted for us, or reliably formed, and whether any of them constitute knowledge. Our epistemologists have noted our worry and vexation, and offered us theories on the matter. To such questions, the medieval philosophers and philosophical theologians offer no answers. No one was raising the questions – not, at least, with any insistence or anxiety. Operating with the received Aristotelian view as to the conditions under which a belief possesses the merit of *being scientific*, they devoted their endeavors to bringing it about that beliefs about God would possess that merit. Let it be added that between us and them, the social practice which we call "science" – "*Wissenschaft*" – has also changed profoundly, with the consequence that none of us today would accept the conditions they laid down for a belief's possessing the merit of being scientific. For a couple of reasons, thus, their work does not speak directly to our concerns. Yet it's not irrelevant: arguments for the existence and character of God which they developed in the course of trying to develop theology as a *scientia* have been offered in the modern world to secure entitlement to belief in God, or to establish that some of our beliefs about God constitute knowledge.

3. The Role of The Doxastic Ideal in Locke's Epistemology of Religion

In the writings of John Locke we find what is indisputably epistemology of religion. In that epistemology, The Doxastic Ideal plays a central role, as it does in his epistemology generally. The role which the Ideal plays in Locke's thought is very different, however, from that which it played in the thought of the medievals. Though in his adherence to the Ideal Locke carries on the long tradition, he now uses the Ideal to formulate an account, not of scientific beliefs, but rather, of belief-*entitlement*, in particular, of entitlement to religious belief; and that is new.[4]

Two considerations lay behind Locke's focus on entitlement. He thought that *scientia* came to very little. A *scientia* of mathematics was possible, he thought, and of logic; and, oddly, of morality. But beyond that, almost nothing. In particular, no significant *scientia* of any substances was possible. More generally, knowledge, as Locke saw things, was, in his famous phrase, "short and scanty." That was one consideration. The other consideration which motivated Locke's focus on entitlement was his vivid awareness of the social and cultural chaos surrounding him, coupled with his conviction that the best hope for peace in the social and culture wars of his day was for the citizenry to cease holding religious and moral beliefs to which they were not entitled, or to cease holding them with a firmness to which they were not entitled.

Locke offered no general account of entitlement. Though he rather often formulates the account he gives in ringingly universal rhetoric, he makes it clear in a number of passages that a general account was not in fact his aim or concern. It was his conviction that all of us every now and then find ourselves in situations where we are obligated to do the human best to find out the truth on a certain matter. If we fail to do so, then such beliefs as we may have on the matter – or indeed, such ignorance – are lacking in entitlement for us. We *ought* not to have those beliefs, or that ignorance; we're not permitted. Locke's persistent question then was this: what determines entitlement in such situations of "maximal concernment"? It was further his conviction that matters of religion and morality are always for all of us matters of maximal concernment. Of course it would be implausible to hold that *all* matters of religion and morality are always matters of maximal concernment for all of us. But since Locke made no attempt to tell us *which* of such matters are of maximal concernment, we will just have to leave it there.

To understand the account Locke offers of what determines entitlement on issues of maximal concernment, we must take note of the fact that Locke's use of The Doxastic Ideal is intertwined with his adherence to what Thomas Reid called "The Way of Ideas." Reid was somewhat inconsistent in his account of exactly which complex of theses he wished to call "The Way of Ideas." But let me on this occasion understand by "The Way of Ideas" no more than a thesis about what it is that we are acquainted with, namely: one is never acquainted with anything else than one's own mind and its "modifications." Only one's own mind and its "modifications" are ever present to us.

His embrace of this thesis led Locke to adopt the representational theory of perception. As noted earlier, perception obviously has *some* sort of intuitional content. On Locke's view, what we are acquainted with in perception – what is presented to us – is never an external object, but only a mental "idea" which represents that external object which is the thing perceived. Likewise, his embrace of the thesis led Locke to adopt the representational theory of memory. Memory also has intuitional content. On Locke's representational account, what one is acquainted with in memory is not the entity remembered, but a present mental "idea" which represents that entity from the past which is the thing remembered.

And now for Locke's account of entitlement on matters of religion and morality – and more generally, on matters of maximal concernment. To be entitled to one's beliefs on such matters, those beliefs must be held on the basis of one's employment of a certain practice of inquiry – specifically, that practice of inquiry which constitutes doing the human best. And incidentally, Locke assumed that, no matter what the topic, it is always the same practice of inquiry which constitutes the best for finding out the truth. The practice which Locke holds to be the best can be thought of as having three stages. First, after formulating a proposition on the matter, one collects evidence concerning the truth or falsehood of that proposition, this evidence, in its totality, to be representative and sufficiently ample, and in its individual items, to consist of beliefs that are certain for one because, in each case, the belief is evoked by one's acquaintance with some fact to which the propositional content of the belief corresponds. Secondly, one appraises the logical force of that evidence, with respect to the proposition under consideration, until one gains acquaintance with the probability of the proposition on that evidence, this acquaintance in turn evoking a belief whose propositional content corresponds to the fact of that probability. And thirdly, one adopts a level of confidence, in the proposition under consideration, which is proportioned to what one has come to believe is its probability on that evidence.

Locke was well aware of the fact that very few religious beliefs of very few people have been formed by the employment of this (supposedy optimal) practice. It was his view, according, that very few religious beliefs are entitled. It was also his conviction, however, that this situation could be remedied. By the employment of the practice we could arrive at a substantial body of beliefs about God – a "rational religion." We could first employ the practice to develop natural religion, using cosmological and teleological arguments. Then we could employ the practice to develop revealed religion, first acquiring evidence for the reliability of the biblical writers, and then using the miracles they report as evidence for the occurrence of revelation. Kant's development of a "rational religion" was a variant on this program: where Locke used cosmological arguments for God's existence, and where his followers used teleological arguments, Kant used moral arguments.

It has rather often been said in recent years (also by this present writer), that the significance of Locke for the epistemology of religion is that he influentially espoused *evidentialism* concerning theistic belief – that is, that he influentially espoused the thesis that theistic beliefs are lacking in truth-relevant merits, especially in entitlement, unless they are held on the basis of other, nontheistic, beliefs. And certainly Locke was one of the great influential exponents of that position. But Locke was just as unhappy with *mediate* theistic beliefs not formed by employing his practice ("mediate" beliefs being those formed or held *on the basis of* other beliefs), as with *immediate* theistic beliefs. So one has to dig deeper, and ask why Locke espoused evidentialism concerning theistic beliefs. The answer is that he, assuming that beliefs formed by probabilistic arguments can satisfy The Doxastic Ideal, embraced the Ideal by incorporating it into his account of entitlement to religious belief – *everybody's* entitlement to *any* religious belief.

The medieval philosophers, as we saw, embraced the Ideal by incorporating it into their account of scientific belief; they held, as a corollary, that theistic belief which measures up to the demands of *scientia* is superior to ordinary theistic belief which does not measure up to those demands. But they did not launch a blanket criticism of the theistic beliefs of ordinary people; they did not say that, just by virtue of not being scientific, those beliefs are deficient in a way such that the person is obligated to try to remove that deficiency. What is new about Locke and his Enlightenment cohorts is that the Ideal is now used to launch exactly such an attack on the ordinary religious believer – on life in the everyday. The ordinary religious believer has not formed his beliefs by employing the (supposedly) optimal method. That marks a deficiency in those beliefs, which the ordinary believer is under obligation to remove.

4. Reformed Epistemology's Rejection of The Doxastic Ideal

It has rather often been said, about that recent development in epistemology of religion which has come to be known as "Reformed epistemology" (of which the present writer is a representative), that its fundamental significance is that it rejects *classically modern foundationalism*. As observed earlier in our discussion, beliefs possess a variety of distinct truth-relevant merits and defects. Classically modern foundationalism concerning one or another of such merits amounts to the claim that a belief, to possess the merit in question, must measure up to The Doxastic Ideal – with the Way of Ideas being regarded as correctly specifying the scope of acquaintance. It's true, indeed, that the Reformed epistemologists reject classically modern foundationalism. Holding that it's possible for human beings to have acquaintance with God, they deny that the Way of Ideas correctly specifies the scope of acquaintance. But their rejection is more fundamental yet. They reject The Doxastic Ideal itself. The failure of the religious beliefs of the ordinary person to measure up to the demands of The Doxastic Ideal does not, so far forth, indicate any sort of deficiency, any sort of impropriety, in those beliefs or in the person holding them. The beliefs are not, just for that reason, lacking in entitlement; nor are they, just for that reason, lacking in warrant. Neither is the person, just for that reason, lacking in intellectual virtue.[5]

How are religious beliefs formed – and sustained? Typically they are evoked by experience of some sort, or by believing what is said in some discourse, or by reflection on the implications of some complex of beliefs that one has previously acquired. Perhaps not always; it may sometimes happen that a person one day just finds herself believing in God, or believing something about God, without there being any experience, discourse, or reflection which she can identify as having evoked the belief. Furthermore, it may be the case that when some experience, discourse, or reflection does evoke the belief, it does not do so by its activation of some indigenous belief-forming mechanism; rather, some direct action of God, or of the Spirit of God, may be the agency. Be that as it may, however, reflection, discourse, and experience – that is, something with intuitional content – are what typically evoke religious beliefs. The experience may be uncanny in one way or another. Uncanny in its character; witness all the reports of mystical experiences, and of experiences of the holy, the numinous. Or it may be uncanny in its jolting and coincidental timeliness – witness Augustine's conviction that by way of the uncanny propriety of the child's chanting "*tolle lege, tolle lege,*" God was telling him to pick up his copy of St. Paul's letters and start reading, or St. Anthony's conviction that by way of the uncanny propriety of the church lector just happening to read, when he, Anthony, stepped into the church, the words from St. Matthew's Gospel, "Sell all that you have and give to the poor," God was telling him, a wealthy young Egyptian, to sell all his possessions and give the proceeds to the poor. Alternatively, the experience may be of something amazing in one way or another, or a complex of beliefs about something amazing. Dwelling, one day, on what one has discovered about the intricacy, complexity, and precariousness of some physical, chemical, or biological process, one may find oneself overwhelmed with the conviction that it didn't just evolve, that it must have been created. Or perhaps, like Schleiermacher, one begins one day to experience everything around one as dependent on something of another order all together.

This is how religious beliefs actually get formed. What emerges, mixed in with the noble, the elevating, and the inspiring, is, by anyone's lights, a great deal of nonsense, often vicious and appalling nonsense – though our century has made it abundantly clear that religion scarcely has a monopoly on vicious and appalling nonsense. Surveying the totality, even the religious person will feel some rapport with those who feel weary or vexed at the prospect of winnowing the wheat from the chaff, and who instead propose imposing The Doxastic Ideal on the whole of it, noble and ignoble alike.

Let's see why such a move should be resisted. Consider the structure of an actual case, Augustine's case. He hears a child's voice chanting "take and read, take and read." After some quick reflection, he finds it uncanny. Perhaps he believes that it is uncanny. More likely, he *hears it as uncanny*; that is, he experiences it under the concept of *the uncanny*. It quickly occurs to him that maybe the chant is part of a game; but he can't think of any such game. But that's really a throwaway point; it makes no difference one way or another. He has an intimation that the words, whatever led the child to chant them, may well be appropriate to his condition; thus the chanting acquires an uncanny character for him. And that apparently immediately evokes in him the belief that God is speaking to him.

If this is how it went – Augustine's description is too brief for us to be sure of all the details – the resultant belief, in its mode of formation, certainly does not measure up to The Doxastic Ideal. The belief which gets formed in Augustine is that God is speaking to him. But the fact with which he is acquainted is the fact of a child chanting "*tolle lege.*" The propositional content of the belief does not correspond to the fact of which he was aware. Was it then perhaps fully grounded in acquaintance? Well, not of course if it was formed immediately. If, on the other hand, it was formed on the basis of an argument, it must have been a probabilistic argument; no deductive argument is in sight. But what that probabilistic argument might have been, Augustine does not tell us. An inference to the best explanation? Surely, before drawing any best explanation inferences, Augustine should have gotten in contact with the child and asked him why he was chanting "*tolle lege.*"

The issue of whether the failure of Augustine's belief to measure up to The Doxastic Ideal marks some deficiency in that belief is perhaps best approached indirectly. It was the two great eighteenth-century Scotsmen, David Hume and Thomas Reid, who first attacked, powerfully and directly, The Doxastic Ideal, by arguing that, whatever the philosopher might prefer, our human condition is such that vast numbers of the beliefs we have, and without which we could not live, were neither formed in accord with The Doxastic Ideal nor could be so formed. Reid also argued that the scope of acquaintance is much wider than what the Way of Ideas claims it to be; on this, he disagreed fundamentally with Hume. But he was fully in agreement with Hume that the Ideal itself must be discarded.

Hume argued the case most powerfully for beliefs about the future formed by induction. His analysis of how such beliefs get formed went as follows: nobody is born with dispositions for the formation of inductive beliefs. We are all born, instead, with a fundamental disposition to *acquire* dispositions to form such beliefs. Such acquisition works as follows: we find pairs of events of certain types to be regularly correlated in our experience – for example, in our experience events consisting of an object losing its support are regularly correlated with events of that object falling. Eventually there is ineluctably formed in us the disposition, upon experiencing the occurrence of an event of one of these types, to ineluctably expect the occurrence of an event of the other type – that is, to believe that there will be an event of the other type. Hume describes these dispositions for the formation of inductive beliefs as "habits" and "customs," to highlight their mode of acquisition.

It's obvious that, on Hume's analysis, inductive beliefs do not exemplify The Doxastic Ideal. An inference does takes place, from something that one perceives; the inductively formed belief about the future is in that way *based on* one's perceptual experience. But what accounts for the inference is not (one's awareness of) one's acquaintance with the fact that the conclusion is logically grounded on the perceived facts; what accounts for the inference is just that habit which one has acquired – "blind" habit, we might call it, since no acquaintance is involved.

Hume was well aware of the fact that readers would protest his conclusion that the inner working which produces the inference is blind habit, rather than acquaintance with some fact of logical grounding. We do, after all, have the belief that nature, in the aspect in question, is regular: that released objects do always fall. When we add that belief to our belief that an object has been released, this latter belief evoked by acquaintance with the fact that the object is released, then the immediately forthcoming belief that the object will fall is in fact logically grounded on those beliefs.

But how, Hume asks, did we acquire the belief that nature, in the aspect in question, is regular? It's not a self-evident truth. So the belief must somehow have been acquired from experience. How so? Well, we have observed lots of cases of nature's regularity in this aspect. *That* must be the experience which leads to the emergence of this general belief. But now notice, says Hume: what follows *logically* from one's observations of regularity, is that that small segment of nature which one has experienced has never presented one with a counterexample to this regularity (ignore, on this occasion, all the instances of released objects rising!). It does not follow, by logic, that nature as a whole – unobserved along with observed – is regular in this regard. Yet one needs that more general principle, or something like it, if one's belief that *this* released object will fall is to be grounded in acquaintance. But of course we have no acquaintance with the fact corresponding to the propositional content of the belief that nature as a whole is regular, since of nature as a whole – future as well as present and past, distant as well as near – we have no experience. So acquaintance always comes up short in inductively formed beliefs. Unlike the two types of beliefs constituting The Doxastic Ideal, they cannot be fully grounded in acquaintance. They are of a fundamentally different sort. Yet such beliefs are indispensable to human existence. So the thesis that beliefs which fail to measure up to The Doxastic Ideal are thereby deficient, in such a way that we ought to try to eliminate the deficiency, cannot be sustained.

Reid made the same sort of claim concerning beliefs based on testimony. Someone asserts that P; and I, upon hearing her, come to believe that she asserted that P. My coming to believe that she asserted that P then evokes in me the belief that P. How are we to understand *this* mode of belief-formation – quite extraordinary, when one thinks about it? It seems right to say that my belief that P was *based on* her assertion that P; but did I get from my belief that she asserted that P, to my belief that P, by *logical* inference? If so, presumably the principle involved is something like this: persons of this sort who speak on topics of this sort in this sort of situation almost always tell the truth. But how did I come by this principle? Reid invites us to consider especially the case of the child: does the child come to believe its parent in a certain case because it reasons that eight out of ten times when the parent has spoken on this sort of matter in this sort of situation, it has spoken truth, so probably it is doing so now as well? Reid's own suggestion – which would take more argumentation to establish than I can give it here, but which seems to me definitely correct – is that indigenous to our human constitution is a *principle of credulity*, as he calls it. The workings of this principle get refined in the lives of each of us, so that eventually we no longer believe certain sorts of people on certain sorts of topics in certain sorts of situations, whereas others, we believe more firmly than ever; but at the bottom of all the refinements is the fact that we are all indigenously disposed to believe what we believe people are telling us. If that is right, then we have here another example of belief-formation which fails to fit The Doxastic Ideal. At the same time, believing things on the say-so of others is so fundamental to human existence that it would be absurd to propose that in beliefs produced by the working of the credulity principle there is something deficient in such a way that we ought to try to eliminate such beliefs.

One can see why The Doxastic Ideal has had the appeal which it has had: there is something admirable about beliefs which measure up to the ideal – at least, about beliefs which measure up to the first stage of the ideal. A belief evoked by acquaintance with the fact to which the propositional content of the belief corresponds: what could be better, more satisfying, than that, and more reassuring – if only there were no mimics! A belief evoked by acquaintance with the fact that the propositional content of the belief is entailed by beliefs of the first sort: such a belief is only slightly less satisfying. But the point to be made now is that such beliefs are not ideal *for us human beings, in our situation*. What has been taken to be *the doxastic ideal* is not an ideal *for us*. The failure of a belief to measure up to the Ideal does not, so far forth, point to a deficiency which *we human beings* ought to remove, or even to a deficiency which it would be *desirable* for us to remove. Our belief-forming constitution does not measure up to the supposed ideal in its indigenous workings; nor is it possible to revise its workings so that those workings do all measure up to the supposed ideal. And even if it were possible, even if we could somehow manage to reshape our belief-forming self so that it conformed in its workings to the supposed ideal, we would find ourselves with too scanty a body of beliefs for life to continue.

The implications for our analysis of the truth-relevant merits are obvious. Locke's proposed practice, which has The Doxastic Ideal at its core, is not *the universally best access* to truth; it gives us no access at all to those truths about the future to which inductive inference gives us access. Likewise, the Ideal is irrelevant to an account of *reliably formed* beliefs; inductive inference, suitably restrained, is an eminently reliable type of belief-formation. It is irrelevant as well to an account of beliefs formed by the *proper functioning* of our constitution. And it is irrelevant to an account of what we are *entitled* – permitted – to believe. What we need is accounts of the truth-relevant merits in beliefs which repudiate The Doxastic Ideal, and proceed without assuming that the merit in question is absent if the belief does not measure up to The Ideal. A number of such accounts have emerged in recent years. Insofar as that is the case, there is a "revolution" in epistemology – a Humean–Reidian revolution.

And now back to religious beliefs. Earlier I said that the deepest significance of that recent development in epistemology of religion which has come to be known as Reformed epistemology is its insistence that the failure of the religious beliefs of the ordinary person to measure up to the demands of The Doxastic Ideal does not, so far forth, indicate any sort of deficiency or impropriety in those beliefs or in the person holding them. We can now state why the "Reformed epistemologist" makes that claim. It's not an *ad hoc* thesis concerning religious beliefs; rather, it's part of the recent "revolution" in epistemology. The Reformed epistemologist stands in the Reidian tradition. Religious beliefs, in good measure, are like inductive and testimonial beliefs, in that the latter also do not exemplify The Doxastic Ideal. But that fact, as we have seen, implies nothing at all about the presence or absence of truth-relevant merits in such beliefs; it proves to be a fundamentally irrelevant observation.

5. Wittgensteinian Philosophy of Religion

Moving forward from this stage in the history of the epistemology of religion will require work on two fronts. Primarily the epistemologist of religion will show how general accounts of the conditions under which truth-relevant merits are present in beliefs apply to the specific case of religious beliefs. And let it be said emphatically here that the Reformed epistemologist by no means holds that all religious beliefs have impeccable credentials; though the fact that a religious belief fails to measure up to The Doxastic Ideal does not, by itself, imply that it lacks warrant, or entitlement, or reliable formation, or whatever, it's also not true that anything goes in religion. Secondly, the epistemologist of religion will not just take whatever general accounts happen to be fashionable, but will cooperate in developing those general accounts. In so doing, she will insist that those accounts take cognizance of the presence (and absence) of the truth-relevant merits in *religious* beliefs.

As already indicated, I do assume that, among religious beliefs, there are not only those that lack one and another truth-relevant merit, but those that possess them. Some philosophers appear to be of the contrary opinion: that religious beliefs are entirely – or almost entirely – lacking in truth-relevant merits. The philosopher who thinks they are not entirely lacking in such merits ought to reflect with care on what these others have to say on the matter – and they, on what he has to say! But if, having done so, he remains of the view that some though not all religious beliefs are entitled, some though not all are reliably and/or properly formed, and so forth, then what else is he to do but be faithful to those reflective convictions of his as he formulates a general account? In the same way he must, in developing a general account, be faithful to his reflective convictions concerning the presence of truth-relevant merits in scientific beliefs, in artistic beliefs, in everyday beliefs, and so forth. It's possible (though not inevitable) that the outcome will be a general account which is unacceptable to those who disagree with him on the distribution of the truth-relevant merits in one or another of these domains. But one of the consequences of no longer working under the spell of The Doxastic Ideal is that epistemology is to be practiced as an attempt to illuminate, rather than to sit in judgment on, our everyday practices of making judgments about knowledge, entitlement, and so forth in the various spheres of human life; and about such judgments, we have our disagreements.

Work in this new stage of the epistemology of religion is well begun, but no more than that. One sees the beginnings in, for example, William Alston's *Perceiving God*, in the two volumes thus far published of Alvin Plantinga's *Warrant*, in Nicholas Wolterstorff's *Divine Discourse*, in Linda Zagzebski's *Virtues of the Mind*, and in the collective volume edited by Plantinga and Wolterstorff, *Faith and Rationality*. But rather than trying to summarize these beginnings, let me bring another contemporary movement in epistemology of religion into the picture – namely, the Wittgensteinian.[6]

Wittgenstein never developed a sustained account of religion. His published comments on religion are scattered about in various of his writings; and much of what he thought on the matter is available to us only from notes taken by auditors of lectures he gave. Furthermore, much of what he said and thought is cryptic; on one central issue there have been, for some time, two distinct traditions of interpretation among his readers and followers. This much is clear, however: Wittgenstein was also firmly opposed to any attempt to impose The Doxastic Ideal on religion. Let us see how that opposition was worked out in his case.

Wittgenstein's polemical partner was Logical Positivism. At the heart of the positivist program was the attempt to demarcate that which was deemed worthy of the honorific title, "science," from all those forms of intellectual activity not deemed worthy of that title – these latter often called, dishonorifically, "metaphysics." The positivists made it clear that under what they called "metaphysics" they meant to include not only what would ordinarily be called metaphysics, but also theology and religion.

How was the demarcation to be made? The suggestion of the positivists was that what demarcated "science" from "metaphysics" was that the discourse of the former had meaning, whereas that of the latter lacked meaning. This suggestion begged, of course, for a criterion of *meaningfulness*. The positivists obliged: a piece of discourse has meaning if and only if it is either analytically true or false, or capable of empirical verification or disverification.

Shortly after this criterion was initially proposed, in the 1920s of our century, it was observed that the criterion appears to have the consequence that ethical discourse lacks meaning; yet surely ethical discourse is not to be tossed into the dustbin, along with metaphysics and theology! The response of the positivists was to add a qualification to their criterion: the criterion, they said, is to be understood as a criterion of *cognitive* meaningfulness. A piece of discourse is *either true or false* if and only if it satisfies the criterion. This qualification to their criterion committed the positivists to interpreting ethical discourse as not making true–

false claims; they energetically set out on the enterprise of developing such an interpretation.

Wittgenstein was deeply opposed to the positivist dismissal of religion. He himself appears to have been a deeply religious person – albeit of an unconventional sort.[7] And his reflections on religion are clearly shaped by the following rule of thumb: if an interpretation of religion makes religion seem silly, pointless, or outmoded, that interpretation should be dismissed out of hand as not understanding what it is talking about. In particular, any interpretation of religion which understands religious beliefs as explanations or predictions – thus, as competing with science – is to be dismissed out of hand.

The large issue of interpretation over which readers and followers of Wittgenstein divide is how Wittgenstein proposed answering the positivist challenge to religion. One interpretation, the one toward which I myself incline, is that Wittgenstein's strategy was to exploit the opening offered by revised positivism: religious discourse is like moral discourse in that it's not cognitive in character; hence the criterion of cognitive meaningfulness does not apply. Religious "belief" and the language used to express it, these often pictorial in character, give expression to one's religious form of life and are at the same time a component therein. "Why shouldn't one form of life culminate in an utterance of belief in a Last Judgement?" asks Wittgenstein (p. 58).[8] Thus, to verbalize a religious "belief" is to express, often in pictorial language, some aspect of one's religious form of life – while at the same time engaging in that form of life. On the alternative interpretation, Wittgenstein not only challenged positivism's dismissal of religion, but its criterion of cognitive meaningfulness as well: religious discourse is cognitively meaningful, even though it fails to satisfy the positivist criterion for such discourse.[9]

On this latter interpretation, there are striking similarities between the way in which Wittgenstein rejects The Doxastic Ideal and the way in which Reformed epistemology does so – the chief difference being that Wittgenstein talks more about what it is that differentiates religious beliefs from others, whereas the Reformed epistemologist talks more about what it is that evokes religious beliefs. On the former interpretation, such similarities as there are, are in good measure overshadowed by this fundamental difference, that whereas the Reformed epistemologist interprets the religious believer, when she says, for example, "God created the world," as making a claim on how things are (a true–false claim), the Wittgensteinian interprets her as doing no such thing.

We cannot undertake here to resolve this issue of interpretation (nor the issue of whether religious beliefs have propositional content); instead, let me simply cite the sorts of passages which each side takes as the center of its interpretation. First, the noncognitivist interpretation.

Wittgenstein insists that the nonbeliever does not *contradict* the believer. The obvious interpretation is that he does not contradict the believer because the believer has not presented anything *to be* contradicted: the believer has not asserted any proposition.

> Suppose that someone believed in the Last Judgement, and I don't, does this mean that I believe the opposite to him, just that there won't be such a thing? I would say: "not at all, or not always."
>
> Suppose I say that the body will rot, and another says "No. Particles will rejoin in a thousand years, and there will be a Resurrection of you."
>
> If someone said: "Wittgenstein, do you believe in this?" I'd say: "No." "Do you contradict the man?" I'd say: "No." (p. 53)

Add to that the following passage, in which Wittgenstein suggests that to be a religious believer is to live with, and be guided by, certain "pictures":

> You might be surprised that there hasn't been opposed to those who believe in Resurrection those who say "Well, possibly."
>
> Here believing obviously plays much more this role: suppose we said that a certain picture might play the role of constantly admonishing me, or I always think of it. Here, an enormous difference would be between those people for whom the picture is constantly in the foreground, and the others who just didn't use it at all. (p. 56)

And finally, this, in which the two ideas are put together:

> Take two people, one of whom talks of his behaviour and of what happens to him in terms of retribution, the other one does not. These people think entirely differently. Yet, so far, you can't say they believe different things.
>
> Suppose someone is ill and he says: "This is a punishment," and I say: "If I'm ill, I don't think of punishment at all." If you say: "Do you believe the opposite?" – you can call it believing the opposite, but it is entirely different from what we would normally call believing the opposite.
>
> I think differently, in a different way. I say different things to myself. I have different pictures. (p. 55)

Whereas these passages, with their definite noncognitivist tone, differentiate religious beliefs from others in terms of their character and function, the passages which lack that tone differentiate religious beliefs from others in terms of the firmness with which they are held.

> Suppose somebody made this guidance for this life: believing in the Last Judgment. Whenever he does anything, this is before his mind. In a way, how are we to know whether to say he believes this will happen or not?
>
> Asking him is not enough. He will probably say he has proof. But he has what you might call an unshakeable belief. It will show, not by reasoning or by appeal to ordinary grounds for belief, but rather by regulating for in all his life.
>
> This is a very much stronger fact – foregoing pleasure, always appealing to this picture. This in one sense must be called the firmest of all beliefs, because the man risks things on account of it which he would not do on things which are by far better established for him. Although he distinguishes between things well-established and not well-established. (pp. 53–4)

The thought is continued in this passage. Controversies in religion

> look quite different from any normal controversies. Reasons look entirely different from normal reasons.
>
> They are, in a way, quite inconclusive.
>
> The point is that if there were evidence, this would in fact destroy the whole business.
>
> Anything that I normally call evidence wouldn't in the slightest influence me.
>
> Suppose, for instance, we knew people who foresaw the future; make forecasts for years and years ahead; and they described some sort of a Judgement Day. Queerly enough, even if there were such a thing, and even if it were more convincing than I have described, belief in this happening wouldn't be at all a religious belief.
>
> Suppose that I would have to forgo all pleasures because of such a forecast. If I do so and so, someone will put me in fires in a thousand years, etc. I wouldn't budge. The best scientific evidence is just nothing. . . .
>
> A man would fight for his life not to be dragged into the fire. No induction. Terror. That is, as it were, part of the substance of the belief.
>
> That is partly why you don't get in religious controversies, the form of controversy where one person is *sure* of the thing, and the other says: "Well, possibly." (p. 56)

And finally, this:

> In a religious discourse, we use such expressions as: "I believe that so and so will happen," and use them differently to the way in which we use them in science.
>
> Although there is a temptation to think we do. Because we do talk of evidence, and do talk of evidence by experience.
>
> We could even talk of historic events.
>
> It has been said that Christianity rests on an historic basis. . . .
>
> It doesn't rest on an historic basis in the sense that the ordinary beliefs in historic facts could serve as a foundation.
>
> Here we have a belief in historic facts different from a belief in ordinary historic facts. Even, they are not treated as historical, empirical, propositions. . . .
>
> Here we have people who treat this evidence in a different way. They base things on evidence which taken in one way would seem extremely flimsy. They base enormous things on this evidence. Am I to say they are unreasonable? I wouldn't call them unreasonable.
>
> I would say, they are certainly not *reasonable*, that's obvious. (pp. 57–8)

In this last passage (and a good many others) there is sounded a theme which became characteristic of Wittgenstein's followers. In religion, we operate with different criteria for *reasonableness* – and presumably for the other doxastic merits as well – from those with which we operate in science and ordinary life. The Wittgensteinians have often been understood as claiming that religious language games are completely insulated from other language games: considerations which arise from outside the religious form of life are simply irrelevant to religious belief, counting neither for nor against it. It's not at all evident what is to be taken as inside here and what as outside; for example, is the charge that a pair of religious beliefs are contradictory a consideration from inside the religious form of life or from outside? But let that pass; D. Z. Phillips, the foremost of the present-day Wittgensteinians, makes clear that he is not of the view that considerations drawn from outside some religious form of life are *per se* irrelevant to that form of life and its language game.[10] So perhaps the best way to understand the Wittgensteinians, at least on the cognitivist interpretation, is that they are *pluralists* when it comes to criteria for the presence and absence in beliefs of the various truth-relevant merits: the criteria in religion are different from those in science, different from those in art, different from those in ethics, and so forth. To quote Wittgenstein: "Whether a thing is a blunder or not – it is a blunder in a particular system. Just as something is a blunder in a particular game and not in another" (p. 59). If that is the right interpretation, then this is another point of divergence between the Wittgensteinians and the "Reformed epistemologists." (Of course, on the noncognitivist interpretation, "reasonableness" and so forth do not even name *truth-relevant* merits when used in religious language games.)

6. Alston on Acquaintance with God

The main theme of my discussion has been the role of what I called "The Doxastic Ideal" in epistemology of religion. I described its positive role in the medieval philosophical theologians, and in the paradigmatic Enlightenment figure, John Locke; and I have argued that fundamental to the two major recent movements in epistemology of religion, Wittgensteinianism and Reformed epistemology, has been the repudiation, each in its own way, of the imposition of the Ideal on religious belief. In closing, let us consider an important recent contribution to epistemology of religion in which it is not so much The Doxastic Ideal itself which is under attack, as the thesis, regularly combined with the Ideal, that God cannot be an object of acquaintance. The contribution I have in mind is William P. Alston's book, *Perceiving God: The Epistemology of Religious Experience*.[11]

It has been a point of near-consensus among philosophers that we human beings, here in this life, do not have acquaintance with God. God is never the intuitional content of our mental acts; God is never presented to us, never puts in his appearance to us. Those who, like Locke, embraced the Way of Ideas, held, of course, that God shares this fate with human beings other than oneself, and with material objects. Given this near-consensus, religious experience has usually been analyzed by philosophers as either some special sort of subjective experience from which the recipient draws inferences about God, the Infinite, or such, or as the perception of an ordinary object or person under some special religious concept.

Alston's contention is that the most plausible analysis of the typical mystical experience is that the person *perceives* God. And as to the structure of perception, Alston embraces what he calls "the Theory of Appearing," explaining it thus:

"For S to perceive X is simply for X to appear to S as so-and-so." That is, for X to be given, or presented, to S's experience as so-and-so. The examples of beliefs about God that the traditional philosopher would have offered as satisfying The Doxastic Ideal were beliefs held on the basis of satisfactory arguments. The novelty of Alston's contribution is to cite, as exemplifying the Ideal, beliefs *held immediately.*

Or so it would seem. For not everything is quite as it appears. Though Alston calls perception a mode of *direct* awareness of the object, nonetheless it is, on his view, *mediated* direct awareness, in contrast to the awareness of one's own conscious states, which is *unmediated* direct awareness. "Our own states of consciousness," says Alston, "are *given* to us with maximum immediacy, not given to us *through* anything. Whereas in direct perception of external objects, though the object is not presented through the *perception* of anything else, it is presented through a state of consciousness that is distinct from the object of experience and of which we can become explicitly aware in the more direct way" (p. 21).

The major questions of interpretation here are these: what are these mediating states of consciousness, how are they related to the perceived object, and how we are to understand being mediately aware of some object *through* one's immediate awareness of one's states of consciousness? On these important matters, Alston is atypically cryptic. What an object *presents itself as* are its *phenomenal qualities*: "sensory experience is essentially a matter of something's 'appearing' or 'presenting itself' to a subject, S, as bearing certain phenomenal qualities" (p. 56). And phenomenal qualities, in turn, are one's mode of consciousness when perceiving the object, this mode of consciousness being, of course, distinct from the object: the mode of consciousness in perception, in distinction from the object, is "most fundamentally . . . characterized by what the object is appearing *as* – as good and powerful, loving, or whatever" (p. 23).

But if, in perception, how an object *presents itself as* consists of one's mode of consciousness when perceiving the object, and if we are aware of that mode of consciousness, what is there left for us to be aware of in the object? We are supposedly aware of the object *through* our awareness of the perceiving state of consciousness; but it looks as if that state of consciousness has swallowed up into itself everything that we could possibly be aware of. So is Alston a defender of the claim that in mystical experience one is aware of God, and of facts of which God is a constituent? Quite clearly he intended to be. But whether he is in fact, remains unclear to me.

Notes

1 The same point has recently been made in an essay by William P. Alston, "Epistemic Desiderata," *Philosophy & Phenomenological Research* LIII/3 (Sept. 1993).
2 An interesting example of the application of epistemological concepts to religious *hope* is the essay by Robert Audi, "Faith, Belief, and Rationality," in James Tomberlin,

ed., *Philosophical Perspectives, 5: Philosophy of Religion 1991* (Atascadero, CA: Ridgeview Publ. Co., 1991).

3 I give a much more elaborate discussion of the medieval concept of *scientia* in my essay "The Migration of the Theistic Arguments: from Natural Theology to Evidentialist Apologetics," in Audi and Wainwright, eds., *Rationality, Religious Belief, and Moral Commitment* (Ithaca: Cornell University Press, 1986).

4 I discuss Locke's account of entitlement much more elaborately in my *John Locke and the Ethics of Belief* (Cambridge: Cambridge University Press, 1996).

5 For a good general introduction to Reformed epistemology, see Kelly Clark, *Return to Reason* (Grand Rapids, MI: Eerdmans Publishing Co., 1990).

6 Richard Swinburne, who allies himself with neither of these two movements, has also made important contributions to philosophy of religion over the past quarter century. Swinburne has not focused, however, on the *epistemology* of religion; his work has been in philosophical theology, and in the offering of arguments for various aspects of theism and Christianity. Thus his work is very similar to that of the medieval philosopher-theologians – though he certainly is not committed to their project of *scientia*.

7 See the biography by Ray Monk, *Ludwig Wittgenstein: The Duty of Genius* (New York: Free Press, 1990).

8 The quotations are taken from *Wittgenstein's Lectures and Conversations on Aesthetics, Psychology, and Religious Belief* (n.d.). The page references inserted in the text are to that volume.

9 A good statement of this latter interpretation can be found in chs. 7 and 8 of Hilary Putnam, *Renewing Philosophy* (Cambridge, MA: Harvard University Press, 1992). The foremost follower of Wittgenstein who embraced a cognitivist interpretation of religious belief was O. K. Bouwsma. See especially his *Without Proof or Evidence* (Lincoln: University of Nebraska Press, 1984). The foremost follower who embraces a noncognitivist interpretation is D. Z. Phillips. From among many books, see especially *Religion without Explanation* (Oxford: Blackwell, 1976).

10 See especially D. Z. Phillips, *Belief, Change, and Forms of Life* (Atlantic Highlands, NJ: Humanities Press International, 1986).

11 Ithaca: Cornell University Press, 1991. Page references will be inserted into the text.

Part IV
New Directions

Chapter 14

Feminist Epistemology

Helen E. Longino

Feminist epistemology is both a paradox and a necessity. Epistemology is a highly general inquiry – into the meaning of knowledge claims and attributions, into conditions for the possibility of knowledge, into the nature of truth and justification, and so on. Feminism is a family of positions and inquiries characterized by some common sociopolitical interests centering on the abolition of sexual and gender inequality. What possible relation could there be between these two sets of activity? Furthermore, feminist inquiry results in substantive claims and analyses of whose adequacy and correctness feminists hope to persuade nonfeminists as well as other feminists. How could such persuasion occur without some highly general and shared conceptions of knowledge and rationality to set the ground rules within which this persuasion will occur? How could this be anything but a general and uniformly applicable epistemology? A feminist epistemology is oxymoronic. On the other hand, feminist scholars have demonstrated the gender bias infusing most other academic disciplines – a gender bias that is expressed in particular claims and facilitated by disciplinary first principles. Women's experience is made invisible or distorted, as are gender relations. What reason have we for thinking philosophy and its subdisciplines might be immune? And how can feminists pursue philosophical inquiry without subjecting our own discipline and subdisciplines to the same kind of searching scrutiny to which other feminist scholars have subjected their disciplines? Indeed, since the traditional academic disciplines have rested on philosophical presuppositions that may be implicated in sexist or androcentric outcomes, it is imperative that we do so. Feminist epistemology is a necessity.

Perhaps some of the air of paradox comes from thinking of "feminist" as modifying "epistemology," rather than "epistemologist." Feminists must not stop being feminists when we start doing philosophy, but neither can we give up entirely on philosophy's constraints and aspirations. Of course, what these properly are is itself a philosophical matter, so we need not expect that doing philosophy as a feminist will leave conceptions of philosophy or of its key terms untouched. Feminist epistemologists make common cause at various junctures with other philosophers who reject or are critical of current mainstreams in Western philosophy, for example, Marxist and pragmatist philosophers, African and African-American philosophers, as well as with philosophers pursuing new directions with old or familiar tools, for example, naturalizers, socializers, and contextualizers in philosophy.

In this essay, I will first outline the background from which feminist work in epistemology has emerged. Then I will review some of the distinctly feminist contributions to rethinking the knowing subject and to rethinking justification. In the fourth section of the paper I will defend one line of argument regarding context and justification from some criticisms, and finally make some observations about the consequences of taking feminist epistemology, or the practice of doing epistemology as a feminist, seriously for our conceptions of philosophical epistemology.

1. The Background

Feminist philosophers turned to epistemology after addressing gaps in ethics and social and political philosophy. The character of this attention to epistemology carries traces of its multiple origins. These include the issues raised in feminist critiques of the sciences, feminist readings of the history of philosophy, and research in educational psychology, as well as concern about the assumptions and presuppositions of analytic epistemology.

Feminist critique of the natural sciences has had the greatest impact in the life sciences, although there has been work in the physical sciences as well.[1] In the life sciences, the representation of explicitly gendered subject matter has been an obvious target of critique, but feminist scientists' exposure of gendered metaphors in the analysis both of natural processes and of the nature of scientific knowledge has been influential in setting an agenda for feminist epistemologists. Donna Haraway, Ruth Bleier, Ann Fausto-Sterling, and Ruth Hubbard analyzed gender bias in primate studies, ethology, and human biology.[2] An early topic of feminist concern was the consistent representation of males of a species as dominant, and as possessing socially valued traits in greater degree than females. If these representations were the outcome of "good science," then surely, the argument went, there must be something wrong with "good science." Was acceptable methodology yielding these results or were social and political biases preventing scientists from employing good methodologies effectively?

The identification of gendered metaphors and their role in scientific theories raised this question even more acutely. Evelyn Keller has shown how belief in a master molecule shaped research in cell biology, developmental biology, and genetics.[3] She also drew attention to the triple conjuncture of ideologies of masculinity, control over nature, and scientific knowledge, using psychoanalytic object relations theory to argue that standard conceptions of scientific objectivity incorporated or were shaped by ideals of masculinity.[4] Our cognitive orientation is affectively inflected, Keller argued. Typical male psychosocial development results in an attitude of "static autonomy," characterized by a rigid separation of self and world. This translates into the cognitive orientation of "static objectivity" characterized by an exaggerated and fiercely maintained distance between the knower and the object of knowledge and an identification of knowledge with domination. The need to maintain distance and to know by control produced flawed understandings of natural processes, Keller claimed, using the resistance to and ultimate triumph of geneticist Barbara McClintock's research on genetic transposition to illustrate her point. She then argued for an alternative understanding of objectivity – as flexible and able to move between distance and intimacy.

Keller's criticism of what she took to be standard conceptions of objectivity and her advocacy of McClintock's form of empathic identification with her objects of study put the topics of objectivity and of relations between subjects and objects on the table for feminist theorists, including philosophers. Her placement of case studies like that of McClintock and of her own work on slime mold aggregation within a larger framework suggested that there might be a comparable framework within which to understand the convergence of conventional gender stereotypes and scientific representations of gender relations. The feminist critiques of science, then, challenged feminist philosophers to address the links between theories of knowledge like empiricism and the perpetuation in many levels of scientific inquiry of gender stereotypes perceived as harmful and distorting.

In addition to such work in the natural sciences, feminist scholars in the social sciences were also reassessing epistemological concepts operating in their disciplines. Sociologist Dorothy Smith argued that men and women experienced the world quite differently, since men encountered a world already processed whether in the form of meals prepared and clothes laundered, or data tabulated and statistics summarized, while the work of women was the processing of the raw material of the world, food, dirty clothes, the testimony of interview subjects, into a form suitable for consumption and use.[5] This notion that there is a fundamental difference in the experience of men and women has haunted feminist thinking about knowledge, although it is no longer clear that the difference I've just delineated reflects a clear sexual division of cognitive labor. Instead, one might speak of a position in a gendered division of labor, and the position of encountering and processing raw data as being a feminized position regardless of the anatomical sex of the person in that position, and that of receiving and disposing of processed materials, data, etc., as well as specifying how the raw materials are to be processed, as a masculinized position.[6]

Political scientists also felt a need for a theory of knowledge that would enable them to reject political theories that sanctioned the domination of women and to advance theories that mandated equality. Sociologists and political scientists labeled their philosophical enemy positivism (sometimes empiricism). The particular views they rejected were views held by prominent theorists in their disciplines, often variants of the nineteenth-century positivism of Auguste Comte, and only loosely related to the twentieth-century philosophical movement known as logical positivism. To the extent that logical positivism was understood as effectively endorsing a scientistic world view and in particular the social sciences of the mid-twentieth century, it became the doctrine to reject and for which to find alternatives.[7] As a result, much early work that was labeled feminist epistemology is actually work done by feminist social scientists and political theorists who need alternative accounts of knowledge and of justification in order to overthrow presuppositions in their disciplines which functioned as obstacles to necessary change.

The notion that epistemological concepts were tainted by masculinist ideologies received further support from work in the history of philosophy. Not only have women philosophers been excluded from the canon, but those philosophers occupying a central place in it both derided female intellectual capacity and offered analyses of concepts like rationality that drew on stereotypes of masculinity. Genevieve Lloyd's *The Man of Reason* traced the association of masculinity and rationality in the work of philosophers from Plato to Kant and Hegel.[8] Phyllis Rooney has analyzed the masculinization of reason through metaphor in the work of contemporary philosophers.[9] The identification of these mutually reinforcing moves (reason is masculine; masculinity includes reason) fuels a suspicion that the epistemological concepts that are the heritage of Western philosophy are overly constricted by the double duty – epistemological and political – that they have been required to perform. Elisabeth Lloyd, in slightly different vein, has analyzed the multiple meanings of "objectivity" and demonstrated the equivocations on that concept which underlie many responses by mainstream philosophers to feminist philosophical analysis.[10] There is, therefore, work to be done in analyzing epistemic evaluation in freedom from the constraints of double duty.

Finally, work in educational psychology has suggested that approaches to learning and problem-solving might be gendered, that the acquisition of gender identity and gendered norms of behavior might include the acquisition of gendered cognitive norms. The psychologist Carol Gilligan criticized her colleague Lawrence Kohlberg's account of moral development as resting too much on a pattern ascertained from male samples (from which deviating female responses were thrown out).[11] The Kohlbergian account stressed independence and rule-governed decision-making as characterizing full moral maturity, while Gilligan identified an alternative pattern that culminated in a relationally defined self making decisions governed by assessments of responsibility rather than by rules. These themes resonate with Keller's view that a learned form of masculinity includes a conception of scientific knowledge as entailing detachment and distance from, as well as control of, objects of knowledge, while a learned form of femininity includes a mode of relating to others, including objects of knowledge, through identification. Educational psychologist Mary Belenky and her colleagues suggested that women learn through connection rather than separation, i.e. that women acquire knowledge through experiencing connectedness or relatedness to rather than difference from objects of knowledge.[12] To call this a *way of knowing*, of course, begs the question "what is knowledge?" In addition, the work of the Belenky team has been called into question as based on too restricted a sample, and as not really engaging in controlled comparative study of men and women. Nevertheless, their work has been influential among feminist educators and, because of the connections with other lines of analysis, among feminist scholars looking for alternative ways to think about knowledge.[13]

This then, serves as the background against which reflection on knowledge became an imperative for feminist philosophers: our own discipline's history of arrogating cognitive capacities, or what was purported to be their most fully developed form, to men or of gendering them in such a way that their expression in women is unseemly or monstrous; the persistence of gender-laden and androcentric patterns of description and explanation in the natural sciences; modes of theorizing in the behavioral and social sciences that make women invisible as social actors and cognitive agents, and their subordination inevitable and natural. Feminist philosophers ask what conceptions of knowledge and the knower support or facilitate these analyses? Are there conceptions of knowledge that can block sexist moves? Are there concepts of justification that show both why the gender representations found in natural, social, and behavioral sciences seemed correct and yet were not? How did knowledge acquire a gender and can it be degendered? How must concepts of truth, rationality, objectivity, certainty, etc., be rethought in order to rid them of the taint of masculinism? This is a delicate task. The cultural inheritance that seems so problematic seems so in light of epistemic concepts and forms of valuation that are also inherited from our tradition, concepts like truth and objectivity, for instance. It seems that it is certain conjunctures of concepts and attitudes or perhaps partial and historically inflected contents of concepts that are at fault rather than the entire tradition. In this case what is required is a careful sorting through of what should be retained, what should be transformed, and what jettisoned in the epistemological tradition. Feminist epistemology is like the rest of philosophy. Certain topics get taken up, considered from different angles, analyzed in contesting, competing ways. Certain problems emerge as central, are worried at for a time, then recede into the background. Certain theoretical formulations get examined, anatomized, and used or discarded. There is no single feminist epistemology. Instead there are a plethora of ideas, approaches, and arguments that have in common only their authors' commitment to exposing and reversing the derogation of women and the gender bias of traditional formulations.

2. Rethinking the Subject

One of the consistent themes running through the feminist rethinking of the subject of knowledge is the insistence on its embodiment. Several consequences of embodiment have received extended attention: the locatedness or situatedness of the knower, the interdependence of knowers, and the ontological parity of subject and object of knowledge. Descartes is the main foil here, as feminist and other critics have identified Cartesian themes throughout subsequent Western theory of knowledge and Descartes is the acknowledged founder of the modern form of epistemology.

Philosopher Naomi Scheman has suggested in a series of essays that the preoccupations inherited from Descartes constitute a kind of collective and profoundly gendered psychosis.[14] These preoccupations she identifies as the quest for certainty and the unity and self-transparency of the subject. Scheman argues that Descartes was oriented to an analysis of genuine knowledge as achieved free from external influence and determination. This required identifying guarantees of truth within himself, i.e. constituting himself (as distinct from church or state) as epistemically authoritative. Descartes found the source of certainty in reason, but a reason purified and disembodied. The body, both as source and subject of doubt, is shorn away from the essential self, as for example Descartes argues in the passage about the ball of wax in Meditation II. Its sensible properties are unstable and hence less knowable than its quantitative, intelligible properties, thus showing the body to be an unreliable source of knowledge, and it is itself, as material substance, analogous to Descartes's body in what can be known about it. Scheman analyzes this in psychoanalytic terms as projection, detaching from and treating as other than the self one of its (former) parts and vilifying it. The embodied self is prone to deceptions and entanglements. The disembodied self can perform acts of pure reason, like the Cogito. The disembodied self, the real self, is the seat of reason and will, cognition and action, while the repudiated body becomes a mere mechanism. The problems of philosophy are the consequence of this self-splitting. "These problems – namely, the mind-body problem, problems of reference and truth, the problem of other minds, and skepticism about knowledge of the external world – all concern the subject's ability or inability to connect with the split-off parts of itself – its physicality, its sociability."[15]

The purified subject that emerges from the disavowal of the body is a masculine and white European subject, and all that it is freed of when freed from the body, argues Scheman, is displaced onto the bodies of feminized and primitivized Others – European women and nonwhite women and men – who are thereby epistemologically disfranchised. To analogize this mode of self-constitution to paranoia is to imply that it is an inappropriate response to the occasioning situation. Feminists make common cause with Wittgensteinians here, in claiming that the acts of separation required involve incoherence and that the unitary, purified self pronouncing the Cogito is not just a fantasy, but a suppression of all that makes it possible. Feminists' reclamations of the body, therefore, assume that knowledge is possible for the embodied subject and that the victims of Cartesian doubt not only misconceived the conditions of meaningful cognitive action but missed significant aspects of cognitive experience, of knowing.

The need for independence and concomitantly for certainty results in a disavowal of the body and of embodiment. It also sets a standard for knowledge against which subsequent theorists will measure their analyses. The empiricists, for example, are forced to accept a very narrow domain as properly the object of knowledge, because they operate against a Cartesian standard. Skepticism and its refutation occupy the lion's share of philosophical attention because of the failure to challenge the Cartesian identification of knowledge and certainty. Repudiating the separation from body, affirming the embodiment of cognitive agents, enables feminist analysts to devote their attention to a range of epistemological issues other than the refutation of skepticism.

a) Situatedness

Embodiment means location. Bodies are in particular places, in particular times, oriented in particular ways to their environments. This places limitations on aspirations to universality, but the particular locations of subjects afford them particular advantages. As Miriam Solomon notes, the rubric of situations emerged first in the work of philosophers of language Barwise and Perry, who used the concept of situation to develop a theory of meaning that locates meaning in the interaction of living (and language-using) things and their environment.[16] Feminists tend to trace their usage of the term to Donna Haraway's essay "Situated Knowledges" and the standpoint epistemology she was discussing.[17] Haraway's essay touches on both the social and physical aspects of situations.

Standpoint epistemology – one major analysis of situatedness – is a reworking of some Marxist ideas, especially as developed by Georg Lukács, which reverse traditional assignments of both social and cognitive privilege. Marxist theorists understand capitalist societies as constituted of two social classes in opposition to each other: the capitalist, or owning, ruling, or managerial class, and the working class. Since material life is structured in opposing ways for the two groups, the vision of each will be an inversion of the other. The capitalist sees the world in ways that confirm the rightness of the capitalist's position of power. The worker sees the world from a different vantage point – one that affirms the essential humanity of the worker and her/his necessity to the productive process and that includes the limited and distorted perspective of the capitalist. That is, the worker knows that from the perspective of the capitalist the worker is simply a replaceable part of the production process and knows that this is a necessary distortion of the worker's humanity. Because the worker's standpoint includes the perspective of the capitalist, and because the worker's standpoint is the basis for a vision of liberation, it is superior to that of the capitalist. This superiority is epistemological as well as political.

Political scientist Nancy Hartsock reworked Marxist standpoint theory as a feminist theory.[18] She emphasized the sexual division of labor in childbearing as providing the basis for the opposed structuring of material life for women and men. Women's life activities provide the basis for a specifically feminist historical materialism and the basis for a better – less partial and less perverse – understanding of the social and natural worlds. Specifically, Hartsock argued that a masculine point of view (a consequence of masculine developmental processes) involved a devaluation of all that is associated with the female, and elevated mind over body, culture over nature, the abstract over the concrete. A feminist standpoint by contrast opposed dualisms, valued the concrete and the relational, and produced a different representation of natural and social worlds.

Feminist standpoint theory fell afoul both of the recognition of women's diversity and of postmodernist suspicions of epistemological notions like truth. A central feature of the theory as Hartsock reworked it was the mutual constitution of masculinist and feminist standpoints and their grounding in the material relations of sex. This requires a constancy of sex relations throughout human societies and cultures. Once their diversity is recognized, once, that is, there are no longer just two opposing standpoints but many, some coexisting in the same society and in multiple relations with each other, it is no longer possible to think of them as generating fully generalizable masculinist or feminist standpoints. Philosopher Sandra Harding has attempted to turn this shortcoming into a virtue by arguing that there are multiple standpoints and that objectivity is achieved by being reflexively aware of the limitations of one's own position and by incorporating ("starting thought from") all standpoints in one's theorizing.[19] Standpoints, as multiple and as assumable, become more like perspectives and the materiality of the original standpoint theory is lost.[20]

Haraway, while sympathetic to the political dimensions of standpoint theory, eschews the aspiration to completeness manifested in Harding's approach and focuses instead on partiality as an ineluctable consequence of situation.[21] Our social situations, our experience, histories, and interests make us partial in the sense of taking a side, but these factors, along with our physical situation, also give us partial perspectives, as in singular, incomplete, limited, shaped and framed by. Haraway elaborates this theme through an extended discussion of vision. Vision has acquired a bad name through its association with an appropriating masculine gaze and its use in universalizing conceptions of knowledge and reason. These latter remove vision from its embodiment in optic nerves and organs and treat the mind as having a relation like vision to concepts and propositions. Haraway reflects on the materiality of vision and of the prostheses – from reading glasses to the Hubble telescope – that we have constructed to assist and enhance our visual senses. We see from particular locations and what we see is a function of our orientations in our surroundings, the direction we face, the variety of wavelengths our eyes and instruments admit. Seeing is very much embodied and its accuracy goes hand in hand with its partiality. Deprived of its appropriative and universalizing potential, vision becomes once again a useful metaphor for knowledge. For Haraway, objectivity is partial perspective.

b) *Subject and object*

A second dimension to the embodiment of the knower is the denial of any essential difference between subjects and objects of knowledge. This has been taken to mean many things. One important interpretation is reflexivity. Feminist theorists, most notably Sandra Harding, have argued that an important component of objectivity is the knower's awareness of her own assumptions and values and of the ways in which these affect her beliefs and theorizing.[22] Another interpretation is a kind of naturalism – a denial that knowers stand outside the world we seek to know and a denial that knowers must satisfy certain conditions of transcendence in order to know. Knowers interact with, are affected by, changed by, the objects of their knowledge. A third interpretation is responsibility: if knowers are not different in kind from the known, then their relations will come under moral guidelines similar to those operating among knowers as persons. While this has obvious implications in social and behavioral sciences, some theorists have extended it to our relations with nonhuman animal research subjects.[23]

Because knowing subjects are not characterized by transcendence of the body with all its entanglements, knowledge or cognitive relations can be charged with affect. An emotional engagement with the objects of one's knowledge does not *ipso facto* disqualify one's beliefs about and perceptions of those objects from counting as knowledge. Alison Jaggar argues that our emotions are sources of knowledge about their objects.[24] Other feminists have argued that one must love the objects of knowledge (whether these are persons or other sorts of entity) in order to know them fully. Once the separation of subject and body is reversed, then the attributes, such as emotion, repudiated along with the body do not characterize only that which can be known (the unruly other) but the knower as well.

Another version of the claim that cognition is affective can be outlined as a modification of Evelyn Keller's earlier-noted analysis of objectivity. She argues that the detachment claimed to be involved in objectivity is a distortion of the concept of knowledge. This distortion is grounded in an affective orientation to the world rooted in fear and the consequent desire to dominate. She advocates an alternative orientation which involves the ability to move in and out of intimacy with objects, in which control is exercised over one's own attitudes toward and degree of relatedness with objects and not over the objects themselves. Instead of labeling one form distorted and one more objective or knowledge-producing, one could say that our knowledge of objects is partially mediated by our affective orientation whether that be fear, the desire to dominate, love, or indifference. Our affective orientation becomes another aspect or dimension – along with place, time, social location – of our situatedness.

The shift from a transcendent and disembodied subject to empirical, embodied, and differentiated subjects is often represented as a loss, encouraging a representation of the aspects of situatedness as interfering with knowledge or cognitive access. Following Haraway's treatment of vision, however, we might better think of them as focusing devices, or cognitive resources, directing our attention to features of that which we seek to know that we would otherwise overlook.

c) *Dependence and interdependence*

One further consequence of acknowledging the embodied character of knowers that feminists have explored is the dependence or interdependence of knowers. Epistemic dependence is taken to be such a consequence, because the claims of autonomy on behalf of knowers are grounded in their characterization as disembodied. Re-embody them and autonomy becomes less plausibly attributed to knowers. There are several dimensions of dependence with epistemological implications.

Annette Baier's naturalistic theory of persons stresses the developmental aspect.[25] Persons as humans are individuals who start out small, helpless, and inarticulately ignorant. They are dependent on adults for language learning and for acquiring the "essential arts of personhood," including the habits of reasoning and standards of epistemic evaluation whose presence is taken for granted in adults. Whatever degree of autonomy we experience in these matters as adults is a function of our having learned such habits and standards as children. Lorraine Code locates additional epistemological implications of the second persons view in conceptions of knowledge. She states that "epistemological positions developed around a 'second persons' conception of subjectivity represent the production of knowledge as a communal . . . activity."[26] This point will be further developed below. She also claims that within the second persons view it becomes possible to understand knowledge claims as claims, that is, as statements made in an interpersonal context. "A knowledge claimant positions herself within a set of discursive possibilities which she may accept, criticize or challenge: positions herself in relation to other people, to their responses, criticisms, agreements, and contributions."[27]

The proposal to treat knowledge claims in this way converges interestingly with some recent suggestions in analytic epistemology. Stewart Cohen, in several articles, worries over the question whether knowing that p requires ideally good reasons or merely good reasons.[28] If an undermining defeater is a statement whose truth would rebut a reason r's status as a reason, and a restoring defeater responds successfully to the undermining defeater, ideally good reasons would be those for which a knower S has a restoring defeater for every undermining defeater. What Cohen tries to sort out is whether S must be aware of these defeaters in order to be said to know. Defeaters must be "intersubjectively evident," that is, evident to S's community, in order to be relevant to S's reasons and knowledge claims, but not all possible defeaters will be intersubjectively evident, so knowledge does not require ideally good reasons, but only good reasons. Good reasons are those for which S has a restoring defeater for every intersubjectively evident defeater. Because the degree of evidence or opacity required for relevant defeaters depends on social standards, argues Cohen, knowledge is dependent on social standards. More precisely, Cohen has established that knowledge attribution is dependent on social standards. What his arguments leave open is whether it makes sense to speak of knowledge as a property or quality of persons different from attributed knowledge, i.e. whether knowledge exists outside of contexts in which standards of knowledge, i.e. sufficiently justified belief, are determined. Another way to read this is as a challenge to those who would extricate knowledge from conversational, dialogic, social, contexts.

Both Cohen's and Code's considerations converge, then, in suggesting that "knowledge" is a term of ratification claimed and ascribed, rather than a natural kind, or state of a subject that obtains independently of facts about the knower's community and relations with her or his community. "Know" is a verb of use primarily within a community, whose meaning is determined in a context of criticism, concurrence, assent, and dissent. To think of cognitive agency in this way is to open the way to conceiving of subjectivity, thought, and perhaps even consciousness, as dialogic and conversational in structure rather than ideally independent of any attachment to others.

The dependence of the child on the adult is transmuted into adult *interdependence*. Social epistemologists have been exploring the role of trust in knowledge.[29] In reality our beliefs originate in the testimony of others at least as much as, if not more than, in our direct perceptual experience. We trust the newspapers, our car mechanic, the scientists in the next building, our doctor. Philip Kitcher treats the division of cognitive labor, i.e. the pursuit of diverse projects by different individuals and communities characterized by different methodological practices, as occasioning a need to determine an optimum assignment or distribution of tasks within that division.[30] The related problem of cognitive authority or deference owed to the expertise of others requires developing methods for weighing authority. Distribution and authority are treated as formal problems by Kitcher.[31] For John Hardwig, the role of trust in knowledge, particularly in complex and corporate inquiries like experimental physics, poses more qualitative philosophical problems. Hardwig asks us to consider who in such cases knows.[32] Can we say individual members of a team of interdependent researchers know or must we say that only the whole team knows?

Neither of these approaches takes up the problem of expert knowledge from the point of view of those who have historically been epistemologically disfranchised. Kathryn Addelson has argued that in an advanced society like ours, we already operate in an institutionalized hierarchy of cognitive authority.[33] This carries the danger that not only the surface pronouncements of designated experts will be granted uncritical credence, but that metaphysical assumptions that support the hierarchized organization of knowledge production will also be thus deferred to. For Code, the role of trust reinforces the interdependence of subjects. "[T]he issue of establishing and relying on authority and expertise, morally, politically, and epistemically, turns on questions about how to be appropriately judicious and circumspect in granting and withholding trust. Like all cooperative enterprises, the division of intellectual labor depends on the cooperators' ability to *trust* one another to play their parts responsibly."[34] She, too, recognizes the problem posed by differences in power, noting how the reports of those in lesser positions of organizational authority, like nurses in relation to physicians in a hospital, manual laborers in relation to managers, or homemakers in relation to efficiency experts, are systematically treated as less credible than those in positions of greater authority. Nurses, workers, homemakers, are described as having experience; physicians, managers, efficiency experts, as having knowledge. This asserts a principled distinction between kinds of knowledge, privileging one at the expense of the other. Code remarks, "The alleged neutrality of judgments that confer epistemic warrant [i.e. judgments as to what counts as knowledge and what not] sounds increasingly like a confirmation of the subjectivity – that is, the values and practices – of the possessors of professional power, who are usually white, middle class, and male."³⁵ The problem, says Code, is not that masculine subjectivity is valorized, so much as that "institutionalized objectivism disavows its subjective dimension," i.e. that any subjectivity should be masked as objectivity.

3. Rethinking Justification

The features of knowing subjects highlighted by feminist epistemologists require some rethinking of justification. The situatedness of subjects means there is no place of transcendence, of unsituatedness for which epistemic privilege can be claimed. It also means that beliefs will be mediated by the spatial, temporal, and social and affective features of situations. One response to the situatedness of subjects is to try to identify an epistemically privileged or authoritative situation, such that being in that situation is either a necessary or sufficient element of epistemic justification. Other theorists reject the strategy of epistemic privileging for alternative approaches to justification.

a) Standpoint theory: privileging the margins

As is clear from the last section, feminist epistemologists think that current social arrangements in fact assign epistemic privilege to occupants of one social position, but that this assignment is masked in the rhetoric of expertism. Feminist standpoint theory seeks to reverse the assignment and grants epistemic privilege to those in subordinated, socially unprivileged positions. This aspect of standpoint theory is manifestly unsatisfactory. First of all, both the delineation of the domain with respect to which occupation of a standpoint is epistemically authoritative and the identification of the privileged situation or standpoint would presumably have to be done from a noninterested position. But according to standpoint theory there is none such. In addition, some of the problems in classical standpoint theory's conception of the subject discussed in the prior section transfer over to its theory of justification. The assignment of epistemic privilege seems most plausible when there are two complementary, exclusive, and exhaustive standpoints. But even in classical Marxist theory society is not constituted of just two opposing classes; the lumpenproletariat are a third element even if disregarded as a social force. Feminists from racial and ethnic minorities compelled the advocates of standpoint theory to recognize that the material conditions and experiences of women differed sufficiently to undermine any notion of a unified standpoint. Thus, if only one standpoint can be epistemically authoritative, that standpoint must be identified. But such identification will require social investigation which itself proceeds from and is subject to assessment from a standpoint. This seems viciously, rather than benignly, circular.³⁶ Harding, as we have seen, attempts to remedy this problem by claiming that the multiplicity of women's situations and standpoints (indeed those of oppressed persons in general) means that one should "start thought" from as many standpoints as possible and that the greatest objectivity and ideal epistemic authority is achieved by incorporation of all standpoints produced by positions of oppression. I noted above that such a proposal dematerializes an originally materialist theory, since it presupposes one can assume standpoints unrelated to one's experience and material situation. It is also a recipe for futility – how does one know if one has properly understood the situation of another? Rather, the standpoint one so achieves is not that of the other but really a more complex standpoint: that of a person with her or his own particular history understanding and reconstructing in a way shaped by that history the standpoint of another. If we take the social and historical conditioning of the subject seriously, then one's assumption of another's standpoint is always mediated by the conditions of one's own subjectivity.

Harding's hope to identify a maximally objective, least distorted standpoint or subject position betrays a strong metaphysical realism – a commitment to the view that there is a way the world is and that it is possible to produce a single unified and complete description of the world. Feminists concerned to make feminist analysis persuasive to nonfeminists often fall back on such a metaphysical monism, as though believing that only if there's one right way to describe a state of affairs is it possible to engage in effectively persuasive discourse. Even Haraway in "Situated Knowledges" insists on the need for "simultaneously an account of radical historical contingency for all knowledge claims and knowing subjects, a critical practice for recognizing our own 'semiotic technologies' for making meanings, *and* a no-nonsense commitment to faithful accounts of a 'real' world."[37]

It is that "no-nonsense commitment" that undermines feminists' attempts to introduce any real differences into epistemology. As long as feminists remain committed whether explicitly or covertly to the idea of a uniquely correct, unified, complete, and coherent description of the world the epistemological innovations we introduce are either inadequate to support that metaphysics or get pushed in the direction of conventional epistemological thought. Is there a way both to embrace the inescapably conditioned nature of subjectivity and to eschew the search for privileged forms of subjectivity; to affirm the meaningfulness of critical interaction without grounding it in metaphysical monism? Some feminists argue that these are indeed reconcilable positions, but that their reconciliation requires a more thorough socializing of epistemology. Others argue that a better understanding of the possibilities of individualist epistemologies drawing on Quine or Peirce offer the best options for feminists. These different approaches involve different ways of thinking about the relation of values and biases to knowledge and hence different ways of thinking about justification.

b) *From situation to context*

The arguments about the conditioned nature of subjectivity can be understood as making a point parallel with and converging with arguments about the role of context in justification. Context can be invoked in at least three ways. In one sense "context" means the background of assumptions in light of which individuals assess data and assign evidential relevance. These assumptions are theory- and value-laden. They include but are not limited to assumptions flowing from or expressive of those features of conditioned subjectivity to which feminists have drawn attention: androcentrism (or a male-centered point of view) which facilitates interpreting data in one way as well as gynecentrism (or a female-centered point of view) or other points of view which facilitate interpreting those same data differently.

One of the classic examples of gendercentric theorizing is the set of theories of human evolution centered around postulated hominid behaviors in the evolutionarily relevant periods. The theorists who attributed the development of distinctive human anatomical features to male behavior could imagine only one use for the sharpened stones which are part of the fossil data: hunting. Those who attributed the development of distinctive human anatomical features to female behavior suggested the stones might have been used for digging roots and smashing seeds. The members of this latter group of theorists deliberately set out to construct a model of human evolution that put females at the center. While most anthropologists now think some mix of hunting and gathering behaviors or perhaps other nongendered behaviors provided the behavioral crucible for human evolution, the articulation of Woman-the-gatherer was important to showing the bias in the affirmation of Man-the-hunter's unique contribution. It could persist as the main theory of human evolution in a context in which male dominance and superiority were rarely challenged cultural assumptions and in which few women participated as researchers. Woman-the-gatherer made her appearance when women entered physical anthropology and the second wave of the women's movement was underway.[38] Other notable examples of the relation of alternative models to context include analyses of research on fertilization, of gene action versus gene activation, of individualism in evolution.[39]

As background assumption context functions as a feature of and modulator of individual belief and inference. A second use of context refers to background assumptions and methodological rules that are not individual but are shared in a community – those assumptions that form the context within which members of a community pursue inquiries and engage in critical interactions in the course of those inquiries. Man-the-hunter and the other examples cited above implicate this notion of context as well. Prior to the development of female-centered alternatives, interpretation of fossil data took place against shared assumptions of male dominance, male centrality to evolution, male activity in contrast to female passivity. Until challenged by those female-centered alternative models, androcentric assumptions were invisible as assumptions. As long as they were shared in the culture and especially in the culture of those pursuing physical anthropology research, there was no challenge to them and they simply formed the consensual background against which other issues could be seen as contentious.

Feminist philosophers of science, arguing for the interaction of normative and empirical, have outlined various ways in which contextual factors play a role in hypothesis justification. In *Science as Social Knowledge*, I argued that questions, categories, local background assumptions, global frameworks, could incorporate social values.[40] Elizabeth Anderson, in developing what she calls a dual track model of theoretical justification, argues that standards of significance and completeness for theories, the definition of meaningful classifications and the criteria of their satisfaction, and the methods needed to answer a question are all determined by contextual values, while evidence determines whether a theory meets standards of significance, whether anything meets the criteria of classification, and whether there are data such as the methods require.[41] In addition to substantive theory- and value-laden assumptions, methodological and heuristic rules and values form part of the common context within which a community pursues its inquiry, but these are not wholly an internal matter and methodological rules and norms often carry social weight.[42]

One way to identify a cognitive or scientific community is by the commitments – substantive, normative, and procedural – that constitute the taken-for-granted context of inquiry. Lynn H. Nelson expands Quine's rejection of the analytic/synthetic distinction and his embrace of meaning holism by arguing that theories, including social and political beliefs and values, no less than sensory data, count as evidence for hypotheses.[43] Knowledge is produced and held by communities constituted by their shared commitments. A community justifies its belief in h by showing that h coheres with its entire gamut of commitments. Nelson thus effectively denies distinctions between constitutive and contextual considerations.

A third use of context refers to features of situations in which beliefs are formed/acquired. Rather than the subjectivity of cognitive agents or cognitive communities, circumstances of the situations in which agents form and use or rely on their beliefs are proposed to have a bearing on matters of justification. David Annis proposes contextualism as an alternative to foundationalism and coherentism.[44] On the view he proposes, a cognitive agent A is justified in some belief b if A is able to meet objections to b – objections regarding the cognitive competence of A with respect to b or objections regarding the truth of b.[45] But A does not have to meet all possible objections – only those based on current evidence to which challengers assign better than low probability. Furthermore, what Annis calls an issue-context determines the kinds of objections that are relevant and the level of understanding and knowledge required to raise them. This in turn determines the appropriate objector challenger group. If the context is conversation about developments in astrophysics gleaned from a science weekly, the expected and relevant objections will be much less rigorous than if the context is an astrophysics seminar at the Jet Propulsion Laboratory. The appropriate objector group for A's belief that b in context C will be a subset of the larger group G to which A belongs. This is the group relative to whose standards issue contexts are differentiated, e.g. informal discussion groups from professional astrophysics seminars, police inquiries from casual gossip. So, says Annis, if A is justified in believing b then A is able to meet relevant objections in a way that satisfies G's practices and norms, i.e. A is able to meet objections deemed by G appropriate to A's issue context in ways that satisfy G's norms for responding to objections.

Jane Duran adopts Annis's form of contextualism in her elaboration of a gynecentric theory of justification.[46] Duran's view is that the context and communicativeness emphasized in Annis's account are homologous with features attributed to female cognitive agents in some feminist theory, i.e. sensitivity to context, relational rather than autonomous sense of self. This way of conceiving of feminist epistemology is as a theory that reverses the traditional derogation of female intellectual and cognitive capacities. Duran uses Annis's account to argue for a theory of knowledge in which women are the better cognitive agents. However appealing such reversals are, they are vulnerable to criticisms that they endorse cultural stereotypes and ignore the very real diversity among the world's women. Patricia Hill Collins has offered an account of what she calls the black feminist standpoint which partially converges with Duran's approach.[47] The black feminist standpoint is one that takes its model of inquiry from the patterns of cognition and interaction Collins attributes to African-American women. These include not just reliance on personal experience and intuition, but responsiveness and dialogic interaction. While it also assigns epistemic advantage to practices rather than to situation, the scope of the claims is not clear. For example, it is not clear whether Collins is recommending the behaviors she describes to everyone regardless of sex or race, or is assigning epistemic privilege to African-American women on the basis of their presumed facility with the patterns of practice described. If the former, some demonstration of their epistemic relevance is required, and if the latter, then the view shares the problems of any standpoint theory.[48] Gynecentric epistemology is not, however, the only way in which to incorporate the contextualism advanced by Annis (and Cohen) into feminist epistemology.

c) *Socializing justification*

Each of the three ways of contextualizing justification has a different bearing on the sociality of knowledge. The first, which treats context as the background of assumptions each agent brings to epistemic justification, poses the following problem. If there is no place outside of some set of assumptions from which to judge independently the relative merits of different sets of assumptions, how can we avoid subjectivism? I have argued that subjectivism can only be avoided by incorporating critical interaction into one's notion of justification.[49] Knowledge is the outcome not just of the cognitive agent's encounter with the world, but of cognitive agents' encounters with one another. The latter encounters bring assumptions to the surface for criticism and then endorsement, rejection, or modification. A recalcitrant agent will not defend or modify her beliefs in response to criticism. Such recalcitrance amounts to opting out of membership in an epistemic commnity.[50] A parallel point can be made in relation to the second form of contextualization. This treats as context the shared values, assumptions, and social experiences in light of which members of a community engage in critical interaction, the background sharing of which is constitutive of community membership. As a naturalizer in epistemology, Nelson argues that the implications of this degree of contextual involvement include both holism and the collective nature of the knower.[51] Nelson's approach seems to treat everything that is causally relevant to belief as evidentially relevant. The approach I favor sees the dependence of justification on contextual factors not as itself an alternative to traditional normative approaches like foundationalism or coherentism, but as requiring a new formulation of normative questions – one that begins with contextual dependence. In particular, I argue that the role of shared values, etc., means that the knowledge produced in communities is at best partial and that communities must themselves develop sites of critical discourse about their assumptions both through incorporating diverse perspectives within themselves as internal resources for criticism and by engaging with communtities whose shared background is different. That is, the community must open itself to the kind of critical interactions that (ideally) occur within it. This level of shared interaction requires some shared values or assumptions, appeal to which grounds criticism across communities, but it does not require a fully shared set of values.[52]

Finally, the third way of contextualizing justification also points to the necessity of making a further socializing move. If a group makes distinctions about the kinds of standards that are appropriately imposed in different contexts, then those distinctions and the standards, practices, and norms involved in drawing them are themselves subject to challenge. The group will be justified in relying on those standards to the extent that it can respond adequately to objections. There is no higher authority determining what counts as an adequate response, thus the group's justification is always provisional and subject to revocation. If a challenge is brought to which no adequate response is possible or if a response is challenged and no adequate response to that challenge is forthcoming, the group is no longer justified in relying on the standard, norm, practice, or distinction in question.

The contextualizing of justification is a naturalizing move in epistemology that acknowledges certain features of everyday reasoning as ineliminable aspects of cognitive practices. It also opens the way to an alternative to foundationalist or coherentist theories of justification. Because these latter theories are offered both as descriptive and as normative theories, it is tempting to treat contextualism as also being something of both. But, as indicated above, contextualism is not itself a normative theory. It is rather a descriptive and analytic account of normative epistemic practices. If proposed as a normative theory, it is hard to distinguish from relativism. Some feminists seem willing to accept this consequence.[53] Others, however, refuse the assumed exhaustiveness of the dichotomy between the orderly epistemic security offered by foundationalism and coherentism and the anarchy of relativism. Thus, while contextualism is the alternative to foundationalism and coherentism as descriptive theories, socialism is the alternative to foundationalism and coherentism as normative theories. Socialism grounds justification not in indubitable or basic foundations nor in systematic coherence of a set of beliefs, but in the survival of criticism from opposing or different points of view.[54] Because such survival carries no protections from future criticism, and because criticism is effective when related to an epistemic goal or cognitive value held by the receiver of criticism, justification will always be provisional and partial. Judgments are always open to revision but the embedding of justification in the tissue of critical interaction offers stability, criteria by which to judge beliefs and practices better and worse, and the possibility of persuasion.

This relationship between contextualism and socialism also allows us to understand why feminists have claimed social epistemology as a feminist epistemology or as an epistemology for feminists. Feminist scholars have argued that traditional epistemological theories have served to legitimate, by masking, the role that assumptions about gender play in scientific theorizing and in the construction of epistemological concepts like reason. Contextualism, especially the first two kinds discussed, incorporates or is suborned in feminist insights into the situated or conditioned character of cognitive agency. The individualist response to contextualism is relativism – either endorsed or presented as a *reductio ad absurdum* of the contextualist analysis. Grounding justification in dialogic interaction, in critical discursive interaction, socializes justification, making the full exercise of cognitive agency dependent on relations with others. Thus social epistemology restores a measure of normative prescription to contextual theories of justification.

There is a second way in which feminist epistemology and social epistemology converge. To the extent that concepts of masculinity are metaphorically bound up with notions of epistemic/cognitive autonomy, commitment to masculinist gender ideology makes epistemic interdependence an untenable or at least unpalatable epistemological position.[55] Feminist philosophical analysis, by liberating the conceptions of cognitive agency from the grip of (unconscious) masculinist ideology and by centering interdependence and interaction in the analysis of personhood, in the manner of Baier's second person analysis, makes socialism in epistemology more palatable. The necessity of dialogic interaction does not follow from the interactionist and interdependent analysis of persons, but the epistemological and metaphysical analyses converge in social epistemology. Of course, not all feminist philosophers concur with this judgment, so I would like to turn to some objections to the kind of position I've just outlined.

4. Meeting objections

Much of the philosophical response to feminist epistemology is unfairly dismissive.[56] But there are interesting objections to the line of analysis just offered coming from feminists. Both Louise Antony and Susan Haack have argued against the social turn in feminist epistemology. Antony rejects the turn in general and as an epistemological approach distinctive of or uniquely valuable to feminists. Antony, however, writes as a feminist epistemologist who endorses a different approach. Haack thinks feminism ought to remain a political position only. She argues against the meaningfulness of the rubric "feminist epistemology" altogether. She further argues both against the social turn in general and offered as a species of feminist epistemology. While there is much to be learned from and to agree with in the papers to be discussed, I do not think they succeed in reducing the social turn (or any acceptable form thereof) to familiar nonsocial themes, nor in showing that feminist epistemology or the social turn in philosophy undermine feminism or epistemology.

Antony's rejection takes the form of a defense of epistemological individualism against a series of challenges.[57] Distinguishing various forms of individualism, she takes methodological individualism to be under attack in arguments I have offered in various papers about the sociality of knowledge. Methodological individualism is the claim that the individual is the primary epistemic subject. This seems to mean both that the individual is the primary cognitive agent and that individuals are the primary objects or targets of epistemological norms. Antony advances several considerations intended to save methodological individualism from socializing arguments.

1. Even if objectivity requires critical interaction, she says, an individual can achieve some degree of objectivity by being reflective about her beliefs, assumptions, etc., i.e. the critical interaction can be internal to the individual, so the individual can to some extent meet the criterion of objectivity without social interaction. To this point the social epistemologist can respond that such reflectivity on the part of individuals (a) is limited in its scope only to those assumptions of which the individual is aware and (b) is in any case the internal rehearsal of a social practice of criticism. It is therefore dependent on and derivative from those patterns of interaction through which the individual learns to reason.

2. Social knowledge presupposes individual epistemic agency. No individual can leave their subjective position, and epistemic processes involve individualistic judgment and perception, so individuals are epistemologically basic. The social epistemologist can agree with all this, but note that the kind of individual agency described is necessary but not sufficient. Of course social knowledge involves individuals; the social is constituted of individuals in interaction, but the interaction is as necessary as the individuals. In the case of scientific inquiry, what is being claimed is that interactive practices (a) make personal, individual beliefs [NB: not private sensations or experiences] into knowledge and (b) transform belief in the process of challenge and response either because the content changes through that process or because the content becomes more firmly anchored in a network of experiential and doxastic states.[58]

3. Antony proposes that the sociality thesis properly understood amounts to nothing more than the claim that human beings use each other to enhance their own individual epistemic situations. This is no challenge to epistemological individualism. But there are at least two meanings of "enhancement." In one, quantitative, sense it means increasing the range of epistemic capacity. So we are one another's cognitive prostheses – extending one another's cognitive range as telescopes and stethoscopes do. In this sense social interaction is not necessary for knowledge *per se*, though we could not know as much without each other. In a second, qualitative, sense, however, the enhancement means the transformation

of belief into knowledge. In this sense the sociality thesis is a challenge to epistemological individualism. It is not (nor is it intended as) a challenge to psychological individualism. The claim is not that we could not have the beliefs we have absent our critical interactions with others. The claim is rather about the status of those beliefs, in particular whether or not they qualify as knowledge. This is a function of social interaction. In rejecting individualism, I am not claiming with Nelson that the community is the primary subject of knowledge, but rather that the ratification of belief which warrants labeling it knowledge is an interactive process.

Antony continues her defense by considering Miriam Solomon's social empiricism. Solomon has argued that scientific reasoning is better understood as a social than an individual process.[59] If science is the most successful cognitive venture, there is a puzzle regarding the individual irrationalities of scientists. Using case studies Solomon argues that communities in which scientists are individually irrational (in the sense of acting on cognitive biases) are collectively rational (in the sense of ultimately arriving at the correct, i.e. empirically successful, theory). Antony says that even if this is the case, Solomon's approach does not show that epistemology can dispense with individualistic norms or divest itself of traditional canons of rationality or objectivity. But Solomon could surely reply that this depends on what epistemology is about. If epistemology is about individual practices, then she has not shown this. But perhaps she has shown the irrelevance of epistemology to understanding the success of science. If, on the other hand, epistemology is about what is required for the ultimate achievement of true (or good) theories, then she has shown that epistemology can dispense with individualistic norms. Part of Antony's response to Solomon is that epistemology just is about individual practices. Her case for individual norms is twofold.

One argument is phenomenological: I seem to myself to be deliberating when coming to believe, and "as long as rational deliberation is a part of the story of how my epistemic commitments are made, there is a role for individual norms."[60] But this presupposes that individuals follow or attend to norms in reasoning or deliberating. Contrary to Antony, I don't think the phenomenological or introspective approach can sustain this presupposition. Indeed, I think it is false. The rules and norms developed over the years are not wholly idle, however. I agree with the suggestion made by Mark Kaplan that the role of epistemological rules and norms is to regulate or set guidelines for criticism, to indicate, that is, the kinds of questions to which it is legitimate to expect a claimant to knowledge to respond.[61] But this, of course, returns us to the social.

Antony's second argument is a rejection of what she sees as Solomon's permissiveness with respect to bias. This argument depends on an analogy with justice. Two complementary wrongs do not cancel each other out, but simply add up to two wrongs. Just as justice is served when individuals try to act fairly, so she says "there is reason to think that we may get the best results collectively when individuals try to reason impartially."[62] But in transferring the ethical case to the doxastic, Antony at best shows that it would be irresponsible for an individual to persist in a belief that is the result of an acknowledged disabling bias. And the analogy is itself partial: in the United States Court system the presupposition seems to be that justice is served when attorneys do the best for their clients. More importantly, it's not clear that "Reason impartially," as an injunction, can mean anything more than "Reason." A naturalist, assuming individuals do the best we can, ought to understand reasoning as a neutral form of cognitive processing that can of course have biasing inputs. Antony gives no account of how one avoids or manages biasing inputs. The social epistemologist does: subject beliefs, assumptions, etc., to interpersonal scrutiny and criticism.

Antony's concern seems to be that socializing epistemology swamps individual cognitive agency and that the effects of socially consensual misogyny have been so deleterious that women need to be independent cognizers. But, as she herself notes, it is a mistake to see the social and the individual as opposed to each other. There is no contradiction in both urging that one think for oneself and claiming that knowledge is an outcome of social processes. To think for oneself is to risk being wrong, but the social processes of justification – challenge, no less than response – depend on individuals taking such risks.

Susan Haack shares some of Antony's concerns, but develops her critique in a different way. She also argues against the sociality of knowledge, but, unlike Antony, opposes the very rubric of feminist epistemology. Feminist epistemology, she says, stands either for an unacceptable politicizing of inquiry or, to the extent it offers acceptable claims, is not distinctively feminist in the claims it advances. Similarly, if science is social, it is so only in a modest sense that does not subvert conventional epistemology. More radical positions can only undermine feminist political goals. The general argument strategy Haack adopts is to offer several interpretations of a given claim and argue that one or more of these is tenable but inconsequential, while the rest are consequential but untenable.

In "Epistemological Reflections of an Old Feminist" (EROF) Haack interprets feminist epistemology as an epistemology serving the interests of women.[63] If this means getting rid of sexism in science, feminism, and *a fortiori* feminist epistemology, is not necessary to get rid of false beliefs. If, on the other hand, the point of feminist epistemology is to legitimate the idea that feminist values should determine what theories are accepted, then it rests on falsehoods. These falsehoods are interpretations of underdetermination theses and contextualist claims about the value-ladenness of science. The criticism of feminist uses of underdetermination and of contextualism is more fully developed in "Science as Social – Yes and No" (SSYN).[64] Here again her strategy is to articulate different interpretations of claims made by feminist epistemologists and argue that they are either trivially true or false. In what follows I will take a path through her arguments to show that there are interpretations of these claims that are neither false nor trivial and that also legitimate a concept of feminist epistemology.

Haack's principal fulcrum in SSYN is the distinction between acceptance and warrant. Warrant is an epistemological notion (warranted belief is belief based on good evidence) in contrast to acceptance which is a psychological and sociological notion. In general, she says, the radical and false interpretations of "science is social" confuse acceptance with warrant. One interpretation is that social values are inextricable from inquiry. This claim rests on underdetermination arguments, i.e. arguments that theories and hypotheses are underdetermined by data. Haack points out that if evidence is insufficient to warrant an hypothesis, one can simply refrain from believing it. Even if some form of underdetermination is true, one needn't decide between alternatives on the basis of which is politically preferable. Furthermore, choosing a theory is not equivalent to deciding it's true; one may only decide to act as if it is true. So social values are not inextricable from inquiry. In EROF she also argues that if underdetermination is true it only applies to wholly theoretical hypotheses. Haack's arguments apply only to the most superficial understanding of underdetermination and she treats the value-laden thesis as an essentialist claim about science. These are easy targets, made of straw. One of the main lessons of the underdetermination argument is that there are no formal rules, guidelines, or processes that can guarantee that social values will not permeate evidential relations.[65] If this is so, then it is a contingent matter whether a given theory is value-laden or not. There are two consequences: 1) it can be asked about any given theory whether it is value-laden and if so with which values, and 2) it becomes imperative to produce an analysis of objectivity (understood as social value management rather than absence of social values) that does not invoke formal rules. By addressing only the most simplistic versions of the theses she rejects, Haack's arguments ignore three different points. Value-ladenness does not mean that social values outweigh other considerations, but that they interact with data and hypotheses in determining evidential relevance. If the value-ladenness of a theory is a contingent matter, then whether values are extricable or inextricable from inquiry is not a matter for a priori argument. Contextual or social values are not just negative features in inquiry, but can have a positive role in grounding criticism of background assumptions and in fostering the development of empirical investigation in directions it would not otherwise go.

Regarding the feminist character of the thesis that science is social, Haack again offers a number of interpretations one of which is that the thesis makes room for feminist values in science. Since this relies on a radical interpretation of the sociality of science thesis which is false, it is an unsound claim. But I've just offered an interpretation of the sociality thesis which escapes Haack's argument *and* which makes room for feminist values. What makes inquiry feminist is that it advances feminist cognitive aims. These aims are not the acceptance or warranting of theses to which a feminist investigator is already committed, but revealing the dynamics of gender oppression. This cognitive goal is context-dependent and what will count as acceptable evidence is also context-dependent, but once aims and criteria are specified evidence is still required to warrant any particular hypothesis about gender oppression.

Haack's arguments require us to ignore the fact that inquiry takes place in a value-saturated context and that inquiries are judged by how satisfactorily they answer questions. Elizabeth Anderson in the passages cited above argues that such judgment involves both social norms and evidence. Haack herself acknowledges that the aim of inquiry is not just truth, but significant and substantive truth. Significance and substantiveness are a matter of context and not given by the material apart from context. Haack has not shown that there is no acceptable radical interpretation of "science is social." Nor has she shown that there can be no interpretation of the concept of feminist epistemology that is not either misleading or a dangerous politicization of inquiry. Her failure to perceive interpretations that escape her criticisms is, I think, a function of a dichotomous bifurcation of value-laden and disinterested ("honest") inquiry. She seems to think that value-laden inquiry cannot be honest inquiry. But this is just false: one can be honest and value-laden. The problem for epistemologists and philosophers of science should be how to articulate norms of inquiry (and warrant) in the face of this fact, rather than to deny it.

Conclusion

I have argued that feminist rethinking of the subject of knowledge reinforces views about the conditioned nature of subjectivity and is well accommodated by a contextualist and social analysis of justification. But feminist epistemology, as discussed here, refers not to a particular doctrine, but to an approach to the theory of knowledge that places feminist concerns at its center. Thus one might better speak of doing epistemology as a feminist. This has the salutary effect of eliminating the suggestion that an epistemological thesis must have distinctively feminist or gender-related content in order to be a feminist thesis. Theses adopted by feminists may be shared with other philosophical approaches. Furthermore, there are significant differences among feminist philosophers regarding specific epistemological theses, just as there are significant differences among philosophers generally. There are also differences as to just what practicing epistemology as a feminist ought to consist in.[66]

Much of feminist epistemology has to date focused on issues regarding scientific knowledge, but there are other epistemological challenges arising from feminist social and political engagement. One of these which is beginning to attract the attention of feminist philosophers is the problem of understanding across difference, where difference is not just in belief, but in forms of life.[67] Feminist epistemology is still in process. Feminist philosophers have, however, succeeded in placing on the agenda of contemporary philosophy questions about the nature of the knowing subject, about justification, and about the influence of masculinist bias in the articulation of conventional philosophical concepts. They have engaged in a sustained discussion of the relations of knowledge, inquiry, and social values. These are issues that were by and large neglected in recent analytic epistemology. By elaborating the philosophical dimensions of these matters, feminists have ensured that such topics will continue to attract philosophical attention.

Notes

1. Evelyn F. Keller, *Reflections on Gender and Science* (New Haven: Yale University Press, 1985) and *Secrets of Life, Secrets of Death* (New York: Routledge, 1992); Sharon Traweek, *Beamtimes and Lifetimes* (Cambridge, MA: Harvard University Press, 1988); Margaret Wertheim, *Pythagoras's Trousers: God, Physics, and the Gender Wars* (New York: Random House, 1995); Karen Barad, "Meeting the Universe Halfway," in Lynn H. Nelson and Jack Nelson, eds., *Feminism, Science, and the Philosophy of Science* (Boston: Kluwer Academic Publishers, 1996), pp. 161–94; Kristina Rolin, "Gender, Emotion, and Knowledge in Science," Ph.D. Dissertation, Department of Philosophy, University of Minnesota, 1996; Mary Tiles, "A Science of Mars or of Venus?" *Philosophy* 62 (1987): 293–306.
2. Ruth Bleier, *Science and Gender* (New York: Pergamon Press, 1984); Ann Fausto-Sterling, *Myths of Gender* (New York: Basic Books, 1985); Donna Haraway, *Primate Visions* (New York: Routledge, 1989).
3. Evelyn F. Keller, *A Feeling for the Organism* (New York: W. H. Freeman, 1983) and *Refiguring Life* (New York: Columbia University Press, 1995). See also Emily Martin, "Egg and Sperm," *Signs: Journal of Women in Culture and Society* 16, no. 3 (1991), and Bonnie Spanier, *Im/partial Science: Gender Ideology in Molecular Biology* (Bloomington, IN: Indiana University Press, 1995).
4. Keller, *Reflections on Gender and Science*, pp. 77ff.
5. Dorothy Smith, *The Everyday World as Problematic: A Feminist Sociology* (Boston: Northeastern University Press, 1988).
6. For approaches to gender that support this analysis, see Rachel Hare-Mustin and Jean Maracek, eds., *Making a Difference: Psychology and the Construction of Gender* (New Haven: Yale University Press, 1990). See also Phyllis Rooney, "Methodological Issues in the Construction of Gender as a Meaningful Variable in Scientific Studies of Cognition," in David Hull, Mickey Forbes, and Richard Burian, *PSA 1994*, Vol. 2 (East Lansing, MI: Philosophy of Science Association, 1995).
7. The relation of philosophical doctrines and disciplinary methodologies is complicated. Contemporary research in the history of twentieth-century positivism shows that it can be read as much friendlier to the concerns of feminists than previously thought. See Nancy Cartwright, Jordy Cat, and Thomas Uebel, eds., *Between Science and Politics: The Philosophy of Otto Neurath* (Cambridge: Cambridge University Press, 1997), and Ronald N. Gieve and Alan Richardson, eds., *Origins of Logical Empiricism* (Minneapolis: University of Minnesota Press, 1996).
8. Genevieve Lloyd, *The Man of Reason* (Minneapolis, MN: University of Minnesota Press, 1984).
9. Phyllis Rooney, "Gendered Reason: Sex Metaphor and Conceptions of Reason," *Hypatia* 6, no. 2 (1991): 77–103, and "Rationality and the Politics of Gender Difference," *Metaphilosophy* 26, nos. 1&2 (1995): 22–45.
10. Elisabeth Lloyd, "Objectivity and the Double Standard for Feminist Epistemologists," *Synthese* 104 (Sept., 1995): 351–81.
11. Carol Gilligan, *In a Different Voice* (Cambridge: Harvard University Press, 1982).
12. Mary Belenky, Blythe Clinchy, Nancy Goldberger, Jill Tarule, *Women's Ways of Knowing* (New York: Basic Books, 1986).

13 For critical discussion see Longino, "Gender and Education" (unpublished manuscript, available from author). Also Lorraine Code, *What Can She Know?* (Ithaca: Cornell University Press, 1991), pp. 250–62.
14 These are collected in Naomi Scheman, *Engenderings* (New York: Routledge, 1995).
15 Scheman, "Though This Be Method, Yet There Is Madness in It," in Louise Antony and Charlotte Witt, eds., *A Mind of One's Own* (Boulder, CO: Westview Press, 1993). Susan Bordo has offered a similar argument, attributing the need for a false kind of objectivity to psychological needs fostered by a certain kind of masculinist ideal. See Susan Bordo, *The Flight to Objectivity* (Albany, NY: State University of New York Press, 1987).
16 Miriam Solomon, "Situated Knowledge," Symposium Paper, American Philosophical Association, Eastern Division, Meetings, Atlanta, GA, Dec. 28, 1996. See also Jonathan Barwise and John Perry, *Situations and Attitudes* (Cambridge: Cambridge University Press, 1983).
17 Donna Haraway, "Situated Knowledges: The Science Question in Feminism and the Privilege of Partial Perspectives," *Feminist Studies* 14, no. 3 (1988): 575–600.
18 Nancy Hartsock, "The Feminist Standpoint: Toward a Materialist Feminism", in Sandra Harding and Merrill Hintikka, *Discovering Reality* (Dordrecht, Netherlands: D. Reidel, 1983).
19 Sandra Harding, "What is Strong Objectivity?" in Linda Alcoff and Elizabeth Potter, eds., *Feminist Epistemologies* (New York: Routledge, 1993).
20 I owe this point to discussions with Celeste Friend.
21 Haraway, "Situated Knowledges." Partiality was one of the advantages of taking a situation perspective for Barwise and Perry.
22 Harding has also used the ontological equivalencing of subject and object to support attributing human/social qualities to the entities in the inanimate realm. Together with her proposal to treat social sciences as the model of science, this suggests a major change in the physical sciences. This suggestion has not attracted much of a following.
23 See Linda Birke and Ruth Hubbard, eds., *Reinventing Biology* (Bloomington, IN: Indiana University Press, 1996).
24 Alison Jaggar, "Love and Knowledge: Emotion in Feminist Epistemology," in Alison Jaggar and Susan Bordo, eds., *Gender/Body/Knowledge* (New Brunswick, NJ: Rutgers University Press, 1989).
25 Annette Baier, "Cartesian Persons," in *Postures of the Mind* (Minneapolis, MN: University of Minnesota Press, 1985), pp. 74–92.
26 Code, *What Can She Know?*, p. 121.
27 Ibid., p. 122.
28 Stewart Cohen, "Knowledge and Context," *Journal of Philosophy* 83 (1986): 574–83, and "Knowledge, Context, and Social Standards," *Synthese* 73 (1987): 3–26.
29 C. A. J. Coady, *Testimony: A Philosophical Study* (Oxford: Oxford University Press, 1992); John Hardwig, "Epistemic Dependence," *Journal of Philosophy* 82 (1985): 335–49.
30 Philip Kitcher, "The Division of Cognitive Labor," *Journal of Philosophy* 87 (1990): 5–22.
31 Philip Kitcher, *The Advancement of Science* (New York: Oxford University Press, 1993), pp. 303–89.
32 Hardwig, "Epistemic Dependence."

33 Kathryn Addelson, "The Man of Professional Wisdom," in Harding and Hintikka, eds., *Discovering Reality*.
34 Code, *What Can She Know?*, pp. 182–3 (emphasis in original).
35 Code, *What Can She Know?*, p. 249.
36 If a standpoint S is to be generally authoritative, rather than only for those sharing S, then it must be acknowledged as such by those who do not share it. But, if they don't share it, then what grounds do they have for acknowledging S's epistemically privileged status? How could they validate S from within their standpoint S_1, if S and S_1 are opposed?
37 Haraway, "Situated Knowledges," p. 579.
38 For more analysis see Haraway, *Simians, Cyborgs and Women*, chs. 2 and 3 (New York: Routledge, 1991), and Helen E. Longino and Ruth Doell, "Body, Bias, and Behavior: A Comparative Analysis of Reasoning in Two Areas of Biological Science," *Signs* 9 (1983): 206–27.
39 Emily Martin, "Egg and Sperm"; Keller, *Refiguring Life* and *Secrets of Life, Secrets of Death*. See also Spanier, *Im/partial Biology*.
40 Longino, *Science as Social Knowledge*, esp. ch. 5.
41 Elizabeth Anderson, "Knowledge, Human Interests, and Objectivity in Feminist Epistemology," *Philosophical Topics* 23, no. 2 (1996): 27–58.
42 See Longino, "Cognitive and Non-cognitive Values in Science: Rethinking the Dichotomy," in Nelson and Nelson, *Feminism, Science, and the Philosophy of Science*.
43 Lynn Hankinson Nelson, *Who Knows: From Quine to a Feminist Empiricism* (Philadelphia: Temple University Press, 1990).
44 David Annis, "A Contextualist Theory of Justification," *American Philosophical Quarterly* 15 (1978): 213–29.
45 Annis's overall position thus bears a strong resemblance to Cohen's discussed above, but Annis focuses on the ways in which differences in contexts have a bearing on standards of justification, while Cohen focuses on the implications of variability in such standards for defining "good reasons."
46 Jane Duran, *Toward a Feminist Epistemology* (Savage, MD: Rowman and Littlefield, 1991). *Editor's note*: contextualism is also treated in the essays by Williams and DeRose, this volume.
47 Patricia Hill Collins, *Black Feminist Thought* (Boston: Unwin Hyman, 1990).
48 Of course, she may be making a quite different claim. She may be recommending to African-American feminist scholars that they preserve a continuity with modes of interaction characteristic of women in African-American communities. Each of these three interpretations of Collins's proposals has different epistemological relevance.
49 Longino, *Science as Social Knowledge*, ch. 4. Critical interaction alone is not sufficient to solve the problem of subjectivism. This chapter also spells out conditions a community must meet for criticism to be epistemically effective.
50 For further discussion of dissent and responsibility in epistemological communities, see Heidi Grasswick, "Knowers as Individuals-in-Community," Ph.D. Dissertation, Department of Philosophy, University of Minnesota, 1996.
51 Nelson, "Epistemological Communities," in Alcoff and Potter, *Feminist Epistemologies*.
52 See Longino, *Science as Social Knowledge*. The conditions mentioned in n. 49 also hold for interactions between communities. For another approach to communication across difference, see Lisa Bergin, "Communicating Knowledge Across Epistemic Difference," Ph.D. Dissertation in progress, Department of Philosophy, University of Minnesota.

53 Code is difficult to read on this question. She endorses what she describes as "mitigated relativism" which both "takes different perspectives into account" and "affirms that there is something there, in the world, to know and act on" (*What Can She Know?*, p. 320). This embrace of bifurcation recalls Haraway's similar insistence quoted above. See also Code, *Rhetorical Spaces* (Ithaca: Cornell University Press, 1996).
54 This socialism is also different from Miriam Solomon's social empiricism. See the discussion below.
55 Rooney, "Gendered Reason"; Lloyd, *The Man of Reason*; Longino, "To See Feelingly: Reason, Passion and Dialogue in Feminist Philosophy," in Domna Stanton and Abigail Stewart, eds., *Feminisms in the Academy* (Ann Arbor, MI: University of Michigan Press, 1994). *Editor's note*: social epistemology is discussed at further length in the essay by Schmitt, this volume.
56 See Lloyd, "Objectivity and the Double Standard."
57 Louise Antony, "Sisters, Please, I'd Rather Do It Myself: A Defense of Individualism in Feminist Epistemology," *Philosophical Topics* 23, no. 2 (1996): 59–94.
58 Antony also discusses my more specific claims that observation and reasoning are social ("Sisters, Please," p. 79). Her arguments, however, are directed against misinterpretations of those claims. She thinks, for example, that I claim an individual must intend that her observations be replicable, whereas my point is that in accepting an individual's observations without attempting to replicate them, the community presupposes that they would be replicated if an attempt were made to repeat the experiment.
59 Miriam Solomon, "Social Empiricism," *Nous* 28 (1994), and "Toward a More Social Epistemology," in Frederick Schmitt, ed., *Socializing Epistemology* (Lanham, MD: Rowman and Littlefield, 1994).
60 Antony, "Sisters, Please," p. 86.
61 Mark Kaplan, "Epistemology Denatured," *Midwest Studies in Philosophy* XIX (1994).
62 Antony, "Sisters, Please," p. 87.
63 Susan Haack, "Epistemological Reflections of an Old Feminist," *Reason Papers* 18 (1993): 31–43.
64 Susan Haack, "Science as Social – Yes and No," in Nelson and Nelson, eds., *Feminism, Science, and the Philosophy of Science*, pp. 79–94.
65 This argument is developed in Longino, *Science as Social Knowledge*, chs. 2 and 3. There I argue that there is a semantic gap between statements describing data and statements describing hypotheses which must be bridged by substantive background assumptions establishing the evidential relevance of the data to hypotheses. The *de re* version of the point is that the facts which we seek to explain and which serve as evidence are different from the facts and processes postulated as explaining or supported by them. Bubble tracks in a compressed gas are different from the particles whose passage is postulated as producing them.
66 For a proposal as to how values identified as feminist might guide feminist epistemological thinking, see Alison Wylie, "Doing Philosophy as a Feminist," *Philosophical Topics* 23, no. 2 (1996): 345–58.
67 See Maria Lugones, "Playfulness, 'World'-Traveling, and Loving Perception," *Hypatia* 2, no. 2 (Summer 1987): 3–19; Kathleen Lennon, "Feminist Epistemology as a Local Epistemology," *Aristotelian Society Proceedings Supplementary Volume* LXXI (1997): 37–54; and Bergin, "Communicating Knowledge Across Epistemic Difference."

Chapter 15

Social Epistemology

Frederick Schmitt

1. Social Epistemology: The Questions

Social epistemology may be defined as the conceptual and normative study of the social dimensions of knowledge. It studies the bearing of social relations, interests, roles, and institutions – what I will term "social conditions" – on the conceptual and normative conditions of knowledge.[1] It differs from the sociology of knowledge in being a conceptual and normative, and not primarily empirical, study, and in limning the necessary and not merely the contingent social conditions of knowledge. The central question of social epistemology is whether, and to what extent, the conditions of knowledge include social conditions. Is knowledge a property of knowers in isolation from their social setting (and in what sense of "isolation"), or does it involve a relation between knowers and their social circumstances? This question can take various forms and admit diverse answers, depending on the kinds of knowers, knowledge, and social relations we ask about.[2]

It is natural to divide social epistemology into three branches: the role of social conditions in individual knowledge; the social organization of cognitive labor; and the nature of collective knowledge. The first branch concerns the knowledge possessed by *individuals* and asks whether social conditions enter into the conditions of individual knowledge. The second branch concerns the *social organization of cognitive labor* among individuals and groups of individuals – that is, the epistemically optimal distribution and profile of cognitive efforts and responsibilities across a population: how ought cognitive tasks, responsibilities, and privileges be distributed among knowers, and in what way does this distribution depend on social relations? The third branch of social epistemology concerns the nature of *collective knowledge*: is knowledge possessed by groups of individuals, communities, or institutions; is such collective knowledge a mere sum of the knowledge of the members of the group, or does it involve more than this, and if so, in what way does the knowledge depend on social relations?

Although these three branches explore diverse issues, they may all be categorized as revolving around the question whether the conditions of knowledge are, in various senses, individualistic or social. Rather than review all three branches, I will focus on the first branch and address the question in social epistemology that has historically received the most attention, the role of testimony in knowledge or justification. This happens to be the question I regard as the most fundamental test of epistemological individualism. By this I mean that if individualism about testimony is defensible, then epistemology will remain in an important sense individualistic; and if it is not defensible, then epistemology will have to be deeply social, whatever view we may take about the questions in other branches of social epistemology. The issue of testimony is therefore an appropriate choice for illustrating social epistemology.

Before turning to the particular issue of testimony, I would like to clarify what is at issue in general between individualism and socialism concerning individual knowledge. There are numerous uncontroversial ways in which individual knowledge is social, and we have not yet reached an interesting dispute between individualism and socialism until we have gotten past these ways. Let me list some of these ways in order to set them aside. It has always been recognized that social conditions *support* knowledge by making perception, memory, and reasoning materially possible. People cannot acquire much knowledge without socially given language. Most knowledge depends for its acquisition on teaching, playing, reading, conversation, and other social activities. And all sorts of human communication can inspire new observations, experiments, and theories. Equally, it has been recognized that social relations can *prevent* us from acquiring knowledge by encumbering us with improper methods and bad ideas or by distracting us from proper methods and good ideas. It has also been conceded, at least since Hume, that social relations – those involved in teaching, received wisdom, common sense, expert authority, and testimony – can *extend* our perceptual faculties in somewhat the way telescopes do, by supplementing our experience vicariously.

Moreover, it is uncontroversial that our common system of epistemic evaluation is social. We learn the concept of knowledge and the standards of epistemic evaluation from others. Epistemic evaluation itself is typically a socially directed act, since we evaluate the cognitive states of others. And epistemic evaluation is able to improve cognition in the way it does only because it operates through a social system of approbation and sanction. It would now be widely conceded that the common system of epistemic evaluation serves key social purposes. For example, it is plausible that the concept of knowledge is employed by us in such a way as to facilitate social goods like the flow of information across individuals, consensus among members of society, and the consequent coordination of behavior in society. Finally, it is widely agreed that the content of epistemic evaluations is intimately related to the cognitive functions of these systems. These uncontroversial points, while significant, may be conceded by the veriest individualist in epistemology. For they do not entail that the conditions of knowledge are themselves social.

To enter the domain of social epistemology, we must consider whether there are reasons for insinuating social factors in the conditions of knowledge or epistemic justification. I will distinguish here three versions of socialism, each with its opposing version of individualism, defined as the negation of socialism. According to the first version, *socialism₁*, social conditions enter into the conditions of justification in a straightforward way:

> The conditions of justification (for at least some kinds of justified beliefs) refer to (or, more weakly, entail) social conditions.[3]

A weaker version of socialism, *socialism₂*, maintains that social conditions enter into the conditions of justification in an indirect, rather than straightforward, way:

> The conditions that *make* a belief justified (for at least some kinds of justified beliefs) include social conditions.

Here the notion of making a belief justified is a formal rather than a causal notion. As I have already emphasized, an individualist of any kind may accept that social conditions can *cause* subjects to acquire justified beliefs. The socialist₂ claims more than this: the conditions of justification are satisfied *in virtue of* some social conditions. On one understanding of "in virtue of," a condition A is satisfied in virtue of a condition B when B realizes A. For example, on a reliabilist account of justification (according to which a belief is justified just in case it results from a reliable belief-forming process), the conditions of justification are realized by the psychological events and psychophysical relations involved in exercising a reliable process. On socialism₂, the conditions of justification are realized by social conditions. Though it is a difficult philosophical problem to say just what it takes for a condition to realize the conditions of justification, I believe that we have an intuitive grasp of the notion of realization. Claiming that the conditions of justification are realized by social conditions is clearly claiming more than that the former conditions are caused by the latter.[4] (A socialist₂ might claim that the conditions of justification are *necessarily* realized by social conditions, or only that they are merely *contingently* so realized. I will advocate only the weaker, contingent version of socialism₂). A final version of socialism, *supervenience socialism*, maintains:

> The conditions of justification (for at least some kinds of justified beliefs) *supervene* on social conditions.

Roughly, the idea is that, in a case of justified belief, there is some social condition such that, if we subtract it from the case while holding other particulars of the case fixed, the belief will no longer be justified.

Socialism₁ clearly entails supervenience socialism and also socialism₂ (both the necessary and the contingent versions), but not conversely. It is a difficult matter to say whether socialism₂ entails supervenience socialism, or vice versa, and I will not attempt to judge the matter here. Rather, I will settle on socialism$_2$ (contingent version) as the version of socialism I wish to advocate in this paper. I do regard the other versions of socialism as plausible as well, but I will not defend them here. To simplify discussion, I will drop the subscript and refer to socialism$_2$ simply as "socialism." And by "individualism," I will mean the negation of socialism$_2$. I will momentarily introduce some more specific versions of individualism, versions which entail individualism$_2$ restricted to the domain of testimonial justification, but rather than introduce further subscripts, I will simply keep these specific versions distinct from individualism$_2$ by attaching qualifiers to them (namely, "weak" and "strong").

2. Testimony: Versions of Individualism

I wish to focus now, and for the remainder of the paper, on one issue that may help us adjudicate between individualism and socialism, the issue of the role of testimony in justification. In due course, I will argue against a version of individualism regarding justification on the basis of testimony (or "testimonial justification," as I will call it). Rejecting this version does not mandate rejecting individualism in favor of socialism, as I have defined them above, since there are other versions of individualism about testimony that would need to be rejected as well. But since the version I will address is, in my view, the most attractive version of individualism about testimony, a successful argument against it gives us good reason to embrace socialism.

The key question regarding testimonial justification is whether we are to conceive of testimony as a mere *causal instrument* in the production of justified belief, one whose role must be approved by prior nontestimonially justified beliefs, or conceive of it instead as a *primary source* of justification in the sense that it supplies justification without any such approval. Does testimony merely extend our perceptually justified belief in somewhat the way a telescope does, as the received view since Hume would have it, by providing new sources of information that must be sanctioned by justified beliefs we already possess? Or is it a source of justified belief independent of perceptually justified belief, one that need not be sanctioned by any perceptually justified beliefs we already possess? Plausibly, someone could be said to be justified in believing that Jupiter has moons by looking through a telescope only if the telescope is a source of information sanctioned by perceptual knowledge the subject already possesses, in the sense that the subject justifiedly believes that the telescope is reliable for such observations, and indeed accepts that Jupiter has moons on the basis of the latter belief about reliability. Is it similarly necessary for testimonially justified belief (e.g., the belief that Jupiter has moons, on the authority of an astronomy text) that one justifiedly believe that the testifier is reliable on the topic and that one hold the belief on the basis of the latter belief about reliability? In this case testimony would be a *secondary*, derivative source of knowledge. By contrast with belief based on telescopic observation, it is plausible that beliefs based on unaided sight can be justified without one's justifiedly believing that one's vision is reliable, or at any rate without basing one's visual belief on the latter belief about the reliability of one's vision. Might one similarly be justified in a belief on testimony without justifiedly believing that the testimony is reliable (or without basing one's testimonial belief on the reliability belief)? In this case, testimony would be a *primary* source of justified belief analogous to sense perception. Here, then, are two very different models of testimonial justification, an individualistic view on which testimonial justification is derivative from perceptual justification and a socialist view on which it is primary. We will look into the relative plausibility of these views. If it should turn out that testimonial justification is primary, then the social conditions of testimonial justification would have to enter into the conditions of justification, in the sense specified above, and socialism as defined above would be vindicated.

Let us distinguish two versions of individualism about testimonial justification. *Strong individualism* is the view that all beliefs must be justified first-hand; no beliefs are justified on testimony. Locke subscribed to the analogous view of testimonial knowledge.[5] Whether applied to justified belief or to knowledge, strong individualism is hard to take seriously, since it rules out my knowledge of my own name, my place of birth, who my parents are, and what country I live in. It also rules out knowledge of propositions people can know only on testimony. If, for example, "the President" is defined as the winner of a national election, then even the President can know that he or she is President only on the basis of the testimony of election judges. Finally, strong individualism excludes knowledge of inductive generalizations – e.g., that grass is generally green and snow is generally white – when an individual's sample is too small for a justified induction to the universal generalization. For in this case, one must depend on testimony for a broad enough sample of grass or snow. Strong individualism therefore has counterintuitive skeptical implications and may well entail a sweeping inductive skepticism.

A more palatable view is *weak individualism*. This view allows that a subject may know or be justified in a belief by testimony. But it maintains that such a belief must be justified on the basis ultimately of perceptually justified or other nontestimonially justified beliefs – i.e., beliefs not themselves justified on the basis of testimony. There are at least three versions of weak individualism. First, the *inductive* version holds that a belief based on testimony (a "testimonial belief," as I will call it) is justified on the basis of the belief that the testimony is trustworthy or reliable, but the latter belief is justified in turn by induction from a first-hand observed correlation between testimonial beliefs of this sort and the truth of the propositions testified to.[6] Second, the *a priori* version proposes an a priori, rather than empirical, justification for testimonial beliefs: my testimonial beliefs are justified by an epistemic parity between my own beliefs and those of others.[7] Third, there is a *coherentist* version of weak individualism, according to which testimonial beliefs are justified in virtue of their coherence with nontestimonially justified beliefs.[8] I will focus here on inductive weak individualism, both because it has been the received view of testimonial justification ever since it was endorsed by Hume, and because I regard it as the most plausible version of weak individualism.

3. Inductive Weak Individualism

As far as I am aware, no one has ever offered a convincing motivation for inductive weak individualism. The view emerged from revision of the epistemic status of testimony in the seventeenth and eighteenth centuries. In the course of the scientific revolution, testimony was gradually elevated from its medieval status as something akin to faith, to a source of justified belief and knowledge. The rise in the status of testimony resulted from its assimilation to perceptual belief, which was also elevated in status but received top billing for its work in the new science. But why was the justification of testimonial belief made derivative from that of perceptual belief, rather than testimony being made a primary source of justification?

The chief motivation for making testimonial justification derivative from perceptual justification was, I suspect, a worry about the reliability of testimony. Testimony was regarded as less reliable than perception, depending as it does on the word of testifiers in addition to the reliability of their perception. Since justification was assumed proportional to reliability, perception was preferred to testimony. To achieve the reliability required for justified belief on testimony, testimonial belief has to be constrained in a way that perceptual belief was not. Accordingly, it was proposed that testimonial belief must be justified on the basis of first-hand perceptually justified beliefs. There was, in addition to this worry about the reliability of testimony, a related worry that testimony differs from perception in needing to be monitored if it is to achieve the reliability required for justified belief. In general, subjects need to check the reliability of their sources if they are to acquire true beliefs by testimony. They need not generally check the reliability of perception in order to acquire true perceptual beliefs.

These points in favor of an asymmetry between perception and testimony no longer carry conviction. We have come to view perception as less reliable than it was viewed as in the seventeenth century, while social strictures on communication and publication have increased the reliability of testimony, at least in institutional and scientific settings. Nor is it clear that perception needs less monitoring than testimony, or that monitoring must be promoted by a concept of justification that imposes a requirement of monitoring. In short, the motivation for weak individualism is wanting.

I would like now to turn from the motivation for inductive weak individualism to an objection to the view.[9] The objection I have in mind is the one I regard as most persuasive: that we have too little first-hand experience to provide a nontestimonial basis for an induction to the reliability of testimony in all instances in which testimonial belief is intuitively justified. This is clearly the case for young children, but it is arguably true for older children and adults as well. People do not generally check the truth of testimonial reports by their own first-hand experience, and indeed they lack the time and resources to check more than a tiny fraction of such reports. Consequently, for most if not all kinds of testimonial reports, people have only a very slim basis of first-hand perceptually justified beliefs from which to infer the reliability of the reports of a kind. Of course, people do acquire a broader basis for an induction to the reliability of testimony of various kinds as they develop cognitively and gain greater experience. But their justification for the premises of such inductions is in general not merely experiential but testimonial as well. In the course of early education, and throughout schooling, people accept the testimony of their parents, caretakers, and teachers without having much basis for ascribing reliability to their testimony beyond the corroboration of a few other adults and the texts for their classes. And they have little first-hand basis for trusting this corroborating testimony. In the typical case of corroboration by a text, the teacher vouches for the text. Of course, the school vouches for the teacher, and it is plausible that the child is justified in believing that the school chooses teachers whose testimony is reliable. But on what basis is the child justified in believing this? Not by a first-hand check on the reliability of the teachers' testimony. Typically, parents or caretakers vouch for the school. Of course children acquire some inductive basis for believing in the reliability of parents' or caretakers' testimony, but they are able to check first-hand only a miniscule fraction of the propositions they accept from their parents and precious few claims that their parents make for the reliability of any other people. In the end, the child's justification for belief in the reliability of teachers' testimony rests on trust of parents.

To be sure, this radical dependence on testimony is reduced in the course of further experience, but it is never eliminated. For most testimony, there is at best a slim first-hand basis for an induction to the reliability of the testimony. We rely on first-hand experience to check the reliability of testimony, but judgments based on first-hand experience are typically also based in part on testimony. A single example will have to suffice for illustration here, though I believe that many different sorts of examples can be mustered in support of the same point. I rely on taxi drivers to take me to my destination; I am justified in believing what the taxi drivers tell me about street locations. And I am justified in believing this in part because they have usually gotten me to my destination. This is as close as I will come to cobbling together even a modest first-hand basis for an induction to the reliability of the testimony of taxi drivers. But what justifies me in believing that taxi drivers have usually gotten me to my destination? I am justified in believing this only because I am justified in believing that my map is accurate, that the street signs I see accurately name their streets, that my hosts really live in the house I am visiting, as they claim to, that the airline pilots accurately announce the cities at which I take myself to have arrived, and so on – all beliefs which are justified at least in part on testimony. My belief in the reliability of the testimony sometimes has what passes for a first-hand inductive basis, but this passing first-hand basis is itself indebted to testimony for its justification.

The inductive weak individualist might hope to trace my justification for these beliefs to my first-hand experience. It might be proposed, for example, that

I am justified in believing that the airline pilots accurately announce destinations, on the basis of my justified belief that airline pilots are able to judge their destinations accurately (since the commercial success of the airline depends on such judgments, and the airline is commercially successful), and that they have a vested interest in reporting these destinations to passengers (since the commercial success of the airline depends on its passengers having accurate beliefs about destinations). But again, what justifies me in believing that pilots are able to judge their destinations accurately, that the airline is commercially successful, etc.? It would seem that I am justified in believing these propositions only on the basis (in part) of testimony.

The inductive weak individualist might propose that my belief that the testimony of airline pilots on destinations (or for that matter, of taxi drivers on street location) is accurate could be justified on the basis of a justified generalization like the following: the testimony of experts tends to be reliable on the topics of their expertise. And one might further propose that my belief in this generalization could be based on *first-hand* justified beliefs about the reliability of samples of expert testimony. But do I have first-hand reason to accept the reliability of more than a tiny sample of expert testimony (namely, the testimony of those in my own field of expertise)? Alternatively, one might propose that my belief in the generalization that the testimony of experts tends to be reliable on the topics of their expertise is justified on the basis of the testimony of various people about the reliability of expert testimony, and these are people whose reliability on the topic of the reliability of expert testimony I have first-hand reason to accept. But this alternative succumbs to the same difficulty as the preceding. I have little first-hand basis for ascribing to anyone reliability on the topic of the reliability of expert testimony. It might be suggested that my belief that others are reliable on the reliability of expert testimony is justified on the basis of a belief that others are reliable on other topics. But while I may have a first-hand basis for ascribing reliability on some topics to some individuals (family members, colleagues), the number of such individuals is small; their reliability on these topics lends slim support to their reliability on the reliability of expert testimony; and their reliability on the reliability of expert testimony provides only modest support for the reliability of others on the reliability of expert testimony. In sum, I would seem to have little first-hand basis for ascribing reliability to airline pilots on destinations or taxi drivers on street locations.

Reflection on examples like this makes a *prima facie* case that, for many if not most testimonial beliefs that are intuitively justified, people lack a broad ultimately first-hand justified basis for an induction to the reliability of the testimony.[10] There is, however, one important reply to inferring from this result the conclusion that inductive weak individualism is mistaken. This reply deserves careful consideration, and since it leads on to several fundamental issues I want to take up later, I will discuss it at length. I have in mind the point that induction does *not* require a large number of confirming instances in order to be justifying. If a justifying induction to the reliability of testimony requires only a small number of confirming instances, then it is reasonable to hope that we have enough first-hand justified premises to make an induction to the reliability of the testimony, and inductive weak individualism will be vindicated. To return to the example of the taxi driver, I have first-hand justification that taxi drivers have delivered me to my house on several occasions. My beliefs to this effect are arguably first-hand justified. If I can infer from this small sample to the reliability of taxi drivers' testimony on other occasions, then I have a justifying induction to the conclusion of reliability that is based on first-hand justified beliefs.

How persuasive is this response on behalf of inductive weak individualism? It will be admitted by everyone that an induction from a single case *can* in certain circumstances be justifying. For example, we need only examine the melting point of one sample of copper to confirm the melting point of copper in general. But arguably, this inference is justifying only because we are already justified in believing that the melting point of a kind of metal is constant across its instances. If we have no such justified background belief, then it is no longer clear that we can infer from a single sample of copper to the generalization; we may need numerous instances.

Now, it is possible to take a stand here and insist that single-case or small-sample inductions are justifying even in the absence of such background beliefs, if we project the right properties. Hilary Kornblith has urged that small-sample inductions are sometimes justifying. For inferences are justifying when they are reliable (i.e., Kornblith assumes reliabilism about inductive justification), and small-sample inductions are reliable when the properties projected are natural kind properties.[11] Natural kind properties suffice for reliability, on Kornblith's view, because natural kinds are homeostatic clusters of properties – i.e., stable or self-maintaining clusters of properties that are well correlated with one another. Because properties belonging to a natural kind are well correlated with one another, one can infer reliably from the correlation of natural kind properties in a small sample of the kind to a *general* correlation of those properties. In Kornblith's view, a justifying induction to the general correlation does not require that one already believe justifiedly that these properties are natural kind properties or that the instances in the induction are samples of a natural kind. All that is required for the justification of the generalization is that the samples belong to a natural kind and the properties belong to the homeostatic cluster that constitutes the kind. This is sufficient to ensure the reliability of the induction. And, Kornblith assumes, the reliability of the induction is sufficient to make it a justifying induction.

If what Kornblith says here is correct, the question arises whether something like his proposal might not apply to *testimonial belief*. Could testimonial belief be justified on the basis of a small-sample induction to the reliability of testimony, an induction that is justifying because it is reliable despite the small sample? If so, the inductive weak individualist could appeal to this proposal to defend the view against the small-sample objection to the inductive justification of testimonial beliefs. The proposal is to treat the properties projected in a small-sample induction to the reliability of testimony analogously to natural kind properties projected in small-sample inductions, so that a small-sample induction to reliability can be similarly justifying. The key feature of natural kind properties from a reliabilist standpoint – the feature which makes an induction projecting these features from a small sample of the kind reliable – is *their being well correlated*. What is crucial for an analogy between small-sample inductions to the reliability of testimony and small-sample natural kind induction, then, is that the properties projected in a small-sample induction to the reliability of testimony be well correlated. In other words, people must select testimony on the basis of properties of the testimony that are well correlated with reliability on the subject matter of the testimony. The child, for example, must select the testimony of teachers on the basis of parental reference, or on the basis of the teachers' reputation, accreditation, or institutional status associated with reliability on the testimonial subject matter. If children believe what parents say about safety, what police officers say about crime, classroom teachers about arithmetic, taxi drivers about the location of streets, doctors and nurses about health, and so on, then they are selecting properties on which to project reliably to the conclusion of the reliability of the testimony. Their inductions will be reliable on the basis of small samples testing the truth of such testimony. The proposal, then, is that small-sample induction will be reliable if children select testimony in this way, and thus testimonial belief can be justified by a small-sample induction to the reliability of testimony. If this proposal is correct, then inductive weak individualism may surmount the small-sample objection.

This is an interesting defense of inductive weak individualism, but it faces a significant problem. It is not very plausible to suppose, as Kornblith does, that a small-sample induction will be justifying just because it projects on well-correlated natural kind properties. Reliability of the sort to which Kornblith appeals is not plausibly sufficient for justification. Suppose a subject happens luckily to select a small sample of the same natural kind without realizing that these are kind members, and happens to select well-correlated properties of the sample that are natural kind properties without realizing that these are kind properties. This subject will inductively generalize in a way that is in some sense reliable: the conditional probability of the generalization given the premises will be high. But is this the kind of reliability relevant to justification? To see the problem, reflect on what we would say about a subject who had arbitrarily but luckily picked two well-correlated properties from a huge random collection of properties and then performed an induction on a small sample to the generalization that the properties are correlated. I do not think we would want to allow this induction to be justifying. But then it seems that we should deny that a small-sample induction from well-correlated natural kind properties will necessarily be justifying even when reliable. It follows that simple reliabilism needs qualification: not just any reliable induction is justifying; not just any induction from a small sample on well-correlated properties is justifying.

What, then, is required for a justifying induction beyond selecting the samples and well-correlated properties belonging to a natural kind? It seems that the selection of the small natural kind sample and properties must itself result from a *nonaccidental selection process.* Kornblith may well have something like this in mind. Indeed, it is possible that he chooses natural kind properties as the properties on which small-sample inductions are justifying, rather than arbitrary pairs of well-correlated properties (which, after all, afford reliability just as well), precisely because it is plausible to suppose that we *do* nonaccidentally select natural kind samples and properties (while selecting pairs of well-correlated properties outside of natural kinds is in general an accidental affair). In other words, Kornblith may prefer small-sample induction on natural kinds to small-sample induction on arbitrary well-correlated properties because he assumes that a nonaccidental selection process is necessary for justification. Let us adopt the obvious account of "nonaccidental selection process": process that tends to lead to the selection of reliable processes for exercise. Presumably, in the case of induction, this will be a process that tends to lead to the selection of reliable inductions. (Of course, the reliability of an induction will vary with sample size and with how well correlated the projected properties are.)

When "nonaccidental selection process" is so understood, adding to reliabilism the requirement of a nonaccidental selection process yields a two-tiered reliabilism that resembles to some extent the two-tiered reliabilism of Alvin Goldman in *Epistemology and Cognition*.[12] According to Goldman's view, there is a distinction between *acquired belief-forming methods* (e.g., algorithms for computing sums) and *native belief-forming processes* (e.g., naive perceptual processes and enumerative induction). A native process is one that is not acquired by learning. Native processes are justifying if reliable, but in the case of acquired methods, reliability does not suffice for justification; it matters how the method was acquired. A reliable acquired method will be justifying only if selected by a *proper method-selecting second-order process.* Goldman suggests that a proper method-selecting process must be metareliable: it must tend to select reliable methods.

Now, it is possible to object to Goldman's two-tiered account on various grounds. I have elsewhere objected to requiring a metareliable selection process for all justifying acquired methods, for reasons I cannot go into here (but see section 5 below).[13] My point about small-sample induction, however, poses the converse objection to Goldman's account: it appears that we must require a metareliable selection process not just for *acquired methods,* but for some *native processes* as well. In particular, a native process of small-sample induction on well-correlated properties is not justifying, despite its reliability, unless the sample and the properties have been selected by a process that tends to give rise to reliable inductions. Presumably, a process can be native in being unlearned, even though it is selected for exercise. (As I will observe below, the requirement of a metareliable selection process for these cases could be reconciled with a simple reliabilism if the selection process were fused in the right way with the selected methods and processes to make a single process that is reliable just in case the selection process is metareliable and the selected method or process is reliable.)

The requirement of a metareliable selection process is satisfied for small-sample inductions precisely because we do choose to perform inductions on natural kinds. Even young children employ a metareliable selection process when they go about their small-sample inductions. For, as Kornblith has argued, they select samples and properties in such a way that their small-sample inductions tend to be reliable. That is because they tend to select samples from the same natural kind and they tend to project properties that belong to the same natural kind, and inductions on such samples and properties tend to be reliable because the properties tend to be well-correlated and the samples sensitive to the general correlation of the properties. Relying on results of recent developmental and cognitive psychology, Kornblith has assembled a probative empirical case in favor of these points. There is a case that young children prefer to categorize objects by natural kind membership, rather than by superficial features. There is also evidence that people sample objects using a strategy, *focused sampling*, that enhances the chance that they will take their samples from the same natural kind when they perform an induction. In focused sampling, objects are examined for properties, and an object is more likely to be examined for further properties if it has properties which figure in covariation hypotheses that have proven successful. If properties P and Q have been discovered to covary in the sample searched, then objects having P and those having Q are more likely to be examined for further properties. In cases where there are more than two covarying properties, this strategy increases the rate of detection of covariation over random sampling of objects – an effect called *clustered feature facilitation*. For this reason, it increases the rate of detection of natural kinds, since we detect natural kinds by detecting clusters of covarying properties. At the same time, focused sampling increases the likelihood that objects in a sample on which an induction is performed will belong to the same natural kind, since the sampled objects are more likely to possess covarying properties belonging to a cluster. It also increases the likelihood that the properties on which an induction is performed will belong to the same natural kind. In short, there is evidence that inductions are selected by a selection process that is itself metareliable in the sense required by the two-tiered view we are now considering. Kornblith does not actually discuss the question of a metareliable selection process and may not view it as necessary for justification, but in any event his evidence for our capacity for successful induction is equally evidence that our inductions satisfy the requirement of a metareliable selection process.

Where does this leave the analogy between testimonial justification and small-sample induction, and how does the point we have made bear on the success of a response to the small-sample objection to inductive weak individualism? Well, if the analogy is good, then a small-sample induction to the reliability of testimony is subject to the same requirements as a small-sample induction on natural kind properties. The induction must be reliable – the property of the testimony on which the induction is based (e.g., taxi drivers on street location) must correlate well with the reliability of testimony that has the property – and the induction must be selected by a metareliable selection process. The latter condition requires that the property of the testimony be selected by a process that tends to select properties well correlated with the reliability of testimony that has the property.

The analogy will establish that a small-sample induction to the reliability of testimony is justifying if these conditions hold. However, appeal to the analogy requires the inductive weak individualist to admit that induction is not sufficient for justification; the induction must be selected by a metareliable process.

The question concerning the success of the response to the small-sample objection to inductive weak individualism is thus whether small-sample inductions to the reliability of testimony are selected by a metareliable process. Unfortunately for the inductive weak individualist, the answer appears to be No. More accurately, the answer is No if the conditions of justification (precisely, what makes the conditions of justification satisfied) are understood in the individualistic spirit of inductive weak individualism. The empirical evidence in favor of a metareliable selection process for natural kind inductions does not support a similar metareliable selection process for testimonial reliability inductions. To be sure, the properties in the testimonial reliability inductions could be called natural kind properties. The property of being the testimony of a taxi driver on street location does correlate with the reliability of testimony having that property (and perhaps this is even a homeostatic property cluster). But despite this, focused sampling could not possibly speed the detection of this kind (or of testimonial kinds in general) or increase (over random sampling) the likelihood of performing inductions on samples of this kind or on the two properties here. For focused sampling can do these things only when the natural kind is deeper than two properties. And this is not so in the case of the properties involved in testimony. Moreover, the properties P and Q that are sampled in focused sampling must be *independent* properties if focused sampling is to help. But in the case of the properties involved in testimony, this is not so. Let P be the property of being the testimony of a taxi driver on street location and Q be the property of testimony's tending to be true when it is the testimony of a taxi driver on street location. These properties are not independent in the required way. For to sample further objects for Q is nothing different from sampling for P and checking the reliability of the testimony sampled. In short, the empirical case in favor of a metareliable selection process for natural kind inductions does not carry over to testimonial reliability inductions.

Now, I would not deny that *some* sort of metareliable selection process is involved in selecting some small-sample inductions to the reliability of testimony. But this selection process is a *social* process, and thus what makes the conditions of justification satisfied is a social condition – in violation of individualism, as I defined it at the outset of this paper. It is plausible to suppose that people often select testimony (or testimonial uptake processes) in a metareliable way (and it is also plausible that they similarly often metareliably select small-sample inductions to the reliability of testifiers). But as the objection to inductive weak individualism shows, not all testimonial justification can be traced to selecting testimony by relying on a belief in the reliability of the testimony based on first-hand justified beliefs. Mature selection processes employing beliefs about the reliability of testimony are possible only because of a prior accumulation of testimonial beliefs that result from processes not selected by an induction to the reliability of testimony based on first-hand justified beliefs.

What sort of selection process, then, selects these prior testimonial beliefs? The selection process in young children is most naturally understood as a *social* process of learning. Children are so constituted psychologically that they tend to prefer their caretakers or parents as sources of information, and also as sources of information about where to get information. The process of selecting testimony is a social process in which the child's disposition to prefer caretakers as sources of information causes the child to defer to the caretaker's choices of testimonial sources for the child. And this social selection process is metareliable. For parents tend to tell children the truth and to refer them to reliable authorities on various topics – maps on geography, street signs on street location, dictionaries on word meanings, teachers on facts, police officers on crime, taxi drivers on street location, and so on. Parents have a powerful practical incentive to provide their children with true information and to refer them to reliable testifiers. The selection processes here involve a system in which the child identifies, by certain incidental traits, its caretakers, who in turn choose testimony for the child. Taken in isolation from this social setting, the young child has no resources to select reliable testimony. And what holds for selecting testimony also goes for selecting inductions by selecting the samples or properties on which to perform inductions to the reliability of testimony. But the social system in which children defer to caretakers does steer the child to reliable testimony and reliable inductions. If we are allowed to expand the selection processes from the psychological mechanisms in individuals that Kornblith evidently has in mind – focused sampling – to the social mechanisms of deference by which culture is transmitted, then there are metareliable processes that select the child's inductions to the reliability of testimony.[14]

It is plausible that the social selection process operative in children also operates in adults, albeit less forcefully and with more frequent intentional preemption. Adults tend to rely less critically on the testimony of friends, relatives, and associates than on that of others. Of course adults are often able to select testimony without having to rely on the referrals of others, but, as we have argued, the premises adults use to judge the reliability of testimony derive largely from the testimony accepted as a result of the social selection process.

Returning now to the question whether the inductive weak individualist may embrace small-sample inductions as justifying and in this way respond to the small-sample objection, the answer would appear to be No. True, a reliabilism that requires a metareliable selection process allows small-sample inductions to be justifying. But the inductive weak individualist is in no position to accept this requirement. For it requires admitting that what makes the conditions of justification satisfied includes a social condition – namely, the working of a social process that selects the samples and properties for the induction to the reliability of testimony. And that is inimical to individualism.

Now, I have said that the selection process here is most *naturally* understood as a social process, and I prefer to theorize about the conditions of justification using the most natural descriptions of the processes involved. At the same time, I would not deny that the selection process whereby children select testifiers (devolving from their tendency to believe caretakers) *could* be described as an *intraindividual psychological process* (namely, as gullibility in the presence of certain incidental personal traits of caretakers). And one might object that on this understanding, what makes the conditions of justification satisfied is *not* a social condition. But this objection is mistaken. First, what makes the process *metareliable* is a social arrangement in which the child participates. (This point is analogous to the point that in the case of perceptual justification, what makes the process reliable is an external relation between the process and the environment; consequently, what makes the conditions of justification satisfied, according to reliabilism, is more than a merely internal, psychological condition.) Second, even if the selection process is understood as an intraindividual psychological process of gullible acceptance, the very identification of this process as the epistemically relevant selection process would seem to require adverting to social conditions: what tells us to look at gullibility in the presence of certain traits of caretakers is nothing other than the difference between caretakers and others as sources of information for children. The conditions of process individuation and the related matter of the identification of epistemically relevant selection processes in particular cases are social conditions. For these two reasons, even if we describe the selection process individualistically, what makes the conditions of justification satisfied are social conditions. And this is contrary to individualism, hence unavailable to the inductive weak individualist.

Thus, the inductive weak individualist does not in the end have an adequate defense from the small-sample objection. It is possible to insist, as the inductive weak individualist does, that all testimonial justification depends on a justifying induction to the reliability of the testimony, but this insistence comes at the cost of admitting the further requirement of a metareliable selection process and hence a nonindividualistic element in the conditions of justification. We should therefore reject inductive weak individualism. My own view is that it is plausible enough that much mature testimonial justification depends on an induction to the reliability of the testimony, and such inductions can be small-sample inductions. But a metareliable selection process is typically needed for the small-sample inductions. And when an induction is needed, the testimonial belief need not be *based on* the induction to the reliability of the testimony; the latter is part of the business of *monitoring* testimony for reliability – itself a process of selecting the process that yields the testimonial belief.

I have defended the small-sample objection to inductive weak individualism. While the objection may fall short of decisive, I believe it gives us some reason to reject the view. Admittedly, the objection is specific to inductive weak individualism and does not strike down other versions of weak individualism about testimonial justification (such as a priori or coherentist weak individualism); still less does it rule out versions of individualism weaker than weak individualism (such as a holistic coherentism). I will not attempt any objection to these other versions of individualism here, but I would like to note that if what I have said about the need for a metareliable selection process in cases of inductive justification, and about the social character of such a process, is correct, then individualism (and supervenience individualism as well) are mistaken. However this may be, I believe we have said enough to motivate taking seriously socialist alternatives to individualism about testimonial justification.

4. Versions of Socialism: Transindividual Reasons

There are several socialist positions on testimonial justification that deserve serious consideration: *the testimonial rules account, the transindividual reasons account, contextual reliabilism,* and *a virtue-theoretic account of testimonial justification.* These four positions take different approaches to testimonial justification, though, in my view, they are, formulated abstractly enough, logically consistent with one another. I will say nothing here about the first or fourth position, a bit about the second, and I will develop the third position more fully.[15]

On the *transindividual reasons* account, a belief p that is justified on the testimony of a certain testifier T is justified on the basis of reasons for p *possessed by T*. This approach is strongly externalist in entailing that a subject is justified in believing p on testimony only if there really is a testifier and the testifier's reasons for p are sufficient to make the belief p justified (for the testifier or for the subject – the account could impose either condition). The subject's belief p is based on the testifier's reasons for p. Within the transindividual reasons approach, there are two different (but mutually consistent) models of the basing relation between the testifier's reasons for p and the subject's belief p. The basing relation could be modeled on *inference*: the relation could be conceived as involving inference from the reason to the belief. That is, the subject could be conceived as related to the testifier in such a way that the belief p is inferred from the testifier's reasons for p. Alternatively, the relation could be modeled on *remote memorial basing*: the relation could be conceived as analogous to the relation that obtains when a belief is based on reasons no longer remembered. Just as beliefs based on memory are based (on one view, at least) on the reasons for which they were originally believed, even when these reasons have been forgotten, so testimonial beliefs might be said to be based on the testifier's reasons, even though these reasons are not possessed by the subject. I said that these two models – an inferential relation and remote memorial basing – are consistent because it would be possible to conceive of remote memorial basing as inferential, albeit an extremely slow inference from reasons now forgotten to the current belief. One could thus model transindividual testimonial justification on both inferential justification and remote memorial justification.

There is, however, a powerful objection to the transindividual reasons account. The account is overly externalist in entailing that a testimonial belief is justified only if there are testimonial reasons that justify the target proposition for the testifier or for the subject. It seems possible for a subject's testimonial belief to be justified even when the testifier's reasons do *not* justify the belief – indeed, even when there are *no* testimonial reasons, and even when there is no testifier. To see this, begin with a paradigmatic case of testimonial justification: a doctor performs a thorough test to determine whether you have strep throat and tells you that it's certain that you do; you then believe that you have strep throat on the basis of the doctor's testimony. Now modify the case in such a way that it merely *appears* to you that the test is thorough; in reality the doctor is irresponsibly guessing and saying that the result is certain. Alternatively, modify the case even further, so that it merely appears to you that the doctor is performing the test when in fact he is faking its performance. We might even imagine a case in which the doctor appears to be performing the test, but in fact you are just hallucinating the whole thing: there is no test, or even a doctor. On the transindividual reasons account, your belief in either of these modified cases fails to be justified. But intuitively your belief is (at least in the first modified case and perhaps in the second as well) as justified as in the paradigmatic case. Of course, the proponent of the transindividual reasons account might refuse to call your belief in these cases a *testimonial* belief and might attempt to skirt the objection by pointing out that the transindividual reasons account is an account only of the justification of *testimonial* beliefs, not of beliefs of other kinds. In the case of hallucination, the doctor clearly does not testify, since there is no doctor, and one might accordingly deny that you believe what you do on the basis of testimony. But this response to the objection is ineffective. For even if these modified cases are not cases of testimonial belief, what makes your belief justified in each case is arguably the same as what makes your belief justified in the paradigmatic case. Thus, the transindividual reasons account gives the wrong explanation of what makes your belief justified in the paradigmatic case. The objection does not turn on whether we call your belief a testimonial belief. It depends only on the point that what makes your belief justified in the modified cases is also what makes your belief justified in the paradigmatic case. Of course, the belief might in all these cases be justified on the basis of an induction from first-hand premises, but suppose not. Then there is a nonindividualist justification of the belief, but this justification does not depend on transindividual reasons. So testimonial justification in the paradigmatic case cannot depend on transindividual reasons either. The requirement of transindividual reasons is too externalist.[16]

To handle the case of hallucinated testimony, the proponent of transindividual reasons could retreat to the idea that what makes the belief justified on the basis of testimony is the mere appearance of testimony, not its actuality: testimonial justification requires only *virtual* transindividual reasons, not actual ones. However, this virtualist view entails individualism about testimonial justification. To avoid individualism, the proponent of transindividual reasons could retreat to a different view: that what makes the belief justified in the case of hallucination is virtual testimony, but what makes it justified in ordinary cases is actual testimony.

I do not find these weakened versions of the transindividual reasons account attractive, but I will not assess them here.

5. Contextual Reliabilism

We turn now to socialist reliabilist approaches to testimonial justification. My primary interest here will be to sketch several alternative reliabilist accounts and ask which best handles our intuitions about cases. According to reliabilism, a belief is justified just when it results from a reliable belief-forming process. Such an account can easily be modified so that it is consistent with inductive weak individualism by requiring that the reliable process that justifies testimonial belief involve an induction to the reliability of testimony from ultimately first-hand justified premises. There is, however, nothing in reliabilism that mandates that premises be *first-hand* justified, as weak individualism requires. Indeed, there is nothing in it that requires the process to be a *psychological* process in the subject. Thus, reliabilism equally lends itself to a nonindividualistic account of testimonial justification. I can think of three interestingly different nonindividualistic versions of reliabilism. I will discuss these in turn.

1. Transindividual process reliabilism

This is a reliabilist analogue of the transindividual reasons approach. According to this account, testimonial beliefs are justified when they result from a transindividual process of communication between the testifier and the subject, involving testimonial transmission and uptake, and this process is justifying because it is reliable. Of course testimonial communication may be unreliable for a variety of reasons: the testifier may lack good reason for the proposition, the testifier may be deceptive, and the communication channel may be noisy, giving rise to miscommunication. But according to this account, when the process is reliable, the testimonial belief that results is justified.

Unfortunately, this account does inherit the drawback of the transindividual reasons account: it is overly externalist. It is not quite as externalist as the transindividual reasons account is. For example, it does not clearly entail, as the transindividual reasons account does, that the testifier's reason must be justifying for the testifier (or for the subject), and that is perhaps a merit of the account, since it is not obvious that this must be so. In fact, the account does not clearly entail even that the testifier must *have* a reason for the proposition. Whether the testifier must have a reason and whether the reason must be justifying for the testifier (or for the subject) will depend on what it takes for testimonial communication to be reliable. Certainly if the testifier has a justifying reason for the proposition, that will generally increase the chance that the proposition is true. But it does not follow that having a justifying reason is necessary for reliability. It could be that testimonial processes are individuated in such a way that testimony without justifying reasons is input to a process that is reliable because its output generally includes testimonial beliefs based on testimony accompanied by justifying reasons, and these beliefs are true with sufficient frequency to make the process reliable. Even if this is so, however, transindividual process reliabilism will still be too externalist. For it requires a communication between the testifier and the subject, and that is too strong a requirement, if the examples we gave earlier against the transindividual reasons account have force. So I am inclined to move on to other versions of reliabilism.

2. *Contextual intraindividual process reliabilism*

On this account, a justified testimonial belief need not result from a transindividual communication process; it need only result from a reliable intraindividual psychological process – presumably a process of testimonial uptake. In this way, the account avoids the excessive externalism of transindividual process reliabilism: it does not entail that justified testimonial belief must result from a communication process. How does the account propose to explain the justification of testimonial beliefs when the individual does not possess a first-hand basis for the beliefs? It explains the justification of these beliefs by appeal to their resulting from intraindividual processes of testimonial uptake that are reliable because social and psychological conditions make people apt to speak the truth in certain circumstances, and social and psychological conditions make it possible for people to exploit this fact in their testimonial beliefs in such a way as to arrive generally at true beliefs. The view is socialist because what makes the intraindividual process reliable is a social condition.

As I suggested earlier in our discussion of small-sample induction, this socially dependent reliability pertains even to young children, who are luckily gullible in just the right way: they are psychologically so constituted as to tend to believe those who are most likely to tell them the truth. Young children believe what their parents and teachers tell them, and what they believe as a result of this tends to be true. The belief-forming process of uptake from caretakers is not an inductive one (at least, it does not involve large-sample inductions). Rather, human psychology inclines young children to trust their caretakers more than they trust others (their peers, for example). Their caretakers have a vested interest in raising children to believe the truth and accordingly tell children what they (the caretakers) believe to be true on relevant topics. Assuming that these beliefs are generally true, it follows that the process that inclines children to believe their caretakers is a reliable one. The reliability of the process of believing caretakers is a consequence of the social structure in which young children learn.

There are various points to make in qualification and defense of these suggestions. It is true that young children sometimes believe their peers, and it cannot be denied that they have some natural inclination to do so – part of the phenomenon of peer pressure. But on the whole, the inclination to believe peers is overridden in young children by the inclination to believe caretakers. (This may not be true of teenagers, but by the time of adolescence, children have already arrived at their larger picture of the world, and most of their beliefs are fixed.) Beliefs based on peer testimony are not in general justified (or not as justified as those based on caretaker testimony). The reason such beliefs are not justified, according to the present account, is that the process that leads to them is not reliable (or at any rate, not as reliable as that which leads to beliefs on caretaker testimony).

It is true, too, that caretakers occasionally have an interest in deceiving children, but for the most part, these deceptions are intended to be temporary (e.g., belief in Santa Claus), to be corrected later either by further testimony or by first-hand discovery. Again, caretakers are bound to believe a good deal that is false, and the preservation of social relations depends on and reinforces false belief (e.g., belief in the generosity of others). Moreover, caretakers are concerned to instill in their charges common and consensual beliefs, as much as they are concerned to instill true beliefs. Nevertheless, with some exceptions, these consensual beliefs would not be as valuable as caretakers assume them to be if they were not also true. And it is plausible that on the whole caretakers select the most probable beliefs to instill in young children, and these beliefs are generally true.

Clearly, the explanations offered by this reliabilist account hang on tricky matters of the individuation of processes. If the process that leads children to believe their peers is counted as the *same* process as the one that leads children to believe their caretakers, then the account will not be able to distinguish beliefs on the testimony of peers from beliefs on caretaker testimony with respect to justification, since beliefs that result from the same process are, on reliabilism, equally justified or unjustified. It is possible that the two processes – uptake from peers and uptake from caretakers – are *psychologically* different, and this psychological difference could be relevant to the epistemic individuation of processes. However, it is likely that contextual differences will also be highly significant for individuation. Looking to contextual differences, it is quite possible that the two processes may be distinguished on the contextual ground that an individuation of processes follows natural divisions along the lines of frequency of truths in the outputs of the processes, and there is such a natural division here, between the testimony of caretakers, with its high frequency of truths, and that of peers, with its low frequency of truths.[17]

Does contextual intraindividual process reliabilism avoid the problem with virtual testimony that confronted transindividual reliabilism? I think it does. In our earlier case of virtual testimony, you believe that you have strep throat on the apparent testimony of a doctor, but in fact there is no testimonial reason or even a testifier. The contextual intraindividual process reliabilist could allow that you are justified on the ground that your virtual testimonial belief is produced by the same intraindividual process that operates when there is uptake of actual testimony, and this process is reliable across its entire output. Assimilating virtual testimonial justification to actual testimonial justification in this way has the advantage over transindividual process reliabilism of permitting virtual testimonial belief to be justified while recognizing that what makes virtual testimonial belief justified is the same as what makes actual testimonial belief justified – the reliability of the intraindividual process.

3. *Contextual metareliabilism*

My favorite way of accounting for testimonial justification is contextual metareliabilism. This view turns on an idea that emerged in our discussion of small-sample induction chez Kornblith. The idea bears some resemblance to the contextual intraindividual process reliabilism just scouted. When we discussed Kornblith's proposal, we focused on the question whether small-sample induction could be justifying, and we observed that even if small-sample induction is reliable, it would be implausible to say that it's sufficient for justification: justification requires in addition a metareliable selection process, one that tends to choose reliable inductions. The same would seem to hold for *noninductive* testimonial justification. Young children are gullible, but they are still selective in the testimony they accept, preferring caretakers to peers as sources of testimony. We could view them as selecting from among various processes that form testimonial beliefs, individuated in the manner of contextual intraindividual process reliabilism. We could then say that the justification of these beliefs requires, not the reliability of the processes they exercise, but rather the *metareliability* of this selection process. What makes the selection process metareliable is of course the fact that young children tend to select testifiers who are motivated to tell them the truth and possess the resources to succeed in doing so. (A parallel suggestion could be made about mature testimonial belief.) Contextual metareliabilism, then, says that a belief is justified just when it results from a belief-forming process that is selected by a metareliable selection process. We could view the selection process as an *intraindividual* psychological process, as we suggested earlier in our discussion of Kornblith. But it would still be a process that is metareliable because of social conditions. Or we could view the selection process as a social process. Either way, there is a social element in the account.

Contextual metareliabilism differs from contextual intraindividual process reliabilism in one important respect (at least if we individuate processes as we have been doing), and this difference between the two views favors contextual metareliabilism. Satisfying contextual intraindividual process reliabilism does entail satisfying contextual metareliabilism, but the converse does not hold.

A belief that satisfies contextual intraindividual process reliabilism must satisfy contextual metareliabilism. There are two reasons for this. First, there is a contingent reason. A belief that satisfies contextual intraindividual process reliabilism results from a process that is reliable in context. The intraindividual psychological process is reliable because social conditions make it so. In the case of juvenile testimonial belief, the child's gullibility in the presence of people with the features caretakers have leads to reliable uptake processes because caretakers tend to refer children to sources who give reliable testimony. Reliable intraindividual psychological uptake processes are, as a matter of contingent social and psychological fact, selected by social conditions. We can view these social conditions as metareliable selection processes. Thus, satisfying contextual intraindividual process reliabilism entails satisfying contextual metareliabilism.

There is a second, deeper, formal reason why a belief that satisfies contextual intraindividual process reliabilism must also satisfy contextual metareliabilism. If a belief satisfies contextual intraindividual process reliabilism, then it results from a reliable process of uptake. But a process of uptake does not even count as reliable unless it results from a metareliable selection process. To take the case of juvenile testimonial belief again, the child can accidentally and luckily choose to believe a testifier who happens to be reliable, but this does not count as exercising a reliable process of uptake unless the choice of testifier results from caretaker referral and the reliability of the choice of testifier is explained by the metareliability of such referral. The reliability of the testifier is not inherited by the uptake process unless the testifier is chosen in virtue of the metareliable selection process. So, again, and this time for a formal reason, contextual intraindividual process reliabilism entails contextual metareliabilism.

The converse, however, does not hold, and this is the source of my preference for contextual metareliabilism over contextual intraindividual process reliabilism. A belief that satisfies contextual metareliabilism need not satisfy intraindividual process reliabilism. For a metareliable process might select an intraindividual process that is unreliable. This is because metareliable selection processes are fallible; they do not invariably select reliable processes, but merely tend to do so. In the case of the young child's testimonial belief, a selection process might select an unreliable process for several reasons. First, the child might make a mistake about who the child's caretaker or teacher is and as a result accept unreliable testimony. Second, the child's caretaker might be unreliable in referring the child to sources on various topics. So the child might end up selecting an unreliable source of testimony. Note that testimonial beliefs that result from uptake from such sources would be justified on contextual metareliabilism but not on contextual intraindividual process reliabilism. Intuitively, contextual metareliabilism gets the correct result here. Even if the child makes a mistake about who its caretaker is, or if the caretaker is unreliable about sources, but the child follows the advice of the caretaker in selecting testifiers, the resulting testimonial beliefs are nevertheless justified. Thus, the divergence here between contextual metareliabilism and contextual intraindividual process reliabilism favors the former view.

Let it be noted, however, that the argument for a divergence between the two accounts depends on a particular way of individuating processes. I have assumed that we are individuating processes narrowly, so that (for example) uptake from a single testifier counts as a single intraindividual process. Processes could no doubt be individuated more broadly, amalgamating the beliefs of diverse testifiers. And under this broader individuation, the intraindividual belief-forming process will be reliable when the caretaker's advice is heeded, since most testifiers to whom a caretaker would refer the child will be reliable. Under the broader individuation, the two accounts are equivalent and equally plausible: both accounts allow that the subject's belief can be justified even when the testimony is unreliable. Thus, if we wish to avoid choosing between a broad and a narrow individuation of processes, we will have to opt for contextual metareliabilism over contextual intraindividual process reliabilism.

Readers familiar with reliabilism will be curious about the relation between contextual metareliabilism for testimonial justification and Alvin Goldman's similar version of reliabilism for beliefs formed by methods.[18] As I reported above, Goldman distinguishes acquired methods from native processes and argues (in my view, persuasively, up to a point) that being formed by a reliable method is not enough for justification; the method must also be selected by a proper selection process. A reliable algorithm for calculating square roots would not form justified beliefs if the algorithm were selected by randomly drawing from a hat. Goldman suggests that a proper selection process is a metareliable one, a process that tends to select reliable methods.

Contextual metareliabilism for testimonial justification resembles Goldman's reliabilism for methods in important respects. The former view can be conceived as extending Goldman's requirement of a metareliable selection process, from cases of beliefs formed by acquired methods to cases of beliefs formed by native processes which form beliefs on testimony. At the same time, contextual metareliabilism can be conceived as extending Goldman's notion of a selection process to cover not only intraindividual psychological selection processes that select methods but *social* selection processes that select native testimonial uptake processes as well. Note, however, that contextual metareliabilism differs from Goldman's reliabilism for methods in omitting the requirement that the selected process itself be reliable; all that is required is the metareliability of the selection process.

As I mentioned in section 3, I have elsewhere criticized Goldman's reliabilism for methods on the ground that the requirement of a metareliable intraindividual psychological process selecting a method is too strong. I observed that intuitively a person who acquired the common algorithm for arithmetical sums could form justified beliefs by using it even if he or she acquired it by an accident like bumping his or her head and thus even if its use did not result from a metareliable selection process. It should also be said that Goldman's requirement that the method be reliable appears to be too strong: an unreliable method for multiplication could be justifying if selected by a metareliable selection process. In earlier work, I appealed to these two criticisms of Goldman's reliabilism to support in its place a simple reliabilism capable of explaining our intuitions here: a reliable method can be sufficient for justification, and a combination of a metareliable selection process and an unreliable method can together make a single reliable process sufficient for justification.[19]

Since contextual metareliabilism closely resembles Goldman's reliabilism for methods, the question arises whether my criticisms of that view, and the simple reliabilism supported by them, are at odds with contextual metareliabilism. In fact, my second criticism fits nicely with contextual metareliabilism, since it points out that intuitively a justifying method need not be reliable, so long as it is selected by a metareliable selection process, and this parallels my point in favor of contextual metareliabilism over contextual intraindividual psychological process reliabilism. But it might be thought that my first criticism, if good, ought to carry over to contextual metareliabilism. For according to that criticism, a metareliable selection process is not necessary for justification; a reliable method is sufficient. And if this is so, the question arises why a metareliable selection process should be necessary for testimonial justification, as contextual metareliabilism requires.

However, I do not believe that my first criticism of Goldman's proposal carries over to contextual metareliabilism for testimonial justification. For there is an important difference between beliefs formed by methods and beliefs on testimony. The difference is that in the case of beliefs on testimony, unlike that of beliefs formed by methods, it is impossible to exercise a reliable testimonial belief-forming process unless the process results from a metareliable selection process. There is no testimonial analogue of accidentally acquiring a reliable algorithm for sums. The reasons for this are the same as the reasons already given for saying that contextual intraindividual process reliabilism entails contextual metareliabilism. For both contingent and formal reasons, a process of testimonial uptake can be reliable only if it is selected by a metareliable selection process. Even when the testifier is reliable, the process does not count as reliable unless the reliability of the testifier is made relevant to the reliability of the uptake process, and this requires selection by a metareliable selection process. Thus, there is nothing in testimonial uptake analogous to accidentally acquiring a reliable algorithm for sums – by a bump on the head, for example – without employing a metareliable selection process. In other words, in naive testimonial belief, there is no gulf between a reliable belief-forming process and a metareliable selection process analogous to that between a reliable method and a metareliable selection process. If there were such a gulf, then we would have to consider whether testimonial uptake processes need not result from a metareliable selection process. But as it happens, exercising a reliable uptake process just entails using a metareliable selection process (though, as I observed earlier, the converse is not true, on a narrow individuation of the belief-forming process). Thus, there is not opportunity for a reliable uptake process to be justifying without being selected by a metareliable selection process, as there is an opportunity for a reliable arithmetical method to be justifying without being selected by a metareliable selection process.[20] For this reason, we can assimilate contextual metareliabilism to simple reliabilism, up to a point.[21]

Summarizing, we might say that, on contextual metareliabilism, all that is required for the justification of a testimonial belief is the reliability of a combination of selection process and belief-forming uptake process. The combination must be reliable, even if the uptake process at the end of it is not. If the uptake process is not reliable, then the selection process grants reliability because it is metareliable. If the uptake process is reliable, then it must have been selected by a metareliable selection process. The result is, approximately, a simple reliabilism for testimonial justification.

It is worth noting at this point that testimonial justification and justification by acquired methods substantially overlap. For acquired methods are often, perhaps typically, acquired by testimony as to the reliability of the methods (or more broadly, by emulating the example of others using the methods). Often justifying acquired methods are selected by testimony. Conversely, and more importantly, most testimonially justified beliefs are not beliefs in propositions picked up from testifiers one by one but rather *indirectly* testimonially justified – beliefs that result from methods acquired by testimony or emulation. Indeed, it is plausible that a great many testimonially justified beliefs are of this sort. We use a standard method for calculating products or square-roots, and this method was selected by testimony. Similarly, we use electronic calculators, and the methods of forming beliefs in accordance with calculator displays are selected by testimony. It is natural to speak of the beliefs that result from using these methods as justified on the basis of testimony, but in any case the methods are acquired by testimony, and we can speak of the beliefs as indirectly testimonially justified. If we think of such beliefs as justified by testimony, then testimonial justification is even broader and more significant for human cognition than we have so far suggested.

The question arises how the accounts of testimonial justification we have canvassed can cover, or be extended to cover, indirectly testimonially justified belief. I will focus here on what contextual metareliabilism should say about these beliefs. The contextual metareliabilist could subsume these beliefs either under testimonially justified beliefs or under justified beliefs that result from acquired methods. If they are subsumed under the former heading, then contextual metareliabilism treats them as justified when they result from an intraindividual process of testimonial uptake selected by a metareliable selection process. Presumably the intraindividual process of testimonial uptake will involve both the recognition that the method has received endorsement from the testifier and the use of the method to form the belief. The selection process will involve accepting the testimony of that kind of testifier (caretaker, teacher, or referred source). If, by contrast, the beliefs in question are subsumed under the heading of resulting from an acquired method, then they are treated as justified when they result from an acquired method selected by a metareliable selection process. In this case, the selection process involves recognizing that the method has been approved by a testifier who tends to select reliable methods.

These are, on the face of it, different accounts of indirectly testimonially justified beliefs. Quite possibly there is nothing to choose between the two accounts. On either account, the process is described as a combination of a process (including at least an acquired method) and a selection process, and the difference lies in where to divide the one from the other. But if the overall reliability of the process is what matters, the difference in the descriptions may not matter. The process may well be the same however described, and what makes the process reliable may well be the same. Whether this is so will depend on how processes are individuated under the two accounts, but it is clear that processes could be individuated in the same way – e.g., by individuating the acquired methods and the selection process in the same way.

This brings to a close my discussion of socialist approaches to testimonial justification. I regard contextual metareliabilism as the most promising socialist approach.

To review our discussion in this paper, I have taken the central question of social epistemology to be whether knowledge and justification are, in various senses, individualistic or social. I have focused here on individual justification, defining socialism as the view that what makes the conditions of individual justification satisfied includes social conditions, and individualism as the denial of this view. Most of our attention has gone to testimonial justification, and I have argued against the historically dominant and, in my view, most plausible individualist view about it, inductive weak individualism, according to which testimonial beliefs are justified on the basis of a belief about the reliability of testimony, itself justified ultimately on the basis of nontestimonially justified beliefs. The failure of inductive weak individualism warrants taking socialism seriously. I considered several versions of socialism about testimonial justification and settled on contextual metareliabilism as the most promising. Though testimonial justification is only one sort of justification, my objection to inductive weak individualism, if good, shows that our reliance on testimony is pervasive. Consequently, the case for socialism about testimonial justification supports a broad role for social conditions in the conditions of individual justification. If my argument has force, then there is reason to regard justification and knowledge as deeply social.[22]

Notes

1 I will rely throughout the paper on an intuitive grasp of what makes a condition *social*. In a minimal sense of "social," a social condition is one that entails that there is more than one person. In a stronger and more interesting sense of "social," it is a condition that entails that there are two or more persons related by some intentional relations (e.g., friendship, mutual admiration, etc.). For discussion of the question what makes a condition social, see David-Hillel Ruben, *The Metaphysics of the Social World* (London: Routledge, 1985); Margaret Gilbert, *On Social Facts* (London: Routledge, 1989); and John R. Searle, *The Construction of Social Reality* (New York: Free Press, 1995).

2 For a general review of the issues in social epistemology, see my "Socializing Epistemology: An Introduction Through Two Sample Issues," in *Socializing Epistemology: The Social Dimensions of Knowledge* (Lanham, MD: Rowman and Littlefield, 1994) and Steve Fuller, "Recent Work on Social Epistemology," *American Philosophical Quarterly* 33 (1996): 149–66. For articles on social epistemology, see the other articles in *Socializing Epistemology* and in the special issue of *Synthese* I edited on social epistemology (*Synthese* 73 (1987)); Philip Kitcher, "The Division of Cognitive Labor," *Journal of Philosophy* 88 (1991): 5–22; and the articles on social epistemology in Alvin Goldman, *Liaisons: Philosophy Meets the Cognitive and Social Sciences* (Cambridge: MIT Press, 1992). For work on social issues in the epistemology of science, see J. R. Brown, *The*

Rational and the Social (London: Routledge, 1989); Helen Longino, *Science as Social Knowledge: Values and Objectivity in Scientific Inquiry* (Princeton: Princeton University Press, 1990); and Ernan McMullin, ed., *The Social Dimensions of Science* (South Bend, IN: Notre Dame Press, 1992). For work on consensus, see Keith Lehrer and Carl Wagner, *Rational Consensus in Science and Society* (Dordrecht: Reidel, 1981); the articles in Barry Loewer, ed., *Synthese*: Special Issue on Consensus 62, (1985); and Nicholas Rescher, *Pluralism: Against the Demand for Consensus* (Oxford: Clarendon Press, 1993). For work on testimony, see Michael Welbourne, *The Community of Knowledge* (Aberdeen: Aberdeen University Press, 1986); F. Schmitt, "Justification, Sociality, and Autonomy," *Synthese* 73 (1987): 43–86; C. A. J. Coady, *Testimony: A Philosophical Study* (Oxford: Oxford University Press, 1992); and B. Matilal and A. Chakrabharti, eds., *Knowing from Words* (Dorchrecht: Kluwer, 1995).

3 For an example of socialism$_1$, see Edward Craig, *Knowledge and the State of Nature* (Oxford: Oxford University Press, 1990).

4 William Alston has already made a plausible case for socialism$_2$, in a version employing a minimal sense of "social," by pointing out that, on a reliability theory of justification, what makes a belief justified, the reliability of the belief-forming process, is a social condition because reliability is defined as the frequency of true beliefs over the whole output of the process, and this in fact includes the beliefs of diverse individuals ("Belief-forming Practices and the Social," in Schmitt, *Socializing Epistemology*). In this paper, I advocate that what makes testimonial beliefs justified is a social condition in a stronger sense, involving intentional relations among individuals.

5 See John Locke, *An Essay Concerning Human Understanding*, 2 vols., ed. A. C. Fraser (New York: Dover, 1959), I, p. 58 and IV, xv and xvi, ss. 10 and 11.

6 We need not assume that the reliability or trustworthiness of the testifier about which the subject must have a justified belief is defined in the same way as the reliability of a process necessary for the justification of a belief.

7 Allan Gibbard, Keith Lehrer, and Richard Foley have exploited the idea of epistemic parity – in the case of Lehrer and Foley, in the service of what they regard as nonindividualistic views of testimonial justification. See Gibbard, *Wise Choices, Apt Feelings* (Cambridge, MA: Harvard University Press, 1990), pp. 179–81; Lehrer, *Self-Trust: A Study of Reason, Knowledge, and Autonomy* (Oxford: Oxford University Press, 1997), ch. 6; and Foley, "Egoism in Epistemology," in Schmitt, *Socializing Epistemology*.

8 This may be Jonathan Adler's view in "Testimony, Trust, Knowing," *The Journal of Philosophy* 91 (1994): 264–75. Alternatively, Adler may intend an individualist view weaker than weak individualism – namely, a holistic coherentist account of testimonial justification on which any given testimonial belief need only cohere with all other beliefs, testimonial as well as nontestimonial; it need not be, as on coherentist weak individualism, that a testimonial belief coheres with nontestimonial beliefs taken alone.

9 For other objections, see Alvin Plantinga, *Warrant and Proper Function* (Oxford: Oxford University Press, 1993), ch. 4, sec. 2, and Coady, *Testimony: A Philosophical Study*, chs. 4 and 8.

10 I should observe here that, to refute inductive weak individualism, it is not necessary to show that people actually lack a sufficient first-hand basis for such an induction. All that need be shown is that we would still ascribe justified belief on testimony to people even if they lacked a first-hand basis for an induction. And this does seem to

be the case. To see this, reflect that our willingness to ascribe justification on testimony seems not to depend on the assumption that people have a first-hand basis for an induction. We are, it seems, willing to ascribe testimonial justification without having resolved whether people have such a basis. In fact philosophers have not resolved this issue, but I doubt whether any philosophers would be inclined to withdraw the ascription of testimonial justification should it turn out that people lack such a basis. And this is enough to refute inductive weak individualism.

11 *Inductive Inference and Its Natural Ground: An Essay in Naturalistic Epistemology* (Cambridge, MA: MIT Press, 1993), chs. 4 and 5.
12 (Cambridge, MA: Harvard University Press, 1986), pp. 81–95, 115–16, and ch. 17.
13 See my *Knowledge and Belief* (London: Routledge, 1992), ch. 6, s. 2.
14 Indeed, in light of the existence of these social mechanisms, I would urge Kornblith to reconsider whether focused sampling is really needed to explain how successful induction is possible. Small-sample induction could depend instead on the guidance of parents and teachers in the selection of natural kind properties on which to perform inductions. Of course the antecedent selection of these properties must be explained historically, but the explanation might not need focused sampling. History is long, and we might collectively have gone through enough samples in the past, and discarded enough properties that fail in inductions, that we do not need focused sampling. The accumulation of samples over time by culture might make the selection process metareliable. This is not to say that focused sampling could not be part of the selection process, but only that it would not be a necessary part. Of course, whether an explanation of the metareliability of the selection process can really do without focused sampling will depend on whether it is possible for children to learn from their elders without themselves using focused sampling.
15 For discussion of the testimonial rules approach, see my "Socializing Epistemology," in *Socializing Epistemology*. For the proposal that a virtue-theoretic account of knowledge can accommodate social aspects of knowledge, see Linda Trinkhaus Zagzebski, *Virtues of the Mind: An Inquiry into the Nature of Virtue and the Ethical Foundations of Knowledge* (Cambridge: Cambridge University Press, 1996).
16 One might wonder whether a socialist can endorse this objection to the transindividual reasons account, since it allows there to be testimonial justification without social conditions being satisfied. But first, a socialist does not have to say that *all* testimonial justification entails social conditions, only that social conditions enter into the conditions of testimonial justification in a significant range of cases. Second, the case is merely one in which the subject's testimonial justification does not entail that the subject is related to a testifier *in this case*. It does not follow that the subject does not have to satisfy any social conditions *at all*, or that what makes the conditions of justification satisfied is not a social condition. It could be that the subject must be related to a broad social condition (e.g., testimony on other occasions, as on contextual reliabilism).
17 See my *Knowledge and Belief*, ch. 6, for discussion of the individuation of processes for purposes of a reliabilist account of justification.
18 See Goldman's *Epistemology and Cognition*, pp. 81–95, 115–16, and ch. 17.
19 See my *Knowledge and Belief*, ch. 6.
20 However, I argue in *Knowledge and Belief* that the reason why a reliable algorithm for sums acquired by a bump on the head can be justifying may have to do with social

conditions – in particular, the fact that algorithms for sums typically result from metareliable selection processes (namely, instruction). So there is yet a similarity between methods and testimony. Though testimonial belief needs a metareliable selection process in order to be justified, and beliefs that result from certain methods do not, nevertheless, in both cases the reason why the belief is justified turns on social conditions that make it likely that the process or method is reliable.

21 The question remains, however, *why* a reliable algorithm for sums is sufficient for justification without resulting from a metareliable selection process, while a reliable uptake process must always result from a metareliable selection process. The answer may be that, as a matter of fact, people tend to acquire reliable algorithms for sums as a consequence of the social conditions of learning, and these conditions are deeply entrenched, so that there is no need to promote the use of a metareliable selection process for selecting algorithms for sums. In the case of testimonial uptake processes, however, there are no comparable entrenched social conditions that enforce the selection of reliable uptake processes. Children have some tendency to accept the testimony of peers and must be dissuaded from doing so in a range of cases if their uptake processes are to be reliable. Thus, the selection of reliable uptake processes needs to be promoted by epistemic evaluation. This is accomplished by requiring a metareliable selection process for testimonial justification. See *Knowledge and Belief*, ch. 6, for further discussion of these issues.

22 I would like to thank John Greco for extensive written comments that greatly improved the paper.

Chapter 16

Procedural Epistemology – At the Interface of Philosophy and AI

John L. Pollock

1. Epistemic Justification

Epistemological theories

Epistemology is about how we can know the various things we claim to know. Epistemology is driven by attempts to answer the question, "How do you know?" This gives rise to investigations on several different levels. At the lowest level, philosophers investigate particular kinds of knowledge claims. Thus we find theories of perceptual knowledge ("How do you know the things you claim to know directly on the basis of perception?"), theories of induction and abduction ("How do you know the general truths you infer from observation of particular cases?"), theories of our knowledge of other minds, theories of mathematical knowledge, and so forth. At an intermediate level, topics are investigated that pertain to all or most of the specific kinds of knowledge discussed at the lowest level. Theories of reasoning, both deductive and defeasible, occur at this level. At the highest level we find general epistemological theories that attempt to explain how knowledge in general is possible. At this level we encounter versions of foundationalism, coherentism, probabilism, reliabilism, and direct realism. One can be doing epistemology by working at any of these levels. The levels cannot be isolated from each other, however. Work at any level tends to presuppose something about the other levels. For example, work on inductive reasoning at least presupposes that reasoning plays a role in the acquisition or justification of beliefs and normally presupposes something about the structure of defeasible reasoning.

Work in epistemology divides in another way as well. The central concept of epistemology is the concept of epistemic justification. The question "How do you know?" is a question about what justifies you in believing. The lowest level theories are about the justification of particular kinds of knowledge claims. The mid-level theories are about general cognitive procedures that contribute to epistemic justification. The highest level theories can be regarded as theories about epistemic justification itself. However, the highest level theories can be viewed in two different ways. On the one hand, they can be regarded as descriptions of the overall structural relations that give rise to epistemic justification. They tell us how the various constituents of cognition fit together to give us our knowledge of the world. I will refer to these as *structural theories of epistemic justification*. On the other hand, high-level theories can also be proposed as to *why* epistemic justification has the general structure it does. These theories typically take the form of logical analyses of the concept of epistemic justification. I will refer to these as *analytic theories of epistemic justification*.

The distinction between structural and analytic theories of epistemic justification has often been appreciated only vaguely. This is really a distinction between high-level theories and higher level theories. The analytic theories are theories about what would make a structural theory true. Following my 1987 book, I will categorize epistemological theories as versions of foundationalism, coherentism, probabilism, reliabilism, and direct realism.[1] Viewed in this light, it is natural to regard foundationalism, coherentism, and direct realism as structural theories, and reliabilism as an analytic theory. A reliabilist might, for example, endorse a foundationalist structural theory on the grounds that it is a (perhaps the only) reliable way of acquiring knowledge. This suggests that reliabilism and foundationalism have different targets and are not automatically incompatible.

On the other hand, foundationalists and coherentists (and also direct realists and probabilists) have often viewed their theories as analytic theories as well. To do that, they must insist that they are not just giving structural accounts of epistemic justification, but logical analyses as well. The claim would be that not only are their theories true as structural accounts, but also that nothing further *makes* them true. The claim is that these structures are *constitutive of* the concept of epistemic justification – the concept is to be analyzed by giving a detailed account of how beliefs come to be justified rather than by giving some overarching principle (like reliabilism) that *selects* the particular constituents of the correct structural theory. In other words, epistemic justification is to be analyzed by enumerating the principles that give rise to it.

The main objection to treating foundationalist, coherentist, and direct realist theories as analytic theories is that they give at best piecemeal, *ad hoc* seeming, analyses. They characterize epistemic justification in terms of a general structure and a lot of diverse unrelated principles regarding particular kinds of reasoning (perception, induction, other minds, etc.) without any general account of what ties all these principles together. As such, they are at least inelegant, and cannot help but leave us wondering if there isn't something more to be said which would explain how this conglomeration of principles comes to be the correct conglomeration.

As I use the terms, *probabilist theories* propose to assess epistemic justification by appealing to the probabilities of individual beliefs, and *reliabilist theories* propose to do so by appealing to the reliability of cognitive processes. Theories of either sort have been touted as giving general and elegant characterizations of epistemic justification that escape from the *ad-hoc*-ness objection. However, I argued in *Contemporary Theories of Knowledge* that neither kind of theory really accomplishes what it claims to accomplish. Both probabilism and reliabilism make objectionable and often uninformed use of probability. When care is taken to distinguish between the different probability concepts that might be employed in these theories, major logical difficulties arise for each theory. I will not rehash the problems here. The interested reader should consult the book. These objections have never been satisfactorily answered by the proponents of probabilist and reliabilist theories. It must be concluded that these theories do not provide the missing account we seek for what unifies the diverse constituents of a correct structural theory of epistemic justification.

In the end, probabilist and reliabilist theories fail to keep their promise of giving a unified account of epistemic justification, and we are left with no other unifying proposals. This is theoretically unsatisfactory. What is the origin of this complex structure of epistemic principles that gives rise to justified beliefs? Light can be thrown on this question by thinking more carefully about the concept of epistemic justification itself. Here we must be careful. As recently as the 1980s, epistemologists took the concept of epistemic justification for granted and argued among themselves about its analysis. It was assumed without argument that there was a single monolithic concept that people were disagreeing about. But in the 1990s, that has come to seem increasingly dubious. It now seems likely that at least two different concepts have been the focus of epistemological investigation.

Procedural epistemology and the Gettier problem

Epistemology is about the question, "How do you know?" At first blush, this would seem to be about knowledge, but it is so only indirectly. It is about *how* we know. This makes it a question about the rational procedures that give rise to our knowledge of the world – rational procedures for belief formation. In arriving at beliefs, epistemic agents follow various procedures. Some of these procedures are epistemically praiseworthy, and others are epistemically blameworthy. There is a procedural sense of epistemic justification according to which a belief is epistemically justified iff it was arrived at or held on the basis of procedures that are epistemically praiseworthy. This is the traditional concept of epistemic justification – the concept that concerned Descartes, Hume, Kant, and most of their descendants. *Procedural epistemology* is the study of this concept of epistemic justification.

In 1963, Edmund Gettier published his famous paper on the analysis of "S knows that p," and epistemology has never been the same since.[2] The Gettier problem is a seductive one, and a voluminous amount of philosophical ink has been spilled on it.[3] Many young epistemologists have been raised on the idea that this is the central problem of epistemology. But one of the lessons to be drawn from the massive literature on the Gettier problem is just what a perverse concept knowledge is. What the Gettier problem shows is that a person can have a true belief, behave with complete epistemic and rational propriety, and still fail to have knowledge through no fault of their own. What is happening here is indeed an interesting problem, but note that epistemology was originally driven by concern with the notions of epistemic and rational propriety. That is what procedural justification concerns. What the Gettier problem shows is that knowledge is less directly connected with procedural justification than we thought.

Interest in the Gettier problem is not going to go away (nor should it). It is a fascinating problem, although I cannot help but think that it will in the end be only an intriguing side issue in the history of philosophy. However, as long as it is with us it must be recognized that it has somewhat warped the course of epistemology. It has led many epistemologists to focus on a concept of epistemic justification that is characterized by its role in knowledge rather than its role in rational or epistemic propriety. We might refer to this as the "knowledgifying" concept of epistemic justification. Viewed from this perspective, theories that fail as theories of procedural epistemology may gain new life. Reliabilism is, for example, an initially plausible attempt to provide an analysis of an important ingredient of knowledge.

I cannot emphasize too strongly that my concern in epistemology is with procedural epistemology. I want to know how rational cognition works. What role it plays in the analysis of "S knows that p" may be an interesting question, but it is not my question.

2. Two Concepts of Rationality

Let us return to the situation in which we found ourselves before my brief digression on the Gettier problem. It seems undeniable that a correct structural theory of (procedural) epistemic justification is going to posit a complex structure in which is embedded a large number of seemingly unrelated epistemic principles governing reasoning about particular subject matters. What unifies the diverse constituents of this structure and makes them all part of the true theory of epistemic justification? I propose to answer this question by scrutinizing the concept of epistemic justification more carefully. The procedural concept of epistemic justification is in an important sense a first-person concept. It pertains to the directing of one's own cognition. In asking whether a person is justified in this sense, we are asking whether he or she did things right. Procedural epistemology is thus the study of how to do it right when engaging in epistemic cognition. The question that is puzzling us is "What makes a procedure the right procedure for use in a particular epistemic context?"

Some light can be thrown on this question by putting it in a broader perspective. Epistemic cognition is just one part of rational cognition. There is a traditional distinction between epistemic cognition (cognition about what to believe) and practical cognition (cognition about what to do). Rational agents are agents that cognize rationally, and correct epistemic cognition is a subspecies of rational cognition in general. So asking what makes certain epistemic procedures correct is a special case of the more general question what makes cognitive procedures rational. Procedural epistemology is part of a general theory of rationality. In addition to its epistemological elements, a theory of rationality will include at least an account of how goals are to be selected for adoption and how actions are to be selected for performance.

Human rationality

Let us turn then to the question, "What makes rational procedures rational?" This question is made more difficult by the fact that there is more than one concept of rationality. We can illuminate one of these concepts by considering the way in which philosophers have traditionally tried to answer questions about how, rationally, to perform various cognitive tasks (e.g., reasoning inductively). The standard philosophical methodology has been to propose general principles, like the Nicod principle, or principles of Bayesian inference, or the hypothetico-deductive method, and test them by seeing how they apply to concrete examples. In order to test a principle by applying it to concrete examples, we must know how the example should come out. Thus, for example, Nelson Goodman conclusively refuted a version of the Nicod Principle by contriving his famous "grue/bleen" example.[4] The refutation was conclusive because everyone who looks at the example agrees that it would not be rational to accept the conclusions drawn in accordance with the Nicod Principle. But how do people know that? The standard answer is "philosophical intuition", but that is not much of answer. What is philosophical intuition?

Considerable light can be thrown upon this methodology by comparing it with the methodology employed by linguists studying grammaticality. Linguists try to construct general theories of grammar that will suffice to pick out all and only grammatical sentences. They do this by proposing theories and testing them against particular examples. It is a fact that proficient speakers of a language are able to make grammaticality judgments, judging that some utterances are grammatical and others are not. These grammaticality judgments provide the data for testing theories of grammaticality. It is equally undeniable that human cognizers are able to make judgments about whether, in specified circumstances, particular cognitive acts are rational or irrational. These rationality judgments provide the data for testing theories of rationality.

I can imagine a philosopher arguing that rationality has to do with concepts and logic, so our intuitions about rationality are a kind of platonic intuition of universals. But no one would be tempted to say the same thing about our intuitions of grammaticality. After all, the details of our language are determined by linguistic convention. Our language could have been different than it is, and if it were, our grammatical intuitions would have been different too.

When we learn a language, we learn *how to do* various things. Knowledge of how to do something is procedural knowledge. For most tasks, there is more than one way to do them. Accordingly, we can learn to do them in different ways, and so have different procedural knowledge. But a general characteristic of procedural knowledge seems to be that once we have it, we can also judge more or less reliably whether we are conforming to it in particular cases. For example, once I have learned how to ride a bicycle, if I lean too far to one side (and thus put myself in danger of falling), I do not have to wait until I fall down to know that I am doing it wrong. I can detect my divergence from what I have learned and attempt to correct it before I fall. Similarly, it is very common for competent speakers of a language to make ungrammatical utterances. But if they reflect upon those utterances, they have the ability to recognize them as ungrammatical and correct them. I suggest that exactly the same thing is true of cognition. We have procedural knowledge for how to cognize, and that carries with it the ability to recognize divergences from that procedural knowledge. That is what our so-called "philosophical intuition" amounts to, at least in the theory of rationality.

Chomsky introduced the competence/performance distinction.[5] Performance theories are theories about how people in fact behave. A performance theory of language would include, for example, an account of what utterances people actually make under various circumstances, be they grammatical or not. A competence theory, on the other hand, attempts to articulate people's procedural knowledge for how to do various things. A competence theory of language would include a theory of the grammatical rules that people have learned to use in constructing their utterances. Because people do not always conform to their own procedural knowledge, competence and performance can diverge dramatically.

My proposal is that the theories of rationality that philosophers construct by appealing to their intuitions about rationality are best viewed as competence theories of cognition. That is, they are attempts to articulate the rules comprising our procedural knowledge for how to cognize.[6] We have no direct access to those rules themselves, but because we can detect (with fair reliability) divergences from our procedural knowledge, we can tell in real or imagined cases whether it would be rational to draw various conclusions (i.e., whether doing so would conform to our procedural knowledge). We can use such knowledge about particular cases to confirm general principles about the content of our procedural knowledge.

Unlike linguistic knowledge, it seems pretty clear that large parts of our procedural knowledge of how to cognize are built into us rather than learned. This may be required as a matter of logic – it may prove impossible to get started in learning how to cognize unless we already know how to cognize to some extent. But even if that is not true, it is overwhelmingly likely that evolution has built into us knowledge of how to cognize so that we do not come into the world so epistemically vulnerable as we would otherwise be. This way, we at least know how to get started in learning about the world. This is rather strongly confirmed by the overwhelming agreement untutored individuals exhibit in their procedural knowledge of how to cognize.[7] For example, psychological evidence indicates that everyone finds reasoning with modus ponens to be natural and reasoning with modus tollens to be initially unnatural.[8] It is unlikely that this is something we have learned. Once we start supplementing our built-in procedural knowledge with learned principles, we are quick to embrace modus tollens as well.

Notice that the rules comprising our procedural knowledge of how to cognize cannot be viewed as mere generalizations about how we do cognize. That would make them descriptions of cognitive performance rather than cognitive competence. Instead, they are the rules that we, in some sense, "try" to conform to. They are the rules perceived divergence from which leads us to correct our cognitive performance to bring it into conformance.

My proposal then is that *human rationality* is composed of the principles comprising our built-in procedural knowledge of how to cognize. When we turn more specifically to epistemology, this is what unifies the diverse collection of principles that make up a correct structural theory of epistemic justification. They are unified simply by being among the principles that are built into our cognitive architecture as human beings. There need be no overarching general characterization that explains why those are the principles we use. These are the principles comprising our cognitive architecture because we just happen to be built that way.

Generic rationality

Of course, it is not entirely an accident that humans are built the way they are. Environmental pressures have led to our evolving in particular ways. We represent one solution to various engineering problems that were solved by evolution. There is no reason to think that these problems always have a single, or even a single best, solution. For example, human beings have built-in principles of reasoning that enable them to perform deductive reasoning. As I remarked, modus ponens is among the built-in principles, but there is overwhelming psychological evidence that modus tollens is not. Would humans have been less fit for survival had modus tollens been included in our cognitive architecture as well? I see no reason to think so. Certain engineering problems call for arbitrary choices between solutions that work equally well. Our cognitive architecture probably reflects a great many decisions that would be made arbitrarily by an engineer designing a cognitive agent like us.

These considerations simultaneously explain what unifies the various principles comprising our system of epistemic justification (they are unified by being part of the human architecture of epistemic cognition) and indicate that there is a certain arbitrariness to the contents of the system. This also suggests that there is a more general concept of rationality than that of human rationality. Some of the details of the principles comprising human rationality are to varying degrees arbitrary. A cognitive agent that differed from human beings with respect to these arbitrary details (e.g., it used modus tollens) would not thereby be irrational. It would just fail to conform to the standard of *human* rationality. I will refer to this more general concept as *generic rationality*.

Generic rationality emerges from approaching cognition from the design stance. Rationality represents the solution to certain design problems. Approaching rationality from the design stance is more common in artificial intelligence than it is in philosophy. In philosophy, the emphasis has been on human rationality, but in artificial intelligence there has been less concern with mimicking human rationality and more interest in designing intelligent (rational) systems that will accomplish certain cognitive tasks in human-like ways but not necessarily in exactly the way humans do it. If we are to characterize generic rationality as I propose, we must say to what design problem it is the solution. Here I can do no better than I did in my recent book *Cognitive Carpentry*. "The world contains many relatively stable structures. These can be roughly categorized as of two kinds. Some are stable by virtue of being hard to destroy. A rock is a good example of such *passive stability*. Others achieve stability by interacting with their immediate surroundings to make them more congenial to their continued survival. Plants and animals are the obvious examples of such *active stability*. Rationality (in a very general sense) represents one solution to the problem of active stability. A rational agent has beliefs reflecting the state of its environment, and it likes or dislikes its situation. When it finds the world not entirely to its liking, it tries to change that. Its *cognitive architecture* is the mechanism whereby it chooses courses of action aimed at making the world more to its liking."[9] The design problem is *to achieve active stability by using such a cognitive architecture*. An architecture that solves the design problem is a rational architecture.

I argued in *Cognitive Carpentry* that many general features of human rationality are dictated by this design problem. They represent the only or the only obvious way to achieve various cognitive tasks required by the design problem. This includes various aspects of epistemic cognition, like defeasible reasoning, and the general structure of practical reasoning that includes goal selection, plan selection based upon values inherited from the goals achieved, and the directing of actions on the basis of plans.

One can do epistemology either as human epistemology or more generally as the epistemology of arbitrary rational agents. The two may not be all that different if many of the principles of human cognition represent the only solution to elements of the design problem underlying generic rationality. However, where the design of human rationality represents arbitrary design decisions, they will differ. In that case it strikes me as often more interesting to pursue the epistemology of arbitrary rational agents. An anthropocentric bias makes sense if you are doing psychology, but why should philosophy be so constrained?

The OSCAR Project

Reflections of this sort spawned the OSCAR Project in the mid-1980s. The goal of the OSCAR Project is the construction of a general theory of rationality and its implementation in an artificial rational agent. The implemented system will be an artificial intellect (an *artilect*) of the sort constructed in AI, but where it differs from most AI systems is that will be based upon a detailed philosophical theory of rationality. The computer implementation of philosophical theories represents a marked divergence from conventional philosophical methodology. The armchair-trained philosopher may wonder why we should bother with implementation. Of course, the simple answer is that it is fun to build something that actually works. But the more serious answer is that implementing an abstract theory of rational cognition is the only way to be sure that it actually will work. The lesson that any nascent computer programmer learns at his PC's knee is that programs almost never do what you expect them to do the first time around. Writing a computer program that actually does what you want is a matter of making a first attempt and then repeatedly testing it and refining it. When this lesson is applied to philosophical theories of rational cognition, a theory that looks good from your armchair will almost never work the way you expect if you write a program that directly implements your first thoughts on the matter.

Implementation achieves two things. First, it requires the theorist to be precise and to think the details through. Philosophers are much too prone to ignore the details, just waving their hands when the going gets rough. That might be all right if the details were *mere* details and we could be confident that filling them in was a matter of grunt work. But in fact, when philosophical theories fail it is usually because the details cannot be made to work. Grand pictures painted with broad brushstrokes are fine for hanging on the wall and admiring for aesthetic reasons, but if the objective is to discover truth, it is essential to see whether the details can be made to work. So the first thing implementation achieves is that it requires the theory to be sufficiently precise that it can actually be implemented. It is remarkably common when implementing a theory to discover to your chagrin that there are significant parts of the theory that you simply overlooked and forgot to construct. To the armchair-bound philosopher, that may sound remarkably stupid, but that is only because he has never tried implementing his theories and has thereby never had the opportunity to make the same humbling discoveries about his own thought.

The second thing that implementation achieves is that it provides a test of correctness for theories of cognition. A theory of cognition is a theory of how to achieve certain cognitive tasks. Only by implementing the theory can we be certain that the theorized procedures do indeed accomplish their objectives. The armchair-bound philosopher attempts to do this by looking for counterexamples. That is, in effect, what implementation is doing as well. Implementation enables us to use the computer as a tool in searching for counterexamples because it allows us to apply the implemented theory to concrete examples. But this technique far outstrips what can be accomplished searching for counterexamples while firmly implanted in your armchair. The difficulty with the latter is twofold. First, as remarked above, you may simply be wrong about the consequences your theory has for a specific example. The theory may not work the way you expect it to. If it is implemented, you can apply it to the example mechanically and not be misled by your own expectations. Second, the examples to which you can apply your theory from the armchair are severely limited in their complexity. Truly complicated examples are simply beyond our ability to work through them in our heads. But if the theories are implemented, they can be applied mechanically to a much broader range of more complex examples. The armchair philosopher, in his naiveté, may suppose that if a theory is going to fail, it will fail on simple examples. That is just not true. AI has a long history (long for AI at least) of constructing theories and testing them on "toy examples". For example, much early AI work on planning was tested on the blocks world, which is a world consisting of a table top with children's blocks scattered about and piled on top of each other, and the planning problems were problems of achieving certain configurations of blocks. AI learned the hard way that systems that worked well for such toy problems frequently failed to scale up to problems of realistic complexity. There is every reason to expect the same thing to be true of philosophical theories of rational cognition. The only way to give them a fair test is to implement them and apply them to problems of real-world complexity.

3. New Directions in Epistemology

Top-down and bottom-up reasoning

Work on high-level epistemological theories has typically proceeded in a rather abstract fashion. Defenders of theories like coherentism or probabilism have formulated their theories in very general terms, and have usually made only half-hearted attempts to show how they can accommodate the specific kinds of epistemic cognition required for knowledge of concrete subject matters. This can be regarded as a kind of *top-down epistemological theorizing*. Concentration on low-level theories, with an insistence on implementation, is a kind of *bottom-up theorizing*. I want to insist that neither top-down nor bottom-up theorizing can be satisfactory by itself. A necessary condition for the correctness of a low-level theory (e.g., a theory of inductive reasoning, or a theory of inference from perception) is that it must fit into a correct high-level structural theory of epistemic justification, like foundationalism, or coherentism. Focusing on the low-level theory by itself, without reference to a high-level theory into which it must fit, is theorizing in a relative vacuum and imposes too few constraints. Conversely, it is equally a necessary condition for the correctness of a high-level structural theory that it be possible to fill it out with low-level theories of specific kinds of epistemic cognition, and the only way to verify that this can be done is to do it. To be ultimately satisfactory, epistemological theorizing must combine top-down and bottom-up theorizing.

I suspect that little progress can be made on low-level theories without presupposing something about high-level theories. Accordingly, the natural way to proceed in epistemology is to begin by giving general arguments for a high-level theory, and then to fill it out by constructing low-level theories compatible with it. Difficulties in constructing the low-level theories should lead to modification of the high-level theory, or in extreme cases, to its abandonment.

Direct realism

The development of the OSCAR Project follows the course I am proposing. In *Contemporary Theories of Knowledge* I surveyed the different possible high-level structural theories, categorizing them as foundationalism, coherentism, probabilism, reliabilism, and direct realism. I raised what I regarded as compelling objections to all but direct realism, and so concluded that direct realism, as the only survivor, must be correct. As I use the term, direct realism proposes a structure of epistemic justification that is much like that proposed by foundationalism. There is a foundational level, and then beliefs are justified by reasoning from the foundations. However, according to foundationalism, the foundations consist of *basic beliefs*, which are beliefs that do not stand in need of justification (they are *self-justifying*). Direct realism, by contrast, takes the foundation to consist of *mental states*, like the experiencing of percepts, the having of recollections, the occurrent thinking of a thought, the having of a desire, etc. In both foundationalism and direct realism, reasoning proceeds in accordance with the *reason-for* relation. In foundationalism, the reason-for relation is a relation between the *contents* of beliefs, i.e., propositions. In direct realism, the reason-for relation is a relation between mental states rather than their contents. Thus holding one belief may be a reason for holding another, but also having a percept or a desire may be a reason for holding a belief. When holding one belief is a reason for holding another, this can be translated into the foundationalist framework by saying that the content of the first belief is a reason for the content of the second. However, when having a percept or a desire is a reason for holding a belief, there is no way to translate that into the foundationalist framework. This cannot be viewed as a relation between the contents of the states, because a belief, a percept, and a desire may all have the same content (e.g., that there is something red before one), but the reasoning licensed by the belief is quite different from the reasoning licensed by the percept or the desire. Foundationalism tries to accommodate reasoning from percepts, desires, and other nondoxastic states by beginning instead with beliefs *about* percepts, desires, etc.

In *Contemporary Theories of Knowledge* I gave two arguments against the use of basic beliefs in foundationalism. It is generally granted that in order to be self-justifying, basic beliefs must be about mental states (most notably, perceptual states). Such beliefs can usually be cast in the form, "It appears to me as if *P*". Favorite examples are beliefs about things looking red, etc. The simplest objection to the claim that all our justified beliefs must be inferred from such basic beliefs is that we rarely have very many beliefs of this kind. For example, when I walk down the street, I form beliefs about people, buildings, trees, birds, automobiles, etc., but not about color blotches in my visual field. I *can* form beliefs of the latter sort, but usually only by a deliberate change of attention. The immediate doxastic product of perception is normally beliefs about physical objects – not beliefs about my perceptual experiences. But if I don't have the latter, then they cannot provide the basis from which I infer the former.

Note that the preceding is only an objection to foundationalism as a theory of *human* epistemology. I have given no reason to think it impossible to build an artilect having the requisite beliefs about percepts. However, a more general objection can be given. This consists of an argument to the effect that even the most stereotypical examples of basic beliefs are not self-justifying. It is supposed to be the content of a belief that makes it self-justifying. Thus all beliefs with the same content must be self-justifying. Consider the belief that something looks blue to me. That is supposed to be a stereotypical example of a basic belief. If it really is a basic belief, then if someone holds such a belief and has no reason to think they should not, they must be justified in holding it. Consider shadows on snow. As every artist knows, shadows on snow are blue, and indeed, upon close inspection they look that way. But many non-artists think that shadows on snow look grey. They hold this as a general belief, presumably inferred from the beliefs that snow is white and shadows on white objects are grey. (In fact, the light reflected by snow is predominantly blue, but its intensity makes snow look white to us; when the intensity is diminished in shadows, it looks blue.) If a person holding such a general belief is asked what color a particular snow shadow looks to him, he may immediately form the belief that it looks grey without carefully inspecting his percept. He thus has a false belief about what color it looks to him. Furthermore, it would be an unjustified belief if he happened to hold the general belief on some unjustified basis. Thus beliefs with this content are not self-justifying.

A common reaction to the preceding counterexample is that the belief is self-justifying *when held on the basis of perception* rather than on some other basis. But this is not something the foundationalist can say. According to foundationalism, the justification of beliefs is determined exclusively by what beliefs the epistemic agent has (where beliefs are individuated by their contents). No appeal can be made to extra-doxastic considerations like the origin of the beliefs. To appeal to the origin is to say that *having the percept of the shadow looking blue* is what justifies the belief that the shadow is blue. But that is not foundationalism – that is direct realism. The whole point of direct realism is that justified belief is anchored in certain kinds of mental states like percepts, and not in certain privileged kinds of beliefs.

I think that this aspect of direct realism would seem obvious if it did not conflict with philosophical preconceptions about cognition. *Internalism* in epistemology is the view that only internal states of the cognizer can be relevant in determining which of the cognizer's beliefs are justified. Direct realism is a form of internalism, but internalists have generally gone further and endorsed the *doxastic assumption* according to which only the cognizer's beliefs can be relevant in determining which of the cognizer's beliefs are justified. The rationale for the doxastic assumption is simple and initially compelling. Procedural justification has to do with how the cognizer should manage his beliefs. In deciding this, it seems that the cognizer can take account of something only insofar as he has a belief about it. So only beliefs can be relevant.

This argument cannot be correct. If it were, it would follow that the cognizer can only take account of his beliefs insofar as he has beliefs about his beliefs, and then an infinite regress would loom. To "take account of something" in cognition is not necessarily to think about it. It is to make use of it in belief formation. There is no reason belief formation should only be sensitive to other beliefs. Cognitive processes can be responsive to a variety of mental states including belief, perception, memory, introspection, desire, and so forth. This is precisely what direct realism proposes.

The construction of an artilect

Thus I think that the abstract arguments in favor of direct realism are fairly compelling. Accordingly, I propose to take direct realism as the jumping-off point for the construction of low-level epistemological theories. Being able to construct low-level theories consonant with direct realism is a necessary condition for direct realism to be correct. Should it prove impossible to construct the low-level theories, direct realism would have to be abandoned. For this reason, the OSCAR Project takes its principal task to be that of constructing and implementing such low-level theories. The end result will be a functioning artificial intellect. The construction of such an artilect is a challenge that must ultimately be met by any satisfactory epistemological theory. Let me take this opportunity to throw down the gauntlet to other epistemologists who are so perverse as to not agree with me about direct realism. If they are to defend their theories adequately, unrepentant coherentists, probabilists, etc., must not only answer the theoretical objections that I and others have leveled against them – they must show that it is possible to build an artilect founded on their structural theories of epistemic justification. I seriously doubt that any of them can meet this challenge. On the other hand, direct realism is well on its way to meeting this challenge.

Let me turn then to the construction of low-level theories in the OSCAR Project. According to direct realism, justified beliefs are inferred from various mental states and from other justified beliefs. The task of constructing low-level theories is that of describing the various species of reasoning that can lead to justified beliefs about different subject matters. Before we can implement such a theory, however, we must have an implementation of reasoning *per se*. In other words, low-level theories must be implemented on top of an *inference engine*. The nature of the requisite inference engine is the subject of what I earlier called "mid-level theories". Most of the work on the OSCAR Project over the last decade has concerned the formulation and implementation of a general theory of defeasible and deductive reasoning. The resulting theory and implementation is described in detail in my *Cognitive Carpentry* and *The OSCAR Manual*.[10] There isn't time or space to discuss that here, so for the rest of the paper I will just take that theory for granted. Interested readers should peruse the aforementioned publications.

The OSCAR Project has only recently reached the point where the inference engine is reasonably complete and hence attention can be directed at low-level theories. Topics that have thus far been investigated include reasoning from perceptual input, certain kinds of temporal and causal reasoning (including an implemented solution to the frame problem),[11] and work has begun on practical reasoning and planning. I will close this paper with an extended example of low-level theorizing about reasoning from perception.

4. Reasoning from Percepts

The fundamental principle underlying direct realism is that perception provides reasons for judgments about the world, and that the inference is made directly from the percept rather than being mediated by a (basic) belief about the percept. The principle can be formulated very simply as follows:

PERCEPTION
Having a percept at time t with the content P is a defeasible reason for the agent to believe *P-at-t*.

The traditional "problem of perception" was to explain what justifies an inference like this. The answer forthcoming from the account of human rationality proposed above is that nothing justifies this. This is one of the basic principles of rational cognition that make up the human rational architecture. This is partially constitutive of our knowledge of how to cognize. It cannot be derived from anything more basic. This principle, or something like it, must be present in the rational architecture of any agent that is capable of reacting to the way the world is. By definition, rational agents direct their activity in response to their beliefs about the way the world is, so some such principle is an essential ingredient of the rational architecture of any rational agent.

When giving an account of a species of defeasible reasoning, it is as important to characterize the defeaters for the defeasible reasons as it is to state the reasons themselves. One of the central doctrines of that theory of defeasible reasons and reasoning implemented in OSCAR is that there are just two kinds of defeaters – *rebutting defeaters* and *undercutting defeaters*. Any reason for denying *P-at-t* is a rebutting defeater for **PERCEPTION**. An undercutting defeater for an inference from a belief in P to a belief in Q attacks the connection between P and Q rather than merely denying the conclusion. An undercutting defeater is a reason for the formula $(P \otimes Q)$ (read "It is false that P would not be true unless Q were true," or abbreviated as "P does not guarantee Q").[12] The only obvious undercutting defeater for **PERCEPTION** is a reliability defeater, which is of a general sort applicable to all defeasible reasons. Reliability defeaters result from observing that the inference from P to Q is not, under the present circumstances, reliable. To make this precise it is necessary to understand how reason-strengths work in

OSCAR. Some reasons are better than others. In OSCAR, reason-strengths range from 0 to 1. Reason-strengths are calibrated by comparing them with the *statistical syllogism*, according to which, when $r > 0.5$, "Bc & prob $(A/B) = r$" is a defeasible reason for "Ac", the strength of the reason being a function of r.[13] A reason of strength r is taken to have the same strength as an instance of the statistical syllogism from a probability of $2 \cdot (r - 0.5)$. The inference rule **PERCEPTION** will have some strength r, although for artificial agents this may vary from agent to agent. The value of r should correspond roughly to the reliability of an agent's system of perceptual input in the circumstances in which it normally functions. **PERCEPTUAL-RELIABILITY** constitutes a defeater by informing us that under the present circumstances, perception is not as reliable as it is normally assumed to be:

PERCEPTUAL-RELIABILITY
Where R is projectible, r is the strength of **PERCEPTION**, and $s < 0.5 \cdot (r + 1)$, "R-at-t, and the probability is less than or equal to s of P's being true given R and that I have a percept with content P" is an undercutting defeater for **PERCEPTION** as a reason of strength $\geq r$.

The projectibility constraint in this principle is a perplexing one. To illustrate its need, suppose I have a percept of a red object, and am in improbable but irrelevant circumstances of some type C_1. For instance, C_1 might consist of my having been born in the first second of the first minute of the first hour of the first year of the twentieth century. Let C_2 be circumstances consisting of wearing rose-colored glasses. When I am wearing rose-colored glasses, the probability is not particularly high that an object is red just because it looks red, so if I were in circumstances of type C_2, that would quite properly be a reliability defeater for a judgment that there is a red object before me. However, if I am in circumstances of type C_1 but not of C_2, there should be no reliability defeater. The difficulty is that if I am in circumstances of type C_1, then I am also in the disjunctive circumstances $(C_1 \vee C_2)$. Furthermore, the probability of being in circumstances of type C_2 given that one is in circumstances of type $(C_1 \vee C_2)$ is very high, so the probability is not high that an object is red given that it looks red to me but I am in circumstances $(C_1 \vee C_2)$. Consequently, if $(C_1 \vee C_2)$ were allowed as an instantiation of R in **PERCEPTUAL-RELIABILITY**, being in circumstances of type C_1 would suffice to indirectly defeat the perceptual judgment.

The preceding example shows that the set of circumstance-types appropriate for use in **PERCEPTUAL-RELIABILITY** is not closed under disjunction. This is a general characteristic of projectibility constraints. The need for a projectibility constraint in induction is familiar to most philosophers (although unrecognized in many other fields).[14] I showed in Pollock (1990) that the same constraint occurs throughout probabilistic reasoning, and the constraint on induction can be regarded as derivative from a constraint on the statistical syllogism.[15] However, similar constraints occur in other contexts and do not appear to be derivative from the constraints on the statistical syllogism. The constraint on reliability defeaters is one example of this, and another example will be given below. Unfortunately, at this time there is no generally acceptable theory of projectibility. The term "projectible" serves more as the label for a problem than as an indication of the solution to the problem.

PERCEPTUAL-RELIABILITY constitutes a defeater by informing us that under the present circumstances, perception is not as reliable as it is normally assumed to be. Notice, however, that this should not prevent our drawing conclusions with a weaker level of justification. The probability recorded in **PERCEPTUAL-RELIABILITY** should function merely to weaken the strength of the perceptual inference rather than completely blocking it. This can be accomplished by supplementing **PERCEPTION** with the following rule:

DISCOUNTED-PERCEPTION
Where R is projectible, r is the strength of **PERCEPTION**, and $0.5 < s < 0.5 \cdot (r + 1)$, having a percept at time t with the content P and the belief "R-at-t, and the probability is less than s of P's being true given R and that I have a percept with content P" is a defeasible reason of strength $2 \cdot (s - 0.5)$ for the agent to believe P-at-t.

DISCOUNTED-PERCEPTION must be defeasible in the same way **PERCEPTION** is:

PERCEPTUAL-UNRELIABILITY
Where A is projectible and $s^* < s$, "A-at-t, and the probability is less than or equal to s^* of P's being true given A and that I have a percept with content P" is a defeater for **DISCOUNTED-PERCEPTION**.

In a particular situation, the agent may know that a number of facts hold each of which is sufficient to lower the reliability of perception. The preceding principles have the consequence that the only undefeated inference from the percept will be that made in accordance with the weakest instance of **DISCOUNTED-PERCEPTION**.[16]

5. Implementation

Reasoning in OSCAR consists of the construction of natural-deduction-style arguments, using both deductive inference rules and defeasible reason-schemas. Premises are input to the reasoner (either as background knowledge or as new percepts), and queries are passed to the reasoner. OSCAR performs bidirectional reasoning. The reasoner reasons forwards from the premises and backwards from the queries. The queries are "epistemic interests", and backwards reasoning can be viewed as deriving interests from interests. Conclusions are stored as nodes in the inference-graph (*inference-nodes*).

Reasoning proceeds in terms of reasons. *Backwards-reasons* are used in reasoning backwards, and *forwards-reasons* are used in reasoning forwards. Forwards-reasons are data-structures with the following fields:

- reason-name.
- forwards-premises – a list of forwards-premises.
- backwards-premises – a list of backwards-premises.
- reason-conclusion – a formula.
- defeasible-rule – T if the reason is a defeasible reason, NIL otherwise.[17]
- reason-variables – variables used in pattern-matching to find instances of the reason-premises.
- reason-strength – a real number between 0 and 1, or an expression containing some of the reason-variables and evaluating to a number.
- reason-description – an optional string describing the reason.

Forwards-premises are data-structures encoding the following information:

- fp-formula – a formula.
- fp-kind – :inference, :percept, or :desire (the default is :inference)
- fp-condition – an optional constraint that must be satisfied by an inference-node for it to instantiate this premise.
- clue? – explained below.

Similarly, *backwards-premises* are data-structures encoding the following information:

- bp-formula.
- bp-kind.
- bp-condition.

The use of the premise-kind is to check whether the formula from which a forwards inference proceeds represents a desire, percept, or the result of an inference. The contents of precepts, desires, and inferences are all encoded as formulas, but the inferences that can be made from them depend upon which kind of item they are. For example, we reason quite differently from the desire that x be red, the percept of x's being red, and the conclusion that x is red.

Backwards-reasons will be data-structures encoding the following information:

- reason-name.
- forwards-premises.
- backwards-premises.
- reason-conclusion – a formula.
- reason-variables – variables used in pattern-matching to find instances of the reason-premises.

- strength – a real number between 0 and 1, or an expression containing some of the reason-variables and evaluating to a number.
- defeasible-rule – T if the reason is a defeasible reason, NIL otherwise.
- reason-condition – a condition that must be satisfied by the sequent of interest before the reason is to be deployed.

Simple forwards-reasons have no backwards-premises, and *simple backwards-reasons* have no forwards-premises. Given inference-nodes that instantiate the premises of a simple forwards-reason, the reasoner infers the corresponding instances of the conclusions. Similarly, given an interest that instantiates the conclusion of a simple backwards-reason, the reasoner adopts interest in the corresponding instances of the backwards-premises. Given inference-nodes that discharge those interests, an inference is made to the conclusions from those inference-nodes.

In deductive reasoning, with the exception of a rule of reductio ad absurdum, we are unlikely to encounter any but simple forwards- and backwards-reasons.[18] However, the use of backwards-premises in forwards-reasons and the use of forwards-premises in backwards-reasons provides an invaluable form of control over the way reasoning progresses. This will be illustrated at length below. *Mixed* forwards- and backwards-reasons are those having both forwards- and backwards-premises. Given inference-nodes that instantiate the forwards-premises of a mixed forwards-reason, the reasoner does not immediately infer the conclusion. Instead the reasoner adopts interest in the corresponding instances of the backwards-premises, and an inference is made only when those interests are discharged. Similarly, given an interest instantiating the first conclusion of a mixed backwards-reason, interests are not immediately adopted in the backwards-premises. Interests in the backwards-premises are adopted only when inference-nodes are constructed that instantiate the forwards-premises.

There can also be *degenerate backwards-reasons* that have only forwards-premises. In a degenerate backwards-reason, given an interest instantiating the first conclusion, the reasoner then becomes "sensitive to" inference-nodes instantiating the forwards-premises, but does not adopt interest in them (and thereby actively search for arguments to establish them). If appropriate inference-nodes are produced by other reasoning, then an inference is made to the conclusions. Degenerate backwards-reasons are thus much like simple forwards-reasons, except that the conclusion is only drawn if there is an interest in it.

Reasons are most easily defined in OSCAR using the macros **DEF-FORWARDS-REASON** and **DEF-BACKWARDS-REASON**:

(def-forwards-reason *symbol*
   :forwards-premises *list of formulas optionally interspersed with expressions of the form (:kind . . .) or (:condition . . .)*
   :backwards-premises *list of formulas optionally interspersed with expressions of the form (:kind . . .) or (:condition . . .)*
   :conclusion *a formula*
   :strength *number or a an expression containing some of the reason-variables and evaluating to a number.*

```
:variables list of symbols
:defeasible? T or NIL (NIL is the default)
:description an optional string (quoted) describing the reason)

(def-backwards-reason symbol
    :conclusion a formula
    :forwards-premises list of formulas optionally interspersed with expressions of the form
        (:kind ... ) or (:condition ... )
    :backwards-premises list of formulas optionally interspersed with expressions of the form
        (:kind ... ) or (:condition ... )
    :condition this is a predicate applied to the binding produced by the target sequent
    :strength number or an expression containing some of the reason-variables and evaluating
        to a number.
    :variables list of symbols
    :defeasible? T or NIL (NIL is the default)
    :description an optional string (quoted) describing the reason)
```

The use of these macros will be illustrated below.

Epistemic reasoning begins from contingent information input into the system in the form of percepts. Percepts are encoded as structures with the following fields:

- percept-content – a formula, with temporal reference built in.
- percept-clarity – a number between 0 and 1, indicating how strong a reason the percept provides for the conclusion of a perceptual inference.
- percept-date – a number.

When a new percept is presented to OSCAR, an inference-node of kind :percept is constructed, having a node-formula that is the percept-content of the percept (this includes the percept-date). This inference-node is then inserted into the inference-queue for processing.

Using the tools described above, we can implement **PERCEPTION** as a simple forwards-reason:

```
(def-forwards-reason PERCEPTION
    :forwards-premises "(p at time)" (:kind :percept)
    :conclusion "(p at time)"
    :variables p time
    :defeasible? t
    :strength .98
    :description "When information is input, it is defeasibly reasonable to believe it.")
```

The strength of .98 has been chosen arbitrarily.

PERCEPTUAL-RELIABILITY was formulated as follows:

PERCEPTUAL-RELIABILITY

Where R is projectible, r is the strength of **PERCEPTION**, and $s < 0.5 \cdot (r + 1)$, "R-at-t, and the probability is less than or equal to s of P's being true given R and that I have a percept with content P" is an under-cutting defeater for **PERCEPTION** as a reason of strength $\geq r$.

It seems clear that this should be treated as a backwards-reason. That is, given an interest in the undercutting defeater for **PERCEPTION**, this reason-schema should be activated, but if the reasoner is not interested in the undercutting defeater, this reason-schema should have no effect on the reasoner. However, treating this as a simple backwards-reason is impossible, because there are no constraints (other than projectibility) on R. We do not want interest in the undercutting defeater to lead to interest in every projectible R. Nor do we want the reasoner to spend its time trying to determine the reliability of perception given everything it happens to know about the situation. This can be avoided by making this a degenerate backwards-reason (no backwards-premises), taking $R\text{-}at\text{-}t$ (where t is the time of the percept) and the probability premise to be forwards-premises. This suggests the following definition:

```
(def-backwards-undercutter PERCEPTUAL-RELIABILITY
  :defeatee PERCEPTION
  :forwards-premises
  "((the probability of p given ((I have a percept with content p) & R)) ≤ s)"
  (:condition (and (s < 0.99) (projectible R)))
  "(R at time)"
  :variables p time R s
  :defeasible? t
  :description "When perception is unreliable, it is not reasonable to accept its representations.")
```

(**DEF-BACKWARDS-UNDERCUTTER** is a variant of **DEF-BACKWARDS-REASON** that computes the reason-conclusions for us.) For now, I will take the projectible formulas to be any conjunctions of atomic formulas and negations of atomic formulas, although it must be recognized that this is simplistic and will ultimately have to be refined.

A problem remains for this implementation. **PERCEPTUAL-RELIABILITY** requires us to know that R is true at the time of the percept. We will typically know this only by inferring it from the fact that R was true earlier. The nature of this inference is the topic of the next section. Without this inference, it is not possible to give interesting illustrations of the implementation just described, so that will be postponed until section 7.

6. Temporal Projection[19]

The reason-schema **PERCEPTION** enables an agent to draw conclusions about its current surroundings on the basis of its current percepts. It is natural to suppose that this suffices to provide an agent with the basic data it needs to reason about the world, and if we supplement this with "higher level" reason-schemas enabling it to reason inductively, together perhaps with some special purpose reason-schemas pertaining to reasoning about particular subject matters like other minds, then the agent will be able to reason its way to a rich model of the world.

However, there is a gap in this reasoning that has been overlooked by epistemologists. The problem is that perception is really a form of sampling. It is not possible to continually monitor the entire state of the world perceptually. All we can do is sample small space–time chunks of the world and then make inferences from combinations of these samplings. There is a surprising difficulty connected with making inferences from combinations of perceptual samplings. This can be illustrated by considering a robot whose task is to visually check the readings of two meters and then press one of two buttons depending upon which reading is higher. This should not be a hard task, but if we assume that the robot can only look at one meter at a time, it will not be able to acquire the requisite information about the meters using only the reason-schema **PERCEPTION**. The robot can look at one meter and draw a conclusion about its value, but when the robot turns to read the other meter, it no longer has a percept of the first and so is no longer in a position to hold a justified belief about what that meter reads *now*. The cognitive architecture of the robot must be supplemented with some reason for believing that the first meter still reads what it read a moment ago. In other words, the robot must have some basis for regarding the meter reading as a *stable property* – one that tends not to change quickly over time.

One might suppose that a rational agent that can reason inductively would be able to discover that properties like meter readings are stable over at least short intervals. However, it turns out to be impossible to perform the requisite inductive reasoning without already presupposing the stability at issue. To say that a property is stable is to say that objects possessing it tend to retain it. To confirm this inductively, an agent would have to reexamine the same object at different times and determine whether the property has changed. The difficulty is that in order to do this, the agent must be able to reidentify the object as the same object at different times. Although this is a complex matter, it seems clear that the agent makes essential use of the perceptible properties of objects in reidentifying them. If the perceptible properties of objects fluctuated rapidly and unpredictably, it would be impossible to reidentify them. The upshot of this is that it is epistemically impossible to investigate the stability of perceptible properties inductively without presupposing that most of them tend to be stable.[20] Some such assumption of stability must be built into the cognitive architecture of an agent capable of learning about the world perceptually. On the other hand, given an assumption of stability, the agent can use induction to refine it by discovering that some perceptible properties are more stable than others, that particular properties tend to be unstable under specifiable circumstances, etc. Apparently, a rational agent must come equipped with reason-schemas of the following sort for at least some choices of P:

(1) If $t_0 < t_1$, believing $P\text{-}at\text{-}t_0$ is a defeasible reason for the agent to believe $P\text{-}at\text{-}t_1$.

A stable property is one such that if it holds at one time, the probability is high that it will continue to hold at a later time. Let ρ be the probability that P will

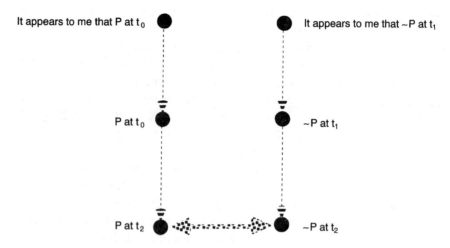

Figure 16.1 The perceptual updating system

hold at time $t+1$ given that it holds at time t. Assuming independence, it follows that the probability that P will hold at time $(t + \Delta t)$ given that it holds at time t is $\rho^{\Delta t}$. In other words, the strength of the presumption that a stable property will continue to hold over time decays as the time interval increases. This has very important consequences for perception. Consider *the perceptual updating problem* in which an agent has a percept of P at time t_0, and a percept of $\sim P$ at a later time t_1. What an agent *should* conclude (defeasibly) under these circumstances is that the world has changed between t_0 and t_1, and although P was true at t_0, it is no longer true at t_1 and hence no longer true at a later time t_2. If we attempt to reconstruct this reasoning using principle (1) without taking account of decaying reason strengths, we get the wrong answer. We get the resoning diagrammed in figure 16.1, where the dashed arrows represent defeasible inferences and the "fuzzy" arrows represent defeat relations. This inference-graph is a straightforward case of collective defeat. That is, the conclusion P-at-t_2 and the conclusion $\sim P$-at-t_2 are both inferred defeasibly, but they contradict each other, so each constitutes a rebutting defeater for the other. On any theory of defeasible reasoning, this has the consequence that both conclusions are defeated. This would make perceptual updating impossible. However, once we take account of reason strengths, the problem evaporates. A probability of $\rho^{\Delta t}$ corresponds to a reason-strength of $2 \cdot (\rho^{\Delta t} - .5)$. $\rho^{\Delta t} > .5$ iff $\Delta t < \log(.5)/\log(\rho)$, so we can build decaying reason strengths into principle (1) by reformulating it as follows:

(2) When $\Delta t < \log(.5)/\log(\rho)$, believing P-at-t is a defeasible reason of strength $2 \cdot (\rho^{\Delta t} - .5)$ for the agent to believe P-at-$(t + \Delta t)$.

Principle (2) has the consequence that the support for P-at-t_2 is weaker than the support for $\sim P$-at-t_2, and hence the former is defeated and it is defeasibly reasonable to accept the latter.

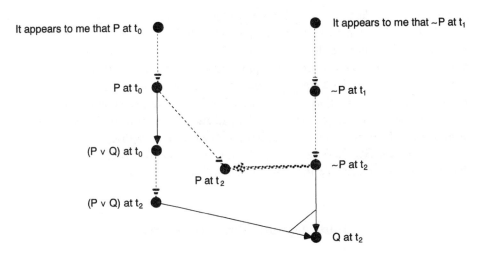

Figure 16.2 The need for a temporal projectibility constraint

Although principle (2) handles the example of figure 16.1 correctly, it is not yet an adequate formulation of a reason-schema for temporal projection. The difficulty is that it is subject to a projectibility problem, much like that discussed above in connection with **PERCEPTUAL-RELIABILITY**. This is illustrated by the example diagrammed in figure 16.2, where solid arrows symbolize deductive inferences, and bars connecting arrows indicate that the inference is from multiple premises. In this example, the conclusion $Q\text{-}at\text{-}t_2$ comes out undefeated. But this is intuitively preposterous. $Q\text{-}at\text{-}t_2$ is inferred from $(P \vee Q)\text{-}at\text{-}t_2$. $(P \vee Q)$ is expected to be true at t_2 only because it was true at t_0, and it was only true at t_0 because P was true at t_0. This makes it reasonable to believe $(P \vee Q)\text{-}at\text{-}t_2$ only insofar as it is reasonable to believe $P\text{-}at\text{-}t_2$, but the latter is defeated. The source of the difficulty here is that temporal projection is being applied to $(P \vee Q)$. Apparently it should only be applied to P, and then $(P \vee Q)$ inferred *from* P. To accomplish this we must build a projectibility constraint into principle (2):

TEMPORAL-PROJECTION
If P is temporally-projectible and $\Delta t < \log(.5)/\log(\rho)$ then believing $P\text{-}at\text{-}t$ is a defeasible reason of strength $2 \cdot (\rho^{\Delta t} - .5)$ for the agent to believe $P\text{-}at\text{-}(t + \Delta t)$.

It is unclear precisely what the connection is between the projectibility constraint involved in temporal projection and that involved in induction, so I have referred to it neutrally as "temporal-projectibility". Notice that in temporal-unprojectibility, disjunctions are not the only culprits. The ascriptions of properties to objects will generally be projectible, but the negations of such ascriptions need not be. For instance, "x is red" would seem to be temporally projectible. But "x is not red" is equivalent to a disjunction "x is blue or green or yellow or orange or ...", and as such it would seem to be temporally unprojectible. On the other hand, there are "bivalent" properties, like "dead" and "alive" for which the negation of an ascription is projectible because it is equivalent to ascribing the other (temporally-projectible) property. For a complete theory of this reasoning, we must supplement TEMPORAL-PROJECTION with an analysis of temporal-projectibility. Unfortunately, that proves no easier than providing an analysis of projectibility as it occurs in induction. I do not, at this time, have an analysis to propose.

TEMPORAL-PROJECTION must also be supplemented with an account of defeaters for this defeasible inference, but I will not pursue that here.[21]

7. Implementing Temporal Projection

In order to implement TEMPORAL-PROJECTION, we must have a test for the temporal-projectibility of formulas. Lacking a theory of temporal-projectibility, I will finesse this by assuming that atomic formulas, negations of atomic formulas whose predicates are on a list *bivalent-predicates*, and conjunctions of the above, are temporally projectible. This will almost certainly be inadequate in the long run, but it will suffice for testing most features of the proposed reason-schemas.

It seems clear that TEMPORAL-PROJECTION must be treated as a backwards-reason. That is, given some belief P-at-t, we do not want the reasoner to automatically infer P-at-$(t + \Delta t)$ for every one of the infinitely many times $\Delta t > 0$. An agent should only make such an inference when the conclusion is of interest. For the same reason, the premise P-at-t should be a forwards-premise rather than a backwards-premise — we do not want the reasoner adopting interest in P-at-$(t - \Delta t)$ for every $\Delta t > 0$. Making TEMPORAL-PROJECTION a backwards reason has the effect that when the reasoner adopts interest in P-at-t, it will check to see whether it already has a conclusion of the form P-at-t_0 for $t_0 < t$, and if so it will infer P-at-t. This produces a degenerate backwards-reason:

```
(def-backwards-reason TEMPORAL-PROJECTION
   :conclusion "(p at time)"
   :condition (and (temporally-projectible p) (numberp time))
   :forwards-premises
      "(p at time0)"
      (:condition (and (time0 < time*) ((time* - time0) < log(.5)/log(*temporal-decay*))))
   :variables p time0 time
   :defeasible? T
   :strength (- (* 2 (expt *temporal-decay* (- time time0))) 1)
   :description
   "It is defeasibly reasonable to expect temporally projectible truths to remain unchanged.")
```

To illustrate this implementation, consider the perceptual updating problem:

```
===========================================================================
```
First, Fred looks red to me. Later, Fred looks blue to me. What should I conclude about the color of Fred?

Forwards-substantive-reasons:
    PERCEPTION

Backwards-substantive-reasons:
    TEMPORAL-PROJECTION
    INCOMPATIBLE-COLORS

Inputs:
    (the color of Fred is red) : at cycle 1 with justification 1.0
    (the color of Fred is blue) : at cycle 30 with justification 1.0

Ultimate epistemic interests:
    (? x)((the color of Fred is x) at 50)   degree of interest = 0.5
```
===========================================================================
```
THE FOLLOWING IS THE REASONING INVOLVED IN THE SOLUTION
Nodes marked DEFEATED have that status at the end of the reasoning.

                # 1
                interest: ((the color of Fred is y0) at 50)
                This is of ultimate interest
||||||||||||||||||||||||||||||||||||||||||||||||||||||||||||||||||||||||||
It appears to me that ((the color of Fred is red) at 1)
||||||||||||||||||||||||||||||||||||||||||||||||||||||||||||||||||||||||||
1
It appears to me that ((the color of Fred is red) at 1)
2
((the color of Fred is red) at 1)
Inferred by:
    support-link #1 from { 1 } by PERCEPTION
undefeated-degree-of-support = 0.98
3
((the color of Fred is red) at 50)   DEFEATED
undefeated-degree-of-support = 0.904
Inferred by:
    support-link #2 from { 2 } by TEMPORAL-PROJECTION defeaters: { 7 } DEFEATED
This discharges interest 1
                # 5
                interest: ~((the color of Fred is red) at 50)
                Of interest as a defeater for support-link 2 for node 3
```
=========================================
```
Justified belief in ((the color of Fred is red) at 50)
with undefeated-degree-of-support 0.904
answers #<Query 1: (? x)((the color of Fred is x) at 50)>
```
=========================================
```
||||||||||||||||||||||||||||||||||||||||||||||||||||||||||||||||||||||||||
It appears to me that ((the color of Fred is blue) at 30)
||||||||||||||||||||||||||||||||||||||||||||||||||||||||||||||||||||||||||
4
It appears to me that ((the color of Fred is blue) at 30)
5
((the color of Fred is blue) at 30)
Inferred by:
    support-link #3 from { 4 } by PERCEPTION
undefeated-degree-of-support = 0.98
6
((the color of Fred is blue) at 50)
Inferred by:
    support-link #4 from { 5 } by TEMPORAL-PROJECTION defeaters: { 8 }
undefeated-degree-of-support = 0.960
This discharges interest 1

```
# 9
    interest: ~((the color of Fred is blue) at 50)
    Of interest as a defeater for support-link 4 for node 6
==========================================
    Justified belief in ((the color of Fred is blue) at 50)
    with undefeated-degree-of-support 0.960
    answers #<Query 1: (? x)((the color of Fred is x) at 50)>
==========================================
# 7
~((the color of Fred is red) at 50)
Inferred by:
        support-link #5 from { 6 } by INCOMPATIBLE-COLORS
undefeated-degree-of-support = 0.960
defeatees: { link 2 for node 3 }
        vvvvvvvvvvvvvvvvvvvvvvvvv
        #<Node 3> has become defeated.
        vvvvvvvvvvvvvvvvvvvvvvvvv
==========================================
    Lowering the undefeated-degree-of-support of ((the color of Fred is red) at 50)
    retracts the previous answer to #<Query 1: (? x)((the color of Fred is x) at 50)>
==========================================
================ ULTIMATE EPISTEMIC INTERESTS ==================
Interest in (? x)((the color of Fred is x) at 50)
is answered by node 6: ((the color of Fred is blue) at 50)
-------------------------------------------
```

Now let us return to the problem noted above for **PERCEPTUAL-RELIABILITY**. This is that we will typically know R-at-t only by inferring it from R-at-t_0 for some $t_0 < t$ (by **TEMPORAL-PROJECTION**). **TEMPORAL-PROJECTION** is a backwards-reason. That is, given some fact P-at-t, the reasoner only infers P-at-t^* (for $t^* > t$) when that conclusion is of interest. Unfortunately, in **PERCEPTUAL-RELIABILITY**, R-at-t is not an interest, and so it will not be inferred from R-at-t_0 by **TEMPORAL-PROJECTION**. This difficulty can be circumvented by formulating **PERCEPTUAL-RELIABILITY** with an extra forwards-premise R-at-t_0 which is marked as a *clue*, and a backwards-premise R-at-t:

```
(def-backwards-undercutter PERCEPTUAL-RELIABILITY
    :defeatee *perception*
    :forwards-premises
      "((the probability of p given ((I have a percept with content p) & R)) ≤ s)"
      (:condition (and (projectible R) (s < 0.99)))
      "(R at time0)"
      (:condition (time0 < time))
      (:clue? t)
    :backwards-premises "(R at time)"
    :variables p time R time0 s
    :defeasible? t
    :description "When perception is unreliable, it is not reasonable to accept its
    representations.")
```

The difference between ordinary forwards-premises and clues is that when a clue is instantiated by a conclusion that has been drawn, that conclusion is not included in the list of conclusions from which the new conclusion is inferred. The function of clues is only to guide the reasoning. Thus in an application of **PERCEPTUAL-RELIABILITY**, if R-at-t_0 is concluded, this suggests that R-at-t is true and leads to an interest in it, which can then be inferred from $R\text{-}at\text{-}t_0$ by **TEMPORAL-PROJECTION**.

The implementation of these rules can be illustrated by the following example:

===
The agent wants to know the color of Fred at time 10. Fred looks red at time 10. This provides a strong defeasible reason for thinking Fred is red at time 10. But at time 15 the agent learns that it was wearing red tinted glasses at time 1, and it knows that the probability of something being red given that it appears red when one is wearing red tinted glasses is ≤ .8. By TEMPORAL-PROJECTION it can infer that it was still wearing red tinted glasses at time 10, and so the inference to the conclusion that Fred is red at time 10 is defeated by PERCEPTUAL-RELIABILITY. DISCOUNTED-PERCEPTION reinstates the inference, but with a weaker degree of justification. Then at time 30 the agent learns that its surroundings were illuminated by red light at time 1, and it knows that the probability of something being red given that it appears red when its surroundings were illuminated by red light is ≤ .8. By TEMPORAL-PROJECTION the agent can infer that its surroundings were still illuminated by red light at time 10, so the second inference to the conclusion that Fred is red at time 10 is defeated by PERCEPTUAL-UNRELIABILITY. Again, DISCOUNTED-PERCEPTION reinstates the inference, but with a still weaker degree of justification. Finally, at time 50 the agent learns that its surroundings were not illuminated by red light at time 8. By the reasoning involved in perceptual updating, this defeats the inference to the conclusion that its surroundings were still illuminated by red light at time 10, thus reinstating the second inference to the conclusion that Fred is red at time 10.

Forwards-substantive-reasons:
    PERCEPTION
    DISCOUNTED-PERCEPTION

Backwards-substantive-reasons:
    PERCEPTUAL-RELIABILITY
    PERCEPTUAL-UNRELIABILITY
    TEMPORAL-PROJECTION
    NEG-AT-INTRO

Inputs:
    (the color of Fred is red) : at cycle 10 with justification 1.0

Given:
    ((the probability of (the color of Fred is red) given ((I have a percept with content (the color of Fred is
        red)) & my surroundings are illuminated by red light)) ≤ 0.7) : with justification = 1.0
    ((the probability of (the color of Fred is red) given ((I have a percept with content (the color of Fred is
        red)) & I am wearing red tinted glasses)) ≤ 0.8) : with justification = 1.0
    (I am wearing red tinted glasses at 1) : at cycle 15 with justification = 1.0
    (my surroundings are illuminated by red light at 1) : at cycle 30 with justification = 1.0
    (~my surroundings are illuminated by red light at 8) : at cycle 50 with justification = 1.0

Ultimate epistemic interests:
    ((the color of Fred is red) at 10)   degree of interest = 0.5
===
THE FOLLOWING IS THE REASONING INVOLVED IN THE SOLUTION
Nodes marked DEFEATED have that status at the end of the reasoning.

\# 1
((the probability of (the color of Fred is red) given ((I have a percept with content (the color of Fred is red))
    & my surroundings are illuminated by red light)) ≤ 0.7)
given
\# 2
((the probability of (the color of Fred is red) given ((I have a percept with content (the color of Fred is red))
    & I am wearing red tinted glasses)) ≤ 0.8)
given
                    \# 1
                    interest: ((the color of Fred is red) at 10)
                    This is of ultimate interest
|||||||||||||||||||||||||||||||||||||||||||||||||||||||||||||||||||
It appears to me that ((the color of Fred is red) at 10)
|||||||||||||||||||||||||||||||||||||||||||||||||||||||||||||||||||

3
It appears to me that ((the color of Fred is red) at 10)
4
((the color of Fred is red) at 10)
Inferred by:
    support-link #3 from { 3 } by PERCEPTION defeaters: { 7 } DEFEATED
This node is inferred by discharging interest 1
    # 2
    interest: (((it appears to me that (the color of Fred is red)) at 10) $\otimes$ ((the color of Fred is red) at 10))
    Of interest as a defeater for support-link 3 for node 4
==
Justified belief in ((the color of Fred is red) at 10)
with undefeated-degree-of-support 0.98
answers #<Query 1: ((the color of Fred is red) at 10)>
==
5
(I am wearing red tinted glasses at 1)
given
    # 5
    interest: (I am wearing red tinted glasses at 10)
    For interest 1 by DISCOUNTED-PERCEPTION
    For interest 2 by PERCEPTUAL-RELIABILITY
    This interest is discharged by node 6
6
(I am wearing red tinted glasses at 10)
Inferred by:
    support-link #5 from { 5 } by TEMPORAL-PROJECTION
This discharges interest 5
4
((the color of Fred is red) at 10)
Inferred by:
    support-link #6 from { 2 , 3 , 6 } by DISCOUNTED-PERCEPTION defeaters: { 10 }
    support-link #3 from { 3 } by PERCEPTION defeaters: { 7 } DEFEATED
This node is inferred by discharging interests (1 1)
    # 8
    interest: ((((the probability of (the color of Fred is red) given ((I have a percept with content (the color of Fred is red)) & I am wearing red tinted glasses)) $\leq$ 0.8) & (((it appears to me that (the color of Fred is red)) at 10) & (I am wearing red tinted glasses at 10))) $\otimes$ ((the color of Fred is red) at 10))
    Of interest as a defeater for support-link 6 for node 4
7
(((it appears to me that (the color of Fred is red)) at 10) $\otimes$ ((the color of Fred is red) at 10))
Inferred by:
    support-link #7 from { 2 , 6 } by PERCEPTUAL-RELIABILITY
defeatees: { link 3 for node 4 }
This node is inferred by discharging interest 2
    vvvvvvvvvvvvvvvvvvvvvvvvvvv
    The undefeated-degree-of-support of #<Node 4> has decreased to 0.6
    vvvvvvvvvvvvvvvvvvvvvvvvvvv
8
(my surroundings are illuminated by red light at 1)
given
    # 12
    interest: (my surroundings are illuminated by red light at 10)
    For interest 1 by DISCOUNTED-PERCEPTION
    For interest 2 by PERCEPTUAL-RELIABILITY
    For interest 8 by PERCEPTUAL-UNRELIABILITY
    This interest is discharged by node 9
9
(my surroundings are illuminated by red light at 10)   DEFEATED
Inferred by:
    support-link #9 from { 8 } by TEMPORAL-PROJECTION defeaters: { 13 } DEFEATED
This discharges interest 12

14
interest: ~(my surroundings are illuminated by red light at 10)
Of interest as a defeater for support-link 9 for node 9

4
((the color of Fred is red) at 10)
Inferred by:
    support-link #10 from { 1 , 3 , 9 } by DISCOUNTED-PERCEPTION   DEFEATED
    support-link #6 from { 2 , 3 , 6 } by DISCOUNTED-PERCEPTION defeaters: { 10 }
    support-link #3 from { 3 } by PERCEPTION defeaters: { 7 }   DEFEATED
This node is inferred by discharging interests (1 1)

7
(((it appears to me that (the color of Fred is red)) at 10) ⊗ ((the color of Fred is red) at 10))
Inferred by:
    support-link #11 from { 1 , 9 } by PERCEPTUAL-RELIABILITY   DEFEATED
    support-link #7 from { 2 , 6 } by PERCEPTUAL-RELIABILITY
defeatees: { link 3 for node 4 }
This node is inferred by discharging interest 2

10
((((the probability of (the color of Fred is red) given ((I have a percept with content (the color of Fred is red)) & I am wearing red tinted glasses)) $\leq$ 0.8) & (((it appears to me that (the color of Fred is red)) at 10) & (I am wearing red tinted glasses at 10))) ⊗ ((the color of Fred is red) at 10))   DEFEATED
Inferred by:
    support-link #12 from { 1 , 9 } by PERCEPTUAL-UNRELIABILITY   DEFEATED
defeatees: { link 6 for node 4 }
This node is inferred by discharging interest #8

vvvvvvvvvvvvvvvvvvvvvvvvvvv
The undefeated-degree-of-support of #<Node 4> has decreased to 0.4
vvvvvvvvvvvvvvvvvvvvvvvvvvv

==
Lowering the undefeated-degree-of-support of ((the color of Fred is red) at 10) retracts the previous answer to #<Query 1: ((the color of Fred is red) at 10)>
==

19
interest: (~my surroundings are illuminated by red light at 10)
For interest 14 by NEG-AT-INTRO
This interest is discharged by node 12

11
(~my surroundings are illuminated by red light at 8)
given

12
(~my surroundings are illuminated by red light at 10)
Inferred by:
    support-link #14 from { 11 } by TEMPORAL-PROJECTION defeaters: { 14 }
This discharges interest 19

21
interest: ~(~my surroundings are illuminated by red light at 10)
Of interest as a defeater for support-link 14 for node 12

13
~(my surroundings are illuminated by red light at 10)
Inferred by:
    support-link #15 from { 12 } by NEG-AT-INTRO
defeatees: { link 9 for node 9 }
This node is inferred by discharging interest #14

vvvvvvvvvvvvvvvvvvvvvvvvvvv
The undefeated-degree-of-support of #<Node 4> has increased to 0.6
vvvvvvvvvvvvvvvvvvvvvvvvvvv
#<Node 9> has become defeated.
vvvvvvvvvvvvvvvvvvvvvvvvvvv
#<Node 10> has become defeated.
vvvvvvvvvvvvvvvvvvvvvvvvvvv

==
Justified belief in ((the color of Fred is red) at 10)
with undefeated-degree-of-support 0.6
answers #<Query 1: ((the color of Fred is red) at 10)>

```
========================================
================ ULTIMATE EPISTEMIC INTERESTS ====================
Interest in ((the color of Fred is red) at 10)
is answered affirmatively by node 4
----------------------------------------
```

This reasoning can be diagrammed as in figure 16.3.

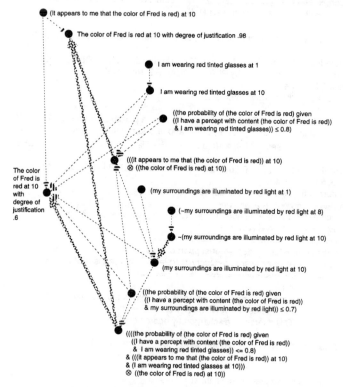

Figure 16.3 Perceptual reasoning

8. Conclusions

I have defended a large number of fairly controversial theses in this paper. First, I have distinguished procedural epistemology from the kind of epistemology that is driven by the Gettier Problem, and maintained that the former is the true descendant of traditional epistemology. I argued that structural theories of epistemic justification can be understood as partial theories of human rationality, where the latter are to be understood as competence theories of human cognition, i.e., theories of the content of our built-in procedural knowledge for how to cognize. I also proposed that sense can be made of a generic concept of rationality that is more general than human rationality, and this generates a more general epistemological endeavor – the epistemology of arbitrary rational agents. A complete epistemological theory must combine a high-level structural theory of epistemic justification, a mid-level theory of defeasible and deductive reasoning, and low-level theories of the species of reasoning required for reasoning about specific subject matters. One of the most important points of the paper is that we should not be confident of our epistemological theories without testing them on a large number of examples of realistic complexity, and the only feasible way of doing that is to implement the theories in the form of AI systems. The OSCAR Project begins with direct realism as its structural theory of epistemic justification, builds an inference engine by constructing and implementing a general architecture based upon defeasible and deductive reasoning, and then undertakes the construction of an artilect by formulating and implementing low-level theories within that architecture. The paper gave as an extended example a theory of perceptual reasoning.

I want to urge that this general approach, including both high-level theorizing and lower level implementation, is the only legitimate way to do procedural epistemology. I encourage other philosophers to experiment with this approach by downloading the OSCAR architecture from my website (http://www.u.arizona.edu/~pollock) and using its tools to construct and implement their own low-level theories. The system of perceptual reasoning described in this paper can be downloaded as well.

Notes

This work was supported by NSF grant no. IRI–9634106.

1 John Pollock, *Contemporary Theories of Knowledge* (Lanham, MD: Rowman and Littlefield, 1987).
2 Edmund Gettier, "Is Justified True Belief Knowledge?" *Analysis* 23 (1963): 121–3.
3 Robert K. Shope's *The Analysis of Knowing* (Princeton: Princeton University Press, 1983) contains a good collection of essays on the Gettier problem.
4 Nelson Goodman, *Fact, Fiction, and Forecast* (Cambridge, MA: Harvard University Press, 1955). The version of the Nicod Principle in question proposes that sets of premises of the form "$(Ac\ \&\ Bc)$" confirm the generalization "All A's are B's," for any choice of A and B.
5 Noam Chomsky, *Syntactical Structures* (The Hague: Mouton and Co., 1957).
6 In *Contemporary Theories of Knowledge* I called the rules "epistemic norms."
7 This is not to say that everyone is equally good at cognizing. Cognitive performance varies dramatically. But insofar as people make cognitive mistakes, they can generally be brought to recognize them as such, suggesting that their underlying procedural knowledge is the same.
8 See P. Wason, "Reasoning," in B. Foss, ed., *New Horizons in Psychology* (Harmondsworth, England: Penguin, 1966), and P. W. Cheng and K. J. Holyoak, "Practical Reasoning Schemas," *Cognitive Psychology* 17 (1985): 391–406.
9 John Pollock, *The OSCAR Manual* (http://www.u.arizona.edu/~pollock, 1996), p. 6.
10 John Pollock, *Cognitive Carpentry* (Cambridge, MA: MIT Press, 1995).
11 See John Pollock, "Reasoning about Change and Persistence: a Solution to the Frame Problem," *Nous* 31 (1997): 143–69.

12 There is an asymmetry between defeasible reasons from beliefs and those from percepts. The undercutting defeater for the former is "The truth of the content of the belief does not guarantee the truth of the conclusion", whereas the form of the latter is "Having the percept does not guarantee the truth of the conclusion".
13 This is a slight oversimplification. See my *Nomic Probability and the Foundations of Induction* (New York: Oxford University Press, 1990) for a detailed discussion of the statistical syllogism.
14 The need for the projectibility constraint on induction was first noted by Goodman in *Fact, Fiction, and Forecast*.
15 The material on projectibility in my *Nomic Probability* has been collected into a paper and reprinted in Pollock, "The Projectibility Constraint," in Douglas Stalker, ed., *Grue! The New Riddle of Induction* (La Salle, IL: Open Court, 1994).
16 In such a case, we might also know that the reliability of perception on the combination of facts is higher than it is on the individual facts (interfering considerations might cancel out). In that case, we should be able to make an inference from the percept to its content in accordance with that higher probability. However, that inference can be made straightforwardly using the statistical syllogism, and does not require any further principles specifically about perception.
17 NIL is "the false", sometimes written "⊥".
18 This is discussed at greater length in ch. 2 of *The OSCAR Manual*.
19 The material in this section is drawn in part from Pollock, "Reasoning about Change and Persistence."
20 A more detailed presentation of this argument can be found in ch. 6 of Pollock, *Knowledge and Justification* (Princeton: Princeton University Press, 1974).
21 For more on this, see Pollock, "Reasoning about Change and Persistence."

Chapter 17

Hermeneutics as Epistemology

Merold Westphal

Now no more useful inquiry can be proposed than that which seeks to determine the nature and scope of human knowledge... Neither ought it to seem such a toilsome and difficult matter to define the limits of [human] understanding...
Descartes[1]

For I thought that the first step toward satisfying several inquiries the mind of man was very apt to run into, was to take a survey of our own understandings, examine our own powers, and see to what things they were adapted... Whereas, were the capacities of our understandings well considered, the extent of our knowledge once discovered, the horizon found which sets the bounds between the enlightened and dark parts of things; between what is and what is not comprehensible by us, men would perhaps with less scruple acquiesce in the avowed ignorance of the one, and employ their thoughts and discourse with more advantage and satisfaction in the other.
Locke[2]

I know no inquiries which are more important for exploring the faculty which we entitle understanding, and for determining the rules and limits of its employment, than those which I have instituted...
Kant[3]

Richard Rorty announces the end of epistemology in Part 3 of *Philosophy and the Mirror of Nature*, entitled "From Epistemology to Hermeneutics." He makes it clear that he is not offering, with help from Quine and Sellars, a new and better epistemology but a complete abandonment of the whole idea of a theory of knowledge, for which no legitimate task can be identified.[4]

What Rorty repudiates as epistemology he associates strongly with Descartes, Locke, and Kant. As is clear from the above citations, the three of them contribute toward identifying epistemology with the broad, generic task of reflecting on the nature and limits of human knowledge. It is entirely unclear why Rorty identifies as epistemology not this generic task but certain features of the specific way these three and others go about it; ultimately this identification is seriously misleading.

Among the most important of the specific notions that Rorty identifies with epistemology are the following:

1) The notion of knowledge as accurate representation, as correspondence. It is here that the "mirror of nature" image plays its role.

2) The demand for certainty in knowledge.

3) The notion of epistemology as a neutral, a priori tribunal whose task is to show how to achieve the desired apodicticity of accurate representation.

4) The special role of privileged representations as providing the foundations of knowledge so construed. Sellars' critique of the myth of the given and Quine's argument for the contingency of necessity, along with Kuhnian philosophy of science and its argument against the possibility of theory-free data – these are all attacks on the notion of "representations which cannot be gainsaid."[5]

It is clear that where Rorty says "epistemology" one might just as well say "modernity" or, to be more precise, "the Enlightenment project" or, to be still more precise, "foundationalism."[6] Over against the foundationalist epistemologies of modernity, whose twentieth-century paradigms are to be found in Russell's knowledge by acquaintance and Husserl's intuition of essences, Rorty offers a paradigm shift to an understanding of understanding that he calls hermeneutics. It is holistic, historicist, and pragmatic; it construes truth as conversational agreement, rationality as practical, self-corrective capacity, and intuition as linguistic capacity.

But hermeneutics, so conceived, is a reflection on the nature and limits of human knowledge; for it is no longer limited to the interpretation of texts but interprets all cognition as interpretation. In terms of the nature of knowledge, it emphasizes the embeddedness of knowledge in historically particular and contingent vocabularies (Rorty calls them "optional"); in terms of the limits of knowledge, it emphasizes our inability to transcend that embeddedness in order to become pure reason or absolute knowledge or rigorous science. In other words, *hermeneutics is epistemology*, generically construed. It is a species diametrically opposed to foundationalist epistemologies, but it belongs to the same genus precisely because like them it is a meta-theory about how we should understand the cognitive claims of common sense, of the natural and social sciences, and even of metaphysics and theology. By failing to distinguish the generic epistemological task from the specifically modern foundationalist projects, Rorty obscures the fact that hermeneutics is not the replacement of epistemology as such but the replacement of one type of epistemology with another.

The issue of self-reference arises here. Especially because Rorty denies that epistemological reflection can occur in a privileged space prior to that of first-order knowing and immune from the conditions of the latter, hermeneutics must be understood to be a theory about itself and not just about various kinds of first-order knowing. If hermeneutics presents itself as a particular language game whose truth consists not in accurate representation but in conversational agreement, it is hard to see how it falls immediately into performative or self-referential contradiction.

But isn't hermeneutics hopelessly relativistic? Yes and No. As already noted, hermeneutical historicism offers no hope that we can escape from the particular and contingent life world or language game to which our beliefs are relative into anything other than another particularity and contingency. Against Cartesian foundationalism it denies that we can start at some Alpha point from which it is possible to view the world *sub specie aeternitatis*; and against Hegelian holism it denies that we can achieve this same goal by arriving at some Omega point of transubstantiation in which the totality of particularity becomes universality and the totality of contingency becomes necessity.

Still, Rorty is not content to leave us with a "these language games are played" relativism. Hermeneutical understanding is needed not merely to illuminate conversations occurring within a given paradigm but especially to highlight the conditions under which conversations between apparently incommensurable paradigms can occur.[7] Hermeneutical "arguments" will not be foundationally constructed, but will be conversational attempts to generate anomalies for other paradigms. To say that this is a matter of rhetoric rather than of logic is simply to say that there is no neutral language game in which the conversation can be played.

Rorty is not the theme of this essay. My assignment is to discuss epistemological currents in continental philosophy, and I have chosen to do so by focusing on hermeneutical themes in Heidegger and then, briefly, on their "right-wing" development in Gadamer and their "left-wing" development in Derrida. Rorty serves as a useful introduction for two reasons:

1) By presenting hermeneutics as an alternative to epistemology he makes it easy to specify the sense in which it is rather an alternative epistemology. To repeat, *hermeneutics is epistemology*.[8]

2) Since the search for alternatives to foundationalism (in the strong sense that requires privileged representations to give security to the foundations and thus the whole edifice of knowledge) is widespread outside continental philosophy,[9] and since Rorty himself draws heavily not only on Heidegger but also on Wittgenstein, Dewey, Quine, Sellars, and Kuhn, starting with him points to the common problematic that runs through many different philosophical traditions, methodologies, and vocabularies. If the Enlightenment project is quintessentially modern, then not only is Gadamer as "postmodern" as Derrida, but analytic philosophy in many of its current forms is as "postmodern" as contemporary continental philosophy. As I turn to Heidegger, Gadamer, and Derrida, I hope to have given at least initial plausibility to the claim that although they do not describe themselves as epistemologists, they are addressing some of the same large questions discussed by those who do.

1

Heidegger's account of the hermeneutical circle at work in all understanding is a critique of "the myth of the given" and a repudiation of foundationalist epistemologies. It is not that Heidegger denies that knowledge has foundations; it is just that the kinds of foundations he discovers render the ideals of foundationalist epistemologies futile.

Originally the hermeneutical circle had to do with interpreting texts. One comes to a text with a sense of the whole (this is a poetic tragedy, this is a historical narrative) which guides the interpretation of specific passages. But the understanding of the whole is revised in the light of specific readings. At the very least, it becomes more specific and precise. But it may be modified quite dramatically. What at first seemed to be a children's story may turn out to be a political satire or a theological reflection; and an apparent historical narrative may turn out to be a hoax of some sort. What makes the relation circular is the fact that neither one's sense of the whole nor one's reading of the parts is an independent variable. X is (at least in part) a function of Y and vice versa.

We are familiar with such circles in post-positivist philosophy of science. Theories, of course, are supposed to be dependent upon observational data. But suppose there are no theory-free data because, as Hanson writes, "There is a sense, then, in which seeing is a 'theory-laden' undertaking. Observation of x is shaped by prior knowledge of x."[10] In that case the relation between theories and the data that suggest and confirm them would be circular. Each could be modified in light of the other.

This same circle is at work in what Rawls calls reflective equilibrium in ethical theory. We try to formulate general principles that will account for our firmest considered convictions about particular (types of) situations. These convictions are only "provisional fixed points" because "there is no point at which an appeal is made to self-evidence in the traditional sense either of general concepts or particular convictions."[11] In case the theory under consideration conflicts with our pre-theoretical convictions, we may either revise the theory or amend our convictions. Since neither general theory nor particular judgment is an independent variable, the relation between them is circular; each is subject to modification in the light of the other.

Like Hanson and Rawls, Heidegger gives us a revised Kantianism. The hermeneutical circle is Kantian because it stresses the role of the a priori in all cognition. Nothing is simply given, pure and unaffected by our receptive posture. "By showing how all sight is grounded primarily in understanding . . . we have deprived pure intuition of its priority . . . 'Intuition' and 'thinking' are both derivatives of understanding, and already rather remote ones" (187/147).[12] Every cognitive act presupposes a prior understanding of the matter at hand. Heidegger details this preunderstanding in terms of fore-having, fore-sight, and fore-conception (*Vorhabe, Vorsicht,* and *Vorgriff*), concluding, "Interpretation is never a presuppositionless grasping of something previously given . . . Any interpretation which is to contribute understanding, must already have understood what is to be interpreted" (191–2, 194/150, 152).

But this is a revised Kantianism because, by speaking of the circular structure of understanding and interpretation, Heidegger makes it clear that the a priori elements do not have the fixed and final character Kant gave to the forms and categories.[13] They are not simply given any more than the interpretations they make possible. At the same time, by insisting that this circularity is not to be construed as vicious, Heidegger makes it clear that he is simply abandoning the Euclidian, syllogistic models of knowledge (194–5/152–3). Rather, we are to see in the circle "a positive possibility of the most primordial kind of knowing" (195/153).

But Heidegger's account of the hermeneutical circle is a far more radical revision of the Kantian scheme and thus of the Enlightenment project than we have seen to this point. On his view the a priori elements in knowledge are not only corrigible but also pretheoretical. According to Hanson's formula, "Observation of x is shaped by prior *knowledge* of x," which means that all seeing is "*theory*-laden" (emphasis changed). But Heidegger thinks the deepest levels of preunderstanding do not consist of knowledge or belief or representation. For this reason his account of the hermeneutical circle in terms of fore-having, fore-sight, and fore-conception "includes, but goes beyond, the insight of theoretical holism that all data are already theory laden."[14] He signals this by presenting knowing as a "founded mode" of being-in-the-world in ¶13 of *Being and Time*, and by entitling ¶33, "Assertion as a Derivative Mode of Interpretation." If knowing is "founded" and assertion is "derivative," theoretical cognition has precognitive presuppositions that can nevertheless be called understanding and interpretation.

There is a religious background to Heidegger's protest against the primacy of the theoretical that dominates so much of the philosophical tradition. His philosophy of religion lecture courses of 1920–1 are a sustained argument that the life of faith is not primarily a concern over the correctness of assertions.[15] He summarizes his findings in a lecture first given in 1927, the year *Being and Time* was published. After quoting Luther, "Faith is permitting ourselves to be seized by the things we do not see," he claims that faith "is not some more or less modified type of knowing" and that theology "is not speculative knowledge of God."[16]

But in *Being and Time* he makes a more general argument for the founded character of knowing and the derivative nature of assertion. It involves a double movement from the secondary to the primary: from theory to practice and from theory to affect. For Husserl, the phenomenological reduction abandons the natural standpoint of empirical consciousness in the midst of a surrounding real world. By bracketing the question of the relation of thought to reality, the phenomenologist is to focus on the ways in which the contents of consciousness, whatever their ontological status, are given to pure or transcendental consciousness, that is, consciousness which intends a world of which it is not a part. But for Heidegger the task is not a move from the natural standpoint to a realm of pure consciousness where presuppositionless, apodictic intuitions of essences can occur; it is a move from all theoretical postures (scientific, theological, philosophical, etc.), now understood as abstractions from primordial, everyday experience, back to the fullness of the natural standpoint, or to be more precise, to a reflective understanding of the natural standpoint in all of its practical and affective concreteness.

Following a tradition that goes back to Plato and his own Orphic-Pythagorean religious roots, Husserl's reduction is a rite of purification. By contrast, Heidegger's reduction is a rite of repentance and conversion, turning away from the cult of such self-purification. The tradition we can call Platonic, though it has a wide variety of footnotes, is a kind of Gnostic or Manichean dualism that treats embeddedness, the epistemological form of embodiment, as intrinsically evil. Heidegger's theological analogue is the Jewish or Christian affirmation that embodiment, and thus embeddedness, is good because it is part of God's creation. It is a sign of our finitude, but it is not evil; and every attempt to flee that finitude is a self-defeating, Luciferian hybris that says, "I will make myself like the Most High" (Isaiah 14:14).

2

Heideggerian hermeneutics is a three-story universe in which assertion is doubly derivative; it rests upon interpretation which in turn rests upon understanding. In attempting to understand what it means to say that both understanding and interpretation are more basic than assertion, we can deliberately adopt two hypotheses to serve as heuristic preunderstandings to guide us. In the process, of course, they will be put to the test.

The first will be the hypothesis that Heidegger seeks to dethrone the theoretical in the same way that speech-act theory does. In Austinian language, making an assertion is performing a constative speech act, one whose *raison d'être* and primary virtue relate to the truth or falsity of what is said. But this is only one of the many things we can do with words, one of the many illocutionary acts we can perform by the locutionary acts of uttering or inscribing sentences. Others, such as promising, commanding, comforting, complaining, and so forth, have different rationales and can fail to be apt other than by being false.

Heidegger's account has obvious affinities with speech-act theory. He speaks the language of assertion (*Aussage*) and judgment (*Urteil*) rather than the Platonizing language of proposition (*Satz*). The foundation of language (*Sprache* = *langue* = language as system) is discourse (*Rede* = *parole* = language in use) and not the reverse (203/160). The logos (semantic field, intelligible space) to which he links assertion is an earthly and temporal logos rather than a heavenly and eternal one (195–6/153–4). Furthermore, he makes it equivalent to "categorical statement" and "theoretical judgment," and in doing so links it tightly to constative speech acts and thus to truth as correctness (196/154, 200/157).

But there is a crucial difference. Speech-act theory challenges the primacy of theoretical reason by making assertion or the constative speech act just one of the many things we can do with words. Among many other illocutionary acts, which do not have correct information or accurate representation as their essential mission, assertion has no special privilege. At the same time, there is nothing in speech-act theory to resist the Husserlian move that makes theoretical intentions primary and basic to all nontheoretical intentions.[17]

But such a resistance is explicitly present in Heidegger's account, precisely when he insists that assertion is "a derivative form in which an interpretation has been carried out" and that "in concernful circumspection there are no such assertions 'at first' [*zunächst*]... Interpretation is carried out primordially [*ursprünglich*] not in a theoretical statement but in an action of circumspective concern – laying aside the unsuitable tool, or exchanging it, 'without wasting words'. From the fact that words are absent, it may not be concluded that interpretation is absent" (200/157); for the interpretation is expressed in the action even in absence of any assertion. Assertion is not just one mode of interpretation among many; it is less basic than some mode of interpretation it presupposes.

Heidegger immediately (re)introduces his distinction between the ready-to-hand [*Zuhandenheit*] and the present-at-hand [*Vorhandenheit*] as crucial to his point. If I see what is before me as merely present-at-hand or objectively present, I see it was a fact about which true or false assertions can be made.[18] If I see it as ready-to-hand I see it, to use his most famous example, as a hammer available for my use, or perhaps for some reason unusable. The world initially gives itself to us in this latter mode, on Heidegger's view, and it requires a severe abstraction from experience to see things as objectively present, as what is merely the case, as facts or events waiting to be accurately represented. "The kind of dealing which is closest to us is as we have shown, not a bare perceptual cognition, but rather that kind of concern which manipulates things and puts them to use; and this has its own kind of 'knowledge' " (95/67) or sight (98–9/69).[19]

In light of this distinction, Heidegger makes his point this way. If what we interpret

> becomes the "object" of an assertion, then as soon as we begin this assertion, there is already a change-over in the fore-having. Something *ready-to-hand with which* we have to do or perform something, turns into something *"about which"* the assertion that points it out is made. Our fore-sight is aimed at something present-at-hand or objectively present in what is ready-to-hand. Both *by* and *for* this way of looking at it, the ready-to-hand becomes veiled as ready-to-hand... Only now are we given any access to *properties* or the like... The as-structure of interpretation has undergone a modification. (200/157–8)

How shall we interpret this distinction and the "modification" it signals? If we take as our clue Heidegger's claim that prior to assertion is a mode of interpretation that can occur "without wasting words" and from which "words are absent," we can give ourselves a second heuristic hypothesis, this time from Rorty. In his attack on the "myth of the given," Sellars seems to argue that there is no prelinguistic awareness, and Rorty seeks to show why this is not "unfair to babies," since babies clearly have pains and some sort of awareness of colored objects.

Sellars and Rorty distinguish "awareness-as-discriminative-behavior," which children, rats, amoebas and even computers may be said to have, from awareness "in the logical space of reasons, of justifying and being able to justify what one says" (Rorty quoting Sellars), which is only found among language users. "In this latter sense awareness is justified true belief – knowledge – but in the former sense it is the ability to respond to stimuli."[20]

It is Sellars' view that prelinguistic discriminative awareness is a causal condition of knowledge but not a justifying ground. On this view "there is no such thing as a justified belief which is nonpropositional, and no such thing as a justification which is not a relation between propositions ... knowing what things are like is not a matter of being justified in asserting propositions."[21] Knowing that such-and-such is the case presupposes linguistic competence; knowing what things are like does not.

Our second hypothesis can be that Heidegger makes assertion derivative because, like Sellars and Rorty, he wants to distinguish linguistic interpretation from prelinguistic interpretation. Let us see if this is how to draw the line between assertion as derivative and the understanding and interpretation that are the a priori conditions for the possibility of assertion.

Interpretation is seeing-as. Every act of interpretation apprehends something as something, as "a table, a door, a carriage, or a bridge" (189/149). It comes as no surprise that a prior understanding is already at work in every interpretation. We've been going around in hermeneutical circles for a while now. What goes beyond the merely formal structure of the hermeneutical circle is Heidegger's claim that the understanding presupposed by every act of interpretation is our understanding, not of the table, the door, the carriage, or the bridge, but of ourselves.

Heidegger calls this self-understanding a kind of "knowing" (184/144; cf. 186/146).[22] But he repeatedly denies that it is theoretical knowing, the kind of knowing with which philosophy has been so preoccupied. Thus, understanding oneself does not mean "gazing at a meaning" (307/263). Nor are we dealing here with the understanding, as distinct from explanation, with which neo-Kantianism sought to put the *Geisteswissenschaften* on the sure path to science (182/143). Nor are we dealing with introspection, as if the self were some entity objectively present that could be known by an "immanent self-perception" in which the self would grasp itself thematically (183–5/143–5). Self-understanding is "not a matter of perceptually tracking down and inspecting a point called the 'Self' ..." as if, to repeat, the self were something objectively present to itself (187/146-7).

Every act of interpretation presupposes our understanding of ourselves as thrown projection or thrown possibility in our concernful dealings with things and our solicitude for other persons. But we "know" ourselves as such, not by reflectively observing these characteristics inhering in us but by being them. To be a thrown projection for whom the beings we encounter in the world matter is to understand oneself as such, and all explicit acts of interpretation, including self-interpretation, presuppose this primordial understanding.

So far Heidegger would seem to be innocent of the "unfair to babies" charge. Nothing he has said about understanding as the most basic form of "knowing" requires linguistic competence.

Between understanding and assertion there lies interpretation. Self-understanding as so far specified is mostly unspecified; it is vague and general. Like the preunderstanding of a whole text as belonging to a particular genre, it needs to be filled out and concretized with specific interpretations. Accordingly, Heidegger presents interpretation as the "development" of understanding in which the beings which matter to us are "explicitly" understood (188–9/148–9). As already noted, each specific interpretation is a seeing-as, an apprehension of something as something (189–90/149–50).

But this "pre-predicative seeing" is not to be identified with assertion or judgment (189–90/149); for assertion has been defined, in part, as predication (196/154). According to our working hypothesis, prepredicative here means prelinguistic. Can we confirm the suggestion that assertion or judgment is derivative because it is a linguistic act that presupposes prelinguistic experience? Is it sufficient to point out that babies can interpret the mother's breast as a source of satisfaction and, when hungry, can interpret the pacifier as a poor substitute?

The answer depends on Heidegger's understanding of our primal encounter with things as ready-to-hand. What we encounter in this way we can call "Things 'invested with value' " or "equipment," but both of these expressions are liable to serious misinterpretation. What is ready-to-hand matters to us in modes more immediate and concrete than as being objectively present as possible topics for truthful assertions. As such they are not bare things, tractarian facts whose mission in life is simply to be the case. In the ways they matter to us they are value-laden facts, something welcome or unwelcome or irrelevant. But to speak of them as "invested with value" suggests a value added interpretation of them as if we first encounter them as bare facts and only later endow them with value. It is not "as if some world-stuff which is proximally objectively present in itself were 'given subjective colouring' . . . In interpreting, we do not, so to speak, throw a 'signification' over some naked thing which is objectively present, we do not stick a value on it; but when something within-the-world is encountered as such, the thing in question already has an involvement . . . which gets laid out by the interpretation" (101/71; 190–1/150).

Heidegger is aware of the broader Gestalt form of this argument. "It requires a very artificial and complicated frame of mind to 'hear' a 'pure noise'. The fact that motor-cycles and wagons are what we proximally hear is the phenomenal evidence that in every case Dasein, as Being-in-the-world, already dwells *alongside* what is ready-to-hand within-the-world; it certainly does not dwell proximally alongside 'sensations' " (207/164).[23]

There is also a danger with describing the ready-to-hand as "equipment" (*das Zeug*), that which is "manipulable in the broadest sense and at our disposal" (97–8/68–9), as distinct from the object of a theoretical gaze. First, in spite of Heidegger's famous example of the hammer, we must avoid identifying equipment with tools; for he also presents the room as equipment for dwelling and shoes as equipment for wearing. In addition, he tells us that Nature too first comes to us as ready-to-hand and not as "pure objective presence" (100/70). Thus, for example, the honey is to be eaten, but the angry bees are to be avoided.

Reference to the angry bees, not a Heideggerian example, points to a second danger. Heidegger wants to define the ready-to-hand in terms of our activity, our practical behavior in the world (98–9/69). But by focusing on what is manipulable and usable he gives insufficient attention to negative instances where the value in which things come already wrapped is negative. It is stretching language too far to speak of angry bees as equipment.

If we avoid narrowing the notion of the ready-to-hand to that of tools or the positively useful, we have a concept of things, all the way from hammers to angry bees, that are meaningful to us in valuational terms in relation to our practices. We have seen that Heidegger describes the interpretation at work in these practices as prepredicative and pretheoretical. Does this mean that it is prelinguistic?

We can see in what sense we must answer this question Yes and in what sense No if we return to a passage considered earlier. "Interpretation is carried out primordially not in a theoretical *statement* but in an *action* of circumspective concern – laying aside the unsuitable tool, or exchanging it [or rejecting the pacifier], 'without wasting words'. From the fact that words are absent, it may not be concluded that interpretation is absent" (200/157, emphasis added). It is clear that interpretation is prelinguistic in that neither linguistic expression nor linguistic competence is required for it to occur. So far we must say Yes, our hypothesis is confirmed.

But linguistic expression and, *a fortiori*, linguistic competence, may very well belong to interpretation; and this means that we must say No. If interpretation is not *necessarily* linguistic, neither is it *necessarily* prelinguistic. Immediately before the passage just cited, Heidegger writes that interpretation, being prior to assertion, does not have the form of the " 'categorical statement' . . . 'The hammer is heavy' " nor the form of a "theoretical judgment" such as " 'This Thing – a hammer – has the property of heaviness.' " But the practice embedded interpretation of the hammer as too heavy "may take some such form as 'The hammer is too heavy', or rather just 'Too heavy!, Hand me the other hammer!' "[24]

According to Heidegger's epistemology, knowledge has foundations. But at the basis of the linguistic expressions that are the bearers of truth or falsity are not those representations that are epistemically privileged, guaranteed to be true by being given (Sellars) or necessary (Quine) or self-evident or incorrigible or evident to the senses (Plantinga). At the basis of our truth-bearing assertions are practices that are not truth bearing, whether or not they are accompanied by speech acts. Relative to such foundations, the dominant epistemological ideals of the philosophical tradition from Plato to Husserl, Russell, and the early Wittgenstein, are pipe dreams.

The reason it has been both possible and necessary to speak of Heidegger as an epistemologist is that such claims plainly constitute a theory about the nature and limits of human knowledge. It is precisely because his theory opens up a realm of understanding and interpretation prior to that of truth in the usual sense that Heidegger looks for a more primordial conception of truth as unconcealment. Just as the claim that assertion is derivative is not meant to abolish assertions but to specify (in a kind of Kantian manner) the conditions under which they are possible, so the quest for a more fundamental notion of truth is not meant to replace the usual notion but to specify its conditions.[25]

This account of the radically conditioned nature of our truth as correspondence, agreement, adequation, etc., is a humbling of philosophy's pride in the light of which the empiricist traditions appear less as the humblers of rationalist hybris than as co-revelers in it.[26] While repudiating the value added understanding of the ready-to-hand, Heidegger insists, "*Readiness-to-hand is the way in which entities as they are 'in themselves' are defined ontologico-categorically*" (101/71). The Kantian reference is unmistakable, and it means that our theoretical accomplishments, which reduce the world to objective presence, never get beyond appearances or phenomenal knowledge, whether we construe them in rationalist or empiricist terms.

3

Because of the way Heidegger makes practice foundational to theory, Dreyfus calls his hermeneutics a form of practical holism as distinct from the theoretical holism of, say, postpositivist philosophy of science.[27] This provides a nice segue to his own interest in the way Foucault will give foundational epistemological significance to social practices, similarly denying the autonomy of knowledge.[28] But it leaves us with a seriously incomplete account of Heidegger's "phenomenological reduction" from theoretical (constative, truth asserting) modes of being-in-the-world to the primordial experience from which they are derivative. For Heidegger treats state-of-mind or attunement (*Befindlichkeit*) as equi-primordial with understanding and a prior condition of cognition. Since this is the ontological (a priori) structure that expresses itself ontically (empirically) in moods, it becomes clear that Heidegger is an affective holist as much as a practical holist. His "reduction" is from theoretical cognition both to the practices in which beings are meaningful as ready-to-hand and to the moods in which an equally "primordial disclosure" takes place (173/134).

We are "*delivered over*" to our moods. They are tightly tied to the "*thrownness*" of our existence as thrown projection, our "*facticity*" (173–4/134–5). In this respect Heidegger conforms to the tradition that identifies our affective life with passivity, with the passions. But where much of the tradition treats feeling and emotion as subjective addenda whose only cognitive significance is that they might interfere with clear thinking, Heidegger stresses the disclosive function of moods as a priori conditions of theoretical thought. They are "*prior to all cognition and volition and beyond* their range of disclosure" (175/136). In addition, they are conditions of the possibility that anything, including ourselves, should 'matter" to us. '*The mood has already disclosed, in every case, Being-in-the-world as a whole, and makes it possible first of all to direct oneself towards something*" (176–8/137–9). Intentionality presupposes mood.

We are not surprised when Heidegger tells us once again that the conditions for the possibility of theoretical (assertive, constative) engagement with the world are pretheoretical. This is because "the possibilities of disclosure which belong to cognition reach far too short a way compared with the primordial disclosure belonging to moods... 'To be disclosed' does not mean 'to be known as this sort of thing' " (173/124). We should not compare what is disclosed to one in moods with what one "is acquainted with, knows, and believes" or measure it "against the apodictic certainty of a theoretical cognition of something merely objectively present" (175/135–6). It is when the world shows itself "in accordance with our moods, that the ready-to-hand shows itself... By looking at the world theoretically, we have already dimmed it down to the uniformity of what is merely objectively present" (177/138).

Does this primacy of mood over cognition mean that for Heidegger as for Hume, reason "is and ought only to be the slave of the passions"?[29] Surely not if this means the attempt "to surrender science ontically to 'feeling' " (177/138) in which phenomena are falsified by being "banished to the sanctuary of the irrational" (175/136). The Stoics, and following them, Spinoza, emphasize the dependence of the passions on our beliefs.[30] Heidegger clearly wants to give a priority to the passions, but not simply by reversing this relationship so as to make the propositional content of our assertions a function of our moods. He has no interest in a world in which the cat is on the mat for happy folks but not for sad sacks.

His point is rather that theory commits the fallacy of misplaced concreteness, at least as traditionally conceived. The world comes to us as value-laden by our moods as by our practices and we kid ourselves if we think we can reflect ourselves out of this condition, for "when we master a mood, we do so by way of a counter-mood; we are never free of moods" (175/136). Theory has its own mood, just as it is a certain kind of practice. What is more, we kid ourselves if we think we would get closer to the way things "really" are if we could strip away our moods and our practices in order to become pure reason. As we saw at the conclusion of the previous section of this essay, if we wish to be in touch with things in themselves and not with mere appearances, we must let them show themselves to us in the light of our moods and our practices.

4

And in the light of our prejudices. Which brings us to Gadamer. At the heart of Gadamer's hermeneutics is the claim that

> the fundamental prejudice of the Enlightenment is the prejudice against prejudice itself, which denies tradition its power... The overcoming of all prejudices, this

global demand of the Enlightenment, will itself prove to be a prejudice, and removing it opens the way to an appropriate understanding of the finitude which dominates not only our humanity but also our historical consciousness . . . *the prejudices of the individual, far more than his judgments, constitute the historical reality of his being.* (270, 276–7)[31]

Heidegger's account of the hermeneutic circle and of the fore-structure of understanding is Gadamer's point of departure (265). In urging us not to flee the hermeneutical circle, Heidegger stresses its positive role. "In the circle is hidden a positive possibility of the most primordial kind of knowing" (195). Gadamer shares this emphasis. "Prejudices are not necessarily unjustified and erroneous, so that they inevitably distort the truth. In fact, the historicity of our existence entails that prejudices, in the literal sense of the word [prejudgments], constitute the initial directedness of our whole ability to experience. Prejudices are biases of our openness to the world. They are simply conditions whereby we experience something . . . "[32] The prejudices Gadamer seeks to rehabilitate are not ugly attitudes toward people who are different from ourselves, but the preunderstandings presupposed by every understanding. Just as embodiment is a condition for being either Jack the Ripper or Mother Teresa, so prejudgment is a condition for seeing those who are different from me either as inferior or as my sisters and brothers.

But there are at least two important differences from Heidegger. First, Gadamer stands in closer relation than Heidegger to Kuhnian philosophy of science and Rawlsian reflective equilibrium. For rather than reflect on our affects and practices as conditions for the possibility of assertion or judgment, Gadamer returns us to a theoretical holism in which prior to every judgment (*Urteil*) there is a pre-judgment or pre-judice (*Vor-urteil*). Thus, while Heidegger points to modes of preunderstanding that are prior to assertion or judgment, Gadamer points to modes of preunderstanding that already have the form of judgment (assertion, constative speech act).

In close relation to this first difference is a second. "Tradition" ceases to be a dirty word. In Robinson and Macquarrie's Index of English Expressions in *Being and Time*, the only three subheadings are to the traditional conception of time, the traditional conception of truth, and traditional ontology. One needn't know *Being and Time* very well to know that all three signify a danger from which we are to be rescued. Nor is this surprising in the light of what Heidegger says about tradition in general.

> When tradition becomes master, it does so in such a way that what it 'transmits' is made so inaccessible . . . that it rather becomes concealed. Tradition takes what has come down to us and delivers it over to self-evidence; it blocks our access to those primordial "sources" from which the categories and concepts handed down to us have been in part quite genuinely drawn . . . Dasein has had its historicality so thoroughly uprooted by tradition that . . . it has no ground of its own to stand on. (43/21)

It is ironical to hear Heidegger sounding so much like Descartes. Gadamer wants to make a more radical break with the spirit of the Enlightenment by breaking not only with the substantive content of the Cartesian worldview but also with the repudiation of the authority of tradition that motivates Descartes's resort to method. For, to allow ourselves a bit of historical freedom, Gadamer views Descartes as following Kant's advice to grow up by shaking off his "self-incurred tutelage," the "inability to make use of his understanding without direction from another,"[33] only by adopting a thoroughly adolescent rebellion according to which whatever one's intellectual parents say is *ipso facto* discredited.

One of Gadamer's subheadings is "The Rehabilitation of Authority and Tradition" (277). He might well have spoken of the authority of tradition, for on his view tradition has considerable though not absolute authority. His attitude is like that Socrates had to the laws of Athens as his parents. Even when one is sharply critical of tradition, as Gadamer is critical of the Cartesian/Enlightenment tradition, one must recognize one's embeddedness in tradition and one indebtedness to it. Tradition is the primary source of the prejudices without which understanding, including critical understanding, would not be possible. When Rorty says that criticism is never possible in terms of eternal standards but only in terms of those "of our own day,"[34] Gadamer will agree only if "of our own day" means not "those currently dominant in our culture" but "those currently available, thanks, for the most part, to tradition."

Gadamer's critics are usually willing to concede "that there are legitimate prejudices" (277). But the weight he gives to tradition has led many, reviving a distinction from the aftermath of Hegel, to portray Gadamer as a "right-wing" Heideggerian, distinct from such "left-wing" developers of Heideggerian hermeneutics as Derrida and Foucault.[35] Both in the Gadamer – Habermas debate and in the Gadamer – Derrida debate,[36] Gadamer's opponents, failing to pay much attention to tradition as a source of critique, portray him as tilting too much away from critique in favor of tradition.

For example, Jack Caputo describes Gadamer's hermeneutics as "a reactionary gesture,"[37] too comforting in relation to the truth of tradition. He cites the passage from the section on "The Rehabilitation of Authority and Tradition" in which Margolis finds the key to Gadamer's "closet essentialism":

> That which has been sanctioned by tradition and custom has an authority that is nameless, and our finite historical being is marked by the fact that the authority of what has been handed down to us – and not just what is clearly grounded – always has power over out attitudes and behavior... The real force of morals, for example, is based on tradition. They are freely taken over but by no means created by a free insight or grounded on reasons. This is precisely what we call tradition: the ground of their validity... tradition has a justification that lies beyond rational grounding and in large measure determines our institutions and attitudes. (280–1)[38]

Is this equivalent to the claim that reason is and ought to be the slave of tradition? Any careful reading of this passage will notice that it is explicitly an "is" statement, describing what actually happens. It needs to be read in the light of Gadamer's warning in the second edition foreword to *Truth and Method*, "My real concern was and is philosophic: not what we do or what we ought to do, but what happens to us over and above our wanting and doing" (xxviii).[39] Also relevant here is Gadamer's very Heideggerian claim about the limits of reflection. "Reflection on a given preunderstanding brings before me something that otherwise happens *behind my back*. Something – but not everything, for what I have called the *wirkungsgeschichtliches Bewusstsein* is inescapably more being than consciousness, and being is never fully manifest."[40] In other words, the reflection that critically thematizes some presupposition will itself be guided by a preunderstanding not yet subjected to criticism. Gadamer agrees with the pragmatists that we can subject any of our beliefs to criticism, but not all at once. We are, as a matter of fact, always given over to our belonging to history, not so absolutely as to be but pawns, but so thoroughly that the dream of cognitive autonomy is a pipe dream and the anxiety of influence a neurosis. "Does being situated within traditions really mean being subject to prejudices and limited in one's freedom? Is not, rather, all human existence, even the freest, limited and qualified in various ways? If this is true, the idea of an absolute reason is not a possibility for historical humanity" (276).

There is an "ought" implicit in this analysis. Since foundationalist justifications are unavailable, we ought not to seek them; and since our commitments always exceed what we can rationally justify in any absolute sense, we ought not to pretend differently.

So reason is and ought to be, not the slave of tradition, but honest about its ineluctable dependence on tradition. Finitude is not fate. I am not bound over inexorably to this tradition or that one. The hermeneutical circle always means that one's foundations, which cannot eliminate tradition in favor of pure insight, are contingent and corrigible. The earth rests on the back of a turtle, and it's turtles all the way down. Where is the excessive comfort in this unflinching acknowledgement of reason's inability to become self-sufficient by escaping the hermeneutical circle?

5

Finally, an all too brief look at Derrida's "left-wing" or radical hermeneutics.[41] Already with Heidegger hermeneutics goes way beyond the interpretation of texts. Everything, including ourselves, our artifacts, and the world of nature, is apprehended in interpretation. The whole world is a text, or better, a library of texts. Gadamer makes explicit his own commitment to this ubiquity of interpretation in the opening essays of *Philosophical Hermeneutics*.[42] One of the ways Derrida affirms the universal scope of interpretation, and thus the textual character of the world, is in his (in)famous claim, "*There is nothing outside the text.*"[43]

There are two meanings to this thesis, one Kantian and one Hegelian. Neither implies that we are free to make up the world as we go; instead, both signify textuality as a limit within which we have whatever freedom we have. The Kantian sense is merely the affirmation of the hermeneutical circle in its theoretical dimension, the claim that before we say anything "Being must always already be conceptualized." This " 'must always already' precisely signifies the original exile from the kingdom of Being . . . signifies that Being never is, never shows *itself*, is never *present*, is never *now*, outside difference (in all the senses today required by this word."[44] In its Kantian form, this denial of presence (and the metaphysics of presence) is not a denial of the claim that there is a computer in front of me as I write. It is a denial of all philosophies according to which either meanings or facts can be merely and directly present to me, unmediated essentially (and not just causally) by that which is absent. There are no atomic facts, no instantaneous nows.

Of course there are intuitions and there is acquaintance. But such cognitions lose their epistemic privilege when we pay attention to the mediations that make them possible and render their highly valued immediacy illusory. It goes without saying that Derrida's is a post-Kantian Kantianism in which those mediations are themselves diverse and contingent, like Rorty's optional vocabularies, not universal and necessary.

But when introducing his "nothing outside the text" thesis, Derrida focuses on the Hegelian meaning of his claim. The point is not primarily that we have access to, in this case, persons "only in the text," that is, in some particular interpretation of them, "and we have neither any means of altering this, nor any right to neglect this limitation. All reasons of this type would already be sufficient, to be sure, but there are more radical reasons." The more radical reasons concern the nature of the things themselves, not our access to them. "What we have tried to show . . . is that in what one calls the real life of these existences 'of flesh and bone,' beyond and behind what one believes can be circumscribed as Rousseau's text, there has never been anything but writing . . ."[45]

What does it mean to say that "beyond and behind" the text of Rousseau's *Confessions*, through which we have access to Rousseau, Mamma, and Thérèse, they themselves, and whatever else gets written about or interpreted, are texts? Most simply put, "*The thing itself is a sign.*" Like signs, things essentially point beyond themselves. We must abandon the search for the transcendental signified, and, what is the same, the distinction between sign and signified. For there is no signified that "would place a reassuring end to the reference from sign to sign" by failing to refer beyond itself.[46] Things are not substances or atoms that stand alone. Their very being is constituted by their relations. This is the Hegelian theme that the English idealists labeled the doctrine of internal relations, and it is an important part of what Derrida means by calling his "mediation on writing" Hegelian.[47]

In summary, radical hermeneutics finds that "there is nothing outside the text" and this means both, epistemologically, that "Being must always already be conceptualized" and, ontologically, that "The thing itself is a sign."

This theory of double mediation signifies our exile from sheer immediacy, pure presence. But it leaves open the possibility of "two interpretations of interpretation."[48] One is associated with the rabbi and Rousseau, the other with the poet and Nietzsche. Both experience interpretation as exile, texts as a veil that separates them from Truth as directly and fully present. For both "we have ceased hearing the voice [of God] from within the immediate proximity of the garden ...Writing is displaced on the broken line between lost and promised speech. The *difference* between speech [immediacy, presence] and writing [mediation, absence] is sin, the anger of God emerging from itself, lost immediacy, work outside the garden."[49] Interpretation is what we do east of Eden, after the fall, prior to the beatific vision.

But the world of the rabbi is that of a *"sacred text surrounded by commentaries."*[50] The task of interpretation is to retrieve the divine voice in the written word, to return as nearly as possible, to the garden where truth is immediately present. The broken immediacy and the inevitable incompleteness of interpretation evoke nostagia, and even guilt for Rousseau, but he "dreams of deciphering a truth or an origin which escapes play and the order of the sign." In other words, he dreams "of full presence, the reassuring foundation, the origin and end of play."[51] This is the (possibly regulative) ideal of the Transcendental Signified.

The Nietzschean poet, by contrast, rather than seeking to retrieve the voice of God takes the silence of God to be an invitation to speak ourselves. God allowed the Tables of the Law to be broken "in order to let us speak...we must take words upon ourselves...must become men of vision because we have ceased hearing the voice from within the immediate proximity of the garden."[52] The silence or death of God is experienced, not in nostalgia and guilt but in "the joyous affirmation of the play of the world and of the innocence of becoming, the affirmation of a world of signs without fault, without truth, and without origin which is offered to an active interpretation. *This affirmation then determines the noncenter otherwise than as the loss of the center*. And it plays without security."[53]

If one understands that for Derrida the overcoming of metaphysics is not its abolition but its delimitation, one will not be surprised to find that he does not simply reject the first interpretation of interpretation in order to affirm the second. He thinks it is foolish to talk of choosing between them and talks instead of living them simultaneously and trying to discover their common ground.[54] For "there will always be rabbis and poets. And two interpretations of interpretation."[55] "Rabbinical" hermeneutics is indeed like metaphysics in the Kantian dialectic: it is a project we can neither accomplish nor abandon.

But the hermeneutical turn in both its nostalgic and its Nietzschean modes is a recognition that absolute knowledge is not in the cards for us; it is an abandonment of the quest for certainty and of the Cartesian (foundationalist) and Hegelian (totalizing) strategies for achieving it. But this is just as true of Heidegger and Gadamer. Even if some hermeneutical turns are sharper, and thus more radical, than others, we should not lose sight of the common ground that unites the hermeneutical traditions as an alternative to those epistemologies that seek to locate knowledge in some Alpha or Omega point beyond interpretation.

Notes

1. Descartes, *Rules for the Direction of the Mind*, in *The Philosophical Works of Descartes*, trans. Haldane and Ross (n.p.: Dover Publications, 1955), I, 26 (discussion of Rule 8).
2. Locke, *An Essay Concerning Human Understanding* (New York: Dover Publications, 1959), I, 31 (Introduction, section 7).
3. Kant, *Critique of Pure Reason*, trans. Norman Kemp Smith (New York: St. Martins, 1961), A xvi.
4. Richard Rorty, *Philosophy and the Mirror of Nature* (Princeton: Princeton University Press, 1979), pp. 10, 180, 210, and 315.
5. Rorty, p. 315.
6. By 'foundationalism' I shall always mean the strong variety which requires foundational apodicticity from privileged representations "which cannot be gainsaid." See note 9.
7. Rorty, p. 347.
8. This is not to say that it is *only* epistemology or that for any given thinker it is *primarily* epistemology.
9. For example, in his critique of classical foundationalism, Al Plantinga identifies three types of privileged representations. "The only properly basic propositions [according to classical foundationalism] are those that are self-evident or incorrigible or evident to the senses." Quine's critique of necessity addresses the first of these, while Sellars' attack on the given addresses the other two. See "Reason and Belief in God," in *Faith and Rationality: Reason and Belief in God*, eds. Alvin Plantinga and Nicholas Wolterstorff (Notre Dame: University of Notre Dame Press, 1983), p. 59. See note 6.
10. N. R. Hanson, *Patterns of Discovery: An Inquiry into the Conceptual Foundations of Science* (Cambridge: Cambridge University Press, 1961), p. 19. It is worth noting that Hanson, drawing on Gestalt psychology and Wittgensteinian analyses of seeing-as, makes the point about seeing in general. Scientific observation is but one case in point.
11. John Rawls, *A Theory of Justice* (Cambridge, MA: Harvard University Press, 1971), pp. 20–1. Cf. 48–51.
12. Passages from Heidegger's *Being and Time* will be cited by A/B references in the text. "A" stands for the translation by Macquarrie and Robinson (New York: Harper and Row, 1962). "B" stands for the pagination in the seventh German edition, given in the margins of Macquarrie and Robinson and the more recent translation of Joan Stambaugh (Albany: SUNY Press, 1996). I will sometimes use or draw on Stambaugh's renderings.
13. For a similar account of the a priori from the same decade as *Being and Time*, see C. I. Lewis, "A Pragmatic Conception of the A Priori," in *Readings in Philosophical Analysis*, ed. Herbert Feigl and Wilfrid Sellars (New York: Appleton-Century-Crofts, 1949). This essay anticipates major themes in Quine's "Two Dogmas of Empiricism," in *From a Logical Point of View* (New York: Harper and Row, 1963), as well as Rorty's joint appeal to Heidegger and American pragmatism.
14. Hubert Dreyfus, "Holism and Hermeneutics," *The Review of Metaphysics*, XXXIV (1980–1): 10. Where Dreyfus says "theoretical holism" we can read "a theoretical interpretation of the hermeneutical circle." Like Rorty, Dreyfus links hermeneutics to holism at least in part because in the absence of either a fixed a priori form or a given empirical content for knowledge, the whole fabric of knowing is in question whenever one of its parts is in question.

15 *Einleitung in the Phänomenologie der Religion* (WS 1920–1) and *Augustinus und der Neuplatonismus* (SS 1921) in *Gesamtausgabe* (GA), vol. 60, *Phänomenologie des religiösen Lebens* (Frankfurt: Klostermann, 1995).

16 "Phenomenology and Theology," in *The Piety of Thinking*, trans. James G. Hart and John C. Maraldo (Bloomington: Indiana University Press, 1976), pp. 10 and 15.

17 See Husserl's *Logical Investigations*, trans. J. N. Findlay (New York: Humanities, 1970), pp. 556, 636–40, and 648–51. Heidegger appropriately calls *Logical Investigations* "a phenomenology of the theoretical logos" (GA 9 35 = *Wegmarken*). Also see *Ideas Pertaining to a Pure Phenomenology and to a Phenomenological Philosophy, First Book*, trans. F. Kersten (The Hague: Martinus Nijhoff, 1983), ¶¶ 116–21. It is difficult not to read Wittgenstein's critique of his own *Tractatus* as other than at least the intention of such a resistance. See *Philosophical Investigations*, trans. G. E. M. Anscombe (Oxford: Blackwell, 1958), section 23.

18 Where Macquarrie and Robinson translate *vorhanden* as "present-at-hand," Stambaugh renders it as "objectively present." What Heidegger has in mind is very much like the facts of the early Wittgenstein, that which is simply the case, so I shall go with Stambaugh's translation from here on.

19 The scare quotes are in the German original.

20 Rorty, pp. 181–3. Heidegger's focus is on human understanding. He might be willing to extend his analysis of preassertive understanding to rats and amoebas, but would surely balk at computers. But that will not be the issue here.

21 Rorty, pp. 183 and 185. It is worth noting that in the previous paragraph Rorty ties knowledge to linguistic awareness, while here he refers to prelinguistic awareness as "*knowing* what things are like" (emphasis added). He might well have put this latter "kowing" in scare quotes. Heidegger will make a similar distinction between knowing and knowing. See notes 19 and 22.

22 The scare quotes are in the German original of both passages cited. See previous note.

23 In developing his hermeneutic understanding of natural science, Hanson (p. 9) makes a similarly general Gestalt appeal: "one does not first soak up an optical pattern and then clamp an interpretation on it."

24 Cf. the opening paragraphs of Wittgenstein's *Philosophical Investigations*, where he critiques the primacy of the theoretical in the *Tractatus* in terms of a simple language game in which "Slab!" means "Bring me a slab!" It would seem that Heidegger is mistaken in suggesting that linguistic *communication* first arises at the level of assertion (197/155 and 203/160).

25 See Section 44 of *Being and Time*; *On the Essence of Truth* (1930), in *Basic Writings*, ed. David Farrell Krell (New York: Harper & Row, 1977); and *Plato's Doctrine of Truth* (1942), trans. John Barlow, in *Philosophy in the Twentieth Century*, vol. 3, eds. William Barrett and Henry D. Aiken (New York: Random House, 1962).

26 Hume's appeal to custom and the passions would be an exception. So would Hempel's reluctant acknowledgment that the verification criterion of meaning is a policy and not a truth. See "Problems and Changes in the Empiricist Criterion of Meaning," in *Semantics and the Philosophy of Language*, ed. L. Linsky (Urbana: University of Illinois Press, 1952).

27 In doing so he links Heidegger to Wittgenstein and Merleau-Ponty. "Holism and Hermeneutics," p. 7. He might well have followed Rorty and added Dewey to the list. See the passages cited from Hanson at nn. 10 and 14 above.

28 See Hubert L. Dreyfus and Paul Rabinow, *Michel Foucault: Beyond Structuralism and Hermeneutics*, 2nd ed. (Chicago: University of Chicago Press, 1982, 1983). A brief introduction to this motif in Foucault is found in chs. 5–9 of *Power/Knowledge*, ed. Colin Gordon (New York: Pantheon Books, 1980).
29 Hume, *A Treatise of Human Nature*, ed. L. A. Selby-Bigge (Oxford: Clarendon Press, 1960; repr. of 1888 ed.), p. 415 (II, III, III).
30 For helpful discussion of the Stoics on this point, see Martha Nussbaum, *The Therapy of Desire: Theory and Practice in Hellenistic Ethics* (Princeton: Princeton University Press, 1994).
31 Gadamer references in the text will be to *Truth and Method*, trans. Joel Weinsheimer and Donald G. Marshall, 2nd ed. rev. (New York: Crossroad, 1991).
32 *Philosophical Hermeneutics*, trans. David E. Linge (Berkeley: University of California Press, 1976), p. 9.
33 Kant, "What is Enlightenment," in *On History*, ed. Lewis White Beck (Indianapolis: Bobbs-Merrill, 1963), p. 3.
34 Rorty, pp. 178–9.
35 By far the best accounts of Derrida and Foucault in this light are, respectively, Jack Caputo, *Radical Hermeneutics* (Bloomington: Indiana University Press, 1987) and Dreyfus and Rabinow, *Michel Foucault: Beyond Structuralism and Hermeneutics*. See note 28 above.
36 A good introduction to the former, with references to the primary sources, is found in Thomas McCarthy, *The Critical Theory of Jürgen Habermas* (Cambridge, MA: MIT Press, 1978). For the latter see Diane P. Michelfelder and Richard E. Palmer, eds., *Dialogue and Deconstruction: The Gadamer – Derrida Encounter* (Albany: SUNY Press, 1989).
37 *Radical Hermeneutics*, pp. 5–6.
38 Quoted in Caputo's essay, "Gadamer's Closet Essentialism: A Derridian Critique," in *Dialogue and Deconstruction*, p. 258, from the older translation, which I have replaced with the second, 1991 edition.
39 Elsewhere I have shown that Gadamer repudiates the Hegelian strategy for achieving absolute knowledge as vigorously as he rejects the Cartesian strategy. See "Hegel and Gadamer," in *Hegel, Freedom, and Modernity* (Albany: SUNY Press, 1992). I am not convinced by Caputo's claim that Gadamer is more Hegelian than Heideggerian. See *Radical Hermeneutics*, p. 6 and "Gadamer's Closet Essentialism," p. 259.
40 *Philosophical Hermeneutics*, p. 38.
41 For a much fuller treatment, see Caputo, *Radical Hermeneutics*.
42 "The Universality of the Hermeneutical Problem" and "On the Scope and Function of Hermeneutical Reflection." The latter is an explicit response to Habermas's attempt to delimit hermeneutics.
43 *Of Grammatology*, trans. Gayatri Chakravorty Spivak (Baltimore: Johns Hopkins Press, 1976), p. 158.
44 "Edmond Jabès and the Question of the book," in *Writing and Difference*, trans. Alan Bass (Chicago: University of Chicago Press, 1978), p. 74. See "Différance," for the spatial and temporal meaning of this key term, in *Margins of Philosophy*, trans. Alan Bass (Chicago: University of Chicago Press, 1982). The temporal sense of the term derives from the deconstructive reading of Husserl on internal time consciousness

45 *Of Grammatology*, pp. 158–9.
46 *Of Grammatology*, p. 49. This notion that things refer in a sign-like way is built into Heidegger's account of the ready-to-hand.
47 *Of Grammatology*, p. 26. Derrida immediately adds that his Hegelianism is without the closure that comes by moving from finite, sign-like things to the infinite totality which would be the transcendental signified, in Spinoza's language, the only substance. Gadamer can also be described as a Hegelian without totality, without the Absolute.
48 Derrida develops this theme both in "Edmond Jabès and the Question of the Book," p. 67, and in "Structure, Sign, and Play in the Discourse of the Human Sciences," *Writing and Difference*, p. 292.
49 "Edmond Jabès," p. 68.
50 Ibid., p. 67. The phrase is quoted from Jabès.
51 "Structure, Sign, and Play," p. 292. For Derrida play is more something that happens to us than something we do. It is the constant reference of signs, including things, from one point to another without any point being privileged as center or origin. For an attempt to counter widespread misreadings of this theme, see my "Deconstruction and Christian Cultural Theory: An Essay on Appropriation," in *Pledges of Jubilee*, ed. Lambert Zuidervaart and Henry Luttikhuizen (Grand Rapids, MI: Eerdmans, 1995).
52 "Edmond Jabès," p. 68.
53 "Structure, Sign, and Play," p. 292.
54 "Structure, Sign, and Play," p. 293.
55 "Edmond Jabès," p. 67.

(Note: entry 45 continues from previous page; preceding text: "that Derrida gives in *Speech and Phenomena*, trans. David B. Allison (Evanston, IL: Northwestern University Press, 1973).")

Select Bibliography of Epistemology by Topic

Scepticism (Michael Williams)

Annas, Julia and Jonathan Barnes, *The Modes of Scepticism* (Cambridge: Cambridge University Press, 1985).
Ayer, A. J., *The Problem of Knowledge* (London: Pelican, 1976).
BonJour, Laurence. *The Structure of Empirical Knowledge* (Cambridge, MA: Harvard University Press, 1985).
Burnyeat, M. F., ed., *The Skeptical Tradition* (Berkeley: University of California Press, 1983).
Fogelin, Robert, *Pyrrhonian Reflections on Knowledge and Justification* (Princeton: Princeton University Press, 1994).
Hadot, Pierre, *Philosophy as a Way of Life* (Oxford: Blackwell, 1995).
Hankinson, R. J., *The Sceptics* (London: Routledge, 1995).
Nozick, Robert, *Philosophical Explanations* (Oxford: Oxford University Press, 1981).
Popkin, Richard, *Scepticism from Erasmus to Spinoza* (Berkeley: University of California Press, 1979).
Strawson, P. F., *Skepticism and Naturalism: Some Varieties* (London: Methuen, 1985).
Stroud, Barry, *The Significance of Philosophical Scepticism* (Oxford: Oxford University Press, 1984).
——, "Skepticism and the Possibility of Knowledge," *Journal of Philosophy* (1984), p. 550.
——, "Understanding Human Knowledge in General," in Marjorie Clay and Keith Lehrer, eds., *Knowledge and Skepticism* (Boulder, CO: Westview Press, 1989).
Williams, Bernard, *Descartes: The Project of Pure Enquiry* (Harmondsworth: Pelican, 1978).
Williams, Michael, *Unnatural Doubts* (Princeton: Princeton University Press, 1996).
——, "Understanding Human Knowledge Philosophically," *Philosophy and Phenomenological Research* (1996).
——, "Scepticism Without Theory," *Review of Metaphysics* (1988).

Realism and Objectivity (Paul Moser)

Alston, William P., "Epistemic Circularity," in Alston, *Epistemic Justification* (Ithaca: Cornell University Press, 1989).
——, *The Reliability of Sense Perception* (Ithaca: Cornell University Press, 1993).

——, *A Realist Conception of Truth* (Ithaca: Cornell University Press, 1996).
Cornman, James, *Skepticism, Justification, and Explanation* (Dordrecht: Reidel, 1980).
Davidson, Donald, "A Coherence Theory of Truth and Knowledge," in Dieter Henrich, ed., *Kant oder Hegel* (Stuttgart: Klett-Cotta, 1983).
Devitt, Michael, *Realism and Truth* (Oxford: Blackwell, 1984).
Foley, Richard, *Working Without a Net* (New York: Oxford University Press, 1993).
Fumerton, Richard, *Metaepistemology and Skepticism* (Lanham, MD: Rowman and Littlefield, 1995).
Goldman, Alan, *Empirical Knowledge* (Berkeley: University of California Press, 1988).
Lycan, William, *Judgement and Justification* (New York: Cambridge University Press, 1988).
Moser, Paul K., *Knowledge and Evidence* (New York: Cambridge University Press, 1989).
——, "A Dilemma for Internal Realism," *Philosophical Studies* 59 (1990): 101–6.
——, *Philosophy After Objectivity* (New York: Oxford University Press, 1993).
——, "Beyond Realism and Idealism," *Philosophia* 23 (1994): 271–88.
Moser, Paul K. and David Yandell, "Against Naturalizing Rationality," *Protosociology* 8/9 (1996): 81–96.
Putnam, Hilary, *The Many Faces of Realism* (LaSalle, IL: Open Court, 1987).
Quine, W. V. O., *Word and Object* (Cambridge, MA: MIT Press, 1960).
——, "The Nature of Natural Knowledge," in S. Guttenplan, ed., *Mind and Language* (Oxford: Clarendon Press, 1975).
——, "Things and Their Place in Theories," in Quine, *Theories and Things* (Cambridge, MA: Harvard University Press, 1981).
Rorty, Richard, *Consequences of Pragmantism* (Minneapolis: University of Minnesota Press, 1982).
——, *Contingency, Irony, and Solidarity* (New York: Cambridge University Press, 1989).
——, "Antirepresentationalism, Ethnocentrism, and Liberalism," in Rorty, *Objectivity, Relativism, and Truth: Philosophical Papers, Volume 1* (New York: Cambridge University Press, 1991).
——, "Putnam and the Relativist Menace," *The Journal of Philosophy* 90 (1993): 443–61.

What is Knowledge? (Linda Zagzebski)

Alston, William P., *Epistemic Justification* (Ithaca: Cornell University Press, 1989).
BonJour, Laurence, *The Structure of Empirical Knowledge* (Cambridge, MA: Harvard University Press, 1985).
Chisholm, Roderick, *Theory of Knowledge* (Englewood Cliffs, NJ: Prentice-Hall, 1966; 2nd ed. 1977; 3rd ed. 1989).
Craig, Edward, *Knowledge and the State of Nature* (Oxford: Clarendon Press, 1990).
Fogelin, Robert, *Pyrrhonian Reflections on Knowledge and Justification* (New York: Oxford University Press, 1994).
Gettier, Edmund, "Is Justified True Belief Knowledge?" *Analysis* 23 (1963): 121–3.
Goldman, Alvin, "A Causal Theory of Knowing," *Journal of Philosophy* 64 (1967): 357–72.
——, *Epistemology and Cognition* (Cambridge, MA: Harvard University Press, 1986).
Klein, Peter, "A Proposed Definition of Propositional Knowledge," *Journal of Philosophy* 67 (1971): 471–82.

Kornblith, Hilary, ed., *Naturalizing Epistemology*, 2nd ed. (Cambridge, MA: MIT Press, 1994).
Lehrer, Keith, *Theory of Knowledge* (Boulder, CO: Westview Press, 1990).
Moser, Paul K., *Knowledge and Evidence* (Cambridge: Cambridge University Press, 1989).
Plantinga, Alvin, *Warrant and Proper Function* (Oxford: Oxford University Press, 1993).
Pollock, John, *Contemporary Theories Of Knowledge* (Totowa, NJ: Rowman and Littlefield, 1986).
Sosa, Ernest, *Knowledge in Perspective: Selected Essays in Epistemology* (Cambridge: Cambridge University Press, 1991).
Zagzebski, Linda T., "The Inescapability of Gettier Problems," *Philosophical Quarterly* 44, no. 174 (1994): 65–73.
———, *Virtues of the Mind: An Inquiry into the Nature of Virtue and the Ethical Foundations of Knowledge* (Cambridge: Cambridge University Press, 1996).

Foundationalism and Coherentism (Laurence BonJour)

Alston, William P., *Epistemic Justification* (Ithaca: Cornell University Press, 1989).
Audi, Robert, *The Structure of Justification* (New York: Cambridge University Press, 1993).
Bender, John, ed., *The Current State of the Coherence Theory* (Dordrecht: Kluwer, 1989).
Blanshard, Brand, *The Nature of Thought* (London: Allen & Unwin, 1939).
BonJour, Laurence, *The Structure of Empirical Knowledge* (Cambridge, MA: Harvard University Press, 1985).
Butchvarov, Panayot, *The Concept of Knowledge* (Evanston, IL: Northwestern University Press, 1970).
Chisholm, Roderick, *The Foundations of Knowing* (Minneapolis: University of Minnesota Press, 1982).
———, *Theory of Knowledge* (Englewood Cliffs, NJ: Prentice-Hall, 1966; 2nd ed. 1977; 3rd ed. 1989).
Davidson, Donald, "A Coherence Theory of Truth and Knowledge," in Dieter Henrich, ed., *Kant oder Hegel* (Stuttgart: Klett-Cotta, 1983).
Haack, Susan, *Evidence and Inquiry: Towards Reconstruction in Epistemology* (Oxford: Blackwell, 1993).
Lehrer, Keith, *Knowledge* (Oxford: Oxford University Press, 1974).
———, *Theory of Knowledge* (Boulder, CO: Westview 1990).
Moser, Paul K., *Knowledge and Evidence* (Cambridge: Cambridge University Press, 1989).
Quinton, Anthony, *The Nature of Things* (London: Routledge & Kegan Paul, 1973).
Rescher, Nicholas, *The Coherence Theory of Truth* (Oxford: Oxford University Press, 1973).
———, "Foundationalism, Coherentism, and the Idea of Cognitive Systematization," *Journal of Philosophy* 71 (1974): 695–708.
———, *Methodological Pragmatism* (New York: New York University Press, 1977).
Sellars, Wilfrid, "Empiricism and the Philosophy of Mind," reprinted in Sellars, *Science, Perception and Reality* (London: Routledge & Kegan Paul, 1963).
———, "Givenness and Explanatory Coherence," *Journal of Philosophy* 70 (1973): 612–24.
———, "Some Reflections on Language Games," reprinted in Sellars, *Science, Perception and Reality* (London: Routledge & Kegan Paul, 1963).
Sosa, Ernest, *Knowledge in Perspective: Selected Essays in Epistemology* (Cambridge: Cambridge University Press, 1991).

Internalism and Externalism (Ernest Sosa)

Alston, W. P., "An Internalist Externalism," in *Epistemic Justification* (Ithaca: Cornell University Press, 1989).

BonJour, L., *The Structure of Empirical Knowledge* (Cambridge, MA: Harvard University Press, 1985), esp. ch. 3.

Foley, R., *Working Without a Net: A Study of Egocentric Epistemology* (Oxford: Oxford University Press, 1993).

Fumerton, R., *Metaepistemology and Skepticism* (Lanham, MD: Rowman & Littlefield, 1995).

Goldman, A., *Epistemology and Cognition* (Cambridge, MA: Harvard University Press, 1986).

Greco, J., "Internalism and Epistemically Responsible Belief," *Synthese* 85 (1990): 245-77.

Kornblith, H., "How Internal Can You Get?" *Synthese* 74 (1988): 313-27.

Lehrer, K., "Externalism and Epistemology Naturalized," ch. 8 of his *Theory of Knowledge* (Boulder, CO: Westview, 1990).

Moser, P., *Knowledge and Evidence* (Cambridge: Cambridge University Press, 1989).

Plantinga, A., *Warrant: the Current Debate* (Oxford: Oxford University Press, 1993), esp. chs. 1-3.

Sosa, E., "Reflective Knowledge in the Best Circles," *Journal of Philosophy* 94 (1997).

Naturalized Epistemology (Richard Feldman and Hilary Kornblith)

Armstrong, D. M., *Belief, Truth and Knowledge* (Cambridge: Cambridge University Press, 1973).

Cerniak, Christopher, *Minimal Rationality* (Cambridge, MA: MIT Press, 1986).

Dretske, Fred, *Knowledge and the Flow of Information* (Cambridge, MA: MIT Press, 1981).

Gettier, Edmund, "Is Justified True Belief Knowledge?" *Analysis* 23 (1963): 121-3.

Goldman, Alvin, "Epistemic Folkways and Scientific Epistemology," repr. in *Naturalized Epistemology*, 2nd ed., ed. by Hilary Kornblith (Cambridge, MA: MIT Press, 1994).

——, "Epistemics: The Regulative Theory of Cognition," *The Journal of Philosophy* 75 (1978): 509-23.

——, "Naturalistic Epistemology and Reliabilism," in *Midwest Studies in Philosophy* XIX, eds. Peter A. French et al. (Notre Dame, IN: University of Notre Dame Press, 1994).

——, *Epistemology and Cognition* (Cambridge, MA: Harvard University Press, 1986).

——, *Liaisons: Philosophy Meets the Cognitive and Social Sciences* (Cambridge, MA: MIT Press, 1992).

Harman, Gilbert, *Change in View: Principle of Reasoning* (Cambridge, MA: MIT Press, 1986).

Haack, Susan, *Evidence and Inquiry* (Oxford: Cambridge University Press, 1993).

Kitcher, Philip, "The Naturalists Return," *Philosophical Review*, 101 (1992): 53-114.

Kornblith, Hilary, *Inductive Inference and Its Natural Ground: An Essay in Naturalized Epistemology* (Cambridge, MA: MIT Press, 1993).

——, ed., *Naturalizing Epistemology*, 2nd ed. (Cambridge, MA: MIT Press, 1994).

——, "Natural Epistemology and Its Critics," *Philosophical Topics* 23 (1995): 237-55.

Lycan, William, *Judgement and Justification* (Cambridge: Cambridge University Press, 1988).

Plantinga, Alvin, *Warrant and Proper Function* (Oxford: Oxford University Press, 1993).
Quine, W. V. O., *Ontological Relativity and Other Essays* (New York: Columbia University Press, 1993).
Sosa, Ernest, *Knowledge in Perspective: Selected Essays in Epistemology* (Cambridge: Cambridge University Press, 1991).
Stein, Edward, *Without Good Reason: The Rationality Debate in Philosophy and Cognitive Science* (Oxford: Oxford University Press, 1996).
Stich, Stephen, *The Fragmentation of Reason: Preface to a Pragmatic Theory of Cognitive Evaluation* (Cambridge, MA: MIT Press, 1990).
—— and Richard Nisbett, "Justification and the Psychology of Human Reasoning," *Philosophy of Science* 47 (1980): 188–202.

Contextualism (Keith DeRose)

Annis, David, "A Contextualist Theory of Epistemic Justification," *American Philosophical Quarterly* 15 (1978): 213–19.
Cohen, Stewart, "How to be a Fallibilist," *Philosophical Perspectives* 2 (1988): 91–123.
DeRose, Keith, "Contextualism and Knowledge Attributions," *Philosophical and Phenomenological Research* 52 (1992): 913–29.
——, "Solving the Skeptical Puzzle," *Philosophical Review* 104 (1995): 1–52.
Hambourger, Robert, "Justified Assertion and the Relativity of Knowledge," *Philosophical Studies* 51 (1987): 241–69.
Lewis, David, "Scorekeeping in a Language Game," *Journal of Philosophical Logic* 8 (1979): 339–59, esp. Example 6, "Relative Modality," pp. 354–5.
——, "Elusive Knowledge," *Australasian Journal of Philosophy* 74 (1996): 549–67.
Schiffer, Stephen, "Contextualist Solutions to Scepticism," *Proceedings of the Aristotelian Society* 96 (1996): 249–61.
Unger, Peter, *Philosophical Relativity* (Minneapolis: University of Minnesota Press, 1984).
——, "The Cone Model of Knowledge," *Philosophical Topics* 14 (1986): 125–78.
Williams, Michael, *Unnatural Doubts: Epistemological Realism and the Basis of Scepticism* (Cambridge, MA: Blackwell, 1991).

Rationality (Keith Lehrer)

Aristotle, *Nicomachean Ethics*, tr. David Ross (Oxford: Oxford University Press, 1991).
——, *On the Soul*, tr. W. S. Hett (Cambridge, MA: Harvard University Press, 1986).
Audi, Robert, *Belief, Justification and Knowledge* (Belmont, CA: Wadsworth, 1988).
Baccarini, Elvio, "Rational Consensus and Coherence Methods in Ethics," *Grazier Philosophische Studien* 40 (1991): 151–9.
Baird, Davis, "Lehrer-Wagner Consensual Probabilities Do Not Adequately Summarize the Available Information," *Synthese*, 62 (1985): 47–62.
Baker, Lynne Rudder, *Saving Belief* (Princeton: Princeton University Press, 1987).
Bartlett, Steven, ed., *Reflexivity: A Source-Book in Self-Reference* (New York: Elsevier Science, 1992).
Bender, John W., ed., *The Current State of the Coherence Theory* (Boston: Kluwer, 1989).
Black, Max, "Self-Supporting Inductive Arguments," *Journal of Philosophy*, 55 (1958): 718–25.

BonJour, Laurence, *The Structure of Empirical Knowledge* (Cambridge, MA: Harvard University Press, 1985).
Braaten, Jane, "Rational Consensual Procedure: Argumentation or Weighted Averaging," *Synthese*, 71 (1987): 347–53.
Brown, Harold I., *Rationality* (London: Westview Press).
Chisholm, Roderick, *Theory of Knowledge* (Englewood Cliffs, NJ: Prentice-Hall, 1966; 2nd ed. 1977; 3rd ed. 1989).
Christiano, Thomas, "Freedom, Consensus, and Equality in Collective Decision Making," *Ethics*, 101 (1990): 151–81.
Cohen, Jonathan L., *The Provable and Probable* (Oxford, Clarendon Press, 1977).
Cohen, Stewart, "Justification and Truth," *Philosophical Studies*, 46 (1984): 279–95.
Descartes, René, *First Meditation*, tr. J. Cottingham et al., *The Philosophical Writings of Descartes*, vol. II (Cambridge: Cambridge University Press, 1993).
De Sousa, Ronald, *The Rationality of Emotion* (Cambridge, MA: MIT Press, 1987).
Dretske, Fred, *Knowledge and the Flow of Information* (Cambridge, MA: MIT Press, 1981).
Feigl, Herbert, "On the Vindication of Induction," *Philosophy of Science*, 28 (1961): 212–16.
Foley, Richard, *A Theory of Epistemic Rationality* (Cambridge, MA: Harvard University Press, 1987).
Forrest, Peter, "The Lehrer-Wagner Theory of Consensus and the Zero Weight Problem," *Synthese*, 62 (1985): 75–8.
Gauthier, David, *Morals By Agreement* (Oxford: Clarendon Press, 1986).
Gibbard, Allan, *Wise Choices, Apt Feelings* (Cambridge, MA: Harvard University Press, 1990).
Goldman, Alvin, *Epistemology and Cognition* (Cambridge, MA: Harvard University Press, 1986).
Harman, Gilbert, *Change in View* (Cambridge, MA: MIT Press, 1986).
Heil, John, "Believing Resonably," *Nous*, 26 (1992): 47–62.
Holton, Richard, "Deciding to Trust, Coming to Believe," *Australiasian Journal of Philosophy*, 72 (1994): 63–76.
Hume, David, *A Treatise Of Human Nature* (Oxford: Clarendon Press, 1978).
Jeffrey, Richard, *The Logic of Decision* (New York: McGraw-Hill, 1965).
Kant, Immanuel, *Critique of Pure Reason*, tr. Norman Kemp Smith (New York: The Humanities Press, 1950).
Klein, Peter, *Certainty: A Refutation of Scepticism* (Oxford: Clarendon Press, 1984).
Kordig, Carl, "Self Reference and Philosophy," *American Philosophical Quarterly*, 20 (1983): 207–16.
Lehrer, Adrienne and Keith Lehrer, "Fields, Networks and Vectors," in F. Palmer, ed., *Grammar and Meaning* (New York: Cambridge University Press, 1995).
Lehrer, Keith, *Metamind* (Oxford: Clarendon Press, 1990).
——, *Self-Trust: A Study of Reason, Knowledge and Autonomy* (Oxford: Clarendon Press, 1997).
Lehrer, Keith and Carl Wagner, *Rational Consensus in Science and Society* (Dordrecht: Reidel, 1981).
Levi, Isaac, "Consensus as Shared Agreement and Outcome of Inquiry," *Synthese*, 62 (1985): 3–12.
Moser, Paul K., *Knowledge and Evidence* (Cambridge: Cambridge University Press, 1989).

Nozick, Robert, *Philosophical Explanation* (Cambridge, MA: Harvard University Press, 1981).
Plantinga, Alvin, *Warrant and Proper Function* (Oxford: Oxford University Press, 1993).
Pollock, John, *Contemporary Theories of Knowledge* (Totowa, NJ: Rowman and Littlefield, 1986).
Reichenbach, Hans, "On the Justification of Induction," *Journal of Philosophy*, 37 (1940): 97–103.
Rescher, Nicholas, *Pluralism: Against the Demand for Consensus* (New York: Oxford University Press, 1993).
Roth, Michael and Glenn Ross, *Doubting: Contemporary Perspectives on Skepticism* (Boston: Kluwer, 1992).
Schmidtz, David, *The Limits of Government* (Boulder, CO: Westview Press, 1991).
——, *Rational Choice and Moral Agency* (Princeton: Princeton University Press, 1995).
Shafir, E. and A. Tversky, "Thinking Through Uncertainty: Nonconsequential Reasoning and Choice," *Cognitive Psychology*, 24 (1992): 449–74.
Simon, Herbert, *Reason in Human Affairs* (Stanford: Stanford University Press, 1983).
Sosa, Ernest, *Knowledge in Perspective: Selected Essays in Epistemology* (Cambridge: Cambridge University Press, 1991).
Suber, Peter, "A Bibliography of Works on Reflexivity," in Peter Suber, ed., *Self-Reference* (Dordrecht: Nijhoff, 1987).
Swain, Marshall, *Reasons and Knowledge* (Ithaca: Cornell University Press, 1981).
Van Cleve, James, "Foundationalism, Epistemic Principles and the Cartesian Circle," *The Philosophical Review*, 88 (1979): 55–91.

Perceptual Knowledge (William Alston)

Alston, William P., *The Reliability of Sense Perception* (Ithaca: Cornell University Press, 1993).
Bender, John W., ed., *The Current State of the Coherence Theory* (Boston: Kluwer, 1989).
BonJour, Laurence, *The Structure of Empirical Knowledge* (Cambridge, MA: Harvard University Press, 1985).
Broad, C. D., *Scientific Thought* (London: Routledge & Kegan Paul, 1923).
——, *The Mind and Its Place in Nature* (London: Routledge & Kegan Paul, 1925).
Chisholm, Roderick M., "The Problem of Empiricism," *Journal of Philosophy* XLV (1948).
——, *Theory of Knowledge* (Englewood Cliffs, NJ: Prentice-Hall, 1966; 2nd ed. 1977; 3rd ed. 1989).
Davidson, Donald, "A Coherence Theory of Truth and Knowledge," in Ernest LePore, ed., *Truth and Interpretation: Perspectives on the Philosophy of Donald Davidson* (Oxford: Blackwell, 1986).
Dretske, Fred I., *Seeing and Knowing* (London: Routledge & Kegan Paul, 1969).
Ginet, Karl, *Knowledge, Perception, and Memory* (Dordrecht: D. Reidel, 1975).
Goldman, Alvin I., "Discrimination and Perceptual Knowledge," *Journal of Philosophy*, 73 (1976).
——, "What is Justified Belief?", *Journal of Philosophy*, 73 (1979).
——, *Epistemology and Cognition* (Cambridge, MA: Harvard University Press, 1986).
Jackson, Frank, *Perception: A Representative Theory* (Cambridge: Cambridge University Press, 1977).

Lewis, C. I., *An Analysis of Knowledge and Valuation* (La Salle, IL: Open Court, 1946).
Lovejoy, Arthur O., *The Revolt Against Dualism* (La Salle, IL: Open Court, 1930).
Moore, G. E., *Philosophical Studies* (London: Routledge & Kegan Paul, 1922).
——, *Some Main Problems of Philosophy* (London: Allen & Unwin, 1953).
Moser, Paul K., *Knowledge and Evidence* (Cambridge: Cambridge University Press, 1989).
Pollock, John L., *Knowledge and Justification* (Princeton: Princeton University Press, 1974).
Price, H. H., *Perception* (London, Methuen, 1932).
Russell, Bertrand, *Our Knowledge of the External World as a Field for Scientific Method in Philosophy* (Chicago: Open Court, 1914).
——, *Mysticism and Logic* (London: Allen & Unwin, 1917).
Swartz, Robert J., ed., *Perceiving, Sensing, and Knowing* (Garden City, NY: Douleday, 1965).
Wittgenstein, Ludwig, *Philosophical Investigations*, tr. G. E. M. Anscombe (Oxford: Blackwell, 1953).

A Priori Knowledge (George Bealer)

Bealer, George, "The Philosophical Limits of Scientific Essentialism," *Philosophical Perspectives*, 1, 1987: 289–365.
——, "The Incoherence of Empiricism," *The Aristotelian Society, Supplementary Volume*, vol. 66, 1992: 99–138. Reprinted in *Rationality and Naturalism*, S. Wagner and R. Warner, eds. (Notre Dame: University of Notre Dame Press, 1993).
——, "*A Prior* Knowledge and the Scope of Philosophy," *Philosophical Studies*, 91, 1996: 121–42.
——, "On the Possibility of Philosophical Knowledge," The Fourth Annual *Philosophical Perspectives* Lecture, *Philosophical Perspectives*, 10, 1996: 1–34.
——, "A Theory of Concepts and Concept Possession," *Proceedings of the Tenth Annual SOFIA Conference*, Enrique Villanueva (ed.), Atascadero: Ridgeview, in press.
——, *Philosphical Limits of Science* (Oxford: Oxford University Press, in preparation).
BonJour, Lawrence. "A Rationalist Manifesto." *Canadian Journal of Philosophy*, Suppl. Vol. 18, 1992: 53–88.
——, "Toward a Moderate Realism." *Philosophical Topics*, 23, 1995: 47–78.
——, *In Defense of Pure Reason* (New york: Cambridge, 1997).
Casullo, Albert. *A Priori Knowledge*. International Research Library of Philosophy (Hanover, Vermont: Dartmouth Publishing Company).
Chisholm, Roderick. *Theories of Knowledge* (Englewood Cliffs: Prentice Hall, 1989), ch. 4.
DePaul, Michael and William Ramsey, eds. *Proceedings of The Notre Dame Intuition Conference* (Totowa: Rowman and Littlefield, 1997).
Gödel, Kurt, "What Is Cantor's Continuum Problem?", Collected Works, vol. II, Solomon Feferman *et al.*, eds. (New York: Oxford, 1990), 254–70.
——, "Some Basic Theorems on the Foundations of Mathematics and Their Implications," Collected Works, vol. III, Solomon Feferman et al., eds. (New York: Oxford, 1995), 304–23.
Goldman, Alvin and Joel Pust. "Philosophical Theory and Intuitional Evidence," in DePaul and Ramsey, eds., 1997.
Katz, Jerrold. *The Metaphysics of Meaning* (Boston: MIT Press, 1990).
——, *Realistic Rationalism* (Boston: MIT Press, 1998).

———, "Analyticity, Necessity, and the Epistemology of Semantics." *Philosophy and Phenomenological Research*, LVI, 1, March 1997: 1–28.
Kitcher, Philip. *The Nature of Mathematical Knowledge* (New York: Oxford University Press, 1983).
Kripke, Saul. "Naming and Necessity," in *Semantics of Natural Language*, Davidson and Harman, eds. (Dordrecht: Reidel, 1972), 253–355 and 763–9. Reprinted as *Naming and Necessity* (Cambridge, MA: Harvard, 1980).
Moser, Paul, ed., *A Priori Knowledge* (Oxford: Oxford University Press, 1987).
Peacocke, Christopher, "How are A Priori Truths Possible." *European Journal of Philosophy*, 1, 1993: 175–99.
Quine, W. V. "Two Dogmas of Empiricism," *From a Logical Point of View* (Cambridge, MA: Harvard, 1953), pp. 20–46.
Sosa, Ernest, "Minimal Intuition," in DePaul and Ramsey, eds., 1997.
Warner, Richard. "Why is Logic A Priori?" *The Monist*, 72, 1, 1989: 40–51.

Moral Epistemology (Robert Audi)

Annis, David, "A Contextualist Theory of Epistemic Justification," *American Philosophical Quarterly* 15 (1978): 213–19.
Audi, Robert, *Moral Knowledge and Ethical Character* (Oxford: Oxford University Press, 1997).
———, *The Structure of Justification* (New York: Cambridge University Press, 1993).
Brandt, Richard B., *A Theory of Good and Right* (Oxford: Oxford University Press, 1979).
Brink, David, *Moral Realism and the Foundations of Ethics* (New York: Cambridge University Press, 1989).
Butchvarov, Panayot, *Skepticism in Ethics* (Bloomington: Indiana University Press, 1989).
Copp, David, and David Zimmerman, eds., *Morality, Reason, and Truth: New Essays on the Foundations of Ethics* (Totowa, NJ: Rowan and Littlefield, 1985).
Dancy, Jonathan, *Moral Reasons* (Oxford: Blackwell, 1993).
Depaul, Michael R., *Balance and Refinement: Beyond Coherence Methods of Moral Inquiry* (New York: Routledge, 1993).
Ewing, A. C., *Ethics* (New York: Macmillan, 1947).
Follesdal, Dagfinn, ed., "Justification in Ethics," in *The Monist* 76, no. 3 (1993).
Gert, Bernard, *Morality* (New York: Oxford University Press, 1988).
Gewirth, Alan, *Reason and Morality* (Chicago: University of Chicago Press, 1978).
Gibbard, Allan, *Wise Choices, Apt Feelings* (Cambridge, MA: Harvard University Press, 1990).
Goldman, Alan, *Moral Knowledge* (New York: Routledge, 1988).
Hare, R. M., *Essays in Etihcal Theory* (Oxford: Clarendon Press, 1989).
Harman, Gilbert, *The Nature of Morality: An Introduction to Ethics* (New York: Oxford University Press, 1977).
Holmgren, Margaret, "Wide and Narrow Reflective Equilibrium," *Canadian Journal of Philosophy* 19 (1989): 43–60.
Mackie, J. L., *Ethics: Inventing Right and Wrong* (New York: Penguin, 1977).
McNaughton, David, *Moral Vision: An Introduction to Moral Theory* (Cambridge, MA: Blackwell, 1988).
Moore, G. E., *Principia Ethica* (London: Cambridge University Press, 1903).

Odegard, D., ed., *Ethics and Justification* (Edmonton, Can.: Academic Printing and Publishing, 1988).
Ross, W. D., *The Right and the Good* (Oxford: Oxford University Press, 1930).
Russell, Bruce, "Two Forms of Moral Skepticism," in *Ethical Theory: Classical and Contemporary Readings*, ed. Louis Pojman (Belmont, CA: Wadsworth, 1989).
Sayre-McCord, Geoffrey, ed., *Essays on Moral Realism* (Ithaca: Cornell University Press, 1988).
Sencerz, Stefan, "Moral Intuitions and Justification in Ethics," *Philosophical Studies* 50 (1986): 77–95.
Sosa, Ernest, "Knowledge and Intellectual Virtue" and "Reliabilism and Intellectual Virtue," both in *Knowledge in Perspective* (Cambridge: Cambridge University Press, 1991).
Sinnot-Armstrong, Walter, and Mark Timmons, eds., *Moral Knowledge?* (New York: Oxford University Press, 1996).
Thomson, Judith Jarvis, *The Realm of Rights* (Cambridge, MA: Harvard University Press, 1990).
Timmons, Mark, ed., Spindel Conference 1990: Moral Epistemology, *Southern Journal of Philosophy* 29, supplement (1990).
Williams, Bernard, *Ethics and the Limits of Philosophy* (London: Fontana Press, 1985).
Zagzebski, Linda, *Virtues of the Mind* (Cambridge: Cambridge University Press, 1996).

Epistemology of Religion (Nicholas Wolterstorff)

Alston, William P., *Perceiving God* (Ithaca: Cornell University Press, 1991).
Audi, Robert, and William Wainwright, *Rationality, Religious Belief, and Moral Commitment* (Ithaca: Cornell University Press, 1986).
Bouwsma, O. K., *Without Proof or Evidence*, eds. J. L. Craft and R. E. Hustwit (Lincoln: University of Nebraska Press, 1984).
Clark, Kelly, *Return to Reason* (Grand Rapids, MI: Eerdmans Publishing Co., 1990).
Phillips, D. Z., *Belief, Change, and Forms of Life* (Atlantic Highlands, NJ: Humanities Press International, 1986).
——, *Faith after Foundationalism* (New York: Routledge, 1988).
——, *Religion Without Explanation* (Oxford: Blackwell, 1976).
——, *Wittgenstein and Religion* (New York: St. Martin's Press, 1993).
Plantinga, Alvin, *Warrant and Proper Function* (Oxford: Oxford University Press, 1993).
Plantinga, Alvin, and Nicholas Wolterstorff, *Faith and Rationality* (Notre Dame, IN: Notre Dame University Press, 1983).
Wittgenstein, Ludwig, *Wittgenstein's Lectures and Conversations on Aesthetics, Psychology and Religious Belief*, ed. Cyril Barrett (Berkeley: University of California Press, n.d.).
Wolterstorff, Nicholas, *Divine Discourse* (Cambridge: Cambridge University Press, 1995).
——, *John Locke and the Ethics of Belief* (Cambridge: Cambridge University Press, 1996).
Zagzebski, Linda, ed., *Rational Faith: Catholic Responses to Reformed Epistemology* (Notre Dame, IN: Notre Dame University Press, 1993).
——, *Virtues of the Mind: An Inquiry into the Nature of Virtue and the Ethical Foundations of Knowledge* (Cambridge: Cambridge University Press, 1996).

Feminist Epistemology (Helen E. Longino)

Addelson, Kathryn, "The Man of Professional Wisdom," in Sandra Harding and Merrill Hintikka, *Discovering Reality* (Dordrecht: Reidel, 1983).

Select Bibliography of Epistemology

Alcoff, Linda and Elizabeth Potter, *Feminist Epistemologies* (New York: Routledge, 1993).

Anderson, Elizabeth, "Feminist Epistemology: An Interpretation and Defence," *Hypatia*, 10 (1995): 50–84.

——, "Knowledge, Human Interests, and Objectivity in Feminist Epistemology," *Philosophical Topics*, 23 (1996): 27–58.

Antony, Louise, "Sisters, Please, I'd Rather Do It Myself: A Defense of Individualism in Feminist Epistemology," *Philosophical Topics*, 23 (1996): 59–94.

—— and Charlotte Witts, eds., *A Mind of One's Own* (Boulder, CO: Westview Press, 1993).

Baier, Annette, "Cartesian Persons," in *Postures of the Mind* (Minneapolis: University of Minnesota Press, 1985).

Belenky, Mary F., Blythe Clinchy, Nancy Goldberger, and Jill Tarule, *Women's Ways of Knowing* (New York: Basic Books, 1986).

Bergin, Lisa, "Communicating Knowledge Across Epistemic Difference," Ph.D. Dissertation in progress, Dept. of Philosophy, University of Minnesota.

Bordo, Susan, *The Flight to Objectivity* (Albany: State University of New York Press, 1987).

Collins, Patricia Hill, *Black Feminist Thought* (Boston: Unwin Hyman, 1990).

Code, Lorraine, *What Can She Know?* (Ithaca: Cornell University Press, 1991): 250–62.

——, *Rhetorical Spaces* (Ithaca: Cornell University Press, 1995).

Duran, Jane, *Toward a Feminist Epistemology* (Savage, MD: Rowman and Littlefield, 1991).

Gilligan, Carol, *In a Different Voice* (Cambridge, MA: Harvard University Press, 1982).

Grasswick, Heidi, "Knowers as Individuals-in-Community," Ph.D. Dissertation, Dept. of Philosophy, University of Minnesota, 1996.

Haack, Susan, "Epistemological Reflections of an Old Feminist," *Reason Papers*, 18 (1993): 31–43.

——, "Science as Social – Yes and No," in Lynn Hankinson Nelson and Jack Nelson, eds., *Feminism, Science, and the Philosophy of Science* (Boston: Kluwer, 1996).

Haraway, Donna, "Situated Knowledges: The Science Question in Feminism and the Privilege of Partial Perspectives," *Feminist Studies*, 14 (1988): 575–600.

Harding, Sandra, *Whose Science? Whose Knowledge?* (Ithaca: Cornell University Press, 1991).

——, "What is Strong Objectivity?" in Linda Alcoff and Elizabeth Potter, eds., *Feminist Epistemologies* (New York: Routledge, 1993).

—— and Merrill Hintikka, eds., *Discovering Reality* (Dordrecht: Reidel, 1983).

Hare-Mustin, Rachel and Jean Maracek, eds., *Making a Difference: Psychology and the Construction of Gender* (New Haven: Yale University Press, 1990).

Hartsock, Nancy, "The Feminist Standpoint: Toward a Materialist Feminism," in Sandra Harding and Merrill Hintikka, eds., *Discovering Reality* (Dordrecht: Reidel, 1983).

Jaggar, Alison, "Love and Knowledge: Emotion in Feminist Epistemology," in Alison Jaggar and Susan Bordo, eds., *Gender/Body/Knowledge* (New Brunswick, NJ: Rutgers University Press, 1989).

—— and Susan Bordo, eds., *Gender/Body/Knowledge* (New Brunswick, NJ: Rutgers University Press, 1989).

Keller, Evelyn F., *A Feeling for the Organism* (New York: W. H. Freeman, 1983).

——, *Reflections on Gender and Science* (New Haven: Yale University Press, 1985).

Lennon, Kathleen, "Feminist Epistemology as a Local Epistemology," *Proceedings of the Aristotelian Society Supplement*, LXXI (1997): 37–54.

—— and Margaret Whitford, eds., *Knowing the Difference* (New York: Routledge, 1994).

Select Bibliography of Epistemology

Lloyd, Elisabeth, "Objectivity and the Double Standard for Feminist Epistemologists," *Synthese*, 104 (1995): 351–81.

Lloyd, Genevieve, *The Man of Reason* (Minneapolis: University of Minnesota Press, 1984).

Longino, Helen E., *Science as Social Knowledge* (Princeton: Princeton University Press, 1990).

——, "Reason, Passion and Dialogue in Feminist Philosophy," in Donna Stanton and Abigail Stewart, eds., *Feminisms in the Academy* (Ann Arbor: University of Michigan Press, 1994).

——, "In Search of Feminist Epistemology," *Monist*, 77 (1994).

——, "Cognitive and Non-Cognitive Values in Science: Rethinking the Dichotomy," in Lynn Hankinson Nelson and Jack Nelson, eds., *Feminism, Science, and the Philosophy of Science* (Boston: Kluwer, 1996).

——, "Feminist Epistemology as a Local Epistemology," *Proceedings of the Aristotelian Society supplement*, LXXI (1997): 19–36.

Lugones, Maria, "Playfulness, 'World'-Traveling, and Loving Perception," *Hypatia*, 2 (1987): 3–19.

Monist 77, no. 4, "Feminist Epistemology – For and Against," Special issue ed. by Susan Haack, 1994.

Nelson, Lynn Hankinson, *Who Knows: From Quine to Feminist Empiricism* (Philadelphia: Temple University Press, 1990).

——, "Epistemological Communities," in Linda Alcoff and Elizabeth Potter, *Feminist Epistemologies* (New York: Routledge, 1993).

—— and Jack Nelson, eds., *Feminism, Science, and the Philosophy of Science* (Boston: Kluwer, 1996).

Nicholson, Linda, ed., *Feminism/Postmodernism* (New York: Routledge, 1990).

Rolin, Kristina, "Gender, Emotion, and Epistemic Values in High Energy Physics," Ph.D. Dissertation, Dept. of Philosophy, University of Minnesota, 1996.

Rooney, Phyllis, "Gendered Reason: Sex Metaphor and Conceptions of Reason," *Hypatia*, 6 (1991): 77–103.

——, "Rationality and the Politics of Gender Difference," *Metaphilosophy*, 26 (1995): 22–45.

——, "Methodological Issues in the Construction of Gender as a Meaningful Variable in Scientific Studies of Cognition," in David Hull, Mickey Forbes, and Richard Burian, eds., *PSA 1994*, vol. 2, Philosophy of Science Association, East Lansing, MI, 1995.

Rose, Hilary, *Love, Power and Knowledge* (Bloomington: Indiana University Press, 1994).

Scheman, Naomi, "Though This Be Method, Yet There Is Madness in It," in Louise Antony and Charlotte Witts, eds., *A Mind of One's Own* (Boulder, CO: Westview Press, 1993).

——, *Engenderings* (New York: Routledge, 1995).

Smith, Dorothy, *The Everyday World as Problematic: A Feminist Sociology* (Boston: Northeastern University Press, 1988).

——, *The Conceptual Practices of Power* (Boston: Northeastern University Press, 1991).

Solomon, Miriam, "Situated Knowledge," Symposium Paper, American Philosophical Association, Eastern Division, Meetings, Atlanta, GA, Dec. 28, 1996.

——, "Social Empiricism," *Nous*, 28 (1994).

——, "Toward a More Social Epistemology," in Frederick Schmitt, ed., *Socializing Epistemology* (Lanham, MD: Rowman and Littlefield, 1994).

Wylie, Alison, "Doing Philosophy as a Feminist," *Philosophical Topics*, 23 (1996): 345–58.

Social Epistemology (Frederick Schmitt)

[For an extensive bibliography of social epistemology, see Schmitt, *Socializing Epistemology*.]

Adler, Jonathan, "Testimony, Trust, Knowing," *Journal of Philosophy*, 91 (1994): 264–75.
Alston, William P., "Belief-forming Practices and the Social," in Schmitt, ed., *Socializing Epistemology*.
Brown, J. R., ed., *The Rational and the Social* (London: Routledge, 1989).
Coady, C. A. J., *Testimony: A Philosophical Study* (Oxford: Oxford University Press, 1992).
Craig, Edward, *Knowledge and the State of Nature* (Oxford: Clarendon Press, 1990).
Foley, Richard, "Egoism in Epistemology," in Schmitt, ed., *Socializing Epistemology*.
Fuller, Steve, "Recent Work on Social Epistemology," *American Philosophical Quarterly*, 33 (1996): 149–66.
Gibbard, Allan, *Wise Choices, Apt Feelings* (Cambridge, MA: Harvard University Press, 1990).
Gilbert, Margaret, *On Social Facts* (London: Routledge, 1989).
Goldman, Alvin I., *Epistemology and Cognition* (Cambridge, MA: Harvard University Press, 1986).
——, *Liaisons: Philosophy Meets the Cognitive and Social Sciences* (Cambridge, MA: MIT Press, 1992).
Kitcher, Philip, "The Division of Cognitive Labor," *Journal of Philosophy*, 87 (1990): 5–22.
Kornblith, Hilary, *Inductive Inference and Its Natural Ground: An Essay in Naturalistic Epistemology* (Cambridge, MA: MIT Press, 1993).
Lehrer, Keith, *Self-Trust: A Study of Reason, Knowledge and Autonomy* (Oxford: Clarendon Press, 1997).
—— and Carl Wagner, *Rational Consensus in Science and Society* (Dordrecht: Reidel, 1981).
Locke, John, *An Essay Concerning Human Understanding*, 2 vols., ed. A. C. Fraser (New York: Dover, 1959).
Loewer, Barry, ed., *Synthese*, special issue on Consensus, 62 (1985).
Longino, Helen E., *Science as Social Knowledge* (Princeton: Princeton University Press, 1990).
Malital, B. and A. Chakrabharti, eds., *Knowing from Words* (Dordrecht: Kluwer, 1995).
McMullin, Ernan, ed., *The Social Dimensions of Science* (South Bend, IN: Notre Dame University Press, 1992).
Plantinga, Alvin, *Warrant and Proper Function* (Oxford: Oxford University Press, 1993).
Rescher, Nicholas, *Pluralism: Against the Demand for Consensus* (New York: Oxford University Press, 1993).
Ruben, David-Hillel, *The Metaphysics of the Social World* (London: Routledge, 1985).
Schmitt, Frederick F., ed., *Synthese*, special issue on Social Epistemology, 73 (1987).
——, "Justification, Sociality, and Autonomy," *Synthese*, 73 (1987): 43–86.
——, *Knowledge and Belief* (London: Routledge, 1992).
——, ed., *Socializing Epistemology: The Social Dimensions of Knowledge* (Lanham, MD: Rowman and Littlefield, 1994).
——, "The Justification of Group Belief," in Schmitt, ed., *Socializing Epistemology*.
——, "Socializing Epistemology: An Introduction Through Two Sample Issues," in Schmitt, ed., *Socializing Epistemology*.
Searle, John R., *The Construction of Social Reality* (New York: Free Press, 1995).
Welbourne, Michael, *The Community of Knowledge* (Aberdeen: Aberdeen University Press, 1986).

Zagzebski, Linda, *Virtues of the Mind: An Inquiry into the Nature of Virtue and the Ethical Foundations of Knowledge* (Cambridge: Cambridge University Press, 1996).

Epistemology and AI (John Pollock)

Cheng, P. W. and K. J. Holyoak, "Practical Reasoning Schemas," *Cognitive Psychology* 17 (1985): 391–406.
Chomsky, Noam, *Syntactical Structures* (The Hague: Mouton and Company, 1957).
Gettier, Edmund, "Is Justified True Belief Knowledge?" *Analysis* 23 (1963): 121–3.
Goodman, Nelson, *Fact, Fiction, and Forecast* (Cambridge, MA: Harvard University Press, 1955).
Pollock, John, *Knowledge and Justification* (Princeton: Princeton University Press, 1974).
——, *Contemporary Theories of Knowledge* (Lanham, MD: Rowman and Littlefield, 1987).
——, *Nomic Probability and the Foundations of Induction* (New York: Oxford University Press, 1990).
——, "The Projectibility Constraint," in Douglas Stalker, ed., *Grue! The New Riddle of Induction* (La Salle, IL: Open Court, 1994).
——, *Cognitive Carpentry* (Cambridge, MA: MIT Press, 1995).
——, *The OSCAR Manual* (http://www.u.arizona.edu/~pollock, 1996).
——, "Reasoning about Change and Persistence: a Solution to the Frame Problem," *Nous* 31 (1997): 143–69.
Shope, Robert K., *The Analysis of Knowing* (Princeton: Princeton University Press, 1983).
Wason, P., "Reasoning," in B. Foss, ed., *New Horizons in Psychology* (Harmondsworth, England: Penguin, 1966).

Postmodernism and Epistemology on the Continent (Merold Westphal)

Caputo, John D., *Radical Hermeneutics* (Bloomington: Indiana University Press, 1987).
Derrida, Jacques, *Of Grammatology*, tr. Gayatri Chakravorty Spivak (Baltimore: Johns Hopkins Press, 1976).
——, *Margins of Philosophy*, tr. Alan Bass (Chicago: University of Chicago Press, 1982).
——, *Speech and Phenomena*, tr. David B. Allison (Evanston, IL: Northwestern University Press, 1973).
——, *Writing and Difference*, tr. Alan Bass (Chicago: University of Chicago Press, 1978).
Dreyfus, Hubert, "Holism and Hermeneutics," *The Review of Metaphysics* XXXIV (1980–1).
—— and Paul Rabinow, *Michel Foucault: Beyond Structuralism and Hermeneutics*, 2nd ed. (Chicago: University of Chicago Press, 1982, 1983).
Foucault, Michel, *Power/Knowledge*, ed. Colin Gordon (New York: Pantheon Books, 1980).
Gadamer, Hans-Georg, *Philosophical Hermeneutics*, tr. David E. Linge (Berkeley: University of California Press, 1976).
——, *Truth and Method*, tr. Joel Weinsheimer and Donald G. Marshall, 2nd ed. rev. (New York: Crossroad, 1991).
Heidegger, Martin, *Being and Time*, tr. Macquarrie and Robinson (New York: Harper and Row, 1962).

Select Bibliography of Epistemology

——, *Phanomenologie des religiosen Lebens, Gesamtausgabe*, Ed. 60 (Frankfurt: Klostermann, 1995).

——, "Phenomenology and Theology," in *The Piety of Thinking*, tr. James G. Hart and John C. Maraldo (Bloomington: Indiana University Press, 1976).

Husserl, Edmund, *Ideas Pertaining to a Pure Phenomenology and to a Phenomenological Philosophy, First Book*, tr. F. Kersten (The Hague: Martinus Nijhoff, 1983).

——, *Logical Investigations*, tr. J. N. Findlay (New York: Humanities, 1970).

Michelfelder, Diane P. and Richard E. Palmer, eds., *Dialogue and Deconstruction: The Gadamer–Derrida Encounter* (Albany: State University of New York Press, 1989).

Rorty, Richard, *Philosophy and the Mirror of Nature* (Princeton: Princeton University Press, 1979).

Westphal, Merold, "Positive Postmodernism as Radical Hermeneutics," in *The Very Idea of Radical Hermeneutics*, ed. Roy Martinez (Atlantic Highlands, NJ: Humanities, 1997).

Index

Main subject references and the authors of chapters are indicated in **bold** print. Page references followed by 'n' mean there is information in the notes at the end of the corresponding chapter. Material in notes is only indexed if there is no reference in the main text.

a posteriori knowledge 20, 244
a priori knowledge 20-1, 164-5, **243-70**; concept possession 255-65; intuition and evidence 246-51; necessity and analyticity 243-5; reliabilism 251-5; role in cognition 30, 418-19
absolute terms: Unger 201-3
Academic skepticism 63n
acceptance: as distinct from belief 347-8
Accessibility of Epistemic Supervenience (AES) 148
Accessibility of the Internal (AI) 147
accidentality: and knowledge 103-4
acquaintance: direct 132; with God 322-3; mimic of 306-7; notion of 24, 305; scope of 314
acquired belief-forming methods: reliabilism 364, 376-8
action, rational: and moral judgment 293-6
Addelson, Kathryn 337
adequacy conditions: perception 228-9
Adler, Jonathan 380n
adverbial theory: perception 19, 233, 234-6

affect: primacy of passions 30-1, 425-6; as source of knowledge 26, 335
Agrippa's Trilemma 3-4, 8, 38-43, 50-4
Aiken, Henry D. 433n
Alcoff, Linda 351n, 352n
Allison, David B. 435n
Alston, William P. 29, 71, 72, 114n, 227, 231, 240-1n, 268-9n, 301n, 317, 323n, 380n; acquaintance with God 322-3; circularity 74, 76-7; *Perceiving God* 322-3; perceptual knowledge 18-20, **223-42**
analytic/synthetic distinction 20, 243-5, 341
Anderson, Elizabeth 341, 348-9
androcentrism 340
animal: knowledge 96, 114n; research 335
Annas, Julia 64n
Annis, David 113n, 190, 341-3
Anscombe, G. E. M. 433n
Anthony, St 313
Antony, Louise 344, 351n; individualism 345-7
appearances: physical-object 136-7
Appearing, Theory of: Alston 322-3

451

Index

Aquinas, St Thomas: *scientia* 23, 307–9
Aristotle 99, 251; definitions 96–7; good 272; morality 273; rationality 16–17, 206, 209; virtue 105, 108, 112
Armstrong, D. M. 167n
artifical intelligence (AI): and epistemology 28–9, 391–415
assent: knowledge as form of 6, 93; skeptical 64n, 65–6n
Assert the Stronger rule 16, 197, 198–9, 200, 202–3
assertability: contextualism 15–16, 195–203
assertion, derivative 30–1, 419, 420–5
assumption, doxastic 394–5
attributor contextualism 190–1, 193
Audi, Robert 298n, 299n, 300n, 302n, 323–4n; moral knowledge 21–3, **271–302**
Augustine, St 92; *tolle lege, tolle lege* 313–14
Austin, J. L. 65n, 66n, 67n
authority, cognitive: hierarchy of 337–8
autonomy: of knowers 335–6
awareness: mediated 323; prelinguistic 421–2; unmediated 322
Ayer, A. J. 62n, 65n

Bacon, Francis 62
Baier, Annette 336
ballpark psychologism 174–6
Barad, Karen 350n
Barlow, John 433n
Barnes, Jonathan 64n
Barrett, William 433n
Barwise, Jonathan 333
Bass, Alan 434n
Bayes' theorem 186n
Bealer, George 168n, 186n, 247, 265n, 267n, 269n, 270n; a priori knowledge 20–1, **243–70**
Beck, Lewis White 434n
Belenky, Mary 330–1
belief and beliefs: acquired methods 364, 376–8; basic 131–2, 119–22, 393–4; cognitively spontaneous 125–6, 129–30; difference from intuition 247–8;

formation of inductive 314–15; ideally formed 304–7; immediate 309, 320; justified true belief (JTB) 97, 99–104, 172–3; and knowledge 6, 93; mediate 312; memory 29, 129; native processes 362, 374–6; religious 23, 303–4, 313–16, 319–22; from sensory experience 120, 136–8, 232; state of 93; and testimony 24, 315–16, 337, 362–3, 378–9
Bennett, Jonathan 241n
Bentham, Jeremy: utilitarianism 272
Bergin, Lisa 352n, 353n
Berkeley, George 138–9, 244
bias in reasoning 346–7
biology: feminist critique of 25, 328–9
Birke, Linda 351n
Black, Max 219n
Blackburn, Simon 299n
Blanshard, Brand 140n
Bleier, Ruth 328
bodies: embodiment of knowledge 25–6, 331–8
BonJour, Laurence 62n, 65n, 139–40n, 141–2n, 168n, 169n, 241n, 298n, 299n, 301n; foundationalism and coherentism 8–9, **117–42**
Bordo, Susan 351n
Bosanquet, Bernard 123
Bouwsma, O. K. 67n, 323n
Brandom, Robert 65n, 68n, 69n
Brandt, Richard B. 297n, 299n, 301n
Broad, C. D. 225, 226; perception 234–7
Brown, Harold I. 219n
Brown, J. R. 379–80n
Buchler, Justus 66n
Burge, Tyler 247, 255
Burian, Richard 350n
Burnyeat, M. F. 63n, 65n
Bury, R. G. 63n, 64n

Caputo, Jack 428, 434n
Carneades 63n, 64n; doctrine of the tested impression 65–6n
Cartesian approaches: epistemology 12, 13, 158, 159–61, 177–8; skepticism 4, 44–9, 55–8

Index

Cartesian internalism 10–11, 147–8
Cartwright, Nancy 350n
Cat, Jordy 350n
categorical imperative: Kantian 272, 273
Cavell, Stanley 66n
certainty 36–7, 416
Chakrabharti, A. 380n
charity: principles of 80
Cheng, P. W. 413n
Cherniak, Christopher 167n
children: peer pressure 372–3; reliability of testimony 28, 359–60, 363, 367, 368, 372–3, 374–5; small-sample inductions 365
Chisholm, Roderick 38, 96, 115n, 132, 136, 137–8, 139n, 140n, 186n, 246; internalism 10–11, 147–51, 152–3; perception 234–7
Chomsky, Noam 388
Church, Alonzo 265n
Churchland, Patricia 168n
Churchland, Paul 168n
circular reasoning 3–4, 39–40, 42
circularity: realism 74, 76–7, 80–2
Clark, Kelly 323n
Clarke, Thompson 66n
Clay, Marjorie 68n
Clinchy, Blythe 350n
closure, epistemic 68–9n
clustered feature facilitation 365
Coady, C. A. J. 351n, 380n
Code, Lorraine 337–8, 351n, 353n
cognition: and direct realism 394–5; epistemic 386–7; and gender 330–1; goals 165–6; practical 386–7; social organization of labor 354
Cohen, Stewart 188, 193, 336
coherent systems objection, alternative 128, 129
coherentism 176, 275; and contextualism 190; and foundationalism 8–9, 117–42; objections to 127–9; perceptual belief 225; response to epistemic regress problem 122–7; as structural theory 384; theories of justification 42–3; theories of truth 64n
collective knowledge: nature of 354

Collins, Patricia Hill 342
communal activity: knowledge as 26, 336–7, 340–1, 342–3
competence theory 388–9
completeness property 261, 264
computers *see* artificial intelligence
Comte, Auguste 329
conceiving: concept of 71
concept possession 20, 21, 255–65, 265
concepts: categorical content 262; noncategorical content 263; semantically stable 262
conceptual analysis, epistemic: and psychology 13–14, 172–80
concernment, maximum 309, 310–11
Conee, Earl 186n
confidence: Locke 310
confirmation: intuition 247–8
consciousness 419–20; perception 322
consensual beliefs: children 373
consequentialist thesis 272
consistency: intuition 248–9; moral 273; probabilistic 124
context, role in justification 26, 339–42
contextual intraindividual process reliabilism 372–6
contextual metareliabilism 374–9
contextualism 9, 14–16, 52–3, 54, 62, 187–205; attributor 190–1, 193; explanation of 187–90; and feminism 26, 341–2, 343–4, 349; history of 191–3; and intuitionism 22–3, 286–7; and knowledge 97; and skepticism 4–5, 58–61, 193–5; subject 190–1, 193; warranted assertability maneuvers (WAM) 15–16, 195–203
contingent/necessary distinction 20, 243–5
conversational context 15, 16, 191, 194–5
Cornman, James 77
correctness property 261, 264
corroboration: intuition 248–9
Cosmides, L. 168n
Cottingham, J. 65n
counterexamples 28, 170, 391–2
Craig, Edward 95, 380n

credulity: principle of 79–80, 315; and skepticim 36
criterion: problem of 39–40

Dancy, Jonathan 300n
Davidson, Donald 67n, 80, 133, 232
default and challenge structure 51–2, 59
defeasibility 100–1; intuitionism 22, 280–1, 291–2; moral knowledge 287–8
defeasible reasoning 29, 395, 396–7
defeaters 51; reliability 396–7; rebutting 396; undercutting 396
defense commitments 52
definitions 243–4, 245; ad hoc 99, 102, 103–4; circular 98; criteria for good 98–9; knowledge 95–9; negative 98; real 95–6
Deontological Conception of Epistemic Justification 149
deontologism, epistemic 11, 148–51
DePaul, M. 168n, 169n
DeRose, Keith 66n, 113n, 203n, 204–5n; contextualism 15–16, **187–205**
Derrida, Jacques 428; hermeneutics 29, 31, 429–31
Descartes, René 2, 58, 64n, 428; epistemology 30, 415–16; Evil Deceiver 10, 45, 49, 145–6, 149, 152, 211; foundationalism 12, 159–61, 163–4, 177; 211; mind/body dichotomy 25–6, 331–2; perception 225; skepticism 44–5, 61, 62; *see also* Cartesian
Descartes's Paradox 10, 145–6
Devitt, Michael 71; naturalized epistemology 78–9
diversity: women 334, 338–9, 342, 349
Doell, Ruth 352n
dogmatism 3, 39–40, 93; in intuitionism 23, 289–91; and skepticism 36
Don't Know Either Way (DKEW) 197
Don't Know Otherwise (DKO) 197
double mediation: theory of 430–1
dreams 10, 146–7; perpetual 44–5
Dretske, Fred 66–7n, 167n, 204n; perception 229–30, 231
Dreyfus, Hubert L. 425, 432n, 434n
Dummett, Michael 65n

Duran, Jane 342
duty: final 288–9; *prima facie* 22, 277–8, 287–8, 292

education: reliable testimony in 360, 363
egocentric rationality 81–2
Ellis, R. 69n
embodiment of knowledge 25–6, 331–8
emotions *see* affect
empathy 26, 329
empirical knowledge: case for 164–7; continuous with epistemology 12–13, 158, 163–4; preceded by epistemology 12, 159–61; relevance to epistemology 13–14, 176–80; *see also* psychology
empiricism 332; and intuitionism 21, 247–9, 263–4, 285–6; perception 226–7; social 346; utilitarian 22, 272–5
ends: people treated as 273; rationality of 16–17, 207–9
Enlightenment foundationalism: rejection of 30, 415–17
entitlement: religious belief 23, 303, 309, 310–11
epistemics 171–2
epistemology: armchair 170–86; central questions in 1–2; feminist 25–6, **327–53**; hermeneutics as 29–31, **415–35**; Humean-Reidian revolution 24, 316; issues covered in 171–2; levels of generality 28–9, 383–4; naturalized 12–13, 78–9, **158–69**; against naturalized 13–14, **170–86**; new directions in 392–6; procedural 28–9, **383–414**; Reformed 311–16, 316, 318, 321; after skepticism 61–2; social 26–8, **354–82**
equality principle: Kantian rationality 273
equipment: Heidegger 423–4
essentialism, scientific: intuitions and 261–2
ethical discourse 317–18
ethics: utilitarianism 182; virtue theories of 106–7, 113–14, 275–6

Index

evaluation, epistemic 9, 10, 355
evidence: and intuition 20–1, 245–50, 251–5; and knowledge 245–6; Locke 311
evidentialism: religion 310–11
Evil Deceiver hypothesis 10, 45, 49, 145–6, 149, 152, 211
exclusion, principle of 145
expected utility maximization accounts of rationality 208–9
experience: men and women 329; mystical 302; nature of 224; perceptual 18, 19, 226–8, 232–7, 237–8; privacy of 46, 47; and reliability of testimony 360–1; religious 302, 312, 321–2
expert knowledge: hierarchy of 337–8
expert testimony 361
external world: Cartesian tradition 159; and foundationalism 134–9; knowledge of 3; perception 18, 225–7, 234–6
externalism **145–57**; and internalism 10–12, 146–8; moral knowledge 285–6; and naturalism 11–12; in perception 18, 229–30, 234, 240, 240–1n; in transindividual process reliabilism 371–2; in transindividual reasons account 369–70; of utilitarian empiricism 275; of virtue ethics 277

fallibilism 37, 54
Fausto-Sterling, Ann 328
Feigl, Herbert 432n
Feldman, Richard 116n, 186n; naturalism in epistemology 13–14, **170–86**
feminist epistemology 25–6, **327–53**; historical background 328–31; justification 338–44; nature of knowing subject 331–8; sociality of knowledge 342–9
Findlay, J. N. 433n
Fine, Kit 265n
focused sampling 365, 366, 367
Fogelin, Robert 63n, 64n, 68n
Foley, Richard 168n; egocentric rationality 80–2
Forbes, Mickey 350n
Foucault, Michel 425, 428

foundationalism 41–2, 55, 57–8; basic beliefs 29, 393–4; classically modern 311; and coherentism 8–9, **117–42**; and contextualism 190; Descartes 12, 159–61, 163–4, 177; Enlightenment 30, 415–17; external world problem 134–9; formal 9; and intuitionism 22, 274–5; perception 228; reconsideration of 130–4; response to epistemic regress problem 119–22; as structural theory 384
Frankena, William K. 297n
Friend, Celeste 351n
Fuller, Steve 379n
Fumerton, Richard 74
future: beliefs about 46

Gadamer, Hans-Georg: hermeneutics 29, 31, 426–9
Gauthier, David 219n
gender bias 25, 327, 328
Gert, Bernard 302n
Gettier, Edmund 63n, 100, 172, 266n, 385
Gettier objections 6–7, 63n, 68n, 111, 99–104, 385–6; ethics 107–8
Gibbard, Allan 299n
Gilbert, Margaret 379n
Gilligan, Carol 330
Ginet, Carl: fake barn example 190–1
Gödel, Kurt 246
Goldberger, Nancy 350n
Goldman, Alvin 77, 96, 97, 115n, 167n, 168n, 169n, 175, 180, 181, 184n, 193, 205n, 230, 379n; acquired belief-forming methods 364, 376–8; epistemics 171–2; knowledge as reliably true belief 162; substantive naturalism 174
good: concept of 99; of knowledge 6, 94–5, 97, 104, 109–11
Goodman, Nelson 387, 412n
Grasswick, Heidi 352n
Greco, John 111–12, 115n, 140n, 141n, 156n, 185n, 186n, 298n, 382n; epistemology **1–31**
Grice, H. P. 198–9

grounding conditions: beliefs 4, 52–3, 54, 58–9, 74–5; prior grounding requirement 4, 9, 50–2, 59, 61
guilt 431
Guttenplan, Samuel 68n
gynecentrism 340

Haack, Susan 136, 184n, 344–5; critique of feminist epistemology 347–9
Habermas, Jürgen 428
habits: blind 313–14
Hadot, Pierre 69n
hallucinations 18, 19–20, 238–40, 370
Hankinson, R. J. 64n
Hansen, P. 166n
Hanson, N. R. 418, 419, 433n
Haraway, Donna 328, 333, 334, 339, 352n, 353n
Harding, Sandra 334, 338–9, 351n
Hare-Mustin, Rachel 350n
Harman, Gilbert 140n, 167n, 184n, 219n, 265n
Harrison, Jonathan 299n
Hart, James G. 433n
Hartsock, Nancy 333–4
Heath, D. 69n
Heidegger, Martin: *Being and Time* 418–26, 427; hermeneutics 30–1, 417–26
Henle, P. 266n
Henrich, Dieter 141n
hermeneutical circle 30, 417–19, 427, 430
hermeneutics: Derrida 29, 31, 429–31; as epistemology 29–31, **415–35**; Gadamer 29, 31, 426–9; Heidegger 30–1, 417–26; Rorty 30, 415–17
Hett, W. S. 218n
Hintikka, Merrill 351n
holism: affective 425; practical 425; theoretical 30–1, 419, 427
Holyoak, K. J. 413n
Hooker, Brad 300n
hopes 303
Howard, Don 350n
Howard-Snyders, Frances and David 103
Hubbard, Ruth 328, 351n
Hull, David 350n

Hume, David 2, 46, 48–9, 64n, 226, 244, 433n; doxastic ideal 23–4, 314–15; empiricism 266n; probabilistic arguments 306; rationality 207; reason 426; skepticism 37, 38, 60
Humean-Reidian revolution 24, 315
Hunter, B. 168n
Husserl, Edmund 416, 419–20
hypotheses: skeptical 47
hypothetico-deductive method 387

ideal: doxastic 23–4, 304–7, 318; in medieval understanding of *scientia* 307–9; rejection by Reformed epistemology 312–17; role in Locke's epistemology of religion 310–12
implementation, epistemic theories 28, 391–2
implicatures 198–200; false 16, 198–200
incommensurability: and intuitionism 288–9; and moral knowledge 294
indignation, moral 285
individual knowledge: social conditions for 355–7
individualism 345–7; a priori weak 358; coherentist weak 358–9; inductive weak 27, 358, 359–69; and social epistemology 26–8; strong 358
induction: problem of 17, 214–15; small-sample 27–8, 362–9, 374
inductive beliefs: formation 313–14
inductive inference: 4, 46, 48–9, 313–14, 315
infallibilism: intuition 246, 252–3
inference to best explanation: 48–9, 77–8
inferences: Bayesian 387; conclusions of 281–2, 297; external 284; inductive 4, 46, 48–9, 313–14, 315; internal 284; moral knowledge 283–4
inquiry: practice of 310
instrumentalist theory of rationality 16, 207–9, 293
interdependence: of knowers 26, 335–8
internal relations: doctrine of 430
internalism 50–1, **145–57**, 394–5; Cartesian 10–11, 147–8; Chisholmian 10–11, 147–51, 152–3;

Index

and externalism 10–12, 146–8; and justification 152–6; Kantian rationality 274; moral knowledge 285–6; virtue ethics 276
internalist approaches: perception 18, 230–1, 232–3, 235, 241, 241–2n
interpretation: circular structure with understanding 30, 417–19; interpretations of 430–1; more basic than assertion 420–5; prelinguistic 422, 423, 424
intrinsic end formulation 272, 273
intuitionism: dogmatism in 290–2; empiricist 285–6; epistemological resources of moderate 278–85; ethical 24–5, 275–7; incommensurability and 289–90; philosophical commitments of 292; prospects and problems of moderate 285–93; rationalist 288–9; Rossian 22, 278–81
intuitions: aesthetic 266–7n; and evidence 20–1, 244–5, 246–51, 251–5; moral 266–7n; philosophical 387–8; physical 247; phenomenology of 247–8; rational 247; self-evident 22, 23, 276
invariantism 188; nonskeptical 192; skeptical 192; warranted assertability objection 195–6, 201–3
involuntariness: and coherence 138–9
isolation problem: coherentism 127

Jackson, Frank 205n
Jaggar, Alison 335
Jeffrey, Richard: expected utility maximization accounts 208
judgments, moral: explanatory and object-level 300n; gap with rational action 23, 292–5
justification, epistemic: analytic theories 384; conditions 237; and contextualism 4–5, 58–61, 189–90; degrees of 223; deontologism 11, 148–51; description of 383–6; evidential 50–1; and feminism 25, 26, 338–44, 349; gynecentric theory of 342; and internalism 9, 118, 152–6; perceptual belief 227–40; personal 52–4; personal aetiology 153;

prima facie 223; *simpliciter* 50, 52–3; procedure 245–6; social aetiology 153; structural 283, 384; theories of 303; and truth 53–4; *see also* regress
justified true belief (JTB) 97, 172–3; Gettier objections 99–104

Kahneman, D. 169n, 248
Kallen, H. H. 266n
Kant, Immanuel 219n, 296, 428; *Anschauung* 304; epistemology 415–16
Kantian rationalism 62, 273–5
Kantianism, revised: Heidegger 30, 418
Kaplan, David 266n
Kaplan, Mark 168n, 169n, 346
Keller, Evelyn 328–9, 330, 335, 352n
Kersten, F. 433n
Kierkegaard, Søren 114n
Kim, Jaegwon 168n, 300n
Kitcher, Philip 69n, 168n, 171, 172, 173, 337, 379n
Klein, Peter 67n, 95, 114n, 115n
knowing, ways of: gendered 25, 330–1
knowledge: a priori 20–1, 164–5, 243–70; by acquaintance 92; as act of intellectual virtue 7–8, 104–13; animal 97, 114n; collective 354; as communal activity 26, 336–7, 340–1, 342–3; concept of 12–14, 97–8, 161, 165–6; defining propositional 95–9; and evidence 245–6; expert 337–8; and Gettier objections 99–104; naturalistic theory of 161–4; object and components of propositional 92–5; perception and memory 94–5, 97, 109–10; phenomenon of 12–14, 161–4, 167; possibility of 36–7, 159, 165; primary 274; priority of experiential 55–7; propositional 6–8, 92–116; reflective 114n; as reliably true belief 162, 180; scientific 161–2; scientific analysis more useful than conceptual analysis 176–80; secondary 274–5; *see also* empirical knowledge
Kohlberg, Lawrence 330
Kornblith, Hilary 96, 115n, 167–8n, 168n, 174, 184n; criticism of 176–8,

177–8; naturalized epistemology 12–13; **158–69**; small-sample induction 362–9, 374
Krell, David Farrell 433n
Kripke, Saul 265n, 266n
Kuhnian philosophy of science 416, 427
Kvanvig, Jonathan L. 156n, 298n

Lackey, Jennifer 156n
Langer, S. K. 266n
language: and interpretation 420–5
learning: gendered approaches to 330–1
Lehrer, Adrienne 219n
Lehrer, Keith 68n, 218n, 219n, 380n; rationality 16–18, **206–19**
Lennon, Kathleen 353n
Leonardi, P. 168n
Lepore, E. 67n
Lewis, C. I. 120–1, 140n, 432n; perception 234–7
Lewis, David 68n, 113n, 188, 189, 192, 204n
limitations, human 186n
Linge, David E. 434n
Linsky, L. 433n
Lloyd, Elisabeth 330
Lloyd, Genevieve 330, 353n
Locke, John 62, 64n, 138–9, 358; doxastic ideal 315; entitlement 23; epistemology 30, 415–16; perception 225; real definitions 95–6; religion 309–11
Loewer, Barry 380n
logical behaviorism 48
logical constructions 235
Longino, Helen E. 204n, 340–1, 342, 351n, 352n, 353n, 380n; feminist epistemology 25–6, **327–53**
Lovejoy, Arthur O.: perception 225
luck: epistemic 7, 59, 100, 107–8, 111
Lugones, Maria 353n
Lukács, Georg 333
Luther, Martin 419
Lycan, William 168n; skepticism 86–8

Macdonald, G. F. 141n
Mackie, J. L. 142n
Macquarrie 427, 432n, 433n
Maffie, James 167n
Malcolm, Norman 192
Maracek, Jean 350n
Maraldo, John C. 433n
Markie, Peter 186n
Marshall, Donald G. 434n
Martin, Emily 352n
Marxism: standpoint theory 333
material world *see* external world
Mates, Benson 63n
mathematics 41–2; self-evidence 307–8
Matilal, B. 380n
McCarthy, Thomas 434n
McClintock, Barbara 329
McDowell, John 64–5n, 69n
McGinn, Marie 66n
McGrath, Matthew 156n
McLaughlin, Brian P. 204n
McMullin, Ernan 380n
meaningfulness, cognitive: religion 318
mediation, double, theory of 430–1
memory: beliefs 29, 130; perceptual and memory knowledge 94–5, 97, 109–10, 383; principles 183, 184; representational theory of 310; testimonial beliefs 369
mental images: perception 239
mental states 393–4
metaphysics: logical positivism 317
metareliabilism, contextual 374–9
metareliable selection process 28, 364–6, 368–9; children 367
Michelfelder, Diane P. 434n
Mill, John Stuart 301n; utilitarianism 272, 273–5
mind/body dichotomy 25–6, 331–8
modernist epistemology: rejection of 30, 415–17
modus ponens 389
modus tollens 389
Monk, Ray 323n
Montmarquet, James 298n
moods: primacy of 30–1, 425–6
Moore, G. E. 146–7, 278; perception 234–7

Index

moral development: gender bias in accounts of 330
moral good: of knowledge 94–5
moral knowledge 21–3, **271–302**; approaches to 271–8; gap between intuitive judgment and rational action 293–7; memorially direct 274; moderate intuitionism 278–85; prospects and problems of moderate intuitionism 285–93; testimonially direct 274
Moser, Paul K. 72, 74, 77, 80, 82, 85, 90; perception 225; realism and objectivity 5–6, **70–90**
multigon example 256–7, 259–60
Myro, George 266n
mystical experience 303

Nagel, Thomas 63n, 107
native belief-forming processes: reliabilism 364, 376–8
natural kind properties 27–8, 362–4, 365, 366
naturalism 11–13, 68–9n, 79–80; as alternative to Cartesian approach 161–4; defense of 12–13, **158–69**; empirical epistemology 164–7; feminism 334–5; methodological 13–14, **170–86**; moral knowledge 285–6; substantive 174
necessary/contingent distinction 20, 243–5
Nelson, Jack 350n, 352n
Nelson, Lynn H. 341, 342–3, 346, 350n, 352n
neurological factors: knowledge 162–3
Nicod principle 387
Nidditch, P. H. 63n
Nietzsche, Friedrich 431
Nisbett, Richard 184n, 248
nonaccidental selection process 363–4
nonaccidentality: and knowledge 104–5
noncognitivism 22, 277–8, 301n
noncognitivist interpretation: religious belief 318–19
normativity 9, 98–9
nostalgia 431

Nozick, Robert 66n, 67n, 219n
Nussbaum, Martha 69n, 434n

object of knowledge: knowing subject and 26, 334–5
objectivity: concepts of 324, 335; and feminism 25, 328–9; and individualism 345; and intelligible realism 70–3; and moderate realism 5–6, **70–90**; static 329; uselessness of questions about 82–90
observational knowledge: role of sensory and perceptual experience in 8, 124–6, 127–8, 129–30
Observational Requirement 126, 129–30
operative agreement 288
opinion: knowledge and 6
OSCAR project 29, 390–2, 396–412

Palmer, F. 219n
Palmer, Richard E. 434n
partiality 334
passions: primacy of 30–1, 425–6
past: beliefs about 46, 47
Peacocke, Christopher 266n
Peirce, Charles Sanders 54
perception 18–20, **223–41**, 359, 393–4; artificial intelligence: low level theory of 29, 396–412; causal theory of 225–6; doxastic conditions 228–9; of God 319–20; nature of 18, 224, 232–7; principles of 180–2, 183, 184; representational theory of 310
perceptual and memory knowledge 94–5, 97, 109–10, 383
perceptual updating 29, 404, 406–8
performance theory 388
Perry, John 333
person: rationality of 17, 209–10; theory of 336
phenomenal quality theory 19, 233, 235, 236, 323
phenomenalism 48
phenomenological reduction 419–20, 425
Phillips, D. Z. 322, 324n
philosophy: a priori investigation 164–5; feminist critiques of 330

Index

physical objects: perception 136–7, 137–8
Plantinga, Alvin 96, 114n, 148, 156–7n, 168n, 298n, 318, 380n, 424
Plato 64n, 113n; doxastic ideal 23–4; knowledge 6, 95, 97; Theaetetus 1–2, 63n, 83, 97, 114n
Pojman, Louis P. 301–2n
political science: feminism 329–30
Pollock, John L. 63n, 113n, 226, 237, 385, 390, 393, 395, 397, 413n, 414n; procedural epistemology 28–9, **383–415**
Popkin, Richard 63n
Popper, Karl 54, 133, 219n, 265
positivism, logical: feminism and 329–30; religion 318–19
Post, John F. 300n
Potter, Elizabeth 351n, 352n
pragmatism: eliminative 82–6; and realism 6, 77, 87
predicative judgment 30–1, 419, 420–5
preference: practical rationality 206–10
prejudices 31, 426–7
presence, denial of 430
present-at-hand: Heidegger 421
presumption, doxastic 43, 126–7, 129
Price, H. H. 67n, 137, 225; perception 234–7
Prichard, H. A. 114n, 285, 299n
prima facie duty 22, 278–9, 288–9, 293
principles, epistemic: identification of 14; intuitionism 293; and psychology 180–3
Prior, A. N. 265n
prior grounding requirement 4, 9, 50–2, 59, 61
priority, epistemic: hierarchy of 4, 55–8
probabilism: epistemic justification 384–5
probabilistic arguments 305, 313
probability: Locke 24, 310
projectibility constraints 397–8, 405–6
propositions, true: in knowledge 92
psychological factors: knowledge, 13, 162–3
psychologism: ballpark 174–6
psychology: and analysis of epistemic concepts 13, 172–80; educational, feminist critiques of 25, 331–2; and epistemic principles 14, 180–3; evaluation of skeptical arguments 14, 183–4; evolutionary 268n; role in epistemology 170–86
Pust, Joel 169n
Putnam, Hilary 247, 263, 265n, 324n; reality 71, 72
Pyrrho of Elis 63n
Pyrrhonian skepticism 63n

questionbegging realism 5–6, 73–5
Quine, W. V. O. 61, 68n, 416, 424, 432n; analytic/synthetic distinction 20, 244–5, 341; naturalism 79–80, 158
Quinton, Anthony 120

Rabinow, Paul 434n
Railton, Peter 297–8n
Ramsey, W. 168n, 169n
rational action: gap with moral judgment 293–6
rationalism: intuitionism and 288–9; Kantian 22, 273–5
rationality 16–18, **206–19**; association with masculinity 330; diachronic 17, 215–16; egocentric 81–2; generic 389–90; human 387–9; Kantian 277, 284–5; personal 206; practical 16, 76–7, 206–10; relationship with reasoning 214–15; scientific 80; social 17–18, 206, 216–18; synchronic 206, 215–16; theoretical 16, 17, 206, 210–14
Rawls, John 418, 427
ready-to-hand: Heidegger 421, 423–4, 425
real world hypothesis 48–9
realism: as analytic theory 384; epistemological 4–5, 57–8, 59, 60, 61; minimal 71; moderate 5–6; ordinary 71; scientific 71
realism, direct 47; and artificial intelligence 29, 393–5; naive 227; perception 18–20, 230, 233–4, 237–40; as structural theory 384

Index

realism, moderate 5–6; intelligibility of 70–3; and objectivity **70–90**; responses to skeptical challenge 76–82; skeptical challenge to 73–5, 82–90
reason-for relation 393
reasonableness: criteria for 321–2
reasons and reasoning: circular 3–4, 39–40, 42; conditional 117; limitations of human 6, 88, 90; in OSCAR 398–402; from percepts 396–8; and rationality 206–7, 214–15; top-down and bottom-up 392–3
reduction 48; phenomenological 419–20, 425
Reed, Baron 156n
reflection 147–8, 149–50; conclusions of 281–2, 297; limits of 429; moral knowledge 22, 284, 297
reflective equilibrium 418
reflexivity 334
Reformed epistemology 319, 322; rejection of doxastic ideal 312–17
regress argument, epistemic 8–9, 16, 117–18, 207–8; coherentism 122–7; foundationalism 118–21; *see also* Agrippa's Trilemma
Reid, Thomas 23–4, 76; testimony 314–15; Way of Ideas 310–11, 312, 314
relativism 26, 343; and contextualism 193; hermeneutics 417; mitigated 353n
relevant alternatives (RA) 192–3
reliabilism 95, 251–2; acquired methods and native processes 364, 376–8; contextual 369, 371–9; contextual intraindividual process 372–4, 374–6; contingent 251–2; modal 246, 253–5, 265; moral knowledge 286; theories 384–5; transindividual process 371–2
reliabilist analyses of knowledge 14, 173–6, 181, 183
reliabilist approach: perception 230–1
religion 23–4, **303–24**; acquaintance with God 322–3; doxastic ideal 304–5; Heidegger 419; Locke's epistemology of religion 309–11; natural 311; rational 311; rejection of doxastic ideal 312–17; revealed 311; Wittgensteinian philosophy of 317–22
religious belief 23, 303–4, 313–16, 319–22
representation, accurate: knowledge as 416
representational theory of memory 311
representational theory of perception 311
representations, privileged: role of 416
Rescher, Nicholas 140–1n, 380n
responsibility: of subjects 335
Robinson, Richard 113n
Rolin, Kristina 350n
Rooney, Phyllis 330, 350n, 353n
Rorty, A. O. 65n, 351n
Rorty, Richard 61, 133, 421–2, 428, 430, 432n; eliminative pragmatism 82–6; reality 71, 72; rejection of modernist epistemology 30, 415–17
Ross, David 218n
Ross, W. D. 285, 286, 287, 291, 292, 298n; intuitionism 278–81
Rousseau, Jean Jacques 431; *Confessions* 430
Ruben, David-Hillel 379n
Russell, Bertrand 37, 114n, 416; perception 225, 234–7
Russell, Bruce 301–2n
Ryan, Sharon 115n

Santambrogio, M. 168n
Sartre, Jean-Paul 82
Savellos, Elias 300n
Scheffler, Israel 114n
Scheman, Naomi 332
Schiffer, Stephen 203n
Schilpp, Paul Arthur 298n
Schleiermacher, Friedrich 313
Schmidtz, David 220n
Schmitt, Frederick 64n, 168n, 353n, 379n, 380n, 381–2n, 382n; social epistemology 26–8, **354–82**
science: acceptance of probability of error 211; and belief 309; continuous with epistemology 12–13, 158, 163–4; empirical investigation 164–5; feminist critiques of 25, 328–31; logical positivism 318; post-positivist

philosophy of 30, 418; preceded by epistemology 12, 159–61; rationality of scientists 346; and realism 6, 78–80; role in epistemology **170–86**
scientia: Aquinas 23, 307–9; and doxastic ideal 307–9; Locke 310
scientific analysis: compared to conceptual analysis 176–80
scientific knowledge 161–2; utilitarianism 271–2
scrutiny: level of 59–60
Searle, John R. 379n
seeing: non-epistemic 230
Selby-Bigge, L. A. 63n
selection processes: metareliable 28, 364–6, 367, 368–9; nonaccidental 363–4
self-defeat arguments 85–6, 248
self-evidence 22, 308–9; immediate 284–5; intuitionism 297; mediate 284–5, 288; moral knowledge 23, 276, 279–80; and understanding 282–3
self-reference: hermeneutics 416
self-understanding 422–3
Sellars, Wilfrid 133, 140n, 141n, 416, 421–2, 424, 432n
sense-datum theory: perception 19, 233, 234–7
sensory and perceptual experience 4, 41–2, 44, 56; and belief 120, 137–9, 232; conceptual formulations 134–7; foundationalism 133–4; role in observational knowledge 8, 124–6, 127–8, 129–30
Sextus Empiricus 40, 63n, 64n, 69n
Sharples, R. W. 63n
Shope, Robert 114n, 413n
signified 430; Transcendental 431
signs 430
Simon, Herbert 219n
Sinnott-Armstrong, Walter 297n, 298n, 299n, 300n, 301n, 302n
situatedness 26, 333–4, 338
skeptical arguments: evaluating 14, 183–4
skeptical assent 64n, 65–6n
skeptical hypotheses 45; brain in a vat hypothesis 45, 55, 145–6

skepticism 3–5, **35–69**, 97–8, 332–3; Academic 63n; Agrippa's Trilemma 3–4, 8, 38–43, 50–4; ancient 61, 63n; Cartesian Arguments 4, 44–9, 55–8; and contextualism 15, 58–61, 193–5; and eliminative pragmatism 82–6; inconsistency of 86–90; and moderate realism 5–6, 73–82; moral 23, 293–6; and natural science 14, 183–4; philosophical 3, 35–8; place in epistemology 61–2; practical 35; Pyrrhonian 63n; radical 36–7, 51; religious 23; theoretical diagnosis 35, 37–8, 50, 62; therapeutic 49–50, 57, 62
skeptics: declarative 88–9; interrogative 88–9
Slovic, P. 169n
small-sample inductions 27–8, 362–9, 374
Smith, Dorothy 329
Smith, Norman Kemp 219n
social aetiology justification 153
social analysis of justification: feminism 349
social conditions 26, 354, 356; small-sample inductions 366–8
social factors: knowledge 13, 25, 26, 162–3, 342–4
social practice approach: moral knowledge 288
social rationality 17–18, 206, 216–18
social sciences: feminist critiques of 25, 329
social standards: knowledge dependent on 336
socialism 26–8, 344, **354–82**; contextual reliabilism 369, 371–9; and individualism 355–7; supervenience 356–7; testimonial rules account 369; transindividual reasons account 369–71; virtue-theoretic account of testimonial justification 369
sociality of knowledge: objections to 344–9
Socrates: *Theaetetus* 6
solipsism 46
Solomon, Miriam 333, 346, 353n

Sosa, Ernest 9, 114n, 139n, 157n, 168n, 297n, 299n; internalism and externalism 10–11, **145–57**
Spedding, J. 69n
speech-act theory 420–1
Spinoza, Baruch 426
Spivak, Gayatri Chakravorty 434n
stability 403–4; active 390; passive 390
Stambaugh, Joan 432n, 433n
standards, epistemic 15, 177–8, 201, 202; contextualism 187–8, 189, 191–2, 194–6
standpoint theory 333–4, 338–9; feminist 333–4; Marxist 333; multiple 334
Stanton, Domna 353n
static autonomy 328–9
static objectivity 329
Stein, Edward 168n
Stewart, Abigail 353n
Stich, Stephen 113n, 168n, 184n, 185–6n
Stillinger, Jack 300n
Stine, Gail 188, 193, 195, 205n
Stoics 426
Strawson, P. F. 63n, 65n, 141n
Stroud, Barry 63n, 65n, 66n, 67n, 68n, 168n, 169n, 192
subject contextualism 190–1, 193
subject, knowing: nature of 25–6, 331–8, 349; and object of knowledge 26, 334–5
subjectivism 26, 342
supervenience principles 243
synthetic/analytic distinction 20, 243–5, 341

Tarski, Alfred 72
Tarule, Jill 350n
testimonial rules account: socialism 369
testimony 26–7; beliefs based on 24, 315–16, 337; contextual reliabilism 371–9; indirectly justified beliefs 378–9; inductive weak individualism 358, 359–69; primary and secondary sources 357–8; principles 182, 183, 184; reliability of 27–8; transindividual reasons account 369–71; versions of individualism 357–9; virtual 370, 373–4

texts: interpretation 30, 31, 418, 429–31
theology: natural 308; sacred 308; *see also* religion
theories, epistemological 28–9, 383–5; levels of 392–3, 395; top-down and bottom-up reasoning 392–3
Thomson, Judith Jarvis 301n
Tidman, Paul 299n
Tiles, Mary 351n
Timmons, Mark 297n, 298n, 299n, 300n, 301n, 302n
Tomberlin, James 323–4n
Tooby, J. 168n
toy examples 392
tradition 427–9
Transcendental signified 431
transindividual process reliabilism 371–3
transindividual reasons account 369–71
Traweek, Sharon 350n
trust 303; role in knowledge 337
truth 111; coherence theories of 64n, 128; and justification 53–4, 236–7; minimal realist definition of 72; objective 72; and realism 72–3; relation of intuition to 21, 245, 251–5; replaced with utility 83–5; and theoretical rationality 210–12; as unconcealment 425
truth condition analysis 96, 99, 104
truth conditions 237
truth-absorption 263
truth-relevant merits 304, 316; religion 311–12, 317–18
Tversky, A. 169n, 248

Uebel, Thomas 350n
uncanny 313–14
underdetermination arguments: feminist epistemology 348–9
understanding: adequate 22, 283; circular structure with interpretation 417–19; hermeneutical circles 30; and self-evidence 282–3
Unger, Peter: absolute terms 201–3; *Ignorance* 192, 201–3; invariantism 188; *Philosophical Relativity* 193

universality: Kantian rationality 273
Urbach, Peter 69n
utilitarianism 182; intuitionism 295; moral knowledge 272–5
utility: replacement of truth with 83–5

valuational thesis 272
value judgements 9
values: conflict between moral and nonmoral 294, 295
van Fraassen, Bas 168n
van Roojen, Mark 299n
Vermazen, Bruce 67n
virtual reality 45
virtue: acts of 7, 108, 109; ethics 105–9, 112–13, 275–7; intellectual 7–8, 105, 109–12
virtue-theoretical account of testimonial justification 369
vision: materiality of 334
visual object recognition: reliability of 175–6
visualism 21, 247–50
Vogel, Jonathan 65n

Wagner, Carl 220n, 380n
Wagner, Steven 168n, 186n, 265n
Wainwright, William 324n
Walker, Margaret 301n
Warner, Richard 168n, 186n, 266n
warrant 347–8

warranted assertability maneuvers (WAM) 15–16; bare 199, 201; conditions for success 198–200; guidelines for 196–7
warranted assertability objection 195–6, 201–3
Wason, P. 248, 413n
Way of Ideas: Reid 310–11, 312, 314
Weinsheimer, Joel 434n
Welbourne, Michael 380n
Wertheim, Margaret 350n
Westphal, Merold: hermeneutics 29–31, **415–35**
Williams, Bernard 66n
Williams, Michael 9, 64n, 65n, 66n, 67n, 68n, 168n, 204n; skepticism 3–5, **35–69**
Witt, Charlotte 351n
Wittgenstein, Ludwig 66n, 226, 237, 433n; religion 303, 317–22
Wolterstorff, Nicholas 318, 324n; epistemology of religion 23–4, **303–24**
women: diversity of 334, 338–9, 342, 349; *see also* feminism; feminist epistemology
Wright, Crispin 69n
Wylie, Alison 353n

Yalcin, Umit 300n
Yandell, David 80, 85

Zagzebski, Linda 114n, 115n, 298n, 318, 382n; knowledge 6–8, **92–116**